IS THE MARKET A TEST OF
TRUTH AND BEAUTY?

Is the Market a Test of
TRUTH AND BEAUTY?

Essays in Political Economy

by
LELAND B. YEAGER

Ludwig von Mises Institute

© 2011 by the Ludwig von Mises Institute and published
under the Creative Commons Attribution License 3.0.
http://creativecommons.org/licenses/by/3.0/

Ludwig von Mises Institute
518 West Magnolia Avenue
Auburn, Alabama 36832
mises.org

ISBN: 978-1-61016-188-6

Contents

Introduction vii

PART I: ECONOMICS

1 Should Austrians Scorn General Equilibrium Theory? 3
2 Why Subjectivism? 19
3 Henry George and Austrian Economics 51
4 The Debate about the Efficiency of a Socialist Economy . . . 72
5 The Debate over Calculation and Knowledge 93
6 Austrian Economics, Neoclassicism, and the Market Test . . . 100
7 Is the Market a Test of Truth and Beauty? 116
8 Macroeconomics and Coordination 128
9 The Keynesian Heritage in Economics 157
10 Hutt and Keynes 173
11 The Image of the Gold Standard 191
12 Land, Money, and Capital Formation 209
13 Tacit Preachments are the Worst Kind 225
14 Tautologies in Economics and the Natural Sciences 263

PART II: POLITICS AND PHILOSOPHY

15 Free Will and Ethics 283
16 Elementos del Economia Politic 307
17 Is There a Bias Toward Overregulation? 321
18 Economics and Principles 349
19 American Democracy Diagnosed 361
20 Civic Religion Reasserted 367
21 A Libertarian Case for Monarchy 375

v

22	Uchronia, or Alternative History	388
23	Hayek on the Psychology of Socialism and Freedom	397
24	Kirzner on the Morality of Capitalist Profit	407
25	Mises and His Critics on Ethics, Rights, and Law	422
26	The Moral Element in Mises's *Human Action*	443
27	Can a Liberal Be an Egalitarian?	462
28	Rights, Contract, and Utility in Policy Espousal	477

Index 516

Introduction

This book's title is the same as the newly chosen title of chapter 7, "Is the Market a Test of Truth and Beauty?" That chapter, along with the one before it, questions a dangerously false argument for the free-market economy sometimes made by its supposed friends. Their argument threatens to discredit, by association, the powerful and valid case for the market. Asked whether the market is a test of truth and beauty—of excellence—Ayn Rand would presumably give the same answer as mine: "No, of course not!" Consider her hero of *The Fountainhead*, Howard Roark.

Political economy is the area of overlap among economics, political science, and philosophy. Beyond its positive content, political economy does bear on policy but not only on policy; it is far from a hodge-podge of different people's policy prejudices. Economics, when not disregarded, is obviously relevant to policy. So are philosophy and psychology, as when they underlie doctrines such as redistributionism and egalitarianism. Policy can affect economics. More exactly, a policy proposal may help clarify a strand of economic analysis even when, considering side-effects, the author does not actually recommend the policy; "Land, Money, and Capital Formation," chapter 12, provides an example. Regrettably, though, policy-driven economists do exist who start with their or their employers' preferred policies and then twist their analysis into supporting them.

Writings in political economy, being interdisciplinary, typically omit the deep technicalities of any specific field. Most of this book's chapters are semipopular pieces that the attentive "general reader" should understand. They deal with intersecting fields rather than with advanced details of any one field. Left out of this book, then, are any of my relatively technical writings, as on monetary theory and international economics. A few semitechnical chapters, including numbers 1 and 12, come close to making an exception. Chapter 12 contributes to a field of particular interest to Austrian economists, capital theory. Yet it too strives for nontechnical language.

Some linkages among the chosen articles may not be immediately obvious. But, for example, "Free Will and Ethics" and "Uchronia, or Alternative History" both illuminate the chance aspects of life. So doing, both bear on political philosophy (as on the role of luck in personal status). Both also underline the difficulty of pinpointing the supposed "deep parameters" of the economy and so to making quantitative predictions, as opposed to what F.A. Hayek (1967) called "pattern predictions." (Far be it from me, however, to say that the necessary achievements of the econometricians are forever downright impossible.)

About half of the articles deal with economics in particular. "The Debate about the Efficiency of a Socialist Economy" and "The Debate Over Calculation and Knowledge" are among them. The latter chapter summarizes points made more fully in my "Mises and Hayek on Calculation and Knowledge," *Review of Austrian Economics* 7, no. 2, 1994, and in the ensuing debate with Joseph Salerno, Guido Hülsmann, Jeffrey Herbener, and Hans-Hermann Hoppe in 1996 and 1997 issues of that *Review*. That debate runs to too many pages for inclusion here (see the *Review*'s issues of 1994, 1996, and 1997, online at the Mises Institute's website).

My "Austrian Economics, Neoclassicism, and the Market Test," chapter 6, also provoked controversy, specifically from David Laband and Robert Tollison in the *Quarterly Journal of Austrian Economics* 3, no. 1, Spring 2000. The reader should read their article (at the Mises Institute's website) along with or before reading my reply in chapter 7.

Chapters on "Macroeconomics and Coordination," "The Keynesian Heritage in Economics," "Hutt and Keynes," and "The Image of the Gold Standard" deal with money-macro topics. The last two of the Economics chapters concern methodology or, rather, countermethodology: they advise against being intimidated by narrow methodological preaching.

Several chapters in the Politics and Philosophy section examine the merits and demerits of democratic government. Two of them are book reviews. One of the books treats the American political system realistically. The other takes the George Stigler/Earl Thompson line that—if I may exaggerate just a bit—whatever institution exists must be optimal or at least satisfactory; otherwise it would already have been replaced. Other chapters in the section deal with political philosophy.

Most chapters are reprinted with only slight editing, particularly to standardize the system of references. Chapter 8 has been expanded (and renamed) to take account of developments in the fifteen years since it first appeared, and chapter 5 (also renamed) has been modified at its beginning to read less like an invited introduction to others' articles. Several pages of chapter 25 have been cut out because they rebut a strained interpretation of Mises's work that is hardly worth attention. Chapter 4, "The Debate about the Efficiency of a Socialist Economy," although and perhaps especially because it dates from 1949, is printed unchanged.

The selection process has just happened to give the book an Austrian flavor not originally intended. The bulk of my work is not particularly Austrian. On whether I count as an Austrian economist, see the opening lines of chapter 6.

ACKNOWLEDGMENTS

For enjoyable and instructive discussions over many years, I am indebted to dozens, even hundreds, of students in my graduate Seminar in Political Economy at the University of Virginia and at Auburn University. (That seminar covered its topics in more scope, detail, and technicalities than the articles included here.) Many persons, including ones both mentioned and unmentioned in the individual papers, have given me valuable instruction, encouragement, provocation, and warnings. I hesitate to list names because any such list would be incomplete and would suffer from my lapses of memory; but it would include Roger Garrison, Luis Dopico, Daniel Edwards, Robert Greenfield, Roger Koppl, Juergen Backhaus, Steven Caudill, Warren Nutter, Edgar Browning, William Breit, Northrup Buechner, Murray Rothbard, James Buchanan, Gordon Tullock, and, to go back many years, Aurelius Morgner, James Waller, and Clarence Philbrook.

The Ludwig von Mises Institute made no suggestion that I moderate any views contrary to its own. For this and other reasons I am indebted to Llewellyn Rockwell, the Institute's chairman, and Douglas French, its president. Jeffrey Tucker, editorial vice president, encouraged and patiently supported this book project from the beginning. Perhaps the Institute's greatest support has been the services of Miss Lauren Barlow. She helped select the papers to reprint; standardized the system of citations (including placement of notes where they belong, at the bottom of each page); questioned errors, undue repetition, and infelicitous formulations; coped with many drafts; and gave invaluable support on the many arduous chores scarcely imaginable by someone who has not tried to assemble diverse articles into a coherent (I hope) book.

For these reasons I extend my special admiration and thanks to Lauren Barlow.

REFERENCE

Hayek, F.A. "Degrees of Explanation" and "The Theory of Complex Phenomena." In *Studies in Philosophy, Politics and Economics*, 3–21, and 22–42. Chicago: University of Chicago Press, 1967.

PART I
Economics

CHAPTER 1

Should Austrians Scorn General Equilibrium Theory?*

Austrian economists try to explain how a whole economic system functions. They do not focus narrowly on the circumstances of the individual household or the geometry of the individual firm. They investigate the coordination of the mutually influencing yet separately decided activities of many millions of individual units;[1] they investigate general interdependence.

General equilibrium is a somewhat narrower concept. ("GE" is a convenient abbreviation for both "general equilibrium" and, as context requires, general-equilibrium *theory* or *approach*.) By GE I mean work by and in the tradition of Léon Walras, Vilfredo Pareto, Gustav Cassel, Gerard Debreu (1959), Robert Kuenne (1963, 1968), Kenneth Arrow and Frank Hahn (1971), and others. Distaste for GE among Austrian economists is familiar, as it was among Chicago economists such as Milton Friedman and George Stigler (who thought that it somehow stood in rivalry with Marshallian partial-equilibrium analysis). Austrians sometimes state explicit reasons for their scorn, but often they take the reasons as too well known to need repeating.[2] I myself have been accused of a GE mindset in a context that takes such a mindset for granted as a bad thing (Salerno 1994, pp. 115–120).

---

*From *Review of Austrian Economics* 11, nos. 1–2 (1999): 19–30.
[1] Austrians pursue a line of research marked out by Adam Smith, trying "to explain how a system of 'Natural Liberty', a market economy based upon private ownership and the self-interested pursuit of utility and profits, could become coordinated in such a way that it generates ever-expanding circles of productivity, efficiency and growth" (Boettke and Prychitko 1998, p. x).
[2] Reasons are reviewed by Boettke and Prychitko 1998 and in several of the articles reprinted in the volumes that they edited. Their Introduction, those articles, and the present article reinforce and supplement each other.

EXAMPLES OF SCORN

Jesús Huerta de Soto provides an example of scorn in his 1992 Spanish book on socialism, economic calculation, and entrepreneurship. It is an excellent and insightful book, apart from some methodological preaching. Huerta de Soto regrets

> the negative effects that mathematical formalism and the pernicious obsession with analyses based on full information and on equilibrium have had on the development of our science. It is likewise necessary to abandon the functional theory of price determination and replace it with a *theory of prices* that explains how these are established dynamically as the result of a sequential and evolving process driven by the force of the entrepreneurial function, that is, by the human actions of the actors involved, and not by the intersection of mysterious curves or functions lacking any real existence, since the information necessary to formulate them does not exist even in the minds of the actors involved. (Huerta de Soto 1992, pp. 34–35)

Jack High (1994) provides another example. Especially since World War II, he says, mainstream economists shifted their attention from actual market prices mainly to their hypothetical counterparts in equilibrium. Those economists could say much about how producers and consumers would react to given prices but little about how prices were formed and adjusted. GE existence proofs supposed that producers and consumers were maximizing with respect to "given" prices. To dodge the question of how prices reach their equilibrium values, the theory brought in a *deus ex machina*, a fictional economywide auctioneer who somehow achieves this result.[3] "The fundamental motivating force of economic theory was absent from the theory of price formation" (High 1994, pp. 151–152, quotation from p. 152).

High invokes the authority of Robert Clower (1975/1986) for a further verdict on GE. Although Clower does not classify himself as an Austrian, overlaps between his and Austrian views justify quoting him also.

> To argue that neo-Walrasian theory has any bearing on the observable behavior of an economy actually in motion, we should have to regard it

---

[3] I cannot find mention of the auctioneer in Walras's own writings; and Donald Walker, the leading living U.S. expert on Walras, assured me (in conversation) that the auctioneer indeed does not appear in them. That prodigious figure is the invention of later theorists trying to make the theory tighter.

as providing a *complete* description of actual behavior rather than a *partial* description of *virtual* behavior—and that we surely cannot do. Strictly interpreted, neo-Walrasian theory is descriptive only of a fairy-tale world of notional economic activities that bears not the slightest resemblance to any economy of record, past, present, or future. It is science fiction, pure and simple—clever and elegant science fiction, no doubt, but science fiction all the same. (Clower 1975/1986, p. 195)

More recently Clower noted

the meretriciousness of the economist's notion of "equilibrium." In every branch of physical science, "equilibrium" refers to a "balance of forces" [citations omitted] such as might be associated with an olive resting at the bottom of a cone-shaped martini glass; and the word misleadingly conjures up analogous images when it is used by economic theorists. Strictly speaking, however, the "equilibria" that neowalrasian theory shows to exist are more correctly called *solutions* [to a system of implicitly-defined algebraic equations]. So understood, the important achievements of neowalrasian equilibrium theory lose much of their apparent lustre, which should in any case adhere to the mathematical geniuses Gauss and Brouwer whose work underlies all modern existence proofs. (Clower 1995, p. 317; the eight words in the second pair of brackets are Clower's.)

Clower justly objects to how some economists have stretched the concept of equilibrium. Robert Lucas and Thomas Sargent (1978, p. 58) appeared to congratulate themselves on the "dramatic development" that the very meaning of the term "equilibrium" had undergone. Sargent (interviewed in Klamer 1983, pp. 67–68) expressed satisfaction with "fancier" notions of equilibrium, "much more complicated" notions of market-clearing, and "fancy new kinds of equilibrium models." Well, to recommend destabilizing the meaning of words, subverting communication, is the kind of methodologizing that needs to be dragged into the open and inspected. If what economists "with proper sensitivity training" call the "computable dynamic general equilibrium model" really is the real-business cycle model, as Bernard Saffran (1995, p. 231) suggests, then I share contempt for it.

KEEPING SCORN FOCUSED

Some strands of GE do perhaps deserve scorn or neglect. But let us keep our scorn well focused. The problem lies not with the theory's central ideas but with some abuses committed in its name. These include parades of sham rigor and mathematical games that make no contact with reality (cf. Buchanan 1983/1988, Allais 1989). More specifically, they arguably include obsession with the mathematical requirements for existence, uniqueness, and stability of GE to the extent of crowding out attention to economic substance. (On the other hand, let the would-be mathematicians amuse themselves as they like, provided they not deceive other people about the significance of their efforts.) A related abuse is pushing the strongest-link principle, the tacit idea that a theory is as strong not as its weakest but as its logically most rigorous link (cf. Mayer 1993, pp. x, 57–63, 80, 127–130, and passim). Still others are frontiersmanship and other varieties of tacit methodological preaching (cf. chapter 13 below).

The correct response to abuses is to pinpoint them. If we appraise a doctrine or approach or technique by whether or not it might be abused, misinterpreted, distorted, set aside, or taught with unduly narrow and exclusive emphasis, we are putting it to a test that no doctrine can pass.

GE is often charged with being static and being preoccupied with an all-around equilibrium in which all plans mesh and all prices, being at their market-clearing levels, convey exact information. The services of the mysterious auctioneer leave no scope for entrepreneurial activity and other actual market processes. The theory ignores complexity, uncertainty, judgment, creativity, and enterprise.

COMPLEMENTARY STRANDS OF THEORY

In a sense these complaints are correct. Of course formalized equilibrium theory does not teach us everything about economics, and perhaps not even the main ideas. No one known to me claims that it is the whole story. Of course GE leaves room for investigating the processes at work in the real world of disequilibrium. We cannot learn everything at once, but we can learn something from a static view and then go on to dynamics and process. The two strands complement each other; GE affords insights into general interdependence. We can better understand market pressures and processes if we have an idea of the state toward which they are working (if indeed they are equilibrating rather than disequilibrating) and if this state helps us, by contrast, to contemplate *dis*equilibrium, the nonmeshing of plans. Ludwig von Mises recognized the usefulness of the "evenly rotating economy" as an analytical benchmark (1949/1966, pp. 244–250 and passim). We need not suppose that the world ever actually reaches

Chapter 1: Should Austrians Scorn General Equilibrium Theory?

equilibrium; we can remain duly scornful of theories (like a recently fashionable brand of macroeconomics) that treat equilibrium-always as a substantive proposition.

I taught a course in GE at the University of Virginia for several years flanking 1960. The professors who had named the course, years earlier, apparently thought that GE was a fancy name for macroeconomics, but I took the course title at face value. Large doses of Austrian economics, including Mises's and Hayek's insights into socialist calculation, were helpful, I think, in rescuing GE from the sterility of its worst versions. I never saw any necessary tension between GE and Austrian economics.

FURTHER CLAIMS FOR GE

1. GE gives us a view of the economic system as a whole. Analysis of the behavior of individual firms and households has little point unless it fits into understanding the system (cf. Eucken 1954, pp. 220–221). For example, the charge that a monopoly firm's output is too small has little meaning unless it is related to the economywide allocation of resources.

2. Especially when bolstered by contemplation of a centrally administered economy, GE illuminates the complexity of the task performed by entrepreneurs and other agents, guided by the price system. It illuminates the logic of decentralized decisions for the sake of a fuller use of knowledge, with prices communicating signals and incentives.

3. Contemplating the immense task ideally performed by economy-wide coordinating processes underlines the attendant scope for things to go wrong. (Compare medical students' attention to the physiology of a healthy body.) The surprising thing is not so much that coordination sometimes fails as that the processes work at all. Failure is most evident in depression, when people keenly desire to trade with one another (although more through multilateral than bilateral exchanges), yet run into frustration. Alerted to the coordination problem, we can better look for disruptive conditions or events.

4. GE illuminates the real significance of the money prices, costs, and incomes confronting households, firms, and governments. It explains opportunity cost in a way not possible with partial analysis alone. All too commonly, opportunity cost is defined in the context of choices made by a particular decisionmaker: the cost of his chosen course of action is the next-best course that he thereby forgoes. That definition, bringing to mind the considerations and even agonies involved in making decisions,

seems familiar to the layman. This deceptive familiarity trivializes the concept. What requires the economist's expertise and the student's alertness to learning something new is opportunity cost in a deeper sense—the wider social significance of money cost. Misunderstanding still abounds. How often do we hear complaints about desired production and services being curtailed or worthwhile projects shelved out of grubby concern with mere money cost? (Even the epithet "greed" gets tossed around.) What needs repeated explanation is how money costs reflect the subjectively appraised values of the other outputs and activities necessarily forgone if resources are withheld from them for the sake of the particular output or activity in question. What further needs explanation is how money costs and prices transmit information and incentives to decisionmakers. (This is not to say that the information conveyed about opportunity cost is completely accurate; for one thing, real-world prices are not GE prices. However, the market process, including entrepreneurial activity, works to weed out gross inaccuracies.)

Explaining opportunity cost in the nontrivial sense is not easy. Even Irving Fisher (1930/1970, pp. 485–487, 534–541) astonishingly denied that one particular price, the interest rate, measures any genuine opportunity cost. Precisely because the expository task is such a demanding one, it is important to beware of deceptively simple and familiar formulations and examples. This is what a GE framework helps to do. It helps portray the variety and diffusion of sacrifices of alternative goods, intangible or subjective as well as tangible, that the money cost of a particular good measures.

5. The GE framework is a necessary background for special strands of theory. Monetary theory is closely bound up with concepts of general interdependence, since money is the one good traded on all markets. GE helps show how price-level determinacy presupposes a nominal anchor, provided either by a commodity standard (or foreign-exchange standard) or by quantitative regulation of a fiat currency. In the theory of saving, capital, and interest, GE helps us understand conceptual distinctions even between magnitudes that are the same in equilibrium (apart from differences in risk, liquidity, and the like), such as the interest rate on loans, rates of return on capital goods and land, the agio of present over future goods, subjective marginal rates of time preference, and the technological marginal productivity of investment in capital goods. It shows the error of quarreling over supposedly rival partial-equilibrium theories of interest.

6. GE triggers alertness to consequences of particular actions, including ones remote in space and time; it alerts one to the Law of Unintended Consequences (cf. Meade's primary, secondary, and tertiary effects in his 1955, esp. chaps. XIII, XXXI, XXXII).

Here are some examples of repercussions that GE helps illuminate: Why monetary expansion lowers interest rates only transitionally; how monetary expansion affects the price level; why survey results on the supposed interest-insensitivity of investment decisions do not prove that monetary policy is ineffective (cf. Wicksell's cumulative process). GE helps us understand how the strength of some relation about which we have inadequate direct empirical evidence may be judged indirectly by empirical evidence on something else that is related to the first, even if not in an obvious way. One example involves import and export supply and demand elasticities and purchasing-power parity.

AVOIDING FALLACIES

My next three claims, numbers 7, 8 and 9, are interrelated and, unfortunately, lengthy. They concern avoiding fallacies.

7. GE analysis helps clarify the distinction between data and variables of the economic system. (More exactly, the distinction pertains not so much to objectively existing reality itself as to analysis of a particular aspect of it, or to a particular strand of analysis. For example, population may count among the givens in a particular strand of analysis yet count among the variables to be explained in another strand.) GE emphasizes, in particular, the distinction between variables that get determined, on the one hand, and "wants, resources, and technology," on the other hand. ("WR&T" also includes social and legal organizations and their rules; cf. Eucken 1950, pp. 81, 202–203, and Vining 1984.) GE shows the error of asking about the effects of a change in a particular magnitude when that magnitude is a determined variable and not a given. It is a mistake, for example, to ask how a change in the interest rate will affect investment or total spending. The question should be rephrased to ask about further consequences of whatever change in the data underlies the interest-rate change (e.g., a change in the productivity of investment, in thrift, or in monetary policy). The error is similar to that of asking about the consequences of a change in the price of wheat whose cause goes unspecified. Nowadays, similarly, we have been hearing much ignorant chatter about the consequences of a deficit in foreign trade or on current account.

Of course, individual-experiments can be legitimate if performed in the proper context. What is a dependent variable for the economy as a whole may be an independent variable or datum for individual units and aggregates of them. Something that is not a datum for the economy as a whole may legitimately be taken as a datum in an individual-experiment (Patinkin 1965 develops the distinction between individual- and market-experiments). But it is important to keep the distinction clear. (Some examples of making the distinction would involve demand schedule and quantity demanded; Friedman's "Marshallian" demand curve, supposedly purified of the income effect; the demand for money; and relations between investment and income.)

It can be legitimate to ask about the consequences for the economy as a whole of a variable's accidentally departing from or arbitrarily being set away from its GE value (even though some theorists, e.g., Archibald and Lipsey 1958 and, more recently, the New Classical macroeconomists, have been mistakenly unwilling to consider disequilibrium). We might suppose such a departure to test for stability of equilibrium, to show inconsistency of plans in a disequilibrium situation, or to show forces at work and reasons why such a disequilibrium could not last. But the theorist must know what he is doing. Although it can be legitimate to postulate a specified kind of departure from equilibrium for a particular analytical purpose, the theorist must not imagine a freedom to postulate just any old change in a variable so as to trace out the consequences for a supposed different equilibrium. As for postulating a price floor or ceiling or a change in the money-supply behavior of the authorities, that can be regarded as a change in one of what are regarded as ultimate data of the system. (Implicitly I am referring to Buchanan 1958 and Eucken 1950, pp. 218–219.)

8. GE shows the error of imagining one-way causation of economic variables when mutual determination is at work. It is a mistake to ask whether price depends on cost or on marginal utility, whether the interest rate depends on the marginal productivity of capital goods or of investment or on a subjective discount of future relative to present goods, and whether the wage rate depends on the marginal value product of labor or on labor's marginal disutility or on the marginal utility of alternative activities forgone to engage in labor.

Avoiding false presuppositions about causality helps give insight into the *identification problem* of econometrics. For example, does a pattern of relations between various prices and quantities of some product reflect a demand function, a supply function, a confused mixture of their properties, or what? We must ask what differences in wants, resources, and technology underlie the different price-and-quantity points. Further such examples concern relations between a country's balance of payments and exchange rate, monetary policy and free reserves, and the interest rate and monetary policy or investment or thrift. Did a change in the interest rate come from the demand-for-credit side or the supply-of-credit side, perhaps as influenced by monetary policy?

Recognizing mutual determination does not preclude a causal-genetic tracing out of response to a particular change in the situation. Compare tracing out the consequences of adding a new ball to Marshall's bowl or a new piece to a Calder mobile.

9. GE helps avoid many specific fallacies sometimes abetted by the partial-equilibrium approach. Some examples follow.

(a) The above-mentioned fallacy about interest-sensitivity and monetary policy.

(b) The purchasing-power argument for artificially boosting particular wage rates (or product prices). This ancient argument illegitimately generalizes from a particular firm or industry. If—if—the conditions for an inelastic derived demand for its labor are satisfied, then a wage-rate increase will indeed increase the purchasing power of the firm's or industry's employees. But what happens to other factor shares? Furthermore, widespread wage increases lead into questions of monetary theory, which cannot be handled by partial analysis alone.

(c) The pro-efficiency "shock" effect supposedly achieved by boosting wage rates through union or government action. Insofar as the greater efficiency is achieved by greater capital investment, either less capital formation is possible elsewhere or else the "shock" somehow promotes saving, in which case the argument ought to explain how.

(d) The economies-of-scale case for advertising or consumer trading stamps. Expanded scale in some operations means shrunken scale in others, unless underemployment of resources prevailed and is somehow remedied by the advertising. What reason is there to suppose that advertising promotes the goods that particularly have economies of scale? Anyway, the argument ought to face up to this general-equilibrium question. If the argument depends on standardization, that ought to be made explicit.

(e) The decreasing-cost/marginal-cost-pricing/consumer-surplus argument for subsidizing a particular industry or running it at a loss. Also to be considered are the conditions in industries from which resources are diverted, as well as the consequences of raising revenue for the subsidies.

(f) Similarly, external-economy (including infant-industry) arguments for protection or subsidies for particular industries, or arguments for government finance of particular industries on the grounds that the government can borrow more cheaply than private enterprise, or arguments for credit allocation toward such industries. As GE teaches us, it is not enough to consider one industry or one aspect at a time.

(g) The idea that government loan guarantees can promote (or rescue) desirable projects or activities at little or no cost to the taxpayers. The argument forgets that "capital"—or whatever we may call the resource whose price is the interest rate and that is further rationed by the decisions of loan officers and bond buyers—is a scarce resource whose diversion to some uses necessarily withholds it from other and possibly more highly desired uses.

(h) Capital-import-and-export arguments for trade interventions. In a developing country, protecting a particular industry will perhaps have a "tariff-factory" effect; but will protection in general promote capital import in general? Agreed, admitting a particular product duty-free may encourage home firms to export capital to produce that good abroad, but it does not follow that removal of protection in general will promote overall capital export.

(i) The fallacious argument for tariffs to the effect that our government collects taxes on incomes generated by domestic production of import-competing goods but not on incomes generated by producing imported goods abroad.

(j) The real-bills doctrine about the absence of inflationary effect of money and credit created to finance productive activities, a fallacy that keeps getting independently reinvented in slightly different versions by incompetent amateur monetary theorists.

(k) Merely superficial attention to secondary or "collateral" effects of a particular activity, such as supposed benefits to local business of a new highway or sports stadium, ignoring the diversion of resources from other places or activities.

(l) A catchall category: other instances of the fallacy of composition and of policy arguments that unduly restrict attention to close and short-run effects to the relative neglect of more remote and long-run effects. GE promotes awareness that the wisdom of a particular measure cannot be judged solely by the intentions of those who recommend it. (This is one of the main themes of Eucken 1952, cf. Frédéric Bastiat on "what is seen and what is not seen.")

EQUATION SYSTEMS

Fully supporting my many claims for GE would require a whole college course. Readers might well contemplate, however, one or more of the systems available in the literature that portray the economy as a whole in many equations and variables. Pondering such a system, purporting to describe what an economy would look like in a state of full coordination, helps one grasp the central fact of general interdependence. It helps one see how greater production of some goods and services requires lesser production of others and how, ultimately and subjectively, greater satisfaction of some desires costs lesser satisfaction of others. It helps one grasp the immensity of the coordination task that the price system works toward performing, although never completely and perfectly.

I doubt that anyone can fully appreciate GE without working his way through one or more such equation systems. While Gustav Cassel deserves criticism for presenting his simplification of Walras's system (1932/1967, chap. IV) without giving credit to Léon Walras, his system nevertheless has pedagogic merit. It envisages n goods and services. The quantity per time period demanded of each is a function of all n prices and is equal to the quantity supplied. Supply functions are represented by the conditions that the price of each good is equal to its cost of production, which in turn is equal to the sum of the prices times quantities of the factors of production required to produce one unit of the good. These technical requirements and the equilibrium quantities of goods permit calculating the total quantity demanded of each of the r factors, which in equilibrium is equal to the quantity available. Cassel shows just enough equations to determine the quantities of the various goods produced, their prices, and the prices of the factors of production.

In this first pass at a simplified equation system, Cassel assumes that the "technical coefficients" (the quantities of each factor required for the production of one unit of each good) are fixed parameters, as is the total quantity available of each factor. The total money expenditure of consumers on the purchase of final goods is also fixed. These simplifying assumptions can be relaxed, however, in ways represented by increasing the number of unknown prices and quantities to be determined, and increasing the number of equilibrium equations also, so that the system remains determinate.

Cassel justifiably claims that his

> equations reveal the true nature of pricing, and the pricing process cannot be accurately presented in any simpler form. The demand for a product represents an attempt to attract certain factors of production to a particular use. Conflicting with this attempt are similar attempts in the form of demands for other products. There arises in this way a struggle for the relatively scarce factors of production, which is decided in the exchange economy by placing uniform prices on the factors, which prices in turn determine the prices of the products and thus form a means of effecting the necessary restriction of demand. The demand for a particular factor of production arising from the continuous demand for each particular product is totalled for each unit period, to form a total demand for that factor of production, ... which must, in a state of equilibrium, equal the given quantity of the factor of production. (1932/1967, p. 145)

In this passage and in the equation system it describes, Cassel thus provides a deep insight into the nature of cost, opportunity cost. He goes on to point out how his system portrays the interplay of both subjective and objective factors in price determination. As he says,

> All these factors are essential in determining prices. An "objective" or "subjective" theory of value, in the sense of a theory that would attribute the settlement of prices to objective or subjective factors alone, is therefore absurd; and the whole of the controversy between these theories of value, which has occupied such a disproportionately large place in economic literature, is a pure waste of energy. (p. 146)

E.H. Phelps Brown presents a general-equilibrium equation system simple enough to be solved numerically, as it was even when Brown first published it in 1936, in the days before computers and even before electronic pocket calculators (though not before mechanical desk calculators). Nowadays, when computers and calculators remove so much grunt work, the value of exercises like Brown's has increased. Much may be said for working one's way not only through simplified systems but also through Walras's *Elements* itself, that landmark in the history of economic thought.

It is easy to say that the points illuminated by GE are "obvious" and that its pretentious equations are unnecessary. Conceivably so. But are

Chapter 1: Should Austrians Scorn General Equilibrium Theory? 15

its critics quite sure that their acquaintance with GE does not help make those points seem obvious? Would they have grasped their full significance even without contemplating the equation systems?

Only rather simple mathematics is required for reaping the benefits claimed for GE. (Understanding work like Gerard Debreu's is another matter.) This brings up a related point. Quite a few Austrians maintain that mathematics is out of place in economics. But how can they be confident? Their not seeing how to do anything useful with it is no reason to suppose that no one else can use it any better. People with different personal abilities, backgrounds, and tastes legitimately pursue different research topics and employ different methods and styles of exposition. An approach lacking appeal to oneself may convey valuable insights to other persons. It is paradoxical for Austrians, especially those who like to expatiate on subjectivity and ineffability and the unpredictability of the future, to predict the usefulness of particular methods and to try practically to legislate on such matters.

Alain Enthoven, then applying economics in the Defense Department, testified to how overlearning or overstudy, as one might call it, can help clinch one's grasp of economic reality. The analytical tools that he and his colleagues used

> are the simplest, most fundamental concepts of economic theory, combined with the simplest quantitative methods. The requirements for success in this line of work are a thorough understanding of and, if you like, belief in the relevance of such concepts as marginal products and marginal costs, and an ability to discover the marginal products and costs in complex situations, combined with a good quantitative sense. The advanced mathematical techniques of econometrics and operations research have not proved to be particularly useful in dealing with the problems I have described. Although a good grasp of this kind of mathematics is very valuable as intellectual formation, we are not applying linear programming, formal game theory, queuing theory, multiple regression theory, nonlinear programming under uncertainty, or anything like it. The economic theory we are using is the theory most of us learned as sophomores. The reason Ph.D.'s are required is that many economists do not believe what they have learned until they have gone through graduate school and acquired a vested interest in marginal analysis. (Enthoven 1963, p. 422)

Partial-equilibrium, process-oriented, and GE approaches are not necessarily rivals. Admittedly, only partial-equilibrium theory is "operational" in the Chicago sense of yielding fairly specific predictions, as of the consequences of a change in an excise tax. And even this admission goes too far; GE is not totally without operational application. Still, its main service is as a conceptual framework accommodating the more readily applicable strands of partial analysis.

True, the Walrasian system is formal. It is absurd to envisage solving a Walrasian system for numerical parameters of reality (*pace* Wassily Leontief's aspirations for his input-output system). "Walras' system was once correctly described as resembling a palace of no relevance to the housing problem" (Eucken 1950, p. 27).

CONCLUDING EXHORTATION

GE is a major strand of, approach to, and integrating factor of the whole body of economic theory. A single correct body of theory is what all creative economists presumably strive for, even though probably no one ever will achieve it complete and error-free. Reality is consistent with itself, and so must the correct theory of it be. To say so is not to deny the value of different schools with their own favorite topics, approaches, research methods, and styles of exposition. A researcher can gain encouragement and stimulus from knowing that he has colleagues out there who are ready to read him sympathetically. They accord him a presumption—defeasible of course—that he is right. Thus, there is legitimate scope for the Austrian School, as for others.

But the Austrians should think of themselves as making their own distinctive contributions, critical as well as positive, to an emerging single correct body of theory. Their objective should not be to differentiate themselves from the mainstream in a hostile manner but rather to contribute to the mainstream and help steer it in the right direction. Correct economic theory does not come in distinct and incompatible brands, one for Austrians, one for Marxians, one for conservatives in the style of William F. Buckley and Russell Kirk, one for libertarians, one for left-liberals, and so forth. To suppose that it does is what Ludwig von Mises (1949/1966, chap. III) eloquently condemned as "polylogism."

REFERENCES

Allais, Maurice. Remarks at McGill University, Montreal. Reported in *IMF Survey* (June 1989): 185.

Chapter 1: Should Austrians Scorn General Equilibrium Theory?

Archibald, G.C., and R.G. Lipsey. "Monetary and Value Theory: A Critique of Lange and Patinkin." *Review of Economic Studies* 26 (1958): 9–17.

Arrow, Kenneth J., and Frank H. Hahn. *General Competitive Analysis*. San Francisco: Holden-Day, 1971.

Boettke, Peter J., and David L. Prychitko. "Introduction: Varieties of Market Process Theory." In *Market Process Theories*, edited by Boettke and Prychitko, vol. 1: ix–xxvii. Cheltenham, U.K., and Northampton, Mass.: Elgar, 1998.

Brown, E.H. Phelps. *The Framework of the Pricing System*. 1936. Lawrence: University of Kansas, Student Union Book Store, 1949.

Buchanan, James M. "*Ceteris Paribus*: Some Notes on Methodology." *Southern Economic Journal* 24 (1958): 259–270.

———. "Political Economy: 1957–1982." Lecture of 20 April 1983. In *Ideas, Their Origins, and Their Consequences*, edited by Thomas Jefferson Center Foundation, 119–130. Washington, D.C.: American Enterprise Institute, 1988.

Cassel, Gustav. *The Theory of Social Economy*. 1932. Translated by S.L. Barron. New York: Kelley, 1967.

Clower, Robert. "Reflections on the Keynesian Perplex." 1975. In *Money and Markets*, edited by Donald A. Walker, chap. 14. New York: Cambridge University Press, 1986.

———. "Axiomatics in Economics." *Southern Economic Journal* 62 (1995): 307–319.

Debreu, Gerard. *Theory of Value*. New York: Wiley, 1959.

Enthoven, Alain C. "Economic Analysis in the Department of Defense." *American Economic Review* 53 (May 1963): 413–423.

Eucken, Walter. *The Foundations of Economics*. Translated by T.W. Hutchison. London: Hodge, 1950.

———. *Grundsätze der Wirtschaftspolitik*. Tübingen: Mohr, 1952.

———. *Kapitaltheoretische Untersuchungen*. 2nd ed. Tübingen: Mohr, 1954.

Fisher, Irving. *The Theory of Interest*. 1930. New York: Kelley, 1970.

High, Jack. "The Austrian Theory of Price." In *The Elgar Companion to Austrian Economics*, edited by Peter J. Boettke, 151–155. Aldershot, U.K., and Brookfield, Vt.: Elgar, 1994.

Huerta de Soto, Jesús. *Socialismo, Cálculo Económico y Función Empresarial.* Madrid: Unión Editorial, 1992.

Klamer, Arjo. *Conversations with Economists.* Totowa, N.J.: Rowman & Allanheld, 1983.

Kuenne, Robert E. *The Theory of General Economic Equilibrium.* Princeton, N.J.: Princeton University Press, 1963.

———. *Microeconomic Theory of the Market Mechanism: A General Equilibrium Approach.* New York: Macmillan, 1968.

Lucas, Robert E., Jr., and Thomas J. Sargent. "After Keynesian Macroeconomics." In *After the Phillips Curve: Persistence of High Inflation and High Unemployment,* 49–72. Boston: Federal Reserve Bank of Boston, 1978.

Mayer, Thomas. *Truth versus Precision in Economics.* Aldershot, U.K., and Brookfield, Vt.: Elgar, 1993.

Meade, James E. *Trade and Welfare.* London: Oxford University Press, 1955.

Mises, Ludwig von. *Human Action.* 1949. 3rd rev. ed. San Francisco: Fox & Wilkes, 1966.

Patinkin, Don. *Money, Interest, and Prices.* 2nd ed. New York: Harper & Row, 1965.

Saffran, Bernard. "Recommendations for Further Reading." *Journal of Economic Perspectives* 9 (Fall 1995): 227–234.

Salerno, Joseph T. "Reply to Leland B. Yeager." *Review of Austrian Economics* 7, no. 2 (1994): 111–125.

Vining, Rutledge. *On Appraising the Performance of an Economic System.* New York: Cambridge University Press, 1984.

Walras, Léon. *Elements of Pure Economics.* Translated by William Jaffé. Homewood, Ill.: Irwin, 1954.

Yeager, Leland B. "Tacit Preachments are the Worst Kind." *Journal of Economic Methodology* 2 (1995): 1–33. Reprinted here as chapter 13.

CHAPTER 2

Why Subjectivism?*

INSIGHTS AND EXAGGERATIONS

Economists of the Austrian School emphasize subjectivism. This article reviews why subjectivist insights are important, but it also warns against exaggerations. The latter part, while briefer, particularly warrants attention in Austrian circles.

Various writers define subjectivism in ways that, though not necessarily inconsistent, do seem quite different. Empirical concepts (as opposed to mathematical concepts, like "triangle") necessarily have an "open texture" (Waismann 1965). An open-textured concept just cannot be defined so precisely and comprehensively as to rule out the possibility of an unforeseen situation or case or example that would require modifying the earlier definition. I feel no duty, then, to start with a definition. Instead, the meaning of subjectivism will emerge from the topics covered and from contrasts with nonsubjectivist attitudes.

MATERIALISM VERSUS SUBJECTIVISM IN POLICY

Subjectivist insights contribute to positive economics—to understanding how the world works (or would work with circumstances changed in specified ways). They do not bear primarily on policy. As an expository device, however, it is convenient to begin by considering subjectivism applied—or ignored—in policymaking.

Perhaps the broadest subjectivist insight is that economics deals with human choices and actions, not with mechanistically dependable relations. The economy is no machine whose "structure" can be ascertained and manipulated with warranted confidence. Economics knows nothing comparable to Avogadro's number, atomic weights and numbers, the speed of light in a vacuum, and similar constants of nature (Mises 1949/1963,

---

*From *Review of Austrian Economics* 1, no. 1 (1987): 5–31.

p. 55). Or if such constants do exist, an economist could earn a great reputation by demonstrating a few of them. No amount of cleverness with econometrics can make the nonexistent exist after all.

One reason why no enduring "structural parameters" characterize the economic system is that how people behave in markets, as in other aspects of life, depends on their experiences and expectations and on what doctrines they have come to believe. (Here is one area of overlap between Austrian economics and the rational-expectations school.) These circumstances are inherently changeable. One implication warns against policies whose success presupposes unrealistic kinds or degrees of knowledge. It warns against overambition in attempting detailed central control.

Subjectivist economics points out, for example, what is lost when policy makes simplistic distinctions between necessities and luxuries or when, unlike voluntary transactions, policy fails to take account of subtle differences between the circumstances and tastes of different people. (I leave personal rights aside not because they are unimportant but because the present topic is rather different.)

Examples abound, in Third World countries and elsewhere, of attempts to conserve scarce foreign-exchange earnings for "essentials" by exchange controls, multiple exchange rates, import quotas, and selective import duties designed to limit or penalize the waste of foreign exchange on "luxury" or "nonessential" imports.

The arguments offered for such controls, like arguments for consumer rationing in wartime, are not always sheer nonsense. But subjectivist considerations severely qualify them. It is impossible to make and implement a clear distinction between luxuries and essentials. Suppose that a government tightly rations foreign exchange for pleasure cruises and travel abroad but classifies oil as an essential import. Some of the oil may go for heating at domestic resorts operating on a larger scale than if the cruises had not been restricted. The restrictions may in effect divert factors of production from other activities into providing recreation otherwise obtainable at lower cost through foreign travel. Because of poor climate at home, it may well be that the marginal units of foreign exchange spent on imported oil go to satisfy wants of the same general sort—while satisfying them less effectively—as wants otherwise satisfied by foreign travel. Restricting travel and supposedly nonessential imports is likely to promote imports of their substitutes and also divert domestic and imported resources or materials into home production of substitutes. The diversions may also impede exports that earn foreign exchange.

It is particularly dubious to try to distinguish between essential and frivolous imports according to whether they serve production (or "economic growth") or mere consumption. All production supposedly aims at satisfying human wants, immediately or ultimately. Producing machinery or building factories is no more inherently worthy than producing restaurant meals or nightclub entertainment, for the machinery or factories are pointless unless they can sooner or later yield goods or services that do satisfy human wants. To favor production-oriented (or export-oriented) imports over consumption-oriented imports is to prefer a roundabout achievement of ultimate consumer satisfactions to their more direct achievement merely because of the greater roundaboutness. It is to confuse ends and means.

People obtain their satisfactions in highly diverse ways (even altruistic ways). Some policymakers evidently do not understand how the price system brings into play the dispersed knowledge that people have about their own tastes and circumstances. A journalist illustrated such misunderstanding when badgering Alan Greenspan, then Chairman of the Council of Economic Advisers, with questions about whether business firms would continue producing essential goods when frivolous goods happened to be more profitable. As Greenspan properly replied (in Mitchell 1974, pp. 74–76), people differ widely in their tastes. Some choose to buy extraordinary things and deliberately deprive themselves of other things generally counted as necessities.

One might conceivably—though not conclusively—urge controls as correctives for specific market distortions. Barring such identified distortions, subjectivist economists would let ultimate consumers appraise "essentiality." Sweeping philosophical comparisons are unnecessary. People can act on their own comparisons of the satisfactions they expect from an additional dollar's worth of this and that. Consumers and businessmen can judge and act on the intensities of the wants that various goods can satisfy, either directly or by contributing to further processes of production.

Standard theoretical reservations about this suggestion—arguments for government discriminations in favor of some and against other particular goods and services—invoke the concepts of externalities, of merit wants and merit goods, and of income redistribution. Yet how can policymakers be confident that supposed externalities are genuine and important, that supposed merit wants really deserve cultivation, or that discriminating among goods will accomplish the desired redistribution of real income? Any one of many goods, considered by itself, might seem deserving of special favor; yet how *relatively* deserving different goods are may remain highly uncertain, particularly when no one knows just how severely the diversion of resources into particular lines of production will impair production in other lines that might even be more meritorious by the policymaker's criteria. (Tunnel vision is a failing of policymakers not thoroughly familiar with the idea of general economic interdependence.)

More fundamentally, particular goods do not possess qualities deserving special consideration globally, or by their very nature. On the contrary, usefulness or desirability is a relation between things and human wants. The usefulness of something—specifically, its marginal utility—is the smaller the more abundant the thing is. Ideally, decisions about adjusting quantities of various things should consider their usefulness *at the margin*. It is easy to imagine circumstances in which an additional dollar's worth or an additional ounce of penicillin or polio vaccine would contribute less to human satisfaction than an additional unit of orchids.

The concept of priorities does not properly apply in the contexts considered here. For the reasons mentioned, and also in view of how the political process works and of ample experience with controls, it is unrealistic to expect the government to choose "social priorities" reasonably. Consider, for example, the botch of energy policy, including the long record of subsidizing energy consumption in travel and transport (through the underpricing of road and airport facilities) and also including tax exemptions and subsidized loans granted to rural electric cooperatives, even while government officials plead for energy conservation.

Policies adopted or advocated during the energy crises of 1974 and 1979 betray ignorance of subjectivist insights. Examples are rationing of gasoline not so much by price as by the inconvenience and apprehension of having to hunt around for it and wait in long lines to buy it, or being allowed to buy gasoline only on odd- or even-numbered days according to one's license-plate number. A former chairman of Inland Steel Company (Joseph L. Block in Committee for Economic Development 1974, pp. 79–80) suggested requiring each car owner to choose one day of the week when he would be forbidden to drive. That prohibition, enforced with appropriate stickers, would supposedly have eliminated some needless driving and encouraged use of public transportation. Another example was a decision by the California Public Utilities Commission banning natural-gas heating of new swimming pools (Charlottesville *Daily Progress*, 29 February 1976, p. E11).

Such measures and proposals underrate the value of freedom and flexibility. Arbitrary measures burden some people lightly and others heavily because different people's lives afford different scopes of substituting away from the restricted consumption and make advance scheduling of activities difficult and unrestricted flexibility important in widely differing degrees. In unrestricted voluntary transactions, by contrast, people can allow for such differences.

A narrowly technological outlook is often linked with puritanical moralizing. (I remember my maternal grandmother, who used to bewail the waste of using a teabag only once if it could be made to serve twice and of using and washing a large plate if the food could be crammed onto a small plate.) Recovery techniques left too much oil and gas in the ground, natural gas on the continental shelf was flared, and the prevailing practice in coal mining left half of a seam in the ground merely because it was needed there as a supporting column or because getting it all out was too expensive—so went one complaint (Freeman 1974, pp. 230–232). Energy has been wasted by "too little" insulation of buildings.

Yet so-called waste was probably sensible at the lower energy prices of the past. There can be such a thing as too much conservation; for example, producing aluminum for storm windows installed under tax incentives even consumes energy in other directions. Ample heat and air conditioning brought comfort, and fast driving saved valuable time. Not having to concentrate on ferreting out ways to conserve energy saved mental capacity for other purposes. Now, at today's higher prices, a dollar spent on energy no longer buys as much comfort or saves as much time or thought as before; and people respond accordingly. Conceivably, of course, the energy prices of the past, distorted downward by interventions, may have led people to consume more energy than they would have done at free-market prices; but if so, the specific distortions should have been identified and addressed. Moralizing about ways of consuming less was off the track.

Such moralizing almost regards waste as something perpetrated only with material resources, not with people's time or comfort or peace of mind. Ironically, this strand of materialism sometimes occurs among people who announce Galbraithian scorn for the alleged materialism of the affluent society. Another apparent strand sometimes found in the attitude of such people is self-congratulation on heroic hard-headedness in recognizing necessary austerities. (Speaking at a conference in Beverly Hills on 26 April 1975, Senator Gaylord Nelson welcomed the challenge of helping to create the new and simpler lifestyles of the future.)

Materialistic energy-conservation proposals illustrate a kind of thinking related to what F.A. Hayek (1952) has called *scientism*. It is something quite different from science or the scientific outlook. One aspect of scientism is the feeling that results somehow do not count unless they have been deliberately arranged for. A person with the scientistic attitude does not understand how millions of persons and companies, trading freely among themselves, can express and arrange for satisfying the wants they themselves consider most intense. He does not appreciate self-adjusting processes, like someone's decision to forgo a gas-heated swimming pool, or any pool at all, in view of the prices to be paid. He assumes that a grandmotherly state must take charge, and he performs feats of routine originality in thinking of new ways for it to do so—as by requiring that cars get 30 miles to the gallon, by imposing standards for building insulation, or by banning pilot lights in gas appliances. Tax gimmicks and ideas are a dime a dozen—incentives for storm windows and solar heating and the plowback of profits into oilfield development and what not. The current, or recent, vogue for partial national economic planning under the name of "industrial policy" provides further examples.

Subjectivist insights illuminate the issue of the military draft. (For early discussions by University of Virginia Ph.D. graduates and graduate students, see Miller 1968.) Many persons have advocated the draft on the grounds that an all-volunteer force is too costly. They understand cost in an excessively materialistic and accounting-oriented way. In truth, costs are subjective—unpleasantnesses incurred and satisfactions forgone. In keeping down monetary outlays, the draft conceals part of the costs and shifts it from the taxpayers being defended to the draftees compelled to serve at wages inadequate to obtain their voluntary service. Furthermore, the draft increases total costs through inefficiency. It imposes unnecessarily large costs on draftees who find military life particularly unpleasant or whose foreclosed civilian pursuits are particularly rewarding to themselves and others. At the same time it wastes opportunities to obtain relatively low-cost service from men who happen to escape the draft but would have been willing to serve at wages below those necessary to obtain voluntary service from men in fact drafted. The opposite method—recruiting the desired number of service men and women by offering wages adequate to attract them as volunteers—brings to bear the knowledge that people themselves have of their own abilities, inclinations, and alternative opportunities. So doing, the market-oriented method holds down the true, subjectively assessed, costs of staffing the armed forces. (Of course, considerations in addition to these also figure in arguments over the military draft.)

Subjectivist insights help one understand why compensation at actual market value for property seized under eminent domain probably will not leave the former owner as well off as he had been. His having continued to hold the property instead of having already sold it suggests that he valued it more highly than the sales proceeds or other property purchasable with those proceeds.

Neglect of subjectivism is central to the fallacy of "comparable worth." According to that doctrine, fashionable among feminists and interventionists, the worth of work performed in different jobs can be objectively ascertained and compared. People performing different jobs that are nevertheless judged alike, on balance, in their arduousness or pleasantness, their requirements in ability and training, the degrees of responsibility involved, and other supposedly ascertainable characteristics should receive the same pay; and government, presumably, should enforce equal pay. Formulas should replace wage-setting by voluntary agreements reached under the influences of supply and demand.

This idea ducks the questions of how to ration jobs sought especially eagerly at their formula-determined wages and how to prod people into jobs that would otherwise go unfilled at such wages. It ducks the questions of what kind of economic system and what kind of society would take the place of the free-market system, with its processes of coordinating decentralized voluntary activities. (Though writing before comparable worth became a prominent issue, Hayek 1960, chap. 6, aptly warned against displacing market processes by nonmarket assessments of entitlements to incomes.) The comparable-worth doctrine neglects the ineffable individual circumstances and subjective feelings that enter into workers' decisions to seek or avoid particular jobs, employers' efforts to fill them, and consumers' demands for the goods and services produced in them. Yet wages and prices set through market processes do take account of individual circumstances and personal feelings (a point I'll say more about later on).

Subjectivist economists recognize the importance of intangible assets, including knowledge, a kind of "human capital." They recognize the scope for ingenuity in getting around government controls of various kinds, whereas the layman's tacit case for controls involves a mechanistic conception of the reality to be manipulated, without due appreciation of human flexibility. Controls, and responses to them, destroy human capital by artificially hastening the obsolescence of knowledge; they impose the costs of keeping abreast of the artificially changing scene and divert material and intellectual resources, including inventiveness, from productive employments. Credit-allocation measures and other controls on financial institutions, for example—even reserve requirements and interest-rate ceilings—have bred innovations to circumvent them. Managers have to be trained and other start-up costs borne for new institutions and practices, and customers must spend time and trouble learning about them. Price and wage controls and energy-conservation rules provide further illustrations of such wastes.

Arbitrariness and unfairness figure among the costs of controls intended to buck market forces. As controls become more comprehensive and complex, their administrators are less able to base their decisions on relatively objective criteria. Bureaucratic rules become more necessary and decisions based on incomplete information less avoidable. Multiplication of categories entitled to special treatment invites the pleading of special interests. Even morality, another intangible asset, is eroded.

The complexity of detailed monitoring and enforcement suggests appealing for voluntary compliance, compliance with the spirit and not just the letter of the regulations. (Controls over foreign trade and payments for balance-of-payments purposes, such as President Johnson attempted in the mid-1960s, provide still further examples; see Yeager 1965.) Whether compliance is avowedly voluntary, or whether ease of evasion makes compliance voluntary in effect, such an approach tends to penalize public-spirited citizens who do comply and gives the advantage to others. Exhorting people to act against their own economic interest tends to undercut the signaling and motivating functions of prices. How are people to know, then, when it is proper and when improper to pursue economic gain? To exhort people to think of compliance as in their own interest when it plainly is not, or to call for self-sacrifice as if it were the essence of morality, is to undercut the rational basis of morality and even undercut rationality itself.

A kind of perverse selection results. Public-spirited car owners who heed appeals for restraint in driving thereby leave more gasoline available, and at a lower price than otherwise, to less public-spirited drivers. Sellers who do comply with price ceilings or guidelines must consequently turn away some customers unsatisfied, to the profit of black-marketeers and other less scrupulous sellers. Eventually such effects become evident, strengthening the idea that morality is for suckers and dupes.

Subjectivists know better than to erect efficiency, somehow conceived, into the overriding criterion either of particular processes or institutions or of entire economic systems. The principle of comparative advantage discredits the idea that each product should necessarily be produced wherever it can be produced most efficiently in the technological sense. No presumption holds, furthermore, that any particular line of production necessarily should be carried on in the technologically most advanced way; for the resources required in such production are demanded by other industries also, where they may well contribute more at the margin to consumer satisfactions, as judged by what consumers are willing to pay.

Efficiency in the sense of Pareto optimality is often taken as a criterion of policy. Pareto efficiency is indeed a useful concept in teaching and studying microeconomic theory. It is useful in contemplating outcomes of the market process in the form of particular—but abstractly conceived—allocations of resources and goods. Economists seldom if ever face an occasion or opportunity to appraise concrete, specific allocations, in the real world. As Rutledge Vining properly emphasizes, legislators and their expert advisors necessarily are choosing among alternative sets of legal and institutional constraints rather than among alternative specific results or allocations. (See Vining 1985 and Yeager 1978.) Such constraints are rules of the game within which people strive to make the most of their opportunities amidst ceaseless change in wants, resources, and technology. The very point of having rules and institutions presupposes their having a certain stability and dependability, which would be undermined by continual efforts to make supposedly optimal changes in them.

What is useful in policy discussions, then, is not the supposed benchmark of Pareto efficiency but, rather, comparison of the economic and social systems that alternative sets of rules lead to. If we must have a standard against which to appraise reality, we might well adopt the view of a competitive market economy as a collection of institutions and practices for gathering and transmitting information and incentives concerning not-yet-exhausted opportunities for gains from trade (including "trade with nature" through production or rearrangements of production).

KNOWLEDGE AND COORDINATION

Subjectivists recognize the many kinds of information that market prices and processes bring to bear on decisions about production and consumption.

These kinds include what F.A. Hayek (1945) called "knowledge of the particular circumstances of time and place," knowledge that could hardly be codified in textbooks or assembled for the use of central planners, knowledge that can be used, if at all, only by numerous individual "men on the spot." It includes knowledge about all sorts of details of running business firms, including knowledge of fleeting local conditions. It includes what people know about their own tastes and particular circumstances as consumers, workers, savers, and investors. Subjectivist economists recognize how such factors not only underlie the prices that consumers are prepared to pay for goods but also underlie costs of production.

Each consumer decides how much of each particular good to buy in view of the price of the good itself, the prices of other goods, his income and wealth, and his own needs and preferences. Subject to qualifications about how possible and how worthwhile precise calculation seems, he leaves no opportunity unexploited to increase his total satisfaction by diverting a dollar from one purchase to another. Under competition, the price of each good tends to express the total of the prices of the additional inputs necessary to supply an additional unit of that good. These resource prices tend, in turn, to measure the values of other marginal outputs sacrificed by diversion of resources away from their production. Prices therefore tell the consumer how much worth of other production must be forgone to supply him with each particular good. The money values of forgone alternative production tend, in turn, to reflect consumer satisfactions expectedly obtainable from that forgone production. (I say "reflect"—take account of—in order not to claim anything about actual measurement of what is inherently unmeasurable. I speak only of tendencies, furthermore, for markets never fully reach competitive general equilibrium.)

With prices bringing to their attention the terms of choice posed by the objective realities of production possibilities and the subjective realities of other persons' preferences, consumers choose the patterns of production and resource use that they prefer. Their bidding tends to keep any unit of a resource from going to meet a less intense willingness to pay for its productive contribution (and thus the denial of a more intense willingness). Ideally—in competitive equilibrium, and subject to qualifications still to be mentioned—no opportunity remains unexploited to increase the total value of things produced by transferring a unit of any resource from one use to another. Changes in technology and consumer preferences always keep creating such opportunities afresh, but the profit motive keeps prodding businessmen to ferret them out and exploit them.

To determine how resources go into producing what things in what quantities, consumers need freedom to spend their incomes as they wish, unregimented by actual rationing. But they need more: opportunities to make choices at unrigged prices tending to reflect true production alternatives.

We could speak then of "consumers' sovereignty," but the term is a bit narrow. Insofar as their abilities permit, people can bring their preferences among occupations as well as among consumer goods to bear on the pattern of production. In fact, investors' preferences, including notions about the morality and the glamor of different industries and companies, also have some influence; and we might speak of "investors' sovereignty" as well. (See Rothbard 1962, p. 452 n. 12, and pp. 560–562 on what Rothbard calls "individual sovereignty.")

Suppose that many people craved being actors strongly enough to accept wages below those paid in other jobs requiring similar levels of ability and training. This willingness would help keep down the cost of producing plays, and cheap tickets would draw audiences, maintaining jobs in the theater. Suppose, in contrast, that almost everyone hated mining coal. The high wages needed to attract miners would enter into the production cost and price of coal, signaling power companies to build hydroelectric or nuclear or oil-burning rather than coal-burning plants and signaling consumers to live in warmer climates or smaller or better-insulated houses than they would do if fuel were cheaper. Such responses would hold down the number of distasteful mining jobs to be filled. The few workers still doing that work would be ones whose distaste for it was relatively mild and capable of being assuaged by high wages.

No profound distinction holds between workers' sovereignty and consumers' sovereignty or between getting satisfactions or avoiding dissatisfactions in choosing what work to do and what goods to consume. Consumer goods are not ultimate ends in themselves but just particular means of obtaining satisfactions or avoiding dissatisfactions. People make their personal tastes and circumstances count by how they act on the markets for labor and goods alike.

Our broadened concept of consumers' and workers' sovereignty by no means upsets the idea of opportunity cost. We need only recognize that people choose not simply among commodities but rather among *packages* of satisfactions and dissatisfactions. The choice between additional amounts of *A* and *B* is really a choice between satisfactions gained and dissatisfactions avoided by people as consumers and producers of *A* and satisfactions gained and dissatisfactions avoided by people as consumers and producers of *B*. Choosing package *A* costs forgoing package *B*. Ideally, the prices of products *A* and *B* indicate the terms of exchange, so to speak, between the entire combinations of satisfactions gained and dissatisfactions avoided at the relevant margins in connection with the two products. Prices reflect intimately personal circumstances and feelings as well as physical or technological conditions of production and consumption.

None of this amounts to claiming that different persons' feelings about goods and jobs (and investment opportunities) can be accurately measured and compared by price or in any other definite way. However, people's feelings do count in the ways that their choices are expressed and their activities coordinated through the price system, and changes in their feelings do affect the pattern of production in directions that make intuitively good sense.

Clearly, then, economic theory need not assume that people act exclusively or even primarily from materialistic motives. Pecuniary considerations come into play, but along with others. As the laws of supply and demand describe, an increase in the pecuniary rewards or charges—or other rewards or costs—attached to some activity will increase or decrease its chosen level, other incentives and disincentives remaining unchanged. Money prices and changes in them can thus influence behavior and promote coordination of the chosen behaviors of different people, even though pecuniary considerations do not carry decisive weight and perhaps not even preponderant weight.

ADVANCES IN ECONOMIC THEORY

The role of subjectivism in solving the diamond-and-water paradox, replacing the labor theory or other real-cost theories of value, and accomplishing the marginalist revolution of the 1870s, is too well known to require more than a bare reminder here. Subjectivism must be distinguished from importing psychology into economics (Mises 1949/1963, pp. 122–127, 486–488). Diminishing marginal utility is a principle of sensible management rather than of psychology: a person will apply a limited amount of some good (grain, say, as in Menger 1871/1950, pp. 129–130) to what he considers its most important uses, and a larger and larger amount will permit its application to successively less important uses also.

Subjectivists do not commit the error of John Ruskin, who thought that "Whenever material gain follows exchange, for every plus there is a precisely equal minus" (quoted in Shand 1984, p. 120). They recognize that wealth is produced not only by physically shaping things or growing them but also by exchanging them. In the words of Henry George (1898/1941, pp. 331–332), who independently achieved several Austrian insights, "Each of the two parties to an exchange ... [gets] something that is more valuable to him than what he gives.... Thus there is in the transaction an actual increase in the sum of wealth, an actual production of wealth."

Subjectivists recognize nonmaterial elements in costs as well as demands. Every price is determined by many circumstances classifiable under the headings of "subjective factors" and "objective factors" (or "wants" and "resources and technology"). An alternative classification distinguishes between demand factors and supply factors. This alternative is not equivalent to the first classification because there is no reason to suppose that subjective factors operate only on the demand side of a market while objective factors dominate the supply side.

On the contrary, subjective factors operate on both sides. The supply schedule of a good does not reflect merely the quantities of inputs technologically required for various amounts of output, together with given prices of the inputs. The input prices are themselves variables determined by bidding among various firms and lines of production in the light of the inputs' capabilities to contribute to producing goods valued by consumers. Consumers' subjective feelings about other goods thus enter into determining the money costs of supplying quantities of any particular product.

Subjective factors operate in both blades of Marshall's scissors. (Misleadingly, Marshall 1920/1947, pp. 348, 813ff., had referred to a utility blade and a cost blade, as if utility and cost were quite distinct.)

By the logic of a price system, then, money cost brings to the attention of persons deciding on production processes and output volumes in any particular line—and ultimately to the attention of its consumers—what conditions prevail in all other sectors of the economy, including persons' attitudes toward goods and employments. Money prices and costs convey information about subjective conditions outside the direct ken of particular decisionmakers.

At this point the subjectivism of Austrian economists reinforces their awareness of general economic interdependence and their concern with coordination among the plans and actions of different people. They are wary (as many textbook writers seem not to be) of focusing so narrowly on the choices of the individual household and individual firm as to detract attention from the big picture.

Recognizing the subjective aspects of cost, we gain insights into the dubiousness of expecting prices to correspond to costs in any precise way. Costs represent values of forgone alternatives: costs are intimately linked with acts of choice.

Cost curves are no more objectively given to business firms than are demand curves for their products. A large part of the task of entrepreneurs and managers is to learn what the cost (and demand) curves are and to press the cost curves down, so to speak, through inspired innovations in technology, organization, purchasing, and marketing. Outsiders are in a poor position to second-guess their decisions.

Subjectivists appreciate the role of expectations. Well before the vogue of "rational expectations" in macroeconomics, Ludwig von Mises (1953/1981, pp. 459–460) recognized that an inflationary policy could not go on indefinitely giving real "stimulus" to an economy; people would catch on to what was happening, and the supposed stimulus would dissipate itself in price increases. Mises also argued (1949/1963, p. 586) that disorders such as the corn-hog cycle would be self-corrective. Unless the government protected farmers from the consequences of unperceptive or unintelligent behavior, farmers would learn about the cycle, if it did in fact occur; and by anticipating it would forestall it. (Those who did not learn would incur losses and be eliminated from the market.)

Much expressed nowadays are notions such as "the market's" expectation of some future magnitude—the dollar-mark exchange rate in three months, or whatever. Subjectivists are skeptical. They understand that "the market" does not form expectations or change light bulbs ("How many right-wing economists does it take to change a light bulb?") or do anything else. *People* do, people acting and interacting on markets. Since expectations are formed by people, they are understandably loose, diverse, and changeable.

All this intertwines with the inherent unpredictability of future human affairs. It is not even possible to make an exhaustive list of all possible outcomes of some decision, let alone attach probability scores to outcomes (Shackle 1972, esp. p. 22). Policymakers should take this point to heart and restrain their optimism about being able to control events.

This is not to deny that some predictions can be made with warranted confidence, notably the if-this-then-that predictions of economic theory and of science in general. Foretelling the future is quite another matter. Economists, like other people, have only limited time and energy. It is reasonable for each one to stick to work exploiting his own comparative

Chapter 2: Why Subjectivism? 33

advantages and hunches about fruitfulness and not let himself be badgered into foretelling the unforetellable.

James Buchanan achieved one of the greatest triumphs of subjectivism in demonstrating (1958/1999) that the burden of government spending can indeed be largely shifted onto future generations by deficit financing through issue of bonds. The conventional wisdom among economists (shared even by Ludwig von Mises, though not by the general public) had been unduly materialistic: the burden cannot be shifted through time, since resources are used when they are used. Buchanan recognized that a burden is something subjectively perceived. Persons who voluntarily give up current command over resources in exchange for government bonds that they find attractive suffer no burden in doing so. It is in the future that people—in general, people other than the original bond-buyers—will bear the burden of paying taxes to service the debt or of losing through its inflationary or outright repudiation. Furthermore, bond-financed government deficits do affect allocation of resources in time by trenching on private capital formation, thereby worsening future economic opportunities.[1]

FURTHER POLICY IMPLICATIONS

The ultrasubjectivist view of cost put forward by James Buchanan (1969) and writers in the London School tradition (some of whose articles are reprinted in Buchanan and Thirlby 1973/1981) has been largely adopted by Austrian economists (Vaughn 1980 and 1981; Seldon 1981).

In examining this view, we must avoid false presuppositions about how words relate to things. It is not true that each word has a single definite and unequivocal meaning and that it labels a specific thing or action or relation objectively existing in the world. On the contrary, many words have wide ranges of meaning. One way to learn what writers mean by a word is to see what implications they draw from propositions containing it.

This is true of "cost" as interpreted by Buchanan and the London economists. Those writers associate particular policy positions with the fuzziness that they attribute to cost. They heap scorn on cost-oriented rules for managing enterprises.

---

[1] Unaccountably, I somehow forgot to mention this achievement of Buchanan's until it was too late to change this article while it was being originally published.

Advocates of such rules typically attribute important welfare properties to them. Probably the most prominent such rule is the one requiring the output of an enterprise to be set at such a level that price equals marginal costs. (In the same general cost-oriented family, however, would be rules like the one that total revenue should just cover total cost.) One strand of argument for socialism, in fact, is that socialized enterprises could be made to follow such rules, unlike unregulated private enterprises. Even under capitalism, such rules supposedly might be useful in framing antimonopoly policy and regulating public utilities. They might also figure in other government economic interventions and in simulating market results in nonmarket settings, as in tort settlements.

The case for socialism and milder government economic interventions can be weakened, then, by discrediting the measurability and even the conceptual definiteness of "cost." This, I conjecture, is a clue to the ultrasubjectivist view of the concept. "Cost," says Buchanan (1969, pp. 42–43), "is that which the decisionmaker sacrifices or gives up when he makes a choice. It consists in his own evaluation of the enjoyment or utility that he anticipates having to forego as a result of selection among alternative courses of action." If cost can thus be portrayed as a thoroughly subjective concept or magnitude, if no one but the individual decisionmaker (entrepreneur or manager) can know what cost is or was, and if such knowledge is ineffable and practically incommunicable, then no outside authority can reasonably impose cost-oriented rules on him. The case for displacing or overriding the market dissolves.

This line of argument has some merit. As already observed, cost curves do not objectively exist. Instead, business decisionmakers have the task of discovering or inventing them and modifying them by happy innovations. Unfortunately, as a later section of this article shows, Buchanan and the London economists carry their subjectivist line too far and so tend to discredit it.

Subjectivist insights about expectations have other notable policy implications. The history of energy policy, and of politicians' demagogy, provides reason for expecting future repetition of past infringements on property rights. Firms and investors must recognize that if they make decisions that turn out in some future energy crisis to have been wise—for example, stockpiling oil, cultivating nonconventional energy sources, adopting conservation measures, or building flexibility into their facilities and operations to be able to cope relatively well with energy squeezes—then they will not be allowed to reap exceptional profits from their risk-bearing, their correct hunches, and their good luck. They will be victimized by seizure of oil stocks, by adverse treatment under rationing schemes, by price controls, or in other ways. Government reassurances, even if made, would nowadays not be credible. The benefits of diverse private responses to diverse expectations about energy supplies are thus partly forestalled.

This example reminds subjectivists of a broader point about remote repercussions of particular policies, repercussions remote in time or in economic sector. A violation of property rights may seem the economical and expedient policy in the individual case. Yet in contributing to an atmosphere of uncertainty, it can have grave repercussions in the long run.

Because expectations influence behavior, a policy's credibility conditions its effectiveness, as the rational-expectations theorists, and William Fellner (1976) before them, have emphasized. The question of the withdrawal pangs of ending an entrenched price inflation provides an example. When money-supply growth is slowed or stopped, the reduced growth of nominal income is split between price deceleration and slowed real production and employment. Expectations affect how favorable or unfavorable this split is. If the anti-inflation program is not credible—if wage negotiators and price-setters think that the policymakers will lose their nerve and switch gears at the first sign of recessionary side effects—then those private parties will expect the inflation to continue and will make their wage and price decisions accordingly; and the monetary slowdown will bite mainly on real activity. If, on the contrary, people are convinced that the authorities will persist in monetary restriction indefinitely no matter how bad the side-effects, so that inflation is bound to abate, then the perceptive price-setter or wage-negotiator will realize that if he nevertheless persists in making increases at the same old pace, he will find himself out ahead of the installed inflationary procession and will lose customers or jobs. People will moderate their price and wage demands, making the split relatively favorable to continued real activity.

It is only superficially paradoxical, then, that in two alternative situations with the same degree of monetary restraint, the situation in which the authorities are believed ready to tolerate severe recessionary side-effects will actually exhibit milder ones than the situation in which the authorities are suspected of irresolution. Subjectivists understand how intangible factors like these can affect outcomes under objectively similar conditions.

CAPITAL AND INTEREST THEORY

Capital and interest theory is a particular case or application of general value theory, but its subjectivist aspects can conveniently occupy a section of their own. Subjectivist insights help dispel some paradoxes cultivated by neo-Ricardians and neo-Marxists at Cambridge University. These paradoxes seem to impugn standard economic theory (particularly the marginal-productivity theory of factor remuneration), and by implication they call the entire logic of a market economy into question.

Reviewing the paradoxes in detail is unnecessary here (see Yeager 1976 and Garrison 1979). One much-employed arithmetical example describes two alternative techniques for producing a definite amount of some product. They involve different time-patterns of labor inputs. In each technique, compound interest accrues, so to speak, on the value of invested labor. Technique A is cheaper at interest rates above 100 percent, B is cheaper at rates between 50 and 100 percent, and A is cheaper again at rates below 50 percent.

If a decline of the interest rate through one of these two critical levels brings a switch from the less to the more capital-intensive of the two techniques, which seems normal enough, then the switch to the other technique as the interest rate declines through the other switch point is paradoxical. If we view the latter switch in the opposite direction, an increased interest rate prompts a more intensive use of capital. Capital intensity can respond perversely to the interest rate.

Examples of such perversity seem not to depend on trickery in measuring the stock of capital. The physical specifications of a technique, including the timing of its inputs and its output, stay the same regardless of the interest rate and regardless of whether the technique is actually in use. If one technique employs physically more capital than the other in relation to labor or to output at one switch point, then it still employs more at any other interest rate. This comparison remains valid with any convention for physically measuring the amount of capital, provided only that one does not change measurement conventions in mid-example. If the capital intensities of the two techniques are such that the switch between them at one critical interest rate is nonparadoxical, then the switch at the other must be paradoxical—a change in capital intensity in the *same* direction as the interest rate. We cannot deny perversity at both switch points—unless we abandon a purely physical conception of capital.

The paradox-mongers commit several faults. They slide from comparing alternative static states into speaking of *changes* in the interest rate and of *responses* to those changes. They avoid specifying what supposedly determines the interest rate and what makes it change.

The key to dispelling the paradoxes, however, is the insight that capital—or whatever it is that the interest rate is the price of—cannot be measured in purely physical terms. One must appreciate the value aspect—the subjective aspect—of the thing whose price is the interest rate. It is convenient to conceive of that thing as a factor of production. Following Cassel (1903/1971, pp. 41ff. and passim), we might name it "waiting." It is the tying up of value over time, which is necessary in all production processes. (This conceptualization is "convenient" not only because it conforms to reality and because it dispels the paradoxes but also because it displays parallels between how the interest rate and other factor prices are determined and what their functions are: it brings capital and interest theory comfortably into line with general microeconomic theory.)

In a physically specified production process, a reduced interest rate not only is a cheapening of the waiting (the tying up of value over time) that must be done but also reduces its required value-amount. It reduces the interest element in the notional prices of semifinished and capital goods for whose ripening into final consumer goods and services still further waiting must be done. Increased thrift is productive not only because it supplies more of the waiting required for production but also because, by lowering the interest rate, it reduces the amount of waiting required by any physically specified technique.

The amounts of waiting required by alternative physically specified techniques will in general decline in different degrees, which presents the possibility of reswitching between techniques, as in the example mentioned. When a decline in the interest rate brings an apparently perverse switch to a technique that is less capital-intensive by some physical criterion, the explanation is that the decline, although reducing the waiting-intensities of both techniques, reduces them differentially in such a way as to bring a larger reduction in the overall expense of producing by the adopted technique.

Preconceived insistence on measuring all factor quantities and factor-intensities in purely physical terms clashes with the fact of reality—or arithmetic—that the amount of tying up of value over time required in achieving a physically specified result does indeed depend on that factor's own price. Not only the waiting-intensity of a physically specified process but also the relative waiting-intensities of alternative processes really are affected by the interest rate. When a switch of technique occurs, the technique adopted really is the more economical on the whole, the inputs, waiting included, being valued at their prices. When a rise in the interest rate triggers a switch of techniques, the displaced one has become *relatively* too waiting-intensive to remain economically viable. It is irrelevant as a criticism of economic theory that *by some other, inapplicable, criterion* the displaced technique counts as less capital-intensive.

Further discussion of the supposed paradoxes would display parallels between reswitching and the conceivable phenomenon of multiple internal rates of return in an investment option, which is hardly mysterious at all (Hirshleifer 1970, pp. 77–81). Already, though, I've said enough to show how a subjectivist conceptualization of the factor whose price is the interest rate can avoid fallacies flowing from a materialist or objective conceptualization.

"I AM MORE SUBJECTIVIST THAN THOU"

On a few points, some Austrian economists may not have been subjectivist enough. Murray Rothbard (1962, pp. 153–154) seems to think that a contract under which no property has yet changed hands—for example, an exchange of promises between a movie actor and a studio—is somehow less properly enforceable than a contract under which some payment has already been made. Blackmail is a less actionable offense than extortion through application or threat of physical force (1962, p. 443 n. 49). If a villain compels me to sell him my property at a mere token price under threat of ruining my reputation and my business by spreading vicious but plausible lies, his action is somehow less of a crime or tort than if he had instead threatened to kick me in the shins or trample one of my tomato plants (Rothbard 1982, esp. pp. 121–127, 133–148, and personal correspondence). The material element in a transaction or a threat supposedly makes a great difference.

I may be at fault in not grasping the distinctions made in these examples, but it would be helpful to have further explanation of what superficially seems like an untypical lapse from subjectivism into materialism.

Far more common is the lapse into overstating the subjectivist position so badly as to risk discrediting it. F.A. Hayek is not himself to blame, but a remark of his (1952, p. 31) has been quoted *ad nauseam* (for example by Ludwig Lachmann in Spadaro 1978, p. 1; Walter Grinder in his introduction to Lachmann 1977, p. 23; and Littlechild 1979, p. 13). It has had a significance attributed to it that it simply cannot bear. "It is probably no exaggeration to say that every important advance in economic theory during the last hundred years was a further step in the consistent application of subjectivism."

This proposition of doctrinal history could be strictly correct without implying that every subjectivist step was an important advance. Moreover, past success with extending subjectivism in certain degrees and directions does not imply that any and all further extensions constitute valid contributions to economics.

A theorist is not necessarily entitled to take pride in being able to boast, "I am more subjectivist than thou." More important than subjectivism for its own sake is getting one's analysis straight.

The most sweeping extensions of subjectivism occur in remarks about a purely subjective theory of value, including a pure time-preference theory of the interest rate. Closely related remarks scorn the theory of mutual determination of economic magnitudes, the theory expounded by systems of simultaneous equations of general equilibrium. The ultrasubjectivists insist on monocausality instead. Causation supposedly runs in one direction only, *from* consumers' assessments of marginal utility and value and the relative utilities or values of future and present consumption *to* prices and the interest rate and sectoral and temporal patterns of resource allocation and production (Rothbard 1962, pp. 302–303).

Taken with uncharitable literalness, the ultrasubjectivist slogans imply that people's feelings and assessments have *everything* to do and the realities of nature, science, and technology have *nothing* to do with determining prices and interest rates and all interrelated economic magnitudes. Actually, these objective realities do interact with people's tastes. They condition how abundant various resources and goods are, or could be made to be, and so help determine *marginal* utilities.

For two reasons I know that the ultrasubjectivists do not really believe all they say. First, the propositions in question, taken literally, are too preposterous for *anyone* to believe. Second, subjectivist writings sometimes discuss production functions, the principle of diminishing marginal physical product, and other physical relations, conceding some importance to such matters.

What I object to, then, is not so much substantive beliefs as misleading language, language that sometimes misleads even its users, language adopted on the presupposition that subjectivism is good and more of it is better.

Subjectivists may contend that physical reality counts only *through* people's subjective perceptions of it and the valuations they make in accord with it. But that contention does not banish the influence of objective reality. Businessmen (and consumers) who perceive reality correctly will thrive better on the market than those who misperceive it. A kind of natural selection sees to it that objective reality does get taken into account.

Full-dress argument for purely subjective value and interest theory and for unidirectional causality appears rarely in print. It keeps being asserted in seminars, conversation, and correspondence, however, as I for one can testify and as candid Austrians will presumably acknowledge. Furthermore, such assertions do appear in authoritative Austrian publications. (For example, see Rothbard 1962, pp. 117, 122, 293, 307, 332, 363–364, 452 n. 16, 455 n. 12, 457 n. 27, 508, 528, 557, 893 n. 14; Rothbard, introduction to Fetter 1977; Taylor 1980, pp. 26, 32, 36, 47, 50; and Shand 1984, pp. 23, 44, 45, 54, 56.) Garrison (1979, pp. 220–221) avoids the word "pure" in recommending a time-preference theory of interest and a subjectivist theory of value in general, but he does contrast them favorably with what he calls "eclectic" theories, such as the "standard Fisherian" theory of interest. For outright avowal of a pure time-preference interest theory, see Kirzner's manuscript.)

The point repeatedly turns up in Austrian discussions that goods that people consider different from each other are indeed different goods, no matter how closely they resemble each other physically. This point is not downright fallacious, but the significance attributed to it is excessive, and its use in question-begging ways is likely to repel mainstream economists. An example is the contention that when a manufacturer sells essentially the same good under different labels at different prices, he is nevertheless not practicing price discrimination; for the goods bearing the different labels are considered by the consumers to be different goods, which *makes* them different goods in all economically relevant senses. The manufacturer is supposedly just charging different prices for different things.

Quite probably his practice is not one that perceptive economists and social philosophers would want to suppress by force of law; but we should not let our policy judgments, any more than our subjectivist methodological preconceptions, dictate our economic analysis or remove certain questions from its scope. It may be more fruitful to recognize that price discrimination is indeed going on, with the different labels being used to separate customers according to their demand elasticities.

Crypticism sometimes accompanies insistence on pure subjectivism. An example is a line of attack taken against mainstream interest theory, which enlists considerations of intertemporal transformability (that is, the *productivity* of investment) as well as the subjective time-preference element. This theory is epitomized by Irving Fisher's diagram (1930/1970, pp. 234ff.; Hirshleifer 1970, passim) showing a transformation curve between present and future goods (or consumption), as well as a map of indifference curves between present and future goods. A familiar Austrian objection is to insist that the diagram, specifically the transformation curve, fails to make the required distinction between physical productivity and value productivity.

If not deliberate obscurantism, this objection does indicate misunderstanding of Fisher's theory (or impatience with or prejudice against it). Of course, some technological change that increases the physical productivity of investment in some specific line of production, say widgets, may not increase the value productivity of such investment. The increased physical amount of future widgets obtainable for a given present sacrifice may indeed have a reduced total value relative to other goods and services in general (the future demand for widgets may be price-inelastic). Some of the new opportunities created by technological change will indeed be unattractive to investors. In invoking the greater productivity of more roundabout methods of production, Böhm-Bawerk (1884/1889/1909–1912/1959, vol. II: pp. 82–84; vol. III: pp. 45–56) was referring to "well-chosen" or "skillfully chosen" or "wisely selected" methods; and a similar stipulation applies to the present case. Technological changes that increase the physical productivity of particular roundabout methods broaden the range of opportunities among which investors can exercise wise choice, and implementing some of those choices does add to the demand for waiting, tending to bid up the interest rate.

The ultrasubjectivist objection is open to another strand of reply. It is illegitimate to invoke a contrast between physical productivity and value productivity by restricting the discussion to examples of sacrificing *specific* present goods to get more future goods of the same kind. What is conveyed by borrowing and lending (and other transactions in waiting) is not command over investible resources that would otherwise have gone into producing specific present goods but command over resources in general.

It *is* legitimate to do what Fisher's diagram helps us to do: to conceive of present goods in general being sacrificed for larger amounts of future goods in general.

With their admirable general emphasis on process and on the decisions and actions of individual persons, Austrian economists should not rest content with attacks on mainstream capital and interest theory that rely on cryptic allusions to a distinction between physical productivity and value productivity (or, similarly, to assertions that factor prices will adjust). They should defend their pure subjectivism on this topic, if they can, with a detailed process analysis of how persons act.

Next I turn to exaggerations in the subjectivist cost doctrines of Buchanan and the London School. These theorists interpret the cost of a particular course of action as the next-best course perceived and forgone by the decisionmaker. Ronald Coase (quoted with approval in Buchanan 1969, p. 28) says that "The cost of doing anything consists of the receipts which would have been obtained if that particular decision had not been taken.... To cover costs and to maximize profits are essentially two ways of expressing the same phenomenon."

Well, suppose the best course of action open to me is, in my judgment, to open a restaurant of a quite specific type in a specific location. The next-best course, then, is presumably to open a restaurant identical in all but some trivial detail, such as the particular hue of green of the lampshades. If so, the cost of the precise restaurant chosen is presumably an all but identical restaurant worth to me, in my judgment, almost fully as much. Generalizing, the cost of a chosen thing or course of action is very nearly the full value that the decisionmaker attributes to it.

My counterexample to the Coase-Buchanan cost concept may seem frivolous, but it raises a serious question. How far from identical to the chosen course of action must the next best alternative be to count as a distinct alternative? The point conveyed by questions like this is that either radical error or sterile word-jugging is afoot. (Nozick 1977, esp. pp. 372–373, expresses some compatible though not identical doubts about subjectivist concepts of cost and preference.)

More ordinary concepts of cost, however, are meaningful, including the interpretation of money cost in a particular line of production as a way of conveying information to decisionmakers in it about conditions (including personal tastes) in other sectors of the economy.

Buchanan (1969, p. 43) draws six implications from his choice-bound conception of cost, and Littlechild (in Spadaro 1978, pp. 82–83) quotes them all with apparent approval. I'll quote and comment only on the first, second, and fifth.

> 1. Most importantly, cost must be borne exclusively by the decisionmaker; it is not possible for cost to be shifted to or imposed on others.
>
> 2. Cost is subjective; it exists in the mind of the decisionmaker and nowhere else....
>
> 5. Cost cannot be measured by someone other than the decisionmaker because there is no way that subjective experience can be directly observed.

As for the first word and second implications, of course cost can be imposed on others in quite ordinary senses of those words; it is not always kept inside the mind of the decisionmaker. What about adverse externalities—smoke damage and the like? What about losses imposed on stockholders by an incompetent business management? What about the costs that a government imposes on a population by taxation or inflation (or its command of resources, however financed)? Isn't it notoriously true that a government official need not personally bear all the costs of his decisions? What about involuntarily drafted soldiers? Even an ordinary business decision has objective aspects in the sense that the resources devoted to the chosen activity are withdrawn or withheld from other activities.

Of course the costs incurred in these examples have subjective aspects also—in the minds or the perceptions of the draftees and of persons who would have been consumers of the goods from whose production the resources in question are competed away. What is odd is the contention that no cost occurs except subjectively and in the mind of the decisionmaker alone.

As for the fifth implication, it is true that cost cannot be measured—not measured precisely, that is, whether by the decisionmaker or someone else. But measurability itself is evidently what is at issue, not the admitted imprecision of measurement of cost, as of other economic magnitudes. The money costs of producing a definite amount of some product, or the marginal money cost of its production, can indeed be estimated. Estimates of money cost take into account, in particular, the prices multiplied by their quantities of the inputs required to produce specified marginal amounts of the good in question. True, cost accounting has no objective and infallible rules and must employ conventions. For this and other reasons, estimates of money cost are just that—estimates. But they are not totally arbitrary; they are not meaningless.

Money costs of production, as well as the input prices that enter into estimating them, play a vital role in conveying information to particular business decisionmakers about conditions in other sectors of the economy. Money costs and prices reflect—do not measure precisely, but reflect—the values and even the utilities attributed by consumers to the goods and services whose production is forgone to make the required inputs available to the particular line of production whose costs are in question. (Money costs and factor prices also reflect, as noted above, the preferences and attitudes of workers and investors.)

It is therefore subversive to the understanding of the logic of a price system to maintain that cost is entirely subjective, falls entirely on the decisionmaker, and cannot be felt by anyone else.

Perhaps this risk of subversion is being run in a good cause. A healthy skepticism is in order about socialism, nationalization, and the imposition of cost rules on nationalized and private enterprises. However, we should beware of trying to obtain substantive conclusions from preconceptions about method or about policy. Sound conclusions and policy judgments incur discredit from association with questionable verbal maneuvers.

Valid subjectivist insights join with the fact that general equilibrium never actually prevails in recommending skepticism about policies that would unnecessarily impose imitation markets or the mere feigning of market processes. The fact of disequilibrium prices does not, of course, recommend junking the market system in favor of something else. Market prices, although not precise indicators of the trade-offs posed by reality, are at least under the pressures of supply and demand and entrepreneurial alertness to become more nearly accurate measures.

The recommended skepticism does have some application, however, with regard to compensation for seizures under eminent domain, damage awards in tort cases, and the development of case law. It also has some application in cost-benefit studies. Personal rights, not such exercises, should of course dominate many policy decisions.

Again, though, I want to warn against overstatement. Admittedly, costs and benefits are largely subjective, market prices are at disequilibrium levels, and other bases of making estimates are inaccurate also. But what is to be done when some decision or other has to be made—about a new airport, a subway system, a dam, or a proposed environmental regulation? Does one simply ramble on about how imponderable everything is, or does one try in good faith to quantify benefits and costs? Of course the estimates will be crude, even very crude, but perhaps the preponderance of benefits or costs will turn out great enough to be unmistakable anyway. In any case, expecting the advocates of each of the possible decisions to quantify their assertions and lay them out for scrutiny will impose a healthy discipline on the arguments made. It will weaken the relative influence of sheer poetry, oratory, demagogy, and political maneuvering.

My last example of subjectivism exaggerated and abused is what even some members of the Austrian School have identified as a "nihilism" about economic theory. Nihilistic writings stress the unknowability of the future, the dependence of market behavior on divergent and vague and ever-changing subjective expectations, the "kaleidic" nature of the economic world, and the poor basis for any belief that market forces are tending to work toward rather than away from equilibrium (if, indeed, equilibrium has any meaning). Some of these assertions are relevant enough in particular contexts, but ultrasubjectivists bandy them sweepingly about as if willing to cast discredit not merely on attempts to foretell the future but even on scientific predictions of the if-this-then-that type. It is hard to imagine why an economist who thus wallows in unknowability continues to represent himself as an economist at all. (One hunch: he may think he has an all-purpose methodological weapon for striking down whatever strand of analysis or policy argument he happens not to like. But then his own analysis and arguments—if he has any—would be equally vulnerable.)

There is no point trying to conceal from knowledgable Austrian readers what economist I particularly have in mind, so I'll refer to the writings of Ludwig Lachmann listed in the references (including his articles in Dolan 1976 and Spadaro 1978), as well as Lachmann's admiration of Shackle's writings on the imponderability of the future. Also see O'Driscoll's refreshing criticism (in Spadaro 1978, esp. pp. 128–134) of Lachmann for practically repudiating the concepts of the market's coordinating processes and of spontaneous order.

Most recently, Lachmann has shown evident delight in the phrase "dynamic subjectivism." "[A]t least in the history of Austrian doctrine, subjectivism has become progressively more dynamic" (1985, p. 2). "To Austrians, of all people, committed to radical subjectivism, the news of the move from static to dynamic subjectivism should be welcome news" (1985, pp. 1–2). The word "committed" is revealing. Instead of the scientific attitude, Lachmann evidently values commitment—commitment to a doctrine or to a methodology. Recalling Fritz Machlup's essay on "Statics and Dynamics: Kaleidoscopic Words" (1959/1975), I wish Machlup were alive today to heap onto "dynamic subjectivism" the ridicule it deserves.

CONCLUDING EXHORTATIONS

As Gustav Cassel wrote in a book first published in English long ago, it was an absurd waste of intellectual energy for economists still to be disputing whether prices were determined by objective factors or subjective factors (1932/1967, p. 146). Referring to interest theory in particular, Irving Fisher (1930/1970, p. 312) called it "a scandal in economic science" that two schools were still crossing swords on the supposed issue. Prices, including interest rates, are determined by factors of both kinds. As noted earlier, saying so does not mean identifying objective factors with the supply side and subjective factors with the demand side of markets, nor vice versa. Both sorts of factors operate on both sides.

For a grasp of how subjective and objective factors thoroughly intertwine in a system of economic interdependence, a study of the simplified general-equilibrium equation system presented in Cassel's (1932/1967) chapter 4 is well worth while. The reader should pay attention, among other things, to the role of the technical coefficients, ones indicating the amounts of each input used in producing a unit of each product. Cassel does not need to suppose, of course, that these coefficients are rigidly determined solely by nature and technology. On the contrary, an elaboration of his system can take account of how many of these coefficients are themselves variable and subject to choice in response to prices, which are themselves determined in the system of mutual interdependence.

Study of Cassel's chapter (or similar expositions) should also disabuse the open-minded reader of any lingering belief in unidirectional causality. Mutual determination of economic variables is a fact of reality; and no blanket prejudice against general-equilibrium theory, which does afford important insights, should blind one to that fact.

Of course, when one investigates the consequences of a specified change—say in tastes, technology, taxes, or a fixed exchange rate—it is not enough (nor, realistically, is it possible) to solve a general-equilibrium equation system with one or more parameters changed and then compare the new and old solutions. An adequate analysis traces out, perhaps even sequentially, the reactions of the persons involved and shows the reasonableness of their theorized reactions from their own points of view. But insisting on such a causal analysis does not presuppose belief in monocausality. The specified disturbance does indeed impinge on a system of mutual determination. Both the new and old constellations of economic activities result from multidirectional interactions of a great many subjective and objective factors.

Austrian economists have important messages to convey about subjective elements that, on all sides, pervade market behavior, signals, and outcomes. Their insights have important implications for policy. It is a shame to impede communication by remarks about purely subjective value theory, pure time-preference interest theory, and the alleged fallacy of multidirectional causality.

Austrians cannot really mean what such remarks, taken literally, convey. They mislead and repel people outside the inner circle. The main goal of the Austrians is presumably not to recite slogans that reinforce cozy feelings of camaraderie among members of an elite. Instead, their goal, shared with other economists who wish well for mankind, is presumably to gain and communicate understanding of economic (and political) processes in the world as it is, has been, and potentially could be. They want to extend and communicate such knowledge so as to increase whatever chance there may be that man's deepest values will ultimately prevail. Respect for the straightforward meanings of words will aid in that endeavor.

Besides shunning deceptive slogans, Austrian economists should beware of surrounding their doctrines with a fog of methodological preachments, preachments suggestive, moreover, of pervasive sniping and sour grapes (as, for example, about the elegant formal theory that some mainstream economists rightly or wrongly delight in). Above all, Austrians should avoid discrediting the sound core of their doctrine by contaminating it with bits of downright and readily exposable error (or what comes across as error on any straightforward reading of the words used). Austrians have positive contributions to make and should make them.

REFERENCES

Böhm-Bawerk, Eugen von. *Capital and Interest*. 1884, 1889, 1909–1912. Translated by G.D. Huncke and H.F. Sennholz. 3 vols. South Holland, Ill.: Libertarian Press, 1959.

Buchanan, James M. *Cost and Choice*. Chicago: Markham, 1969.

———. *Public Principles of Public Debt*. 1958. Indianapolis: Liberty Fund, 1999.

Buchanan, James M., and G.F. Thirlby, eds. *L.S.E. Essays on Cost.* 1973. New York: New York University Press, 1981.

Cassel, Gustav. *The Nature and Necessity of Interest.* 1903. New York: Kelley, 1971.

———. *The Theory of Social Economy.* 1932. Translated by S.L. Barron. New York: Kelley, 1967.

Committee for Economic Development. *Achieving Energy Independence.* New York: CED, 1974.

Dolan, Edwin G., ed. *The Foundations of Modern Austrian Economics.* Kansas City, Kans.: Sheed and Ward, 1976.

Fellner, William. *Towards a Reconstruction of Macroeconomics.* Washington, D.C.: American Enterprise Institute, 1976.

Fetter, Frank A. *Capital, Interest, and Rent.* Edited with an introduction by Murray N. Rothbard. Kansas City, Kans.: Sheed Andrews and McMeel, 1977.

Fisher, Irving. *The Theory of Interest.* 1930. New York: Kelley, 1970.

Freeman, S. David. *Energy: The New Era.* New York: Walker, 1974.

Garrison, Roger. "Waiting in Vienna." In *Time, Uncertainty, and Disequilibrium*, edited by Mario J. Rizzo, 215–226. Lexington, Mass.: Lexington Books, 1979.

George, Henry. *The Science of Political Economy.* 1898. New York: Schalkenbach Foundation, 1941.

Hayek, Friedrich A. "The Use of Knowledge in Society." *American Economic Review* 35 (September 1945): 519–530.

———. *The Counter-Revolution of Science.* Glencoe, Ill.: Free Press, 1952.

———. *The Constitution of Liberty.* Chicago: University of Chicago Press, 1960.

Hirshleifer, Jack. *Investment, Interest, and Capital.* Englewood Cliffs, N.J.: Prentice Hall, 1970.

Kirzner, Israel M. "Pure Time-Preference Theory: A Post Script to the 'Grand Debate'." New York: New York University, manuscript, undated but early 1980s.

Lachmann, Ludwig M. *Capital, Expectations, and the Market Process.* Edited with an introduction by Walter E. Grinder. Kansas City, Kans.: Sheed Andrews and McMeel, 1977.

———. Review of *The Economics of Time and Ignorance*, by Gerald P. O'Driscoll and Mario J. Rizzo. *Market Process* 3 (Fall 1985): 1–4, 17–18.

Littlechild, Stephen C. *The Fallacy of the Mixed Economy*. San Francisco: Cato Institute, 1979.

Machlup, Fritz. "Statistics and Dynamics: Kaleidoscopic Words." 1959. In *Essays in Economic Semantics*, 9–42. New York: New York University Press, 1975.

Marshall, Alfred. *Principles of Economics*. 1920. 8th ed. London: Macmillan, 1947.

Menger, Carl. *Principles of Economics*. 1871. Translated by J. Dingwall and B.F. Hoselitz. Glencoe, Ill.: Free Press, 1950.

Miller, James C., III, ed. *Why the Draft? The Case for a Volunteer Army*. Baltimore: Penguin, 1968.

Mises, Ludwig von. *Human Action*. 1949. 2nd ed. New Haven, Conn.: Yale University Press, 1963.

———. *The Theory of Money and Credit*. 1953. Translated by H.E. Batson. Indianapolis: Liberty Classics, 1981.

Mitchell, Edward J., ed. *Dialogue on World Oil*. Washington, D.C.: American Enterprise Institute, 1974.

Nozick, Robert. "On Austrian Methodology." *Synthese* 36 (November 1977): 353–392.

Rothbard, Murray N. *Man, Economy, and State*. 2 vols. Princeton, N.J.: D. Van Nostrand, 1962.

———. *The Ethics of Liberty*. Atlantic Highlands, N.J.: Humanities Press, 1982.

Seldon, James R. "The Relevance of Subjective Costs: Comment." *Southern Economic Journal* 48 (July 1981): 216–221.

Shackle, G.L.S. *Epistemics and Economics*. New York: Cambridge University Press, 1972.

Shand, Alexander H. *The Capitalist Alternative: An Introduction to Neo-Austrian Economics*. New York: New York University Press, 1984.

Spadaro, Louis M., ed. *New Directions in Austrian Economics*. Kansas City, Kans.: Sheed Andrews and McMeel, 1978.

Taylor, Thomas C. *The Fundamentals of Austrian Economics*. San Francisco: Cato Institute, 1980.

Vaughn, Karen I. "Does It Matter That Costs Are Subjective?" *Southern Economic Journal* 46 (January 1980): 702–715.

———. "The Relevance of Subjective Costs: Reply." *Southern Economic Journal* 48 (July 1981): 222–226.

Vining, Rutledge. *On Appraising the Performance of an Economic System.* New York: Cambridge University Press, 1985.

Waismann, Friedrich. "Verifiability." In *Logic and Language*, Anchor ed., edited by Antony Flew, 122–151. Garden City, N.Y.: Doubleday, 1965.

Yeager, Leland B. "Balance-of-Payments Cure Worse than the Disease." *Commercial and Financial Chronicle* 202, no. 2 (September 1965): 3, 29.

———. "Toward Understanding Some Paradoxes in Capital Theory." *Economic Inquiry* 14 (September 1976): 313–346.

———. "Pareto Optimality in Policy Espousal." *Journal of Libertarian Studies* 2, no. 3 (1978): 199–216.

CHAPTER 3

Henry George and Austrian Economics*

Henry George has been widely pigeonholed and dismissed as a single taxer. Actually, he was a profound and original economist. He independently arrived at several of the most characteristic insights of the Austrian School, which is enjoying a revival nowadays. Yet George scorned the Austrians of his time, and their present-day successors show scant appreciation of his work. An apparent lapse in intellectual communication calls for repair.

AUSTRIAN ECONOMICS

The Austrian School traces to the work of Carl Menger, one of the leaders of the marginal-utility revolution of the 1870s, and his fellow countrymen, Eugen von Böhm-Bawerk and Friedrich von Wieser. Notable contributors of a later generation include Ludwig von Mises, F.A. Hayek, and Ludwig Lachmann, each of whom worked first in Austria or Germany and later in the United States, and also the American Frank A. Fetter. In a still later generation, eminent Austrians—the word no longer carries any implications about nationality or mother tongue—include Murray Rothbard and Israel Kirzner. Some eminent young members of the school are Dominick Armentano, Gerald O'Driscoll, Mario Rizzo, Steven Littlechild, and Karen Vaughn; and apologies are in order for not extending the list further.[1]

---

*From *History of Political Economy* 16 (Summer 1984): 157–174. This article derives from a talk given at St. John's University, Jamaica, New York, on 29 March 1982. I am indebted to my hosts there, and particularly to Professor M. Northrup Buechner, for suggestions and encouragement.

[1]Since this article chiefly concerns Henry George, I am assuming that the reader has enough acquaintance with contemporary Austrian economics to make detailed citations unnecessary. In addition to the specifically cited works of Menger, Böhm-Bawerk, Mises,

What follows is an impression of the leading characteristics of Austrian economics.

(i) Austrians are concerned with the big picture—with how a whole economic system functions. They avoid tunnel vision; they do not focus too narrowly on the administration of the individual business firm and the individual household. They investigate how the specialized activities of millions of persons, who are making their decisions in a decentralized manner, can be coordinated. These diverse activities are interdependent; yet no particular agency takes charge of coordinating them, and none would be competent to do so. The relevant knowledge—about resources, technology, human wants, and market conditions—is inevitably fragmented among millions, even billions, of separate human minds.

(ii) Austrians take interest in how alternative sets of institutions can function. Mises in particular, and later Hayek, demonstrated the impossibility of economic calculation—scheduling of economic activities in accordance with accurate assessment of values and costs—under socialism. Centralized mobilization of knowledge and planning of activities is admittedly conceivable. In a Swiss Family Robinson setting, the head of the family could survey the available resources and technology and the capabilities and needs and wants of family members and could sensibly decide on and monitor production and consumption in some detail. In a large, modern economy, however, sensible central direction is not possible. Austrians are alert to possibilities of unplanned order and to what Hayek (1967) has called "the results of human action but not of human design." They investigate how the market and prices function as a vast communications system and computer, transmitting information and incentives and so putting to use scattered knowledge that would otherwise necessarily go to waste.

(iii) Not only do Austrians appreciate the implications of incomplete, imperfect, and scattered knowledge; they also appreciate the implications of change, uncertainty, and unpredictability in human affairs. They take these facts of reality seriously not only in confronting supposed theoretical and econometric models of the economy but also in assessing alternative sets of institutions and lines of policy.

(iv) In connection with the implications of fragmented knowledge, change, and unpredictability, Austrians pay attention to disequilibrium,

---

Hayek, and Rothbard, he might well consult, for orientation, books written or edited by Dolan, Moss, O'Driscoll, and Spadaro; see the bibliography.

process, and entrepreneurship. While not totally scornful of elaborate analysis of the properties of imaginary equilibrium states and of comparative-static analysis, they recognize how incomplete a contribution such analyses can make to the understanding of how economic systems function. They do not suppose, for example, that cost curves and demand curves are somehow "given" to business decisionmakers. On the contrary, one of the services of the competitive process is to press for discovery of ways to get the costs curves down—if one adopts such terminology at all. Austrians tend to accept the concept of X-efficiency[2] and to appreciate the role of competition in promoting it. Far from being an ideal state of affairs with which the real world is to be compared—unfavorably—competition is seen as a process. Entrepreneurs play key roles in that process; they are men and women alert to opportunities for advantageously undertaking new activities or adopting new methods.

(v) As already implied, Austrians have certain methodological predilections. They are unhappy with the tacit view of economic activity as the resultant of interplay among objective conditions and impersonal forces. They are unhappy with theorizing in terms of aggregates and averages (real GNP, the price level, and the like). They take pains to trace their analyses back to the perceptions, decisions, and actions of individual persons: methodological individualism is a key aspect of their approach. Austrians recognize introspection as one legitimate source of the facts underpinning economic theory. They emphasize subjectivism: not only do personal tastes help determine the course of economic activity, but even the objective facts of resources and technology operate only as they are filtered through the perceptions and evaluations of individuals. Insofar as Austrians recognize macroeconomics as a legitimate topic at all, they are concerned to provide it with microeconomic underpinnings.

(vi) Although Austrians like to think of their economics as value-free and although some of them, at least, emphasize that it is not logically linked with any particular policy position, Austrian insights into positive economics, coupled with plausible value judgments of a humanitarian and individualistic nature, undeniably do tend toward a particular policy position—non-interventionistic, laissez-faire, libertarian. More about this later.

---

[2] See, in particular, Leibenstein 1976. (Leibenstein himself, however, is not usually considered an Austrian.)

GEORGE'S INDEPENDENCE

I shall try to show Henry George's affinities with the Austrians by citing passages from his writings. The demonstration proceeds from partial agreement on theoretical points to agreement on major questions. First, however, we should note George's misunderstanding of and even scorn for the Austrians of his time, suggesting that his Austrian-like insights were original with him.[3] George did not understand the marginal revolution in value theory that was getting under way in the last decades of his life. He regretted that "the classical school of political economy" seemed to have been abandoned:

> What has succeeded is usually denominated the Austrian School, for no other reason that I can discover than that "far kind have long horns." If it has any principles, I have been utterly unable to find them. The inquirer is usually referred to the incomprehensible works of Professor Alfred Marshall of Cambridge, England ... ; to the ponderous works of Eugen V. Böhm-Bawerk, Professor of Political Economy, first in Innsbruck and then at Vienna ... ; or to a lot of German works written by men he never heard of and whose names he cannot even pronounce.
>
> This pseudoscience gets its name from a foreign language, and uses for its terms words adapted from the German—words that have no place and no meaning in an English work. It is, indeed, admirably calculated to serve the purpose of those powerful interests dominant in the colleges ... that must fear a simple and understandable political economy, and who vaguely wish to have the poor boys who are subjected to it by their professors rendered incapable of thought on economic subjects. (*SPE*, p. 208)[4]

Later, as quoted below, George complains about the "grotesque confusions" of the Austrian School.

---

[3]One referee hypothesizes that George and some of the Austrians, including Mises, were deriving inspiration in common from French liberals such as Bastiat and Dunoyer. Investigating that hypothesis must be left for another occasion—or for another researcher.

[4]Citations are made to George's works by abbreviated titles. The abbreviations, in the same order as the titles in the bibliography, are *P&P, SP, PFT, PPH,* and *SPE*.

Referring in particular to confusion over the meaning of wealth, George complains that "the 'economic revolution' which has in the meanwhile displaced from their chairs the professors of the then orthodox political economy in order to give place to so-called 'Austrians,' or similar professors of 'economics,' ha[s] only made confusion worse confounded" (*SPE*, p. 121).

Chapter 3: Henry George and Austrian Economics 55

The Austrians, for their part, have not adequately appreciated George. Böhm-Bawerk criticized the natural-fructification theory of interest presented in *Progress and Poverty*, apparently unaware of the advance (discussed below) that George achieved in *The Science of Political Economy* (Böhm-Bawerk 1884/1959, vol. 1: pp. 336–339, 366, 474). Among present-day Austrians, Murray Rothbard shows the greatest acquaintance with George's writings, or some of them. (For example, he recognizes George as a free trader and applauds his "excellent discussion" of the distinction between patents and copyrights.) Yet Rothbard is mostly concerned with what he considers the unsatisfactory moral and economic arguments used in favor of the single tax.[5] With the Austrians, as with other present-day economists, George's reputation does seem to suffer from his being pigeonholed as a propagandist for dubious reforms.

VALUE THEORY: SUBJECTIVISM, PRODUCTIVITY, AND TIME

George held a kind of labor-in-exchange or exertion-saved theory of value, following Adam Smith, but not a Marxian labor-cost theory (*SPE*, pp. 212–256, 503). Still, he had some Austrian-like subjectivist insights:

> the value of a thing in any time and place is the largest amount of exertion that any one will render in exchange for it; or to make the estimate from the other side, ... it is the smallest amount of exertion for which any one will part with it in exchange.

> Value is thus an expression which, when used in its proper economic sense of value in exchange, has no direct relation to any intrinsic quality of external things, but only to man's desires. Its essential element is subjective, not objective; that is to say, lying in the mind or will of man, and not lying in the nature of things external to the human will or mind. There is no material test for value. Whether a thing is valuable or not valuable, or what may be the degree of its value, we cannot really tell by its size or shape or color or smell, or any other material quality, except so far as such investigations may enable us to infer how other men may regard them....

> Now this fact that the perception of value springs from a feeling of man, and has not at bottom any relation to the external world—a fact that

---

[5] Rothbard 1962, vol. 1: pp. 148–149, 152, 410, 442; vol. 2: pp. 512–513, 813–814, 888, 915, 930, 933, 944–945; Rothbard 1970, pp. 37, 57, 91–100, 200, 201, 204, 209, 210; Rothbard 1973, pp. 333–335.

has been much ignored in the teachings and expositions of accepted economists—is what lies at the bottom of the grotesque confusions which, under the name of the Austrian school of political economy, have within recent years so easily captured the teachings of pretty much all the universities and colleges in the English-speaking world. (*SPE*, pp. 251–252)

George goes on to say that the Austrians have drawn wrong inferences from

> the truth that value is not a quality of things but an affectation of the human mind toward things....
>
> What is subjective is in itself incommunicable. A feeling so long as it remains merely a feeling can be known only to and can be measured only by him who feels it. It must come out in some way into the objective through action before any one else can appreciate or in any way measure it....
>
> ... what value determines is not how much a thing is desired, but how much any one is willing to give for it; not desire in itself, but ... the desire to possess, accompanied by the ability and willingness to give in return.
>
> Thus it is that there is no measure of value among men save competition or the jiggling of the market, a matter that might be worth the consideration of those amiable reformers who so lightly propose to abolish competition.
>
> It is never the amount of labor that has been exerted in bringing a thing into being that determines its value, but always the amount of labor that will be rendered in exchange for it. (*SPE*, pp. 252–253)

Actually, George and the Austrians were not as far apart as he thought when alleging "grotesque confusions." Admittedly, though, some present-day Austrians do invite misunderstanding by insisting that value in general, as well as the interest rate in particular, is *entirely* a subjective phenomenon, instead of being determined—as of course it is—by interaction between objective reality and subjective perceptions and appraisals.

The valid subjective element in George's doctrine also appears in his recognition that wealth can be produced not only (1) by physically shaping things and (2) by growing things but also (3) by *exchanging* things:

> this third mode of production consists in the utilization of a power or principle or tendency manifested only in man, and belonging to him by virtue of his peculiar gift of reason....

... [I]t is by and through his disposition and power to exchange, in which man essentially differs from all other animals, that human advance goes on.... [I]n itself exchange brings about a perceptible increase in the sum of wealth.... Each of the two parties to an exchange aims to get, and as a rule does get, something that is more valuable to him than what he gives—that is to say, that represents to him a greater power of labor to satisfy desire. Thus there is in the transaction an actual increase in the sum of wealth, an actual production of wealth.... Each party to the exchange gets in return for what costs it comparatively little labor what would cost it a great deal of labor to get by either of the other modes of production. Each gains by the act.... [T]he joint wealth of both parties, the sum of the wealth of the world, is by the exchange itself increased. (*SPE*, pp. 331–332)

George had some glimmerings of the marginalist and Austrian idea of *imputation*: the values and remunerations of the factors of production are imputed to them according to what they contribute to producing outputs valued by consumers. Labor, George explained, does not transmit value into whatever it is applied to. Instead, labor derives its wages from its productive contribution and from the value that consumers attribute to the output produced. This insight refuted the wages-fund doctrine (*P&P*, pp. 23, 50–70). Even labor employed on a project of long duration is effectively deriving its wages from the project's growth in value as it comes gradually closer to completion.

Some authorities credit George with contributing to development of the marginal-productivity theory of functional income distribution.[6] Even John Bates Clark recognized his contribution:

It was the claim advanced by Mr. Henry George, that wages are fixed by the product which a man can create by tilling rentless land, that first led me to seek a method by which the product of labor everywhere may be disentangled from the product of cooperating agents and separately identified; and it was this quest which led to the attainment of the law that is here presented, according to which the wages of all labor tend, under perfectly free competition, to equal the product that is separately attributable to the labor. The product of the "final unit" of labor is the same as that of every unit, separately considered; and if normal tendencies could work in perfection, it would be true not only of each unit, but

---

[6] See Charles Collier, pp. 223–226, and Aaron Fuller, pp. 298–300, both in Andelson 1979.

of the working force as a whole, that its product and its pay are identical. (1899/1908, p. viii)

George did not see how his marginal-productivity theory of the wages of labor applied in a similar way to all factor remunerations (Collier in Andelson 1979, p. 228). Neither did the early Austrians; it was left to Wicksteed to make that contribution in 1894.

Regarding land rent, George was avowedly a follower of Ricardo (*P&P*, pp. 165–172). His conceptions of capital and its productivity were incomplete. He had a fructification theory of interest, centering around a supposed "reproductive or vital force of nature," illustrated by the growth of crops, the reproduction of animals, and the maturing of wine in storage (*P&P*, esp. pp. 179–182).

He did share insights with the Austrians, however, on the vital role of time in the productive process. He devotes a whole chapter of *SPE* to this topic:

> if I go to a builder and say to him, "In what time and at what price will you build me such and such a house?" he would, after thinking, name a time, and a price based on it. This specification of time would be essential.... This I would soon find if, not quarreling with the price, I ask him largely to lessen the time ... I might get the builder somewhat to lessen the time ... ; but only by greatly increasing the price, until finally a point would be reached where he would not consent to build the house in less time no matter at what price. He would say [that the house just could not be built any faster]....
>
> The importance ... of this principle that all production of wealth requires time as well as labor we shall see later on; but the principle that time is a necessary element in all production we must take into account from the very first. (*SPE*, pp. 369–370)

The implication, which practically cries out to be made explicit, is that output is not even ultimately attributable to labor (and land) alone; the tying up of wealth over time is also necessary. Since this service is both productive and scarce—since it is demanded and is limited in supply—one can hardly expect it to be free. In short, George was on the right track in capital and interest theory; but his achievement was incomplete.

MONEY

George and the Austrians shared insights even on such relatively specific topics as money and the analogy that money and language bear to each other. They were not simply agreeing with everyone else that both are useful social institutions. They recognized both, in Hayek's words, as "results of human action but not of human design." (That insight may be familiar nowadays, but it was not so when George and Menger and even when Hayek were developing it.) Instead of being deliberately invented and instituted, money evolved spontaneously. George explains that it evolved from the most readily exchangeable commodities, which individuals employed in indirect barter because doing so afforded them economies in conducting their transactions. The medium of exchange naturally drifted into being also used as the measure of value or unit of account.

George anticipated the analogy more recently developed by Hayek and others:

> While the use of money is almost as universal as the use of languages, and it everywhere follows general laws as does the use of languages, yet as we find language differing in time and place, so do we find money differing. In fact, as we shall see, money is in one of its functions a kind of language—the language of value. (*SPE*, p. 494)

George anticipated, in at least a rudimentary way, the cash-balance approach to monetary theory later developed independently by Mises (1912/1981) and others. The demand for cash balances is accounted for by the services that they render to their holders (George presents examples in *SPE*, pp. 484–487). The development of credit promotes economics in the holding and transfer of the actual medium of exchange. "Money's most important use today is as a measure of value."[7]

KNOWLEDGE, COORDINATION, AND UNPLANNED ORDER

So far this study has reviewed points on which George shared or anticipated Austrian insights only incompletely. Now it turns to some major points of agreement.

---

[7]The quotation is taken from a subheading in *SPE*, p. 504. The insight expressed there brings to mind present-day proposals for achieving monetary reform and macroeconomic stability by defining a stable measure of value distinct from the medium of exchange, with the choice and the supply of the latter being left to unregulated private enterprise. Describing such proposals, however, would carry us too far from our present topic.

He and the Austrians agree that a central task of economics is to explain how specialized human activities may be coordinated without deliberate direction. First he distinguishes two kinds of cooperation, each of which increases productive power. One kind is the combination of effort, illustrated by men joining forces to remove a rock or lift a log too heavy for any one to move alone. The other is the separation of effort—the division of labor, specialization. Next George distinguishes two ways of arranging cooperation itself. The first is conscious direction by a controlling will, illustrated (ideally) by the deployment of an army.

The second way, achieving "spontaneous or unconscious cooperation," draws George's chief attention. One example, reminiscent of Bastiat's essay, "Natural and artificial social order" (1850/1964, pp. 1–19), is

> The providing of a great city with all the manifold things which are constantly needed by its inhabitants.... This kind of cooperation is far wider, far finer, far more strongly and delicately organized, than the kind of cooperation involved in the movements of an army, yet it is brought about not by subordination to the direction of one conscious will, which knows the general result at which it aims; but by the correlation of actions originating in many independent wills, each aiming at its own small purpose without care for or thought of the general result. (*SPE*, p. 383)

As further examples of the two kinds of coordination, George offered, respectively, the sailing (arrangement of sails and so forth) and the construction and equipping of a large ship. He elaborated on the latter example in rather poetic passages:

> Consider the timbers, the planks, the spars; the iron and steel of various kinds and forms; the copper, the brass, the bolts, screws, spikes, chains; the ropes, of steel and hemp and cotton; the canvas of various textures; the blocks and winches and windlasses; the pumps, the boats, the sextants, the chronometers, the spy-glasses and patent logs, the barometers and thermometers, charts, nautical almanacs, rockets and colored lights; food, clothing, tools, medicines and furniture, and all the various things, which it would be tiresome fully to specify, that go to the construction and furnishing of a first-class sailing ship of modern type, to say nothing of the still greater complexity of the first-class steamer. Directed cooperation never did, and I do not think in the nature of things it ever could, make and assemble such a variety of products, involving as many of them do the use of costly machinery and consummate skill, and the existence of subsidiary products and processes. (*SPE*, p. 389)

When he receives an order for such a ship, the builder does not send men out with detailed instructions for doing all the necessary work—cutting various woods, mining and refining various metals, planting hemp and cotton and breeding silkworms:

> Nor does he attempt to direct the manifold operations by which these raw materials are to be brought into the required forms and combinations, and assembled in the place where the ship is to be built. Such a task would transcend the wisdom and power of a Solomon. What he does is to avail himself of the resources of a high civilization, for without that he would be helpless, and to make use for his purpose of the unconscious cooperation by which without his direction, or any general direction, the efforts of many men, working in many different places and in occupations which cover almost the whole field of a minutely diversified industry, each animated solely by the effort to obtain the satisfaction of his personal desires in what to him is the easiest way, have brought together the materials and productions needed for the putting together of such a ship. (*SPE*, pp. 389–390)

Deploying insights later also achieved by F. A. Hayek (1945), George goes on to speak of the mobilization of knowledge that is inevitably dispersed and that simply could not be centralized and put to use by a single mind or a single organization:

> So far from any lifetime sufficing to acquire, or any single brain being able to hold, the varied knowledge that goes to the building and equipping of a modern sailing-ship, already becoming antiquated by the still more complex steamer, I doubt if the best-informed man on such subjects, even though he took a twelvemonth to study up, could give even the names of the various separate divisions of labor involved.
>
> A modern ship, like a modern railway, is a product of modern civilization ... ; of that unconscious cooperation which does not come by personal direction ... but grows ... by the relation of the efforts of individuals, each seeking the satisfaction of individual desires. A mere master of men, though he might command the services of millions, could not make such a ship unless in a civilization prepared for it. (*SPE*, pp. 390–391)

The cooperation required for sailing a ship is relatively simple. The kind required for building one is beyond the power of conscious direction to order or improve. "The only thing that conscious direction can do to aid it is to let it alone; to give it freedom to grow, leaving men free to seek the gratification of their own desires in ways that to them seem best" (*SPE*, p. 391).

George has more to say on the spontaneous mobilization of dispersed knowledge. Physical force can be aggregated, but not intelligence:

> Two men cannot see twice as far as one man, nor a hundred thousand determine one hundred thousand times as well.... No one ever said, "In a multitude of generals there is victory." On the contrary, the adage is, "One poor general is better than two good ones." (*SPE*, p. 392)

In spontaneous cooperation, however,

> what is utilized in production is not merely the sum of the physical power of the units, but the sum of their intelligence.
>
> ... while in the second kind of coöperation the sum of intelligence utilized is that of the whole of the coöperating units, in the first kind of coöperation it is only that of a very small part.
>
> In other words it is only in independent action that the full powers of the man may be utilized. The subordination of one human will to another human will, while it may in certain ways secure unity of action, must always, where intelligence is needed, involve loss of productive power. (*SPE*, pp. 392–393)

George understands the roles of exchange, markets, prices, and money in accomplishing spontaneous coordination; and he is skeptical (*SPE*, pp. 445–446) that government regulation of prices and wages and interest rates can achieve its intended purposes:

> Exchange is the great agency by which ... the spontaneous or unconscious coöperation of men in the production of wealth is brought about and economic units are welded into that social organism which is the Greater Leviathan. To this economic body, this Greater Leviathan, into which it builds the economic units, it is what the nerves or perhaps the ganglions are to the individual body. Or, to make use of another illustration, it is to our material desires and powers of satisfying them what the switchboard of a telegraph or telephone or other electric system is to that system, a means by which exertion of one kind in one place may be transmitted into satisfaction of another kind in another place, and thus the efforts of individual units be conjoined and correlated so as to yield satisfactions in most useful place and form, and to an amount exceeding what otherwise would be possible. (*SPE*, pp. 399–400)

SOCIALISM

George rejects socialism, understood as collective or state management of all means of production (*SPE*, p. 198), on the grounds that it would restrict the scope of spontaneous coordination. Attempting conscious coordination of work requiring spontaneous coordination

> is like asking the carpenter who can build a chicken-house to build a chicken also.
>
> This is the fatal defect of all forms of socialism—the reason of the fact, which all observation shows, that any attempt to carry conscious regulation and direction beyond the narrow sphere of social life in which it is necessary, inevitably works injury, hindering even what it is intended to help.
>
> And the rationale of this great fact may ... be perceived when we consider that the originating element in all production is thought or intelligence, the spiritual not the material. This spiritual element, this intelligence or thought power as it appears in man, cannot be combined or fused as can material force. (*SPE*, pp. 391–392)

The last sentences quoted remind us of the emphasis of present-day Austrians on the creative role of entrepreneurship. They also remind us of Julian Simon's emphasis, in a recent book, on *The Ultimate Resource*—human intelligence and ingenuity.

To develop his points further, George asks us to imagine that "the very wisest and best of men were selected" to direct a socialist economy. Consider

> the task that would be put upon them in the ordering of the when, where, how and by whom that would be involved in the intelligent direction and supervision of the almost infinitely complex and constantly changing relations and adjustments involved in such division of labor as goes on in a civilized community. The task transcends the power of human intelligence at its very highest. It is evidently as much beyond the ability of conscious direction as the correlation of the processes that maintain the human body in health and vigor is beyond it. [The human body functions without being consciously directed by the mind.] ...
>
> And so it is the spontaneous, unconscious cooperation of individuals which, going on in the industrial body, ... conjoins individual efforts in the production of wealth, to the enormous increase in productive power,

and distributes the product among the units of which it is composed. It is the nature and laws of such cooperation that it is the primary province of political economy to ascertain. (*SPE*, pp. 394–396)

These passages remind us again of Hayek's conception of the chief task of economics and of his and Mises's analyses of why accurate economic calculation would be impossible under full-fledged socialism.[8]

METHODOLOGY

George's views on methodology are remarkably similar to those of Carl Menger and of the modern Austrians.[9] George and Menger agree that the economist's job is not merely to catalogue economic phenomena but to search for cause-and-effect relations among them, to formulate laws expressing dependable coexistences and sequences, and to discover uniformities underlying superficial diversities.

Perhaps the leading methodological tenet of both men is that these elementary uniformities cannot be found solely in panoramic study of the economic system as a whole. They must be sought by penetrating to the level where decisions are actually made, the level of the individual person, family, firm, and agency. This approach, recommended by today's Austrians as *methodological individualism*, recognizes the legitimacy and necessity of appealing to purpose and motive. The relevant facts include not only the objective characteristics of resources and activities and products but also the characteristics attributed to them by fallible human beings, as well as human preferences and intentions. Again the subjectivism of George and the Austrians comes to the fore. Both recognize that economics does, after all, concern human action (and these two words form the title of Mises's *magnum opus*).

George asserts a basic principle that people seek to satisfy their desires with the least possible exertion, and Menger expresses similar ideas. This

---

[8] For other comments by George on socialism, though earlier and less insightful ones, see his *PFT*, pp. 320–334. Although an emphatic opponent of socialism, George did advocate not only public schools but also government ownership of what he conceived to be natural monopolies. In these he included railroads, the telegraph and telephone, and urban systems of water, gas, heat, and electricity (*SP*, p. 198ff.).

[9] George's remarks on the topic occur mostly in *SPE*, with a chapter in *PFT* and scattered observations in *P&P*. Menger develops his views in 1871/1950 and in 1883. An earlier discussion, with more detailed citations, appears in Yeager 1954.

is not an assumption that people behave like the economic man of the familiar caricature or that they act only on selfish motives.[10]

George and Menger, as well as Mises and other later Austrians, help clarify the nature of so-called armchair theorizing. Economists can discover basic facts by observation of their own and other people's decisionmaking. They even have the advantage of being able to observe the basic elements of their theoretical generalizations (human individuals and their strivings) directly, while the natural scientists must postulate or infer their basic but not directly observable elements from whatever phenomena they can observe directly. Much as geometers deduce many theorems from a few axioms, so economists deduce a powerful body of theory from a relatively few empirical generalizations, ones so crushingly obvious that their failure to hold true is almost inconceivable in the world as we know it. The axioms underpinning economic theory include ones like George's least-exertion principle and the fact that labor continued beyond some point becomes irksome (as well as others that could be added to George's list, such as the fact of scarcity itself and the principle of eventually diminishing marginal returns). (The banality of empirical observations is not related inversely to the scope and importance of their implications in economics; indeed, one might argue that a direct relation is the more plausible.) Armchair theorizing need not be the mere sterile juggling of arbitrary assumptions; it can have a sound empirical basis.

George considers how economists can disentangle the complex intermingling of many causes and many effects that occurs in the real world. He explains the method of "mental or imaginative experiment," the method of testing "the working of known principles by mentally separating, combining or eliminating conditions" (*SPE*, p. 100; *PFT*, pp. 27–29).

George and Menger share a skeptical attitude toward the "organic" conception of society. Both recognize how an economic system seems to have a life and purpose and orderliness of its own, as if it had been shaped and were operating by deliberate design. Yet they do not join the holists and institutionalists in supposing that this apparent organic unity requires concentrating research on the system's overall institutional arrangements and supposed evolutionary trends. Instead of taking the coherence and order of a market economy for granted, they regard these as among the

---

[10] See *SPE*, esp. pp. 91, 99. In this respect George anticipated Wicksteed 1910/1933, esp. chap. 5.

chief phenomena crying out for explanation. Both employ methodological individualism in developing their explanations.

George and Menger offer the same two examples of how features of the system as a whole can arise, without being deliberately contrived, from the efforts of individuals to gratify their separate desires: (1) money evolves from the most marketable of commodities under barter; (2) new communities grow and their economic activities evolve into the appearance of a rational pattern, even though settlers move in and take up particular occupations only with a view to satisfying their separate desires.

George and Menger—to summarize—conceive of economic theory as a body of deductions from a few compellingly strong empirical generalizations. They employ methodological individualism because they realize that economists' "inside" understanding of human purposes and decisions is a leading source of empirical axioms. (Not sharing George's and Menger's understanding of how empirical content can enter into armchair theory, many economists of our own day apparently regard theoretical and empirical work as two distinct fields, with adverse consequences for both.)

SOCIAL PHILOSOPHY

A final affinity between George and the modern Austrians concerns social or political philosophy. Austrian economists tend to be libertarians (although several of them insist that there is no *necessary* connection). Many libertarians—to look at the relation the other way around—tend to regard Austrianism as their own "house brand" of economics. This is unfortunate.[11]

Anyway, the ideological affinity between George and the Austrians remains a fact. As C. Lowell Harriss says:

> George could probably have considered himself a libertarian had the term been current in his day.... And such twentieth-century libertarian

---

[11]"Economics is a tool for understanding and possibly reshaping the world—for trying to make one's deepest values prevail, whatever they may be. Everyone, therefore, has an interest in getting his economics straight. The truths of economics, as of any other field of objective research, once discovered, will be the same for everyone. There is no one truth for libertarians, another for collectivists, and so on. Of course, both George and the Austrians have much to contribute toward getting economics straight; and the capacity to contribute is not confined to any particular school. What is unfortunate is a belief in different house brands of truth. Ludwig von Mises (1949) was duly emphatic in attacking this notion, which he called "polylogism."

champions as Albert Jay Nock and Frank Chodorov professed themselves outright Georgists. It was Nock, in fact, who acclaimed George "the philosopher of freedom," "the exponent of individualism as against Statism," "the very best friend the capitalist ever had," and "the architect of a society based on voluntary cooperation rather than on enforced cooperation." (Harriss in Andelson 1979, p. 367; citations omitted here.)[12]

George rejected socialism not only out of concern for economic efficiency but also (anticipating Hayek 1944) out of concern for human freedom:

> The proposal which socialism makes is that the collectivity or state shall assume the management of all means of production, including land, capital and man himself; do away with all competition, and convert mankind into two classes, the directors, taking their orders from government and acting by governmental authority, and the workers, for whom everything shall be provided, including the directors themselves.... It is more destitute of any central and guiding principle than any philosophy I know of.... It has no system of individual rights whereby it can define the extent to which the individual is entitled to liberty or to which the state may go in restraining it. (*SPE*, p. 198)

George, like many libertarian Austrians, champions the concept of natural rights or the rights of man.[13] He emphatically includes property rights. He was no redistributionist.

In a chapter entitled "The Rights of Man," he asserts:

> some facts [are] so obvious as to be beyond the necessity of argument. And one of these facts, attested by universal consciousness, is that there are rights as between man and man which existed before the formation of government, and which continue to exist in spite of the abuse of government; that there is a higher law than any human law—to wit, the law of the Creator, impressed upon and revealed through nature, which is before and above human laws, and upon conformity to which all human laws must depend for their validity. To deny this is to assert that there is no standard whatever by which the rightfulness or wrongfulness of laws and institutions can be measured; to assert that there can be no actions in themselves right and none in themselves wrong; to assert that an edict

---

[12] Harriss goes on to cite passages from *P&P*, pp. 434–436, that make George look like a supply-sider also, passages on the great release of productive energies to be expected if laborer and capitalist alike were allowed, through the abolition of taxes (other than the single tax), to reap the full reward of what they produce.

[13] Besides the passages cited below, see Andelson in Andelson 1979, pp. 386–387.

which commanded mothers to kill their children should receive the same respect as a law prohibiting infanticide.

These natural rights, this higher law, form the only true and sure basis for social organization. (*SP*, p. 92)

He denies any "real antagonism between the rights of men and the rights of property—since the right of property is but the expression of a fundamental right of man." He challenges those who imagine any conflict between human and property rights "to name any denial of the rights of men which is not or does not involve a denial of the rights of property; or any denial of the rights of property which is not or does not involve a denial of the rights of men" (*PPH*, pp. 209–210):

> This is not an accidental, but a necessary connection. The right of life and liberty—that is to say, the right of the man to himself—is not really one right and the right of property another right. They are two aspects of the same perception—the right of property being but another side, a differently stated expression, of the right of man to himself. The right of life and liberty, the right of the individual to himself, presupposes and involves the right of property, which is the exclusive right of the individual to the things his exertion has produced.
>
> This is the reason why we who really believe in the law of liberty, we who see in freedom the great solvent for all social evils, are the stanchest and most unflinching supporters of the rights of property, and would guard it as scrupulously in the case of the millionaire as in the case of the day-laborer. (*PPH*, pp. 210–211)

> I have been an active, consistent and absolute free trader, and an opponent of all schemes that would limit the freedom of the individual. I have been a stancher denier of the assumption of the right of society to the possessions of each member, and a clearer and more resolute upholder of the rights of property than has Mr. Spencer. I have opposed every proposition to help the poor at the expense of the rich. I have always insisted that no man should be taxed because of his wealth, and that no matter how many millions a man might rightfully get, society should leave to him every penny of them.[14] (*PPH*, pp. 70–71)

> This, and this alone, I contend for—that he who makes should have; that he who saves should enjoy. I ask in behalf of the poor nothing whatever that properly belongs to the rich. Instead of weakening and confusing the idea of property, I would surround it with stronger sanctions. Instead

---

[14] Herbert Spencer is the person referred to in the book's title and in the passage quoted.

of lessening the incentive to the production of wealth, I would make it more powerful by making the reward more certain. Whatever any man has added to the general stock of wealth, or has received of the free will of him who did produce it, let that be his as against all the world—his to use or to give, to do with it whatever he may please, so long as such use does not interfere with the equal freedom of others. For my part, I would put no limit on acquisition. No matter how many millions any man can get by methods which do not involve the robbery of others—they are his: let him have them. I would not even ask him for charity, or have it dinned into his ears that it is his duty to help the poor. That is his own affair. Let him do as he pleases with his own, without restriction and without suggestion. If he gets without taking from others, and uses without hurting others, what he does with his wealth is his own business and his own responsibility. (*SP*, pp. 86–87)

SCHUMPETER'S ASSESSMENT

In conclusion I remind the reader, but without quoting the whole passage verbatim, of Joseph Schumpeter's assessment of Henry George. "He was a self-taught economist, but he *was* an economist." He acquired most of the economics taught in the universities of his time. He was at home in scientific economics up to and including Mill's *Principles*, although he did fail to understand Marshall and Böhm-Bawerk. Barring his single tax and the phraseology connected with it, he was an orthodox economist, conservative in method. Whatever else might be said about his panacea, it was not nonsense; and as a competent economist, "he was careful to frame his 'remedy' in such a manner as to cause the minimum injury to the efficiency of the private-enterprise economy." What George said about the economic benefits to be expected if it were possible (as Schumpeter doubted) to remove other taxes was even "obvious wisdom" (Schumpeter 1954, p. 865).

The present article lends support, I hope, to this assessment.

REFERENCES

Andelson, Robert W., ed. *Critics of Henry George*. Rutherford, N.J.: Fairleigh Dickinson University Press, 1979. Articles cited: Andelson, "Neo-Georgism," pp. 381–393; Charles Collier, "Rutherford: The Devil Quotes Scripture," pp. 222–233; Aaron B. Fuller, "Davenport: 'Single Taxer of the Looser Observance,'" pp. 293–302; and C. Lowell Harriss, "Rothbard's Anarcho-Capitalist Critique," pp. 354–370.

Bastiat, Frédéric. 1850. *Economic Harmonies.* Translated by W. Hayden Boyers. Princeton, N.J.: D. Van Nostrand, 1964.

Böhm-Bawerk, Eugen von. *Capital and Interest.* 1884. Translated by George D. Huncke and Hans F. Sennholz. 3 vols. South Holland, Ill.: Libertarian Press, 1959.

Clark, John Bates. *The Distribution of Wealth.* 1899. New York: Macmillan, 1908.

Dolan, Edwin G., ed. *The Foundations of Modern Austrian Economics.* Kansas City, Kans.: Sheed and Ward, 1976.

George, Henry. 1879. *Progress and Poverty.* New York: Robert Schalkenbach Foundation, 1940. P&P.

———. 1883. *Social Problems.* New York: Doubleday Page, 1904. SP.

———. 1886. *Protection or Free Trade.* New York: Doubleday Page, 1905. PFT.

———. *A Perplexed Philosopher.* 1892. New York: Doubleday Page, 1904. PPH.

———. 1898. *The Science of Political Economy.* New York: Robert Schalkenbach Foundation, 1941. SPE.

Hayek, Friedrich A. *The Road to Serfdom.* Chicago: University of Chicago Press, 1944.

———. "The Use of Knowledge in Society." *American Economic Review* 35 (September 1945): 519–530.

———. "The Results of Human Action but Not of Human Design." In *Studies in Philosophy, Politics, and Economics*, 96–105. Chicago: University of Chicago Press, 1967.

Leibenstein, Harvey. *Beyond Economic Man.* Cambridge, Mass.: Harvard University Press, 1976.

Menger, Carl. *Untersuchungen über die Methode der Socialwissenschaften und der politischen ökonomie insbesondere.* Leipzig: Duncker & Humblot, 1883.

———. 1871. *Principles of Economics.* Translated and edited by James Dingwall and Bert F. Hoselitz. Glencoe, Ill.: Free Press, 1950.

Mises, Ludwig von. *Human Action.* New Haven, Conn.: Yale University Press, 1949.

———. *The Theory of Money and Credit.* 1912. Translated by H.E. Batson. Indianapolis: Liberty Classics, 1981.

Moss, Laurence S., ed. *The Economics of Ludwig von Mises.* Kansas City, Kans.: Sheed and Ward, 1976.

O'Driscoll, Gerald P. *Economics as a Coordination Problem.* Kansas City, Kans.: Sheed Andrews and McMeel, 1977.

Rothbard, Murray N. *Man, Economy, and State.* 2 vols. Princeton, N.J.: D. Van Nostrand, 1962.

———. *Power and Market.* Menlo Park, Calif.: Institute for Humane Studies, 1970.

———. *For a New Liberty.* New York: Macmillan, 1973.

Schumpeter, Joseph. *History of Economic Analysis.* New York: Oxford University Press, 1954.

Simon, Julian L. *The Ultimate Resource.* Princeton, N.J.: Princeton University Press, 1981.

Spadaro, Louis M., ed. *New Directions in Austrian Economics.* Kansas City, Kans.: Sheed Andrews and McMeel, 1978.

Wicksteed, Philip H. 1910. *The Common Sense of Political Economy.* Rev. and enlarged ed. London: Routledge, 1933.

———. *An Essay on the Coordination of the Laws of Distribution.* 1894. London: London School of Economics, 1932.

Yeager, Leland B. "The Methodology of Henry George and Carl Menger." *American Journal of Economics and Sociology* 13 (1954): 233–238.

CHAPTER 4

The Debate about the Efficiency of a Socialist Economy*

Non-academic socialists have in general bothered little about how a socialist economy would work. Even Karl Marx preferred to attack capitalism rather than describe socialism. In popular thought, socialist production was to be organized very simply, with sole regard to the needs of the comrades.

The popular slogan "production for use, not for profit" overlooks the fundamental economic problem of scarcity. It is simply impossible to satisfy all of everybody's wants fully. Without some indexes of the intensity and satiability of wants and of the scarcity of resources relative to usefulness, rational economic calculation is out of the question. Suppose ten more small radios could be produced at the sacrifice of one large television set. Would national output thereby be increased or decreased? Without some concept of "value," the question is meaningless. Suppose a certain product could be produced either with ten units of land plus five of labor or with four units of land plus nine of labor. Which method of production is more economical? Without some concept of "value," the question is meaningless.

When socialism became an immediate political issue at the end of World War I, the Austrian economist Ludwig von Mises spoke forth to deny that socialism is economically practicable. Mises's main argument can be summarized—as the socialist H.D. Dickinson (1939, p. 111) has done—in three statements:

1. Rational economic activity requires the pricing of all goods, production goods as well as consumption goods.

---

*Presented in the Department of Economics staff seminar, Texas A&M University (then College), November 1949. Printed here unchanged except for standardization of the format of references.

2. Pricing requires the existence of a market.
3. A market requires the existence of independent owners of the goods exchanged.

Listen to Mises's own words:

> In any social order, even under Socialism, it can very easily be decided which kind and what number of consumption goods should be produced. No one has ever denied that. But once this decision has been made, there still remains the problem of ascertaining how the existing means of production can be used most effectively to produce these goods in question. In order to solve this problem it is necessary that there should be economic calculation. And economic calculation can only take place by means of money prices established in the market for production goods in a society resting on private property in the means of production. That is to say, there must exist money prices of land, raw materials, semi-manufactures; that is to say, there must be money wages and interest rates. (1922/1981, pp. 141–142)

At about the same time that Mises's famous article appeared in 1920, similar ideas came from the pens of Max Weber in Germany and Boris Brutzkus in—of all places—Russia. Brutzkus, for instance, wrote:

> just as capitalism possessed a general measure of value in the rouble, so socialism would have to possess an analogous unit for the evaluation of its elements.... *Without evaluation any rational economic conduct, under whatever kind of economic system, is impossible.* (1935, p. 15; italics in original)

Mises, Weber, and Brutzkus were not the first writers to question the economic efficiency of arbitrary planning. For instance, as early as 1902, the Dutch economist Nicolaas G. Pierson (1935, pp. 41–85) had emphasized that a socialist community would have to face the problem of value. But it was left for Professor Mises to revolutionize academic discussion. This Mises accomplished by his dogmatic insistence that rational economic calculation under socialism would be impossible. In Mises's own words, "Every step that takes us away from private ownership of the means of production and from the use of money also takes us away from rational economics" (1920/1935, p. 104).

Ensuing discussion of how to avoid the pitfalls stressed by Mises became reminiscent of an article published by Enrico Barone in 1908. In his "The Ministry of Production in the Collectivist State," Barone had applied

Pareto's system of equations to demonstrate that "all the economic categories of the old regime must reappear, though maybe with other names: prices, salaries, interest, rent, profit, saving, etc." (1908/1935, p. 289). The Ministry of Production, through deliberate arrangement, would have to satisfy the two conditions that would result automatically from perfect competition, that is, equalization of prices with cost, and minimization of costs of production. The system of equations giving the correct allocation of resources and labor would be identical with the system reflecting the operation of free competition. However, Barone assumed that the Ministry would actually have to formulate and solve such equations, so he referred skeptically to "the laborious and colossal centralization work of the Ministry (assuming the practical possibility of such a system)" (p. 290).

The concept of "optimum conditions" is either explicit or implicit in the work of Barone and many post-Mises writers. If one makes a number of assumptions—such as that people's preferences as workers and consumers are to "count" and that an ethically desirable income distribution can be achieved—then it is possible to deduce certain conditions which must prevail in a situation of maximum welfare as a situation in which no household could be made still better without some other household being made worse off in consequence. Following Vilfredo Pareto, J.R. Hicks, Paul Samuelson, Abram Bergson, M.W. Reder, Abba Lerner, Oskar Lange, and other recent writers have explicitly formulated sets of optimum conditions. The optimum conditions are the heart of modern welfare economics.

To save time, I shall not read a typical set of optimum conditions. The conditions are more easily followed when seen in print than when merely heard, anyway. Suffice to say that Professor Hayek has summed up several of the conditions very neatly: "the marginal rates of substitution between any two commodities or factors must be the same in all their different uses" (1948, p. 77).

The optimum conditions may be restated briefly in terms of "costs." The total cost incurred in the production of the optimum amount of any commodity must be a minimum, that is, the average cost at optimum output must be a minimum. The optimum output of each commodity is specified by the condition that marginal cost equal price. The "prices" used in valuing outputs and measuring costs need not be thought of as market prices; they can—in principle—be mere indexes inversely proportional to the common subjective marginal rates of substitution for households and the common marginal technical rates of substitution for firms.

The point of the discussion so far is that a socialist planning board could formulate a set of optimum conditions and translate these conditions into mathematical equations. If the planning board knew in complete detail the preferences of all people as workers and as consumers, if it knew the production functions of all productive processes, if it had detailed information on the stocks of all resources, and if it could decide on some scheme of income distribution, then—conceivably—it could determine the amounts of each and every sort of good and service which "should" be allocated to each and every use. If the planning board were omniscient, then—as Hayek remarks—the solution of the community's economic problem would be a matter of pure logic (Hayek 1948, p. 77). For the board would embody its omniscience in mathematical equations. As Barone showed, there would be as many equations as unknowns. The equations are to be solved simultaneously, and the solution would be determinate.

Writers before the time of Mises's famous article—notably Wieser, Pareto, and Cassel, as well as Barone—had used the concept of equilibrium determination through simultaneous equations as an expository device. But some socialist writers have envisaged the solution of simultaneous equations as the actual method of socialist resource allocation (for instance, Carl Landauer, and—at one time—H.D. Dickinson).

On this approach, the comments of Lionel Robbins are most pertinent. I quote from Robbins, *The Great Depression* (1934, pp. 150–151).

> On paper we can conceive this problem to be solved by a series of mathematical calculations. We can imagine tables to be drawn up expressing the consumers' demands for all the different commodities at all conceivable prices. And we can conceive technical information giving us the productivity, in terms of each of the different commodities, which could be produced by each of the various possible combinations of the factors of production. On such a basis a system of simultaneous equations could be constructed whose solution would show the equilibrium distribution of factors and the equilibrium production of commodities.

> But in practice this solution is quite unworkable. It would necessitate the drawing up of millions of equations on the basis of millions of statistical tables based on many more millions of individual computations. By the time the equations were solved, the information on which they were based would have became obsolete and they would need to be calculated

anew. The suggestion that a practical solution of the problem of planning is possible on the basis of the Paretian equations simply indicates that those who put it forward have not begun to grasp what these equations really mean. There is no hope in this direction of discovering the relative sacrifices of alternative kinds of investment. There is no hope here of a means of adjusting production to meet the preferences of consumers.

In his article "On the Economic Theory of Socialism," Oskar Lange makes fun of Robbins and Hayek for worrying about whether socialists propose to solve simultaneous equations (Lange and Taylor 1938, p. 88). But before deciding whether Robbins and Hayek deserve this ridicule, lets see what Carl Landauer wrote in a book published as recently as 1944. The following lines are, to me, among the funniest in all economics:

> Price formation on the market is a search for an equilibrium through trial and error. The sellers and buyers change their charges and biddings until a price is established which just equilibrates supply and demand. The planning board can carry this process out on paper with infinitely less cost and loss of time than it can be carried out by sellers and buyers in reality.
>
> ... it is possible to establish a system of simultaneous equations, in which the combined effects, in terms of utility produced, and the physical quantities of each element in each combination appear as the knowns and the unit values of the elements as the unknowns.
>
> There is no difficulty at all in finding as many equations as we wish, since there are almost innumerable combinations of goods and we have always enough to calculate the unknowns.
>
> Instead of following the rules of the mathematical text-book, we may systematically change all the elements of the equations until we arrive at magnitudes which will satisfy the conditions.
>
> The planning board ... applies the trial-and-error process on paper.... This form of experimental variation is an immense economy in time, effort, and material as compared with the experiments in steel and timber, copper and labor, selection of occupation and expenditure of consumer dollars, which is the prevalent form of approaching an equilibrium under the *status quo*.
>
> ... the equations will not reach a fabulous number, but it is quite possible that a few hundred thousand combinations have to be taken into account. Why this should exceed the power of algebraic analysis is difficult to see. It probably does not exceed the amount of calculation work

which a hundred middle-sized engineering firms have to perform in a week.

It is a crude method to search for an equilibrium by experimentally varying all the determinants until they fit together, and, although it is infinitely more economical to carry out these variations on paper than in reality, a further great economy of effort might be achieved through the development of mathematical shortcuts. A future generation may look upon the trial-and-error process very much as a second-year schoolboy, knowing the use of multiplying and dividing techniques, looks at the abacus. But in the meantime, the abacus method serves the purpose of demonstrating that the problem is in any case soluble, practically as well as theoretically.[1] (Landauer 1944, pp. 34–41)

Before proceeding to socialist schemes that assign a large role to prices, let's examine the optimum condition that for every product, marginal cost should equal price. This is Abba Lerner's famous instruction to managers of socialized enterprises. Its implications have been one of the hottest topics of debate in the field of welfare economics.

First, just *why* should marginal cost and price be equal? The marginal cost of commodity A is the sum of the prices of the additional factor-units needed to make an extra unit of commodity A. The price to a producer of commodity A of each factor-unit equals the factor's marginal value productivity elsewhere. If consumers will pay more for commodity A than its marginal cost, this means that the necessary additional factors will produce more satisfaction (as measured by what consumers are willing to pay) in the production of commodity A than in the production of anything else. If, on the other hand, consumers will not pay as much for commodity A as its marginal cost, this means that marginal factors will produce more consumer satisfaction elsewhere. Now, an additional unit of any factor should have the same marginal value productivity—that is, the same marginal productivity of consumer satisfactions—in all its uses. Therefore, production of commodity A should be expanded or contracted to the point at which marginal cost and price are equal.

If average cost of a commodity decreases throughout the relevant range as output expands, marginal cost is less than average cost. The total amount

---
[1] In a footnote Landauer cites the work of Henry Schultz to show that actual demand curves *can* be found.

In the book quoted, Landauer, an old-time socialist, is ostensibly arguing for "planning" rather than for "socialism." However, it would be mere quibbling about the use of words to deny that Landauer's proposals are socialism.

paid for the commodity on the basis of marginal-cost pricing will thus fall short of total costs. But since price should equal marginal cost, the industry should run at a loss, and the government should make up the loss out of general taxation.

Alfred Marshall had already in his *Principles* (1890/1920, pp. 469–473) championed subsidies to decreasing-cost industries in the old-fashioned language of "consumers' surplus." In recent years Harold Hotelling (1938, pp. 242–269) and Abba Lerner (1947, esp. pp. 194–199) have insisted vigorously on the proposition; and though the conclusion is startling, the Hotelling-Lerner logic, summarized above, seems impeccable.

The disconcerting thing is that another chain of reasoning leads to a seemingly opposite conclusion. R.H. Coase (1946, pp. 169–182, esp. p. 172) states two principles of optimum pricing:

1. For each individual consumer the same factor should have the same price in whatever use it is employed. Otherwise consumers would not be able to choose rationally, on the basis of price, the use in which they preferred to have the factor employed.

2. The price of a factor should equate its supply and demand and should be the same for all consumers and in all uses.

From these principles Coase draws the implication that the amount paid for a product should be equal to the total value that the factors used in its production have in another use or to another user. In other words, the price of a product should be equal to its full cost.

Coase argues that if certain factors of production can be obtained free in one use (because they do not enter into marginal cost), but have to be paid for in another use (because they do enter into marginal cost), then consumers may choose to employ these factors in the use in which they are free, even though they would in fact prefer to employ them in some other way. If the Hotelling-Lerner solution were adopted, there would be only one way out of the difficulty. That would be for the state to decide whether or not each consumer should be supplied with the particular good in question. This would be done by estimating whether or not each consumer *would* be willing to pay the full cost of supplying him if he were called upon to do so. Coase further argues that no government could estimate individual demands accurately; that if all pricing were on a marginal-cost basis, there would be less information available by which such an estimate could be made; and that the incentive to correct forecasting would suffer if there were no subsequent market test of whether such estimates of individual demand were correct or not.

Coase's second objection to Hotelling-Lerner pricing is that it would redistribute income in favor of patrons of decreasing-cost industries. It is not easy to imagine how such a redistribution might be considered ethically desirable. For instance, Harry Norris (1947, pp. 54–62) imagines two countries which are identical except that one is lighted by a constant-cost gas industry and the other is lighted by a decreasing-cost electric industry. In each country ten percent of the taxpayers are backwoodsmen living beyond the range of utility service. In the gas-lit country, each household pays for its lighting in full. But according to the Hotelling-Lerner solution, the backwoods taxpayers in the electric country should subsidize the lighting of the city dwellers. Yet this arrangement could hardly be defended on ethical grounds.

A third objection to Hotelling and Lerner is that the taxation necessary to raise subsidy money would have the familiar disincentive effects where imposed.

A fourth set of objections to marginal-cost pricing is mentioned, strangely enough, by a champion of the Hotelling-Lerner solution and opponent of Coase's proposals. William Vickrey (1948, pp. 218–238) points out that in some instances the application of Hotelling-Lerner pricing might involve serious political and sociological consequences. Vickrey may have in mind the dangers of any new excuse for raids on the United States Treasury.

R.H. Coase (1946, pp. 169–182, esp. pp. 173ff.) seeks to reconcile the implications of his own and the Hotelling-Lerner reasoning by the ingenious device of multi-part pricing. Patrons of decreasing-cost industries are charged a lump sum or series of lump sums which are supposed to cover intra-marginal costs. Each consumer is then allowed to obtain additional units of product at the marginal cost. The advantage of multi-part pricing is that consumers can be asked to pay a total amount which is equal to the total cost. Therefore, it is possible to discover whether consumers value the total supply at least the total cost of supplying them. (Under a pricing system, whether consumers are willing to pay an amount equal to total cost can be discovered only by actually asking them to pay this amount.) At the same time, additional units are supplied at additional cost, and so the right output can be obtained; that is, the Lerner allocation of factors can be achieved.

William Vickrey (1948, pp. 218–238) raises a number of practical objections to multi-part pricing. But—to put it mildly—a number of practical objections could be leveled against Hotelling-Lerner pricing also. In summary, I believe that Coase's multi-part pricing scheme remains at least as intellectually respectable as marginal-cost pricing.

Writers who were unhappy about the prospect of actually having to solve millions of simultaneous equations formulated the so-called "competitive" or "trial-and-error" solution to the problem of socialist resource allocation. There is a large measure of agreement in the ideas of Oskar Lange and Fred W. Taylor (1938), A.C. Pigou (1937), R.L. Hall (1937), H.D. Dickinson (1939), and Burnham P. Beckwith (1949).

According to the "competitive solution," households have freedom of choice in regard to jobs and consumer goods. Households receive and spend actual cash. The central authority instructs the manager of each production unit to operate in accord with two basic rules. For any given scale of output, he must combine the factors of production in such a way as, at the established prices, to minimize average cost per unit of output. Secondly, he must fix output so that marginal cost of the product equals its established price.

The question arises: How do the prices of consumer goods, intermediate goods, and productive resources *get* "established"? Answer: the central authority does it. (Incidentally, the prices for all things except labor and consumer goods need not be market prices; they can be mere *accounting* prices.) The central authority decrees a price for each good. If the managers of productive units follow the rules, they will—like entrepreneurs under perfect competition—regard the prices as parameters. Of course, the prices decreed by the central authority will not be correct at first. There will be shortages of some things and surpluses of others. Consequently, the authority will raise the prices of things in excess demand, and lower the prices of things in excess supply. By constant experimenting—by trial-and-error—the central authority is supposed to make everything work out all right.

Similarly, the central authority could make capital freely available to the socialist enterprises at an established rate of interest. Interest would be reckoned among the elements in cost. In many socialist blueprints, the central authority would arbitrarily fix the total amount of liquid capital available. In any case, the authority could conceivably equate the demand and supply of capital by manipulating the interest rate, just as it would manipulate other prices. Incidentally, Enrico Barone had already mentioned the idea of setting the interest rate by trial and error in his essay of 1908 (pp. 268–269).

The main feature of the Competitive Solution, then, is that some Board, rather than the market, adjusts prices to bring supply and demand into line.

Several questions about this Lange-Taylor "solution" are obvious:

1. How would the Board force managers to obey the "rules"? For instance, enterprises that were large in relation to their market might profit by taking into account the effects of their actions on the Board's price-setting decisions. The managers might restrict output in much the same way as monopolists do under capitalism. Even assuming away all questions of monopolistic motives, there still remains the problem of whether managers should be allowed to act upon their *anticipations* of price changes by the Board.

2. How would the Board judge the efficiency of managers?

Of course, in coping with those two difficulties, the Board might look into the books of the individual production units. But if carried to any length, this practice would conflict with the essential aim of decentralizing decisionmaking.

3. How would the Lange-Taylor solution apply to the prices of commodities that cannot be standardized, such as large units of capital equipment which must be made to order? In all such cases there would be no basis for centralized fixing of prices so as "to equalize demand and supply." Socialist writers simply ignore the various complications that would arise.

4. If the price-setting authority perceives, for example, that the demand for rubber exceeds the supply, how is it to know whether this indicates too low a price for rubber or too high a price for tires? If the demand for sheet aluminum is less than the supply, is the price of aluminum too high, or is the price of plywood too low? If the demand for gasoline falls short of the supply, is this due to too high a price for gasoline or too high a price for automobiles? The point is that the central authority would have to work with Walrasian, and not merely Marshallian supply and demand functions. The authority could not change a single price without changing the equilibrium prices of other goods. Trial-and-error would not be simply a matter of making particular prices higher or lower; it would be a problem involving at least many millions of possible patterns of price increases or decreases. And for each increase or decrease there would be the problem of how much.

Furthermore, continual shifts and changes in supply and demand functions themselves would blur the central authority's view of the effects of its trials-and-errors.

Still further comments on Lange-Taylor socialism are in order. Like some of the foregoing points, they are stated most cogently in the writings of Professor Hayek (1948, chaps. IX and IV). For instance, by the very nature of administrative decisions, such price changes as were made would occur later than if the prices were determined on a free market. Secondly, the central price authority would differentiate much less than a free market would between the prices of commodities according to differences of quality and the circumstances of time and place. This means that managers of production would have no inducement, and even no real possibility, to make use of special opportunities, special bargains, and all the little advantages offered by special temporary or local conditions. Society could not make full use of the sort of dispersed knowledge that cannot be collected in the form of statistics, for example, knowledge of vacant space in the hold of a tramp steamer about to sail, knowledge of a machine that is not being fully used, knowledge of a particular person's skill that might be better utilized.

Furthermore, theorists of the Lange-Taylor school err in regarding cost curves as "given." One function of capitalist price competition is to reduce costs to a minimum. Under socialism, the new man with the new idea is not able to enter an industry and undercut old producers unless the central authority approves his projects und provides him with capital.

Further comments on Lange-Taylor socialism apply to an even more decentralized type of socialism as well. I will save these comments until the discussion of that other type.

Professor Pigou, for one, recognizes the difficulties that would beset any attempt to apply his Competitive Solution to the problem of socialism. He says: "Evidently ... the practical difficulty of working such a process will be enormous.... Far-reaching errors are almost inevitable." Nevertheless, Pigou congratulates himself on the fact that his "analysis shows that the allocation problem is soluble *in principle*" (1937, p. 115). This brings me to remark that I cannot understand the common charge that critics of socialism base their case on "merely practical" objections. As Lionel Robbins observes, "it is one thing to sketch the requirements of the plan. It is another thing to conceive of its execution" (1934, p. 150). Of course the allocation problem is soluble *in principle*. But it is just as possible, *in principle*, to breed winged elephants. Anyone who doubts this can find out how from me later.

Some socialist writers, notably Maurice Dobb, find it hard to take seriously the suggestion that plant managers should "play an elaborate game of bidding for capital on a market, instead of transmitting the information (about productivities) direct to some planning authority" (1946, p. 302). Dobb and his school take refuge in a large measure of central planning of the Soviet type. Paul Sweezy, also, favors comprehensive planning; indeed, he agrees with H.D. Dickinson that centralization is all but inevitable under socialism. Yet Sweezy (1949, pp. 232–239) cites Lange's *On the Economic Theory of Socialism* "as having finally removed any doubts about the capacity of socialism to utilize resources rationally," and he seems not to realize the inconsistency of his own position.

Since the centralized-planning approach is unquestionably vulnerable to the criticisms advanced long ago by Mises, I find it a peculiarly uninteresting form of socialism. Therefore, let's go on to an extremely decentralized form of socialism.

Abba Lerner, in *The Economics of Control* (1947), and Lerner and Oskar Lange, in a pamphlet published in 1944, advocate "free enterprise." By this, Lerner and Lange mean that both government and private entrepreneurs should be free to enter any line of business not reserved to the government. Perhaps this arrangement would be the famous "mixed economy" rather than full-blown socialism. Franco Modigliani (1947, pp. 441–514) advocates a decentralized socialism in a lengthy article published in 1947, though he does not go nearly as far towards so-called "free enterprise" as do Lerner and Lange.

Lerner and Lange recognize that

> what the manager of every factory needs is some simple indication of the usefulness for alternative production of each of the goods that he might use. Such an indication of the alternative productivity of each factor is provided by its *price*. For this we must have markets for the factors in which the price equates the supply to the demand, with appropriate rules governing the demand for the factors of production by the various managers in charge of the public enterprises. (1944, p. 18)

Incidentally, I cannot help but interpret that quotation from two of the most competent socialist writers as anything less than an outright concession of at least two-thirds of Professor Mises's original argument.

It is also noteworthy that Lange has abandoned the position he held in *On the Economic Theory of Socialism*.

Of the various instructions which Lerner, Lange, and Modigliani address to the managers of production, the most important is our old friend: equate marginal cost and price. But the central planning board now seems to have lost its job of setting prices by trial and error.

In *The Economics of Control*, Lerner writes:

> In each market, whether for factors or for products, prices are raised whenever the demand for any product or factor is greater than the supply and lowered when the supply is greater than the demand until a set of prices is reached in which each demand is equal to the corresponding supply. (p. 63)

It is not clear who is to do the raising and lowering. Lerner seems to leave the task to a market rather than to a Board. But if prices are not parameters either established by atomistic competition or by some Board, then the rule "equate marginal cost and price" is not unambiguous.

Professor Morgner has suggested to me that perhaps the idea is to have each manager operate at the output and sell at the price indicated by the intersection of his average revenue and marginal cost curves. Some remarks by Paul A. Samuelson suggest that this interpretation may be correct:

> the decentralized operators in a planned society should refrain from a literal aping of atomistic, passive, parametric price behavior. Instead of pretending that demand curves are infinitely elastic when they are not, the correct shape of that curve is to be taken into account. This does not mean that the decentralized operators should take account of their influence on price as a monopolist would. (1948, p. 232)

Assuming that the equating of marginal cost and average revenue is what Lerner, Lange, and Modigliani have in mind, let's see how this system would work:

1. Barring extreme coincidences, different enterprises would be trying to charge different prices for the same product. There is no reason for assuming that the marginal-cost-average-revenue intersections of different enterprises would be at the same price.

2. If managers receive prestige, power, or bonuses according to the prosperity of their enterprises, they would have an incentive to take

advantage of imperfect competition by overcharging buyers and underpaying suppliers. If the central authority tried to enforce rigorous adherence to the "rules," there would have to be duplication of management and so perhaps centralized planning after all.

3. Managers might not know their own marginal cost curves, even if determinate. Most important, managers almost certainly could not know their average revenue curves for the simple reason that such curves would not exist as independent entities. To be specific, the socialized enterprises would almost certainly be oligopolies, and the outstanding characteristic of oligopoly is absence of any *determinate* average revenue curve. Notice that I am not talking about "mere practical difficulties" of measurement. My point is that neither the most powerful statistical techniques nor the fact of government ownership could provide an oligopolistic firm with something nonexistent, that is, with a determinate average revenue curve.

Thus it appears that the Lerner-Lange-Modigliani rules do not yield any determinate price-output situation at all. The socialist economy would simply have to wallow in chaos.

Several observations apply both to Lange-Taylor socialism and to Lerner-Lange-Modigliani socialism:

1. The adoption of competition or quasi-competition means giving up whatever advantages centralized planning might afford (if those advantages were considered worth the price in terms of grave disadvantages). For example, competitive socialism has no sure cure for the business cycle. Dickinson, Modigliani, and others who discuss the problem pin their faith on what are essentially the sort of Keynesian fiscal policies that capitalism could adopt. But Beckwith has the most elegantly simple device for getting rid of unemployment: just cut wage rates to whatever extent may be necessary. With regard to wages, Dickinson and Beckwith declare themselves for piece-rates and the other trappings of Taylorism. Incidentally, few socialist price-theorists try to pretend that their systems hold any place for unionism as we know it today. To my knowledge, only Lerner and Lange cannot bear to stop mouthing the shibboleths of contemporary unionism.

2. It is questionable whether the diligence and the decisions of socialist managers of production would be governed by suitable incentives. As Mises points out, the capitalist entrepreneur

> does not just invest his capital in those undertakings which offer high interest or high profit; he attempts rather to strike a balance between his desire for profit and his estimate of the risk of loss. He must exercise

foresight. If he does not do so then he suffers losses—losses that bring it about that his disposition over the factors of production is transferred to the hands of others who know better how to weigh the risks and the prospects of business speculation.

Capitalists and speculators cannot be expected to act as mere agents of the community, for

> the function which capitalists and speculators perform under Capitalism, namely directing the use of capital goods into that direction in which they best serve the demands of the consumer, is only performed because they are under the incentive to preserve their property and to make profits. (1922/1981, pp. 140–141)

Furthermore, there is no reason to think that the recklessness of some socialist managers would compensate for the over-cautiousness of others. Two wrongs don't make a right.

3. As I have already implied, the schemes of price-theory socialists have an extreme static bias. We may well join with Professors Hayek, Mises, and Robbins in asking: What is to be the independent business unit? Who is to be the manager? What resources are to be entrusted to him? How is his success or failure to be tested? On what principle is the control of productive facilities to be transferred from one manager to another (Hayek 1948, esp. pp. 172, 196–197)? The idea of instructing the controllers of various industrial units to act *as if* they were capitalist entrepreneurs ignores the fundamental problem of a dynamic economy, the problem of deciding what resources should be risked in what ventures under the control of what men. As Robbins says,

> For competition to be free the *entrepreneur* must be at liberty to withdraw his capital altogether from one line of production, sell his plant and his stocks and go into other lines. He must be at liberty to break up the administrative unit. It is difficult to see how liberty of this sort, which is necessary if the market is to be the register of the varying pulls of all the changes in the data, is compatible with the requirements of a society whose *raison d'etre* is ownership and control at the centre. (1934, pp. 153–154)

Mises remarks that when socialist theorists assume stationary conditions, the essential function of economic calculation has *by hypothesis* already been performed (1949, pp. 137ff.).

R.L. Hall worries about how anyone could tell whether a socialist monopoly were as efficient as it might be. In Hall's words,

If a world champion has no one against which to measure himself, how can he tell of what he is capable? A runner can run against himself by means of a stop-watch: will a state concern be prepared to make continuous efforts to reduce its own costs? If it does not do so, no one else can. In a capitalist state Nemesis is always waiting for the lethargic monopoly, as the calamity of the internal combustion engine fell upon the railways. But it is doubtful whether anyone in a collectivist state would have any hope of starting a rival department. (1937, pp. 138–139)

4. Few blueprints of socialism make much specific provisions for economic development. Even Franco Modigliani's meager remarks are unusual in the literature (1947, pp. 463–465). Modigliani faces squarely the disadvantage that decisions about new products would have to be made by an administrative body. He perceives the twin dangers of inertia due to lack of a profit incentive and of recklessness due to lack of a loss-penalty. (Modigliani feels that the tendency toward inertia is probably more characteristic of bureaucracy.) To avoid these dangers, Modigliani proposes a Research Commission to decide on new big investments and on new products requiring new plants. The Research Commission and the various industrial managers are to share the responsibility for mere product modifications, and the managers are to receive bonuses for successful innovations.

Doubts about the progressiveness of socialism do not rest on any supposed lack of incentives for scientists. As Brutzkus writes,

> Scientific discoveries, it is true, are not made out of a desire for profit but in answer to humanity's unquenchable search for truth. In the case of inventions the scientific interest recedes in favour of practical motives. But neither scientists nor even inventors are directly responsible for economic progress; it is the organizers and practical men who stimulate development.
>
> Even supposing ... that the highest posts were filled in the best possible manner, there would still remain the danger that each innovation could only be tested in a definite place....
>
> If ... the socialist organization succeeded in assuming stable forms it would be distinguished by immense indolence and conservatism. It would offer nothing which could be compared to the unceasing movement of economic life under capitalism. (1935, pp. 67–69)

In his essay *On Liberty*, John Stuart Mill uses his arguments for freedom of expression as a case for freedom of enterprise:

> The management of purely local business by the localities, and of the great enterprises of industry by the union of those who voluntarily supply the pecuniary means, is further recommended by all the advantages which have been set forth in this Essay as belonging to individuality of development, and diversity of modes of action. Government operations tend to be everywhere alike. With individuals and voluntary associations, on the contrary, there are varied experiments, and endless diversity of experience. (1859/1929, p. 131)

Modigliani's Research Commission would hardly be an adequate substitute for Mill's "diversity of modes of action," even if it were staffed entirely by scientific and technical experts. The very essence of innovation is that it embodies ideas divergent from prevailing thought. Progress cannot be completely plotted and blueprinted in advance; that is why it is progress. Often discovery can be identified only in retrospect (cf. Harper 1949, pp. 72–76). If the government Research Commission decided not to "waste" resources on some new idea, it would be ruled out; that's all. But in a competitive enterprise system, an idea discarded by ninety-nine companies still has a chance with a hundredth company. And no company can afford to be too rash in rejecting innovations, for fear that its competitors will "get the jump" on it. In a competitive system, a research worker who feels frustrated in one job can take his ideas to another employer. Under socialism things would be different.

With regard to invention, R. L. Hall writes:

> there does not seem to be any criterion by which the Socialist state can decide the amount of resources which it is proper to spend: so that they cannot rationally create a profession of inventors. On the other hand, if these matters are left to the chance on which they depend the path of the innovator will be even harder than it is in the capitalist state. In the interests of economy it is necessary to discourage cranks; but it is probable that the leaders of industry will consider that all innovators are cranks. In the capitalist state the inventor is free to devote any resources which he inherits, or can earn or can wheedle from patrons, to his researches. In a socialist state he will get nothing which he does not earn and he may find himself in a labour camp if he neglects his work. The progress of spontaneous invention may well be slowed unless care is devoted to preserving a receptive frame of mind in the higher officials. But if they are too receptive there may be dissipation of the national resources in grandiose projections doomed to failure. It is difficult to follow a middle course when no one knows where the middle is: the socialist state will

have no certainty, nor can any other form of organization give it. (1937, pp. 192–193)

In summary, innovations start out in a progressive economy as the whim of the few and are adopted only later by the inert masses. Innovation would be slowed in an economy which did not allow the widest possible scope for variety, whims, even eccentricities.

It may be objected that the foregoing considerations are *political* objections to socialism, but do not constitute an *economic* argument. I do not think this is so. Whether an economic system is efficient or not is very largely a matter of whether it is progressive or not. The mere fact that we cannot handle questions of economic development by the precise and elegant techniques of price theory does not mean that such questions fall outside the scope of economics.

The political case against socialism is quite different. It would emphasize, among other matters, the danger that pressure groups could sabotage progress. Suppose, for instance, that the automobile had not yet been invented, but that some men had ideas for developing "horseless carriages." Now which pressure group would have the ear of the government Research Commission—the buggy makers, with their thousands of votes, or the would-be automobile makers, with their mere handful of votes?

This paper does not handle the political case against socialism or the question of freedom or serfdom under socialism. I'll leave these matters for discussion afterward. But I do want to record my conviction that political and cultural considerations about socialism rival in importance the purely economic considerations. It does seem futile to worry about whether a socialist government could manage the economy efficiently and in accord with people's wishes, when the more immediate question is whether powerful rulers could at all times be forced to want to rule in the interests of all the people.

It seems to me that the history of socialist literature is a history of continual attempts to get rid of the difficulties in socialist blueprints. And as these difficulties are eliminated, socialism comes to look more and more like competitive enterprise. Therefore, it is not without some justification that Professor Mises, with his characteristic dogmatism, now claims final victory in the debate over the efficiency of socialism. In his latest book Mises writes:

> It is ... nothing short of a full acknowledgment of the correctness and irrefutability of the economists' analysis and devastating critique of the

socialists' plans that the intellectual leaders of socialism are now busy designing schemes for a socialist system in which the market, market prices for the factors of production, and catallactic competition are to be preserved. The overwhelmingly rapid triumph of the demonstration that no economic calculation is possible under a socialist system is without precedent indeed in the history of human thought. The socialists cannot help admitting their crushing final defeat. They no longer claim that socialism is matchlessly superior to capitalism because it brushes away markets, market prices, and competition. On the contrary. They are now eager to justify socialism by pointing out that it is possible to preserve these institutions even under socialism. They are drafting outlines for a socialism in which there are prices and competition.

What these neosocialists suggest is really paradoxical. They want to abolish private control of the means of production, market exchange, market prices, and competition. But at the same time they want to organize the socialist Utopia in such a way that people could act *as if* these things were still present. They want people to play market as children play war, railroad, or school. They do not comprehend how such childish play differs from the real thing it tries to imitate. (1949, pp. 702–703; footnote omitted)

Perhaps the culmination of the free-enterprise trend in socialist thinking is James E. Meade's *Planning and the Price Mechanism* (1948). Meade calls himself a socialist, but his proposals amount to scarcely more than a program for the reconstruction of competitive capitalism, including a moderate amount of government enterprise.

The implication of my remarks should be clear by now. If economists are bent on seeing socialism substituted for capitalism, they should leave the task to their colleagues who are better qualified for the job, namely, to the lexicographers.

REFERENCES

Barone, Enrico. "The Ministry of Production in the Collectivist State." 1908. In Hayek 1935.

Beckwith, Burnham P. *The Economic Theory of a Socialist Economy*. Stanford, Calif.: Stanford University Press, 1949.

Brutzkus, Boris. *Economic Planning in Soviet Russia*. London: Routledge & Sons, 1935.

Coase, R.H. "The Marginal Cost Controversy." *Economica* (August 1946): 169–182.

Dickinson, H.D. *The Economics of Socialism*. London: Oxford University Press, 1939.

Dobb, Maurice. *Political Economy and Capitalism*. London: Routledge, 1946.

Hall, R.L. *The Economic System in a Socialist State*. London: Macmillan, 1937.

Harper, F.A. *Liberty*. Irvington-on-Hudson, N.Y.: Foundation for Economic Education, 1949.

———. *Individualism and Economic Order*. Chicago: University of Chicago Press, 1948.

Hayek, F.A., ed. *Collectivist Economic Planning*. London: Routledge & Kegan Paul, 1935.

Hotelling, Harold. "The General Welfare in Relation to Problems of Taxation and of Railway and Utility Rates." *Econometrica* (July 1938): 242–269.

Landauer, Carl. *Theory of National Economic Planning*. Berkeley and Los Angeles: University of California Press, 1944.

Lange, Oskar, and Fred M. Taylor. *On the Economic Theory of Socialism*. Edited by Benjamin E. Lippincott. Minneapolis: University of Minnesota Press, 1938.

Lerner, Abba. *The Economics of Control*. New York: Macmillan, 1947.

Lerner, Abba, and Oskar Lange. *The American Way of Business*. Washington: National Education Association, 1944.

Marshall, Alfred. *Principles of Economics*. 1890. 8th ed. London: Macmillan, 1920.

Meade, James E. *Planning and the Price Mechanism*. London: Allen & Unwin, 1948.

Mill, John Stuart. *On Liberty and Other Essays*. 1859. New York: Book League of America, 1929.

Mises, Ludwig von. "Economic Calculation in the Socialist Commonwealth." 1920. In Hayek 1935.

———. *Human Action*. New Haven, Conn.: Yale University Press, 1949.

———. *Socialism: An Economic and Sociological Analysis*. 1922. Translated by J. Kahane. Indianapolis: Liberty Fund, 1981.

Modigliani, Franco. "L'organizzazione e la direzione della produzione in un'economia socialista." *Giornale degli Economisti* (September/October 1947): 441–514.

Norris, Harry. "State Enterprise Price and Output Policy and the Problem of Cost Imputation." *Economica* (February 1947): 54–62.

Pierson, Nicolaas G. "The Problem of Value in the Socialist Community." 1902. In *Collectivist Economic Planning*, edited by F.A. Hayek. London: Routledge & Kegan Paul, 1935.

Pigou, A.C. *Socialism versus Capitalism*. London: Macmillan, 1937.

Robbins, Lionel. *The Great Depression*. London: Macmillan, 1934.

Samuelson, Paul A. *Foundations of Economic Analysis*. Cambridge, Mass.: Harvard University Press, 1948.

Sweezy, Paul. *Socialism*. New York: McGraw-Hill, 1949.

Vickrey, William. "Some Objections to Marginal-Cost Pricing." *Journal of Political Economy* (June 1948): 218–238.

CHAPTER 5

The Debate over Calculation and Knowledge*

Peter Boettke and Roger Koppl join a discussion launched by Murray Rothbard, Joseph Salerno, Jeffrey Herbener, Hans-Hermann Hoppe, and Jörg Guido Hülsmann. Those five contributors to the *Review of Austrian Economics* seek, as they say, to "dehomogenize" Ludwig von Mises and F. A. Hayek, differentiating between their doctrines. Subtly or not so subtly, these "chasmologists," as Koppl calls them, often disparage Hayek.

In many writings Hayek portrayed social institutions—notably, language, the common law, money, and the market economy itself—as "spontaneous" products of evolutionary processes. Though these institutions were unplanned as wholes, they have benefited from a kind of natural selection tending to weed out their most inexpedient forms, leaving their relatively successful ones still in the running.

Salerno (1990a) attacks these aspects of Hayek's work. Some of Hayek's formulations, taken out of context, may admittedly seem exaggerated. Some disciples have indeed sometimes perverted Hayek's ideas, erecting the fact of or capacity for "spontaneous" emergence into a test of

---

*Originally entitled "Introduction to Papers by Boettke and Koppl," from a "Symposium: Did Mises and Hayek Have Conflicting Views of the World?" This paper comes from Peter Boettke and Sanford Ikeda, eds., *Advances in Austrian Economics* (1998): 123–129. Peter Boettke and Roger Koppl originally wrote their contributions for a session at the meetings of the Southern Economic Association in Washington, November 1996. Boettke addresses the calculation issue specifically. Koppl probes beneath it, examining philosophical, psychological, and methodological aspects of Mises's and Hayek's work. They both find the positions of Mises and Hayek largely reconcilable.

My introduction, slightly modified here, summarizes points made by Boettke and Koppl in the Symposium, by me in "Mises and Hayek on Calculation and Knowledge," *Review of Austrian Economics* 7, no. 2 (1994): 93–109, and by Joseph Salerno, Jörg Guido Hülsmann, Jeffrey M. Herbener, Hans-Hermann Hoppe, and me in the *Review of Austrian Economics* (1996 and 1997): vols. 9 and 10. For the calculation-not-knowledge (Mises-not-Hayek) side of this debate in its members' own words, see their papers available at http://mises.org/periodical.aspx?Id=5.

93

whether particular institutions are desirable. Hayek's own insight is consistent, though, with points made by Mises and reiterated by Salerno: however unplanned as a whole the evolution of an institution may be, most steps in the process were taken by individuals acting rationally in the light of their own purposes and information. Human rationality must not be disparaged and blind impersonal processes exalted. Surely, however, there is no need to imagine a rationalist Mises and irrationalist Hayek at loggerheads with one another. Nor is there any warrant for imputing to Hayek the view that "Whatever is, is right"; his writings on economic and political reform demonstrate the contrary. The two men's insights are mutually reinforcing.

The dehomogenizers particularly disparage Hayek's elaborations on Mises's analysis of why accurate economic calculation is impossible under socialism. An early example appears in Salerno's 1993 article, which criticizes several Austrian economists' diverse contributions to a *Festschrift* for Hans Sennholz. Salerno distinguishes between two paradigms. The "Hayekian" one "stresses the fragmentation of knowledge and its dispersion among the multitude of individual consumers and producers as the primary problem of economic and social cooperation and views the market's price system as the means by which such dispersed knowledge is ferreted out and communicated to the relevant decision-makers in the production process" (1993, p. 115). The "Misesian" paradigm "focuses on monetary calculation using actual market prices as the necessary precondition for the rational allocation of resources within an economic system featuring specialization and the division of labor" (p. 125). Surely, though, no sharp contrast is warranted. Both strands enter into a full description of the problem and process of economic calculation.

Salerno emphasizes that numerical data, especially market prices, are necessary for economic calculation; qualitative information is not enough (1993, p. 121). Without genuine exchanges of factors and genuine market determination of their prices, central planners could not "cost" resources and allocate them efficiently or purposefully (p. 130). Agreed: quantitative results—suitable product and factor quantities—presuppose quantitative inputs. These must include, somewhere in the calculation process, the numerical specifics of utility and production functions. But these, along with the qualitative information also necessary, could never all be available for centralized, nonmarket decisions.

Market prices, though necessary for calculation, are not ultimate data. Prices represent intermediate steps in taking account of the more nearly ultimate data (often labeled "wants, resources, and technology"). By "costing," Salerno presumably (and if so, correctly) means taking account both of how much of other outputs would have to be forgone to make incremental quantities of a resource available for the line of production contemplated and also of how highly consumers would have valued the forgone alternative outputs. Costing includes, then, taking account of innumerable bits of information about production opportunities and processes and about consumer tastes. Calculating the worth a prospective action requires knowing "the importance to others of the goods and services one commits to that action, and the importance to others of the goods one will obtain from that action" (Kirzner 1996, p. 150; quoted in Boettke's Symposium contribution, note 22).

Already it is clear that the calculation problem cannot be distinct from the knowledge problem.

Unlike Friedrich von Wieser and Hayek, according to Salerno, "Mises held that the social appraisement of productive factors via entrepreneurial competition in resource markets, which is the very basis of economic calculation and purposive action, can only proceed in monetary terms" (1993, p. 135). As if Hayek would deny that, as if his stress on the knowledge problem disparaged money prices and appraisals in money!

Strangely, the "chasmologists" fail to give a clear, precise, and compact statement of just how they conceive the problem of economic calculation. Their writings have a curiously allusive tone, at best alluding to points that they and their readers alike are presumed to have in mind. To demonstrate—not just assert—that the knowledge and calculation problems of socialism are distinct, one would first have to state the calculation problem adequately. Surely it involves more than bits of arithmetic performed on money prices. I am tempted to speculate—but perhaps the speculation is wild if not forbidden—that absence of a full statement of the problem reflects an inadequate grasp of it.

Sure, the dehomogenizers do emphasize that calculation includes comparing benefits and costs and estimating prospective profits and losses and that these comparisons and estimates require arithmetic done with cardinal units of value. Echoing Mises and Hayek both, they place well-warranted emphasis on the crucial importance of genuine prices expressed in money, including prices of privately owned factors of production and capital goods exchanged on genuine markets. Yet their writings are curiously inadequate in explaining what real circumstances are reflected, and how, in money prices, costs, and incomes. Behind the transactions and abstentions and bids and offers of current and would-be owners of the things exchanged lie these traders' purposes and their knowledge and estimates of and entrepreneurial conjectures about resource availabilities, technical possibilities, including complementarities and substitutabilities in production, and their own and other persons' tastes. Money prices embody or reflect *knowledge*, knowledge brought through them to bear on production and consumption decisions without being centralized and, for much of it, without even being articulated in words and numbers.

I won't repeat my 1994 description of the economic-calculation problem, but I'll add a bit to what I have already said here. Accurate calculation would assign productive resources to their most highly valued uses, taking account of people's diverse tastes (as consumers, workers, and investors), as well as of production technologies, resource availabilities, and the principles of diminishing marginal utility and marginal productivity. Ideally, each consumer is informed how much worth of other things must be forgone to supply him with an increment of each particular product. Thus informed about alternatives, each consumer ideally leaves no opportunity unexploited to increase his expected total satisfaction by diverting any dollar from one purchase to another. In this sense consumers choose the pattern of production and resource use that they prefer. Ideally, their bidding keeps any unit of a resource from going to satisfy a less intense effective demand to the denial of a more intense one.

The result of fully successful economic calculation is a state of affairs in which—apart from changes in wants, technology, and resource availabilities—no further rearrangement of patterns of production and resource allocation could achieve an increase of value to consumers from any particular good at the mere cost of a lesser sacrifice of value from some other good. (Even if a dictatorial central planner totally disregarded consumers' tastes and was concerned only with gratifying his own, he would still need vast amounts of other information.)

In a competitive market economy, patterns of resource allocation, production, and consumption get established on a decentralized basis. Of course, the market does not work with all imaginable perfection; nor does any other human institution. But entrepreneurs have incentives to ferret out price discrepancies and unexploited opportunities.

Things are different under socialism. When Mises first wrote about the calculation problem in 1920 and 1922, socialism was generally understood as a centrally directed (or "planned") economy, with government ownership (or the equivalent) of the means of production. Mises maintained that socialist planners could not adequately duplicate the results of a market economy.

In a series of articles beginning in the 1930s and culminating in his 1945 article on "The Use of Knowledge in Society," Hayek spelled out and elaborated on Mises's argument. This, anyway, is the interpretation of the discussion that I share with Professors Boettke and Koppl. How could central planners know, for each resource, its potential contribution to the value of output at all possible margins, in all possible combinations with other factors of production, in all possible lines of production?

The planners would need to know more than the technical aspects of production and more than the actual and potential tastes of consumers and workers. Efficient use of resources would further require their bringing to bear of what Hayek called "knowledge of the particular circumstances of time and place." Examples are knowledge of a machine often standing idle, of whom to call on for emergency repair of a leaking boiler, of an employee's skills that could be put to more valuable use, of stocks of materials that might be drawn on during an interruption of supplies, of empty space in a freighter about to set sail, and of fleeting inter-local differences in commodity prices. Such localized and temporary knowledge can be used only by decisionmakers on the spot and would go to waste under centralization.

But decentralized decision makers cannot work with this particular knowledge alone, or with it combined with technological knowledge. Efficient decisions must also take account of conditions in the whole rest of the economic system—the availabilities and value-productivities of resources in the innumerable lines of production that compete for them. Here Hayek's story brings in the role of the price system as a vast computer and as a communicator of information and incentives, in abbreviated form, to all consumer and business decisionmakers to whom particular bits are relevant. Here, also—if the example were not already so familiar—would be the place to recite Hayek's example of the role of changed prices in motivating appropriate responses to an increased scarcity of tin, whether caused by a blockage of normal supplies or by development of new uses for tin.

A vaguely expressed misunderstanding sometimes attributes to Hayek the claim that prices convey all the information necessary for well-calculated economic decisions. Yet prices are no substitute for knowledge of production techniques in various industries and firms. Nor are prices a substitute for "knowledge of the particular circumstances of time and place," which is not so much conveyed by prices as, rather, reflected in the actions of the decentralized decision makers who possess it.

But prices do convey much knowledge, though not all. They play an essential role in the economywide coordination of innumerable decentralized decisions. They are essential to economic calculation in the narrowest sense—the evaluation of benefits and costs and the calculation of past and prospective profits and losses.

In emphasizing the role of knowledge in economic calculation, Hayek was making explicit and elaborating on points already implicit in the arguments of Mises. In no way was he creating a "chasm" between two rival positions. This, in agreement with Kirzner (1987, 1996), is what I have argued in my 1994 article and my 1996 and 1997 replies to the contrary interpretations of Salerno, Herbener, Hülsmann, and Hoppe. To try to drive a wedge between Mises and Hayek on this issue, especially to the disparagement of Hayek, is unfair to these two great men, unfaithful to the history of economic thought, subversive of understanding an important strand of economic analysis and the nature and ultimate collapse of the communist economies of Eastern Europe, and subversive of analytical and historical understanding that is vital for future policymaking.

REFERENCES

Boettke, Peter, and Sanford Ikeda, eds. *Advances in Austrian Economics* 5, Greenwich, Conn.: JAI Press, 1998. Includes the Symposium contributions of Peter Boettke and Roger Koppl, pp. 131–158 and 159–179.

Hayek, F.A. "The Use of Knowledge in Society." *American Economic Review* 35 (September 1945): 519–530.

Herbener, Jeffrey M. "Ludwig von Mises and the Austrian School of Economics." *Review of Austrian Economics* 5, no. 2 (1991): 33–50.

———. "Calculation and the Question of Arithmetic." *Review of Austrian Economics* 9, no. 1 (1996): 151–162.

Hoppe, Hans-Hermann. "Socialism: A Property or Knowledge Problem." *Review of Austrian Economics* 9, no. 1 (1996): 143–149.

Hülsmann, Jörg Guido. "Knowledge, Judgment, and the Use of Property." *Review of Austrian Economics* 9, no. 1 (1997): 23–28.

Kirzner, Israel. "The Economic Calculation Debate: Lessons for Austrians." *Review of Austrian Economics* 2 (1987): 1–18.

———. "Reflections on the Misesian Legacy in Economics." *Review of Austrian Economics* 9, no. 2 (1996): 143–154.

Mises, Ludwig von. "Economic Calculation in the Socialist Commonwealth." 1920. Translated by S. Adler. Auburn, Ala.: Ludwig von Mises Institute, 1990.

———. *Socialism: An Economic and Sociological Analysis.* 1922. Indianapolis: Liberty Fund, 1981.

———. *Human Action.* 3rd ed. Chicago: Henry Regnery, 1949.

Rothbard, Murray N. "The End of Socialism and the Calculation Debate Revisited." *Review of Austrian Economics* 5, no. 2 (1991): 51–76.

Salerno, Joseph T. "Ludwig von Mises as Social Rationalist." *Review of Austrian Economics* 4 (1990): 26–54.

———. "Postscript: Why a Socialist Economy is 'Impossible'." Postscript to *Economic Calculation in the Socialist Commonwealth*, by Ludwig von Mises. Auburn, Ala.: Ludwig von Mises Institute, 1990.

———. "Mises and Hayek Dehomogenized." *Review of Austrian Economics* 6, no. 2 (1993): 113–146.

———. "Reply to Leland B. Yeager on 'Mises and Hayek on Calculation and Knowledge'." *Review of Austrian Economics* 7, no. 2 (1994): 111–125.

———. "A Final Word: Calculation, Knowledge, and Appraisement." *Review of Austrian Economics* 9, no. 1 (1996): 141–142.

Yeager, Leland B. "Mises and Hayek on Calculation and Knowledge." *Review of Austrian Economics* 7, no. 2 (1994): 93–109.

———. "Salerno on Calculation, Knowledge, and Appraisement." *Review of Austrian Economics* 9, no. 1 (1996): 137–139.

———. "Calculation and Knowledge: Let's Write *Finis*." *Review of Austrian Economics* 10, no. 1 (1997): 133–136.

CHAPTER 6

Austrian Economics, Neoclassicism, and the Market Test*

During a conference in 1987, a member of the audience asked me what school of economics I belonged to. Instead of repudiating this label-mongering, as perhaps I should have, I answered that I was a card-carrying member of no school but a fellow-traveler of the Chicago and Austrian schools both—if that is possible. Yes, it is possible, said Fred Glahe, another member of the panel; for he too was a fellow-traveler of both schools. I have been studying works in the Austrian tradition ever since happening onto writings by Ludwig von Mises and F.A. Hayek in 1946 or 1947. Only a small part of my own work, however, has had a deliberately Austrian character. I say this because two things might otherwise suggest, wrongly, that I am a spokesman for the Austrian School: my academic title and my being asked to comment on an earlier version of Sherwin Rosen's paper at the Mont Pélerin Society meeting in Vienna in September 1996 and again on its revision in this journal.

Rosen recognizes, in broad strokes, some contributions of Austrian economics, especially its insights into decentralization and competition. However, his recognition of Austrian strengths should be amplified and his criticisms softened. I will also argue that his appeal to a market test for judging academic work risks encouraging anti-intellectual attitudes and practices.

AUSTRIAN STRENGTHS

I'll list some Austrian strengths that merit more attention, cautioning, however, that not all Austrians cultivate every one of the themes mentioned.

Austrians are concerned with the big picture, with how a whole economic system functions, and with alternative sets of institutions. This is

*From *Journal of Economic Perspectives* 11 (Fall 1997): 153–165.

Chapter 6: Austrian Economics, Neoclassicism, and the Market Test

what Rosen presumably means by curiously labeling Austrian economics a "macro" rather than "micro" theory. Austrians investigate how the specialized activities and decentralized decisions of millions or billions of persons and business firms are coordinated. Decentralization allows use of what Hayek called "knowledge of the particular circumstances of time and place"—information that would otherwise go to waste or not even emerge in the first place. In bringing further information even about remote parts of the economy to the attention of decentralized decisionmakers and by applying incentives for its use, the market system and prices function as a vast computer and communications system. No particular agency takes charge of this coordination, and none would be competent to do so. In what Rosen calls "their finest hour," Mises and Hayek demonstrated that efficient economic calculation was impossible under centrally planned socialism. To most neoclassical economists with whom Rosen identifies, however, and as he acknowledges, the recent collapse of communist economies came as a surprise.

Austrians understand how useful institutions, including the market system itself, money, the common law, ethics, and language, can evolve "spontaneously," by a kind of natural selection, rather than by conscious implementation of any overall design. Of course, individual participants in unplanned processes act rationally by their own lights. Austrians treat institutions not as givens that can be captured by a parameter or two in an economic model but rather as complex social arrangements whose evolution requires serious thought. While not asserting that "whatever is, is right" and without rejecting possible reforms, Austrians do counsel a certain humility against temptations to overthrow spontaneously evolved institutions and practices merely because their rationales have not been fully understood and articulated.

Austrians recognize the time dimension in economic life. They take change, uncertainty, and unpredictability seriously not only in confronting theoretical and econometric models but also in assessing institutions and policies. They recognize that complex structures of heterogeneous capital goods reflect not only diverse and changeable consumption patterns and production processes but also diverse time horizons adopted in specific investment decisions.

Austrians are not obsessed with contemplating and comparing equilibrium states. They pay attention to disequilibrium and process. They do not suppose that demand curves and cost curves, nor even tastes and technologies, are somehow "given" to decisionmakers. They recognize that such entities emerge within the processes of making and implementing decisions. They see how competition presses toward reducing costs. They value the activity of entrepreneurs alert to profit opportunities in arbitraging away imperfections of coordination and in trying new products and methods. They reject policies aimed at making reality conform to textbook models of pure and perfect competition.

Austrians are relatively resistant to the methodological fads and half-tacit sermons of the academic mainstream. Austrians stress the subjective element in value: economics is primarily about people and their purposes, not about things and quantities. They push their analysis to the level where decisions are actually made, the level of the individual person, family, firm, and agency. However, they do not get trapped in a narrow perspective; they remember that the real challenge is to understand economywide coordination.

Austrians, or many of them, correctly distinguish between value judgments and value-free propositions of positive economics. They understand how the corpus of economic propositions can itself remain positive, even though it combines with plausible humanitarian value judgments in supporting a libertarian political philosophy.

Is Rosen's focus on the processes of competition a fair sketch of what is central to Austrian economics and differentiates it from neoclassicism? The two schools' treatments of competition do characterize their differences but hardly exhaust them. In neoclassical competition, buyers are typically price-takers, while sellers face flat demand curves (in pure competition) or downsloping demand curves (in imperfect competition) and maximize profits accordingly. The Austrian conception is closer to the everyday understanding of competition: rivalry to gain customers by better service, and not necessarily in price alone but in other dimensions as well. Machovec (1995) reviews how classical and Austrian insights into the competitive process became lost from the neoclassical mainstream.

Where does lack of the Austrian perspective take neoclassical economics furthest off track? Neoclassicism downplays the reality of fragmentary, scattered, unarticulated, and undiscovered knowledge. Neoclassicals tend to treat information as something objective, bought and sold on the market, in carrying out maximization decisions. They tend to ignore the role of knowledge that simply does not exist before entrepreneurs discover or create it (Huerta de Soto, 1996, p. 5). The big economic problem comprises more than just scarcity and choice. Equilibrium is not automatic and is in fact never reached. Entrepreneurs have wide scope and play a central role. All this gets shunted aside by fascination with the maximization of an objective function subject to known constraints.

CRITICISMS OF AUSTRIAN ECONOMICS

As a mere fellow-traveler of the Austrian School, and not even of it alone, I am bound by no party line and am free to reject some favorite positions held by many (but certainly not all) Austrians. These include the specifics of their business-cycle theory, their ultra-subjectivism in value theory and particularly in interest-rate theory, their insistence on unidirectional causality rather than general interdependence, and their fondness for methodological brooding, pointless profundities, and verbal gymnastics. Provoked by mainstream abuses of mathematics, including the frequent merely decorative and pretentious use of symbols, some Austrians have wanted to ban mathematics from economics. But is it not arrogant for someone who does not see how to use certain techniques constructively to suppose that no one else will ever see how either? These Austrians should remember how, in other contexts, they emphasize the openness of the future and scope for novelty.

My next complaint presupposes knowing that fairly distinct groups of Austrians are active or have studied at New York University, George Mason University, the University of Georgia, and California State University at Hayward. Others are associated with, though not necessarily located at, Auburn University's Ludwig von Mises Institute. Still other Austrians are scattered elsewhere in the United States and abroad, with a few even in Austria. Some of these groups severely criticize not only mainstream economics but each other. Interpreted optimistically, their mutual criticisms betoken a dynamic research program. On the other hand, infighting among the various Austrian sects sometimes threatens to make the whole school look ridiculous, especially as some of the combatants, fortunately few, employ questionable tactics of scholarly controversy. While not all is well in the Austrian camp, the same is true, for different reasons, in the neoclassical camp—more on this later.

Rosen stresses a criticism related to the Austrians' distaste for mathematics. He prefers the mainstream practice of manipulating precisely specified models to obtain precise results. The Austrians, in contrast, dislike pursuing the consequences of "given conditions," which "greatly limits the empirical scope and consequences" of their theory. They shun "what they consider to be 'routine' mathematical optimization problems that underlie much of empirical economics." Some Austrians go so far as to suspect an affinity between statism and a passion for statistics. Austrian empirical work consists mainly of historical case studies, but Rosen finds the uniqueness of each case limiting the usefulness of that approach.[1] He expects a more quantitative approach to remain dominant, thus already alluding to a market test and a notion that "dominant" means "better."

If Rosen's critique of Austrian nonempiricism is on target, it hits an outer ring, not the bull's-eye. First, an intellectual division of labor can be legitimate and fruitful; a diversity of research styles is not a weakness but a strength of the discipline. Second, the frequently narrow and honorific use of the term "empirical" is misleading. Austrians do take seriously the most pervasive and dependable facts about empirical reality. These include human purpose and other introspectively known realities, scarcity and the necessity of choice, the phenomenon of diminishing marginal returns, and the fragmentation of knowledge. They include other features of the real world that unavoidably restrict atomistic competition to being the exception rather than the rule and that accord entrepreneurs a large role in the working of markets. Further observed facts are that sellers are typically not selling as much of their output or labor as they would like to sell at prevailing prices, that most prices and wages are not determined impersonally but are consciously set (although set with an eye on supply and demand), and that these and other circumstances cause or reveal price stickiness (a fact crucial to macroeconomics). Facts are facts, regardless of whether they are known in a methodologically fashionable way. Austrians are guilty less often than the neoclassicals of what P.T. Bauer (1987) aptly diagnosed as "the disregard of reality."[2] Austrians do not confine the honorific term "empirical" to propositions dug out by arduous econometric labor and, after all, of doubtful general validity (as distinguished from possible validity in specific historical circumstances).

Readers should not misunderstand Ludwig von Mises's calling economic theory (unlike economic history) an "a priori" science. Mises used the term in an unusual way. He referred to empirical axioms like the ones

---

[1] Yet hear Herbert Simon (1992, p. 1504), reviewing studies of firms and government agencies: "Although case studies are only samples of one, such samples are infinitely more informative than samples of none ... valid hypotheses are more likely to emerge from direct, intimate encounter with organizations than from speculation."

[2] Mathematics and econometrics contribute, says Bauer (1987, p. 36), to inverting the "story of the Emperor's New Clothes. Here there are new clothes, and at times they are haute couture. But all too often there is no Emperor within."

alluded to above, ones inescapably obvious even to mere armchair observation. Rosen himself recognizes that large-scale, gross, nonnumerical evidence often is more secure than quantitative evidence, and often quite useful (compare Summers 1991).

Austrians are also more fact-oriented in recognizing what methods have and what methods have not been relatively fruitful in the progress of economic thought. As for predictions, Austrians take another fact seriously: the economic world is an open rather than closed system and as such has an unknowable future. Except, perhaps, for short-run extrapolations or in identifying wide ranges of possible outcomes, numerical forecasts cannot be reliable. A pretense of satisfying unsatisfiable demands for forecasts is intellectually disreputable. The best that can be supplied are qualitative predictions, recognitions of patterns, and explanations of the likely consequences of contemplated actions. Such predictions are well worth heeding, as their frequent disregard in policymaking illustrates by contrast.

Austrians make too much of defining and interpreting entrepreneurial activities, says Rosen; since we cannot measure them, we cannot assess their importance. My reply is the standard remark about keys and lamppost. Again we see the difference between a narrow empiricism that looks only at numbers and a broader empiricism that draws on direct observation. Rosen does recognize, on the other hand, that ignoring entrepreneurship constrains the neoclassical view of competition, and on this topic he expects the largest gains from intellectual trade.

Rosen faults the Austrians for not spelling out empirical criteria for assessing the performance of an economic system. While neoclassical welfare economics must respect given preferences and technologies, Austrians are willing, as he notes, to ask "what kinds of social institutions and rules of the game make for a good society." Well, good for the Austrians. The concepts of theoretical welfare economics, though applicable in certain exercises, are no substitute for no-holds-barred analysis of how alternative sets of institutions are likely to facilitate or impede people's pursuit of happiness.

THE NEOCLASSICAL MAINSTREAM

Neoclassicism is mainly concerned with establishment of equilibrium under known conditions. With the choice set, technology, preferences, and the number and varieties of goods all given and known, it investigates a well-defined solution to the resource-allocation problem. Rosen admires this approach. As he explains, neoclassical economists often apply the welfare theorems to describe an optimum or central-planning solution consistent with specified technology and tastes and then, "without studying individual maximizing decisions at all," suppose that markets somehow "must do it" that way. Rosen also notes that disequilibrium analysis is not possible in the neoclassical scheme, and the entrepreneur has nothing to do.

James Buchanan, who acknowledges Austrian influence but is no card-carrying member of the school, has noted such neoclassical features by way of severe criticism. He deplores the mainstream tendency to trivialize the economic problem by forcing all analyzable behavior into the straitjacket of maximizing an objective function under known constraints. Utility functions are presumed to exist independently of the processes whereby persons make actual choices. Concern with processes of voluntary agreement among trading parties gives way to the concept of an "efficient" allocation of resources existing "out there," against which all institutional arrangements are to be tested. Economics turns into applied mathematics or engineering. Actually, the economy does not have a single objective function to be maximized, nor does it have a single maximizer. No wonder Buchanan said that an article chosen at random out of any economics journal is unlikely "to have a social productivity greater than zero." "Academic programs almost everywhere are controlled by rent-recipients who simply try to ape the mainstream work of their peers in the discipline." (Quotations, paraphrases, and citations appear in Yeager 1990, esp. pp. 209–211.)

The academic respectability of various ideologies has shifted so much in recent decades that some self-conscious neoclassicals have now carried their free-marketry, along with their methodological prejudices, to the extent of its contaminating their positive analysis. This phenomenon is particularly evident in one of my own favorite fields, macroeconomics.

Unfortunately, many Austrians venture beyond such criticisms to make a bugbear of what they blanket under the label of "general-equilibrium theory." Yet there need be no tension between it and Austrian economics. Mises's and Hayek's insights about socialist calculation illuminate general interdependence and the various tasks to be accomplished somehow or other in any economic system. General equilibrium illuminates opportunity cost—a favorite Austrian concept—in a way not otherwise possible. All too commonly, opportunity cost is defined in the context of choices

Chapter 6: Austrian Economics, Neoclassicism, and the Market Test   107

made by a particular decisionmaker: the cost of a chosen course of action is the next best course thereby forgone. That definition, bringing to mind the considerations and even the agonies involved in making a decision, seems familiar to the layman. This deceptive familiarity trivializes the concept. What requires the economist's expertise is explaining opportunity cost in a deeper sense—the wider social significance of money cost. What needs repeated explanation is how money costs reflect the subjectively appraised values or utilities of the other outputs and activities necessarily forgone if resources are withheld from them for the sake of the particular output or activity in question, as well as how money costs and prices transmit information and incentives. The mainstream apparatus can deepen the understanding of subjectivist insights so dear to Austrian hearts.

SUCCESS AND FAILURE IN THE MARKETPLACE OF IDEAS

Entrepreneurial ventures undergo a market test, and Rosen would put ideas to the same test. He sees "an enormous amount of evolutionary Austrian competition in the marketplace for ideas," even though "fashion and peer pressure" are sometimes at work. Austrians fare poorly in this competition. Their approach "excludes most of the things that most economists do"; few Austrians belong to today's professional economics community. "What is the fact that neoclassical economics has scored higher than Austrian economics on the evolutionary/survival test telling us?" Rosen rhetorically asks. He evidently holds it against the Austrians that they do not pass his market test in the intellectual atmosphere created by members of his own camp, an atmosphere pervaded by narrow yet tacit methodological preaching. (Tacit preachments are the worst kind, or so my thus-entitled article reprinted below argues.)

My colleague Roger Garrison is probably right in warning against "counting notches on academic armchairs." Partly for this reason, I have omitted capsule descriptions of work by contemporary Austrian economists. Since Rosen has raised the issue, however, I should mention the trouble that authors have generally had in the last 40 years or so in getting articles on Austrian themes into prestigious journals. Peter Boettke (1994, p. 604) notes some consequences:

> Most of the articles by the younger generation of Austrians that have appeared in the top professional journals are strategic articles. These articles take the form of either "tenure articles" (that is, articles which do not even pretend to advance Austrian ideas but rather pass the professional

test needed to earn tenure) or "synthesis articles" (articles which find a sympathetic trend within the mainstream and then try to build a bridge to Austrian ideas—which are usually hidden in the footnotes).... Despite their strategic importance, however, these articles in themselves do not represent the kind of scientific work required to advance an Austrian understanding of the economic and social world.

Boettke and David Prychitko (1994, pp. 290–291) further explain pressures faced by young economists with Austrian inclinations:

> to meet the formal, positivistic canons of the mainstream, Ph.D. candidates and especially untenured economists still committed to free market liberalism tend to switch their human capital investment to neoclassicism, to create and maintain a relative degree of professional respectability and acceptance.... Time and again young intellectuals born from the ideological womb of Austrian economics mature years later as scholars in the halls of the University of Chicago or UCLA. Reswitching back to Austrian economics seems all too costly once one's professional reputation has been established.

The central lessons of Austrian economics do not readily lend themselves to the kinds of embroidery that win high scores in the academic game as currently played. Yet this does not mean that those lessons are unimportant for understanding the real world. Reality embraces more than the academic game. At times, as P.T. Bauer has said (1984, pp. 160–161, 179; 1987, pp. 41–42), the most important duty of an academic is to keep on insisting on the obvious.

Rosen retells a lightbulb story which, in the version I heard, goes: "How many right-wing economists does it take to change a light bulb?" "None, because the free market will take care of everything." I wonder whether Rosen has fully absorbed the story's point. It takes a jab at theorists who tacitly regard the market as an entity in its own right, distinct from and superior to the mere human beings who interact on it. It takes a jab at the depersonalization of economics, as in neglect of the entrepreneur and as in a conception of competition that abstracts from rivalry. On my interpretation, the story's targets also include persons who see the supposed intellectual marketplace as a mechanism for differentiating between admirable and disreputable theories and methods. Actually, it is individuals who make appraisals. To rely on the supposed market test instead is to ride piggyback on the appraisals of other people, who may in turn be doing the same thing.

An example of appeal to the market test of merit occurred when board members of a professional association were discussing whether to nominate a particular economist for office. One member said in effect: "It doesn't matter what we here think of his work; let the market decide." He went on to name journals that had printed the candidate's work. I once served on a promotions committee whose members spent much time discussing the supposed prestige of the journals listed on the candidates' vitas. Not only had the other members evidently not looked through the articles themselves; they had not even noticed that one candidate had failed to make copies of his articles available.[3]

A broadly similar appeal to the "market" occurs in a rebuff to calls for better writing in economics. Their numerical evidence persuades the authors that effort spent on better writing does not pay off in greater success on the market for acceptances and citations of articles (Laband and Taylor 1992; McCloskey 1992 responds appropriately).

FALLACIES AND PERVERSITY OF THE MARKET TEST

At least two things are wrong with such appeals to "the market." First, the metaphorical academic market is less responsive to the wishes of whoever the ultimate consumer may be than is the actual market in goods and services. The subscriber to journals has an influence more attenuated and more subject to manipulation by others than the influence of the consumer of ordinary goods and services. Editors and referees have scope for heeding fads and cliquish and personal considerations. They are not risking their own money. Subscribers face tie-in sales, which include association memberships and the supposed prestige of subscribing; and they have reason, anyway, to learn even about disagreeable fads. Customers have a harder time in the supposed academic market than in the real market knowing whether they got what they paid for. The analogy between the academic and business markets is further dissected in Bartley (1990, chaps. 6 and 7), Mirowski (1992, pp. 239, 247), and Mayer (1993, pp. 10ff., 84).

Appealing to the metaphorical market test is a variant of the fallacy of argumentum ad populum. Some kindergartners were studying a frog, wondering whether it was a boy frog or a girl frog. One child piped up:

---

[3] The Department of Economics at the University of Virginia was better in this respect: it appointed committees to actually read the writings of promotion candidates and report back on their contents and merits.

"I know how we can tell!" "All right," said the teacher, expecting the worst, "how?" The child beamed, "We can vote" (Fumento 1993, p. 283). In another variant of this approach, an editorial in the *Wall Street Journal* drew an admiring analogy between the "market" of voting and the market in financial instruments ("Toward 2000" 1996, p. A22).

I do not deny that the market metaphor can have some application. But as Roger Garrison asks, is the academic market more like the market for wheat in Chicago or the market for tulips in 17th-century Holland?

A second objection to the metaphorical market test is deeper than that the metaphor is defective. Since when, anyway, was the market, even the actual business market, the arbiter of excellence in consumer goods, literature, art, music, science, or scholarship? Since when does the market decide truth and beauty? A particular good or service passes a rather literal market test if the quantity produced finds buyers willing to pay at least its full costs. That result suggests that resources are not being diverted from alternative uses in which they could have yielded greater value to consumers. Success in a market niche, even a large one, has no deeper significance. All of us can name business successes achieved by catering to execrable tastes, and analogues occur in the academic world. (A healthy society affords scope for noncoercive criticism even of tastes; see Wright 1951/1962, chap. 2.)

The case for the free market is something quite other than that it constitutes the very criterion of what should be admired. An economist ignorant of the valid case is in real trouble.

The attitude of the board and committee members mentioned above, and of the child in the frog story, is the very prototype of the "secondhandism" diagnosed by Ayn Rand. The villains in her novels are secondhanders themselves or trade on the prevalence of that mindset among other people. An ambitious secondhander seeks fame, prestige, admiration, envy—greatness in other people's eyes. The secondhander seeks not so much actual achievement as the reputation for achievement. Secondhandism means taking one's values from other people, especially people thought to be successful, admired, and well-connected. It makes a virtue out of conformity to their standards or examples. A case in point is fawning over celebrities and the market value of their product endorsements. Secondhandism enters into "groupthink" ('t Hart 1990). Discussions of the two phenomena differ largely in emphasis: those of groupthink focus on contexts in which it is likely to occur, those of secondhandism on the characters and attitudes of persons prone to it.

Chapter 6: Austrian Economics, Neoclassicism, and the Market Test

One variety of academic secondhandism is the quest for perceived influence on policy. A practitioner of the "realism" dissected by Philbrook (1953) compromises between advising the policy that he, as an expert, really thinks best and giving the advice he thinks most likely to be heeded. Philbrook sets forth several reasons why such "realism" is immoral. Furthermore, it promotes "[c]onfusion between advancement of knowledge and promotion of policy," which in turn "contributes to indifference to reality" (Bauer 1987, p. 37). Confusion between the two quite different kinds of result also impedes assessment of professional competence (Bauer 1959, esp. p. 107).

A probably more prevalent and insidious variety of academic secondhandism makes a virtue out of aping the people who congratulate each other on working at the supposed frontiers of the discipline.[4] It affects judgments about what questions are worth pursuing, what methods are worth using, and how much merit individual professors have acquired. Young professors do respond to the indicators of success applied (as noted by Boettke and Prychitko 1994, quoted above), even if these indicators may sometimes lead to dysfunctional outcomes, just as manufacturers in the Soviet Union responded, often wastefully, to the success indicators applied by central planners. Heeding the criteria of the secondhanders obstructs the act of an independent mind trying to understand and teach how the real world operates. It undercuts the value and the joy of academic work.

I know a department head who unabashedly practices secondhandism. He awards points to journals for their supposed prestige. He awards points to articles for their length—the wordier the better—and for his prestige scores of the journals where they appear. He awards points to their authors according to these scores of their articles and to citation indexes. This supposed measurement, which spares its practitioners actually having to read people's writings and come to grips with ideas, joins with academic politics in decisions on salaries and promotions. The person in question even does supposed research of his own on this sort of measurement, as if it were equivalent to investigating the real economic world. Academic narcissism joins academic secondhandism.

---

[4] 't Hart 1990, p. 35, notes how "rituals and symbolism" reinforce a sense of "we-ness." In economics, the ritual of the model and use of mathematical symbols come to mind. So do psychological experiments in which group pressure seems to affect an individual's very perceptions, or reported perceptions, as of motions of an actually stationary point of light in a dark room or of differences between the lengths of two lines (Tajfel 1968, p. 574).

Ideally, scholars build on and criticize each other's work in their efforts to advance knowledge. Counting citations to measure excellence is something else again. It is parasitic on the pursuit of knowledge, and even subversive of it if the workers in a field take account of extraneous influences that citations may have. Of course, not all ideas and approaches deserve equal attention. As P.T. Bauer has remarked somewhere, if everyone has his say, no one can be heard. Scholars must have some notions of standards and of fruitful allocations of their own time and energy. The pernicious thing is subversion of genuine standards by outsiders practicing parasitical secondhandism, sometimes garbed in spuriously scientific quantification.

Rosen, with his notions of success in the marketplace of ideas, unintentionally aids and abets that sort of thing. He aids and abets resulting pressures to climb onto bandwagons.[5] He now qualifies his notions with reference to the long run: eventually the market test works and correct doctrines and fruitful methods tend to prevail. I too want to believe so. Examples come readily to mind, however, of false but long-dominant ideas in natural science, medicine, geography, and even economics. Anyway, no impersonal market achieves the eventual triumph of truth. That result depends on honest and competent men and women exercising their own independent judgment even against prestigious opinion. Furthermore, invoking the long run in defense of the market test is an example of what Karl Popper would call an immunizing stratagem: evident failures can be talked away with the claim that they will turn into successes eventually.

First-hand appraisals are not always possible. In everyday life we must take most of our beliefs and bases of action from other people. Time is scarce and division of knowledge necessary. Academic administrators and committees may understandably feel a need for outside help in assessing the qualifications and character of a candidate for a post. In certain circumstances, however, we as individuals have a duty to express judgments of our own. Then we are derelict if we subordinate our own direct knowledge (as of candidates' personal and professional characters) to the opinions of other people. If an element of secondhandism sometimes seems necessary, we must recognize it as a shortcut and seek to reduce its influence, rather than praise our expediency in the name of some sort of market test. Above all, we academics have the professional duty of treating secondhandism,

---

[5]Machovec's story (1995) of what happened to the concept of competition illustrates the harm done by bandwagonry, by obsession with what is thought most publishable thanks to attunement to contemporary notions of the frontier of research.

groupthink, anti-intellectualism, phony quantification, diversionary narcissism, and perverse success indicators with the contempt they deserve.

COMPLEMENTARY SCHOOLS

Schools in academe—groups of scholars working on favorite topics and with favorite methods—have value. Scrutiny within and across schools can shoot down bad ideas and empty fads. Schools can help motivate research by giving their members the presumption of a sympathetic audience.

Scholars should approach each school (and each sect) for what they can learn from it, not as a target of polemics for polemics' sake and not as a foil for self-congratulation. The neoclassical and Austrian schools, each stripped of excrescences, are complementary. Aspiring Austrian economists should indeed take the standard Ph.D. courses. Austrian economics is ready again to contribute, as it once did, to the mainstream. Contemporary Austrians have been setting good examples in their work on comparative systems, economic history, and entrepreneurial history, industrial organization, labor economics, monetary and financial theory and institutions, other market institutions for coping with ignorance and uncertainty, the history of thought, and political philosophy. Austrian macroeconomics has much and could develop more in common with new Keynesianism (which in its fundamentals, despite its label, is neither new nor Keynesian). Even in fields usually considered remote from distinctively Austrian interests, criticism from an Austrian perspective, like scientific criticism generally, can exert healthy discipline.

If the neoclassicals who are obsessed nowadays—apparently without even realizing it—with methodology, prestige, and frontiersmanship can shake off these obsessions, and if, further, they can resist the badgering of parasitical secondhanders, they can reap gains from trade with the Austrians.

REFERENCES

Bartley, W.W., III. *Unfathomed Knowledge, Unmeasured Wealth: On Universities and the Wealth of Nations.* La Salle, Ill.: Open Court, 1990.

Bauer, P.T. "International Economic Development." *Economic Journal* 69 (March 1959): 105–123.

———. "Further Reflections on the State of Economics," In *Reality and Rhetoric*, chap. 10. Cambridge, Mass.: Harvard University Press, 1984.

———. "The Disregard of Reality." *Cato Journal* 7 (Spring/Summer 1987): 29–42.

Boettke, Peter J., ed. *The Elgar Companion to Austrian Economics*. Aldershot, U.K., and Brookfield, Vt.: Elgar, 1994.

Boettke, Peter J., and David L. Prychitko, eds. *The Market Process: Essays in Contemporary Austrian Economics*. Aldershot, U.K., and Brookfield, Vt.: Elgar, 1994.

Fumento, Michael. *Science under Siege*. New York: Morrow, 1993.

't Hart, Paul. *Groupthink in Government: A Study of Small Groups and Policy Failure*. Amsterdam, Rockland, Mass., and Berwyn, Pa.: Swets & Zeitlinger, 1990.

Huerta de Soto, Jesús. "The Ongoing *Methodenstreit* of the Austrian School." Comment on papers by Sherwin Rosen and Erich Streissler. Presented at the meeting of the Mont Pélerin Society, Vienna, September 1996.

Laband, David N., and Christopher N. Taylor. "The Impact of Bad Writing in Economics." *Economic Inquiry* (October 1992): 30, 673–688.

Machovec, Frank M. *Perfect Competition and the Transformation of Economics*. London and New York: Routledge, 1995.

Mayer, Thomas. *Truth versus Precision in Economics*. Aldershot, U.K., and Brookfield, Vt.: Elgar, 1993.

McCloskey, D.N. "Writing as a Responsibility of Science: A Reply to Laband and Taylor." *Economic Inquiry* 30 (October 1992): 689–695.

Mirowski, Philip. "Three Vignettes on the State of Economic Rhetoric." In *Post-Popperian Methodology of Economics*, edited by Neil de Marchi, 235–259. Boston: Kluwer, 1992.

Philbrook, Clarence. "'Realism' in Policy Espousal." *American Economic Review* 43 (December 1953): 846–859.

Rosen, Sherwin. "Austrian and Neoclassical Economics: Any Gains from Trade?" *Journal of Economic Perspectives* 11 (Fall 1997): 139–152.

Simon, Herbert A. "Review of *Organization Theory*", edited by O.E. Williamson. *Journal of Economic Literature* 30 (September 1992): 1503–1505.

Streissler, Erich W. "Methodenstreit: The Austrian vs. Neo-Classical Approaches to Economics." Paper presented at the meeting of the Mont Pélerin Society, Vienna, September 1996.

Summers, Lawrence H. "The Scientific Illusion in Empirical Macroeconomics." *Scandinavian Journal of Economics* 93, no. 2 (1991): 129–148.

Tajfel, Henri. "Social Perception." In *International Encyclopedia of the Social Sciences*, vol. 11: 567–575. New York: Macmillan and Free Press, 1968.

"Toward 2000." *Wall Street Journal*, 7 November 1996.

Wright, David M. *Capitalism.* 1951. Chicago: Regnery, 1962.

Yeager, Leland B. "Buchanan on Scope and Method." *Constitutional Political Economy* 1, no. 2 (1990): 197–220.

———. "Tacit Preachments Are the Worst Kind." *Journal of Economic Methodology* 2, no. 1 (1995): 1–33. Reprinted here as chapter 13.

CHAPTER 7
Is the Market a Test of Truth and Beauty?*

MARKET TESTS

In this Journal of Spring 2000, Robert Tollison joins David Laband in reiterating a stretched conception of market test. Laband and Tollison recommend grading academic performance by the sorts of statistics that Laband compiles, which involve article and page counts, impressions of journal quality, and citations. As I said in the 1997 article that Laband and Tollison attack (the preceding chapter here), not even the actual commercial market is a test of truth and beauty or excellence. Granted, if the quantity produced of some good or service finds willing buyers at a price at least covering all costs, that fact implies that resources have not been diverted from alternative outputs that consumers would have valued more highly. Losses are a retrospective sign of waste (apart from a quasi-exception for business owners who derive satisfaction from using their own wealth even in money-losing ways). Such a market test exerts healthy discipline.

Furthermore, social cooperation through the market and in other ways itself has moral value. The market method of organizing economic activity is indeed better, by the standard of human happiness, than alternative methods. But financial success in some broad or narrow market niche has no deeper philosophical significance; in itself, it is no further sign of excellence or virtue. (The lesson of Hayek 1960, chap. 6, is well worth taking to heart.) Market success does not prove that the tastes catered to, the

---

*Originally entitled "The Tactics of Secondhandism," this paper comes from the *Quarterly Journal of Austrian Economics* 3 (Fall 2000): 51–61. It replies to a comment that David N. Laband and Robert D. Tollison had made on my article reprinted just above. For Laband and Tollison's own words, see their "On Secondhandism and Scientific Appraisal," *Quarterly Journal of Austrian Economics* 3, no. 1 (Spring 2000): 43–48, http://mises.org/journals/qjae/pdf/qjae3_1_4.pdf.

116

goods and services provided, or the providers themselves are admirable. Facts alone do not yield appraisals (you can't get an "ought" from an "is"). "The market" is a metaphor. It makes no appraisals. "Choices are made only by humans rather than by personified abstractions such as 'the market'" (James M. Buchanan 1995, quoted in Lee 1996, p. 787; here and in his article of 2000, Lee makes the point eloquently). Overreaching claims for the market, especially as a transpersonal arbiter of truth, decency, and excellence, tend to discredit the valid and quite different case for a free society. (On backlash from exaggerated claims of market perfection, compare Heyne 2000, first full paragraph of p. 138.) He is a poor champion of the market system who cannot defend it as it really is, "warts and all." It is sad to see public understanding of the case for the market undercut by the market's would-be friends.

Laband and Tollison invite such backlash, unintentionally. They identify their own position on "secondhandism and scientific appraisal" with "the free-market side of the discipline"; they impute belief in "market failure" to their critics (2000, p. 43). The market system, far from being a substitute for good judgment and morality, presupposes morality. Yet secondhandism has morally questionable aspects in some of its applications (cf. McCloskey 1992, commenting on Laband and Taylor 1992).

If the fairly literal test of the commercial market has limited (though great) significance, even less significant is its supposed analogue in the metaphorical market for science and scholarship. There, truth, not marketability, is the goal—and truth as such, not different, incompatible brands of truth for different consumers. (In the commercial market, by contrast, businesses do cater to widely divergent tastes and do, appropriately, satisfy even demands for inexpensive goods of relatively low quality.) To speak of truth is not to traffic in metaphysics about Truth with a capital T. I mean merely that scientific endeavor is the pursuit of propositions of generality and depth corresponding to the way things actually are (to borrow words from Peter Bauer and George Will separately).

TRUTH AND GAMES

Scientific or scholarly or academic life has at least two strands. First is trying to find and communicate truth or knowledge. Second is the academic game itself—the pursuit of prestige, admiration, and money. Self-promotion and gamesmanship enter in. Of course, the two aspects of academic life overlap. Even someone overridingly concerned with truth desires admiration, wants to deserve it, and cares about its sources and reasons. Furthermore, hope for fame and fortune can indeed be a strong and respectable incentive to the pursuit of scientific truth (as well as a temptation to politicking and the like).

Still, how closely the two aspects of scientific activity correspond is affected by the tone and policies prevailing in the academic world. The preachings of Laband and Tollison, if heeded, would impair the correspondence and increase tension between the two aspects.

"The truth is not relevant if it is not a shared truth," they write (Laband and Tollison 2000, p. 43). I am not sure just what they mean by "relevant" or in how broad or how narrow a context they apply their remark. Perhaps they mean relevance to scoring well in the academic game. Their remark does sound like relativism. Yet reality is what it is, regardless of how many or how few people share a correct perception of it. Being influential or enjoying prestige may sometimes carry a presumption that one's ideas are right, but it is not the same as their actually being right.

Sharing truth—communicating ideas—is important, of course. Curiously, Laband and Tollison seem to value communication only in a narrow "market" associated with a notion of prestigious journals. But how narrow or how broad a market properly "counts"—how small or large a set of persons addressed? No market answers that question by itself. Does the appropriate market include all employers and potential employers of economists or all actual and potential consumers of economic information? Or is it a much narrower set of appraisers, people inclined to receive and transmit bandwagon effects relating to the supposed frontiers of the discipline? More comes later about questions like these.

STANDARDS AND ERSATZ STANDARDS

I want to forestall misinterpretation. If we had to rank economists of the past, if all copies of their writings and of others' discussions of their writings had been irrecoverably lost, if no information about them survived other than statistics of the kinds that Laband compiles, and if we waive the question of what purpose a ranking under such circumstances might serve, then I do suppose that consulting those statistics would be more plausible than any alternative that comes to mind. Saying so is not much of a concession. Acting on a hunch with some slight basis is more plausible than acting at random. Actually, we do *not* have to rank economists under such circumstances and by such a method.

Chapter 7: Is the Market a Test of Truth and Beauty?

Two other points, which are not even *semi*concessions, already appeared in my 1997 article.[1] First, some standards must apply in science and scholarship; not all scribblings can command equal respect and attention. Partly in unavoidable consequence, unfashionable ideas face an uphill battle. Second, life requires much reliance on secondhand knowledge. Wholly firsthand appraisals (as of academic candidates' qualifications, accomplishments, and characters) are scarcely possible; often one's own direct knowledge must be supplemented by the judgments of other people.

Laband and Tollison's ersatz standards partly crowd out sounder ones. Far from being apologetic, Laband and Tollison make an actual virtue of exaggerated secondhandism and their stretched conception of market test. Such thinking and attitudes, to the extent that they have influence, worsen the defects of the already weak analogy between the academic quasi-market and the real market. Academe is not immune from fads and bandwagon effects such as occur in many areas of life, for example, the adulation of celebrities. Analogues of the Keynesian beauty contest appear in economic research and styles of exposition under pressures to do not so much what the individual economist thinks best as what is thought to win acclaim.[2] Such tendencies tilt the playing field more steeply against unfashionable ideas.

Laband and Tollison make much of citations as indicators of influence or fame.[3] Admiring influence so registered, even independently of substance, is analogous to admiring the political "realism" justly attacked by Clarence Philbrook (1953)—admiring perceived influence on policy

---

[1] On these and other matters, I am struck by how little attention Laband and Tollison pay to what I actually wrote in the article under attack and to the writings I cited. My and other observers' reasons for concern about secondhandism and groupthink may perhaps be mistaken, but they are relevant to the issues under discussion.

[2] Brown (1948/1950, pp. 51–53, 63–64), provides an early and eloquent diagnosis of faddism in economics. More recently, macroeconomics provides glaring examples. The impact of "big players" has been analyzed chiefly in actual markets, but the analysis can be extended to fads and bandwagon effects in other activities. "A Big Player is anyone who habitually exercises discretionary power to influence the market while himself remaining wholly or largely immune from the discipline of profit and loss." Koppl and Yeager 1996, p. 368; also see works cited there, as well as Butos and Koppl 1995.

[3] Or even of notoriety, as noted in the text below. Ronald Coase remarked many years ago (in conversation, so I quote only from memory): "In the academic game, the important thing is to have been heard of. People may forget in just what connection they heard of you, but they're likely to remember whether they heard of you. It is better to have been heard of for murdering your wife than not to have been heard of at all."

even when obtained by the advisor's compromising with his own honest judgments. Citations properly serve any of several purposes: They steer the reader to facts and arguments supporting the author's points or to supplementary discussions. They give credit to other authors for ideas or findings or particularly apt formulations. When one researcher is criticizing another's ideas or results, citations give the reader a chance to check the attacked work and see whether it is being dealt with fairly. Less admirably, citations may be used as moves in the academic game—to borrow the prestige of the other writers cited, to signal that one's own work is à la mode, on the supposed frontier of the discipline, or to signal familiarity with recondite sources or areas of knowledge. If an author expects citations to be put to the uses of Laband and Tollison, he might even give or withhold them for that reason. The parasitic use of citations can corrupt their primary use.

Laband and Tollison even claim more for citations as they use them than for the actual market (2000, p. 46):

> dollar votes are an imprecise measure of value. More accurately, they reflect minimum expected value. Citations, by contrast, clearly reveal that the academic consumer received value from the product cited, irrespective of whether the citation was positive or negative. This is because the citations are issued only after purchase and consumption of the product. Thus, a case can be made that the academic market conveys product information even more accurately through citations than do markets for goods and services using dollar voting.

The terminology and the whole analogy are strained; the claim is bizarre. I know someone whose idea of economic research—as I have told him—is to ransack the literature for passages that express or can be interpreted as expressing fallacies, then triumphantly to pounce on and demolish those fallacies. According to the Laband and Tollison test, even perpetrators of crude fallacies, far from deserving scorn for cluttering up the literature, deserve the positive points that their citations bring them; for the fallacy-hunters have "received value" from the works cited.

Laband and Tollison make excuses for assessing people by Labandian numbers. Some such method is a practical necessity. It possesses objectivity (or so Laband and Tollison seem to suggest on p. 47). Yet personal judgment necessarily enters into constructing the numerical indexes. Conformably with their secondhand nature, the indexes fail to show who judged whose work up or down and for what reasons. Furthermore, publication indexes cannot realistically be the sole measure of academic performance. Professors have other duties, even teaching; and subjective judgment unavoidably enters into assessing and weighting various kinds of performance.

In Laband and Tollison's view, "the alternative to relying on markets to assign value to scientific contributions is that we must rely on the ostensibly firsthand knowledge of some central authority, such as Yeager" (p. 46). Never mind the insinuation that I aspire to the role of central authority. Notice again the notion that "markets," impersonal markets, make judgments and that some mechanism or statistical process should "assign value to scientific contributions." Yet such value does not exist in the abstract. A researcher learns from the actual substance of his colleagues' work, not from mere summary numbers pertaining to journal quality and citations. Writings have value for the persons who use the reported facts and ideas, such as other scientists, engineers and technicians, consumers who ultimately benefit from technological progress, and citizens in general who benefit from progress in economic knowledge (to the extent that such knowledge is actually heeded in policymaking).

In grading academics for appointments, promotions, and so forth, the alternative to Laband's approach is not reliance on some supposed central authority, such as me. No, the alternative is that the decisionmakers and their informed consultants frankly lay out their own judgments, for which they take responsibility, and the reasons for them. Let them not hide behind some sort of statistical precipitate of the anonymous judgments of other people. Let these appraisers discuss their tentative judgments with one another and possibly revise them. An academic department might name a committee to actually read candidates' writings, perhaps seeking supplementary information from outside, and to report its members' assessments and reasons to the broader decisionmaking group.

FURTHER WORRIES

Economists should understand that people, including academics, respond to incentives and that inappropriate incentives can bring unintended consequences. Responses to "success indicators" in the Soviet planned economy provided examples. As caricatured in the humor magazine *Krokodil*, if a nail factory's output was measured in number of units, the factory would produce very many tiny nails; but if total weight counted instead, it would produce few but huge nails. (Compare Tullock 1965, chap. 23, on how bureaucrats react to attempts to measure their performances numerically.) Standardized tests of school children reportedly elicit "teaching to test"; certain measures of performance steer the attention of the police to violators easy to catch.

The individually sensible response of young professors under Laband-and-Tollison-type pressures may well be to toil away in some prevalent fad on one of the supposed frontiers of the discipline, which may well involve work addressed to some small in-group, resistant to informed evaluation by outsiders and enjoying scant wider relevance—all in hopes of being prestigiously published. (There is no necessary contradiction in identifying both faddism and narrow specialization. Numerous small modish topics may exist, as well as methodological, rhetorical, and stylistic fads infecting many specialties at once.)

It is perverse to push academics lacking a comparative advantage in modish work to waste their energies on it anyway. Why prod them to write articles in which few people are really interested (except perhaps as a basis for Brownie points or as inputs to more such work by other similarly motivated academics)?[4] They might make more solid contributions in other ways; the principle of opportunity cost applies even in academe. Even within an academic department, diversity of talents and specializations has value.

Let's face it: few economists are capable of frequently finding important new knowledge. At the same time, widespread ignorance prevails about the core of economics, the very logic of a market economy. Long-exploded errors persist among policymakers and the general public. The quasi-market works less well for knowledge in economics than for knowledge in the natural sciences (especially than for industrially applicable, as distinct from politically applicable, scientific knowledge). Even economists far apart on the ideological spectrum do agree on important issues about which the general public and even noneconomist intellectuals are ignorant.

If economics has much of value to teach, the persistence of ignorance and error over the decades and centuries suggests a lapse of communication worth trying to remedy. Room remains for devising improved ways to

---

[4] However the points are calculated, only x percent of candidates can wind up in the top x percent; yet much effort and talent may be misdirected into trying to wind up there anyway. Economists should understand the differences between a race for positional values and the creation of values of other kinds.

make economic principles clear and to communicate them widely. Why should such efforts be disdained? Proficiency in some advanced technique or work on the frontier of some narrow specialty may indeed be valuable, but it is no proof in itself of understanding the very basics of economics. (I have encountered a few economists who constitute examples of this point.)

These thoughts make me wonder how consistent Laband and Tollison are in their faith in the market test. Are they prepared to rank publications by their circulation numbers? Or, as in some circles, do skillfully written contents and wide readership affect appraisals negatively?

As for appraising persons, it is one thing to make appraisals responsibly when choices must be made, as among candidates for employment, promotion, and professional honors. It is another thing to make appraisals in a vacuum, out of the context of necessity—secondhand appraisals that may even be abused for thirdhand appraisals. Turning academic economics into its own subject matter is narcissism. I wonder whether the apparent popularity of articles ranking departments and journals and persons traces to their appeal as material for gossip, like the appeal of tabloids sold at supermarket checkouts. (Similar thoughts come to mind about some strands of economic imperialism, as in writings that strain to attribute rent-seeking motives to ever more institutions and officials.)

IS LABAND-AND-TOLLISON-TYPE THINKING IN FACT INFLUENTIAL?

So far I have been worrying about the Laband and Tollison market test to the extent that it is applied. But do Laband and Tollison in fact have influence? I do not know. Conceivably, almost everybody ignores them; on the other hand, they are not unique in thinking as they do. What I do know is that they try to have an impact. Their numerical systems of rating persons and departments and journals are intended to affect what people do. Even in their article, they preach at economists. They preach about publishing in prestigious journals, which implies (perhaps unintentionally) preaching about research on topics considered most acceptable to prestigious journals, preaching about what to emphasize and what not, preaching about research methods, preaching about styles of exposition (sometimes even involving strategic obscurity), and preaching about trying to associate oneself (as by judicious citations) to current fashions in the profession. The message, in short, is: compromise your standards. Put less effort into the kinds of work that you consider important, in which you have a comparative advantage, and that you enjoy. (Joy is a legitimate incentive, but one eroded by Laband-and-Tollison-type attitudes and practices.) Switch toward catering to editors and referees (who themselves operate under similar pressures to the extent that Laband and Tollison prevail).

Such preaching distresses me not merely because it is or might become influential but because it is officious and repellent in itself.

STYLE OF ARGUMENT

Laband and Tollison beg the question they purportedly discuss: as unabashed secondhanders, they simply assert or assume that their supposed market test is indeed the correct measure of excellence. But what justification is it of certain criteria that the players try to satisfy them when they are applied? Laband and Tollison, citing earlier papers coauthored by Laband, argue, for example, that journal editors try to publish "high-impact papers." Well, it is no surprise that people respond to incentives, but to offer this fact as justifying a particular structure of incentives is circular reasoning.

A further sign of the weakness of Laband and Tollison's case is their resort to emotive words like "sour grapes" and "crybabyism." Such name-calling hardly applies to the eminent economists, including Nobel laureates, who have expressed concern about the state of much of the academic literature, including what might be called its narcissistic or incestuous aspects.[5] What opinion of the literature may we infer, by the way, precisely among economists who excuse neglecting actually to read the work even of candidates being appraised?

The personal nature of Laband and Tollison's attack further appears in how they characterize an alternative to secondhand appraisals, namely, reliance "on the ostensibly firsthand knowledge of some central authority,

---

[5] Examples of concern are cited in my articles of 1995 and 1997. Another example is McCloskey 1995. I cannot resist requoting from McCloskey (p. 414) an exchange between George Borts and Harry Johnson when both were journal editors. Borts: "[W]e get more good articles than we know what to do with!" Johnson: "Then why don't you publish a few?"

The tragedy of misdirected efforts is even worse than one might think from what actually gets into the journals. Economists with experience in refereeing manuscripts could testify to this point.

such as Yeager."[6] Yet this is not the alternative, as I have explained above. Further, Laband and Tollison make a snide remark about "the literature that Professor Yeager dotes on"—the literature of a cult for which "up is down and down is up," for which "failing a market test is really passing it," and whose members are content just to chat among themselves, forgoing Wimbledon in hopes of winning the Austrian Open (p. 45). How do they know that I "dote" on such literature or that I "dote" on any literature? As I made clear in 1997, I am no spokesman for any particular school or sect. I have a low opinion of much Austrian literature, as well as a high opinion of some of it, opinions that I have formed myself and have not taken over secondhand. Of course much crummy work, along with excuses for it, is knocking around in economics, as in other fields. What does that fact have to do with the issue under discussion—appraisal by a supposed market test?

Are Laband and Tollison willing to let their remark about what I "dote" on remain as an example of their standards of accuracy and relevance? Their analogy with tennis tournaments reflects, by the way, their obsession with the game aspect of academic life.

CONCLUSION

Let me be clear about what I am not saying. I never questioned the need for standards, nor the uphill battle that unpopular ideas necessarily and even appropriately face, nor the necessity of secondhandism of some kinds and degrees and for some purposes. I am not sweepingly condemning the literature of academic economics. Economists continue making solid contributions despite everything.

I regret the perversion of standards through glorification of secondhandism. When appraisals are necessary, they should be kept as close as practicable to persons who have the most direct knowledge and who bear responsibility for their judgments. I regret the strengthening of incentives to jump onto bandwagons. I implore readers to learn lessons from the characters in Ayn Rand's novels who either are secondhanders themselves

---

[6]I do not know whether the following remark (2000, p. 43) is also directed against me personally, but it is a sneer at someone, if only a straw man: "It is not enough for the individual qua scientist to maintain that he has been enlightened and *knows* the *truth*."

While unhappy about the likely consequences of Laband and Tollison's attitudes and practices, I am not angry about being personally attacked. Their attack helps reveal the nature and weakness of their case.

or exploit other people's secondhandism and their susceptibility to intellectual intimidation.[7] (Rand provides insights into the craving for prestige that I could scarcely hope to reproduce here.)

We should beware of relativism about truth. Beyond the game-like or fame-and-fortune side of academic careers, the truth-and-beauty side deserves cultivation. Communication is important, even including skillful communication of knowledge to students and to the broad public.

Above all, I warn against discrediting the valid case for the free society by misconstruing the market as an entity in its own right that transcends the mere men and women who trade on it, an entity that makes superior judgments even about good and bad. Obstacles to understanding the logic of a market economy are great enough already. A spurious linkage in people's minds between a twisted version of free-marketry and the serious, valid, and quite different case for the free market can only harm the cause of freedom. Overreaching boomerangs.

REFERENCES

Binswanger, Harry, ed. *The Ayn Rand Lexicon*. New York: New American Library, 1986.

Brown, Harry Gunnison. "Two Decades of Decadence in Economic Theorizing." 1948. In *Some Disturbing Inhibitions and Fallacies in Current Academic Economics*, pp. 37–64. New York: Robert Schalkenbach Foundation, 1950.

Buchanan, James M. "The Metamorphosis of John Gray." *Constitutional Political Economy* 6, no. 3 (1995): 293–295.

Butos, William N., and Roger Koppl. "Big Players and Entrepreneurial Traditions: How Keynesian Policies May Create a Kaleidic Economy." Paper for the Southern Economic Association Meetings, New Orleans, 1995.

Hayek, F.A. *The Constitution of Liberty*. Chicago: University of Chicago Press, 1960.

Heyne, Paul. Review of *The Moral Economy*, by John P. Powelson. *Independent Review* 5 (Summer 2000): 137–140.

---

[7] Consider the way Laband and Tollison draw a scarcely veiled contrast between work at the supposed frontier of the discipline and inferior work, as well as the general tone of their writing. A whiff appears of "the argument from intimidation," so identified by Ayn Rand (Binswanger 1986, pp. 32–34).

Koppl, Roger, and Leland B. Yeager. "Big Players and Herding in Asset Markets: The Case of the Russian Ruble." *Explorations in Economic History* 33 (1996): 367–383.

Laband, David N., and Christopher N. Taylor. "The Impact of Bad Writing in Economics." *Economic Inquiry* 30 (October 1992): 673–688.

Laband, David N., and Robert D. Tollison. "On Secondhandism and Scientific Appraisal." *Quarterly Journal of Austrian Economics* 3 (Spring 2000): 43–48.

Lee, Dwight R. "The Market Didn't Do It." *The Freeman: Ideas on Liberty* 46 (December 1996): 787–789.

———. "Economics with Romance." *Independent Review* 5 (Summer 2000): 121–129.

McCloskey, D.N. "Writing as a Responsibility of Science: A Reply to Laband and Taylor." *Economic Inquiry* 30 (October 1992): 689–695.

———. "Kelly Green Golf Shoes and the Intellectual Range from M to N." *Eastern Economic Journal* 21 (Summer 1995): 411–414.

Philbrook, Clarence E. "'Realism' in Policy Espousal." *American Economic Review* 43 (December 1953): 846–859.

Tullock, Gordon. *The Politics of Bureaucracy*. Washington, D.C.: Public Affairs Press, 1965.

Yeager, Leland B. "Tacit Preachments Are the Worst Kind." *Journal of Economic Methodology* 2, no. 1 (1995): 1–33. Reprinted here as chapter 13.

———. "Austrian Economics, Neoclassicism, and the Market Test." *Journal of Economic Perspectives* 11 (Fall 1997): 153–165. Reprinted here as chapter 6.

CHAPTER 8

Macroeconomics and Coordination*

A more exact, though wordy, title for this chapter would be "Macroeconomics, Coordination, and Discoordination." Macroeconomics studies disruptions to the economywide coordination processes that microeconomics explains. An emphasis, instead, on aggregate demand facing aggregate supply is hopelessly superficial.

DISARRAY AND OPPORTUNITY

It is standard nowadays to bewail disarray in macroeconomics and monetary theory. Fundamentalist Keynesianism, as we might call it, dominated textbooks and policy circles for roughly three decades. Experience and theory then discredited it. The fundamentalists brooded about inadequacy of total spending (or occasionally the reverse), about the propensity to consume out of real income, and about a saving gap that grows with income and wealth and so becomes all the harder to fill with investment spending, especially as real capital formation leaves fewer attractive opportunities for still further private investment. Even nowadays, policymakers and a few economists still cling to some such doctrine by default and still recommend expanding "aggregate demand" to "stimulate" national and world economies, albeit at the risk of price inflation implied by the equally discredited notion of the Phillips curve.

An alternative school of Keynesian interpretation stems from Robert Clower (1984) and Axel Leijonhufvud (1968, 1981). As history of economic thought it may be questionable, but its substance deserves ample attention.

---
*Originally entitled "Austrian Themes in a Reconstructed Macroeconomics," this chapter derives from a conference presentation in Amsterdam, January 1995, published in *Austrian Economics in Debate*, eds. Willem Keizer et al. (London and New York: Routledge, 1997): 22–41. It is considerably updated here.

It features such concepts as absence of the (supposed) Walrasian auctioneer, incomplete and costly and imperfect information, false price signals, sluggish price adjustments, quantity changes as well as price adjustments, the duality of people's decisions about particular transactions according as they are or are not frustrated in accomplishing other desired transactions, and the "income-constrained process" of infectious recession and recovery.

A quite different group of self-styled Keynesians centered at Cambridge University expresses sweeping skepticism about market-oriented economic theory. In the United States, economists associated with the *Journal of Post Keynesian Economics* form still another school.

Some "monetarists" or "monetary-disequilibrium theorists" continue active in the tradition of David Hume, Henry Thornton, Clark Warburton, Milton Friedman, Anna Schwartz, Karl Brunner, and Allan Meltzer. Their influence has been eroded, however, by developments that have made their formerly suggested policy of steady monetary growth no longer applicable and also by misinterpretations of experience. Monetarism has also suffered from attention paid to two schools that have distorted and exaggerated certain of its tenets. The New Classical economists (including Robert Lucas, Thomas Sargent, and Robert Barro) proclaimed rational expectations and equilibrium always. (In effect, everything is always coordinated, or almost so.) Their position gained attention more because of its coherence with theoretical and methodological fashion than because of its empirical substance, later widely questioned (Howitt 1990, chap. 4).

The real-business-cycle school carried the exaggerations of New Classical economics still further. It interpreted macroeconomic fluctuations as efficient responses to underlying real changes (as in technology) rather than as consequences of monetary disturbances. Robert King, Charles Plosser, and Edward Prescott have written along this line; Strongin (1988) and Stockman (1988) provide convenient surveys. Gary Hansen and Randall Wright (1992) provide an example of tinkering with this theory to rescue it from recalcitrant facts; they would do well to remember about Ptolemy and epicycles. Gary Hansen and Edward Prescott conveyed the impression, without explicitly saying so, that they were answering "yes" to the question posed by the title of their 1993 article, "Did Technology Shocks Cause the 1990–1991 Recession?"

Both the New Classical and real-business-cycle schools tacitly attributed near-perfection to markets (including "efficient markets" in securities), as if their members were congratulating themselves on being "more free-market-oriented than thou." (I am reporting my impression of doctrines, not conjecturing about anyone's motives nor saying that exaggeration crowds out scholarly substance; still, fads do come and go in the academic world.)

Self-parodying free-marketry has handed an opportunity to look sensible by contrast to self-styled New Keynesians, who share several perceptions of reality with the monetarists and who take imperfect competition and price and wage stickiness seriously. (Examples of the work of this misleadingly named school appear in Mankiw and Romer 1991.) As Axel Leijonhufvud (1986) has noted in a more general context, macroeconomists have been playing musical chairs with doctrinal positions and labels.

Nowadays (around 2010), a new-classical/new-Keynesian synthesis, also called dynamic (or dynamic *stochastic*) general-equilibrium theory, enjoys academic prestige. It explores the properties of mathematical models and tweaks them to remove blatant contrasts with statistics of the real world. It assumes rational expectations, which is sensible enough if taken to mean no more than that people will not persist in making recognized mistakes. It assumes that markets are always in or near equilibrium—in some stretched sense of that word—so showing scant attention to the issues of coordination and discoordination that concern Austrian economists.[1]

This disarray in macroeconomics gives Austrian-school economists, as well as monetarists and New Keynesians, an opportunity to set the main stream of macroeconomics on a sounder course. Two major characteristics, besides others mentioned below, especially equip Austrians to seize this opportunity. First, it focuses on the central problem bridging micro and macro economics, the problem of economywide coordination. (Gerald O'Driscoll aptly entitled his doctoral dissertation *Economics as a Coordination Problem*.) Second, it is readier than other free-market-oriented schools to face reality as it is, "warts and all."

COORDINATION

Robert Clower (1984, p. 272) observed that

the approaches of the Keynesians, monetarists, and new classical economists to monetary theory and macroeconomics will get us exactly nowhere

---

[1] Some might consider this characterization unfair. For an enthusiastic textbook treatment, see Wickens 2008.

because each is founded, one way or another, on the conventional but empirically fallacious assumption that the coordination of economic activities is costless.

As this remark suggests, the key question of money/macro theory is not "What determines whether aggregate demand for goods and services is deficient or excessive or just right?" but "What determines whether the processes of exchange and coordination in an economy of decentralized decisionmaking are working smoothly?"

Austrian economists recognize the disaggregated character of economic activity. They take seriously the profound differences between an advanced economy of fine-grained division of labor and the nearly self-sufficient miniature economy of a medieval monastery or manor or of Swiss family Robinson on its desert island (cf. Eucken 1950). Knowledge of wants, resources, technology, and market opportunities, including knowledge of temporary and local conditions, is radically decentralized and simply could not be made available to central planners in anything approaching its fullness. If knowledge is not to go to waste, production and consumption decisions must be radically decentralized (Hayek 1945/1949). Specialization greatly enhances productivity. People produce their own particular goods and services to exchange them away, thereby exercising demand for what other specialists are producing. But what coordinates all these fragmented activities?

The debates over economic calculation under socialism and capitalism initiated by Ludwig von Mises and Friedrich Hayek illuminate the scope of this question (cf. the literature reviewed in Yeager 1994). Even the mere physical meshing of activities as portrayed in a self-consistent input-output table is hard enough to achieve in the absence of genuine markets and prices, as Soviet experience testifies. Full coordination is a still more demanding task. It requires taking account of physical and subjective substitutabilities and complementarities among goods and services and factors of production in their various uses in consumption and production so that no unit of a productive resource goes to satisfy a less intense effective final demand to the denial of a more intense demand. Market bids and offers for resources and final goods play a central role in this process, but its very complexity permits glitches.

Forces of unbalanced supply and demand tend, to be sure, to press disequilibrium prices toward their market-clearing levels. What ensures, however, that these coordinating forces operate rapidly enough and that impediments to transactions do not reinforce each other in the meanwhile to a degree that shows up as recession or depression? Because the fundamental insight of Say's Law is correct—supplies of particular goods and services constitute demands for others, sooner or later—the *fundamental* macroeconomic problem cannot be a deficiency of aggregate demand. However, anything that impairs the processes of market exchange also impairs production. People work and produce in the expectation of being able to exchange their outputs away, and they will not persist indefinitely (especially not in buying inputs for unsalable outputs) if their attempted exchanges keep on being frustrated. Goods and services exchange for each other not directly but through the intermediaries of money and of credit denominated in and ultimately to be settled in money. Monetary disorder can snarl up the process of exchange and so impede production. Austrians, like monetarists, are prepared to take this snarl seriously.

These considerations help argue, incidentally, for putting the micro semester of a Principles of Economics course before the macro semester. Students can hardly understand disruptions of coordination until they know that a coordination problem exists in the first place and understand how the market process solves it when it is working well.

Coordination requires more than correct prices. In Walrasian models of general equilibrium, the "auctioneer" not only achieves the whole array of market-clearing prices but also puts trading partners in contact with one another, obviating the costly mutual searches otherwise necessary. In effect he makes all assets equally liquid—equally readily marketable or usable as means of payment—at their general-equilibrium prices. It is questionable whether models featuring such a mythical personage can contribute much to illuminating macroeconomic issues.[2]

In the real world, however, a worker may be unemployed not necessarily because he insists on too high a wage rate but because he and a suitable employer have not yet made contact. Various startup costs of a new employer-employee relation also enter into the story. In the real world, prices are not the only bearers of signals and incentives about potential transactions. Quantities also perform these functions—quantities of goods, services, and factors in accomplished transactions, frustrated transactions, and inventory buildups and rundowns. Inventory management, quality verification, advertising, and informational and other such activities bear on whether transactions can go forward to the mutual benefit of

---

[2]Léon Walras did not postulate the auctioneer explicitly; that secretary of the market, possessing prodigious informational and calculating abilities, is an invention of interpreters. See chapter 1, note 3.

the parties. These activities have "transactions costs" in an inclusive sense of the term. Many of them impede not only actual transactions but even messages of willingness to buy or sell.

Recoordination to recover from recession requires more, then, than just adjusting prices and wages. Business contacts must be restored or revised. Information, including information about market conditions, must be brought up to date and transmitted.

OBSTACLES TO COORDINATION

Costs and complexities of reality help explain the value of habits, routines, and long-term business relations, as between supplier and customer, employer and worker, and borrower and bank. Not every business relation is continuously open to price revision, as abstract equilibrium theory might seem to recommend. The very concept of different degrees of liquidity of various financial and real assets reflects recognition that price is not the only determinant of whether potential transactions get consummated. If all goods were perfectly liquid, as tacitly assumed in the Walrasian model, then impediments to communication would have been removed. Howitt (1990), writing partly under the inspiration of Clower and Leijonhufvud, surveys some of foregoing themes, as does Okun (1981). Howitt, as well as Hall (1991), comments on difficulties of finding trading partners in "thin" as opposed to "thick" markets. By analogy, my installing a telephone benefits people who might want to reach me but imposes a congestion cost on people who might want to reach people talking with me.

Whether a particular transaction can go forward depends on much more than the terms subject to negotiation between the two potential trading partners. Whether a manufacturer and a potential employee could both benefit from their relation depends on more than the wage rate. It depends on prices charged by competitors and by suppliers of materials, on terms on which energy, transportation, and credit are available, on market conditions facing potential customers, on inventories of various kinds, and on much else besides.

Changes affecting such conditions are continually going on, challenging entrepreneurs to cope with them, as by developing new business opportunities to replace fading ones. In ordinary times, entrepreneurs continually accomplish myriads of interdependent microeconomic adjustments without palpable macroeconomic disorder.

When major economywide disruptions occur, however, it is not surprising that the many necessary interlocking adjustments should stretch out painfully over time. Much besides prices and wages must change, for even a purely monetary shock (whatever one might be) has "real" consequences. Knowledge must be transmitted and received, risk allowed for, combinations of factors and products in production and consumption revised, search conducted, trading partners contacted, and new quantities of goods produced and exchanged. Stickiness of prices and wages delays the transmission of appropriate signals and incentives. ("Price stickiness" may serve as a convenient term alluding to myriad obstacles to prompt and painless adjustment. It is a shorthand label for a wide range of circumstances.)

By adopting the fashionable assumption of rational expectations, New Classicals and subsequently even the New Keynesians tacitly assumed away central aspects of the economywide coordination problem. They replaced a vision of people trying to set prices and quantities and strike bargains in a world of fragmentary and dispersed information with an unrealistic vision of remarkably well-informed people—informed, to be sure, not of specific future quantities and prices but well informed on average about probability distributions. To assume rational expectations oversimplifies problems of coordinating people's beliefs: "No one makes systematic errors in guessing the values of variables that depend in turn upon others' guesses" (Howitt 1990, pp. 12–13).

"IMPERFECTIONS" OF REALITY

In using their word, I am defying theorists who judge reality "imperfect" in comparison with textbook chapters on equilibrium under pure and perfect competition and who thereby damn reality for being real. Of course no "Walrasian" auctioneer is at work achieving ideal outcomes. Of course not all imaginable intertemporal markets and contingent-state markets exist. Of course full coordination is never achieved; and it is approached, to the extent that it is, through the piecemeal, asynchronous gropings of myriads of entrepreneurs. Theory relevant to the real world cannot confine itself to equilibrium analysis and comparative statics. Instead of a state of affairs, competition is a process. Except perhaps for organized exchanges for standardized commodities and securities, no impersonal "market" adjusts prices to changed conditions. *People* change prices, and only after they have perceived *reasons* to do so. Reasons include opportunities offered by changes in technology and notably include perceived market imbalances and frustrations of transactions at the old prices. Perceptions and responses are not instantaneous.

Already in his *Theory of Money and Credit* (1912/1981, pp. 186–187), Ludwig von Mises recognized such facts of reality. Many prices are deliberately set, obviously in retail trade, and set by trial and error.

> Now this phenomenon is not accidental. It is an inevitable phenomenon of the unorganized market. In the unorganized market, the seller does not come into contact with all of the buyers, but only with single individuals or groups.... Consequently the seller fixes a price that in his opinion corresponds approximately to what the price ought to be (in which it is understandable that he is more likely to aim too high than too low), and waits to see what the buyers will do.... The sole way by which sellers can arrive at reliable knowledge about the valuations of consumers is the way of trial and error.

Institutional forces work to postpone price changes otherwise called for by small or transitory changes in supply and demand (1912/1981, p. 134). "Every change in the market data has its definite effects upon the market. It takes a definite length of time before all these effects are consummated, i.e., before the market is completely adjusted to the new state of affairs" (Mises 1949/1963, p. 652).

> [C]hanges in the factors which determine the formation of prices do not produce all their effects at once. A span of time must elapse before all their effects are exhausted. Between the appearance of a new datum and the perfect adjustment of the market to it some time must pass.... In dealing with the effects of any change in the factors operating on the market, we must never forget that we are dealing with events taking place in succession, with a series of effects succeeding one another. We are not in a position to know in advance how much time will have to elapse. (p. 246)

Mises recognizes a certain inertia of prices (1912/1981, pp. 133–136). Relatedly, he recognizes that flexible exchange rates tend to move ahead of their purchasing-power parities; relatively, prices of many goods and services are sluggish (1949/1963, pp. 455–456). Mitchell (1908/1966, pp. 259–283) observed the same phenomenon in detail in the U.S. "greenback" period of 1862–1878. Mises also observes more of a historical element in the value of money than in the value of any ordinary good.

[A] historically continuous component is contained in the objective exchange value of money. The past value of money is taken over by the present and transformed by it.... Prices change slowly because the subjective valuations of human beings change slowly.... If rapid and erratic valuations in prices were usually encountered in the market, the conception of objective exchange value would not have attained the significance that it is actually accorded both by consumer and producer.

In this sense, reference to an inertia of prices is unobjectionable. (1912/1981, p. 133)

It is so far as the money prices of goods are determined by *monetary* factors, that a historically continuous component is included in them, without which their actual level could not be explained. (p. 135)

MONEY AND PRICE STICKINESS

Without explicitly saying so, then, Mises clearly implies that money's role as unit of account contributes to the stickiness of prices. People are in the habit of formulating their subjective valuations of goods in terms of the money unit, and subjective valuations ordinarily do not change suddenly. Even if relatively objective developments do call for a change in the market value of any ordinary good or of the money unit itself, people require time to perceive and react to these changes and to reformulate their valuations of goods in money (1912/1981, pp. 133–135; 1949/1963, p. 426).[3]

One might add, as Lerner (1952, pp. 191–193) did, that the most sweeping source of price stickiness lies in the very nature of money. In a money economy, unlike a barter economy, people need not bother about all the real (relative) prices that might concern them, for a thing's money price indicates the value of other things that one might have instead. A price conveys information and guides decisions, however, only if it is reasonably dependable. Imagine how difficult decisions and coordination would be if a thing's price today were only a poor clue to its price tomorrow. Substantial money and price inflation or deflation distorts relative prices and decisions and impairs coordination because not all money prices can be equally flexible. On the other hand, stability in the purchasing power of money tends to reinforce itself and deter accidental or random fluctuations; being the general measure of value supports institutions, habits,

---

[3]Mises is only one of many economists who since long ago have recognized price stickiness. The notion that attention to it is distinctively a contribution of Keynes is just wrong as history of economic thought. See my 1991/1997.

and expectations that work to this effect. In short, thoroughgoing wage and price flexibility would keep money from serving its normal purposes; it could not survive. A degree of price stickiness—or dependability—is no mystery.[4]

A leading theme of Mises's theory is that money is far from neutral in its effects on quantities, incomes, and relative prices (1949/1963, pp. 408ff.). Prices do not automatically set themselves in proportion to the total quantity of money, as a naive interpretation of the quantity-theory equation might suggest. Some changes occur relatively rapidly, others after long delays. People's responses to ongoing monetary and price inflation change as experience accumulates and expectations change accordingly. Mises's discussion of *differential* price changes constitutes emphatic recognition of the stickiness of many prices. This recognition is not a distinctively Keynesian notion, despite remarks by textbook authors neglectful of the history of economic thought.

Mises accepts the concept of general equilibrium—the evenly rotating economy, as he calls it—as a tool of analysis. Using it in no way entails supposing that the

> final prices corresponding to this imaginary conception are ... identical with the market prices. The activities of the entrepreneurs or of any other actors on the economic scene are not guided by consideration of any such things as equilibrium prices and the evenly rotating economy. (1949/1963, p. 329)

Austrians are concerned with process—not merely with functional relations in the mathematical sense but with who does what, why, when, and how. Attention to process bars exclusive infatuation with the equilibrium state. (Austrian scorn for the neo-Walrasian brand of general-equilibrium theory is well known. It might well be better focused, however, than it habitually is.) Austrian economics recognizes the scope for entrepreneurship in disequilibrium. Recognizing disequilibrium is one aspect of Austrian *realism*. Austrians are willing to see the world as it actually is. They are not sidetracked into supposedly "rigorous" theorizing about imaginary worlds that diverge from reality in crucial respects. Austrians recognize that pure and perfect competition, like equilibrium, are abstractions and not reality. These imaginary extreme conditions do

---

[4]Roger Garrison objects to the term "sticky prices" on the grounds that stickiness implies some sort of defect, as of a valve. Perhaps, then, the term "dependable prices" would serve better.

have roles to play in theorizing, but economists should recognize when they are inapplicable. In understanding money/macro phenomena and in building bridges between macro and micro economics, it is essential to recognize that sellers are in general *not* pure price takers and that they are not already selling all of their product or of their labor that they want to sell at the prevailing price. In macroeconomics it is important to recognize that most prices are *set* and not impersonally determined by the interplay of atomistic supply and demand.

The Austrians' concern for facts of reality is often overlooked because of their supposed insistence on a *purely a priori* method. This term, notably as used by Ludwig von Mises, unfortunately invites misinterpretation. So used, *a priori* suggests an unintended sharp contrast with *empirical*. Mises did not mean that all important propositions of economic theory can be spun out of factually empty logical truisms. He relied, rather, on axioms for which factual evidence constantly presses itself on us so abundantly that we can hardly imagine a world to which those axioms did not apply (cf. Rothbard 1957). Austrians do not—or should not—confine the honorific term "empirical" to propositions dug out by arduous labor and of doubtful general validity after all.

In related respects, Austrians are more realistic than self-congratulating "empirical" researchers. They open their eyes to what sorts of method have and what sorts have not brought important results. They look at the facts bearing on whether or not stable functions exist that quantitatively and dependably describe relations among economic magnitudes and that might be relied on for forecasting. They are at least as ready as other economists to accept the facts that call into question overambitious, activist, fine-tuning policies whose success presupposes knowing durable quantitative relations.

BOOMS, SLUMPS, AND CONTAGION

What explains the recessions that interrupt prosperity from time to time?[5] Each recession is a specific historical event. Researchers have the job of investigating each one, asking whether many of them share some dominant feature and discarding hypotheses that do not fit the facts. It is

---

[5] I may seem to give unsuitably less attention to inflation than recession. The reason is not complacency; on the contrary, I am something of an antiinflation hawk. The reason is that the theory of money and price inflation is straightforward and well understood. Incomprehensibility is not the reason why impecunious governments so often disregard it.

premature to start by supposing that one theory fits all, just as it would be to expect a single cause of wars or revolutions or electoral landslides. Macroeconomics is inherently a messier field than micro. Micro describes straightforward principles that bear on decisionmaking, coordination, and possible specific distortions of resource allocation. Macro studies what might go wrong on a large scale. Micro bears an analogy with describing the structure and functioning of a healthy human body; macro resembles the study of what might go wrong—diseases and wounds of innumerable kinds.

Narrative and statistical history has convinced monetarists that most recessions exhibit a monetary disturbance—a shrinkage of the quantity of money or, anyway, its downward deviation from a trend that would accommodate real economic growth without a general fall in prices and wages. Monetarists can cite ample historical and statistical evidence from many times and places. It is unnecessary to review this evidence here, but undue neglect warrants a plug in the list of References for an insightful and prescient article in the monetarist tradition written by Harry Gunnison Brown just a few days before Franklin Roosevelt took office at the depths of the Great Depression in 1933. In articles of 1989 and 1990, Christina and David Romer review recessions evidently caused by monetary policy in the United States since World War II.

Money is not the only thing, however, conceivably disrupting coordination. Severe "real" disturbances might overwhelm entrepreneurial efforts to cope with them. It is instructive to ponder what would happen to total output if the country's telephone system (Hall 1991, p. 23) or, more starkly, if all of its electronic communications and data processing were somehow to fail for several months.

In historical fact, however, it is implausible to put special blame on such "real" disturbances for the major recessions and depressions actually experienced. Instead of being readily attributable to changes in productive capacity, recessions and depressions exhibit what look like pervasive deficiencies of demand, pervasive difficulties in finding customers and finding jobs. A "real" theory assuming continuous market equilibrium is especially hard put to explain eventual macroeconomic recoveries.

Even a real disturbance as great as the shift from war to peace in 1945–1946 brought a surprisingly modest macroeconomic ripple, with low unemployment despite demobilization. The two oil-price shocks of the 1970s might count as real causes of recession, but even these had monetary aspects. They not only made old patterns of quantities and relative prices wrong but also shrank real cash balances and reshuffled their ownership. Furthermore, previous money and price inflation had helped trigger the oil shocks themselves (and this inflation in turn arguably traced to a built-in bias of the Bretton Woods system).

Ludwig von Mises aptly entitles one of his chapter sections "The Fallacies of the Nonmonetary Explanations of the Trade Cycle" (1949/1963, pp. 580–586; cf. pp. 554–555). He particularly criticizes "the two most popular varieties of these disproportionality doctrines": the durable-goods (or echo-effect) doctrine and the acceleration principle. He judges them hard to square with the *general*, economywide character of business expansions and contractions (pp. 583, 585).

The crisis and recession beginning in 2007 had a conspicuous real element—the collapse of a housing boom. In its background, however, lurked a monetary policy of arguably excessive liquidity and too-low interest rates, as well as ill-considered government housing and mortgage policies and private financial imprudence.

This recession illustrates the contagion of distress through several channels. Insolvency or illiquidity of some institutions weakens others holding claims on them. Consider an example. Consumers buy houses, putting up only a very small fraction of the purchase prices in money of their own and obtaining mortgage loans for the rest. Now a financier "packages" these mortgages into bonds. More specifically, he buys these mortgage claims from the original lenders (unless he already owns them by himself being the original lender). He gets the necessary funds only fractionally from resources of his own and issues bonds for the difference. His bonds are in turn bought by further financiers, who also pay only a fraction of the purchase price in cash and obtain the rest by issuing still further bonds. Bonds bought serve as collateral for the loans obtained (that is, further bonds issued) to pay for the bond purchases. And so on. In short, loans are made with borrowed money obtained in turn mostly by borrowing: bond sales finance bond purchases. At the end of the chain are the saver-investors who pay in full, for example, individuals who invest in bonds or bond mutual funds or participate in pension funds.

At some stage in the chain, a financier may issue bonds divided into two or more tranches, some appearing safer by having a primary claim on earnings and ultimate repayment and lower tranches being riskier by having only subordinate claims. Upper-tranche ultra-safe bonds are apparently manufactured, then, out of low-quality mortgage loans.

Investing largely with borrowed money is "leverage." "Deleveraging" shook a multitiered structure of claims based on claims. The marketability of securities declined as their actual values became unknown.

Credit-default swaps are in effect insurance policies issued to cover the risk of default on bonds and so make the bonds more marketable. Ordinarily the insurance providers need not expect having to make good on any substantial fraction of their policies at once, so they hold liquid funds amounting to only a small fraction of their total potential liabilities. "Ordinarily," for in times of crisis the credit-default swaps enter into the crumbling of the leveraged chain.

The chain is more fragile than one might suppose on the grounds that, indirectly and ultimately, houses largely back the bonds held by the investors at the end of the chain. The netting-out of intermediate stages is not reassuring, for financial distress might strike any of the several institutions in the chain and break it.

Even so, compounded leverage is not inherently fraudulent; for it can provide the benefits of sophisticated financial intermediation. It productively allocates the burdens of saving and risk-bearing to the parties most able and willing to bear them in view of prospective returns. Complexity breeds ignorance, however; and unscrupulous operators may exploit it.

Contagion marks booms and slumps. In times of exuberance, things usable as collateral rise in price, permitting bigger loans. Furthermore, lenders grant larger loans relative to collateral. This expanded credit bids up asset prices further. And so on upwards until the spiral goes into reverse. Lenders become more demanding. The troubles of operators holding depreciating assets infect their creditors. The multitiered leverage aggravates the downward spiral (Geanakoplos 2010).

Mortgage foreclosures characterize just one channel of contagion. Houses stand empty, lawns go untrimmed, the neighborhood depreciates, house prices fall further and trigger further defaults, and holders of mortgage-backed bonds suffer.

Structural contagion through these channels, as one might call it, is joined by expectational and psychological effects. The stock market is just one of the things registering and perhaps intensifying optimism or pessimism. Investment fads and herd behavior are evident as people take clues from one another. After a bubble collapses, fear engenders more fear. Geanakoplos (2010) writes repeatedly of "scary bad news," by which he means news that is not merely bad but that intensifies itself by worsening general uncertainty. Gorton (2008) emphasizes information and its absence, as about the degree and location of risk. Financial complexity erodes information.

During the recession that began in 2007, lenders held back from lending; banks accumulated huge excess reserves of base money newly created by the Federal Reserve; and investors and consumers postponed spending. The demand to hold money and near-money assets strengthened relative to income and expenditure: the velocity of money fell. Uncertainty was at work according to interpretations circulating widely toward the end of 2010. Businesses could hardly predict the impact of the mammoth new laws affecting health care and finance. Uncertainty about whether the Bush-era tax cuts would be allowed to expire, extended, or modified contributed to hesitation in hiring and in making major expenditures.

MONETARY DISORDER

To understand what scope disordered money has for doing damage, it helps to recall money's immensely valuable services when it works even halfway properly. It vastly facilitates the exchange of goods and services for one another. Indirect exchange through money takes place not only among people working in different sectors of the economy but also over time. Through building up and drawing down cash balances and through credit transactions, people can arrange to receive what other people produce either before or after they deliver their own outputs. This intertemporal aspect of money facilitates the pooling and mobilization of savings and so promotes real capital formation, which, like specialization, enhances productivity.

Money serves not only as the medium of exchange but also as the unit of account, the unit in which prices are quoted, bookkeeping accomplished, contracts written, debts expressed, subjective evaluations formulated, benefits and costs of activities appraised, prospective and past profits and losses estimated and recorded, and taxes levied. The vital roles of market prices, profits, and losses expressed in money received attention in the debates over socialist economic calculation initiated by Ludwig von Mises. When monetary disturbances require substantial changes in general levels of prices and wages, then, *whether or not* these changes occur promptly, the functions of prices, profits, and losses in conveying signals and incentives suffer disruption. One notable glitch is the debt-deflation aspect of depression described by Irving Fisher (1933). Comparable effects occur when price inflation or deflation turns out substantially greater or slighter than people had allowed for in their borrowing and lending and other plans. Previously scheduled debt and interest payments can become disruptively burdensome when debtors and so their creditors suffer disappointments of kinds other than or in addition to price-level or price-trend changes.

Money is potentially a "loose joint," as F.A. Hayek said (Garrison 1984, 2001), between decisions to produce and sell things on the one hand and decisions to buy on the other hand. In accomplishing exchanges, people (and business firms) routinely receive payments into and make payments from *holdings* of money, a fact whose significance Mises well understood in developing his cash-balance approach to monetary theory (1912/1981). The sizes of cash balances desired are related to the sizes of people's and firms' expected inward and outward flows of payments (among other variables). If desired amounts of money exceed or fall short of actual amounts, then people try to adjust their holdings by modifying their behavior on the markets for goods and services and securities. As Mises wrote,

> A shortage of money means a difficulty in disposing of commodities for money.... Under the present organization of the market, which leaves a deep gulf between the marketability of money on the one hand and the marketability of other economic goods on the other hand, nothing but money enters into consideration at all as a medium of exchange. (1912/1981, p. 157)

Theories of difficulty in making contact with potential trading partners help illuminate the decline of the velocity of money in recessions (see the cited works of Clower, Leijonhufvud, and Hall, and particularly Clower 1990, p. 82). With many desired sales thwarted, people find themselves, more or less by default, holding more money than usual relative to their incomes and expenditures. The grim business scene, together with uncertainty and precaution, counts against acting to get rid quickly of cash balances that would otherwise seem excessive.

In some ways, as just implied, imbalance between money's supply and demand is self-aggravating. More generally, supply and demand stay in equilibrium less readily for money than for ordinary goods and services. Because money is the one thing routinely traded on all markets, its supply and demand do not confront each other on a market of its own and cannot be equilibrated with each other through a price adjustment of its own. Equilibrating processes do operate, but only indirectly, over time, and in a piecemeal manner through trials and errors in adjusting quantities and prices on innumerable specific markets. When an excess demand for money requires widespread cuts in prices and wages, sellers and wage negotiators in many or most of the markets for individual goods and services have reason to delay cuts of their own while waiting for a clearer reading on market conditions and waiting to see what other sellers—competitors, workers, suppliers—will do.

Rapid coping with monetary disequilibrium is difficult because knowledge is scattered in millions of separate minds—knowledge about tastes, resources, production possibilities, exchange opportunities, money and credit conditions, and conditions on specific markets. Because the market is, among other things, a mechanism for conveying signals and incentives, it would be inconsistent both to recognize these functions yet to suppose (as the rational-expectations theorists nearly do) that transactors somehow *already* have the knowledge that the price system works to convey. The market process has no quick and easy substitute.

Mises repeatedly emphasized the delayed and nonuniform responses to money-supply changes (1912/1981, pp. 162–163, where he cites observations of David Hume and John Stuart Mill; Mises 1990, chaps. 4–6). "The essence of monetary theory is the cognition that cash-induced changes in the money relation affect the various prices, wage rates, and interest rates neither at the same time nor to the same extent" (1949/1963, p. 555). Although Mises focuses his critical attention on money and credit expansion and its consequences, he recognizes the damage done to business when a credit expansion ceases (p. 568). "Deflation and credit contraction no less than inflation and credit expansion are elements disarranging the smooth course of economic activities" (p. 567). Mises alludes (p. 568) to the damage done by deflation and credit restriction required by Britain's return to the prewar gold parity of its currency after both the Napoleonic wars and World War I.

CREDIT AND MONEY

Credit disruption accompanies or even seems to overshadow monetary disruption in some episodes. Again the current recession provides an example. When the housing boom fed by cheap credit went into reverse, spreading fear made banks and other lenders, including those in the commercial-paper market, hesitant to lend. Some businesses, deprived of credit, had to curtail their operations, spreading distress to their suppliers and laid-off employees. Others that might still have obtained credit did not seek it for lack of attractive opportunities to employ the money.

Credit contraction may indeed count as a "real," nonmonetary, factor in recession; but it still had monetary aspects. Velocity, as already mentioned, fell, and for any plausible concept and measure of money used in the calculation. Income saved from consumption but not devoted to real investment or to nonmonetary assets was allocated to the one remaining asset, namely money, narrowly or broadly defined. If there were no such asset to latch onto, credit contraction could not have occurred, or not in any familiar way (Cover and Hooks 1989). $MV = PQ$, the familiar tautological equation of exchange, remains a useful check on what implies what.

THE TIME ELEMENT

Perhaps more so than other schools, Austrian economists emphasize one banal fact: economic plans and activities stretch out over time. (Dynamic general-equilibrium theory does formally take account of time in its models, but not in the way Austrians do.) This is one more reason why price flexibility cannot keep markets continuously cleared. People cannot do everything at once; they cannot set all prices at the same time and revise all of them equally often. Long-term contracts fix some prices; principal and interest on debt are in the nature of preset prices. A change in the general level of prices necessarily disrupts previous price relations.

A more general point is that coordination requires intertemporal as well as interindustry meshing of plans and activities. Roger Garrison (1984, 2001) identifies the intersection of the "market for time" and the "market for money" as the subject matter of macroeconomics. Money is not the only Hayekian "loose joint" in a market system. A merely loose relation also holds between a definite assortment of capital goods and the subsequent demand for the corresponding consumer goods. This looseness permits maladies such as "overinvestment" or "underinvestment" or "malinvestment." Once committed to a certain course, people cannot "instantaneously and costlessly change that commitment; thus the passage of time and its irreversibility are matters of paramount importance in understanding economic activity" (Laidler 1975, p. 5).

A further link between the universals of time and money (so called by Garrison 1984, 2001) is that people hold money to cope with Keynes's "dark forces of time and ignorance." To the extent that they want to postpone consumption while keeping their options open about the timing and specific types and amounts of their future consumption and investment, people hold financial claims, including money. Keeping options open is possible for individuals but is not possible for the economy as a whole (or is possible only to a lesser extent, through construction of versatile rather than highly specialized capital goods). Private attempts to do the socially impossible—keeping options open—epitomize the intertemporal "loose joint."

SAVING, INVESTMENT, AND MONEY

Fundamentalist Keynesianism worried about the separation of saving and investment decisions. Since both types of decision concern the future, an imbalance between desired saving and desired investment implies intertemporal discoordination. The interest rate (or array of rates) alone cannot ensure saving/investment equilibrium, for interest is not the price of those two aggregate flow magnitudes. Instead, it is the price of loans, broadly interpreted, or, more comprehensively, the price of "waiting" performed through ownership of claims and other assets.

Imbalance implies monetary disequilibrium; yet the interest rate is not the equilibrator of money's supply and demand, either. To understand the relation between saving, investment, and money, let us focus on the case of oversaving, seen as pervasive deficiency of demand for currently produced or producible goods and services. As follows from the two-sided character of markets and of both actually accomplished and unsuccessfully attempted transactions and as Walras's Law states, supply-and-demand imbalance for some things implies imbalance in the opposite direction for other things. (The aggregate value of all excess demand quantities, due account taken of algebraic sign, is tautologically equal to zero.) In the case considered, excess supply (negative excess demand) for currently produced goods and services implies (positive) excess demand for other things. What might this other thing or things be?

People who are trying to save (instead of fully spending their current incomes on consumption) are by that very token trying to acquire saving*s* ("savings" with the *s*) in the form of real or financial assets. Which assets? If the savers themselves are buying labor and other resources to construct new capital goods, they are not contributing to any deficiency of current total spending. (Hindsight might later reveal the particular mix of capital goods constructed to be inappropriate, but that is a problem different from oversaving.) If, instead, savers are acquiring new stocks or bonds from issuers who use the monetary proceeds (the command over resources released from supplying current consumption) to construct capital goods, again no oversaving occurs. If savers are buying already existing physical assets or securities, the question shifts to what their sellers are trying to do with the proceeds. If those asset sellers are using the proceeds for consumption or new capital construction, again no oversaving occurs. If they are trying to shift wealth into other vehicles of saving, the question reappears of what these other vehicles might be: what is the thing or things whose excess demand matches the deficiency of demand for currently produced goods and services?

How, furthermore, could the excess demand for this something persist? Consider how an excess demand might work itself out. (1) The thing's quantity might increase, as with automobiles and certain claims on financial-intermediary institutions. (2) Its price might rise or its yield fall, as with Old Masters, securities, and claims on financial intermediaries. (3) If its quantity and price are both rigid, frustrated demand for the thing might divert itself onto other things, with macroeconomic consequences much the same as if the diverted demand had run in favor of the substitute goods in the first place. (4) For only one thing does none of these responses to excess demand operate, requiring some quite different process. That thing is money, the medium of exchange. (Even nearmoneys can respond in quantity or price or yield.)

In the current U.S. monetary system, the quantity of money depends on the policy-determined stock of government base money and the circumstances represented in the textbook money-multiplier formula. Of the four supply-and-demand-equilibrating mechanisms, the first, the quantity response, is not free to work "automatically" (not apart from monetary policy, for existing institutions do not allow the actual quantity fully to accommodate itself to changes in the demand for money at the existing price level). Mechanism 2, the price response, does not work because money lacks a price of its own. Mechanism 3, diversion of demand, does not work because money supply and demand do not exhibit their imbalance on a specific market from which excess demand might be diverted. (Besides, what would diversion mean for the medium of exchange itself?) Because money is the medium of exchange, excess demand for it is not clearly apparent. Everyone can obtain as much money as he thinks he can "afford" to hold under his circumstances by restraining his purchases, if not by eagerness in selling whatever he has for sale. (A depressed level of income does affect how much money people think they can "afford.") Market difficulties appear to pertain to sales of goods and services, not to money.

With none of responses 1, 2, and 3 operating, the market process of reequilibrating money's supply and demand has to be the roundabout process of adjusting innumerable prices and wages on the individual markets for goods and services. For reasons already noted, prices and wages cannot immediately jump to their new equilibrium level and pattern. Meanwhile, transactions, production, and employment suffer.

The supposed problem of oversaving boils down, then, to monetary disequilibrium. Unsurprisingly, what looks like oversaving—a general deficiency of demand posing an economywide impediment to transactions—is connected with the medium of exchange, which is also, in our current system, the medium in which prices are correctly or incorrectly set or adjusted or left unadjusted.

Suitable monetary institutions and policy might avoid macro discoordination involving saving and investment and a general deficiency or excess of demand for current output. By themselves, however, they cannot ensure both that a proper share of current income is saved and devoted to capital formation and that resources are properly allocated among capital-construction projects by economic sectors and by degrees of remoteness from final consumption. Nothing can ensure such ideal results—and the very meaning of "proper" in this context is unclear. People do not have perfect foresight, so some capital-construction projects are bound to turn out, in retrospect, to have been unwise, while others will turn out to have been worth expanding. Furthermore, nothing guarantees that the proper share of income will be saved and invested or, in other words, that "society" will discount the future at the proper rate. (These are inherently fuzzy concepts anyway; and again, it is pointless to blame reality for being real.)

Still, avoiding monetary disruption means avoiding a major obstacle to the functioning of the price system. Undistorted by monetary influences, the interest rate is free to play its coordinating role, along with other prices. A well functioning price system allows people to use their own decentralized knowledge and judgments in allocating their resources between current consumption and investment to achieve greater future consumption. Monolithic central decisions that might turn out monstrously wrong are avoided. Entrepreneurs whose judgments turn out consistently sound will acquire greater control over resource allocation than those whose judgments turn out consistently mistaken. Even if the inherited array of capital goods does prove at any time to be what hindsight deems a mistake—as inevitably it will to some extent—market signals and incentives

Chapter 8: Macroeconomics and Coordination   149

will help promote an efficient use of this array. The bond and stock markets play a role in mobilizing information and in facilitating recombinations of the inherited complex of capital goods. A stable unit of account would aid these market processes and the economic calculation that they presuppose.

CAPITAL AND INTEREST

Recognizing the time element as they do, Austrians give great attention to capital and interest and the importance of saving and investment for growth of productivity and real incomes. Understanding that branch of theory is essential to understanding even the basics of economics, especially microeconomics and the logic of a price system. Böhm-Bawerk and writers in his tradition have made indispensable contributions here.

Keynes saw investment spending as a strategic part of the total spending that sustains economic activity, but he did not treat what capital goods are built or not built as a crucial issue.

Monetarists certainly recognize the importance of capital and interest theory. Unlike some Austrians, however, they do not see it as a dominant strand of explaining the fluctuations of boom and recession. Similarly, although a disequilibrium pattern of *relative* prices and wages is important in some contexts, it is not central to explaining cyclical fluctuations. The centerpiece of the monetarist story, instead, is a disequilibrium relation between the nominal quantity of money and the general level of prices and wages. Crucial here are the factors determining the quantity of money and the demand for cash balances.

Central-bank policy has much to do with determining the quantity of money. Trying to keep a target rate of interest below the "natural" rate that would otherwise clear the credit market entails expanding the quantity of money, as Knut Wicksell explained; and (less familiarly) trying to keep a target rate above the natural rate involves shrinking the quantity of money or slowing its growth. True as all this is, however, it does not elevate capital and interest theory to the crucial role specifically in macroeconomics that some Austrians would accord to it.

A QUESTIONABLE BUSINESS-CYCLE THEORY

Partly for such reasons my enthusiasm for Austrian economics does not extend to a theory propounded by Ludwig von Mises and F.A. Hayek early in the twentieth century and still recited by some Austrians as the dominant strand of their macroeconomics. The theory blames recession on a preceding policy of excessively easy money. Artificially low interest rates falsify price signals, exaggerating how much saving is freeing resources from consumption for real investment. The false cheapness of credit lures entrepreneurs into otherwise unattractive long-term-oriented, interest-sensitive projects. In time the scarcity of saved resources for completing uncompleted projects or operating completed ones forces abandoning some of them. Demands for complementary inputs and factors of production, including labor, fall off. The downturn arrives. Nothing can be done about the misallocation and waste of resources except to restructure some of the mistaken projects for whatever alternative uses can be found. The lesson about not repeating the easy money that may have caused such distress is often, sadly, not taken to heart.

This scenario, although conceivable enough, finds little historical support. Overambitious investment projects are typically abandoned or restructured not for lack of real resources to complete and operate them but from disappointingly weak demand for them and for the goods and services into whose production they were meant to enter. Consider gluts in the past several years of fiber-optic cable and of houses and high-rise condominiums.

Strands of the Austrian business-cycle theory may well belong in the tool kit of theories that researchers may draw on in investigating historical episodes. Overemphasis on it, however, is an embarrassment that the Austrian school would well be rid of. (For a fuller critique, see Yeager 1986/1997, pp. 229–235.) Excessively easy money can indeed do damage in various ways, but justified warnings against it had best not be tarred by association with a questionable one.

INSTITUTIONS

Not everything said here is standard Austrian economics. It does fit in well, however, with several leading traits of the Austrian school—its emphasis on the coordination problem, its forthright perception of messy reality and the scope it leaves for entrepreneurial activities, and its putting money and time at the center of macroeconomics. One further trait is concern for institutions. It contrasts in this respect with the hyper-free-marketry of the New Classical and real-business-cycle schools, which have cultivated analysis of abstract models uncontaminated by institutional detail. Austrians practice comparative-institutional analysis, which does not mean comparing the real world unfavorably with the Walrasian vision of general equilibrium. When told that reality is unsatisfactory in this or that respect, Austrians are inclined to ask, "Unsatisfactory compared to what?" Like members of the Public Choice school, Austrians know better than automatically to regard government as superior to private enterprise in accomplishing various tasks.

The aggregate-demand/aggregate-supply analysis still dominating the textbooks almost invites itchy-fingered attempts to fine-tune the macroeconomy. The Austrians' concern with fine-grained specialization and the task of coordination directs attention, by contrast, to the question of what framework of institutions and of more or less steady policies, institutionalized policies, can best allow market processes to operate.

The Austrian concern with institutions shows up in the debate over economic calculation under socialism and capitalism and in discussions of monetary standards and monetary reforms. It shows up in the attention that Ludwig von Mises and Friedrich Hayek paid to history. Distinguishing between theory and history, they warned against misconceiving of economics as numerical aspects of recent or earlier economic history. Aware of how important and how changeable institutions are, Austrians are skeptical that a country's economic "structure" can be pinned down econometrically in functions of stable form and with stable coefficients. Nothing can fully substitute for insights from history.

APPRAISAL AND OPPORTUNITIES

The large institutional and historical element in macroeconomics bars a specific general theory and any well-specified model of the macroeconomy. Emphasizing that element may seem antitheoretical, uninformative, and sloppy; but if that is the way things are, supposing otherwise sabotages understanding. Scarcely conceivable progress in macroeconomics might some day change that condition, but meanwhile we must acknowledge the contrast between micro- and macroeconomics.[6] Devising a general theory is as difficult for macroeconomics as for diseases and wounds of the human body.

In policy, also, a realistic macroeconomics might seem deficient. Unlike what a well-specified model might seem to do, it cannot grind out

---

[6]For an appeal for due modesty in macroeconomics by an eminent mainstream economist, see Summers 1991.

specific recommendations, especially not quantitative ones. The best it can recommend to policymakers is to avoid disrupting an economic environment that facilitates the coordination of private plans. What history particularly warns against is disruptions from excessively contractionary or expansionary monetary policy. The case for dependability in monetary policy—for rules, not episode-to-episode discretion—deserves attention.

Macroeconomics gives scant specific guidance for remedying the fears and uncertainties of late 2010. It is true in principle that a monetary policy even more expansionary than already adopted could revive spending by offsetting the fall in money's velocity—by gratifying the temporarily intensified demand to hold money. Unlike many earlier recessions, however, the current one is not marked by monetary tightness. To ease money and credit further would aggravate the "exit-strategy" problem for the Federal Reserve, the problem of how safely to reverse the great expansion of its balance sheet. Furthermore, such a short-run-oriented expedient might well destroy the Federal Reserve's hard-won reputation as guardian of the value of money.

In summary, Austrian economics, including macroeconomics, recognizes how messy ("imperfect") reality is, with so much depending on radically decentralized knowledge and decisions to be coordinated somehow. Decisions are guided, not only by current conditions but also by changing experience, theories, entrepreneurial spirit (Keynes's "animal spirits"), intuitions, and hunches. Austrian emphasis on the subjective element is amply warranted. Fortunately, attention to the psychological contagion of speculative booms and paralyzing fear is gaining academic respectability.

This cannot all be formalized and rigorized in the way sought by mainstream economic models, with their functional forms and specific parameters informing ambitious and successful policy. Perhaps remarkable intellectual advances will some day satisfy such aspirations. Until then, however, theory and policy must remain modest.

The current disarray in macroeconomics and the exaggerations of lately fashionable free-marketry give Austrian economists an opportunity to earn the attention of the mainstream. In business-cycle theory, their broad time-and-money orientation holds more promise than their specific application of capital and interest theory criticized above, which may have seemed more plausible under certain past historical-institutional conditions than it is in general. Austrian macroeconomics has much in common, and could develop still more in common, with monetarism, with work like that of Clower and Leijonhufvud and Howitt, and even with

New Keynesianism. (We should not be afraid of mere labels, which have been especially misapplied in recent years anyway.)

Rising Austrian economists might well find dissertation topics in the areas of monetary history, monetary reform, alternative market institutions,[7] property rights, and institutional and entrepreneurial history. A search for historical episodes of depression or recession of entirely *non*monetary origin and character could be instructive, whether or not any actually turn up.

Going beyond preservation and transmission of cherished truths, Austrians can exploit their insights to help gain new knowledge and sounder public policy. Macroeconomics as recommended here may offer governments unfashionably little specific advice, little numerically definite, little beyond warning against monetary disorder and against otherwise contributing to uncertainty and fear. But if that is the way things are, what else can one say?

Austrians can also point out the absurdity of our undefined fiat dollar, whose value rests precariously on nothing better than the changeable policies of the Federal Reserve, badgered from all sides with contradictory, changeable, and short-run-oriented advice. They have much to say about how this monetary anomaly abets irresponsible government, reflected in persistent budget deficits. It is unnecessary to identify sound money exclusively with a particular commodity standard of relatively brief historical duration. As F.A. Hayek and several younger Austrian economists have shown, several alternative monetary reforms are of theoretical and practical interest.

REFERENCES

Brown, Harry G. "Nonsense and Sense in Dealing with the Depression." *BGS International Exchange* (Spring 1933): 97–107.

Clower, Robert W. *Money and Markets*. Edited by Donald Walker. New York: Cambridge University Press, 1984.

———. "Keynes's General Theory: A Contemporary Perspective." *Greek Economic Review* 12, Supplement (Autumn 1990): 73–84.

---

[7]Peter Howitt recommends studying how real-world institutions function very differently from the centralized Walrasian auction (1990, p. 51). "Further progress will depend upon supplying institutional detail..., including the inventory-holding, advertising, negotiating, inspection, and even price-quoting services of intermediaries and other market-making institutions of real life" (1990, p. 19).

Cover, James P., and Donald L. Hooks. "Credit versus Monetary Theories of Macroeconomic Fluctuations." *Atlantic Economic Journal* 17 (June 1989): 42–46.

Eucken, Walter. *The Foundations of Economics*. Translated by T.W. Hutchison. London: Hodge, 1950.

Fisher, Irving. "The Debt-Deflation Theory of Great Depressions." *Econometrica* 1 (October 1933): 337–357.

Garrison, Roger W. "Time and Money: The Universals of Macroeconomic Theorizing." *Journal of Macroeconomics* 6 (Spring 1984): 197–213.

———. *Time and Money: The Macroeconomics of Capital Structure*. London: Routledge, 2001.

Geanakoplos, John. "Solving the Present Crisis and Managing the Leverage Cycle." Federal Reserve Bank of New York *Economic Policy Review* 16, no. 1, Special Issue (August 2010): 101–131.

Gorton, Gary. "The Panic of 2007." Paper delivered at Jackson Hole, August 2008. http://www.kansascityfed.org/publicat/sympos/2008/gorton.08.04.08.pdf.

Hall, Robert E. *Booms and Recessions in a Noisy Economy*. New Haven, Conn.: Yale University Press, 1991.

Hansen, Gary D., and Edward C. Prescott. "Did Technology Shocks Cause the 1990–1991 Recession?" *American Economic Review* 83 (May 1993): 280–286.

Hansen, Gary D., and Randall Wright. "The Labor Market in Real Business Cycle Theory." Federal Reserve Bank of Minneapolis *Quarterly Review* 16 (Spring 1992): 2–12.

Hayek, F.A. "The Use of Knowledge in Society." 1945. In *Individualism and Economic Order*, chap. 4. London: Routledge & Kegan Paul, 1949.

Howitt, Peter. *The Keynesian Recovery and Other Essays*. Ann Arbor: University of Michigan Press, 1990.

Laidler, David. *Essays on Money and Inflation*. Chicago: University of Chicago Press, 1975.

Leijonhufvud, Axel. *On Keynesian Economics and the Economics of Keynes*. New York: Oxford University Press, 1968.

———. *Information and Coordination*. New York: Oxford University Press, 1981.

———. "Whatever Happened to Keynesian Economics?" Paper delivered at a conference on The Legacy of Keynes, Gustavus Adolphus College, Saint Peter, Minnesota, 30 September and 1 October 1986.

Lerner, Abba P. "The Essential Properties of Interest and Money." *Quarterly Journal of Economics* 66, no. 2 (May 1952): 172–193.

Lucas, Robert E., Jr. *Models of Business Cycles.* Yrjo Jahnsson Lectures. Oxford and New York: Basil Blackwell, 1987.

Mankiw, N. Gregory, and David Romer, eds. *New Keynesian Economics.* 2 vols. Cambridge, Mass.: MIT Press, 1991.

Mises, Ludwig von. *The Theory of Money and Credit.* 1912. Translated by H.E. Batson. Indianapolis: Liberty Classics, 1981.

———. *Human Action.* 1949. Rev. ed. New Haven, Conn.: Yale University Press, 1963.

———. *Money, Method, and the Market Process.* Selected by Margit von Mises, edited by Richard M. Ebeling. Auburn, Ala., and Norwell, Mass.: Ludwig von Mises Institute and Kluwer, 1990.

Mitchell, Wesley C. *Gold, Prices, and Wages Under the Greenback Standard.* 1908. New York: Kelley, 1966.

O'Driscoll, Gerald P., Jr. *Economics as a Coordination Problem.* Kansas City: Sheed Andrews and McMeel, 1977.

Okun, Arthur M. *Prices and Quantities: A Macroeconomic Analysis.* Washington, D.C.: Brookings, 1981.

Romer, Christina D. and David H. Romer. "Does Monetary Policy Matter? A New Test in the Spirit of Friedman and Schwartz." NBER *Macroeconomics Annual* (1989): 121–170.

———. "New Evidence on the Monetary Transmission Mechanism." *Brookings Papers on Economic Activity*, no. 1 (1990): 149–198.

Rothbard, Murray N. "In Defense of 'Extreme Apriorism'." *Southern Economic Journal* 23 (January 1957): 314–320.

Stockman, Alan C. "Real Business Cycle Theory: A Guide, an Evaluation, and New Directions." Federal Reserve Bank of Cleveland *Economic Review* 24, no. 4 (1988): 24–47.

Strongin, Steven. "Real Boats Rock: Monetary Policy and Real Business Cycles." Federal Reserve Bank of Chicago *Economic Perspectives* 12 (November/December 1988): 21–28.

Summers, Lawrence H. "The Scientific Illusion in Empirical Macroeconomics." *Scandinavian Journal of Economics* 93, no. 2 (1991): 129–148.

Wickens, Michael. *Macroeconomic Theory: A Dynamic General Equilibrium Approach*. Princeton, N.J.: Princeton University Press, 2008.

Yeager, Leland B. "The Significance of Monetary Disequilibrium." 1986. In Yeager, *The Fluttering Veil*, edited by George Selgin, 217–251. Indianapolis: Liberty Fund, 1997.

———. "New Keynesians and Old Monetarists." 1991. In *The Fluttering Veil*, edited by George Selgin, 281–302. Indianapolis: Liberty Fund, 1997.

———. "Mises and Hayek on Calculation and Knowledge." *Review of Austrian Economics* 7, no. 2 (1994): 93–109.

CHAPTER 9

The Keynesian Heritage in Economics*

KEYNES THE SALESMAN

What difference has the *General Theory* made? How do economic theory and policy differ from what they would have been if Keynes had never lived?

Keynes sold the economics profession on concern with the macro problems of employment and demand. This concern was not new. Even—or especially—among Chicago economists in the early years of the Great Depression, it had already led to policy recommendations sounding remarkably Keynesian (Davis 1971). But understanding was far from general, as one can verify by browsing through Joseph Dorfman's *Economic Mind in American Civilisation* (1959) and by considering how experimental and eclectic anti-depression policy was. Keynes saw and provided what would gain attention—harsh polemics, sardonic passages, bits of esoteric and shocking doctrine. It helps a doctrine make a splash, as Harry Johnson (1971) suggested, to possess the right degree of difficulty—not so much as to discourage those who would thrill at being revolutionaries, yet enough to allow those who think they understand it to regard themselves as an elite vanguard.

If anyone should argue that pro-spending policies inspired by Keynesian doctrines contributed to general prosperity in the industrialised countries for roughly two decades after World War II, I would concede the point. It took roughly that long for expectations to become attuned to what was happening, for the Phillips unemployment/inflation trade-off to break down, and for expansionary policies to waste their impact in price

---

*From *Keynes's General Theory: Fifty Years On*, eds. John Burton et al. (London: Institute of Economic Affairs, 1986), 27–44; reprinted in *A Critique of Keynesian Economics*, ed. Walter Allan (New York: St. Martin's Press, 1993), 59–71.

inflation rather than maintain the desired real stimulus. The longer-run effects of Keynesianism are another story.

WHAT KEYNES "CROWDED OUT"

Even in its early years, Keynesianism may have been a misfortune. Sounder developments in economic theory might have gained influence had not Keynesianism crowded them off the intellectual scene. What Clark Warburton has called "monetary disequilibrium theory" already had an honourable tradition, extending back at least as far as David Hume in 1752 and P.N. Christiernin in 1761.[1] Even earlier in that century, a rudimentary version evidently found successful expression in policy in several American colonies (Lester 1939/1970, chaps. III, IV, and V). Warburton's own efforts to extend the theory and the statistical evidence for it in the 1940s and 1950s were robbed of attention by the then-prevalent Keynesianism.

A sound approach to macroeconomics, in my view, runs as follows (it largely overlaps what W.H. Hutt teaches in his own idiosyncratic terminology). Fundamentally, behind the veil of money, people specialise in producing particular goods and services to exchange them for the specialised outputs of other people. Any particular output thus constitutes demand for other (non-competing) outputs. Since supply constitutes demand in that sense, there can be no fundamental problem of deficiency of aggregate demand. Even in a depression, men and women are willing to work, produce, exchange, and consume. In particular, employers are willing to hire more workers and produce more goods if only they could find customers, while unemployed workers are willing and eager to become customers if only they could be back at work earning money to spend.

This doctrine is not just a crude, Panglossian version of Say's Law. It goes on to recognise that something may be obstructing the transactions whereby people might gratify unsatisfied desires to the benefit of all concerned. It inquires into what the obstruction might be. In Hutt's version, villains are obstructing the market forces that would otherwise move wages and prices to market-clearing levels.

Clark Warburton offered a different emphasis. As he argued (e.g., 1966, selection 1, esp. pp. 26–27), a tendency towards equilibrium rather

---

[1] Pehr Niclas Christiernin (1725–1799) was a Swedish philosopher and economist at the University of Uppsala.

than disequilibrium is inherent in the logic of a market economy. Whenever, therefore, markets are quite generally and conspicuously failing to clear, some essentially exogenous disturbance must have occurred, a disturbance pervasive enough to resist quick, automatic correction. In a depression, what bars people from accomplishing all the exchanges of each other's goods and services that they desire is a deficient real quantity of money. Such a deficiency could arise either from shrinkage of the money supply or from its failure to keep pace with the demand for money associated with real economic growth. Even then, the real money supply could remain adequate if people marked down their prices and wages sufficiently and promptly. Price and wage "stickiness" is, however, sensible from the standpoint of individual decisionmakers, even though that stickiness, in the face of monetary disturbances, has painful macroeconomic consequences. (An adaptation of this account, drawing on an analogy between levels and trends of prices, can handle the case of "stagflation." It is unnecessary to assume, as simplistic Keynesian analysis does, that inflation and depression are exact opposites associated respectively with too much and too little aggregate demand.)

REINTERPRETATIONS OF KEYNES

Robert Clower (1965) and Axel Leijonhufvud (1968), and other writers in their tradition, have interpreted Keynes as espousing a good part of the theory just sketched out. (They ignored its earlier expositors.) They emphasise such concepts as the absence of the Walrasian auctioneer, incomplete and costly and imperfect information, false price signals, sluggish or poorly coordinated price adjustments, quantity adjustments besides price adjustments, the dual-decision process (i.e., people's decisions about trying to buy or sell in some markets depend on whether or not they succeed in carrying out desired transactions in other markets), and the "income-constrained process" (the infectiousness of failure or success in accomplishing transactions). In brief, information gaps and other frictions bar the swift, coordinated, and appropriate readjustment of interdependent yet separately decided prices. In the face of pervasive disturbances, notably monetary disturbances, the price system cannot maintain or readily restore equilibrium.

Clower and Leijonhufvud admit that Keynes did not explicitly state what they suppose he meant. They offer excuses for him. In trying to break free from orthodoxy, he was handicapped by unavailability of the required concepts. The orthodox doctrine he was attacking had not yet been spelled out explicitly enough. Still, ample excuses for not having done or said something are not, after all, the same as actually having done or said it.

WAS KEYNES A "KEYNESIAN"?

Despite Clower and Leijonhufvud, much of what Keynes says in the *General Theory* (1936) does indeed resemble the supposedly vulgar Keynesianism of the textbooks. If Keynes really was a disequilibrium theorist, why did he make so much of the possibility *of equilibrium* at underemployment? Why did he minimise and almost deny the automatic forces conceivably working, however sluggishly, towards full-employment equilibrium? Why did he repeatedly worry (as in the *General Theory*, p. 347) about "a chronic tendency throughout human history for the propensity to save to be stronger than the inducement to invest"? "The desire of the individual to augment his personal wealth by abstaining from consumption," Keynes continued (p. 348), "has usually been stronger than the inducement to the entrepreneur to augment the national wealth by employing labour on the construction of durable assets." Why did he say (p. 31) that a rich community would find it harder than a poor community to fill its saving gap with investment? Why did he argue (p. 105) that the more fully investment has already provided for the future, the less scope remains for making still further provision? Keynes's hints at the stagnation thesis and in favour of government responsibility for total investment also suggest that he worried about *real* factors making for a chronic tendency for demand to prove deficient. So does his emphasis on a "fundamental psychological law" of consumption spending and his hints in favour of income redistribution (p. 373) to raise the overall propensity to consume.

His worries about excessive thrift date back to before the *General Theory*. Recall, for example, his parable in the *Treatise on Money* (1930, vol. 1: pp. 176–178) about the devastation wrought by a thrift campaign in an economy of banana plantations; he goes on to compare his own theory with the over-saving or under-consumption theories of Mentor Bouniatian, J.A. Hobson, W.T. Foster and W. Catchings. Keynes's banana parable describes too simple an economy to be amenable to interpretation along the lines of Clower and Leijonhufvud. The parable does not even mention money. Clearly Keynes was worrying about over-saving as such.

Keynes's emphasis in the *General Theory* on a definite multiplier relation between changes in investment and in total income also suggests concern about difficulties more deep-seated than the Clower-Leijonhufvud analysis describes. This analysis interprets Keynes in terms of the dynamics of income-constrained processes associated with deficiencies of information, inadequately adjusted prices, and the attendant discoordination. It seems significant that W.H. Hutt, whose theory of cumulative deterioration in a depression is remarkably similar to that of Clower and Leijonhufvud (Glazier 1970), believes he is expounding a doctrine quite different from what he considers to be the crudities of Keynes.

George Brockway (1986, p. 13) provides an extreme example of crude, popularised Keynesianism. Possibly Keynes's greatest contribution was his demonstration that in a capitalist system (or in any system that is advanced much beyond bare subsistence), glut is not only possible; it is always imminent.

Liquidity preference makes the economy unable "to buy and pay for everything it produces; hence a glut." Brockway finds "disgusting and stupid" the attempt being made in the United States nowadays "to 'balance' the budget and thus reduce government expenditures at the very moment they should be expanded."

"Was Keynes a 'Keynesian'?" Contradicting Leijonhufvud's thesis, Herschel Grossman in effect answers "Yes"—and properly, in my view (Yeager 1973): "Keynes' thinking was both substantially in accord with that of his popularisers and similarly deficient" (Grossman 1972, p. 26). He provided no adequate microeconomic foundation for his macro-theory. His treatment of the demand for labour, in particular, is inconsistent with the Clower-Leijonhufvud interpretation. Instead of focusing on the labour-market consequences of disequilibrium in the market for current output, Keynes accepted the classical view that unemployment in a depression derives from an excessive real wage rate. Keynes had in mind nothing like Clower's interpretation of the consumption function and simply offered an *ad hoc* formulation instead. Neither Keynes's writings nor the ensuing controversy and popularisation accomplished a shift away from a classical analytical with such writers as Patinkin and Clower.

Professor Allan Meltzer is another economist who does not accept the Clower-Leijonhufvud interpretation of the *General Theory* as emphasising the supposedly contagious failure of markets to clear because of sticky or malcoordinated prices (Meltzer 1981, esp. pp. 49, 59; also Meltzer 1983). Keynes was indeed concerned whether investment would be adequate to fill the savings gap at full employment. Investment tended to be inadequate—not always, but on the average over time—because investors' long-term expectations were bedevilled by uncertainty (non-quantifiable contingencies, not mere risks that might be estimated). Because expectations were poorly rooted in objective, measurable circumstances, changes in investors' "animal spirits" tended to be contagious. Because investment thus fluctuated around a sub-optimal level, so did total output and employment. Some sort of government planning of large segments of investment seemed advisable as a remedy.

For Keynes, as also interpreted by Meltzer, then, macroeconomic difficulties were more real than monetary ones. Potted versions of Keynesian theory understandably came to focus on those of its aspects that are relatively easy to build into models—the consumption function, the savings gap to be filled by investment, the multiplier, and various interest elasticities or inelasticities—rather than on the shapeless topic of hesitant and changeable expectations.

Alan Coddington (1976, in Wood 1983, vol. IV: p. 227) commented aptly on Clower's suggestion that Keynes must have had the dual-decision hypothesis, in particular, "at the back of his mind":

> The picture here seems to be one of Keynes with a mind full of ideas, *some* of which he got onto the pages of the *General Theory*, the task being to work out what the remainder must have been. This is a problem of reading not so much between the lines as off the edge of the page.

Early reviews and anniversary reviews of the *General Theory* collected in the volumes edited by Wood, especially volume II, provide little or no support for the Clower-Leijonhufvud interpretation. More recent dissenters from that interpretation, in articles also collected in Wood's volumes, include Ivan Johnson, Robin Jackman, and Victoria Chick.

The distinctive feature of the *General Theory*, says Don Patinkin,

> is not simply its ... concern with changes in output, but the crucial role that it assigns to such changes as an *equilibrating force* with respect to aggregate demand and supply—or, equivalently, with respect to saving and investment.

This is "what Keynes's theory of effective demand is all about" and what lends crucial significance to his "fundamental psychological law" of a marginal propensity to consume less than one (Patinkin 1975, in Wood 1983, vol. I: p. 493). In letters to economists who had written major review articles on the book, Keynes not only failed to reject the interpretation that gave rise to the standard IS-LM apparatus but even criticised reviewers who gave insufficient emphasis to its cornerstone, his theory of effective demand.

So there is no basis for the ... contention ... that the message which Keynes really meant to convey with his *General Theory* has been distorted by this interpretation. (Patinkin 1981, in Wood 1983, vol. 1: pp. 607–608)

WAS KEYNES A MONETARIST?

As a self-taught Keynesian who had read and re-read the *General Theory* before taking any college courses in economics, and also as a self-taught monetarist, I long ago was enthusiastic about the apparently monetarist aspects of chapter 17 in particular. Later I became disillusioned. In describing the "essential properties" that make money a prime candidate for being in excess demand and thereby causing depression, Keynes emphasises money's yield. Its liquidity advantages in excess of carrying costs may well pose a target rate of return that new capital goods could not match, in the view of potential investors. As a result, investment may be inadequate to fill the savings gap. Keynes even considers whether assets other than money, such as land or mortgages, might pose the same sort of troublesomely high target rate of return. He does not perceive the special snarl that results when the thing in excess demand is the medium of exchange, so that the supply of some goods and services can fail to constitute demand for others. He does not perceive the closely related difficulty that money, alone among all assets, has no price of its own and no market of its own. Keynes's context offered him an inviting opportunity to make Clower's point (1967), if he really had it in mind, about a possible hiatus between sales and purchases involving the one thing used in practically all transactions; yet he did not seize that opportunity.[2]

Keynes is not entirely consistent with himself throughout the *General Theory*, but on the whole the book conveys a real, nonmonetary, theory of macroeconomic disorder. It *diverted* economic research and policy away from monetary disequilibrium theory.

DISEQUILIBRIUM THEORY AGAIN

That (sounder) theory can explain the consequences of imbalances between demand for and supply of money when prices and wages are not

---

[2] For further argument that Keynes was preoccupied with oversaving as such rather than with excess demand for holdings of money, see Greidanus 1950, esp. pp. 202–203.

sufficiently flexible promptly to absorb the full impact of a monetary disturbance. It recognises the utter reasonableness of that inflexibility from the standpoint of individual price-setters and wage negotiators. Although myriad prices and wages are interdependent, they are necessarily set and adjusted piecemeal in a roundabout process. Whether a contemplated transaction can take place to the advantage of both potential parties may well depend on prices besides those subject to the decisions of those parties.

H.J. Davenport, to mention just one example from early twentieth-century America, emphasised the monetary nature of depression.

> It remains difficult to find a market for products, simply because each producer is attempting a feat which must in the average be an impossibility—the selling of goods to others without a corresponding buying from others.... [T]he prevailing emphasis is upon money, not as intermediate for present purposes, but as a commodity to be kept.... [T]he psychology of the time stresses not the goods to be exchanged through the intermediary commodity, but the commodity itself. The halfway house becomes a house of stopping.... Or to put the case in still another way: the situation is one of withdrawal of a large part of the money supply at the existing level of prices; it is a change of the entire demand schedule of money against goods. (1913, pp. 319–320)

Davenport also recognised (p. 299) that the depression would be milder and shorter if prices could fall evenly all along the line. In reality, however, not all prices fall with equal speed. Wages fall only slowly and with painful struggle, and entrepreneurs may be caught in a cost-price squeeze. Existing nominal indebtedness also poses resistance to adjustments.[3]

Monetary disequilibrium theory not only has a long and venerable history but was at times the dominant view on macroeconomics (cf. Warburton's writings). Much evidence supports it, including statistical evidence of the sort that present-day monetarists produce.

LINGERING KEYNESIANISM

Unfortunately, that promising line of analysis was largely crowded out for a long time by such Keynesian concepts as the IS-LM apparatus, which

---

[3] Further quotations from and citations to pre-Keynesian writings on the prevalence and reasonableness of price and wage stickiness can be found in my "The Keynesian Diversion" (1973).

for some years trivialised the confrontation between Keynesians and monetarists into supposed differences of opinion about interest elasticities. I confess that personal experience has made me even more weary of such concepts. While a visiting professor at George Mason University in the fall of 1983, I not only had to clean the blackboard after my classes, as a professor should; I also had to clear away what the inconsiderate professor before me had left on the board. Through the entire semester, more often than not, it seemed to me, what was left was the Keynesian cross diagram illustrating the simple-minded Keynesian multiplier.

I blame the Keynesians for lingering notions that government budget deficits, apart from how they are financed, unequivocally "stimulate" the economy. Examples of taking this for granted are Abrams and others (1983) and Eisner and Pieper (1984). The latter authors even argue, in effect, that partial repudiation of the U.S. government debt through its decline in nominal market value as interest rates rise, and then through erosion of the dollar itself, should count as a kind of government revenue, making the *real* budget deficit and its real stimulatory effect slighter than they superficially appear to be.

Buchanan and Wagner (1977) argue that the Keynesian justification of budget deficits in specific circumstances has been illegitimately extended by politicians into a reason for complacency about deficits even in a much-widened range of circumstances.

> Although Keynes advocated government deficits to boost total spending in a slack economy, he also called for government surpluses to restrain inflation during booms. But politicians have selectively recalled their Keynesian theory, perennially invoking the spending rationale while conveniently ignoring the restraint Keynes envisioned. (Bendt 1984, p. 5)

Perhaps, as is often said, Keynes was over-confident of his ability to turn public opinion and policy choices around when his own assessments changed.[4]

OVERREACTION AND LABEL-SHIFTING

I conjecture that Keynesianism, followed by disillusionment with it, has provoked an intellectual overreaction. I refer to doctrines of "equilibrium

---

[4]Professor Hayek recounted just such an expression by Keynes of his belief in his powers of persuasion in a conversation they had "a few weeks before his [Keynes's] death." In Hayek 1966/1978, p. 103.

always," which tend to be associated with the rational-expectations or New Classical school, and which treat disequilibrium theories with scorn.[5]

Why should stickinesses persist and contracts go unrevised, obstructing exchanges, when rational market participants would adjust prices promptly and completely to levels at which mutually advantageous transactions could proceed? Equilibrium-always theorists do not see fluctuations in output and employment as reflecting changing degrees of disequilibrium. They suggest, instead, that markets are still clearing, but with transactors sometimes responding to distorted or misperceived prices. Perceptions of relative prices and relative wages are likely to go awry when price inflation occurs at an unexpectedly high or unexpectedly low rate. In the sense that workers and producers are still operating "on their supply curves," equilibrium, though distorted, continues to prevail. Even this distortion would supposedly be absent if people fully expected and allowed for the underlying changes in monetary policy, as self-interest would lead them to do to the extent that is cost-effectively possible.

Exaggerated notions of how nearly perfect markets are possess a strange appeal for some theorists. Anyway, these exaggerations, together with the exegetical writings of Clower and Leijonhufvud, have given perceptive Keynesians an opportunity to shift their ground gracefully, with an ironic result: something like the venerable monetary-disequilibrium theory, which Keynesianism had crowded out, now finds itself labelled "Keynesian" by leaders in the over-reaction. The very title, "Second Thoughts on Keynesian Economics," of an article by Robert Barro (1979), a recanted disequilibrium theorist, suggests the apparent notion that theories invoking wage and price stickiness are Keynesian.[6] Kenneth Arrow (1980, p. 149) casually refers to "Disequilibrium theorists, ... stemming from Keynes." Stanley Fischer (in Fischer 1980, p. 223) refers to "Keynesian disequilibrium analysis." James Tobin (1980a, p. 789) refers to "the Keynesian message" as dealing with disequilibrium and sluggishness of adjustment.

Frank Hahn (1980, p. 137) notes "the present theoretical disillusionment with Keynes" (which, he conjectures, will be reversed). Arthur Okun's posthumous book (1981) spelling out much of the logic of price and wage stickiness is widely regarded as Keynesian. In a new textbook, Hall and Taylor (1986, pp. 13–14, 325) report that

---

[5]Lucas 1975 and 1980, Lucas and Sargent 1978, and Willes 1980 are examples of writings to this effect. Comments interpreting such writings pretty much as I do include Arrow 1980, Buiter 1980, and Tobin 1980a and 1980b.

[6]Also Barro 1984, esp. chap. 19.

Keynes's idea was to look at what would happen if prices were "sticky".... Macro-economic models that assume flexible prices and wages bear the name *classical*, because it was this assumption that was used by the classical economists of the early twentieth century.... In the 1930s, John Maynard Keynes began to emphasise the importance of wage and price rigidities.

Really! A manuscript once sent me by the authors even referred to the elasticities approach to balance-of-payments analysis as Keynesian.

Among advanced thinkers, or leaders in the overreaction, "Keynesian" apparently serves as a loose synonym for out of fashion and therefore wrong. More generally, though, Keynes enjoys automatic charity. It is widely taken for granted that such a thing as Keynesian economics exists and makes sense. Discussion concerns just what it is to which the label "Keynesian" properly applies. Pro- and anti-Keynesians alike could well use better care in the application of labels and more respect for the history of thought.

KEYNES'S LASTING APPEAL

I do not want to seem too negative. Much can be said in Keynes's favour. He actively pursued interests in the arts, public service, and many other fields. He made contributions in analysing Indian currency and finance, in assessing economic conditions and the peace settlements after World War I, in probability theory, and in the study of monetary history and institutions. He wrote charming biographical and other essays. His contributions in the *Tract* of 1923 ran soundly along lines later called monetarist. Despite unintended influences that his later doctrines may have had, Keynes himself was a lifelong and eloquent opponent of inflation (Humphrey 1981).

Here, however, our concern is mainly with the *General Theory*. In writing it, Keynes was no doubt moved by a benevolent, if perhaps patrician, humanitarianism—he meant well. Assuming that a first-best (monetarist) diagnosis of and policy response to the depression of the 1930s was somehow not in the cards, then the policies seemingly recommended by the *General Theory* would have been a good second-best approach. In the United States, however, what brought recovery was not policies inspired by Keynes but an almost accidental monetary expansion, unfortunately interrupted in 1936–1937, and finally wartime monetary expansion. The ideas of the *General Theory* took several years to filter down through the academic world and did not gain major influence in the policy arena until after the war. Those policy ideas may well have been beneficial in the short run, but their long-run harmfulness started becoming evident in the 1960s, and more so in the 1970s.

Why, even today, after so much academic dissection of Keynesian ideas and so much sorry experience with their results in practice, does the Keynes of the *General Theory* remain for many a fascinating and even heroic figure? The disorganisation, obscurities, and contradictions of the book, together with its apparent profundity and novelty, actually keep drawing attention to it.[7] Writing in 1946, Paul Samuelson found it

> not unlikely that future historians of economic thought will conclude that the very obscurity and polemical character of the *General Theory* ultimately served to maximize its long-run influence. (Wood 1983, vol. II: p. 193)

Different economists can read their own favourite ideas into the *General Theory*. Left-wingers, delighted to learn that no mechanism exists to keep saving and investment equal at full employment, can use that supposed fundamental flaw as one more stick to beat the capitalist system with. Right-wing Keynesians (e.g., Polanyi 1948) rejoice that an easy repair will preserve and strengthen the system.

James Schlesinger (1956, in Wood 1983, vol. II: p. 281) suggested that what makes Keynes so satisfying is not his theoretical structure but his "emotional attractiveness." For many economists whose views were shaped by the events of the 1930s, he "represents the Proper Attitude Toward Social Problems." For them, the symbolic Keynes will retain his present position of veneration, for he is the continuing embodiment of the Dreams of Their Youth—the reforming fervor of ancient days.

APPRAISAL

The discussions, research, and attitudes evoked by the *General Theory* offer much to admire. Even as propaganda for a short-run policy stance, the book may have had merit (as I said above, with heavy qualifications). But does it deserve lasting admiration as a scientific performance? Even from

---

[7]Although I am not directly acquainted with the James Joyce industry, I suspect that *Ulysses* and the *General Theory* are alike in offering employment for academic labourers of a certain kind. My own admittedly lame excuse is that I have never written on Keynes except by invitation.

students writing examination papers under time constraint and stress, we teachers expect adequately clear exposition; and a student's protests about "what he meant..."—about what was "at the back of his mind," to adopt a phrase from Keynes's sympathetic interpreters—do not suffice to get his grade revised upward. Keynes, likewise, hardly deserves credit for what he supposedly may have meant but did not know how to say. If, more than 50 years later, scholars are still disputing the central message of the *General Theory*, that very fact should count against rather than in favour of Keynes's claim to scientific stature. Whatever the *General Theory* was, it was not great science. It was largely a dressing-up of old fallacies. Worse, for many years it crowded better science off the intellectual scene.

If Keynes had never written, I conjecture, experience in the Great Depression would have prodded economists towards rediscovering and perfecting monetary-disequilibrium theory. Researchers like Clark Warburton would have gained respectful attention earlier. Whatever one may say favourably about Keynes's work, it did divert attention away from theories that stand up better to factual experience and critical inspection.

REFERENCES

Abrams, Richard K., Richard Froyen, and Roger N. Waud. "The State of the Federal Budget and the State of the Economy." *Economic Inquiry* 21 (October 1983): 485–503.

Arrow, Kenneth J. "Real and Nominal Magnitudes in Economics." *The Public Interest*, Special Issue (1980): 139–150.

Barro, Robert J. "Second Thoughts on Keynesian Economics." *American Economic Review* 69 (May 1979): 54–59.

———. *Macroeconomics*. New York: Wiley, 1984.

Bendt, Douglas L. "Leashing Federal Spending." *The Chase Economic Observer* 4 (March/April 1984): 3–5.

Brockway, George P. "Choking to Death on Cream." *New Leader* 69 (January 1986): 12–13.

Buchanan, James M., and Richard E. Wagner. *Democracy In Deficit: The Political Legacy of Lord Keynes*. New York: Academic Press, 1977.

Buiter, Willem. "The Macroeconomics of Dr. Pangloss: A Critical Survey of the New Classical Macroeconomics." *Economic Journal* 90 (March 1980): 34–50.

Christiernin, Pehr Niclas. *Summary of Lectures on the High Price of Foreign Exchange in Sweden.* 1761. In *The Swedish Bullionist Controversy*, translated and edited by Robert V. Eagly, 41–99. Philadelphia: American Philosophical Society, 1971.

Clower, Robert W. "The Keynesian Counterrevolution: A Theoretical Appraisal." In *The Theory of Interest Rates*, edited by F.H. Hahn and F.P.R. Brechling, 103–125. London: Macmillan, 1965.

———. "A Reconsideration of the Micro-foundations of Monetary Theory." *Western Economic Journal* 6 (December 1967): 1–9.

Davenport, Herbert J. *The Economics of Enterprise.* New York: Macmillan, 1913.

Davis, J. Ronnie. *The New Economics and the Old Economists.* Ames: Iowa State University Press, 1971.

Dorfman, Joseph. *The Economic Mind in American Civilization.* Vol. 5. New York: Viking Press, 1959.

Eisner, Robert, and Paul J. Pieper. "A New View of the Federal Debt and Budget Deficits." *American Economic Review* 74 (March 1984): 11–29.

Fischer, Stanley, ed. *Rational Expectations and Economic Policy.* Chicago: University of Chicago Press, 1980.

Glazier, Evelyn M. *Theories of Disequilibrium: Clower and Leijonhufvud Compared to Hutt.* MA thesis, University of Virginia, 1970.

Greidanus, Tjardus. *The Value of Money.* 2nd ed. London: Staples Press, 1950.

Grossman, Herschel I. "Was Keynes a 'Keynesian'? A Review Article." *Journal of Economic Literature* 10 (March 1972): 26–30.

Hahn, Frank. "General Equilibrium Theory." *The Public Interest*, Special Issue (1980): 123–138.

Hall, Robert E., and John B. Taylor. *Macroeconomics.* New York: Norton, 1986.

Hayek, F.A. "Personal Recollections of Keynes and the 'Keynesian Revolution'." 1966. In *A Tiger by the Tail*, 2nd ed. London: IEA, 1978.

Hume, David. "Of Money." 1752. In *Writings on Economics*, edited by Eugene Rotwein, 33–46. Madison: University of Wisconsin Press, 1970.

Humphrey, Thomas M. "Keynes on Inflation." Federal Reserve Bank of Richmond *Economic Review* 67 (January/February 1981): 3–13.

Hutt, W.H. *Keynesianism—Retrospect and Prospect.* Chicago: Regnery, 1963.

———. *A Rehabilitation of Say's Law.* Athens: Ohio University Press, 1974.

———. *The Keynesian Episode: A Reassessment.* Indianapolis: Liberty Press, 1979.

Johnson, Harry G. "The Keynesian Revolution and the Monetarist Counter-Revolution." *American Economic Review* 61 (May 1971): 1–14.

Keynes, John Maynard. *A Tract on Monetary Reform.* London: Macmillan, 1923.

———. *A Treatise on Money.* 2 vols. London: Macmillan, 1930.

———. *The General Theory of Employment, Interest and Money.* London and New York: Macmillan and Harcourt Brace, 1936.

Leijonhufvud, Axel. *On Keynesian Economics and the Economics of Keynes.* New York: Oxford University Press, 1968.

Lester, Richard A. *Monetary Experiments: Early American and Recent Scandinavian.* 1939. Reprinted Newton Abbot, U.K.: David & Charles Reprints, 1970.

Lucas, Robert E., Jr. "An Equilibrium Model of the Business Cycle." *Journal of Political Economy* 83 (December 1975): 1113–1144.

———. "Methods and Problems in Business Cycle Theory." *Journal of Money, Credit, and Banking* 12, Pt. 2 (November 1980): 696–715.

Lucas, Robert E., Jr., and Thomas J. Sargent. "After Keynesian Macroeconomics." In *After the Phillips Curve: Persistence of High Inflation and High Unemployment,* 49–72. Boston: Federal Reserve Bank of Boston, 1978.

Meltzer, Allan H. "Keynes's *General Theory*: A Different Perspective." *Journal of Economic Literature* 19 (March 1981): 34–64.

———. "Interpreting Keynes." *Journal of Economic Literature* 21 (March 1983): 66–78.

Okun, Arthur. *Prices and Quantities.* Washington, D.C.: Brookings Institution, 1981.

Polanyi, Michael. *Full Employment and Free Trade.* Cambridge, U.K.: Cambridge University Press, 1948.

Tobin, James. "Are New Classical Models Plausible Enough to Guide Policy?" *Journal of Money, Credit, and Banking* 12, Pt. 2 (November 1980a): 788–799.

———. *Asset Accumulation and Economic Activity.* Oxford: Basil Blackwell, 1980b.

Warburton, Clark. *Depression, Inflation, and Monetary Policy*. Baltimore: Johns Hopkins Press, 1966.

———. "Monetary Disequilibrium Theory in the First Half of the Twentieth Century." *History of Political Economy* 13 (Summer 1981): 285–299.

———. Book-length manuscript on the history of monetary-disequilibrium theory, available in the library of George Mason University, Fairfax, Virginia.

Willes, Mark H. "'Rational Expectations' as a Counterrevolution." *The Public Interest*, Special Issue (1980): 81–96.

Wood, John Cunningham, ed. *John Maynard Keynes: Critical Assessments*. 4 vols. London: Croom Helm, 1983.

Yeager, Leland B. "The Keynesian Diversion." *Western Economic Journal* 11 (June 1973): 150–163.

CHAPTER 10

Hutt and Keynes*

William H. Hutt's career involved work on three continents. Born in London in 1899, he studied at the London School of Economics. From 1928 to 1965, the University of Cape Town in South Africa was his academic base. He subsequently emigrated to the United States, teaching at several American universities. He died in 1988.

Hutt was a wide-ranging scholar. Like John Maynard Keynes, he contributed to topics beyond monetary theory and macroeconomics (see, for example, Reynolds 1986). In *Economists and the Public* and *Politically Impossible ... ?*, he waxed philosophical, exploring the proper role of academic economists in debates over public policy. He counselled academics to cherish their ivory-tower purity, avoiding even the appearance of speaking for political parties or industries or other private interests, in order to preserve their scientific authority. They should not compromise in hope of being influential. Hutt was "sufficient of a realist to know that the chances of ... exercising any influence on policy are small." "Every true economist in this age must be satisfied with great hopes and small expectations" (1952a, p. 53, quoting the preface to his own *Theory of Idle Resources*). When an economist does consider *political* feasibility and so recommends a policy other than the one he considers best on grounds of economics (and avowable value judgments), then he should clearly state the amateur political assessment underlying his recommendation, and also state the policy he truly considers best. Keynes, unlike Hutt, relished active involvement outside academia. He wrote much on policy issues, was confident of his ability to sway public opinion first one way and then another (as he mentioned in a conversation recalled by F.A. Hayek, 1979, pp. 101–102), and was inclined to develop theory to bolster existing policy intuitions. As its title suggests, however, this chapter concentrates on work for which Hutt and Keynes

---

*From *Perspectives on the History of Economic Thought*, vol. 6, Selected Papers from the History of Economics Conference, 1989, ed. William J. Barber (Aldershot, U.K., and Brookfield, Vt.: Elgar, 1991).

are best known and in which they treat the same topics—their money-macro theories.

KEYNES ON DEMAND FAILURE

As the *General Theory* in particular shows, Keynes believed in a deep-seated, recurrent tendency toward deficiency of effective demand, causing unemployment and loss of potential output. Keynes had no particular complaint about how the price mechanism would allocate resources, given adequate total demand. Especially in wealthy communities, however, private investment tended to be inadequate to absorb all the saving that would be attempted at full employment. Although Keynes and his followers sometimes identified the difficulty as characteristic of a monetary economy as opposed to a barter economy, they did not trace deficiency of demand to an unstable and often wrong quantity of money. Even though Keynes waffled a bit on the question of monetary disorder (notably in chapter 17 of the *General Theory*), he definitely was not a monetarist in today's sense of the word. Monetary disequilibrium, if it occurred, reflected *real* troubles; he saw market failure, particularly failures centred in the labour and stock and bond markets. He believed that on average over time, business investment was inadequate for full employment and was prone to fluctuate with the state of business confidence, which in turn was subject to sudden change because estimates of prospective yield had to be made using limited knowledge. Keynes alluded to waves of optimism and pessimism, an antisocial fetish of liquidity, and "dark forces of time and ignorance" enveloping the future (1936, pp. 153–155). For such reasons, he thought that an acceptable approximation to full employment required sustained government action to maintain adequate total spending. (To avoid repeating myself in detail, and for documentation, I refer to my chapter 9.)

HUTT'S MICRO ORIENTATION

Hutt's macroeconomics is more disaggregative and micro-oriented. Hutt adopts a Say's Law, or goods-against-goods, approach. People specialize in producing particular goods and services to trade them away for the specialized outputs of other people. Incomes created in particular lines of production are the sources of demand for the outputs of other lines: supply of some things constitutes demand for other (non-competing) things.

Chapter 10: Hutt and Keynes 175

Fundamentally, then, there can be no deficiency of demand. Any apparent problem of that sort traces to impediments to the exchange of goods and services for each other. Impediments to exchange discourage the production of goods and services destined for exchange and discourage the employment of labour and other productive factors. Diagnosing these impediments is Hutt's overriding concern.

Say's Law, as Hutt interprets and extends it, explains how cuts in production in some sectors of the economy entail cuts in real demands for the outputs of other sectors and so cuts in production in those other sectors also. The rot is cumulative; disequilibrium is infectious; a multiplier process operates, although not in the mechanistic way suggested by Keynes's spuriously precise formulas. In the opposite and more cheerful direction, anything promoting recovery of production in some sectors promotes recovery in other sectors also.

But what are the impediments to exchange and production that trigger the downward movement and whose alleviation triggers cumulative recovery? Hutt points to wrong prices. Prices too high to clear the markets for the outputs of some sectors cause cutbacks in their production and in their demands for the outputs of other sectors. What might otherwise have been equilibrium prices for the outputs of those other sectors are now too high; and unless adjusted downwards, they impede exchanges and production further. Hutt blames wrong pricing, not any inadequacy of "spending." Instead of determining the volume of exchanges, spending gets determined: the flow of money transferred in lubricating transactions depends on their physical volume and on the money prices at which those real transactions are evaluated. It is fallacious to suppose, with the Keynesians, that income is created by transfers of money (Hutt 1979, pp. 90, 381). Hutt does not flatly assert that monetary disorder never plays any role at all in frustrating exchanges and production. His view of the role of money will require further attention later in this chapter. Meanwhile, we may note his remark that "Money is relevant to 'effective demand' only because *unanticipated* inflation can, in a very crude way, cause certain prices which have been forced above market-clearing levels (causing therefore nonuse or underuse of men and assets) to become market-clearing values, thereby releasing 'withheld' potential productive capacity and increasing 'effective demand' in our sense *and* in Keynes' sense" (Hutt 1977, p. 36, emphasis in original).

Hutt scorns the fundamentalist Keynesianism that broods about adequacy or inadequacy of demand, about the propensity to consume out of real income, and about a savings gap that grows with income and wealth and so supposedly becomes all the harder to fill with real investment spending, especially as real capital formation supposedly leaves fewer and fewer attractive opportunities for still further investment. Saving, as such, cannot pose a problem. People cannot save without acquiring some assets or other. If this process, including the associated financial transactions, results in real capital formation, well and good; opportunities for further investment still are not foreclosed. Complementarities exist among capital goods; having more of some expands profitable opportunities to construct more of others. Furthermore, sectors of the economy employing additional capital goods enjoy increased productivity and real incomes, which increase the demands for the outputs of other sectors and for the resources to produce them. If, on the other hand, savers neither acquire real assets themselves nor acquire securities by transferring their command over resources to entrepreneurs who will construct assets, then they must be trying to build up their holdings of money. Yet Keynes, says Hutt, tried to put the blame on an excessive propensity to save as such, obscuring the liquidity-preference or demand-for-money aspect of the disequilibrium. (This charge, it seems to me, overlooks chapter 17 of the *General Theory*. What Keynes might better be charged with is vagueness, along with inconsistency among different parts of his book.)

Actually, says Hutt (1979, p. 295), "saving preference and liquidity preference are as unrelated as demands for monocles and bubble gum." Even when an intensified demand for money balances is contributing to macroeconomic disequilibrium, the blame should fall not on this particular change in preferences but on the failure of prices to accommodate it. With prices insufficiently flexible, *any* change in technology or resources or preferences, including not only a strengthening but even a weakening of savings preference or of liquidity preference, can impede market clearing, exchanges, and production. Diagnosis must thus focus on how well or poorly the pricing process is working, and why.

DISEQUILIBRIUM THEORIES

In emphasizing the infectiousness of the failure of some markets to clear (and, more cheerfully, the cumulative character of recovery when some prices initiate adjustment to market-clearing levels), Hutt's doctrine parallels a line of advance in macroeconomics pioneered by Robert Clower (1965, 1967) and Axel Leijonhufvud (1968) and followed by such other economists as Donald Tucker (1971) and Robert Barro and Herschel Grossman (1971, 1976). Their approach features such concepts as absence of the (supposed) Walrasian auctioneer, incomplete and costly and imperfect information, false price signals, sluggish price adjustments, quantity changes as well as price adjustments, the duality of people's decisions about particular transactions according to whether they do or do not meet frustration in accomplishing other desired transactions, and the income-constrained process (the counterpart of Hutt's infectiousness of disequilibrium and recovery).

Clower and Leijonhufvud offered their approach as spelling out what Keynes "really meant" or "had at the back of his mind" while writing the *General Theory*. In this they were wrong, in my opinion. Actually, they were independently resurrecting an older approach from which the Keynesian revolution had diverted attention (Yeager 1973; cf. Grossman 1972). Hutt believes that his own remarkably similar doctrine stands poles apart from what he considers the crudities of Keynes. In a thesis on *Theories of Disequilibrium: Clower and Leijonhufvud Compared to Hutt*, Mrs. Evelyn Marr Glazier notes but does not actually tackle the question of who more correctly understands what Keynes really meant. She does, however, show that the three economists named in her title "agree more on some of the fundamental issues of disequilibrium than they do on the history of doctrines" (p. 3).

Hutt differs from Clower and Leijonhufvud more in emphasis than on substance. He puts less emphasis than they do on reasons why a considerable degree of price and wage stickiness is understandable and rational. He does not recognize why, after a disturbance, it naturally takes time to achieve a new equilibrium level and coordinated pattern of prices because of incompleteness and costliness of and delays in obtaining up-to-date knowledge of market conditions and the interdependence yet separate and sequential setting and revision of individual prices and wages. (On this latter point, see Cagan 1980 and Yeager 1986.)

Hutt notes that Clower and Leijonhufvud stress "the imperfections of the information and communication process as a cause of the *hiatus*" that money poses between desires to sell and desires to buy.

> But the kind of communication or information required for the coordination of the economy takes the form of market pressures; and these pressures are exerted through loss-avoidance, profit-seeking incentives. Faced with such market signals as shrinking or accumulating inventories, entrepreneurs react by changing the rates of liquidation of different

inventories via the price changes which they forecast will effect the desired results. (Hutt 1974, p. 102, emphasis in original)

MARKET PROCESSES THWARTED

In passages where he seems about to recognize the natural aspect of price and wage stickiness (for example, 1974, pp. 40–41), Hutt does not follow through. He regrets the less than instantaneous operation of market pressures and returns to the theme that wrong prices in other economic sectors "merely" make price cuts necessary for market clearing in a particular sector (1974, pp. 40–41, 89–90). He notes that if an entrepreneur *correctly* expects a decline in demand for his product to prove temporary, then letting its inventory grow will turn out to have been a wise investment. If he proves wrong, then he will have withheld supplies, and his misbehaviour has depressive effects on other sectors. Market processes, however, including the natural selection of entrepreneurs, will generally achieve quick adjustment of prices to market-clearing levels if only they are allowed to work (pp. 44–45, 97). Even if government policy aimed at preventing misbehaviour in the pricing process, it admittedly could not succeed completely. "There would always be defects in the drafting of the required legislation, as well as error in enforcement and judicial interpretations" (pp. 41–42). So saying, Hutt again blames imperfect policy rather than natural conditions. Entrepreneurial pessimism or timidity in depressions has always been "a consequence of the price mechanism having been prevented from fulfilling its co-ordinative role" (p. 99). Note the word "prevented."

Hutt blames government for not suppressing the basic reason—villainy—why prices and wages do not clear markets and assure continuous coordination. He perceives villainy—but the word is mine, not his—on the part of labour unions, business monopolists, and government itself. Villainy includes such things as union control over wages, minimum-wage laws, overgenerous unemployment compensation, and monopoly and collusion. Hutt recognizes that the victims of incorrect pricing are not necessarily the villains. Villainous pricing of particular factors and outputs can reduce the demands for other outputs, rendering their unchanged prices wrong and their producers idle (for example, Hutt 1974, p. 88). However, he is inclined to criticize even these victims of others' malpricing for not adapting to the changed situation by adjusting their own prices promptly and steeply enough (1974, p. 83).

Throughout his many writings (for example, 1973) Hutt denounces union wage scales and strikes. Even the mere possibility of strikes deters productive investment and so the growth of real incomes. Even for me, no great admirer of unions, his repeated fulminations against them become downright boring.

Hutt's book of 1944, containing proposals for postwar Britain in particular, further expounds his diagnosis by displaying his passion for reconstructing the world along idealized competitive lines. Drastic antitrust laws would prohibit strikes, lockouts, and boycotts; contracts or conspiracies to restrain output, trade, or exchange or to take part in collusive monopolies; price discrimination; amalgamations, mergers, and holding companies; acquisition by a corporation of shares or debentures of other corporations or purchase, as a going concern, of the assets of competitors; and interlocking directorates. A State Trading Board would have the right to compete with private enterprise, to expropriate property, to impose schemes for coordination, synchronization, and standardization upon groups of independent firms, to determine hours and conditions of labour in certain circumstances, to certify quality, and to issue cease-and-desist orders. A Labour Security Board might require young people to accept specified training or apprenticeship and might penalize failure to attend regularly and perform with due diligence. A Resources Utilization Commission would require State corporations and owners of public utilities to practise marginal-cost pricing, unless aggregate receipts would be less than fixed cost plus avoidable cost. Hutt gave a definition of marginal cost and added: "In the interpretation of this definition recourse may be had to the text-books of economics" (1944, quotation from p. 62).

I doubt that Hutt would still, late in his career, have advocated such drastic steps toward making reality conform to textbook chapters on pure and perfect competition. In the intervening years he, like so many of the rest of us, presumably learned much about the interrelations between economic freedom and human freedom in general; he presumably became disenchanted about turning to government for solutions to market failures. But his book of 1944 remains symptomatic of an orientation that Hutt apparently did hold throughout his career—a concern to trace macroeconomic difficulties to impediments to the ideal working of markets and to seek remedies through microeconomic reconstructions. In his book of 1974 (pp. 101–102) he still suggested that antitrust action, if not perverted by demagogic vote-seeking, would be an appropriate and important ingredient of policy for full employment. Pre-Keynesian economists whom he admired believed "that unless government performed its classical role *there was an automatic tendency for groups acting in collusion to price their inputs or outputs in such a way that a cumulative tendency for economies to run down could be set in motion*" (1974, p. 120, emphasis in original).

Hutt and the Clower-Leijonhufvud school differ, as we have seen, in their relative emphases on villainy and reasonable behaviour in explaining wage and price stickiness. (I do not want to suggest, however, that the latter school stresses rigidity or even stickiness as the ultimate source of discoordination. Clower and Leijonhufvud probe more deeply into the intricate and prolonged groping necessary to enlist scattered knowledge and achieve a new market-clearing level and pattern of prices after a major shock. On this distinction, see, in particular, Leijonhufvud 1981, pp. 111–112.)

HUTT ON MONEY

Another point on which emphases differ concerns the role of money in economic discoordination. Clower in particular (for example, 1967) emphasizes that goods do not exchange for goods *directly*: money is the medium of exchange, and if people have difficulty obtaining money by selling their own goods or services, that very fact keeps them from expressing their demands for other people's goods and services.

Hutt is sceptical of this notion of money as a hiatus between selling and buying.

> [W]hen a person buys, he normally demands with *money's worth*, not with money. He demands with money only when he happens to be reducing his investment in it (i.e., not concurrently replenishing his money holdings), *for he can always obtain money costlessly by realizing his inputs or outputs (services or assets) as their money's worth.... [T]he acquisition and spending of money... is costless*. It follows that money is as incidental (and as important) as cash registers and cashiers in the demanding and supplying process. (1974, pp. 67–68, emphasis in original; cf. pp. 57–60)

In this passage Hutt seems to be supposing a unified budget constraint, in contrast with the realistic split constraint described by Clower (1967). He also seems to suppose that all goods and services are extremely liquid or readily marketable at their full values. His downplaying of the role of money as medium of exchange may be associated with his defining the quantity of money very broadly so as to include what he calls the "pure money equivalent" of nearmoneys and nonmoneys (Hutt 1974, pp. 17–18; 1979, chap. 8).

The possible frustration of transactions through failure of communications and market signals does not basically trace to the use of money. The hiatus arises from the remoteness of wage-earner and wage-earner, of entrepreneur and entrepreneur. These remotenesses are inevitable consequences of the extreme division of labour that the pricing system and money make possible. Except in this sense, the use of money has nothing whatever to do with the problem. (These sentences closely paraphrase 1974, pp. 58–59.)

Yet one would expect someone who expounds the tremendous services of money as eloquently as Hutt does (for example, 1974, p. 60) to recognize the correspondingly great scope for damage if the real quantity of money comes to deviate seriously from the total of real cash balances demanded. One would expect that recognition from the author of "The Yield on Money Held" (1956), an absolutely fundamental contribution to monetary theory. (Hutt explains the straightforward senses in which business cash balances are productive and consumers' cash balances afford utility. A brilliant exposition and extension by Selgin, 1987, makes further discussion here unnecessary.)

Yet Hutt says he does not understand why the tastes, market processes, and so forth that determine the purchasing power of the money unit should induce "income constraints in the form of the withholding of supplies and hence of demands, except in the sense that, in the presence of downward cost and price rigidities, deflation will aggravate the cumulative withholding process—just as *unanticipated* inflation will mitigate or reverse it" (1974, p. 62, emphasis in original). Whether Hutt realizes it or not, the exception he makes is a mammoth one. He also appears to recognize the damage that an inappropriate quantity of money can do when he quotes Leijonhufvud, with apparent agreement, concerning "recurrent attacks of central bank perversity" (1974, p. 73, quoting Leijonhufvud 1968, p. 399, where, however, Leijonhufvud capitalizes the initial letters of "Central Bank").

Yet Hutt shies away from recognizing the role of money in business cycles and from appreciating the monetary-disequilibrium hypothesis of David Hume, Clark Warburton, Milton Friedman, Karl Brunner, Allan Meltzer, and other monetarists. In an oblique reference to the monetary aspect of depression, Hutt did go so far as to say that the classical orthodoxy of the 1920s and 1930s had warned against "the development of an inflationary situation which, requiring subsequent deflationary ratification *if contractual monetary obligations were to be honored*, would eventually precipitate depression through predictable resistances to the necessary price adjustments" (Hutt 1974, p. 118, emphasis in original). In several places, furthermore, Hutt appears to advocate a policy of accommodating the quantity of money to the demand to hold it at a stable price level.

Even so, he backs away from tracing macroeconomic disorder to money. When he comes as close as he ever does to comparing monetary disturbances and price rigidities as sources of disruption, he almost always puts his emphasis on the rigidities (for example, 1974, p. 69). The nonmonetary view of depression, he says, "is truly the explanation of *all* depression. When deflation is the initiating factor (under downward cost or price rigidity), the economy still runs through the cumulative consequences of the withdrawal of supplies of non-money" (1974, p. 73 n., emphasis in original).

[D]epression is due to the chronic, continuous boosting of costs in occupations and industries where the unions tend to be strongest—because demands for their outputs happen to be most inelastic and consumers therefore most easily exploited. In the absence of inflation it would have been perceived how the withdrawal of labour and output by over-pricing in such activities reduces the source of demands for the outputs of less easily exploitable occupations and activities. (1975, p. 113; footnotes omitted here)

But one might well expect Hutt to explain why a "chronic" and "continuous" problem manifests itself in only occasional depressions, with healthy growth and occasional booms intervening. Later Hutt says that inflation, if unanticipated, can improve price/cost ratios in many sectors of the economy. But this crude remedy attracts resources into unsustainable kinds of production and "creates such basic distortions in the pricing mechanism that *we must often blame the attempt to spend depression into prosperity for aggravating prospective and realised unemployment*" (1975, pp. 113–114, emphasis in original).

Hutt touches on certain crucial questions about money without giving sufficiently explicit answers. In some passages he takes such pains to penetrate behind the veil of money that he practically denies money's routine but momentously important function as the medium of exchange; he actually says that people are buying goods and services with money only when, untypically, they are acting to reduce their cash balances (1979, pp. 238, 295). When inflation appears to be stimulating a depressed economy—a phenomenon supposedly beloved of the Keynesians—does the stimulus come from the monetary expansion as such, with prices lagging and the quantity of money and flow of spending thus growing in real terms, or from the price inflation itself, which may be rectifying wrong relative prices, especially by eroding excessively high real wage rates? Often Hutt appears to give the latter answer, suggesting that the trick of getting real wages down in a relatively politically feasible way is the essence of Keynesian employment policy. Interpreters disagree, but others have also taken Keynes to mean just that. It would be ironic if Hutt and Keynes, when agreeing, agree on an erroneous point.

In a malcoordinated and depressed economy, does the trouble necessarily stem from wrong *relative* prices, such as excessive real wages, or might it stem instead mainly from prices and wages that, although not badly out of line with one another, are *generally* too high (or conceivably too low) in relation to the nominal quantity of money? In some passages (September 1953, p. 224; 1979, pp. 147, 282–283, and passim) Hutt emphasizes *unstable* price rigidities and people's postponement of purchases while waiting for the rigidities to break down and prices to fall, seeming to imply that the particular price level would not matter if its *permanent* rigidity were obviating these expectations and postponements. In other passages (1979, pp. 185–186, 207, and passim) he seems to advocate a policy of flexibly accommodating the nominal quantity of money to the existing price level, as if he were indeed concerned about the painful necessity of otherwise adjusting the price and wage level to the money supply.

Hutt anticipated some of the soundest parts of the present-day doctrine of rational expectations. He emphasizes that when inflation has come to be generally expected and allowed for, it becomes purposeless. Unemployment becomes almost a normal accompaniment of inflation, even accelerating inflation (1977, pp. 37–38; cf. p. 252). In these and other passages, however, it is unclear whether he sees the underlying money-supply expansion itself or instead sees the resulting price inflation as what may initially stimulate or recoordinate an economy (although eventually becoming futile). Apparently he means the latter: price inflation may be a way—an inferior, temporary, Keynesian way—of improving coordination by inflating down excessively high real wage rates. He does not forthrightly grapple with the monetarist point that depression may occur not so much because *relative* prices and wages are wrong as because the whole wage and price level is too high in relation to the nominal quantity of money or, in other words, because the nominal money supply has become too small for the wage and price level.

HUTT'S STYLE OF ARGUMENT

Readers must wish that Hutt had done what he did not do, namely systematically present the doctrines he considered rivals of his own in their strongest versions, criticize them in adequate detail, and show just how they fail where his succeeds. We know Hutt disliked Keynesianism; it would be interesting to know in some detail what he thought about monetarist reasoning and evidence.

Hutt's failure to make his position clear on crucial issues, together with the writing style that is largely responsible, brings to mind his own complaint (for example, in 1979, Prologue) about how little scholarly dialogue his work had elicited, particularly from Keynesians. (Consider, also, the harsh review of Hutt 1974 by Herschel Grossman, 1976, someone who I think would be sympathetic to much of Hutt's message if it were presented clearly.)

Hutt's exposition is a collection of discursive and often cryptic remarks. Strewn over hundreds of pages (in 1979, for example), and in no readily intelligible order, we find bits of positive analysis, jabs at Keynesianism, historical allusions, policy proposals, and autobiographical asides. Hutt had a habit of latching onto remarks by other writers as they were apparently cast up at random by his own reading, even if those writers were not leading or typical authorities or controversialists on the points at issue, and then using their remarks as pegs onto which to string his own observations. This habit gave his writing an unnecessarily polemical tone. (As Pejovich 1978 noted, Hutt had a normative bent and seemed not particularly concerned with non-normative analysis of allocations generated by alternative institutional arrangements.)

Strewn through Hutt's writings are echoes of long-standing obsessions, including, of course, his obsession with labour unions. Another concerns Britain's return to the gold standard in 1925 at the prewar parity, requiring internal deflation if that parity were to remain workable. Repeatedly, though often in cryptic language, Hutt offered apologetics for that policy. He might even have been right, but the way that these apologetics kept intruding in unlikely places and with a moralizing tone is characteristic of his style.

Another characteristic is lengthy brooding over the meanings of terms and concepts. Hutt once recorded his "strong dislike for mere 'terminological innovation'" (September 1953, p. 215), but this is a dislike that he managed to overcome. Some wag once said that he wrote in Huttite. Hutt offered lengthy and sometimes obscure definitions of such concepts as market-clearing prices for inputs (1977, p. 105), competition (1977, p. 154; 1974, pp. 15–16), exploitation (1977, p. 218 n.), money (1977, p. 254), and some nine or ten varieties of idleness (throughout his 1977). Presumably out of aversion to theorizing with aggregates and averages, Hutt avoided the term "price level," saying "scale of prices" instead (for example, September 1953, p. 217; 1979, p. 214).

Hutt used one term so much that I, anyway, became accustomed to it: "withheld capacity." This term suggests that people who, in ordinary language, are having a hard time finding jobs or customers are *withholding* their capacity to work or produce by insisting on wages or prices above market-clearing levels. So doing, they are withholding their demands for the goods and services of other people and thereby causing other prices and wages, if unchanged, to be excessive. This terminological allusion to villainy serves to shunt aside analysis of the nature and reasons for price and wage stickiness, including ways that the interdependence of wages and prices narrows the reasonable options available to individual price-setters and wage negotiators. His terminology helps Hutt to damn reality for being real. Yet he himself briefly recognized (for example, 1977, pp. 136 n., 204) that resistance to wage and price adjustments can be "individually rational" although "collectively irrational."

His terminology would permit him, if pressed, to defend propositions that are startling on their face.

The withholding of capacity which is capable of providing currently valuable services is always a case of restraint on freedom. (1979, p. 371 n.)

[T]he labor of all able-bodied persons was demanded throughout the depression years. *It was not supplied.* (1979, p. 169)

[W]hat is usually called "unemployed labor" could be more realistically called "unsupplied labor." (1974, p. 79)

Individuals actively "prospecting" for remunerative jobs are employed. (italicized section heading in 1977, p. 83)

[In the] phrase "excess supply" of labor ... the word "excess" ... could more appropriately be "deficient" or "insufficient"! (1974, p. 86)

[T]he phrase "willingness to demand" ... simply means "willingness to supply"! (1974, p. 27)

[W]hen there is a "shortage" or rationing, we usually say that "demand exceeds supply," although what we really mean is that, at the price asked, more *would* be demanded if more were supplied. Hence I cannot conceive of any situation in which ... the value and amount demanded in any market fails to equal the value and amount supplied.... [P]eople who *would be* prepared to demand at the price asked if they could get the goods are prevented from demanding. (1974, pp. 80–81)

[C]onsumption is always the *extermination* of power to demand. The failure of the Keynesians to understand this simple truth lies at the root of what I believe to be the most outrageous intellectual error of this age. (1979, p. 341)

Hutt often covered himself against challenge by qualifying apparently egregious propositions with cryptic phrases that are hardly understandable unless the reader is already familiar with his terminology and allusions. For example,

It is quite wrong to assume that unfavorable prospects can deter net accumulations, otherwise than through the discouragement of saving preference, or—indirectly—through the encouragement of the withholding of capacity (although such prospects certainly do influence the *form* taken by accumulation). (1979, p. 349)

A similar habit was to mention government policies not always straightforwardly but rather with reference to the results that Hutt would expect them to have. Thus, in an historical context: "not a single governmental step toward multiplying the wages flow was taken" (italicized in 1979, p. 61), meaning, approximately, that the government did not act against the unions.

THE SELLING OF IDEAS

Besides his terminology, tone, and paradox-mongering, other circumstances help explain why Hutt's work has received less attention than Keynes's. Although the *General Theory* was not Keynes's best-written book, it does contain flashes of clever writing and appealing new concepts and terminology. Keynes presented his message as revolutionary, offering young or adaptable economists the opportunity to march at the vanguard of the profession. Keynes's theory had political appeal. It came as a rationalization (whether sound or unsound) of policies that would have been beneficial under the exceptional circumstances of the mid-1930s. Hutt, though, was recommending micro-oriented policies that would have stepped on toes and whose desired benefits would not have come quickly.

Hutt always maintained that he was expounding old, orthodox doctrine; but, although alluding to Edwin Cannan and the London School tradition, he did not build on his predecessors' work in adequate detail, and he neglected to forge links with pre-Keynesian monetary-disequilibrium theory. So he put himself at a double-barreled disadvantage—confessing that his message was basically old stuff, while not clearly showing how he was extending it. Keynes's theory, in contrast, appealed to academic economists by containing concepts and gimmicks offering possibilities for research and publication, for class lectures and examination questions. (On this matter of the internal dynamic of a field of study, see Colander 1986.)

THE ENDURING VALUE OF HUTT'S MESSAGE

Although I do think that Hutt created unnecessary difficulties for its acceptance, I do not mean to disparage his message itself. Apparent macro disorders can indeed trace partly to micro distortions, particularly in prices and wages. Because market transactions are voluntary and the short side determines the actual quantity traded in any market, frustration of transactions and so of production can cumulate in a quasi-multiplier process. Downward cumulativeness is particularly severe if money and credit undergo an induced or secondary deflation (although I do wish that Hutt had been more emphatic in recognizing the role of money). Like F.A. Hayek and others, Hutt was magnificently right in his strictures against chronically inflationary policies as supposed cures of unemployment.

Because of Hutt's style and tone, his writings are unlikely to persuade readers who lack the background and the will necessary to understand his eccentrically phrased message. For two reasons I myself have been turned off by Hutt's style less than most readers probably would be. First, when I came across Hutt's work decades ago, I happened to be predisposed in favour of the sort of message he was trying to convey. Second, I was privileged in 1955 to attend a two-week conference at which he was one of the main speakers. Later, when he served as visiting professor at the

University of Virginia, we were colleagues. His analytical message, his humanitarian concern for those suffering from restrictions on economic opportunity, his intellectual force and zeal, and his integrity came across better when he had ample opportunity to present his message in person than when he offered it in writing alone.

Whether he realized it or not, Hutt was preaching to the already saved. Doing so, however, is far from pointless. Sympathetic readers can find much in his work to fortify their understanding of how the real world works and could be made to work better. They can find much to deepen their insights into the fallacies of Keynesian doctrines whose former dominance has still not been entirely expunged. Teachers able to give sympathetic expositions can make good use of Hutt's work in their classes. It may serve as the focus of fruitful controversy among sympathetic readers.

REFERENCES

Barro, Robert J., and Herschel I. Grossman. "A General Disequilibrium Model of Income and Employment." *American Economic Review* 61 (March 1971): 82–93.

———. *Money, Employment, and Inflation*. New York: Cambridge University Press, 1976.

Cagan, Philip. "Reflections on Rational Expectations." *Journal of Money, Credit, and Banking* 12, Pt. 2 (November 1980): 826–832.

Clower, Robert W. "The Keynesian Counterrevolution: A Theoretical Appraisal." In *The Theory of Interest Rates*, edited by F.H. Hahn and F.P.R. Brechling, 103–125. London: Macmillan, 1965.

———. "A Reconsideration of the Microfoundations of Monetary Theory." *Western Economic Journal* 6 (December 1967): 1–8.

Colander, David C. "The Evolution of Keynesian Economics." Unpublished manuscript dated 14 October 1986. Prepared for presentation at Glendon College, York University, Conference on Keynes and Public Policy after Fifty Years, 1986.

Friedman, Milton, and Anna J. Schwartz. *A Monetary History of the United States, 1867–1960*. Princeton, N.J.: Princeton University Press, 1963.

Glazier, Evelyn M. *Theories of Disequilibrium: Clower and Leijonhufvud Compared to Hutt*. MA Thesis, University of Virginia, 1970.

Grossman, Herschel I. "Was Keynes a 'Keynesian'?" *Journal of Economic Literature* 10 (1972): 26–30.

———. Review of *A Rehabilitation of Say's Law*, by W.H. Hutt. *The Manchester School of Economic and Social Studies* 44 (June 1976): 196–197.

Hayek, F.A. *A Tiger by the Tail*. San Francisco: Cato Institute, 1979.

Hutt, W.H. *Economists and the Public*. London: Jonathan Cape, 1936.

———. *Plan for Reconstruction*. New York: Oxford University Press, 1944.

———. "The Nature of Money." *South African Journal of Economics* 20 (March 1952a): 50–64.

———. "The Notion of the Volume of Money." *South African Journal of Economics* 20, no. 3 (September 1952b): 231–241.

———. "The Notion of Money of Constant Value." Parts I and II. *South African Journal of Economics* 21 (September and December 1953): 215–226 and 341–353.

———. "The Significance of Price Flexibility." *South African Journal of Economics* 22 (March 1954): 40–51.

———. "The Yield from Money Held." In *On Freedom and Free Enterprise*, edited by M. Sennholz, 196–216. Princeton, N.J.: D. Van Nostrand, 1956.

———. *Keynesianism—Retrospect and Prospect*. Chicago: Regnery, 1963.

———. *Politically Impossible...?* London: Institute of Economic Affairs, 1971.

———. *The Strike-Threat System*. New Rochelle, N.Y.: Arlington House, 1973.

———. *A Rehabilitation of Say's Law*. Athens: Ohio University Press, 1974.

———. *The Theory of Collective Bargaining, 1930–1975*. 1930. London: Institute of Economic Affairs, 1975.

———. *The Theory of Idle Resources: A Study in Definition*. 1939. 2nd ed. Indianapolis: Liberty Press, 1977.

———. *The Keynesian Episode: A Reassessment*. Indianapolis: Liberty Press, 1979.

Keynes, John M. *The General Theory of Employment, Interest and Money*. New York: Harcourt Brace, 1936.

Leijonhufvud, Axel. *On Keynesian Economics and the Economics of Keynes*. New York: Oxford University Press, 1968.

———. *Information and Coordination*. New York: Oxford University Press, 1981.

Pejovich, Svetozar. Review of *Economic Forces at Work*, by Armen Alchian, and *The Theory of Idle Resources*, by W.H. Hutt. *Modern Age* 22 (Winter 1978): 92–94.

Reynolds, Morgan O., ed. *W.H. Hutt: An Economist for the Long Run*. Chicago and Washington, D.C.: Gateway Editions, 1986.

Selgin, George A. "The Yield on Money Held Revisited: Lessons for Today." *Market Process* 5, no. 1 (Spring 1987): 18–24.

Tucker, Donald P. "Macroeconomic Models and the Demand for Money under Market Disequilibrium." *Journal of Money, Credit, and Banking* 3 (February 1971): 57–83.

Warburton, Clark. *Depression, Inflation, and Monetary Policy*. Baltimore: Johns Hopkins Press, 1966.

———. "Monetary Disequilibrium Theory in the First Half of the Twentieth Century." *History of Political Economy* 13 (Summer 1981): 285–299.

Yeager, Leland B. "The Keynesian Diversion." *Western Economic Journal* 11 (June 1973): 150–163.

———. "The Significance of Monetary Disequilibrium." *Cato Journal* 6 (Fall 1986): 369–399.

Carl Menger recognized that the typical European currency was not a gold currency but a "gold-plated" one. It had a core of paper, surrounded by layers of minor coins and silver and then with an outer layer of gold plating. This arrangement was good enough for him, provided the plating was strong enough to resist the acid test of financial crisis. What he wanted was stable exchange rates (p. 247).

In Hungary, István Tisza expressed similar ideas: A paper-money country experiences no significant inflows and outflows of money. "In gold-standard countries, on the other hand, the size of the need for gold is decisive." Rich or populous countries need more media of exchange, poor or less populous ones need less.

> The relation between quantity and need must be such that in both places they are equal; and money even goes from the richest country to the poorest if there is relatively greater need for it there, for then it can be turned to better account there; and the elements of the balance of payments will necessarily change as the relation between the quantity of and need for gold requires.... The tendency of balances of payments will always be ... to equalize the relation between demand and supply in all countries and give all as much gold as they need in relation to the needs of others. (Tisza 1890, pp. 92–93)

Its Austrian supporters saw the gold standard less as a transmitter of foreign disturbances than as a means of cushioning domestic disturbances by linkage with the presumably more stable world economy. Franz Perl wrote in 1887 that

> in the isolation in which our currency places us, we are left to our own resources whenever credit is shaken; that international flow of money which stands helpfully at the side of other money markets in times of need is lacking to us; our securities, which only in rare cases have a real abode abroad, return to us at the least sign of mistrust; we lack that equilibrating help. (1887, p. 64, citing Alfred von Lindheim)

Deputy Anton Menger also believed that business crises were "very considerably intensified" by the inability of money to flow into and out of Austria, a monetary island. The value of Austrian money rested only on a very dangerous basis, its scarcity, for a country should have enough money and not too little (Austria, Parliament, Chamber of Deputies 1892, pp. 7182–7183).

Another deputy (Eim) pointed out that the value of a paper money depended on the need for money and on the amount in circulation. The latter could be controlled, but the need for money could hardly be calculated. Thus, the value of paper money "is subject to continual changes, which depend on the most various circumstances, often on chance, indeed even on speculation" (Austria, Parliament, Chamber of Deputies 1892, p. 6989).

The economist Julius Landesberger likewise saw it as a grave defect of a system of purely fiduciary money that it could not work well "unless it were continuously possible to ascertain most reliably the need of the whole economy for means of circulation at all times and to regulate the monetary circulation correspondingly. To this, however, the resources of science are not adequate today" (Landesberger 1892, p. 68).[5]

Russian supporters of gold also argued that that standard made a country's money supply appropriately elastic. Under a paper system, by contrast, the money supply supposedly did not respond appropriately and automatically to the changing need for means of circulation; yet it was impossible to calculate and deliberately meet that need. In a gold-standard country, though, a deficiency of the domestic money supply would remedy itself through a balance-of-payments surplus and an inflow of gold, and a superabundance of money would remedy itself through a deficit and an outflow. Each country would automatically come to hold the quantity of metallic money appropriate to its wealth and transactions, without anyone's having to try to estimate the required quantity.[6]

Opponents of the gold standard sometimes argued that the sacrifices required to get onto gold would prove to have been in vain in case Austria-Hungary should get into another war. The pro-gold reply was that the country should have hard money in peacetime to save the possibility of paper-money issues—the state's "note credit"—for wartime. With the country having a depreciated paper money even in time of peace, said Perl (1887, p. 29), every economist and patriot must shudder to think of what would happen in time of war or fear of war.

---

[5]Landesberger thus seemed to imply that *if* the supply of a fiat money *could* be regulated appropriately, exchange-rate fluctuations would not count decisively against that system. Some people, he noted, even considered the fluctuations a desirable insulator against price deflation in gold countries.

[6]These arguments are reported in Vlasenko 1963, pp. 85–86; Raffalovich 1896, p. 369; Trakhtenberg 1962, pp. 174ff.; and Finance Minister Witte's bill to authorize contracts in gold currency, quoted in Saenger 1927, p. 16.

In Russia, also, gold-standard opponents argued that monetary reform would not be worth the trouble, since a new war would only make the paper money irredeemable again. The reply was that irredeemable paper money should be abolished now so that new issues could be put into circulation if the occasion arose. The currency reform could be a "reconstruction of war material" (Schultze-Gävernitz 1899, p. 462). Starting from the gold standard, the government would have better wartime financial alternatives than if it started from irredeemability.

Early in 1879, when the world-market price of silver had sunk so low that the Austrian gulden was again worth as much as its supposed silver content, or even slightly more, the coinage of silver on private account threatened to inflate the money supply and price level. The Austrian and Hungarian governments responded by closing their mints to the free coinage of silver. That action had been taken in a legally very informal way, however, leaving the possibility that the silver standard would come alive again. For some years the gulden floated at a value above that of its supposed silver content.

By 1890, a different aspect of the loose link remaining between the gulden and silver—one working through speculation about domestic redemption and coinage policy and American silver-purchase policy—came to the fore, providing one of the strongest motives to reform. The Austrian financial press and Parliament seemed preoccupied with the progress of the Sherman Silver Purchase Bill in the U.S. Congress, and unusual day-to-day jumps in the price of silver and the gulden's exchange rate were generally attributed to news from Washington.

Finance Minister Steinbach warned Parliament on 14 May 1892 that forces supporting and opposing free coinage of silver in the United States were almost evenly balanced; powerful influences on the Austrian currency *could* come from that direction. "*The rate fluctuations of the year 1890*, which you all remember, gentlemen, have brought us a *small foretaste* of what would happen if silver coinage were made free today in the United States of North America" (Austria, Parliament, Chamber of Deputies 1892, p. 5930).

Another aspect of legal untidiness was the existence of four distinct types or concepts of gulden: (1) the ordinary fiat gulden ("gulden of Austrian currency"), in which currency and bank deposits were denominated and in which most prices and debts were expressed; (2) the silver gulden, in which some bonds and preferred stocks were still denominated and which could again become separated from the ordinary gulden if silver rose sufficiently in market value; (3) a gold gulden worth two-and-a-half French francs, in which some bonds and customs payments were expressed; and (4) another gold gulden, worth 1.2 percent less, which had some slight application in government accounting; it was the gold equivalent of the standard silver gulden at the 15.5:1 bimetallic ratio of the Latin Monetary Union. As Josef Kreibig later observed, "if there was one drastic proof of the necessity of a reform, it was this peculiar splitting of the monetary unit" (Kreibig 1899, pp. 61–62).

CLIMATES OF OPINION

Dominant Hungarian interests switched in favor of gold around 1889–1890. Earlier they had opposed it out of fear that it meant appreciation of the paper gulden to equality with the two-and-a-half-franc gold gulden, hampering agricultural exports. But as the Hungarians came to realize that the gulden would not be pegged upward at that rate and that the gold standard might mean resistance to further appreciation, or even a partial reversal of recent appreciation, the sentiment of the country's export-and import-competing interests shifted.[7]

It seems that the experts, so considered by the Establishment, were almost all in favor of the gold standard. Being an expert (and so being invited to testify before the commissions mentioned in footnote 3) apparently presupposed, almost by definition, advocacy of the gold standard. None of the major Austrian political parties, as a party, opposed the gold standard, although many individual deputies did. Even proponents of the gold standard recognized that a large opposition existed—and that opponents might possibly outnumber proponents—but outside the most influential circles. The masses had supposedly become accustomed to the existing currency situation and were apathetic about reform. Among the articulate, though, advocacy of gold dominated. A pro-paper pamphleteer suggested a version of the fable of the emperor's clothes: even people who did not understand the supposed disadvantages of paper money and the supposed advantages of gold nevertheless joined the progold chorus in order not to seem unenlightened (Gruber 1892, pp. 114–115).

---

[7]Vienna Board of Trade 1887, p. 388; Kamitz 1949, pp. 147–148; *Aktionär*, 22 June 1890, first supplement, dispatch from Prague; Silin 1913, pp. 394, 395, 399, quoted and paraphrased at length in Trakhtenberg 1962, pp. 265–266. Tisza 1890, esp. pp. 93–95, explained the incorrectness of the earlier fears and argued that the gold standard would serve Hungarian interests.

Even so, opposition consumed most of the time in the parliamentary debates. This was understandable: the government's position took the form of definite bills, and only so much could be said in their favor without repetition, while opposition views were aired in great variety. Only a minority of the opponents forthrightly favored retaining fiat paper money. Most of them wanted bimetallism, or thought that the time was not ripe for the gold standard, or believed that action should await some sort of international agreement, or wanted a gold standard different from what the government's bills would introduce, or engaged in nit-picking about such issues as the emperor's titles on the new gold coins. The only amendment adopted was one expanding his titles from Imperator et Rex to a long list including King of Bohemia, King of Gallicia, and ending with Apostolic King of Hungary.

Some pamphleteers did state the case for retaining a fiat paper money with floating exchange rates—a case centered around the greater importance of domestic than of exchange-rate stability and the importance of a measure of insulation from foreign deflation and crises. Josef Neupauer predicted that "a slow and steady increase in the means of circulation will without doubt encourage the spirit of enterprise, and all the more remain without influence on the price of the Austrian money as indeed the population grows and the whole economy develops." He proposed that the new money necessary to accompany real economic growth be put into circulation through purchase of securities on the Bourse. He even hazarded a guess about the proper rate of annual increase in the money supply—4 percent (Neupauer 1892, p. 26 and passim).

Dominant trends of opinion were apparently quite different in Russia. The discussions of the Imperial Free Economic Society in St. Petersburg in March/April 1896[8] serve as evidence that advocacy of the gold standard was *not* part of the conventional wisdom among economists and leading thinkers. Even advocates of the gold standard acknowledged that apathy toward the reform was quite general. Schulze-Gävernitz referred to those discussions to justify his assertion that "the State carried out the currency reform *against* public opinion, with few exceptions, *against* the press, *against* the tough resistance of the public" (Schulze-Gävernitz 1899, pp. 461–462, 470–471).

---

[8] Austria, Währungs-Enquête Commission 1892; Imperatorskoe Voljnoe .Ekonomicheskoe Obshchestvo 1896.

Finance Minister Sergei Witte also testified to the climate of opinion. As he said, nearly the whole of thinking Russia was initially opposed to his reform. Even he, while new in office, contemplated abandoning his predecessors' work of moving toward the gold standard.[9]

The opposition to the gold standard was so strong in Russia that in order to enact it, the Tsar had to bypass the usual legislative procedure, which involved various committees. Supporting his finance minister, the Tsar enacted it piecemeal by autocratic decrees.[10]

NONECONOMIC MOTIVES

Before turning to the noneconomic reasons for adoption of the gold standard, particularly in Austria, I want to emphasize that the economic reasons did *not* include poor performance of the fiat paper currency (see Yeager 1969, pp. 61–89). Exchange-rate fluctuations were not extreme by present-day standards, and the paper currency was not suffering price inflation. (In fact, the price trend had been downward since about 1871, though less steeply downward than in the gold-standard world.)

Yet Deputy Anton Menger complained. He said that importers and exporters were able to perceive seasonal tendencies in the exchange rate—very feeble tendencies, so far as the figures show—and profit from them by shrewdly timing their purchases and sales of foreign exchange. This sounds like stabilizing speculation to us—hardly grounds for complaint. Yet Menger implied, without articulating his complaint explicitly, that the gains of the shrewd traders were necessarily coming at the expense of the country as a whole (Austria, Parliament, Chamber of Deputies 1892, p. 7473). The gold standard would put a stop to that.

Apart from the economics of the matter, the fluctuating exchange rate was widely viewed as a symbol of disorder and backwardness, whereas being on the gold standard—the most *modern* monetary system—was the mark of a civilized country. Vienna's leading newspaper deplored the monarchy's confused monetary system—with silver as the basic metal, with irredeemable paper notes in circulation, and with the gulden's value exposed to the vicissitudes of wild international speculation—"while all civilized states have long since assured themselves of a stable measure of

---

[9] Witte 1921, pp. 59–60; cf. Von Laue 1963; Crisp 1967, p. 211; Migulin 1899–1904, pp. 130–131.

[10] Witte 1921, pp. 59, 61; Von Laue 1963, pp. 141–144; Migulin 1899–1904, pp. 284–286; Trakhtenberg 1962, p. 267; Russia, Finance Ministry 1902, vol. 2: pp. 422–425.

value, a money as steady in value as possible" (*Neue Freie Presse*, 7 September 1890).[11]

Considerations of prestige were at work. In the Hungarian Currency Inquiry of 1892, Koloman Szell, a former finance minister and future prime minister, declaimed about "the stigma of a paper economy, unworthy of a civilized nation" (quoted in Gruber 1892, p. 117). The Currency Committee of the Austrian Parliament observed in 1892 that "considerations of state [had] influenced the decision of the government" to proceed with gold-standard legislation. Twenty years before, Austria had not been alone in using paper money; since then the United States, Italy, and even little Rumania had gone onto the gold standard. Russia, the only other major power still with a paper standard, was already making preparations for going onto gold. "Every year it detracts more from the State prestige of Austria that it still belongs to the countries with an unregulated currency" (Austria, Parliament, Chamber of Deputies 1892, *Beilage* no. 491, p. 8).

Deputy Dr. Foregger reminded his colleagues that the "scrap-of-paper economy" degraded Austria economically to a second-rate power. "We demonstrate that our Empire does not have the strength to introduce among us, too, the means of payment, hard money, that holds sway in the civilized world. We thereby incessantly damage our credit, our economic flexibility and competitiveness." Lack of foreign confidence extended beyond the economic sphere into

> all other sides of our international relations; it lessens respect for us, esteem for us; it lessens our power position. We must therefore make all efforts to bring the strength of our Monarchy into full effect again by regulating our monetary system.... We cannot have a separate, an insular, currency continue: if we want to take part in the competition of civilized nations, we too must accept the international means of payment, and the international measure of value is just nowadays gold. (Austria, Parliament, Chamber of Deputies 1892, pp. 7132–7133)

The "scrap of paper" to which Dr. Foregger alluded was itself a source of dismay. The state currency notes (as distinguished from the notes of the Austro-Hungarian Bank) were thought of as an actual debt to be paid off sooner or later. This view found support not only in linkage of the legally permissible quantities of state notes and treasury bills (*Salinenscheine*)

---

[11]Earlier (1 November 1884) the same newspaper had exclaimed, "What enthusiasm it would stir up if at last the warmly longed-for moment had arrived to raise Austria onto the height of the civilized states!"

under a ceiling on their combined amount but also in the inscription on the notes themselves, which acknowledged each note as "a part of the common floating debt of the Austro-Hungarian Monarchy" ("common" here meaning shared by the two governments). The term "floating debt" sounds more ominous in German than in English—*schwebende Schuld*—conveying the impression of a "hovering guilt" still to be expiated. One of the purposes of the monetary reform bills of 1892, the Austrian government said, was to abolish these state notes, which had been issued under the compulsion of "shattering political events" (Austria, Parliament, Chamber of Deputies, *Beilage* no. 436). The reference was to monetary inflation during the Austro-Prussian War of 1866. The yearning to banish an ever-present reminder of the humiliation of Königgrätz was an old one. On 1 November 1884 the *Neue Freie Presse* said that "redeeming the floating debt" was "an old duty of honor of Austria." On 1 January 1892 the newspaper lamented "the dismal legacy of revolution and wars, the irredeemable notes, these hateful stains on the name of Austria.... The paper gulden is ... [a] sad monument that has been erected in our budget to remind us of the sufferings of the past."

Even the analytical Carl Menger "most decidedly" rejected "the opinion of those who deny Austria-Hungary the right to reshape her currency on the pattern of that of the civilized nations. It should not be interpreted as immodesty if we too wish to be counted among the 'nations les plus avancées dans la civilisation,' among the nations that are already 'ready for gold,' and not among the peoples 'of the other currency area,' which should content themselves with silver currency" (Menger 1893/1936, pp. 172–173).

Among its advocates in Russia, the gold standard "had become, in the mid-nineties, more than ever a matter of national respectability and economic advantage.... For Russia (as for any civilized country at that time) it was a prerequisite for sound credit and economic progress in general. Above all it would encourage more foreign investment in Russian industry" (Von Laue 1963, p. 139).

A.N. Gurjev was one of the economists who held such a view. For him, restoration of the ruble to a metallic basis had political and cultural as well as economic significance:

> Membership in worldwide civilization is unthinkable without membership in the worldwide monetary economy.... A country with an isolated monetary economy cannot enter into stable cultural intercourse if it is separated from civilized peoples by the whole complex of economic evils connected with the disorder of the monetary system. (Gurjev 1896, p. 163)

Finally, we have the judgment of an eminent Austrian economist of a later generation. Modern economists will be quite unable to understand, said Joseph Schumpeter, why countries such as Austria-Hungary, Russia, and Italy imposed hardships on themselves to adopt gold parities for their currencies. No important economic interests clamored for that policy. Noneconomic considerations were decisive. Gold symbolized sound practice and honor and decency. "Perhaps this explanation raises more problems than it solves. That it is true is certain" (Schumpeter 1954, p. 770).

THE SEDUCTIVE APPEAL OF THE GOLD STANDARD

Now, in preparation for coming to a conclusion, I want to return to my earlier themes. These themes concern the appeal or the desirability of the gold standard.

As we know, some prominent economists and politicians nowadays are recommending a return to the gold standard—or the adoption of whatever it is that they are marketing under that label. My response is not that we must not turn back the clock. That hackneyed slogan betrays a provincialism about one's own time, a shallow meliorism, a moral futurism. Nor is my message that we *can't* turn back the clock. Rather, my message is a reminder of *what it is* that we would have to turn back to. It is a reminder of the entire situation in which the gold standard flourished. More exactly, perhaps, the gold-standard world is an idealized past state of affairs.

The few, very few, decades during which the international gold standard flourished offered almost uniquely favorable conditions. Mint pars among gold standard currencies, instead of being arbitrarily chosen, expressed an equilibrium that had evolved gradually between themselves and national price levels. Mildly rising world prices after 1896 facilitated relative adjustments of prices and wages, while the uptrend did not last long enough—until war destroyed the system—to dissipate its possible benefits by becoming embodied in expectations. Relative calm in social and political affairs and the absence of excessively ambitious government programs and excessive taxation all favored confidence in monetary stability. The age of the gold standard was an age of peace, relatively.[12]

---

[12] The *Neue Freie Presse* (Vienna) and *Aktiönar* (Berlin), both evident organs of liberal bourgeois thought, repeatedly stressed that peace was good for business.

Hugh Rockoff suggested that the tolerably good performance of the gold standard before World War I hinged on favorable conditions that no longer prevail: a corps of dedicated gold prospectors working in unexplored areas; absence of political interference (a laissez-faire atmosphere); patience with the long and uncertain lags in the response of the gold supply to the changing demand for money.

By and large, people (in countries that happened to be on the gold standard, anyway) were freer from government control than in any age before or since—freer to transact business, to make investments, to transfer funds, to travel. There is a certain charm in the reminiscences of an old German banker of how, during his student days at Heidelberg, he and some friends, one of whom had just come into an inheritance, left on the impulse of the moment for a tour of Italy, where the banker in the first town they stopped at considered it an honor to cash in gold coin the large check written by the young stranger. There is similar charm in Jules Verne's story of Phineas Fogg, who left on short notice for his eighty-day tour of the world, paying his expenses from a carpetbag full of Bank of England notes, accepted everywhere. The civility and internationality prevalent during the age of the gold standard have such charm for us nowadays that it seems almost sacrilege to ask whether these benefits resulted from the gold standard or, instead, coexisted with it by mere coincidence.

The gold standard, in short, evokes the "good old days." This association is well illustrated by two quotations, the first from Benjamin M. Anderson, a lifelong champion of gold, and the second from John Maynard Keynes, his generation's leading critic of that standard.

> Those who have an adult's recollection and an adult's understanding of the world which preceded the first World War look back upon it with a great nostalgia. There was a sense of security then which has never since existed. Progress was generally taken for granted.... We had had a prolonged period in which decade after decade had seen increasing political freedom, the progressive spread of democratic institutions, the steady lifting of the standard of life for the masses of men....
>
> In financial matters the good faith of governments was taken for granted.... No country took pride in debasing its currency as a clever financial expedient. (Anderson 1949, pp. 3–4, 6)
>
> What an extraordinary episode in the economic progress of man that age was which came to an end in August, 1914! ... [A]ny man of capacity or

character at all exceeding the average [could escape from the working class] into the middle and upper classes, for whom life offered, at a low cost and with the least trouble, conveniences, comforts and amenities beyond the compass of the richest and most powerful monarchs of other ages. The inhabitant of London could order by telephone, sipping his morning tea in bed, the various products of the whole earth, in such quantity as he might see fit, and reasonably expect their early delivery upon his doorstep; he could at the same moment and by the same means adventure his wealth in the natural resources and new enterprises of any quarter of the world, and share, without exertion or even trouble, in their prospective fruits and advantages.... He could secure forthwith ... cheap and comfortable means of transit to any country or climate without passport or other formality, could despatch his servant to the neighboring office of a bank for such supply of the precious metals as might seem convenient, and could then proceed abroad to foreign quarters, without knowledge of their religion, language, or customs, bearing coined wealth upon his person, and would consider himself greatly aggrieved and much surprised at the least interference. But, most important of all, he regarded this state of affairs as normal, certain, and permanent, except in the direction of further improvement, and any deviation from it as aberrant, scandalous, and avoidable. (Keynes 1920, pp. 10–12)

Reminiscences like these reinforce my impression that the outbreak of World War I was a momentous turning point and a great tragedy in the history of the world—a tragedy all the more poignant because the war broke out so accidentally. The building in Sarajevo near which the assassin was standing when he fired the fateful shots bears a plaque saying that here, on 28 June 1914, Gavrilo Princip carried out an act expressing resistance to tyranny and the will to freedom. The inscription says nothing about the initiation of a chain of events that may, even yet, carry to the destruction of Western civilization. It says nothing about the start of our present age of wars, of globally expansionist tyrannies, and of the perversion of democratic government into an instrument whereby each interest group seeks to plunder society in general, to the unintended net loss of practically all.

If I were asked for my recommendation, therefore, I would not merely recommend going back to the gold standard. By itself, apart from restoration of its preconditions, that would hardly be a constructive step. My nostalgia is for the whole pre-1914 climate, not for one specific facet of it. I recommend repealing World War I, root and branch. If only we could!

ATTITUDES NECESSARY FOR SOUND MONEY

Repealing World War I would have to include restoring certain attitudes that seem to have been more prevalent in public affairs before 1914 than they are now. Those attitudes favored limitations on the scope of government activity and restraint on seeking special advantage through the instrumentality of government. Broadly speaking, these were liberal attitudes in the nineteenth-century sense. These attitudes have now been undermined in ways analyzed, in part, by Ortega y Gasset in *The Revolt of the Masses* (1930).

Nowadays, we have tyranny in the nondemocratic countries and, in the democratic countries, democracy perverted in such a way that political decisions are made out of short-run expediency and without due regard for long-run consequences. But in the gold-standard era, as Lars Jonung says, "the democratic system had not been fully developed." (Peter Lindert detects signs of the perversion of democracy in the United Kingdom, however, even before World War I.)

Without a return to liberal attitudes and self-restraints, a restored gold standard would not work well and would hardly endure. After all, the gold standard is simply a particular set of rules for policy regarding the monetary system; and these rules are no more inherently self-enforcing than any other set of monetary rules. Michele Fratianni has been telling us of the readiness of Italian politicians to throw out the gold standard, and Peter Lindert has noted the propensity of the gold standard and key-currency systems to collapse when shocked. (Even today, before we have gone back to a supposed gold standard, there is plenty of reason for suspecting that what some of its supporters are advocating is not a real but a pseudo gold standard, to echo a distinction made by Milton Friedman, 1961, pp. 66–79.)

Maybe some hope is to be found in constitutional restraints on government taxing and spending, maybe in the depoliticization of money. It would be outside my assignment to discuss these possibilities tonight. My purpose, rather, has been to set our examination of the classical gold standard into the context of the conditions and attitudes that apparently prevailed at the time.

Given the required attitudes and the related restraints on government, the gold standard is not the only set of monetary arrangements that would function tolerably well. Economists can easily imagine, and have proposed, monetary arrangements that would function better.

Chapter 11: The Image of the Gold Standard

The required attitudes were illustrated in Austria even while the country was still on fiat paper money. The government and the financial press repeatedly agonized even over budget deficits that would seem delightfully small to us today. Although the price level was generally steady or even trending mildly downward (except during wars and immediately afterward), the government and the press worried about the value of money as reflected in the exchange rate. (Nowadays, attention would more suitably focus on a price index.) The *Neue Freie Presse* took exchange rates of 120 guldens or higher for ten pounds sterling as a particularly ominous warning.

I will conclude with three quotations from that newspaper.

> London: 120! A cannon shot cannot shock us more than this figure; and it also forms an urgent warning for the many finance ministers of the Monarchy to maintain moderation, to retrench, to resume the policy of soundness.... When the exchange rates, this manometer of credit, rise, then it is better to reef in the sails a bit. Is it really our fate eternally to bear the mark of shame of a disordered currency? Will there never come a chancellor of the treasury who will have the will and also the power to restore the most important basis of the economy? (14 October 1883)

> The price of foreign bills is the loudest and gravest accusation against the government.... [When the opposition parties] want to depict the sad condition of the state with one stroke, then they need only unfold the Cursblatt [sic] and say: Things have gone pretty far in Austria when one franc equals half of our gulden on the world market.... what the ghosts were for poor Macbeth, the foreign exchanges are for [Finance Minister] Dunajewski; indeed, we are convinced that he often wakes up at night, terrified, and suddenly perceives a figure before him that mockingly hisses at him: London 126.50! (26 April 1885)

To introduce my final quotation, I should explain that the Austrian police from time to time confiscated issues of publications containing articles considered too critical of the government. The *Neue Freie Presse* occasionally carried a notice on its front page saying that its preceding issue had been confiscated. (To compensate its subscribers, the newspaper would either reprint the confiscated issue without the offending material or else make the next issue especially large.) In one of its editorials denouncing the confiscations, the paper complained about discrimination, as well: Unlike itself, the official *Coursblatt* of the Vienna Bourse had *never* been confiscated. Yet its latest issue quoted London exchange at 120.95. "And if we were to write our fingers sore, we could not portray the situation more precisely. Confiscate the Cursblatt [sic], Mr. Attorney General" (26 February 1882).

REFERENCES

Anderson, Benjamin M. *Economics and the Public Welfare.* New York: D. Van Nostrand, 1949.

Austria. Parliament. Chamber of Deputies. *Stenographisches Protokoll,* xi[th] session, 1892.

———. Währungs-Enquête Commission. *Stenographische Protokolle über die vom 8. bis 17. März abgehaltenen Sitzungen.* Vienna: K. k. Hof- und Staatsdruckerei, 1892.

Crisp, Olga. "Russia, 1860–1914." In *Banking in the Early Stages of Industrialization,* edited by Rondo Cameron et al. New York: Oxford University Press, 1967.

Friedman, Milton. "Real and Pseudo Gold Standards." *Journal of Law and Economics* 4 (October 1961): 66–79.

Gruber, Robert. *Nationales oder internationales Geld? Die Quintessenz der Währungsfrage.* Vienna: Lesk und Schwidernoch, 1892.

Gurjev, Aleksandr Nikolaevich. *Reforma Denezhnago Obrashchenija.* St. Petersburg: Kirshbaum, 1896.

Imperatorskoe Voljnoe .Ekonomicheskoe Obshchestvo. *Reforma denezhnago obrashchenija.* Reprinted from the society's *Trudy 3.* St. Petersburg: Demakov, 1896.

Kamitz, Reinhard. "Die österreichische Geld- und Währungspolitik von 1848 bis 1948." In *Hundert Jahre österreichischer Wirtschaftsentwicklung, 1848–1948,* edited by Hans Mayer. Vienna: Springer, 1949.

Keynes, John Maynard. *The Economic Consequences of the Peace.* New York: Harcourt Brace & World, 1920.

Kreibig, Josef Clemens. *Unser Währungs- und Münzwesen während der letzten fünfzig Jahre.* Vienna, 1899.

Landesberger, Julius. *Über die Goldprämien-Politik der Zettelbanken.* Vienna: Manz, 1892.

Menger, Carl. *Collected Works of Carl Menger.* Vol. 4, *Schriften über Geldtheorie und Währungspolitik.* 1893. London: London School of Economics and Political Science, 1936.

Migulin, P.P. *Russkij gosudarstvennyj kredit, 1769–1899.* Vols. 2–3. Kharkov: Pechatnoe Delo, 1899–1904.

Neupauer, Josef Ritter von. *Die Schäden und Gefahren der Valutaregulirung für die Staatsfinanzen, die Volkswirthschaft und die Kriegsbereitschaft.* Vienna: Lesk und Schwidernoch, 1892.

Ortega y Gasset, José. *La Rebelión de las Masas.* Madrid: Revista de Occidente, 1930.

Perl, Franz. *Zur Frage der Valutaregulirung in Oesterreich-Ungarn.* Zurich: Verlags-Magazin, 1887.

Raffalovich, Arthur. "Histoire du rouble-crédit." *Journal de la Société de Statistique de Paris* 37 (October 1896): 369.

Russia. Finance Ministry. *Ministerstvo finansov, 1802–1902.* St. Petersburg: .Ekspeditsija Zagotovlenija Gosudarstvennykh Bumag, 1902.

Saenger, Max. *Die Wittesche Währungsreform.* Vienna and Leipzig: Deuticke, 1927.

Schulze-Gävernitz, Gerhard von. *Volkswirtschaftliche Studien aus Russland.* Leipzig: Duncker & Humblot, 1899.

Schumpeter, Joseph. *History of Economic Analysis.* New York: Oxford University Press, 1954.

Silin, N. *Avstro-vengerskij bank.* Moscow, 1913.

Sowell, Thomas. *Knowledge and Decisions.* New York: Basic Books, 1980.

Tisza, István. "Valutánk rendezéséről." *Budapesti Szemle* 62, no. 160 (1890).

Trakhtenberg, Iosif Adoljfovich. *Denezhnoe Obrashchenie i Kredit pri Kapitalizme.* Moscow: Izdateljstvo Akademii Nauk SSSR, 1962.

Vienna Board of Trade (Handels- und Gewerbekammer in Wien). *Bericht über den Handel, die Industrie und die Verkehrsverhältnisse in Nieder-Oesterreich während des Jahres 1886.* Vienna, 1887.

Vlasenko, Vasilij Evtikhievich. *Teorii deneg v Rossii, Konets XIX-dooktjabrskij period XX v.* Kiev: Izdateljstvo Kievskogo Universiteta, 1963.

Von Laue, Theodore H. *Sergei Witte and the Industrialization of Russia.* New York: Columbia University Press, 1963.

Wicksell, Knut. *Interest and Prices.* 1898. Translated by R.F. Kahn. New York: Augustus M. Kelley, 1965.

Witte, Sergej Juljevich. *The Memoirs of Count Witte.* Edited and translated by Abraham Yarmolinsky. Garden City: Doubleday Page, 1921.

Yeager, Leland. "Fluctuating Exchange Rates in the Nineteenth Century: the Experiences of Austria and Russia." In *Monetary Problems of the International Economy,* edited by R.A. Mundell and A.K. Swoboda. Chicago: University of Chicago Press, 1969.

CHAPTER 12

Land, Money, and Capital Formation*

WAITING THROUGH LANDOWNERSHIP[1]

What service, if any, do landowners perform for the rents they collect? Land, narrowly interpreted as sheer space and the associated pure gifts of nature, is just *there*, available to render services regardless of ownership and of owners' work. Partly with such a thought in mind, Henry George proposed taxing away most pure land rent. Even some fervent defenders of private ownership of land and collection of rent give incomplete and thus feeble accounts of service performed. The landowner, according to Murray Rothbard,

> finds, brings into use, and then allocates, land sites to the most value-productive bidders.... [I]t is not just the physical good that is being sold, but a whole bundle of services along with it—among which is the service of transferring ownership from seller to buyer, and doing so efficiently. Ground land does not simply exist; it must be *served* to the user.... The landowner earns the highest ground rents by allocating land sites to their most value-productive uses, i.e., to those uses most desired by consumers....
>
> The view that bringing sites into use and deciding upon their location [sic] is not really "productive" is a vestige from the old classical view that a service which does not tangibly "create" something physical is not "really" productive. Actually, this function is just as productive as any other, and a particularly vital function it is. To hamper and destroy this function would wreck the market economy. (Rothbard 1962, vol. II: pp. 813–814; attached endnotes on vol. II: pp. 929–930, are omitted here.)

---

*From *Economic Policy in an Orderly Framework: Liber Amicorum for Gerrit Meijer*, eds. J.G. Backhaus et al. (Münster: Lit Verlag, 2003), 455–469.
[1] An omitted introduction contains complimentary remarks about Gerrit Meijer, the honoree of the Festschrift.

This is Rothbard's main explanation of what the landowner does. It is true that elsewhere (vol. II: pp. 503, 509) he briefly likens rental returns on land values to interest, but he does not develop this comparison and apparently either does not see its full significance or considers its significance too obvious to need spelling out.

A fuller account recognizes that landowners, like owners of capital goods, stocks, and bonds, are performing the service of *waiting*, as Gustav Cassel (1903/1956) called it, insightfully interpreting it as an independent factor of production. Instead of selling their assets and spending the proceeds on consumption or other current purposes and instead of never accumulating savings in these forms in the first place, the owners are tying up wealth over time and are waiting for the future incomes and maturity or sale values that their assets will yield. So doing, they free resources otherwise allocated to consumption for construction and maintenance of machines, buildings, and other capital goods (and for formation of human capital); they thereby contribute to productivity and economic growth. Landowners are performing essentially the same service as recipients of interest in the strict sense of the term.

Arbitrage of various kinds tends to press annual net rents, expressed as percentages of land values, and interest rates on loans toward equality (subject to standard qualifications about differences in risk, maturity, liquidity, and so forth).[2] The uniform rate toward which these tendencies press may be seen as the reward or price of waiting in general, waiting performed in various ways by delaying consumption, tying up one's savings in claims or assets, and so freeing resources for capital formation.

But just how does waiting through acquiring and holding land operate? Suppose that people become more thrifty and devote their thrift to buying land. Their purchases tend to raise land prices and reduce percentage yields on land and, through arbitrage, to raise asset prices and reduce percentage yields generally, including the interest rate. The decline in target yields encourages business firms to invest the freed resources in real capital formation, and the rise in real investment contributes to the general decline in rates of return. The increased investment embodies the increased thrift.

Conversely, a decline in thrift restrains real investment. If landowners, becoming less thrifty, decide to sell their holdings and spend the proceeds

---

[2] But these different rates of yield are not identical just because they tend to be equal in equilibrium. Explaining this equality is part of the economist's job, which is only impeded by making rent returns conceptually identical to the interest rate narrowly defined.

on consumption, net rents expressed as percentages of the depressed land values would rise. Arbitrage would communicate this rise in yields to the interest rate in the more specific sense. Investment in time-consuming production processes would suffer, as is already obvious from the reduced freeing of resources for such investments.

Waiting, then, is the social function (along with others mentioned by Rothbard) for which the landowner is "rewarded." Saying so merely notes a parallel with the receipt of interest; it is not meant to *justify* the private ownership of land and receipt of land rent. Maurice Allais has even expressed some worries (examined below) about private landownership and rent collection.

INTERNATIONAL CAPITAL MOVEMENTS THROUGH INVESTMENT IN LAND

Another way in which placement of savings in land can affect the interest rate and real capital formation is instructive. Foreigners' purchase of land in our country does so. The transaction, counted as "capital inflow," contributes toward a balance-of-payments surplus on capital account and deficit on current account. During a period of adjustment, imports of goods and services exceed exports: our people gain the additional real resources embodied in the net imports. The foreigners perform waiting for our country by surrendering these resources currently and waiting for the yields on their newly purchased land. Furthermore, the foreign purchase tends to bid up land prices, slightly reducing percentage yields and, through arbitrage, the general interest rate as well. In this way, capital inflow through foreign purchases of land promotes domestic capital formation much the same as would capital inflow through purchase of securities. This example reinforces the analysis of domestic saving devoted to buying land.

POSSIBLE DIVERSION OF THE WILLINGNESS TO WAIT

One distinction between land and man-made capital goods holds in degree if not in essence. The supply of land given by nature in fixed quantities is highly price-inelastic, while quantities of most capital goods can respond to price. In some circumstances, then, the desire to accumulate wealth in the form of land (wealth, not mere acreage) can be met through mere growth in the market value of a fixed amount, while accumulation of wealth as capital goods ordinarily presupposes an increase at least partly in physical quantity. Maurice Allais finds this distinction important (1947, vol. II: chap. IX and passim; passages on this and related topics reviewed below are widely scattered in his two volumes).

People's overall willingness to wait, *if* it were somehow predetermined, would promote capital formation all the more if people did not have the option of waiting through ownership of land in particular. Accumulation of wealth in bid-up land values partially gratifies the overall willingness to wait, leaving less of that willingness for satisfaction in ways that ultimately result in capital formation.

Allais's point serves a deeper understanding of capital and interest, but no policy conclusions immediately follow. It concerns *how* the taste for waiting is gratified. It does not contradict recognition that waiting performed through landownership makes the interest rate lower and capital construction and maintenance greater than these would be if the waiting so performed did not occur at all, not even through ownership of wealth in other forms.

It does seem plausible that waiting is more attractive and therefore more abundant overall with than without the landownership option. Allais seems to take the overall supply of waiting tacitly for granted, however, and to suppose that if thrift could not find an outlet in landownership, it would all seek an outlet in ownership of capital goods, either directly or through securities, further lowering the interest rate and promoting real capital formation.

The opportunity to accumulate wealth as privately owned land cuts two ways. On the one hand, it broadens the opportunities open to savers, thereby improving the overall attractiveness of waiting and so presumably increasing its total performance (assuming, anyway, a "normal" rather than "backbending" response to its rewards). On the other hand, the landownership option diverts some fraction of total waiting away from capital formation into accumulation of private wealth in the socially rather fictitious form of bid-up land values. The inelasticity of land's supply is relevant: strengthened demand increases its quantity much less than its market value (and not merely nominal price but value relative to other things). It is not obvious whether the absolute volume of waiting devoted to capital formation is larger or smaller than it would be if the growth of land values did *not* accrue to private owners. Allais evidently believes that it is smaller, which is why he wants to restrain that accrual.

A loose analogy holds here with creation and destruction of trade as analyzed by the theory of customs unions. A union opens some trade among member countries that trade barriers had formerly blocked, but it also diverts to within the union some trade formerly carried on with the outside world. In the absence of specific facts, one cannot conclude which dominates—the benefits from trade creation or the damage from trade diversion. In the present context, similarly, it is not obvious which effect of private landownership prevails—the encouragement of total waiting or the diversion of some waiting into accumulation of socially fictitious wealth.

This remark about encouragement and diversion needs to be sharpened. Real resources cannot be diverted into accumulation of fictitious wealth; what can be diverted, rather, is the *willingness* to postpone consumption and accumulate and hold wealth. It is thus inexact in this context to worry over any diversion of saving apart and distinct from its decrease. Allais's worry must mean that the propensity to save or wait is gratified and sopped up by accumulation of wealth that, though genuine from the private point of view, is fictitious from the point of view of society as a whole. This fictitious wealth—values created by competition to own land that would physically exist anyway—makes the economywide propensity to save slighter (as I interpret his view) than it would otherwise be. (The concepts of supply or diversion of waiting and the possible waste of willingness to supply it speak further, by the way, in favor of the view of waiting as a factor of production.)

Emphasizing the divergence of viewpoints further clarifies Allais's point. By owning land, the individual is transferring consumption from the present to the future for himself but not for society except—and the exception is important—insofar as substitution and arbitrage promote capital-goods accumulation and the like because of waiting as such rather than because of waiting performed through landownership in particular. Through landownership, waiting can be done from the private point of view that is not waiting from the social point of view. (Waiting performed through landownership and otherwise not performed at all, however, does promote capital-goods construction through substitution and arbitrage, so that the damage done through diversion of waiting into landownership is partially and conceivably even more than fully offset.)

A *reductio ad absurdum* helps convey Allais's point. If saving and real capital formation were to bring the marginal productivity of investment and the interest rate extremely low, capitalizing land rents at that rate would make land values extremely high. As landed wealth grew from the private point of view, it would deter saving through a positive effect on the propensity to consume. Thus the tentatively supposed great saving, capital accumulation, and reduction of the marginal productivity of investment and the interest rate would not go to such an extreme in the first place. An increase in wealth from the private though not from the social point of view does tend to check saving and real capital formation. That particular check would be absent if savers were denied the opportunity to acquire land.

CHANGES IN TASTES OR POLICIES

Some examples of change may reinforce the analysis. Suppose that people become more thrifty and that they initially direct their increased propensity to wait to landownership. Land rises in price, making more monetary wealth available to be accumulated as land. From the social point of view, however, this increase in opportunities for waiting is spurious. The increased propensity to wait will go partly into holding an unaugmented physical amount of land at higher prices rather than predominantly into holding an increased amount of capital goods.

Suppose that although the overall degree of thrift has not changed, wealth-owners' preferences about the *kind* of wealth they hold does shift—toward land and away from capital goods and securities issued to finance them. The bid-up level of land prices increases the amount of landed wealth from the private point of view—this is a matter of arithmetic—but not from the social point of view.[3] This socially fictitious wealth helps satisfy its owners' desire for accumulated savings and thus competes with satisfying that desire through financing the construction of new real wealth with resources diverted from current consumption. This is not to say that the fictitious landed wealth reduces the willingness to save or wait as described by a schedule or function. Instead, landed wealth from the private point of view forms part of the wealth argument in the saving function. The more wealth people already hold, the weaker is their incentive to accumulate still more. The effect in question is the so-called wealth or Pigou or real-balance effect (an effect reviewed below in connection with how the existence of *money* also affects the interest rate, saving, and real capital formation).

---

[3] Assets from which demand has shifted away presumably decline in price, but they *are* of kinds associated with capital formation.

Suppose a change in policy. A new tax (or, almost equivalently, some sort of new social stigma) makes landownership less attractive than before. The old rate of return on land is inadequate. Landowners try to sell their holdings and shift into securities until, at its reduced price, land bears a percentage rate of return sufficiently higher than the rate on bonds to compensate for the new disadvantages of owning it. Neither land itself nor its services have become any more or less abundant than before, and nothing obvious works unambiguously to raise or reduce the prices of its services. Still, the development that made people want to sell land and buy bonds depresses the bond interest rate and promotes real capital formation. With their prices reduced, the unchanged physical quantities of land absorb less of the overall propensity to wait or save, assumed to remain unchanged.

The following question might seem to discredit Allais's analysis. If the overall propensity to save or wait has not increased, where do the additional resources for capital-goods construction come from? How do additional resources get released from providing current consumption? To answer, we must distinguish between the degree of thrift, in other words, the propensity to save or wait, expressible as a function of several variables, and the actual volume of saving or waiting performed. (Compare the distinction between the schedule of demand for something and the amount demanded or the distinction between the Keynesian consumption function and the actual volume of consumption.) The answer is that the reduced attractiveness of land as an outlet for the propensity to save affects the direction of that propensity at the margin in such a way fewer resources do indeed go into current consumption and more into capital formation.

Two ways of analyzing the result of the new tax or stigma attached to landownership might seem to contradict each other. On the one hand, penalizing waiting in a particular form would presumably help make aggregate waiting less attractive, scarcer, and costlier. On the other hand, the tax or stigma would reduce the land-wealth deterrent to saving and so promote satisfying the propensity to save through financing the construction of real wealth.

The difference in possible conclusions traces to differences in tacit assumptions. One strand of analysis assumes that the penalty on waiting performed through owning land deters waiting overall. It assumes relatively slight substitutability among forms of waiting: not all the waiting displaced from one particular form, land, switches to others; and the total volume goes down. Another strand, Allais's, tacitly assumes high substitutability: the propensity to save will be satisfied in some form or other; and if satisfying it in a socially fictitious way is made less attractive, more will be satisfied through real capital formation.

This second strand of analysis tacitly supposes that land simply exists. If it can be created and destroyed, then the argument is stronger for treating it like any other capital good. If land does not, in fact, go on yielding a stream of services that remains unimpaired forever despite the conditions of ownership, then the signals and incentives transmitted by the price system can usefully guide the exploitation and conservation of depletable resources, whether or not they are straightforwardly replaceable. Restricting private ownership of resources and of incomes from them would impair these signals and incentives. Anthony Scott (1955) develops this point at length. He further argues, among other things, that nothing is sacred about conserving depletable resources in their original, nature-given form; man-made capital goods can often sensibly replace them. Because investments in resource conservation and in man-made capital goods are essentially similar, maintaining greater stocks of natural resources means having less man-made capital goods—given the total volume of investable saving.

None of the above cancels what was said near the start of this paper about how people's willingness to acquire and hold land rather than spend the proceeds of its sale on current consumption does tend to hold down the interest rate and promote capital formation. Nor does anything cancel the reservation, largely attributable to Allais, that, *given the propensity to postpone current consumption*, conceived of as a function of income and wealth, the opportunity to accumulate private wealth in the form of land, as compared with its absence, does tend to absorb the propensity to wait in such a way as to impede capital formation.

Allais is not the only economist to mention land (as well as money; see a later section) in an analysis of unproductive diversion of the willingness to save; so does Maxwell J. Fry (1988, p. 17). The total market value of wealth, including the value of land and collectibles, appears with positive sign as an argument in the economy's consumption function and with a negative sign in its saving function. Other things equal, the larger this wealth term is, the larger is the volume of consumption out of a given real income and the smaller the volume of resources released by saving for real investment. The more people satisfy their desire to hold savings by holding wealth of a privately genuine but socially spurious kind, such as the bid-up value of collectibles and land, the less they satisfy their desires for savings by holding capital goods (or securities issued to finance capital goods).

SIMILAR WORRIES ABOUT COLLECTIBLES

As just suggested, a similar worry applies to collectibles—Old Masters, antiques, rare coins and stamps, and similarly durable and nonreproducible assets. If a change in tastes or circumstances strengthens the demand for them (perhaps as hedges against ongoing inflation), the intensified bidding raises their prices. Their increased value—not merely nominal value but value relative to other goods and services—is an increase in wealth for individual holders, but it corresponds to no physical increase in wealth from the social point of view. Nevertheless, this socially fictitious wealth tends to satisfy and absorb the propensity to accumulate savings. This Old Masters wealth effect makes the volume of saving smaller than it would otherwise be, releasing fewer resources for capital-goods construction. In contrast, a strengthened desire to save and accumulate wealth in bonds tends to lower the interest rate and promote real capital formation; the increase in financial assets (and liabilities of the bond-issuers) is matched by an increased quantity of real assets.

This parable of the Old Masters is an analytical device and not a hint at a policy proposal. It reminds us, though, of one of the costs of severe inflation: disruption of financial markets and diversion of people's propensity to save away from financing the construction of real capital equipment.

... AND ABOUT MONEY

Allais applies his argument about the sidetracking of thrift not only to land but also to money. Of course, the very existence of money influences the real fundamentals; the contrast with a barter economy is sharp. But a Pigou or wealth or real-balance effect (Patinkin 1965, 1987/1992) can have the regretted consequences. Money, and especially a rise in the purchasing power of a given nominal money supply, may constitute wealth or an increase in wealth from the private if not the social point of view and so may increase the overall propensity to consume and reduce the overall propensity to save.

The real-balance effect is probably most familiar in refutation of Keynesian worries about *too great* a propensity to save, which in turn are probably more familiar than Allais's quite different worry. The effect of monetary wealth on the propensity to save can in principle solve any supposed problem of unemployment and idle productive capacity due to oversaving and deficiency of effective demand. In the absence of any other solution, price and wage deflation would eventually make the real value of the nominal money supply adequate to support a full-employment volume of effective demand. (For familiar reasons, of course, this "automatic" solution is not the easiest or best one.)

More important in the present context, the real-balance effect illuminates Allais's worry. Saving and real capital formation may be curtailed not just from a deflationary increase in the real value of a given nominal money supply but even from the availability of money as an alternative to holding capital goods and stocks and bonds. (James Tobin's version of the argument, 1965, is better known than Allais's.)

The reason for this worry about money is similar to the reason for worry about land. If people can postpone consumption by holding money or land or Old Masters as well as by holding man-made capital goods or securities that finance them, then part of their propensity to save or wait is diverted from channeling resources into capital-goods construction. Money is wealth from the point of view of the individual owner, and holding it contributes to satiating his overall propensity to save or wait; but it is not wealth in the same way and to the same extent for the economy at large.

The phrase "in the same way and to the same extent" is a hedge. Even from the social point of view, money is not mere fictitious wealth. It eliminates the frustrations and costs of barter. It facilitates financial intermediation and capital formation. It renders services to its holders. A larger cash balance permits less attention to synchronizing payment inflows and outflows and less use of labor and materials in managing the holder's cash position. What renders these services is real and not merely nominal cash balances. Real money is peculiar in that its quantity is determined on the demand side. There is no way of simply supplying more real money to an economy unless holders are somehow induced to demand more of it (as they would be induced when nominal money expansion helps restore a depressed economy to full employment). (An exception is rather trivial: monetary inflation can increase the real money stock temporarily until prices have caught up.) The just-mentioned hedge applies to land as well as to money. Land is socially useful, of course, as are Old Masters. But they have a socially fictitious wealth aspect also.

Supposing a certain type of change of tastes helps us understand this divergence between private and social viewpoints. Although people remain as willing as before to postpone consumption by holding assets, they desire to hold more of their wealth as money and less in other forms. The resulting initial excess demand for cash balances (and deficient demand for goods and services) tends to deflate prices and wages. The corresponding rise in the real value of the unchanged total nominal money supply is an increase in real wealth for individual holders, but it is less fully so from the social point of view. Yet this increase in private real monetary goes toward satisfying people's willingness to postpone consumption and accumulate wealth; it makes the propensity to consume higher and the propensity to save lower than they would otherwise be. Fewer real resources are released from providing current consumption and made available for capital-goods construction. The more of this quasi-fictitious wealth people hold, the less real wealth (including capital goods) they want to accumulate. In short, the availability of wealth in the form of cash balances diverts some of people's propensity to wait away from the accumulation and construction of real capital goods.

Allais accordingly regrets the opportunity open to savers to accumulate their savings partly in the form of money. The problem would be worse when price-level deflation was actually rewarding the holding of money rather than physical assets (or securities financing them). Growth in the real value of money would be maintaining effective demand for current output by satiating an increased demand for real cash balances, that is, by stimulating consumption and partially neutralizing the public's propensity to save.

Allais's proposed remedy provides further insight into his reasoning. He suggested stamped money (as Silvio Gesell, 1934, did but for a different purpose). The tax thus imposed on cash balances would prod people to accumulate wealth in other forms, such as capital goods or securities. Almost equivalently, a policy of chronic mild price inflation would discourage money-holding and channel propensities to save and accumulate into socially more productive directions. Allais even suggested splitting apart the unit of account and medium of exchange. The "franc," the unit of account, would be defined so as to have a stable value. The "circul," or medium of exchange, would continuously depreciate against the stable franc, discouraging holdings of circul-denominated banknotes and deposits. Use of the circul as unit of account would be "flatly forbidden" (1947, vol. II: pp. 579–585 and passim).

Allais focused on what he considered beneficial allocation effects of mild inflation. What amounts to a tax on real cash balances motivates people to allocate a *given* volume of saving less toward them and more toward real capital formation. The inflationary erosion of wealth held as cash balances further promotes saving insofar as people try to recoup this lost wealth (Mundell 1963; 1971, chap. 2). On the other hand, the loss of real-balance services would itself tend to hamper economic activity (cf. Short 1979).

As for whether the willingness to wait is used productively or is diverted, securities resemble or represent capital goods and contrast with money. Ultimately, securities can be bought only if they are issued; and, by and large, they are issued more to finance real investment than to finance consumption. If either Allais's tax or ongoing price-level inflation prods people away from money balances and into securities, financing capital construction becomes cheaper and more attractive for companies. The resulting larger stock of capital goods, while tending to raise the productivity of complementary factors of production, tends to reduce those goods' own marginal productivity and the marginal productivity of investment, in line with the depressed interest rate.

Despite but not contrary to Allais's analysis, an increase in overall thriftiness, even if initially directed toward acquiring larger real money balances, does tend to promote capital formation, although less so than in the absence of the effect that worried Allais. Don Patinkin's apparatus of CC-BB-LL curves (1965, chaps. IX–XI) is useful in showing how. Although his apparatus, unsupplemented, does not distinguish between consumer goods and capital goods, it does yield conclusions about changes in the interest rate (and price level) that in turn suggest effects on capital-goods construction. A shift of preferences away from goods—from current consumption, specifically—toward holding money tends to lower the rate of interest and thus promote capital construction, although more slightly than if the shift had been in favor of bonds. (A shift of preferences away from money holdings and in favor of bonds would also tend to lower the rate of interest and promote capital construction, as Patinkin's apparatus also illustrates, in agreement with Allais's analysis.) Even when oriented toward money, the willingness to postpone consumption and accumulate wealth favors capital formation, though in a lesser degree than when oriented to capital goods directly or to securities for financing them. In a sense, money itself can be a vehicle of financial intermediation, a means of conveying command over resources from savers to real investors (a role of money explained in McKinnon 1973, Shaw 1973, and Yeager 1997). This possibility hinges on the nature of the particular monetary system.

Allais's objection to nontaxed and noninflationary money is best interpreted, then, not as denying money's financial-intermediary function but as emphasizing that certain types of money perform that function imperfectly. Allais himself recognized that creating new money in ways that tended to favor real investment, as through bank-credit expansion for that purpose, could more or less neutralize the anti-capital-formation effect that he worried about (1947, vol. 1: chap. VIII, esp. pp. 338–340). The very issue of new money to meet a strengthened demand for money (instead of letting price deflation increase the real value of the existing nominal supply) could help convey to real investors the command over resources released by savers acquiring the new money.

This effect is a mild version of "forced saving" (cf. Hansson 1992), although the term may be inexact in the mild and noninflationary case considered here. In the prototypical case, new money loaned to investors enables them to bid resources away from other people, who are forced to consume less as inflation shrinks the purchasing powers of their incomes, money holdings, and other nominal claims. In the present mild case, new money appears merely in amounts that meet a growing demand at the existing price level (for example, a growing demand for real money balances associated with economic growth). The manner in which additional real and nominal money comes into circulation more or less corrects for the consumption-promoting divergence between the private and social views of money as wealth. An increased willingness to wait, even by way of holding money, does then promote capital construction.

This result can arise from the mere *existence* and not just the *expansion* of money that is matched on the asset sides of its issuers' balance sheets by loans to real investors. As new investment-related loans replace old ones being paid off, even with their total amount unchanged, the money matching them continues serving as a vehicle of intermediation. The continuing opportunity to hold savings in that form promotes rather than deters waiting devoted to maintenance or replacement of capital goods. Like other instruments of intermediation, money helps hold down the spread between the effective interest rates (nominal rates plus and minus pecuniary and nonpecuniary advantages and costs) that lenders receive and that borrowers pay.

The alternative method of accommodating a strengthened demand for real money balances in a growth context works through price-level deflation. Allais's worry does apply to that method. It applies most straightforwardly to money based on a commodity, like gold, whose production uses up real resources, to government fiat money of fixed nominal quantity, and to bank money fully backed by such gold or such fiat money. It also applies to money created to finance consumption (including government budget deficits).

In short, Allais's worry about the pro-consumption/anti-saving influence of wealth held in real money balances is not refuted by a different consideration pulling in the opposite direction. Allais himself recognized it: existence and growth of the demand for money provide opportunities for the noninflationary creation of new money to finance investment projects.

It is not clear that the effect that concerned Allais is quantitatively important. Relative to the volumes of saving and investment and financial intermediation routinely accomplished anyway, only presumably small volumes might be frustrated by absence of suitable growth of the nominal money and of Allais's measures to deter money-holding. Still, that effect was worth describing because of its parallel with the similar and supposedly worrisome effect of land.

A DEFECTIVE TELESCOPIC FACULTY?

As is evident from his arguments summarized above, Allais, along with some other economists, thinks that the market-determined overall rate of saving and capital formation is too low. An excessive market rate of interest reflects and implements an inadequate degree of concern for the future. A person's choices between consumption today and consumption ten or twenty years later are made by the present person only. The future person, who might well prefer a more future-oriented allocation, has no say in the matter. The state knows better and might legitimately impose forced saving through taxation (1947, vol. I: pp. 220 n., 221–225; vol. II: pp. 592–593; similar thoughts are scattered widely through both volumes; on individuals' "telescopic faculty" being "defective" or "perverted," compare Pigou 1932/1950, pp. 24–26; and Scott 1955, chap. 8, "A Social Rate of Time Preference"). On all this, remember that Allais was writing back in 1947, before the accumulation of subsequent experience with government economic and budgetary policies and before the development of public choice theory.

CONCLUSION

Private ownership of land has a social function. In freeing resources from serving current consumption while waiting for land's periodic rents and future selling price, the owner is supplying a productive service. It is essentially the same as the waiting for which lenders receive interest. On the other hand, the volumes of this service and of the resulting real capital formation would be still greater if private and social viewpoints of landed wealth did not diverge and if the Pigou or wealth effect did not deter saving. Quite similar remarks apply to some other vehicles of waiting, notably collectibles and money.

The entire foregoing discussion serves an analytical purpose only and is not meant, by itself, either to justify or to condemn the private collection of land rents. It does not claim that the effects described are quantitatively important and detectable amidst all the constantly occurring changes in economic conditions. For this and other reasons, the discussion does not recommend any particular policy. Policy proposals are mentioned to help clarify the analysis that underpins them.

REFERENCES

Allais, Maurice. *Économie et Intérêt*. 2 vols. Paris: Imprimerie Nationale, 1947.

Cassel, Gustav. *The Nature and Necessity of Interest*. 1903. New York: Augustus M. Kelley, 1956.

Fry, Maxwell J. *Money, Interest, and Banking in Economic Development*. Baltimore: Johns Hopkins University Press, 1988.

Gesell, Silvio. *The Natural Economic Order*. San Antonio, Tex.: Free Economy Publishing, 1934.

Hansson, Björn. "Forced Saving." In *The New Palgrave Dictionary of Money & Finance*, edited by Peter Newman, Murray Milgate, and John Eatwell, vol. 2: 140–142. New York: Stockton Press, 1992.

McKinnon, Ronald I. *Money and Capital in Economic Development*. Washington, D.C.: Brookings Institution, 1973.

Mundell, Robert. "Inflation and Real Interest." *Journal of Political Economy* 71 (June 1963): 280–283.

———. *Monetary Theory*. Pacific Palisades, Calif.: Goodyear, 1971.

Patinkin, Don. *Money, Interest, and Prices.* 2nd ed. New York: Harper & Row, 1965.

———. "Real Balances." 1987. In *The New Palgrave Dictionary of Money & Finance,* edited by Peter Newman, Murray Milgate, and John Eatwell, vol. 3: 295–298. New York: Stockton Press, 1992.

Pigou, A.C. *The Economics of Welfare.* 1932. 4th ed. London: Macmillan, 1950.

Rothbard, Murray N. *Man, Economy, and State.* 2 vols. Princeton, N.J.: D. Van Nostrand, 1962.

Scott, Anthony. *Natural Resources: The Economics of Conservation.* Toronto: University of Toronto Press, 1955.

Shaw, Edward S. *Financial Deepening in Economic Development.* New York: Oxford University Press, 1973.

Short, Eugenie Dudding. "A New Look at Real Money Balances as a Variable in the Production Function." *Journal of Money, Credit, and Banking* 11 (August 1979): 326–339.

Tobin, James. "Money and Economic Growth." *Econometrica* 33 (October 1965): 671–684.

Yeager, Leland B. "Injection Effects and Monetary Intermediation." In *The Fluttering Veil,* edited by George Selgin. Indianapolis: Liberty Fund, 1997.

CHAPTER 13

Tacit Preachments are the Worst Kind*

PREACHING AND COUNTERMETHODOLOGY

Some years ago I gave a talk on "The Curse of Methodology." That unfortunate title appeared to deny that methodology comes in good varieties as well as bad. Still, good methodology is mostly countermethodology, which strives to free working economists from methodological pressures. The worst preachments, which were and remain my main target, are the pervasive, tacit, dimly identified kind. Countermethodology can drag them into the open, exposing them to inspection and, when appropriate, to ridicule. As if to ward off this exposure, however, the practitioners of tacit methodology appear to taboo explicit method-talk.[1]

I offer this and other remarks about the state of academic economics not as confident assertions but as conjectures and as possible explanations of what we do observe. We have an opportunity to confess our suspicions and to compare and check them out. I quote and paraphrase scholars whose writings document my points or who share my perceptions and I also use footnotes all more extensively than precepts of good writing style might otherwise recommend. Invoking respectable company itself proves nothing, but it assuages my uneasiness.

In part, admittedly, I'll be expressing personal pique. Even some experiences with explicit methodologizing prod me. They include all too many "Austrian" seminars at two or three universities in which discussion routinely degenerated from the substantive to the methodological. I have seen dissertation-writers (at the University of Virginia) badgered about what their models might be or what hypotheses they were testing (and have

---

*From *Journal of Economic Methodology* 2, no. 1 (June 1995): 1–33.
[1] "[M]ethod-talk is asserted to be taboo in economics, when in fact it is surpassed in its ubiquity only by discussion of other people's salaries" (Mirowski 1992, p. 236).

225

experienced some badgering myself). I have heard all too much praise of methodological articles that did not rise above pointless profundity.[2]

Some economists, then, though a minority, are fascinated with methodology. Why? Could they be delighted with their own breadth of learning, as in epistemology and the philosophy of science? Could they believe that such profundity and wisdom must have great significance, somehow, for their own field? Perhaps it helps make a splash to propose importing into economics, even without reference to any genuine questions or problems, ideas and techniques lifted from other fields. Examples include notions of Newtonian and Bergsonian time, concepts of hermeneutics, psychological notions, and mathematical techniques from engineering.

Far be it from me to taboo such borrowings, but the test should be not whether they confer a supposed cachet on the borrowers but whether they further genuine investigations. Nor do I want to lecture methodologists against the pleasure of wallowing in their favorite profundities—not unless they expect other people admiringly to join in.

Methodologists get a handle on other people as teachers, dissertation supervisors, journal editors and referees, conference organizers, participants in tenure and promotion decisions, writers of letters of recommendation, and members of fellowship and research committees. People in such roles almost necessarily issue advice or apply requirements. Those people may deserve some advice in turn, even though it may sound like methodology itself.

Donald McCloskey (1985, esp. pp. 24–26) distinguishes three levels of methodology. The bottom level, unobjectionable and necessary, consists of teaching nuts and bolts like how to construct an Edgeworth box, run a regression, and punctuate a sentence. The top level, "Sprachethik," also unobjectionable, calls for constructive dialogue. Scholars should try to communicate clearly and avoid shouting and other tricks of intimidation.

On the middle level we find pronouncements about mathematics, econometrics, modeling, empiricism, armchair theorizing, methodological individualism, use of aggregates and averages, use of questionnaires, experimentation, and so on. Methodologists discuss whether the supposed methods of the natural sciences belong in economics, whether

---

[2] Paul Samuelson was avowedly joking, but probably only half-joking, when he reported a negative correlation between the fruitfulness of scientific disciplines and "their propensity to engage in methodological discussion.... [S]oft sciences spend time in talking about method because Satan finds tasks for idle hands to do. Nature does abhor a vacuum, and hot air fills up more space than cold" (1963, in Caldwell 1984, p. 188).

Chapter 13: Tacit Preachments are the Worst Kind   227

economics is more like physics or biology, whether notions from anthropology and literary criticism and other disciplines should be imported, and what should be regarded as the Lakatosian hard core of economics. Such middle-level methodologizing is presumptuous and officious.[3]

Anyone who has refereed for journals knows that hitching onto fads, routine originality, unnecessary polemics, pretentiousness, tedium, and bad writing abound. Methodology will hardly remedy these defects because, for one thing, no single best method is available. The academic division of labor leaves no presumption that all researchers should tackle the same problems in the same way.[4]

---

[3] The methodologist "undertakes to second-guess the scientific community"; he "claims prescience," "pretends to know how to achieve knowledge before the knowledge to be achieved is in place," insists on "an artificially narrowed range of argument," and "lay[s] down legislation for science on the basis of epistemological convictions held with a vehemence inversely proportional to the amount of evidence that they work" (McCloskey 1985, pp. 20, 36, 53, 139).

The particular examples of exhortation and taboo mentioned in the text are more mine than McCloskey's.

[4] K. Klappholz and J. Agassi deplore "the illusion that there can exist in any science methodological rules the mere adoption of which will hasten its progress" and warn against the "belief that, if only economists adopted this or that methodological rule, the road ahead would at least be cleared (and possibly the traffic would move briskly along it)." They will heed only the general "exhortation to be critical and always ready to subject one's hypotheses to critical scrutiny." Additional rules to reinforce this general maxim are "likely to be futile and possibly harmful" (1959, pp. 60, 74).

The physicist P.W. Bridgman liked to say that

> there is no scientific method as such, but that the most vital feature of the scientist's procedure has been merely to do his utmost with his mind, no holds barred. This means in particular that no special privileges are accorded to authority or to tradition, that personal prejudices and predilections are carefully guarded against, that one makes continued check to assure oneself that one is not making mistakes, and that any line of inquiry will be followed that appears at all promising.... The so-called scientific method is merely a special case of the method of intelligence, and any apparently unique characteristics are to be explained by the nature of the subject matter rather than ascribed to the nature of the method itself. (Bridgman 1955, p. 544)

> I think that the objectives of all scientists have this in common—that they are all trying to get the correct answer to the particular problem in hand.... What appears to [the working scientist] as the essence of the situation is that he is not consciously following any prescribed course of action, but feels complete freedom to utilize any method or device whatever which in the particular situation before him seems likely to yield the correct answer. In his attack on his specific problem he suffers no inhibitions of precedent or authority, but is completely free to adopt any course that his ingenuity is capable of suggesting to him. No one standing on the outside can predict

Whether the natural and social sciences are fundamentally similar or fundamentally different is a pointless concern. What does "fundamental" mean? All sciences seek propositions of generality and depth (Bauer 1959), seek uniformity amidst superficial diversity, and try to explain initially puzzling phenomena as examples of familiar or potentially familiar generalizations, so that curiosity rests (evoking Machlup's "aha!"). Success in prediction strengthens the scientist's hunch that he has found the correct explanation of some phenomenon. All sciences presumably involve what Karl Popper called "conjectures and refutations." All presumably presuppose similar ideals of scientific integrity and of openness to critical examination. On the other hand, any two sciences differ in their specific subject matters and so in what kinds of empirical observation enter into arousing curiosity, inspiring conjectures, and sifting hypotheses. Human purposiveness and free choice play a role in the social sciences that they cannot play in the natural sciences. Whether this makes the two fields fundamentally different is a mere semantic question.

TACIT METHODOLOGY AT WORK

Here are some signs of poorly articulated methodological thinking:

- Routine questions such as: What hypothesis are you testing? How could it be falsified? What is your model?

> what the individual scientist will do or what method he will follow ... there are as many scientific methods as there are individual scientists. (pp. 82–83)
>
> Questioning the assumption of one or a few best methods, Fritz Machlup identifies the harmful
>
>> attitude of snubbing, disparaging, excommunicating, and prohibiting the working habits of others and of preaching a methodology that implies that they are inferior in scientific workmanship. [Machlup's footnote below.]
>
> Good "scientific method" must not proscribe any technique of inquiry deemed useful by an honest and experienced scholar. The aggressiveness and restrictiveness of the various methodological beliefs which social scientists have developed—in subconscious attempts to compensate for their feelings of inferiority vis-a-vis the alleged "true scientist"—are deplorable. Attempts to establish a monopoly for one method, to use moral suasion and public defamation to exclude others, produce harmful restraints of research and analysis, seriously retarding their progress.
>
> [Footnote:] ... I have not said anything against the working habits of others and have not questioned anybody's scientific workmanship. I have dealt with their claims of exclusive possession of the one and only scientific method. (Machlup 1956/1978, p. 344 in chap. 13)

- The prestige of falsifiability, with misconceptions about it being reinforced by the slogan against testing a theory by its assumptions to the degree that downright false propositions share in its supposed prestige. (A warning is valid, however, against ostensibly empirical propositions so constructed as to enjoy built-in immunity to any adverse evidence.)

- The prestige of the polar extremes of abstract, high-power theorizing and empirical work, with what counts as "empirical" being practically confined to statistics.

- The associated idea that familiar, dependable facts are by that very token unimportant.

- Knee-jerk insistence on certain styles of argumentation and particularly on "rigor" (about which I'll have more to say).

- The prestige of working on the frontier.

Examples abound of methodological preconceptions practically foreordaining conclusions or shielding shaky argument or dubious assumptions from scrutiny. They include (in my opinion) the "Austrian" theory of the business cycle, the "pure-time-preference" theory of interest, London-School skepticism of cost-oriented business regulation and indeed of any objective content in the very concept of cost, the rational-expectations school's insistence on equilibrium modeling, Milton Friedman's Marshallian demand curve, and widespread mindless recitation of Friedman's slogan about not testing a theory by its assumptions.

In macroeconomics, the shift of fashion from monetarism to its new-classical version and then on to real business cycles appears to exhibit a methodological basis (as well as some factors discussed later). David Laidler (1990) and Karl Brunner (1989) have diagnosed as much, mentioning an impatience with disequilibrium analysis and a shift of priorities away from empirical evidence toward supposed first principles, microfoundations, and rigor.

EXAMPLES FROM THE NEW CLASSICAL MACROECONOMICS

The new classical macroeconomics, or rational-expectations/equilibrium-always school, provides examples. (Citations and fuller discussion appear in my 1986, pp. 386–393.) The Lucas supply function (Lucas 1973) deals with cyclical fluctuations in aggregate output on the basis of the methodological preconception that sellers are responding to prices only, rather than also to how readily they are finding customers. Notions of pure competition lurk below the surface: the seller can sell all he desires at the going price.

Theorists in this camp seem to believe that monetary expansion, for example, and unexpected monetary expansion in particular, can have an impact on real variables only through price changes—unexpected and misinterpreted changes—and not directly, as by giving sellers more customers. The rival monetary-disequilibrium theory can interpret recovery from depression in a more straightforward way than is available to a theorist unwilling to recognize disequilibrium in the first place.

The idea seems to be afoot in certain circles (or was for a while) that equilibrium modeling is the thing—the technically advanced thing—to be doing in macroeconomics. Robert Lucas and admirers (Lucas 1980, pp. 697, 708; Willes 1980, pp. 90, 92) recommended their brand of equilibrium economics for employing technical advances in modeling that simply were unavailable a few years earlier.

Lucas and Sargent (1978, p. 58) appeared to congratulate themselves on the "dramatic development" that the very meaning of the term "equilibrium" had undergone. Sargent (interviewed in Klamer 1983, pp. 67–68) expressed satisfaction with "fancier" notions of equilibrium, "much more complicated" notions of market-clearing, and "fancy new kinds of equilibrium models." Well, to recommend destabilizing the meaning of words, subverting communication, is the kind of methodologizing that needs to be dragged into the open and inspected.

Suggesting the influence of sheer commitment to a cherished theoretical tradition, Herschel Grossman (1983, p. 240) wrote:

> The position that strict application of neoclassical maximization postulates is relevant to macroeconomic developments only in the "long-run" may seem reasonable from an empirical standpoint, but it puts neoclassical economics in a defensive position. It suggests the possibility of a general inability of neoclassical economics to account for short-run economic phenomena.

Yet despite the apparent implication here, disequilibrium is not incompatible with individuals' efforts to maximize.

The idea seems to be in circulation that an economist who talks about disequilibrium is really talking not about market failure but about his own failure as a model-builder. It is methodologically unfashionable to speak of prices and quantities that are not at their equilibrium values but are only tending toward them at speeds specified only in *ad hoc* ways. In this connection, Lucas (1980) scorns models containing "free parameters." Observing and reasoning about disequilibrium processes in a straightforward and therefore relatively nonmathematical manner can be stigmatized as casual and loose, so they escape due attention.

Equilibrium-always theorists presumably know as well as anyone else that atomistic competition is and must be the exception rather than the rule in the real world, that sellers are typically not selling as much of their output or labor as they would like to sell at prevailing prices, that most prices and wages are not determined impersonally but are consciously decided upon (even though decided with an eye on supply and demand), and that these and other circumstances cause or reveal price stickiness. But the theorists do not know these facts officially, not in a methodologically reputable way.

They are inclined to recite the slogan that (in the paraphrase of Willes 1980, p. 91) "theories cannot be judged by the realism of their assumptions," a slogan reasonable enough in certain contexts and under certain interpretations, yet much abused. Actually, it is necessary to distinguish at least between simplifying assumptions that abstract from unimportant details and assumptions on which the conclusions crucially depend. (Alan Musgrave, 1981, makes enlightening distinctions between negligibility, domain, and heuristic assumptions.)

What assumptions are acceptable simplifications and what ones are crucial to the conclusions depends on the question at hand. "[A]n ecologist concerned about pollution may treat the Black Sea as a closed body of water, the Straits of Marmara being sufficiently narrow for that. But someone considering how to ship goods from London to Odessa should not" (Mayer 1993, p. 38). In investigating the long-run effects on relative prices and quantities of a specified change in wants, resources, technology, or taxes, it is convenient to assume that competition is pure and that markets clear. Things are different in *macro*economics, whose very subject matter is the lapses that do sometimes occur from a high degree of coordination of radically decentralized decisions and activities. When one is investigating how and why separate but interdependent markets fall short of working to perfection, it is fatuous to insist that they are always in equilibrium anyway. More generally, it is fatuous to work with assumptions that rule out the questions to be faced. (It is important, by the way, as Karl Popper taught, to have a question or problem to work on, not a mere topic; Bartley 1990, p. 159.)

Robert Clower and Paul Krugman are among the minority of economists who have spoken out emphatically against the methodology-driven excesses of the equilibrium-always approach. "[T]he approaches of the Keynesians, monetarists, and new classical economists to monetary theory and macroeconomics will get us exactly nowhere," Clower writes, "because each is founded, one way or another, on the conventional but empirically fallacious assumption that the coordination of economic activities is costless." While established value theory has indisputable merits, "for some purposes, such as the fruitful analysis of ongoing processes of monetary exchange, models of a very different kind may be required" (1984, "Afterword," p. 272).

The "Lucas Project," as Paul Krugman calls it, tried "to build business-cycle theory on maximizing microfoundations.... The ramshackle, *ad hoc* intellectual structures of the 1950s and 1960s were ruthlessly cleared away, making room for the erection of a new structure to be based on secure microfoundations. Unfortunately, that structure never got built" (Krugman 1993, pp. 15–16). The Lucas Project "destroy[ed] the old regime but failed to create a workable new macroeconomics.... The true believers in equilibrium business cycles shifted to real-business-cycle theory" (p. 16). "[R]ational-expectations macroeconomics ... collapsed in the face of its own internal contradictions," leaving macroeconomics in "a terrible state" (p. 18).

In Krugman's view, "the effort to explain away the apparent real effects of nominal shocks is silly, even if one restricts oneself to domestic evidence. Once one confronts international evidence, however, it becomes an act of almost pathological denial" (1993, p. 17). Krugman mentions tight correlation between nominal and real exchange rates (p. 16). Finding international macroeconomics in a painful dilemma, Krugman alludes to fads and tacit methodologizing: "to write a macroeconomic model with sticky prices is professionally dangerous, but to write one without such rigidities is empirically ridiculous" (p. 17).[5]

---

[5]"It's easy to be cynical about the motivations of the people who write these papers. You don't progress as an economics professor by solving the real problems of the real economy, at least not in any direct way. Instead, you progress by convincing your colleagues that you are clever. In an ideal world you would demonstrate your cleverness by developing blindingly original ideas or producing definitive evidence about how the economy actually works. But most of us can't do that, at least not consistently. So professors look for more surefire approaches. And thus the most popular economic theories among the professors tend to be those that best allow for ingenious elaboration without fundamental

THEMES IN QUASI-TACIT PREACHING: RIGOR

One broad message of Thomas Mayer's book of 1993 is that academic economics is driven not only by economic reality but also by features of the game itself. Economists attuned to the academic game "frequently act as though the strength of their whole argument is equal to the strength of its strongest link" (1993, p. x). (This strongest-link analogy recurs repeatedly and appropriately, as on pp. 57–63, 80, 127–130. I myself have long used it, for it is an obvious one.) One form of the bias toward excessive formalization "is to lavish tender loving care on those steps of the argument that are rigorous, while paying little attention to the other steps" (p. 66). A related strand of tacit methodology is reductionism—the insistence that all macroeconomics be reduced to microeconomics (pp. 90–97; compare the insistence that psychology be reduced to chemistry and ultimately to physics).

"Rigor" is often taken as self-evidently crucial to respectable economics. At a department meeting years ago, discussion of a proposed course in portfolio management did not concern what of substance the students might learn, or how its subject matter might relate to the body of

---

innovation—ways to show that you are smart by putting old wine in new bottles, usually with fancier mathematical labels" (Krugman 1994, p. 8).

"[T]he technicality and difficulty of Lucas's [business-cycle] theory ... was, in the world of academic economics, an asset rather than a liability. It is cynical but true to say that in the academic world the theories that are most likely to attract a devoted following are those that best allow a clever but not very original young man to demonstrate his cleverness. This has been true of deconstructionist literary theory; it has equally been true of equilibrium business cycle theory. It turned out that Lucas's initial theory naturally led to the application of a whole new set of mathematical and statistical techniques. A first set of Lucas disciples made academic reputations developing these techniques; later waves of students invested large amounts of time and effort learning them, and were loath to consider the possibility that the view of the economy to which their specialized training was appropriate might be wrong. Indeed, Lucas himself has in the end seemed more interested in his techniques than in what he does with them" (Krugman 1994, p. 52).

In Krugman's view, political bias also helped make rational-expectations macroeconomics attractive (1994, pp. 52–53).

Mayer also testifies to tacit methodology at work: "New classicals explain business cycles as mostly due to supply shocks because a demand-side explanation is inconsistent with their chosen Walrasian market clearing paradigm" (1993, p. 116).

Mirowski (1992, pp. 241–247) and McCloskey (1992, p. 266) tell the story of the suppression of an invited conference paper by Lawrence Summers (an eminent economist, certainly, associated with New Keynesianism) because of frankness about methodology similar to that of Krugman and Mayer. Summers had entitled his paper "The Scientific Illusion in Macroeconomics" (published elsewhere in 1991).

economic theory or to other courses in the curriculum, or whether it might duplicate existing courses. No, the overriding concern was with whether the prospective instructor would teach the course with due "rigor," meaning, in the context, teach it as an application of advanced mathematics.

Rigor does have its proper place. In mathematics or formal logic—and these of course can enter into an economist's work—one does not want lapses from due rigor; one does not tolerate either mistakes or steps in the argument where crude appeal to intuition substitutes for logical entailment.

Yet even in mathematics, excessive or premature insistence on rigor can impede progress (Lakatos 1976). Davis and Hersh identify a myth of totally rigorous and formalized mathematics (1986, section on "Mathematics and Rhetoric," pp. 57–73). No one knows exactly what constitutes a mathematical proof. All proofs fall short of complete formal logic and so of commanding absolute confidence. A mathematical proof written in complete logical detail would be unreadable and incomprehensible. "Professedly rigorous proofs usually have holes that are covered over by intuition" (p. 69; an example follows). Proof simply means proof in enough detail to convince the intended audience. The competent mathematician knows where his audience should focus their skepticism. There he will supply sufficient detail, abbreviating the rest. Most mathematical articles, Davis and Hersh add, do not get close scrutiny from either referees or journal readers.

Garrett Hardin identifies such a thing as "mathematical machismo" (1986, p. 39). Arrogant numeracy can do harm. Lord Kelvin said, "[W]hen you cannot measure it in numbers, your knowledge is of a meagre and unsatisfactory kind" (quoted in Hardin 1986, p. 39). Yet Kelvin radically underestimated the age of the earth, predicted that man would never fly in craft heavier than air, and predicted that any metal cooled almost to absolute zero would become an electric insulator (p. 40). Many contributions to science, as by Darwin, Pasteur, Kekulé, Harvey, Virchow, Pavlov, and Sherrington, have been much more qualitative than quantitative (p. 41).

Even more so than mathematical proofs, knowledge of the real world simply cannot be totally rigorous; induction is not deduction.

In Karl Brunner's view, the new-classical and "Minnesota" school of macroeconomics, with its insistence on beginning from the supposed beginning, commits what he called the "Cartesian fallacy."

The Cartesian tradition insisted that all statements be derived from a small set of "first principles." "Cogito ergo sum" and everything else follows.... Anything not derived from "first principles" does not count as knowledge. You are not allowed to talk about money if you have not derived from "first principles" a specification of all the items which are money. This methodological position is quite untenable and conflicts with the reality of our cognitive progress over history. Science rarely progresses by working "down from first principles"; it progresses and expands the other way. We begin with empirical regularities and go backward to more and more complicated hypotheses and theories. Adherence to the Cartesian principle would condemn science to stagnation. There are, moreover, as Karl Popper properly emphasized, no first principles. (Karl Brunner interviewed in Klamer 1983, p. 195; compare Brunner 1989, pp. 225–227.)

The Cartesian fallacy appears linked with what W.W. Bartley III (1984) called "justificationism." An often unrecognized trait running through the history of philosophy, justificationism is the expectation that all propositions be justified (demonstrated, proved, warranted) by appeal to some authority, whether reason in the style of Descartes, empirical observation, divine revelation, or some other definitive source. But no interesting propositions can be justified in such a way. The demand for justification is a piece of ancient methodology carried forward uncritically into modern discussion (1984, p. 221 in particular). Bartley rejects justificationism in favor of the Popperian process of conjectures and refutations. Scientists invent laws and theories and devise ways of winnowing out wrong ones. It is reasonable to accept, tentatively, laws and theories not yet rejected on logical or empirical grounds and not yet displaced by more attractive alternatives. Accepting them in that way is not the same, however, as holding them to have been justified or proved; for positive justification is downright impossible. We cannot criticize all of our beliefs all at the same time. Criticism of particular propositions or theories must employ others—notably, standard logic—taken as valid for the purpose at hand. But none of these is exempt from criticism in all contexts. Although we cannot criticize everything at once, nothing is properly immune against any criticism in all circumstances and contexts. (See the many pages on justification and justificationism cited in the index to Bartley 1984.)

ANOTHER THEME: MODELS

Years ago a graduate-student advisee reported to me the expectations of another of his advisors: he must build his dissertation around a model.

"Why?" the student asked. "I don't know," was the reported reply, "you've just got to have a model." The other advisor reportedly went on to say that if the student expected to get his dissertation past certain members of the department, he would have to do work of the kind they expected.

Such sermonizing seldom appears in print and fully articulated, which is why it can be so insidious. Although influential, it escapes critical examination. I wish economists would drag it into the open by recounting their experiences with it. (Mayer makes a good beginning in his 1993, chap. 9, entitled "Model or Die.")

One little episode involved me directly. During the discussion period at a conference, I remarked that a particular monetary reform would eliminate the contagion of bank runs, and I briefly explained why. During the further discussion, and at greater length during the coffee break, another conferee objected that if I and my coauthor expected anyone to understand what we were saying, we would have to argue in the context of a model of bank runs, complete with specification of 100 persons, 47 commodities (or whatever the numbers might be), and so forth. If I had thought fast on my feet, I would have pressed the question "Why?". I would have asked my interlocutor to make his methodological sermon explicit and support it with reasons. Unfortunately, the conversation wandered off.

Months later, in conversation with Donald McCloskey, I wondered about the claims of some economists not to understand arguments presented outside of formal models. McCloskey conjectured that they mean what they say: some of them are so wrapped up in their own models and favorite symbols that they actually cannot understand arguments presented in an unexpected language, English.

Peter N. Ireland (1994) provides another example of what bothers me. After making sensible remarks about relations between money and economic growth, he goes on to give his argument supposed rigor with mathematics and numerical simulations. He elaborates a model of a large number of identical, infinitely lived households possessing perfect foresight. Each consists of a worker and a shopper. Production functions have specific special properties. Perfect competition prevails. A cash-in-advance constraint applies to purchases made without the assistance of a financial intermediary. Yet if these and other special assumptions spelled out in great detail (about transactions costs and so forth) are not necessary for the conclusions reached, what is the point of making them? And if they *are* necessary, is it not a great lapse from the trumpeted rigor to convey the impression that the conclusions reached apply to the messy real world anyway?

In the same journal issue, Steve Williamson and Randall Wright (1994) explain how money, besides providing its familiar services, cuts down the information requirements of exchange, giving transactors a better chance than they would have under barter to wind up with high-quality goods. The authors' model assumes away the noninformational difficulties of barter, leaving no role for money in the absence of private information. Time is discrete and goes on forever. The population is a continuum of immortal agents who can produce both good and bad commodities at positive and zero utility cost, respectively. Consumption of money, of a bad commodity, or of one's own output yields zero utility, while consumption of someone else's good output does yield utility. Detailed assumptions about proportions of good and bad commodities, probabilities of encounters, and so forth create the opportunity for numerous equations and graphs adding nothing to the central message, as far as I can see, except spurious rigor. The authors give no reason for supposing that what is rigorously true of their concocted world is equally true of the real world.

Robert Frank has done much insightful writing at the intersection of economics, psychology, and ethics. His article of 1987, however, provides an example of the merely decorative use of mathematical code, as distinguished from bona fide manipulation requiring symbols. One footnote (1987, p. 595) even promises "a more reader-friendly version" of his model in a then-forthcoming book. Well, why wasn't he friendly to his current readers? Bénassy's article of 1993, which I admire for its actual substance, is similarly discourteous in its use of symbols. Bénassy actually distinguishes between certain concepts by whether the identical double-subscripted letters representing them are topped by a macron or by an only slightly wavy tilde; this is a subtlety likely to escape a reader not wielding a magnifying glass. I suspect that he, like Frank, Ireland, and Williamson and Wright, was bowing to tacit methodological pressures.

As Mayer's strongest-link (or most-rigorous-link) principle suggests, a display of technique can plaster over much. Robert Solow was staying within the bounds of permissible exaggeration when he wrote (1985, p. 330) that a modern economist, dropped with his computer from a time machine into any old time and place, will soon

> have maximized a familiar-looking present-value integral, made a few familiar log-linear approximations, and run the obligatory familiar regression. The familiar coefficients will be poorly determined, but about one-twentieth of them will be significant at the 5 percent level, and the other

nineteen do not have to be published. With a little judicious selection here and there, it will turn out that your data are just barely consistent with your thesis adviser's hypothesis ... , modulo an information asymmetry, any old information asymmetry, don't worry, you'll think of one.

Walter Eucken (1948, Pt. II, esp. pp. 192–193) criticized two rather opposite trends in theory. Often the question is asked how things would go in an a priori model built with little reference to reality. The very framing of the question excludes reality. On the other hand, Eucken continues, analysis may work with crude, sweeping concepts like "capitalism," "laissez faire," or "socialism." But both a priori models and imprecise "blanket" concepts can be of little help in investigating reality.

James Tobin (1980, p. 86) comments on overlapping-generations models of money. Long before, economists had already pointed out how a common medium of payment facilitates multilateral trade, whereas barter would restrict transactions.

The insight tells us why the social institution of money has been observed throughout history even in primitive societies. An insight is not a model, and it does not satisfy the trained scholarly consciences of modern theorists who require that all values be rooted, explicitly and mathematically, in the market valuations of maximizing agents. But I must say in all irreverent candor that as yet I do not feel significantly better enlightened than by the traditional insight.

Let me quote two physicists. Pierre Duhem (1954, esp. chap. IV) does not deny the usefulness of models. He recommends "intellectual liberalism." "Discovery is not subject to any fixed rule.... The best means of promoting the development of science is to permit each form of intellect to develop itself by following its own laws and realizing fully its type" (1954, pp. 98–99). Duhem questions the claim that providing a "mechanical or algebraic model" for each of the chapters of physics satisfies all the legitimate wishes of understanding (p. 100). Perhaps the most fruitful procedure in physics has been the search for analogies between distinct categories of phenomena, but we should not confuse it with modeling (pp. 95–97). The use of mechanical models "has not brought to the progress of physics that rich contribution boasted for it." Its contribution "seems quite meager when we compare it with the opulent conquests of abstract theories. The distinguished physicists who have recommended the use of models have used it [that method] far less as a means of discovery than as a method of exposition" (p. 99).

Ronald Giere (1988, esp. chap. 3, "Models and Theories") describes models as stylizations or idealizations about which propositions hold more rigorously true than they ever could about their possible counterparts in reality (cf. Hausman 1992, pp. 75–82, 273). $F = ma$ and other general "laws" of mechanics are not really empirical claims but more like general schemas that need to be filled in (Giere 1988, p. 76). If the laws of motion, such as the law of the pendulum, were to give a literally true and exact description of even the simplest of physical phenomena, they would have to be incredibly more complex than any that could ever be written down. The nonuniformity of gravity near the earth's surface, the gravitational force of the moon, nonlinearities in air resistance, and so forth would all have to be taken into account. Idealization and approximation are of the essence of empirical science (pp. 76–78). Hooke's law "states that the force exerted by a spring is proportional to the amount it is stretched," the constant of proportionality being "interpreted as a measure of the stiffness of the spring" (p. 68). Such a statement presupposes certain "idealizations," such as that the spring is without mass and subject to no frictional forces, that the force-displacement is linear, that the attached mass is subject to no frictional forces, and that the wall is rigid, so the wall recoil due to motion of the mass may be neglected (Giere, pp. 69–70). In mechanics, "The equations truly describe the model because the model is defined as something that exactly satisfies the equations" (p. 79). (The physicist Henri Poincaré repeatedly insisted on similar points about the role of stylizations and conventions in science; see Yeager 1994, esp. pp. 161–162, and Poincaré's writings cited there.)

> Unlike a model, a theoretical hypothesis is ... a statement asserting some sort of relationship between a model and a designated real system (or class of real systems).... The general form of a theoretical hypothesis is thus: Such-and-such identifiable real system is similar to a designated model in indicated respects and degrees. (Giere 1988, pp. 80–81)

Lucas and Sargent (1978, p. 52) say in effect that anyone uttering any proposition of economics must, whether he realizes it or not, be working with some sort of model in mind. It may be vague or clear, poor or good; but if the economist does not set forth his model explicitly, he is just hiding it from professional scrutiny and criticism.

Is it true, though, that one is necessarily working with a model? If the term "model" is stretched to cover any piece of reasoning, then it seems a mere equivocation to insist after all on a model in a narrower sense. If "model" means a complete set of equations specific enough to be ready for econometric estimation, the answer is pretty clearly that the theorist is not necessarily working with one. He may not want to restrict himself to any specific model because he believes that suitable ones differ widely in their details across times and places. Consider a model of our solar system. For some purposes we are interested in the system's specific, historically accidental, features; and for such purposes, a detailed model is necessary. But for other purposes we want to emphasize propositions of wider application, such as those of gravity; and then it would be pointless to be tied down to a model of a particular solar system.

Similarly in economics, propositions of the sort we hope to develop may not pertain to an economic system of one specific structure; and then a specific model may be mere clutter. As Ludwig von Mises once remarked (orally) about an econometric investigation of the watermelon market, none of the fundamental propositions of economics depends on the existence of such a commodity as watermelons. Nor, one might add, does any depend on the existence of such a country as the United States of America.

In many contexts, by the same token, we are concerned with propositions applicable widely enough not to stand or fall on the existence of railroads or labor unions or negotiable certificates of deposit. What sort of model it may be legitimate to insist on, if on any at all, thus depends on the purpose at hand, including the conceived scope of the propositions under investigation.

The investigator might recognize that he cannot produce a mathematical or econometric model with specific details yet wide applicability. He might be concerned, instead, with the characteristics that any plausibly relevant model would have—if one insists on speaking of models. He might be seeking Bauer's "propositions of generality and depth." Examples in economics include the principle of diminishing marginal returns, the law of demand, and the quantity theory of money. They enter into the construction of widely different specific models. The investigator might legitimately be more concerned with such propositions themselves than with one or another of their particular embodiments. Before one can sensibly construct a model, one must have some idea of what observed or conjectured or even merely postulated features of reality one is trying to embody in it. One needs to know what relations of interdependence or cause and effect one is trying to exhibit. In that sense, propositions (and the concepts they employ) are logically prior to models. (Kosko 1993, pp. 165, 169, 177, makes sensible remarks about models and about the frequent usefulness of "model-free estimation or approximation" and "model freedom.")

Far be it from me to taboo modeling, which can be a way of stimulating, organizing, and presenting one's thoughts.[6] A burst of insistence on modeling may even be justified if it is provoked by someone's argument that is too vague, is phrased in idiosyncratic language, or rests on unstated assumptions. If so, challenging the theorist to put his argument into graphs or equations may force him to make his assumptions and reasoning explicit. More generally, translating an argument from one style into another may serve as a check on one's reasoning and improve communication. (Thomas Hobbes made a noteworthy case for the translation test in 1651/1968, chaps. 8 and 46.) While translation can indeed be beneficial, the logical priority of propositions over models embodying them casts doubt on insistence on modeling as the only legitimate way to develop and communicate propositions. What warrant, then, does a critic have for accusing an investigator of doing something disreputably cryptic—namely, working with a model while protecting it from inspection—when he may not be working at the modeling stage at all?

ECONOMETRIC EVIDENCE

The recent vogue of real-business-cycle models has produced econometric studies purportedly discrediting the more traditional focus on money as a source of business fluctuations. Econometric studies enjoy the recommendations of explicit and tacit methodology both. They enjoy the reputation of coming to grips with reality by high-powered techniques, in contrast with commonplace and mostly qualitative observations of the role of money over the centuries and throughout the world and also in contrast with questions about the nature of the barriers in the channels through which money plausibly would affect output.

---

[6]Jones and Newman 1992 is a good example. The authors argue that technological progress increases potential output but may reduce current output by making current knowledge obsolete and disrupting current adaptations. They adopt the metaphor of goods concealed in holes in the ground in definite amounts each period. Progress increases the amounts of goods available but reshuffles their locations, making knowledge gained from past searches obsolete. A mathematical formulation of this metaphor, with parameters expressing the probability of technological shocks and their effects on productivity, does illuminate questions of welfare and its distribution and of possible policy tradeoffs.

An article by Hansen and Prescott (1993) provides a partial exception to the observation that real-business-cycle theorists do not identify the "real" shocks that their theory presupposes. Ultimately, though, the partial nature of that exception supports the observation. Without explicitly saying so, Hansen and Prescott convey the impression that they are answering "yes" to the question posed by their title, "Did Technology Shocks Cause the 1990–1991 Recession?", thus invoking that episode in support of their theory. In their concluding paragraph (p. 286) they say: "Of course, if technology shocks continue to be above average, the United States will experience a boom; if the shocks in the coming year are below average, we can expect a recession." Earlier (e.g., p. 284), they say that their model economy had a recession roughly matching that of the actual economy in timing, magnitude, and duration.

Hansen and Prescott's method was to construct a model economy, modified from the standard real-business-cycle model and calibrated with figures from the real world. They calculate supposed productivity or technology parameters from employment data and other macroeconomic figures. They find that fluctuations of the model and actual economies match each other fairly well, except for stronger and more rapid reactions to productivity shocks and faster recovery from the recession in the model than in the real world. (Robert Clower's "major objection to the new classical economics," comes to mind: "it equates theoretical progress with improved econometric performance of theoretical models rather than with enhanced understanding of the way in which decentralized economic systems work." 1984, p. 272.)

Lacking space to describe their procedures in detail, Hansen and Prescott nevertheless convey the impression that sophisticated technique went into reaching their results, as if that very fact recommends them. Despite entitling one section "What Are These Technology Shocks?" (pp. 280–282), the authors do not actually name the supposed causes of recession. At most they hint that antipollution regulations may have been involved. This style of exposition—conveying impressions rather than mustering explicit evidence and argument—requires comment that I nevertheless refrain from providing here, except to point out an example of tacit cheerleaders for rigor arguing in quite a nonrigorous way.

Philip Cagan reviews studies that manage to avoid detecting the influence of monetary changes on output (1989, followed by comments by Robert Rasche and others). Cagan criticizes the regression techniques commonly employed, "Granger-causality" tests, and particularly vector-autoregression studies, for the way they handle correlations among the "independent" variables, because of processing of the data (prewhitening, trend removal, and other purifications of time-series data in ways that throw away some of the association that may exist), and because these methods are testing for specific (e.g., linear or log-linear) relations and rigid relations among the variables, whereas money exerts its effects with "long and variable lags." The filtering techniques employed remove much of the cyclical movements in money, and monetary influences are masked by innovations in interest rates, in turn reflecting monetary policy. (Michael Bordo, editor of the volume, adds that observation.) The VAR technique for dealing with spurious correlation eliminates important monetary changes. By removing all serial and cross correlations from economic series, VAR in effect removes all but short-run blips in money, losing the influence of relatively sustained monetary changes that do tend to affect business activity.

Cagan also criticizes the treatment of money's endogeneity. (Monetarists know that connections between monetary changes and business activity can run and evidently have run in both directions.) If the Federal Reserve could override the endogeneity of money and thereby make output behave differently than it behaves in fact, then money does count. There is a difference between being endogenous with no independent effect and a mutual dependence which policy can affect. Those who deny monetary effects on output may be aware of this point but continue to neglect it. Even if money had been in some sense completely endogenous in 1929–1933, the Federal Reserve could have overridden that endogeneity and saved the economy from devastation.

I can only raise, not answer, a few further questions about supposed econometric evidence. Is it really informative to run correlations with time-series figures taken not only from periods of cyclical or "abnormal" change in output, money, prices, and so forth but also from periods of steadiness or relatively steady growth (or relatively undisturbed money-supply-and-demand relations), as if all these figures, taken indiscriminately, constituted observations on a single universe? In other words, can one really examine and compare the effects of monetary and non-monetary disturbances by jumbling together numbers from periods both experiencing and not experiencing such disturbances? The issue is not really what calculated parameters describe ill-defined average-over-time relations among various macroeconomic variables. The issue, instead, is the how the phenomena of recession and recovery may be causally related to contemporaneous and earlier events.[7]

If one would rather not find or see something—like monetary disturbances and their consequences—ways are available. The story comes to mind of Admiral Nelson putting his telescope to his blind eye at the battle of Copenhagen.

More fundamentally, what reason is there to suppose that a definite "structure" of the economy, describable by definite functions and definite coefficients, exists in the first place as an object amenable to econometric investigation? Furthermore, even if a mathematically formulated system were deterministic, with known and fixed parameters, the simplest kinds of nonlinearity could render even its qualitative behavior after several or many "rounds" extremely sensitive to parameter sizes and initial conditions. Still further, the real system being modeled, instead of being isolated, is exposed to innumerable perturbations (including "noneconomic" ones) that in principle require being taken into account. In such a system, numerical prediction is impossible (except, perhaps, for short-run extrapolation); the best that can be done is qualitative prediction, or recognition of patterns. Similar remarks apply to attempts to characterize the "processes" supposedly at work in real economies—whether or not they have unit roots, and so forth.

These are among the lessons for economics of the recently popular mathematical theory of "chaos" or "catastrophe." (See Ekeland 1988, who brings E.N. Lorenz's "butterfly effect" and Henri Poincaré's reservations about quantitative modeling into the story.) I do not want to be misunderstood, however, as issuing methodological taboos of my own. Econometric research into recent or earlier economic history can indeed be informative, and its techniques are worth cultivating for applications outside as well as within economics. I merely want to question insistence on them as both obligatory and decisive across practically the whole broad range of economics. Especially where human action is the subject matter, much can be said for observations described and reasoning conducted largely in

---

[7]William Poole (1994, pp. 60–62) makes a related point: an optimal policy should abolish any observable relation between money growth and GDP growth. He offers an analogy about trying to determine the relation between a car's speed and its gasoline consumption by muddling together observations made at moments when the car was going uphill, going downhill, and proceeding on level ground, even though the driver was trying to hold the car's speed steady throughout.

the terms that people themselves use when they perceive and think about and cope with reality.

EVIDENCE OF OTHER KINDS

Cheerleaders for rigor tacitly imply that only numbers constitute really respectable evidence. Everything else is anecdote; and, in the economist's quip, "a historian is one who believes that the plural of anecdote is data" (Brennan and Lomasky 1993, p. 90). Yet Brennan and Lomasky, undeterred, deny

> that the world is describable exhaustively by numbers or that broad brush descriptions of the political landscape have nothing of relevance to contribute to the collection of evidence.... Anecdote does ... have a role to play, and a good feel for the whole story is a crucial prerequisite for proper empirical judgment.... More than "fitting the facts" is required of a theory; it must also genuinely explain, in the sense of rendering intelligible, the facts it fits. (1993, pp. 90–91; compare Higgs 1987, pp. 31–32)

The history of science shows, with Copernicus and Darwin as examples, that theory can play a powerful role in organizing understanding even before it can provide quantitative predictions. *The Wealth of Nations* contains little quantitative detail but had great impact "as a way of seeing how things fit together qualitatively." Quantitative prediction, though a reasonable goal for science, is not the test of a new theory (Margolis 1982, pp. 10–11).

If an economist is not willing to analyze nonquantitative evidence such as executive orders, statutes, court decisions, and regulatory directives, writes Robert Higgs (1987, p. 32), then perhaps he should abandon

> his pretensions in this field of study.... The keys lost elsewhere will never be found under the lamp post, not even with the aid of the most powerful floodlights. The spectacle of economists bringing their awesome mathematical and statistical techniques to bear on the analysis of irrelevant or misleading data can only disgust those for whom the desire to understand reality takes precedence over the desire to impress their colleagues with analytical pyrotechnics.[8]

---

[8]Higgs further reminds us that people do not act merely out of self-interest in the narrow sense of *homo oeconomicus*. Sometimes they act from loyalty to a cherished ideology and for the satisfaction of shared membership in a set of noble, right-minded persons (1987, pp. 42–43).

Robin Winks collected several historical essays under a suggestive title, *The Historian as Detective* (1969). Like a detective trying to solve a murder case, a good researcher of historical questions does not let methodological prejudice or intimidation[9] narrow the range of kinds of clues he is willing to sift. He is willing to undertake episode-by-episode analysis, or any other kind that appears promising. Economists, we may hope, will become equally open-minded even about novel evidence and argument.

COMPETING HYPOTHESES

The disparagers of money-oriented macroeconomics take few pains to link up their theories with earlier theories and the facts that they appeared to account for. (Yet in the natural sciences this is standard practice. Kepler's astronomy accounted for the observations that the Ptolemaic theory had already accommodated. Einstein's relativistic mechanics assimilates Newtonian mechanics as giving an excellent account of a special case, which happens to be the world of ordinary human observation.) Instead, the disparagers of money continue tinkering with their "real" models, "calibrating" them, ingeniously striving for verisimilitude.

So doing, they disregard or flout the method of multiple competing hypotheses. Actually, this is not a specific method or technique, nor is it a tissue of methodological exhortations and taboos; rather, it is a broad approach or attitude toward research. The biophysicist John R. Platt (1964), echoing and reinforcing the geologist T.C. Chamberlin (1897/n.d.), persuasively argues for developing rival hypotheses and seeking ways to rule each one out, seeing which one or more, if any, stand up to the challenges of the best evidence obtainable.

The contrasting approach or attitude is simply to seek arguments and evidence in defense of one's own favorite hypothesis. "[I]n numerous areas that we call science," Platt observes (p. 352), "we have come to like our habitual ways, and our studies that can be continued indefinitely. We measure, we define, we compute, we analyze, but we do not exclude. And this is not the way to use our minds most effectively or to make the fastest progress in solving scientific questions." A researcher with a parental affection for his own favorite theory, Chamberlin had already

---

[9] On "argument from intimidation," see passages from Ayn Rand's works reprinted in Binswanger 1986, pp. 32–34.

observed (1897/n.d., p. 840), searches especially for phenomena that support it. Unwittingly he presses the theory and the facts to fit each other.

Chamberlin in effect advocated substituting discussion for debate. The two are different in spirit. The debater seeks the decision of the judges for his already adopted conclusion; a discussant searches for truth (F.A. Harper in a "publisher's note" to the reprint of Chamberlin's article). "The conflict and exclusion of alternatives that is necessary to sharp inductive inference has been all too often a conflict between men, each with his single Ruling Theory. But whenever each man begins to have multiple working hypotheses, it becomes purely a conflict between ideas. It becomes much easier then for each of us to aim every day at conclusive disproofs—at *strong* inference—without either reluctance or combativeness." Researchers become excited at seeing how the detective story will turn out (Platt 1964, p. 350).[10]

The foregoing views require qualification. Not every researcher need be testing several hypotheses. Division of labor can be fruitful. Some researchers may legitimately work to give one particular hypothesis its best possible shot. It may be instructive for themselves and others to see what persistence and ingenuity can do toward salvaging even a hypothesis that does indeed seem preposterous on its face. Furthermore, some may flourish in a setting and incentive structure of rivalry not merely

---

[10] Platt insightfully warns of the researcher who is method-oriented rather than problem-oriented.

[A]nyone who asks the question about scientific effectiveness will also conclude that much of the mathematicizing in physics and chemistry today is irrelevant if not misleading....

The great value of mathematical formulation is that when an experiment agrees with a calculation to five decimal places, a great many alternative hypotheses are pretty well excluded.... But when the fit is only to two decimal places, or one, it may be a trap for the unwary; it may be no better than any rule-of-thumb extrapolation, and some other kind of qualitative exclusion might be more rigorous for testing the assumptions and more important to scientific understanding than the quantitative fit....

Measurements and equations are supposed to sharpen thinking, but, in my observation, they more often tend to make the thinking noncausal and fuzzy. They tend to become the object of scientific manipulation instead of auxiliary tests of crucial inferences.

Many—perhaps most—of the great issues of science are qualitative, not quantitative, even in physics and chemistry. Equations and measurements are useful when and only when they are related to proof; but proof or disproof comes first and is in fact strongest when it is absolutely convincing without any quantitative measurement. (1964, pp. 351–352)

among ideas but among persons. Differences not merely of abilities, training, and interests but even of temperaments may be put to good use. But to the extent that some economists do work ingeniously at protecting their favorite theories, the task falls all the more to others to perform the necessary confrontations.

Not only real-business-cycle theorists but monetarists must face the objections voiced by Chamberlin and Platt. Still, monetarism is not irrefutable in the disreputable sense of enjoying built-in protection against any adverse evidence. Observations are readily conceivable that would indeed refute it. If these are merely conceivable, not actual, and if they would run counter to manifest facts about the role of money in the everyday activities of individuals and business firms, well, a theory is scarcely at fault for recognizing those facts.

The method of competing multiple hypotheses scarcely requires that no question ever be settled, not even tentatively, and that multiple hypotheses always remain in active contention on all topics. It would be no scandal if a strong consensus eventually developed on the monetary (or nonmonetary) nature of business cycles. What would be a scientific scandal would be to grant certain questions perpetual immunity to ever being reopened, no matter what new evidence and lines of reasoning might be developed.

FALLACY-MONGERING

Countermethodology, which I distinguish favorably from methodology, does not mean that "anything goes." It in no way exempts any argument or supposed evidence from critical inspection. Critics should point out specific defects, however,—slips in logic and errors of fact—rather than just sneer broadly at the use of some methods but not others.

Despite Donald McCloskey's lack of enthusiasm for what he calls "fallacy-mongering" (1985, pp. 48–49), it can be useful to identify and classify specific types of unsatisfactory argument. McCloskey is emphatically in favor of scholarly dialogue, conversation, or rhetoric. Well, dialogue consists largely of critical examination of arguments and evidence and supposed inferences, and being acquainted with and alert to frequent types of fallacy can help in this examination. McCloskey himself warns against some particular types, such as confusion between statistical significance and substantive significance of coefficients in fitted equations (1986; also 1992, p. 267). Identifying and categorizing fallacies is not at all the same thing as issuing methodological injunctions and taboos. Rather, it resembles the bottom-level, nuts-and-bolts methodology acceptable to McCloskey.

Now, what are some types of fallacy—and, to broaden our target, types of irrelevance—found in economic discourse?

- Standard fallacies that textbooks warn against, such as the fallacy of composition (and reverse fallacies of composition).

- The Ricardian Vice (so called by Schumpeter 1954, pp. 668, 1171): "the habit of establishing simple relations between aggregates that then acquire a spurious halo of causal importance, whereas all the really important (and, unfortunately, complicated) things are being bundled away in or behind these aggregates," in other words, "the habit of piling a heavy load of practical conclusions upon a tenuous groundwork, which was unequal to it yet seemed in its simplicity not only attractive but also convincing."

- "Austrian-style disquisitions on the foundations of human knowledge and conduct and the like," an irrelevancy characteristic of Frank Knight's writings, according to LeRoy and Singell (1987, p. 402).

- Similarly, nonsubstantive brooding over the meanings of concepts, as over the essence of entrepreneurship.

- Assuming constancy of magnitudes that simply cannot remain constant in the face of changes in other magnitudes considered (Buchanan 1958).

- Failure to distinguish between individual and overall points of view or, relatedly, failure to make, when relevant, Patinkin's distinction between individual experiments and market experiments (1965, chap. 1 and appendix).

- Failures to distinguish when necessary between actual and desired changes in holdings of money, between an excess demand for or supply of home money on the foreign-exchange market and an excess demand for or supply of domestic cash balances, and between demand for assets denominated in a particular currency and the demand for holdings of that currency as a medium of exchange.

- The real-bills fallacy, which keeps turning up in new disguises.

- Tacitly supposing that lack of tight short-run correlation between changes in certain magnitudes discredits the broad relation that standard theory indicates between their levels. (Nowadays the technique of cointegration is cultivated as a means of overcoming this fallacy.)
- Mere eloquence that crowds out quantitative considerations. Hardin duly condemns decisions dominated by sheer eloquence, whereas the numerate outlook shows a concern for how big, how important, phenomena and effects are (1986, esp. pp. 42–44).

ATTITUDES AND PRESSURES

Fritz Machlup (1956/1978, chap. 13) listed several signs of an "inferiority complex of the social sciences," including Behaviorism, Operationism, Metromania, Predictionism, Experimentomania, and Mathematosis. Pressure to resemble the physical sciences does seem to be a kind of tacit methodologizing.

Another, apparently, is attunement to fads.

In science, as everywhere else, there are few true creators, people able to leave the beaten track and to come up with new ideas. It is very tempting to deem a problem interesting because half the people you know are working on it. But truly deep and difficult problems promise no easy returns, and do not attract people eager to publish. Poincaré makes a distinction between problems that nature sets up and problems that one sets up (Ekeland 1988, p. 25).

What one might call frontiersmanship is a related attitude. Conjecturably it tends to crowd out due attention to history, both of subject matter and of research and doctrine in one's field. In macroeconomics, older and more straightforward doctrines, whatever their merits, were, well, remote from the frontier. Other fields appeared more suitable for the academic game. On the supposed frontier, business-cycle researchers, whether belonging to the new-classical or the "real" school, tend to neglect historical episodes helping to support (or to discredit) the monetarist explanation of cycles. They also neglect or slight the fact that competent observers in widely diverse times and places saw reason to be persuaded of the monetary nature of cycles. Yet this widespread perception surely counts for something, especially since it does not stand alone but complements a variety of other evidence.

Also at work in contemporary macroeconomics is an attitude that I do not want to label; it can exhibit itself. Referring to New Keynesian economics in particular (which, being mislabeled, has close though inadequately appreciated affinities with monetarism), Robert G. King mentions macroeconomists working "on the banks of the Charles River," whose product he disparages in contrast with "that of macroeconomists at the universities where the cutting-edge research has been done over the past decade." The latter consists of dynamic general equilibrium microeconomic models of macroeconomic phenomena. "It is what most graduate students are now learning and what most undergraduates will soon learn. In two decades or less, it will be hard to find a macroeconomist whose first reactions to policy problems will not be conditioned by sustained exposure to [it]" (King 1990, p. 162). In a later article, King reproaches New Keynesians for attempts at "marketing" a version of macroeconomics resembling a Ford Pinto. "The danger is that macroeconomists and policy-makers will pay too much attention to the new Keynesian advertising, and assume for too long that the old product is a sound one" (King 1993, concluding sentence).

ACADEMIC INCENTIVES AND GAMES

The state of academic economics is far from wholly bad; progress does occur. Critics, though, see grounds for complaint. An article chosen at random out of any economics journal, James Buchanan finds, is unlikely "to have a social productivity greater than zero. Most modern economists are simply doing what other economists are doing while living off a form of dole that will simply not stand critical scrutiny" (1979, pp. 90–91). More recently a young academic superstar has said much the same:

> In America's academic system, professors of economics get tenure and build reputations that give them other academic perks by publishing, and so they publish immense amounts—thousands of papers each year, in scores of obscure journals. Most of those papers aren't worth reading, and many of them are pretty much impossible to read in any case, because they are loaded with dense mathematics and denser jargon. (Krugman 1994, p. 8)

"Academic programs almost everywhere," Buchanan continues, "are controlled by rent-recipients who simply try to ape the mainstream work of their peers in the discipline" (Buchanan 1983/1988, p. 130). Mainstream economists of the 1950s, though wrong on much, were interested in ideas, Buchanan says, and were not frauds or conscious parasites. Since then economics has become a science without ultimate purpose or meaning. It has allowed itself to become captive of the technical tools that it employs without keeping track of just what it is that the tools are to be used for. In a very real sense the economists of the 1980s are illiterate in basic principles of their own discipline.... Their interest lies in the purely intellectual properties of the models with which they work, and they seem to get their kicks from the discovery of proofs of propositions relevant only to their own fantasy lands. (1983/1988, pp. 126–127)

Maurice Allais, a mathematical economist who won the Nobel Prize two years after Buchanan did, shares his skepticism. For almost forty-five years, Allais said in 1989, economic literature has featured "completely artificial mathematical models detached from reality." Allais recommends mathematics to economists not for its own sake "but as a means of exploring and analyzing concrete reality." When neither a theory nor its implications "can be confronted with the real world, that theory is devoid of any scientific interest."

In a broader context, Garrett Hardin (1986, pp. 175–176) observes an information glut. "A substantial and growing proportion of the scientific literature is pure jam [in the sense of traffic jam], the consequence of egotistic scientists putting out multiple, repetitive publications in an effort to be noticed.... Progress is impeded. Society suffers." Referring to the examination system for the Mandarins of imperial China, Michael Walzer (1983, p. 141) notes that "examiners increasingly stressed memorization, philology, and calligraphy, and candidates paid more attention to old examination questions than to the meaning of the old books. What was tested, increasingly, was the ability to take a test." In today's academic world, similarly, what gets rewarded seems to be the ability to get rewarded.

Without charging specific individuals with misconduct or reprehensible motives, we may remind ourselves about gamesmanship. Occasionally the writer of an article will try to butter up prospective referees or otherwise engage in politicking to get it published.[11] What is more

---

[11]Bart Kosko may be exaggerating but not practicing sheer invention:

Career science, like career politics, depends as much on career maneuvering, posturing, and politics as it depends on research and the pursuit of truth. Few know that when they start the game of science. But they learn it soon enough. (1993, p. 40)

Politics lies behind literature citations and omissions, academic promotions, government appointments, contract and grant awards, conference addresses and conference committee-member choices, editorial-board selection for journals and book

relevant to our topic, writers sometimes put on a display of erudition, using techniques more advanced than are helpful,[12] otherwise parading supposed rigor, making forays into other academic disciplines, or citing scarcely relevant but impressively obscure sources. Some of this gamesmanship is no doubt tolerable: even serious researchers are entitled to a little fun. It does little damage when it is evident for what it is. It is less tolerable, however, when it warps the writer's approach to the subject matter and his or his readers' understanding.

This situation traces partly to the incentive structure in academe. We observe something reminiscent of the role of "success indicators" in the Soviet command economy. Meeting the target, satisfying the criteria, becomes the objective, crowding out attention to the wants of the customers or—in the present context—the advancement of knowledge, the pleasure of the quest, and the enlightenment of readers and students. The blame falls partly on administrators desiring easy-to-administer criteria for tenure and promotion. As I have observed on committees and otherwise, some evaluators focus not on the actual merits of scholarly work but on the supposed prestige of the journals where it appeared, a consideration related in turn to attunement to fads and fashions. The "second-handism" duly condemned by Ayn Rand rides high (see the passages from her works reprinted in Binswanger 1986, pp. 438–441).

---

series, reviewer selection for technical papers and contract proposals and university accreditation status, and most of all, where the political currents funnel into a laser-like beam, in the peer-review process of technical journal articles. (p. 42)

Bartley's 1990 book is a sustained expression of doubt about the incentives at work in academe. It explores the intrinsically unfathomable character of knowledge, shows to what a limited extent it can be owned and controlled, and argues that universities are not organized so as readily to advance knowledge (Bartley finds them often working against its growth). Chapters on "The Curious Case of Karl Popper" and on the supposed threat that Popper's philosophy poses to intellectual fashions provide a case study of the book's contentions.

Hausman 1992, p. 262, also mentions perverse incentives at work in academic economics.

[12] Not referring to academic economics in particular, Mark C. Henrie (1987, p. 333) notes that an "ability to argue any side of any question demonstrates the importance of technique; but technique alone does not provide the student any insight into which view is true. Quite the opposite, it encourages virtuosity of argumentation for what is false, since to argue falsehood persuasively more fully demonstrates command of technique than to argue for what is true."

I also suspect some inchoate notion that if falsifiability is a good characteristic of a theory, downright falsity is even better.

Something may well be said for "schools," which can encourage a researcher with the prospect of a sympathetic audience. But a school influential enough to dominate what are considered to be success indicators can have a baneful influence, inhibiting independent thought.

THE MARKET ANALOGY

Sometimes second-handers try to justify their stance by invoking the free market in goods and services. Once, when the board of directors of the Southern Economic Association was discussing whether to nominate a particular economist for some position or other, a member whom I'll identify only as "TS" said in effect: "It doesn't matter what we here think of his work; let the market decide." TS went on to name the journals that had printed the candidate's work. At least two things were wrong with this appeal to "the market." First, the ultimate consumer, the reader of academic journals—or, more exactly, the subscriber—has an influence more attenuated and more subject to manipulation by others than the influence of the consumer of ordinary consumer goods and services. Editors and referees have reason and scope for heeding fads and cliquish and personal considerations. They are not risking their own money. Subscribers face tie-in sales (which include association memberships and the supposed prestige of subscribing) and have reason, anyway, to learn about fads, whether they like them or not. It is harder in the supposed academic market than in the real market for customers to know whether they got what they paid for.

Second, since when was the market, even the actual business market, supposed to be the arbiter of excellence in literature, art, music, science, or scholarship? Since when does it decide truth and beauty? The case for the free market is something quite other than that it constitutes the very criterion of what should be admired, and it ill serves the cause of a free society to misrepresent the case for the market.

Finally, TS's position is the very prototype of the second-handism diagnosed by Ayn Rand. Misbehavior in the "marketplace" for ideas is worse than in the marketplace of goods, suggests W.W. Bartley III, because few penalties against offenders are readily enforceable, while "whistle-blowers" are severely punished (1990, chaps. 6 and 7; the analogy between the academic and business markets is further dissected in Mirowsky 1992, pp. 239, 247, and Mayer 1993, pp. 10ff., 84).

CLARITY VERSUS OBSCURANTISM

Overcoming tacit methodological preachments requires, for one thing, cultivating clarity. An article by Max Eastman (1929/1940) is worth citing if only for its insightful title, "The Cult of Unintelligibility." That label fits not only Eastman's specific target, "modernist" poetry, but much academic activity. Yet contempt for conveying a clear message violates the spirit of science, which "is nothing but a persistent and organized effort to talk sense" (Eastman 1929/1940, p. 366). Bartley found the obscurantism of certain entrenched ideologies occurring in two main forms, inappropriate mathematical formalism and lack of clarity in speech and presentation (1990, pp. 132ff.). As Karl Popper taught, pretentiousness is immoral (Bartley 1990, p. 159). Popper would "always try to dislodge his conversational partners from any habits or tricks that preserve their ability to impress and dominate, and to maintain the pretence of knowledge they do not possess" (Bartley 1990, p. 265).

Authors of books on grammar and writing style do not hesitate to warn their readers about specific errors and stylistic infelicities. In that connection, we do well to remember McCloskey's top level of methodology, the ethics of scholarly discourse. Scientists are supposed to be engaged in an interpersonal endeavor, which includes, as McCloskey says, "conversation."

Well, then, communicate. Do not pervert communication into parading how much you know of mathematics or the philosophy of science or whatever. Instead of striving to impress your reader, be polite to him. Edit; rewrite. Recognize that the form in which your ideas originally occurred to you may not be the most effective way to put them across. Do not suppose that employing symbols automatically confers a papal dispensation from obligations incumbent on any writer.

The offenses I have in mind include writing in code, with symbols replacing words, using symbols defined only haphazardly, omitting meaningful labels from diagrams, and using cryptic expressions with variable meanings (such as "real exchange rate" or "appreciation of the exchange rate"). Perhaps your reader can break your code; perhaps he should be able to figure out your argument even in its original, unedited form. But why should he have to bother? He feels more comfortable with occasional reassurances that you and he are on the same wavelength. After all, you might be making a mistake. I recall places where the writer used a slightly different symbol in a diagram than in the text, such as a lower-case instead of upper-case letter or a curved letter *l* instead of a straight one. Did the writer intend a distinction, and if so, what was it, or was he simply being careless? Such time-consuming puzzles could be avoided if the writer deigned to write clearly in the first place, perhaps even labeling his diagrams in English.

The central fact of economics is scarcity. Your readers' time is scarce, as well as their capacity for attention and effort. Besides figuring your message out, they have other things to do. Many topics within and outside of economics besides your current message are worth their attention, and your own. (As Wilhelm Röpke used to say, economics is a subject in which understanding a part presupposes understanding the whole, and indeed more. An economist who is only an economist cannot even be a good economist.)

Remember that the principle of diminishing marginal returns applies widely, even to time and effort spent on a particular activity or topic. Even for readers who can follow an analysis, unnecessary formalist decorations often consume time that might have had other and better uses (Mayer 1993, p. 78). The principle of portfolio diversification applies not only to investment assets but also to knowledge of topics within and outside of economics.

Encouragingly, the mathematician Paul Halmos similarly exhorts his colleagues. They should write correct and clear English, keeping Fowler, Roget, and Webster at hand. A writer who works eight hours to save five minutes for each of 1000 readers saves over eighty man-hours. Halmos warns that the symbolism of formal logic, though sometimes indispensable, is a cumbersome way of transmitting ideas. Nobody thinks in symbols. Coding by the author and decoding by the reader waste the time of both and obstruct understanding. "The best notation is no notation," Halmos advises. Try to write a mathematical exposition as you would speak it. "Pretend that you are explaining the subject to a friend on a long walk in the woods, with no paper available; fall back on symbolism only when it is really necessary" (Halmos 1973/1981, p. 40). Avoid distracting your reader with irrelevant labels (for example, referring to "the function f" when you will not be using the label f again). When conveniently possible, avoid coining new technical terms. Take care about the appearance of the printed page. Solid prose will have a forbidding, sermony aspect; "a page full of symbols ... will have a frightening, complicated aspect" (p. 44).

It may be that clarity does not pay. (It costs time, but editors and referees have an opportunity to impose discipline on authors in the interest of the wider scholarly community.) Putting heavy demands on your reader may advertise your own learning. It may intimidate him into not questioning your argument. (Mayer 1993, p. 78, suggests that formalist trappings may help protect a paper from criticism by making critical comment on it costly in time and effort.) You may make your message appear fresher and more important than it really is by practicing product differentiation, as opposed to taking care to relate your message to the existing literature, exploiting similarities, parallels, analogies, and contrasts. Perhaps reconditeness and obscurity really do bamboozle editors and readers; and perhaps unintelligibility masquerading as profundity may sometimes ward off identification of what is no more than poor style. If so, a moral aspect enters into writing. (Cf. McCloskey 1986, writing in a slightly different context.) If so, furthermore, questions again arise about the incentive structure prevailing in academia.

At the very least, get your grammar, word usage, spelling, and punctuation right. (Nobody is infallible, certainly not I, but at least one should work at these things.) Why do economists tolerate so much slovenliness in these respects? They do not tolerate its counterpart in the mathematical strands of economics—not, that is, when they notice it (and I have some stories to tell about this qualification). If rigor is prized, why shouldn't it be prized in the cut-and-dried aspects of writing?

If for some reason you cannot get your grammar and so forth right, then hire someone to repair your writing before you ship it off to a journal and perhaps even before you inflict it on colleagues. Beyond getting the mechanics right, strive for a readable style. When you ship your manuscript off to a publisher, have it in a form in which you would be glad to see it in print. Don't count on someone else to improve it.

These exhortations bear on what to do about a national crisis (permit me to exaggerate as Andy Rooney does on the tube). Not even Walter Block, who wrote a whole book (1976) trying to portray the pimp, the drug pusher, the litterbug, and other unsavory types as heroes—not even he attempted any defense of the itchy-fingered copyeditor. That would have been just too preposterous. I wonder whether obscurities, jargon, and symbols may not sometimes help protect authors from tampering: copyeditors may shy away from trying to improve on manuscripts that they cannot even understand. Mere palpable sloppiness, on the other hand, flags the copyeditors on. One of my bitterest complaints against writers who think it beneath them to bother with their grammar, spelling, punctuation, and style is that they create externalities: they inflict the curse of copyediting even onto writers more careful than themselves.

Ideally, the author himself should be known to bear responsibility for what appears in print. If the writing is excessively bad, the publisher should simply reject it. As things now stand, however, sloppy writers provide an excuse of sorts for not straightforwardly solving the copyeditor problem.

CONCLUSION

I hope we are giving each other, and perhaps our students and readers, some moral support, some backbone, so that we can carry on our work in the ways that we ourselves think best suited for learning how the world actually operates. I hope we can carry on despite fads, fashions, perverse success indicators, and preachments about "rigor." I hope we will have the courage to unmask and, when appropriate, to defy methodological preachments of the worst kind, the tacit ones.

REFERENCES

Allais, Maurice. Remarks at McGill University, Montreal. Reported in *IMF Survey* (12 June 1989): 185.

Bartley, William Warren, III. *The Retreat to Commitment*. 2nd ed. La Salle, Ill., and London: Open Court, 1984.

——. *Unfathomed Knowledge, Unmeasured Wealth: On Universities and the Wealth of Nations*. La Salle, Ill.: Open Court, 1990.

Bauer, Peter T. "International Economic Development." *Economic Journal* 69 (March 1959): 105–123.

Bénassy, Jean-Pascal. "Nonclearing Markets: Microeconomic Concepts and Macroeconomic Applications." *Journal of Economic Literature* 31 (June 1993): 732–761.

Binswanger, Harry, ed. *The Ayn Rand Lexicon*. New York: New American Library, 1986.

Block, Walter. *Defending the Undefendable*. New York: Fleet, 1976.

Brennan, Geoffrey, and Loren Lomasky. *Democracy and Decision*. Cambridge, U.K.: Cambridge University Press, 1993.

Bridgman, P.W. *Reflections of a Physicist*. New York: Philosophical Library, 1955.

Brunner, Karl. "The Disarray in Macroeconomics." In *Monetary Economics in the 1980s*, edited by Forrest Capie and Geoffrey E. Wood, 197–233. London: Macmillan, 1989.

Buchanan, James M. "*Ceteris Paribus*: Some Notes on Methodology." *Southern Economic Journal* 24 (January 1958): 259–270.

———. *What Should Economists Do?* Indianapolis: Liberty Press, 1979.

———. "Political Economy: 1957–1982." 1983. In *Ideas, Their Origins, and Their Consequences*, by Thomas Jefferson Center Foundation, 119–130. Washington, D.C.: American Enterprise Institute, 1988.

Cagan, Philip. "Money-Income Causality—A Critical Review of the Literature Since *A Monetary History*." In *Money, History, and International Finance: Essays in Honor of Anna J. Schwartz*, edited by Michael D. Bordo, 117–151. Chicago: University of Chicago Press, 1989.

Caldwell, Bruce J., ed. *Appraisal and Criticism in Economics: A Book of Readings*. Boston: Allen & Unwin, 1984.

Chamberlin, Thomas C. "The Method of Multiple Working Hypotheses." *Journal of Geology* 5, (November/December 1897): 837–848. Reprinted as the pamphlet *Multiple Hypotheses*. Menlo Park: Institute for Humane Studies, n.d.

Clower, Robert. *Money and Markets*. Edited by Donald A. Walker. New York: Cambridge University Press, 1984.

Davis, Philip J., and Reuben Hersh. *Descartes' Dream*. New York: Harcourt Brace Jovanovich, 1986.

Duhem, Pierre. *The Aim and Structure of Physical Theory*. Translated by Philip P. Wiener. Princeton, N.J.: Princeton University Press, 1954.

Eastman, Max. "The Cult of Unintelligibility." 1929. In *America Through the Essay*, edited by A.T. Johnson and Allen Tate, 362–378. New York: Oxford University Press, 1940.

Ekeland, Ivar. *Mathematics and the Unexpected*. Chicago: University of Chicago Press, 1988.

Eucken, Walter. "On The Theory of the Centrally Administered Economy: An Analysis of the German Experiment." Translated by T.W. Hutchison. *Economica* 15, no. 57 (February 1948): 79–100; and no. 59 (August 1948): 173–193.

Frank, Robert H. "If *Homo Economicus* Could Choose His Own Utility Function, Would He Want One with a Conscience?" *American Economic Review* 77 (September 1987): 593–604.

Giere, Ronald N. *Explaining Science: A Cognitive Approach.* Chicago: University of Chicago Press, 1988.

Grossman, Herschel I. Review of *Disequilibrium Economics*, by Katsuhito Iwai. *Journal of Political Economy* 91 (April 1983): 343–344.

Halmos, Paul R. "How to Write Mathematics." 1973. In *How to Write Mathematics*, by N.E. Steenrod, P.R. Halmos, M.M. Schiffer, and J.A. Dieudonné, 19–48. Providence: American Mathematical Society, 1981.

Hansen, Gary D., and Edward C. Prescott. "Did Technology Shocks Cause the 1990–1991 Recession?" *American Economic Review* 83 (May 1993): 280–286.

Hardin, Garrett. *Filters against Folly: How to Survive Despite Economists, Ecologists, and the Merely Eloquent.* New York: Penguin Books, 1986.

Hausman, Daniel M. *The Inexact and Separate Science of Economics.* Cambridge, U.K., and New York: Cambridge University Press, 1992.

Henrie, Mark C. "Reason, Unreason, and the Conservative." *Modern Age* 31 (Summer/Fall 1987): 332–342.

Higgs, Robert. *Crisis and Leviathan.* New York: Oxford University Press, 1987.

Hobbes, Thomas. *Leviathan.* 1651. Baltimore: Penguin Books, 1968.

Ireland, Peter N. "Money and Growth: An Alternative Approach." *American Economic Review* 84 (March 1994): 47–65.

Jones, Robert, and Geoffrey Newman. "Economic Growth as a Coordination Problem." Paper presented at the 1992 Southern Economic Association meetings.

King, Robert G. "The Interaction of Monetary Policy and Public Deficits." In *Monetary Policy for a Changing Financial Environment*, edited by William S. Haraf and Philip Cagan, 160–165. Washington, D.C.: American Enterprise Institute Press, 1990.

———. "Will the New Keynesian Macroeconomics Resurrect the IS-LM Model?" *Journal of Economic Perspectives* 7 (Winter 1993): 67–82.

Klamer, Arjo. *Conversations with Economists.* Totowa, N.J.: Rowman & Allanheld, 1983.

Klappholz, K., and J. Agassi. "Methodological Prescriptions in Economics." *Economica* 26 (February 1959): 60–74.

Kosko, Bart. *Fuzzy Thinking: The New Science of Fuzzy Logic*. New York: Hyperion, 1993.

Krugman, Paul. *What Do We Need to Know about the International Monetary System?* Essays in International Finance, no. 190. Princeton, N.J.: Princeton University International Finance Section, July 1993.

———. *Peddling Prosperity: Economic Sense and Nonsense in the Age of Diminished Expectations*. New York: Norton, 1994.

Laidler, David. *Taking Money Seriously and Other Essays*. Cambridge, Mass.: MIT Press, 1990.

Lakatos, Imre. *Proofs and Refutations: The Logic of Mathematical Discovery*. Edited by John Worrall and Elie Zahar. New York: Cambridge University Press, 1976.

LeRoy, Stephen F., and Larry D. Singell, Jr. "Knight on Risk and Uncertainty." *Journal of Political Economy* 95 (April 1987): 394–406.

Lucas, Robert E., Jr. "Some International Evidence on Output-Inflation Trade-offs." *American Economic Review* 63 (June 1973): 326–334.

———. "Methods and Problems in Business Cycle Theory." *Journal of Money, Credit, and Banking* 12, Pt. 2 (November 1980): 696–715.

Lucas, Robert E., Jr., and Thomas J. Sargent. "After Keynesian Macroeconomics." In *After the Phillips Curve: Persistence of High Inflation and High Unemployment*, 49–72. Boston: Federal Reserve Bank of Boston, 1978.

Machlup, Fritz. "The Inferiority Complex of the Social Sciences." 1956. In *Methodology of Economics and Other Social Sciences*, chap. 13. New York: Academic Press, 1978.

Margolis, Howard. *Selfishness, Altruism, and Rationality*. New York: Cambridge University Press, 1982.

Mayer, Thomas. *Truth versus Precision in Economics*. Aldershot, U.K., and Brookfield, Vt.: Elgar, 1993.

McCloskey, Donald N. *The Rhetoric of Economics*. Madison: University of Wisconsin Press, 1985.

———. "Why Economic Historians Should Stop Relying on Statistical Tests of Significance, and Lead Economists and Historians Into the Promised Land." *Cliometrics Society Newsletter* 2 (December 1986): 5–7.

———. "Commentary" on Philip Mirowski's paper. In *Post-Popperian Methodology of Economics*, edited by Neil de Marchi, 261–271. Boston: Kluwer, 1992.

Mirowski, Philip. "Three Vignettes on the State of Economic Rhetoric." In *Post-Popperian Methodology of Economics*, edited by Neil de Marchi, 235–259. Boston: Kluwer, 1992.

Musgrave, Alan. "'Unreal Assumptions' in Economic Theory: The F-Twist Untwisted." *Kyklos* 34, no. 3 (1981): 377–387.

Patinkin, Don. *Money, Interest, and Prices*. 2nd ed. New York: Harper & Row, 1965.

Platt, John R. "Strong Inference." *Science* 146 (October 1964): 347–353.

Poole, William. "Understanding the Monetary Aggregates Today." Shadow Open Market Committee, *Policy Statement and Position Papers* (March 1994): 59–65.

Schumpeter, Joseph A. *History of Economic Analysis*. New York: Oxford University Press, 1954.

Solow, Robert. "Economic History and Economics." *American Economic Review* 75 (May 1985): 328–331.

Summers, Lawrence. "The Scientific Illusion in Empirical Macroeconomics." *Scandinavian Journal of Economics* 93, no. 2 (1991): 129–148.

Tobin, James. "Discussion." In *Models of Monetary Economies*, edited by John H. Kareken and Neil Wallace, 83–90. Minneapolis: Federal Reserve Bank of Minneapolis, 1980.

Walzer, Michael. *Spheres of Justice*. New York: Basic Books, 1983.

Willes, Mark H. "'Rational Expectations' as a Counterrevolution." *The Public Interest*, Special Issue (1980): 81–96.

Williamson, Steve, and Randall Wright. "Barter and Monetary Exchange Under Private Information." *American Economic Review* 84 (March 1994): 104–123.

Winks, Robin W. *The Historian as Detective: Essays on Evidence*. New York: Harper & Row, 1969.

Yeager, Leland B. "The Significance of Monetary Disequilibrium." *Cato Journal* 6 (Fall 1986): 369–399.

———. "Tautologies in Economics and the Natural Sciences." *Eastern Economic Journal* 20 (Spring 1994): 157–169. Reprinted here as chapter 14.

CHAPTER 14

Tautologies in Economics and the Natural Sciences*

THE TOPIC AND A DISCLAIMER

Quibbles over Walras's Law trace, in my experience,[1] to failure to recognize that the Law is tautologically true. To forestall misunderstanding of this and other pieces of economic theory, it is worth recognizing that useful tautologies are fairly numerous.

This paper issues no methodological exhortations or taboos. It does not urge armchair theory over empirical research. Instead, it looks at a feature shared by several specific examples of successful theorizing. Just as scientists try to explain puzzling phenomena by revealing uniformities hidden beneath superficial diversities, so we may better understand the nature and force of argument on a particular topic by recognizing how it resembles (when it does) arguments on even quite different topics. Elucidating one style or strand or component of argument is not the same as insisting on it as the only proper method of research or exposition.

Tautologies are analytic or logically necessary propositions. They are valid thanks to covering all possibilities ("The world is either round or not round") or thanks to interlocking definitions. A negation of a tautology is self-contradictory. (Consider denying "If A implies B, then not-B implies not-A.") Most of the tautologies mentioned below hinge on the formulation and interlocking of terms and concepts, whose meanings and interrelations they illuminate.

Analytic propositions *can* "give us new knowledge" (or aid us in its pursuit). "They call attention to linguistic usage, of which we might otherwise

---

*From *Eastern Economic Journal* 20 (Spring 1994): 157–169.
[1] I am particularly thinking of trouble in making readers understand Alan Rabin's and my paper on "Monetary Aspects of Walras's Law and the Stock-Flow Problem," subsequently published in 1997.

not be conscious, and they reveal unsuspected implications in our assertions and beliefs" (Ayer 1946/1969, p. 35). Logic and mathematics, although apodictically certain, can sometimes yield surprising results. Analytic propositions help one check that the factual propositions being brought to bear on some problem are mutually consistent (pp. 36, 40–41). Tautologies can be useful in applying the "translation test" (illustrated later) and in exposing error (for nothing contradicting a logically necessary proposition can be correct). Tautologies can be useful in focusing attention and organizing discussion.

The examples reviewed below illustrate John Harsanyi's point (1976, p. 64) that social scientists encounter not only formal or logical problems and empirical problems but also conceptual-philosophical problems. Larry Laudan (1977, chap. 2) calls it "an enormous mistake ... to imagine that scientific progress and rationality consist entirely in solving empirical problems." Grappling with conceptual problems "has been *at least as important* in the development of science as empirical problem solving" (p. 45). One of the most important ways science progresses is "the explication of conceptions" (William Whewell, quoted in Laudan 1977, p. 50).

A theory runs into conceptual problems when it is internally inconsistent or vague or when it conflicts with another theory or doctrine believed to be well founded (Laudan 1977, esp. pp. 48–49). Ptolemy's astronomy managed to avoid most of the empirical anomalies of earlier Greek astronomy, but at the price of *"generating enormous conceptual problems"* with its epicycles, eccentrics, and equants. Its hypothesis that certain planets move around empty points in space, that planets do not always move at constant speed, and the like were in flagrant contradiction with the then accepted physical and cosmological theories (Laudan 1977, pp. 51–52). Methodological norms, in Laudan's view, "have been perhaps the single major source for most of the controversies in the history of science, and for the generation of many of the most acute conceptual problems with which scientists have had to cope" (p. 58; italics omitted). "[I]t is usually easier to explain away an anomalous experimental result than to dismiss out of hand a conceptual problem" (p. 64; italics omitted).

Referring in particular to discussions of absolute and relational theories of space and time, general relativity, and the interpretation of the field equations, W.H. Newton-Smith (1981, p. 89) states, "What is at stake in this debate is largely conceptual." Theories must be assessed "in terms of their power to avoid conceptual difficulties and not just in terms of their power to predict novel facts and explain known facts."

Ernst Mayr (1982, p. 23) rejects seeing "science merely as an accumulation of facts." In biology, "most major progress was made by the introduction of new concepts, or the improvement of existing concepts. Our understanding of the world is achieved more effectively by conceptual improvements than by the discovery of new facts, even though the two are not mutually exclusive."

A.A. Zinov'ev emphasizes how suitably chosen definitions, terms, and symbols render scientific discussion more intuitively obvious, compact, and convenient. In their absence, "the record of knowledge and operating with it become practically impossible. The search for the most convenient forms of abbreviation represents one of the most important tasks in the construction of scientific language in general" (1983, pp. 14–15).

What ultimately counts in an empirical science, says Daniel Hausman (1992, p. 298) is identifying regularities in the world. "But science does not proceed by spotting correlations among well-known observable properties of things. The construction of new concepts, of new ways of classifying and describing phenomena is an equally crucial part of science. Such conceptual work has been prominent in economics."

DEFINITIONS AND EMPIRICS: WALRAS'S LAW AND THE EQUATION OF EXCHANGE

Two notable tautologies in economics illustrate certain relations between definitional truths and empirical reality. Walras's Law illuminates interrelations among supplies of and demands for goods, services, securities, and money and among their supply/demand imbalances. The Law emphasizes that no one thing or group of things can be in excess supply or excess demand by itself. It thereby helps focus attention on the role in macroeconomic disorder of a distinctively functioning object of exchange—money. Similarly, it emphasizes that no change in tastes or technology can affect the supply or demand of a single thing alone; at least two things must be involved.

In one formulation, Walras's Law states that if a general-equilibrium equation system specifies equality between quantities supplied and demanded of all goods in the economy but one, then an equation for the one remaining good would be otiose. Instead of being mathematically independent, it would merely duplicate information already contained in the other equations. Supply-demand equilibrium for all goods but one already implies equilibrium for whatever the remaining good may be.

A second formulation, which straightforwardly implies the first, holds in disequilibrium as well as in equilibrium: the total value of all goods supplied equals the total value of all goods demanded. (The term "goods" is inclusive here, covering not only commodities but also labor and other services, securities, and money.) Quantities are valued at the prices at which exchanges are accomplished or attempted, as the case may be. With excess supplies counted as negative excess demands, the sum of the values of all excess demands is identically zero. ("Excess demand" and "excess supply" refer here to market disequilibrium and frustration of attempted transactions. Someone acting to increase his holdings of some good is *not* said to have an excess demand for it—not if he meets no frustration on the market.) (Lange 1942; Patinkin 1965, pp. 73, 229, 258–262, and passim; Patinkin 1987; Baumol 1965, pp. 340–342.)

Walras's Law is "an identity, ... little more than an accounting relationship" (Baumol 1965, p. 341). Where it does not hold, "people must, by definition, be planning to exchange goods which are not equal in value—an odd assertion for any monetary economy" (Baumol 1960, p. 30). The Law holds because budget constraints operate and market transactions are two-sided. Anyone trying to acquire something is by that very token offering something in exchange of equal value at the price contemplated. Anyone trying to sell something is demanding something of equal value in return. An attempted but frustrated transaction, like a successful one, involves two goods and not just one. Each frustrated transaction leaves two excess demand values, equal in size but opposite in algebraic sign.

Yet complications arise, and Walras's Law has itself sometimes been called into question. In addressing fringe doubts, it is necessary to clarify some of the very concepts that enter into the Law. In particular, one must distinguish between "notional" and "effective" supplies and demands and between stock and flow conceptions of quantities. This paper's purpose does not require rehearsing these technicalities (although comments about the balance of payments in a later section will be suggestive). Its purpose, instead, is simply to cite Walras's Law as one example of a useful tautology.

Another familiar example is the equation of exchange $MV = PQ$. Interpreted as a tautology, the equation is necessarily true because of how its terms are defined. It provides two different but reconcilable ways of looking at nominal income (gross domestic product or some such magnitude). Its left side interprets income as the product of the quantity of money and its income velocity of circulation; its right side, as output in physical units valued at the average price of a unit. (All four terms must be defined in more careful detail, of course, than would serve our purpose here.) The equation focuses attention on questions of how changes in nominal income are split between price and output changes and on the confrontation between the actual quantity of money and the demand for holdings of money. The latter is what velocity relates to, and saying so reminds us of how to make a transition from the tautological equation to the condition for equilibrium between money's supply and demand.

The equation of exchange enters into examples of what I call the translation test.[2] How plausible does the theory of an inflationary wage-price spiral unfueled by monetary expansion look when its implications about Q and V are drawn out? How well does the Keynesian theory of the determinants of aggregate spending, conceptualized with the aid of its tautology that nominal income = consumption + investment + government spending + exports − imports, translate into terms of $MV=PQ$? Conversely, how well does the monetarist formulation translate into the Keynesian formulation? Trying to translate a proposition from one conceptual framework into another can sometimes suggest new insights or expose concealed error.

Suppose someone maintains that the equation of exchange is false—not just trivial, not just lacking in applications, but false. He thereby shows that he does not understand what the equation means and how its terms are defined in interlocking ways. His position would be like that of someone claiming to have met an unusual person, a married bachelor, or a married man who, although not married to any particular woman, is nevertheless married.

The equation of exchange also illustrates the point that whether a particular tautology is useful in illuminating reality hinges on facts of reality. (Compare the discussion of Poincaré's conventionalism below.) Validity and usefulness, falsity and uselessness, are not the same things. A proposition lacking empirical application is not false merely for that reason.

We can readily imagine a "chairs" version of the equation of exchange. In $CV_c=PQ$, P and Q would be the same as before, C would be the number of chairs in existence in the country on average during a year, and V_c would be the "velocity" of chairs, meaning the ratio of nominal income to the number of chairs. Thanks to interlocking definitions, $CV_c=PQ$ is just as formally valid as $MV=PQ$; but because of facts about how money

---

[2]Thomas Hobbes (1651/1968, chaps. 8 and 46) suggested that one might test whether a piece of abstract philosophizing means anything by seeing how readily it could be translated from the original language into another.

functions that are not also true of chairs, the money version of the equation has a usefulness that the chairs version lacks. (One might quibble over exactly what counts as a chair, just as over what counts as money, but such quibbles would be relatively peripheral to the logic and usefulness of either equation.)

As this example illustrates, the tautological validity and empirical applicability of a proposition are not the same thing. Being a tautology ordinarily bars a proposition from being an exact description of reality, although it may be a stylization. The tautologies mentioned so far are tools, guides, reminders, illuminators, organizing devices that may prove useful in coming to grips with reality.

CONVENTIONS IN SCIENCE

The mathematician and physicist Henri Poincaré emphasized the role of conventions in science (Copleston 1985, chap. IX, pp. 271–273; Dantzig 1954, esp. pp. 52–53, 64–68; Poincaré 1952, 1958). He did not maintain, of course, that all scientific propositions are true by mere stipulation, agreement, habit, or custom. He warned of too sharp a dichotomy between convention and empirical fact. He criticized his disciple Edouard Le Roy for maintaining that science consists only of conventions and owes its apparent certitude to this fact (Poincaré 1958, chap. X, esp. p. 112). To suggest that the scientist actually *creates* scientific fact itself is going much too far toward nominalism. Scientific laws are not artificial creations. We have no reason to regard them as accidental, though it is impossible to prove they are not (p. 14).

Poincaré's position, rather, is that conventions fruitfully *stylize* reality (although I am not aware of his using that particular word). Often the scientist sharpens up rough or vague concepts, categories, and principles. He reaches propositions that are true by convention or definition and so are not open to falsification. But neither are they arbitrary. They have proved convenient for dealing with reality, just as a decimal coinage is more convenient (though not truer) than a nondecimal coinage. The properties of reality enter into determining whether a particular definition or convention is useful in dealing with it.

In mathematical physics, what was originally an empirical generalization may be so interpreted as to become a disguised definition, not open to falsification (Copleston 1985, chap. IX, p. 273). When an experimental law has received sufficient confirmation, Poincaré says, we may either

Chapter 14: Tautologies in Economics and the Natural Sciences 269

(1) leave it open to incessant revision, ending in demonstration that it is only approximate or (2) elevate it into *a principle* by adopting conventions that make it certainly true. A crystallized principle "is no longer subject to the test of experiment. It is not true or false, it is convenient" (1958, pp. 124–125). Proceeding that way has often been advantageous, but "if *all* the laws had been transformed into principles *nothing* would be left of science" (p. 125).

Actual bodies become slightly deformed when moved, expand when warmed, and so forth. Yet it would be hopelessly complicated for every statement about the motion of a body to allow for its bending and dilation. (Compare trying to formulate Walras's Law and the principles of balance-of-payments accounting to allow even for misunderstanding whether a particular property transfer was a sale or a gift.) For convenience, we invent rigid bodies and idealized types of motion (Poincaré 1958, pp. 125–126). The propositions of mechanics refer to these idealizations, which are nevertheless useful because they are somehow close enough to reality.[3] They are convenient, but convenience—not only for you or me but for all of us and our descendants—has an objective aspect (p. 140).

Poincaré instructively compares science to a library. Experimental physics buys the books. Mathematical physics—the tautological aspect—draws up the catalogue, making the library much more useful to readers. It also reveals gaps in the collection and so helps the librarian use his limited funds judiciously (1952, pp. 144–145).

The laws of science, then, are far from *mere* conventions. They relate to a reality existing independently of how human beings describe it. However, conventions do enter into stating its laws. Some prove more convenient than their alternatives, and this difference hinges on the nature of reality. Again, compare the "chairs" version with the "money" version of the equation of exchange.

The world of classical mechanics is an imaginary, sharpened world describable by infallibly true propositions that nevertheless aid in understanding the real world. This imaginary world is a model. Model-building involves use of conventional or tautological propositions.[4]

---

[3]For similar remarks about astronomical systems, space, time, and the measurement of time, see Poincaré 1958, pp. 27–28, 30, 36, 69, 140–141; 1952, pp. 90–91; and Dantzig 1954, pp. 52–53, 64–68. On the kinetic theory of gases, see Poincaré 1958, p. 131; 1952, p. 147; and Campbell 1957, pp. 126–131. For a general distinction between "empirical" and "abstract" objects and processes, see Zinov'ev 1983, pp. 57–59, 170–171, and passim).

[4]On relations between models, theories, and reality in economics and on the "category mistake" of trying to test models, see Hausman 1992, pp. 76–79, 245, 273, and passim.

FURTHER TAUTOLOGIES IN THE NATURAL SCIENCES

Mathematics is probably the standard example of a body of useful tautologies.[5] (Conant 1953, p. 105, calls mathematics a vast tautology; for Ayer 1946/1969, p. 331, "the truths of logic and mathematics are analytic propositions or tautologies," and J.S. Mill was wrong in supposing that a situation overthrowing any of them could arise.) Although—or because—the propositions of geometry and trigonometry are tautologically true, they are indispensable in surveying.[6] The concept of zero radically simplifies arithmetic and accounting.

In the natural sciences, classical (Newtonian) mechanics perhaps comes closest to sharing the tautological character of mathematics. The formula "force = mass × acceleration" pertains to reality, to be sure, but it also represents the interlocking of definitions. "[T]he formula which connects static force and acceleration ... is a tautology" (Dantzig 1954, p. 103). "If one wishes, one may say mass is defined in this manner, provided one already knows what force is. One might prefer to assume that mass is the known quantity and define force by this equation. What is seen here ... is the establishing of relations between various concepts in order to define terms. Which comes first and which comes later is often a matter of choice" (Teller 1980, p. 39).[7]

The same formula $f = ma$ illustrates the tautological element in defining units of measurement, whose importance in science is undeniable. In the meter-kilogram-second system, force is measured in newtons, one newton being the force required to give a mass of one kilogram an acceleration of one meter per second per second. (The unit of work or energy, the joule, is a force of one newton operating over a distance of one meter;

The usefulness of model-building in some cases and for some purposes hardly justifies insistence on it as the only acceptable method; it hardly justifies badgering researchers with routine cries of "What is your model?" and "How can your model be tested?"

[5] Sometimes tautologies look deceptively like brute facts of reality. It seems a brute fact that might quite conceivably have turned out otherwise that exactly 143 prime numbers occur in the range of 100 to 1000. Yet this specific count follows rigorously from the very concepts of number and prime number.

[6] Although experience played an indispensable role in its genesis, geometry is not an experimental science. "[E]xperience does not tell us which geometry is true, it tells us which is the most *convenient*" (Poincaré, *Space and Geometry*, quoted without page number in Dantzig 1954, p. 52).

[7] Poincaré 1952, chap. VI, esp. pp. 97–106, makes similar but more detailed remarks on the meanings and interrelations of force, mass, and acceleration. Compare Meyerson 1921/1991, esp. pp. 439–440, on the deductive nature of "rational mechanics."

and 1055 joules = one British thermal unit, a unit of some notoriety in U.S. tax-policy discussions of early 1993.)

Electrical identities are broadly similar in character to the mechanical identities. The definitional interrelations among such units as joule, watt, volt, ampere, coulomb, and newton again illustrate tautologies at work.

Gustav Robert Kirchhoff's laws for direct-current circuits are reminiscent of Walras's Law. They guide the formulation of equations to be solved for the currents and voltages in parts of complicated circuits (Nau 1958, pp. 39–43, 52, 72–73, 213, 305).[8] The current law states that the sum of the currents directed toward a node equals the sum of currents directed away from the node; with algebraic sign given proper attention, the sum of all the currents directed toward a node is zero. According to the voltage law, "the potential difference between two points in a circuit is the algebraic sum of the potential differences (scalar quantities) across each of the elements traced between the points"; the sum of all the voltages around any closed loop is thus zero (Nau 1958, pp. 39–40). Nau remarks (pp. 39, 41) that the voltage law holds "[b]y definition" and that "[b]ookkeeping will be facilitated" by certain conventions of notation.

Biology tells us that organisms possessing traits conducive to survival in their environments tend to survive and reproduce; others do not. This principle of natural selection, though practically a tautology, yields insights.

Classifying organisms into species, genera, and higher orders serves gathering and assessing evidence bearing on heredity and evolution. Ideal conceptualizations (never fully achieved) would make it tautologically true of a particular organism that, on the basis of its characteristics, it falls into predefined classes. Ever since Darwin, taxonomists have recognized that more than mere resemblance—rather, propinquity of descent—is involved in classification. Darwin warned against confusing similarities due to common descent with spurious similarities due to convergent evolution under environmental circumstances (Mayr 1982, pp. 210–212). Controversies have arisen among taxonomists of various phenetic schools, which refrain from taking evidence from descent into consideration, and adherents of cladistics, which does try to consider descent, and by a virtually automatic method that would force careful analysis and proper weighting of all characters. Both groups of taxonomists strive to eliminate subjectivity and arbitrariness from classifications (Mayr 1982, pp. 209–233). The

---

[8] I am indebted to Roger Garrison for calling my attention to Kirchhoff's laws and for this reference.

relevant point is that biologists have found it worthwhile to investigate and argue over the most expedient method of framing classifications, concepts, and tautologies.

Suitable classifications are important in linguistics also. Examples include the structural classification of languages as agglutinating, isolating, and inflecting, in their classification by families or descent, and in the classification of consonants as aspirated or unaspirated, voiced or unvoiced. It is tautologically true that in English the sound of g is the voiced and unaspirated counterpart of k, which is unvoiced and aspirated. The very meaning of "phoneme" implies that in any particular language, two (similar) sounds either do or do not constitute the same phoneme; there can be no in-between degree of resemblance in this respect.

Many more examples of tautology and truth by convention appear available in natural science. The several conservation laws,[9] the principle of least action, and the time-minimizing path of light (Gleick 1992, pp. 361, 366) are worth attention. So is the inverse-square feature common to Newtonian gravitation, Coulomb's law of electrostatic attraction and repulsion, the intensity of sound (subject to interferences), and the intensity of light and other electromagnetic radiation. This property accords with empirical observation, but one wonders whether it may not have a mathematical aspect making it more than a brute fact. The area of a sphere is 4π times the square of its radius, suggesting that the intensity of anything emanating from a central point is diluted over a larger area the greater the distance from that point, and diluted in such a way that the intensity is inversely proportional to that squared distance. Teller 1980, pp. 39–42, speaks in this connection of the thinning out of lines of gravitational force.) The formula for the area of a sphere "implies that the total energy crossing any sphere surrounding a point source is independent of the radius. Thus, the inverse-square law for the intensity of radiation at a distance r from a point source is in accord with the law of conservation of energy—the total energy of a wave remains the same even though the wave is spread over a greater area" (Ditchburn 1981, p. 933).

FURTHER TAUTOLOGIES IN ECONOMICS

Mathematical tautologies are familiar in microeconomics. Maximizations of profit, utility, and welfare entail equalization of various marginal

---

[9] Compare Richard Feynman's view of the conservation laws as sketched in Gleick 1992, p. 361.

Chapter 14: Tautologies in Economics and the Natural Sciences 273

magnitudes. Descriptions of long-run equilibrium under perfect competition are tautological yet illuminating. In macroeconomics, working out interlocking definitions of various quantifiable national income and product concepts has been deemed worthy of the Nobel prize.

The money-multiplier formula of money-and-banking textbooks, which involves various reserve and currency/deposit ratios, is tautologically true when the ratios in it are interpreted as actual ratios. When its ratios are reinterpreted as desired ones and the formula itself reinterpreted as an equilibrium condition, the discussion centering around it becomes a theory rather than a tautology. (Compare the transition, mentioned earlier, between the tautological equation of exchange and the condition of monetary equilibrium.)

The government budget constraint points out the logical, not merely empirical, necessity that government spending be covered by the aggregate of tax and similar revenues, borrowing, and money issue. Any proposition or proposal contradicting this tautology is immediately discredited. Sheer arithmetic, if heeded, should bring some discipline into political discussion. If a politician proposes to increase government spending, reduce taxes, and reduce the budget deficit, he is coming awfully close to implying the issue of money, to be counted as a kind of revenue, unless he can give a plausible Lafferesque explanation of how reduced tax rates will nevertheless increase tax revenues. President Bush's 1992 campaign proposal for letting taxpayers designate 10 percent of their payments to go for reducing the national debt—debt, not deficit—came awfully close, in its context, to implying the issue of new money.

Paul Samuelson reports that the mathematician Stanislaw Ulam

> used to tease me by saying, "Name me one proposition in all of the social sciences which is both true and non-trivial." This was a test that I always failed. But now, some thirty years later, on the staircase so to speak, an appropriate answer occurs to me: The Ricardian theory of comparative advantage; the demonstration that trade is mutually profitable even when one country is absolutely more—or less—productive in terms of every commodity. That it is logically true need not be argued before a mathematician; that it is not trivial is attested by the thousands of important and intelligent men who have never been able to grasp the doctrine for themselves or to believe it after it was explained to them. (1969/1972, p. 683)

Significantly, Samuelson calls the proposition "logically true," in other words, a tautology. The principle of comparative advantage is best seen, in my concurring view, not as a substantive empirical proposition but as a piece of reasoning useful in exposing a common fallacy.[10] That fallacy rejects the possibility of mutually beneficial trade between two countries one of which is more efficient or enjoys greater productivity or lower real cost than the other across the entire range of potentially tradable goods. Instead of quibbling about the meaning or possibility of such comparisons, the principle of comparative advantage concocts, for the sake of argument, an extreme case in which the postulated difference is unequivocal. It goes on to show that even then, in the case supposedly most embarrassing for free trade, gains from trade are available to both parties. It provides an "even-if/even-then" argument.

BALANCE-OF-PAYMENTS CONCEPTS AND ANALYSIS

Further examples in international economics are instructive enough to merit a separate section. The concepts of balance-of-payments accounting, as of ordinary accounting, are tautologies. Just as the two sides of a firm's balance sheet have identical totals, thanks to carefully formulated interlocking concepts, the same is true of the credit or plus and debit or minus sides of a country's balance-of-payments statement for a definite time period. This equality of the two totals presupposes complete and accurate information on all aspects of all relevant transactions. In practice, inadequacy of information plagues presentation of an actual statement. Conceptual difficulties (concerning, for example, the uncertain classification of transactors as residents or nonresidents, the ambiguous dating of some transactions, and the handling of smuggled goods) require adopting somewhat arbitrary conventions.

Quibbles can thus arise. The balance-of-payments concept, like other accounting conventions, the equation of exchange, and Walras's Law, may be defended against quibbles by expounding the nature and rationale of analytical tautologies. An analogy comes to mind with what Stephan Körner calls "more or less near-empirical, but still non-empirical mathematics" (1966, chap. VII, esp. pp. 98, 106–107). In reality, boundaries between various classes may be fuzzy, and a proposition about a particular entity being a member or nonmember of a particular class may be

---

[10]While one might sensibly do empirical research related to comparative advantage in some way or another, it would be a category mistake to embark on *testing* the principle of comparative advantage, just as on testing the Heckscher-Ohlin theorem or the Rybczynski theorem or the equation of exchange.

"neutral" rather than "true" or "false." Still, we may treat inexact predicates and classes as if they were exact, so replacing neutral propositions by nonneutral ones. We can exhibit arithmetical concepts that are naturally and frequently identified—though never identical—with empirical ones. Discussion of these "complexes" is not empirical; it amounts at best to a "near-empirical" arithmetic.[11] In balance-of-payments accounting, we idealize and sharpen the concepts involved, arriving at propositions that are logical rather than brute empirical truths.

No one, to my knowledge, denies that these "near-empirical" categories and propositions are useful in analyzing empirical reality. In particular, if transactions are classified into separate "accounts" of the balance of payments (say current account, private capital account, and official settlements account), then the "principle of compensating balances" comes into play: imbalance in one direction in one or more of the accounts must be matched by opposite imbalance in one or more of the remaining accounts. (Compare Walras's Law: excess demand or supply of one thing must be matched by opposite imbalance of one or more other things.) If a country is running a deficit on current account, the balance-of-payments tautology underscores the question of how that deficit is being "financed." An enlightening truism is sometimes forgotten: no deficit can arise or persist unless it gets financed somehow or other. It is similarly enlightening to recognize a country's balance of payments as the aggregate of the individual balances of payments of the persons, firms, government agencies, and other organizations composing the national economy.

The central formula of each of the three leading approaches to balance-of-payments analysis—the elasticities, absorption, and monetary approaches—is valid because of interlocking definitions of the terms it contains. The question of how these three approaches interrelate points to the application of Niels Bohr's "principle of complementarity" (Teller 1980, pp. 93, 105–106, 138–140) beyond its original range, as Bohr himself had foreseen. He recommended treating the wave and particle theories of light as complementary: physicists could legitimately employ each theory where it seemed to work, even if they did not (yet) know how to reconcile those seemingly contradictory theories. In balance-of-payments analysis, similarly, economists may legitimately draw whatever insights they can

---

[11] Körner maintains that "[d]eductive abstraction, the cutting out of irrelevancies, ... the elimination of inexactness, the drawing of sharp demarcation-lines through indefinite conceptual borders" (1966, p. 167) are applied, for example, in the various systems of geometry (p. 112) and in classical mechanics (p. 159).

from each of the three approaches, if necessary leaving their possible reconciliation until later.

The absorption approach relates a country's international surplus (or deficit) on current account to its excess (or shortfall) of national production in relation to national absorption, the latter being output absorbed in consumption, investment, and government activity. Equivalently, it relates the country's current-account surplus (or deficit) to the excess (or shortfall) of national saving in relation to national investment, a government surplus or deficit counting as part of or as a deduction from national saving.

The monetary approach relates a country's overall international surplus or deficit (roughly, its balance on the official-settlements concept) to changes in the aggregate balance sheet of its monetary institutions. Its central formula, like the absorption-approach formula, hinges on interlocking definitions of its terms. Whether the approach is useful in practice depends largely on whether monetary and nonmonetary accounts can be distinguished clearly enough. One must avoid reading causal significance into mere tautological truths. It is a mistake, in particular, to suppose that growth of a country's money supply necessarily represents *intentional* buildups of cash balances.

The elasticities approach centers around an algebraic expression whose sign supposedly indicates whether currency devaluation "improves" or "worsens" the country's balance of payments. This "stability" formula features terms for demand and supply elasticities of imports and exports. The mathematics of its derivation makes the formula tautologically valid, presupposing in it special though often tacit definitions of the elasticities (involving in what respects they are *mutatis mutandis* rather than *ceteris paribus* elasticities). Whether or not the approach is useful for analysis of the real world depends largely on whether the conceptions of elasticity necessary to make the formula correct are near enough to or too far from ordinary conceptions of price elasticity.

Sidney S. Alexander (1952; 1959) criticized the elasticities analysis of exchange-rate adjustment as mere implicit theorizing. The formula for "normal" response of the balance of payments derives purely from manipulation of definitions and has no operational content, he said, unless the import and export demand and supply functions whose elasticities enter into it are independently specified. Those functions can hardly be specified so that their elasticities are "partial" elasticities, indicating how sensitively the quantities respond to their own prices when incomes and other prices remain unchanged; for exchange-rate adjustment simply cannot leave these other things unchanged. Alternatively, the elasticities might be interpreted as "total," indicating how the quantities respond when not only their own prices but also everything else change as in fact they will change in direct or indirect response to the exchange-rate adjustment. The stability formula then becomes tautologically correct but empty. No one could know the sizes of its "total" elasticities without *already* having a complete analysis of how domestic and foreign economies respond to the exchange rate. Carried to its ultimate degree, the total-elasticities approach would assert—emptily—that what happens depends on the elasticity of the country's balance of payments with respect to the exchange rate (Pearce 1970, passim).

But the futility of an approach carried to its ultimate does not imply futility carried judiciously part way. The analyst seeks some compromise between meaningful but unmanageable realism and detail at one extreme and apparent simplicity but emptiness at the other extreme. In balance-of-payments analysis, such a compromise may well involve ignoring or stripping away complications concerning the exact specification of the elasticities. An admittedly tautological formula does nevertheless prove useful in contemplating what conditions would contribute and what ones would impair "normal" response of the balance of payments to the exchange rate.[12]

CONCLUSION

The examples presented here help one recognize a particular style or ingredient of argument and better understand its application in particular contexts from its perhaps more familiar use in others. This recognition should help a writer forestall or answer illegitimate objections, such as empirical quibbles raised against tautologically true propositions like Walras's Law and the equation of exchange. Concepts may legitimately be formulated so that certain propositions about relations among them are not merely true but necessarily true. Many propositions of science are true as a matter of convention, yet conventions are not arbitrary. Whether a convention is useful and convenient hinges on whether and how it makes contact with reality.

---

[12] Still other examples of tautology in economics may be found. James R. Wible (1982–1983) gives an insightful if unenthusiastic review of tautological strands in the macroeconomic literature of rational expectations.

REFERENCES

Alexander, Sidney S. "Effects of a Devaluation on a Trade Balance." *IMF Staff Papers*, (April 1952): 263–278.

———. "Effects of a Devaluation: A Simplified Synthesis of Elasticities and Absorption Approaches." *American Economic Review* (March 1959): 22–42.

Ayer, Alfred J. "The *A Priori*." 1946. In *Necessary Truth*, edited by L.W. Sumner and J. Woods, 27–43. New York: Random House, 1969.

Baumol, William J. "Monetary and Value Theory: Comment." *Review of Economic Studies* (October 1960): 29–31.

———. *Economic Theory and Operations Analysis*. 2nd ed. Englewood Cliffs, N.J.: Prentice Hall, 1965.

Campbell, Norman R. *Foundations of Science*. 1919. Reprinted New York: Dover, 1957.

Conant, James B. *Modern Science and Modern Man*. Garden City: Doubleday Anchor Books, 1953.

Copleston, Frederick. *A History of Philosophy*. Vols. 7 to 9. New York: Doubleday, Image Book, 1985.

Dantzig, Tobias. *Henri Poincaré*. New York: Scribner's, 1954.

Ditchburn, R.W. "Light." In *Encyclopedia Britannica*, vol. 10: 928–949. Chicago: Encyclopaedia Britannica, 1981.

Gleick, James. *Genius: The Life and Science of Richard Feynman*. New York: Pantheon, 1992.

Harsanyi, John C. *Essays on Ethics, Social Behavior, and Scientific Explanation*. Dordrecht and Boston: Reidel, 1976.

Hausman, Daniel M. *The Inexact and Separate Science of Economics*. Cambridge, U.K., and New York: Cambridge University Press, 1992.

Hobbes, Thomas. *Leviathan*. 1651. Harmondsworth and Baltimore: Penguin, 1968.

Körner, Stephan. *Experience and Theory*. New York: Humanities Press, 1966.

Lange, Oskar. "Say's Law: A Restatement and Criticism." In *Studies in Mathematical Economics and Econometrics*, edited by O. Lange et al., 49–68. Chicago: University of Chicago Press, 1942.

Laudan, Larry. *Progress and Its Problems.* Berkeley and Los Angeles: University of California Press, 1977.

Mayr, Ernst. *The Growth of Biological Thought.* Cambridge, Mass.: Belknap Press of Harvard University Press, 1982.

Meyerson, Émile. *Explanation in the Sciences.* 1921. Translated by Mary-Alice Sipfle and David A. Sipfle. Dordrecht and Boston: Kluwer, 1991.

Nau, Robert H. *Basic Electrical Engineering.* New York: Ronald Press, 1958.

Newton-Smith, W.H. *The Rationality of Science.* Boston and London: Routledge & Kegan Paul, 1981.

Patinkin, Don. *Money, Interest, and Prices.* 2nd ed. New York: Harper & Row, 1965.

———. "Walras's Law." In *The New Palgrave,* vol. 4: 863–868. New York: Stockton Press, 1987.

Pearce, I.F. *International Trade.* New York: Norton, 1970.

Poincaré, Henri. *Science and Hypothesis.* Translated by "W.J.G." New York: Dover, 1952.

———. *The Value of Science.* Translated by G.B. Halsted. New York: Dover, 1958.

Samuelson, Paul A. "The Way of an Economist." 1969. Presidential Address of the International Economic Association. Reprinted in *The Collected Scientific Papers of Paul A. Samuelson,* vol. 3: 675–685. Cambridge, Mass.: MIT Press, 1972.

Teller, Edward. *The Pursuit of Simplicity.* Malibu: Pepperdine University Press, 1980.

Wible, James R. "The Rational Expectations Tautologies." *Journal of Post Keynesian Economics* (Winter 1982/1983): 199–207.

Yeager, Leland B., and Alan Rabin. "Monetary Aspects of Walras's Law and the Stock-Flow Problem." *Atlantic Economic Journal* 25 (March 1997): 18–36.

Zinov'ev, A.A. *Logical Physics.* Translated by O.A. Germogenova. Edited by R.S. Cohen. Dordrecht and Boston: D. Reidel Publishing Company, 1983.

PART II
Politics and Philosophy

CHAPTER 15

Free Will and Ethics*

A PERSISTENT OLD ISSUE

The very topic of ethics requires dipping into metaphysics. Although I cannot settle an old issue, I must recognize it. Are individuals' actions and even their decisions, desires, and characters fully determined by circumstances ultimately outside their own control? If that were true—if people lack free will and true choice—then personal responsibility would lack meaning. Praise and blame, reward and punishment, would have no application; and ethics as a field of study would lack any genuine subject matter.

This position, right or wrong, seems to have been the position of Immanuel Kant. Throughout his *Groundwork* (1785/1964), Kant acknowledges an antinomy between freedom of the will and the prevalence of causal laws of nature. He maintains, however, that freedom of the will is a necessary presupposition of morality. He suggests that the antinomy might somehow be resolved through his distinction between the intelligible and sensible worlds (noumenal and phenomenal worlds, in his technical terminology). Experience, filtered through the Kantian "categories" of perception and understanding, imposes the idea of tight causality; but unknowable characteristics of the noumenal world of things in themselves might make freedom of the human will genuine. Confessedly, all this is quite mysterious to me.

The terms "free will" (or "free choice") and "determinism" have no agreed precise meanings, so I cannot begin by defining them. Exploring what these terms and concepts might mean and how they interrelate is a main task of this appendix.

We must, however, avoid "essentialism." As criticized by Karl Popper (e.g., 1985, pp. 88–94), essentialism means focusing on one or more pieces

---

*Appendix to Chapter 2, pp. 40–58 and endnotes, in my *Ethics as Social Science* (Cheltenham, U.K., and Northampton, Mass.: Elgar, 2001).

of terminology, supposing that each one labels a definite aspect of reality, brooding over these aspects or concepts to grasp the "essence" of each, and perhaps brooding further over whether the realities corresponding to two or more concepts could exist together.[1] Trying to gain knowledge in this way proceeds backward. Perceiving uniformities and diversities in the real world belongs ahead of brooding over words to label them. Conceivably, traditional formulations of the whole supposed issue of free will versus determinism will prove misconceived.

SCHLICK ON THE ISSUE

My admiration for two ethicists in particular, Moritz Schlick and Henry Hazlitt, predisposed me toward their solutions; yet in the end I find them incomplete or otherwise unsatisfying. Schlick regarded the supposed issue as a mere pseudo-problem: determinism and free will reconcile (1930/1961, chap. VII). Causality can operate while leaving individuals some freedom not only over what acts they perform but also over what choices they make. The opposite of freedom is compulsion, and determination does not mean compulsion. In the words of R.E. Hobart, whose views are discussed below, compulsion implies causation but causation does not necessarily imply compulsion.[2]

Schlick identifies a confusion between descriptive and prescriptive laws. Scientific laws *describe* how the world works; they do not *prescribe* events; they do not resemble totally enforced legislation *making* events unfold as they do. Kepler's Laws describe how the planets revolve around the sun; they are not prescriptions compelling them to revolve as they do. The law of demand describes how buyers respond to alternative levels of an item's price (apart from other overriding influences); it does not compel buyers to behave in the way it describes.

---

[1] Walter Eucken (1950, pp. 50–51, 329–330) effectively blasts such essentialism or conceptual realism in economics.

[2] Just what is compulsion? How may we distinguish acts done under compulsion from free acts for which a person is responsible? In a sense, as Gerald Dworkin (1970/1984) notes, a person does his every act because he prefers it to any alternative open to him under the circumstances—even submitting to a highwayman. Dworkin distinguishes, then, between two sorts of desires or reasons for action. A free act is one motivated by a reason that the agent finds acceptable. A person acts under compulsion when responding to a reason that he does not want to have.

Although Dworkin may be on the right track, his distinction is inexact. One may undergo an operation, free from compulsion, while wishing that the reason for the operation did not exist.

These distinctions help explain, then, how a person could conceivably be choosing and acting free from compulsion even when his choices and actions are causally determined and in principle predictable. The opposite, presumably, would be choices made and actions taken by sheer chance or baseless caprice. Choices and actions need not be stochastic or capricious to be properly called free.

If their choices and actions were totally unfree, people could not properly be held answerable for them. We do not blame a person for firing a shot if someone stronger forced the gun into his hand and pulled his finger against the trigger. We do not hold someone guilty of a crime if he was genuinely insane and lacked any control over his decision and action. It would be pointless to hold the man whose hand was forcibly manipulated or the insane person accountable for an action not truly his own. Neither is responsible because neither enjoyed freedom of choice and will over his act. (Clear-cut examples like these should not, however, invite multiplying excuses to relieve persons of responsibility for their actions.)

Responsibility presupposes a point for applying a motive, such as desire to avoid blame or punishment or to win praise or reward. Frequently it makes eminent sense to apply motives to people and hold them responsible for their choices and actions. This could not be true if no grounds existed for attributing freedom to people. Hence there *are* grounds for belief in freedom in some sense associated with responsibility.

More exactly, perhaps, the whole free-will/determinism controversy is a chimerical basis for questioning ordinary ethical concepts. Schlick's argument comes across to me as I have summarized it.

C.A. Campbell (1951/1966) finds Schlick's distinction between descriptive and prescriptive laws irrelevant. The usual reason for thinking that moral freedom presupposes some breach in causal continuity is not a belief that causal laws compel in the way legislation compels but instead is the belief that an unbroken causal chain leaves no one able to choose and act other than as he does.

Moral responsibility is *not* the same, says Campbell, as scope for sensibly applying motives. Dogs can be trained with punishments and rewards; yet we do not hold dogs morally responsible for what they do. We can judge dead men morally responsible for particular actions without being able to affect those past actions. Perhaps we might reinterpret Schlick as meaning that a person is morally responsible when his motive could *in principle* be affected by reward or punishment, whether or not the judges or observers are in a position to apply it. But this modification would change Schlick's theory, which links the whole meaning and importance of moral responsibility "to our potential control of future conduct in the interests of society" (Campbell 1951/1966, p. 115).

Schlick identifies "Who is morally blameworthy?" with "Who is to be punished?"—paradoxically, given his view of punishment as a purely educative measure, without retributive content. We often think it proper to "punish" a person, in Schlick's educative sense, even without holding him morally blameworthy (Campbell 1951/1966, p. 116). We punish the dog. We punish demonstrators who may be obstructing traffic from motives that even we, the judges, may think noble.

I'll try to rephrase or interpret Campbell's objection. Schlick sees instrumental, educative, value in applying rewards and punishments, which he identifies with holding people morally responsible. We could hardly do so unless we attributed some freedom to people. But is this a valid linking of ideas? Perhaps rewards and punishments and their generally good consequences are just particular events in the unbroken causal chain. Metaphysical freedom cannot be established by pointing to the apparent or genuine good consequences of reward and punishment.

Campbell suspects that Schlick and many other philosophers cannot recognize contracausal freedom as prerequisite to moral responsibility because, while denying that freedom, they do accept the commonsense belief in moral responsibility (Campbell 1951/1966, p. 117).

His own purpose, Campbell concludes (p. 135), has been not actually to defend free will but rather to show "that the problem as traditionally posed is a real, and not a pseudo, problem."

HAZLITT'S RECONCILIATION

Henry Hazlitt (1964/1972, chap. 27) tries to reconcile free will and responsibility with determinism, interpreted as omnipresent cause and effect. He agrees "that everything that happens is a necessary outcome of a preceding state of things" (p. 269). Like Schlick, however, he stresses that causation is not compulsion. Absence, not presence, of causation is what would exempt people from moral responsibility. "It is precisely because we do not decide or act without cause that ethical judgments serve a purpose.... The knowledge that we will be held 'responsible' for our acts by others, or even that we will be responsible in our own eyes for the consequences of our acts, must influence those acts, and must tend to influence them in the direction of moral opinion" (p. 275).

Hazlitt warns against confusing determinism with materialism, interpreted as the dogma that all causation, even in human affairs, operates ultimately through physical and chemical processes alone. He especially warns against confusing determinism with fatalism, which he interprets as the dogma that events will unfold as they are bound to do, regardless of how people try to promote or prevent them. Fatalism in this peculiar sense is obviously false. Human decisions, choices, wishes, reflection, and will clearly *do* influence the course of events. If, contrary to fact, they did not do so, or if they operated only stochastically, outside of causal chains, then notions of responsibility and ethics would have no application.

Hazlitt accepts universal causation, then, but distinguishes sharply between its supposed operation solely in material ways and its operation in ways leaving scope for human decision and will. But can this distinction carry all the weight Hazlitt places on it?

TWO FURTHER ATTEMPTS AT RECONCILIATION

Michael Slote (1990) explains how making and implementing ethical judgments could be sensible *even if* determinism prevailed, a question he does not tackle. Here I interpret Slote's argument together with a commentary by Peter van Inwagen (1990) and forgo trying to paraphrase each separately.

We may label a person or a dog and certain actions as "vicious" and guard against and "punish" them. Yet we may recognize that the person's or dog's disposition and actions trace to unfortunate genes or mental illness or previous maltreatment, which attenuates or dispels moral culpability. We are not necessarily inconsistent in both recognizing the dispositions and actions as determined yet judging and punishing them as vicious. Our judging and punishing can themselves be links in the chain of deterministic causation and may make the dispositions and actions less vicious than they would otherwise be.

Similarly, we tend to judge actual murder "more wrong" than a failed attempt; we revile and punish an actual murderer more severely than an attempted murderer. Both culprits may have had the same intentions, and only sheer luck may have frustrated one attempt. Still it may make sense to condemn and punish the successful murderer more severely. How a person is judged and punished may thus reasonably depend on more than what he freely willed. Several considerations may warrant distinguishing between actual and attempted murder. Evil intentions may be harder to prove in a failed attempt. The gradation in punishments may help emphasize the public's solemn condemnation of murder, and in subtle psychological ways it may cause more murder attempts to fail than otherwise would.

An analogy of sorts holds between these considerations and F.A. Hayek's argument (1960, chap. 6) about merit versus value in determining a person's income. Even though the market value of a person's efforts probably does not correspond closely to his moral merit, powerful reasons argue for allowing market supply and demand to establish his income anyway. Such remuneration may usefully guide individuals on how to use their special talents and knowledge, and it may motivate appropriate kinds and degrees of risk-bearing. Above all, perhaps, alternative institutions intended to attune remunerations to moral merit appear very unattractive upon close analysis. Again, a person's free will and intentions should not be the only factors governing how other people treat him.

Admittedly, full-fledged determinism still poses embarrassment for consequentialist considerations like these. If we recognize that our making and implementing ethical judgments and adopting this or that set of institutions are themselves fully caused and are mere links in a tight causal chain, we run into awkward paradoxes. These pertain to the whole free-will/determinism issue itself, however, rather than to ethical issues in particular.

DETERMINISM AS FATALISM

Determinism in its most extreme version (commonly attributed to Pierre-Simon de Laplace) is fatalism even more comprehensive than the variety rejected by Hazlitt. It recognizes human will and decision as elements in one grand chain of universal causation. Everything that is happening or has happened or will happen has been fated from the beginning of time to happen exactly as it does or did or will. Causation operates tightly in every detail. Even all of a person's thoughts as he deliberates whether to accept a new job or break off a love affair, and even all other persons' reactions to his decision, were fated to be exactly as they turn out. Even all philosophical controversies over the free-will issue itself take an exactly predetermined course. Far from denying that ideas and choices have consequences, extreme determinism maintains that even these are links in the great causal chain.

Laplace regards the present state of the universe as the effect of its anterior state and the cause of its next state. Ineluctable necessity rules.

Nothing would be uncertain for a sufficiently vast intelligence; the future and the past alike would be present to its eyes. A true act of free will is impossible. Without a determinative motive, not even the nearest thing to a free will could originate even actions considered indifferent. The contrary opinion is an illusion of the mind (Meyerson 1921/1991, pp. 563–564, citing Laplace's *Théorie analytique des probabilités*). (Boyle et al. 1976, pp. 57, 86, give apt quotations from Laplace; further discussion of Laplacean determinism occurs in Popper 1982, pp. xx–xxi, 123–124, and passim; and Georgescu-Roegen 1971, p. 170 and passim.)

Clarence Darrow used to defend his clients with such an argument. The accused criminal is a mere link in the chain. Even his character and his ability or inability to reshape it trace ultimately to causes outside himself, and he is therefore not responsible and not properly punishable for his crimes (Hospers 1961/1966, p. 41).

Can anyone really believe in such tight universal causation? If only Queen Victoria had been a man, the Salic Law would not have separated the hitherto linked crowns of Great Britain and Hanover upon her—his—accession in 1837; and the subsequent history of Germany, Europe, and the world would probably have unfolded much differently from how it actually did. (Reflection on the events of 1866, 1870–1871, 1914, and 1917 helps explain why.) Much depended, then, on which particular sperm happened to fertilize her mother's ovum at Victoria's conception in 1818.[3] Yet this micro event and all its momentous consequences were bound to occur exactly as they did. Thus must strict determinism maintain.

No one, to my knowledge, espouses this position consistently. It is just too preposterous—though I may be mistaken in saying so.

INCREASING COMPLEXITY

One reason for calling full determinism preposterous is that the world seems to be getting more complicated over time. It is hard to imagine how the less complicated past might contain all the information necessary

---

[3]This particular example is my own, to the best of my recollection; yet it is in the spirit of essays collected in Squire 1931. There, for example, Winston Churchill speculates on what would have happened if Lee had not [sic] won the battle of Gettysburg, Hilaire Belloc on what would have happened if the cart that in fact blocked Louis XVI's escape at Varennes in June 1791 had gotten stuck before reaching the crucial place, and Emil Ludwig on what would have happened if German Emperor Frederick III had lived to reign until 1914 and not just for his actual 99 days in 1888.

Such examples mesh nicely with currently popular theories of "chaos" or "complexity."

to specify the more complicated present and future in complete detail. Such complete specification would constitute at least an equal degree of complexity *already* prevailing.

The world is getting "more complicated" by any ordinary standard of judgment. More people are living than in the past, with all their individual characteristics and thoughts and actions. The number and intricacy of the works of man are increasing, including the texts of all the books and articles ever written. The state of the world at any instant includes all the information and all the misprints in all these documents, and even the slightest details of all the flyspecks and coffee stains in individual copies.

Affairs on earth interact with affairs throughout the universe. Men or man-made instruments have disturbed the surfaces of the moon and Mars, and rockets have escaped our solar system. Eclipses, comets, planetary movements, and supernovas have affected human activities directly and through popular, religious, and scientific beliefs.

If a later state is fully determined by an earlier state, then that earlier state must contain aspects or properties or patterns or whatever—whose totality I am calling "information"—specifying that later state in complete detail. And if the world is generally getting more complicated over time, then more information is required to specify a later state than an earlier state. It is hard to imagine how all the detailed information necessary to specify the more complicated later state already existed in the simpler earlier state. It is hard to believe that even the tiniest fraction of a second after the Big Bang, the universe already contained detailed coded information about everything that would ever happen thereafter, including the exact configuration of every wisp of cloud I observed during my last airplane trip and including the exact times at which and pressures with which I would strike each key during my current session at my computer keyboard. Full determinism seems still more incredible because it involves each state's specifying not only one subsequent state but also all the infinitely many intervening states ("infinitely many" if time is continuous).

These points tell against complete causal determination.[4] Its being hard to conceive of does not, however, constitute disproof. Perhaps increasing

---

[4]Considerations resembling these appear in Peirce 1958, selection 9, an article I had read and then forgotten many years before first drafting this appendix.

My appeal to increasing complexity and information content may admittedly appear to run afoul of the second law of thermodynamics, the entropy law, and I may be quite wrong. On the other hand, that law in its central context pertains to energy and its degradation; and its rationale is perhaps most clearly set forth with reference to the statistical properties of crowds of nonliving molecules. The law may not fully carry over to the present context.

overall complexity is a mere illusion. Perhaps greater complexity in some dimensions—in the products of the human mind and in the details of flyspecks on published pages—is offset somehow by reduced complexity in other dimensions. If so, what might they be? Perhaps greater complexity on our earth, which, like our whole solar system, is an open system, is offset somehow by reduced complexity elsewhere in the universe. Even so, wouldn't the point still hold that increasing complexity on our earth implies incomplete predictability of human affairs? By what mechanism, if any, could any offsetting reduced complexity elsewhere save the complete predictability of human affairs, if only in principle? But perhaps I am wrong about my notion of information required for complete causal specification.

Speaking of total causal determination, we may well pause to ask just what "cause" and "causality" mean. Trying to frame objection-free definitions is a sobering challenge. This very difficulty throws some slight extra embarrassment onto doctrines of a great unbroken causal chain.

In arguing for indeterminacy or openness in the universe, Karl Popper distinguishes among "three worlds."[5] World 1 contains physical objects—rocks, trees, structures, living creatures, and physical fields of force. World 2 is the psychological world of fears and hopes, of dispositions to act, and of subjective experiences of all kinds. World 3 contains products of the human mind—art works, ethical values, social institutions, the intellectual contents of books (books as physical objects belong to World 1), scientific problems, theories, including mistaken theories, and solved and unsolved puzzles. Especially characteristic of World 3 is human knowledge put into words.

Autonomous objects exist even in World 3. Human beings originally conceived of the prime numbers and conjectured about their properties, but the primes and their properties have taken on an objective existence. It is a bare fact, but a logical truth rather than a contingent empirical fact,

---

One difference from the context of inanimate processes is that in the evolution of information, as in biological evolution, selection may accomplish a kind of inner directedness. It may be that on our earth and perhaps even in the universe as a whole, neither kind of evolution violates the second law.

[5] See, for example, Popper 1985, selections 4 and 21; 1982, section 38; and his 1972 lecture, reprinted 1982. Earlier (1908, reprinted 1958, pp. 358–379; and 1908, reprinted 1958, pp. 404–405), Charles S. Peirce had distinguished among "three Universes of Experience." Popper's World 3 and Peirce's first universe correspond fairly well, as do Popper's World 1 and Peirce's second universe, but the remaining world and universe correspond loosely at best.

that 143 prime numbers, no more and no fewer, exist in the range of 100 to 1000. Euclid already proved the infinitude of prime numbers: no largest one exists. But is there a largest *pair* of *twin* primes (like 17 and 19, 521 and 523, 1451 and 1453)? No one, the last I heard, has actually proved either a "yes" or a "no" answer. The problem objectively exists as a challenge to human intelligence.

The autonomous objects of World 3 interact with World 1 through the human perceptions, feelings, dispositions, and decisions of World 2. The challenges of pure mathematics lead to results that find applications in computer hardware and software, which in turn function in changing the physical world. Some challenges of her field lead a mathematician to results that enhance her reputation and win her an appointment at a prestigious university, where she has a house—a physical object—built in accordance with her tastes and increased income.

World 3 is intrinsically open or emergent, says Popper (1972/1982, p. 5); any theory holding scientific and artistic creation ultimately explainable by physics and chemistry seems absurd to him. Moreover, interrelations among the three Worlds render the whole universe partly open and emergent.

I am not sure that Popper would agree, but his concept of World 3 in particular, the world of things like scientific theories, does help underline how preposterous it is to suppose that each later state of affairs is totally specified by earlier states. Scientific progress does occur. New knowledge, by its very meaning, was not available in advance; the notion of something being known before it is known is self-contradictory. Is it plausible, then, to maintain that all the mathematical and physical knowledge not yet achieved but that will be achieved in the next hundred years somehow already exists in latent form, already somehow coded into the current state of the universe, along with the date and other details of the discovery of each bit of that future knowledge? (Many of the associated challenges already exist as problems belonging to Popper's World 3, but this is not the same as the preexistence of solutions both to unsolved problems and to problems not yet even formulated.)

CHANCE

Gerd Gigerenzer and coauthors (1989/1993, esp. pp. 59–68, 276–285) review apparent and supposed implications of probability theory and statistics for free will versus determinism. These disciplines have been successfully

Chapter 15: Free Will and Ethics

applied on the assumption that some sheer random processes do operate in the world, which is some evidence, if weak, that determinism in nature is incomplete. Scientists and philosophers such as James Clerk Maxwell and Charles Peirce have believed that airtight causality does not operate in every little detail of the universe, that some element of randomness remains, and that free will might occupy this gap somehow. And such gaps might not be confined to the subatomic level that quantum theory deals with. (Here I insert the obligatory allusion to Heisenberg's indeterminacy principle concerning subatomic randomness.) Maxwell and Peirce (1877, reprinted 1958, p. 95; articles of 1891, reprinted 1955, pp. 9, 319) pointed to the statistical or probabilistic aspect of the kinetic theory of gases, which envisages the constituent molecules moving at different randomly determined velocities and changing velocities as they collide with one another and with the sides of the container. Peirce also noted the random nature of the biological mutations on which natural selection operates.

Karl Popper also argued for the genuineness of chance events even above the subatomic level or even the molecular level. What explains the statistical stability of the heads and tails produced by a penny-tossing machine? Or consider Alfred Landé's conception of dropping ivory balls onto the center of a suitably positioned steel blade, very nearly half of the balls falling on each side. For a determinist, barred by his doctrine from appealing to randomness and reduced to imagining the mutual cancellation of many small causes, the lawlike statistical process must remain ultimately irreducible and inexplicable (Popper 1982, pp. 96–104).

Quantum-level and other small-scale indeterminacies gain relevance from the fact that micro differences can have macro consequences. Erwin Schrödinger gave the hypothetical example of a cat whose survival or death in an experiment depends on an apparatus detecting particles emitted randomly and infrequently in the decay of a radioactive element. The far-reaching consequences of Queen Victoria's sex, already mentioned, provide another example. This micro-to-macro principle is further illuminated by the mathematics of chaos, even though the (hypothetical) systems used in expounding chaos theory are fully deterministic.

An element of sheer chance in the universe appears to operate, then, along with the causality that is also evident. Admittedly, the pervasive *appearance* of chance or randomness does not rigorously rule out complete Laplacean causality. (Laplace himself made contributions to probability theory.) My statistics professor at Columbia University around 1948, Frederick C. Mills, avoided speaking of "chance," period; he always used some such expression as "the complex of unknown causes called chance." Perhaps he had good reason for speaking so carefully. (In his 1938 book, p. 436, he lists three assumptions underlying the derivation of the normal curve of error: "(1) The causal forces affecting individual events are numerous, and of approximately equal weight. (2) The causal forces affecting individual events are independent of one another. (3) The operation of the causal forces is such that deviations above the mean of the combined results are balanced as to magnitude and number by deviations below the mean.")

Another reservation about sheer chance or randomness requires mention. Chance poses no less difficulty for commonsense notions of human freedom and responsibility than tight causality would. To the extent that a person's actions, decisions, deliberations, inclinations, feelings, experiences, capabilities, and character traits occur by sheer chance, they are no more meaningfully his own, and he is no more truly responsible for them, than would be true if they all traced fully to external causes. Actions and thoughts governed by sheer chance are no more compatible with human dignity and responsibility, as ordinarily conceived, than their being dominated by external causes. Dignity and responsibility, if genuine, presuppose something beyond chance linking events; they presuppose a causal link in which the individual plays some independent part.

While elements of sheer chance in the world do not imply freedom of the will, "the presence of random phenomena at the quantum level does take the sting out of the argument that man cannot will freely because the material world is governed by determinism. Clearly, a completely deterministic world and a man with an absolutely free will are incompatible conditions" (Georgescu-Roegen 1971, p. 177, in part citing H. Margenau, Hermann Weyl, and A.S. Eddington). (I'll add that not merely an "absolutely" but even a partially free will is incompatible with complete determinism.) The point so far is not that indications of sheer chance in the world establish the case for free will but only that they defuse one particular kind of argument against it.

Causality as opposed to chance is required for any predictability in human behavior. Yet predictability does not rob human beings of the dignity usually associated with free will and responsibility. If anything, the contrary is true. Suppose that a friend of yours had an opportunity to steal $10,000 while escaping suspicion. In fact the money remains unstolen. Which would your friend rather hear from you: "I was sure that you would not steal the money" *or* "I didn't have a clue whether or not you would steal it"? Would your friend be insulted by your thinking that his behavior is predictable? (Compare Hobart 1934/1984, p. 81).

Far from being vitiated by elements of stable relations—of causality—among events and circumstances, including character traits and actions, the very concepts of free choice and responsibility presuppose such elements. Often these elements make confident predictions possible, all without undercutting notions of free choice and responsibility.

Sheer chance, in short, not only does not establish the case for human freedom and responsibility but even poses difficulties of its own. Its role in my argument is different and slighter: it undermines one particular argument against freedom of the will.

Once chance has shaken the notion of total causal determination, the path remains open for considering whether something besides chance might also contribute to the evident openness or indeterminacy of the universe. Everyday evidence, considered next, testifies to some sort of free will. That evidence can be questioned, but the questions rely precisely on the determinist doctrine that is itself open to question.

THE EXPERIENCE OF FREE WILL

Everyone's experience suggests that people's decisions, talk, writings, and thoughts do influence the course of events. The thoroughgoing determinist or fatalist would not deny this personal experience, but he would question its significance. Our decisions and thoughts, influential though they are, are mere links in unbroken causal chains. Each decision, utterance, and thought is caused by other events and circumstances, including physical conditions, the previous thoughts and utterances of oneself and other people, and one's own and other people's character traits, genetic makeups, and current and past environments—according to the determinist. Each of these causal links traces to contemporaneous and earlier links—and so on, presumably, back to the Big Bang.

A hardened habitual criminal could have avoided committing each of his crimes *if* he had willed not to commit it. But could he have so willed? Well, yes, *if* his character had been different. Furthermore, it would have been different *if* his earlier actions and decisions and circumstances had been different. But could they have been different? These earlier character-influencing events and circumstances, perhaps especially including his childhood environment and his genetic makeup, were themselves links in an unbroken causal chain.

The complete determinist is unimpressed, then, by the observation that the criminal could contingently have avoided committing his crimes. Far from proving his responsibility for them, that observation is an uninformative truism. It merely says that *if* the links in a causal chain had been different from what they actually were and had been fated to be, then the outcome of the chain would have been different from what it in fact was.

Despite these assertions of the (imaginary) fatalist, we all have personal experience with making decisions *ourselves*. We decide, true enough, largely in the light of external circumstances. Often these include the expected reactions of other people. But it is we ourselves who weigh the considerations pulling one way and another. We know from our own experience with decisions, furthermore, and from what observation suggests about the decisions of other people, that people do respond to prospects of reward and punishment, approval and disapproval. (Surely economists understand about incentives.) Holding people responsible does affect their behavior.

A fatalist could accept this conclusion without abandoning his doctrine. He could agree that if juries, judges, and legislatures generally accepted the Clarence Darrow defense, crime would be more rampant than it is in fact, and the world a more miserable place. Society is fortunate, he could agree, that juries, judges, and legislatures, usually ignoring Clarence Darrow, as they are fated to ignore him, do hold criminals responsible and do punish them. We are fortunate, in other words, that his determinist theory is not generally accepted and implemented. Yet the fatalist could maintain that his theory is correct, that he is fated to propound it exactly as he does, and that—probably fortunately—you and I and most of the rest of us are nevertheless fated to reject it.

How would the theory of strict determinism interpret academic disputes over that theory itself? Taken literally, it would regard each move in the dispute—each conversation, lecture, journal article, criticism of an article, reply to the criticism, and every slight detail in each of these—as simply a particular link in the great causal chain. The determinist philosopher would agree that his latest paper on the topic was fated in every slightest detail to say what it does say, fated not only by what he had heard and read on the topic but by his genes and childhood experiences and innumerable other circumstances. All reactions to his paper are similarly fated. Yet this consideration does not necessarily lead him to abandon the whole issue and turn to some other branch of philosophy or some other line of work. He could stick to the issue, recognizing that he is fated to do so and that his work on it, and others' reactions to it, are fated to turn out exactly as they do.

This determinist position, then, may not be downright inconsistent with itself, not downright self-refuting. Rather, it is practically incredible.

THE SELF-REFERENTIAL PROBLEM OF DETERMINISM

Joseph M. Boyle, Jr., Germain Grisez, and Olaf Tollefsen (1976) expose the self-contradictory position of one who "rationally affirms" full determinism or, as they say, denies that anyone has any "free choice." (To "rationally affirm" a proposition goes beyond merely mentioning it or considering it possible; it means holding that it is true or at least more reasonably acceptable than its contradictory.) A philosopher who argues that persons interested in the issue ought rationally to accept the no-free-choice position must believe that although they are not compelled to accept it, they *can* rationally accept it ("ought implies can"); they have some freedom of choice in the matter. Yet the determinist proposition being urged denies that the persons addressed have any freedom. Either the determinist is thus contradicting himself or else is pointlessly urging people to do what by his own doctrine they cannot do—make the free choice of rationally accepting that doctrine.

Boyle and his coauthors do in effect recognize the possibility, mentioned in the preceding section, that determinism is true and that participants in controversy over it versus free choice are behaving like fully programmed robots whose every slightest verbal move in the game is a fully determined rather than rationally chosen action. "To affirm [the determinist] position in this way, however, is to withdraw from the philosophical controversy" (p. 169).[6]

THE IRREFUTABILITY OF DETERMINISM

Besides being practically incredible and besides putting its proponents in the position of either contradicting themselves or avowing themselves to be mere robots rather than rational controversialists, determinism is irrefutable or unfalsifiable—in the bad sense. It has a built-in immunity to any adverse evidence; its claim to say anything definite about how

---

[6]The argument of Boyle et al. is extremely complex, detailed, and repetitious, contains many cross-references and other obstacles to comprehension, and does, after all, occupy an entire book; so I cannot guarantee that my summary is entirely faithful to their argument.

the world actually works is a sham. No perceptions of persons that they are more than mere cogs in tightly working machinery, that they have some scope for making decisions not *totally* predetermined by their genetic makeups and past experiences, count for anything; for these very perceptions have themselves been predetermined. Similarly, no number of episodes in which unexpected, astonishing, or unpredictable decisions of particular persons brought major consequences count for anything. Apparent examples of formidable exertions of will count for nothing. The theory itself rules such episodes out as evidence on the grounds that the cited decisions and exertions, as well as their being unexpected, astonishing, or apparently unpredictable, are themselves mere links in the universal causal chain. Examples in which a person seems to have changed his very character by effort of will would not faze the determinist. He would maintain that the person's exertion of will, and with what degree of success, were themselves predetermined. Determinism does not deny that praise and blame, reward and punishment, can be efficacious in influencing behavior; it simply maintains that these in turn are predetermined.

What adverse evidence of any sort is even conceivable, then, from which the theory does not protect itself in advance? A theory that can accommodate absolutely any evidence does not specify any genuine restrictions on how the real world actually works; its ostensible empirical character is a sham.

Furthermore, the theory does not carry any actual implications for how to live one's own life or for public policy. Should individuals cultivate a sense of control over their own decisions and actions or, at the other extreme, cultivate a fatalistic outlook? Some psychologists may offer the one line of advice and others the opposite line; but in any case, each is merely offering the advice he is fated to offer. A determinist philosopher is not necessarily bound to advise the fatalistic outlook; for he may recognize the benefits of feelings of autonomy and responsibility and himself feel, furthermore, that he is fated *not* to undercut such feelings and the benefits flowing from them. Each ordinary individual, similarly, is receiving the advice he is fated to receive and will respond to it, along with other influences, as he is fated to respond.

Should criminals be held more responsible for their actions and more liable to punishment than they currently are or, on other hand, should the Clarence Darrow defense be given greater heed? The first policy shift may reduce crime and make for a healthier society on that account, although it would be unfair to criminals who are, on the determinist theory, mere unfortunate links in a causal chain. (Incidentally, doesn't determinism undermine even the concept of unfairness?) In either case, policymakers will hear the arguments they are fated to hear and respond as they are fated to do.

In short, the determinist theory not only has built-in immunity to adverse evidence but also lacks implications about how to apply it in practice. It is empty. Individuals, by and large, cannot bring themselves to regard it as meaningful and to conduct their own lives and public policy in accordance with it.

I am saying not that full determinism is wrong but that it is an empty, meaningless doctrine. This conclusion is not, I believe, one of the airy dismissals of philosophical issues that used to characterize a crude logical positivism.

EXTREME POSITIONS AND PARTIAL DETERMINISM

I have tried to show that total fatalistic determinism is empty, perhaps even absurd. We might now try to focus on the opposite extreme position, except that complete free will and absolute *in*determinism are downright inconceivable. No conceivable self is free of a biological nature and of the influences imposed by an external world. Still, let us see how far we can get in imagining a self whose will is *essentially* free.

A self whose character had been determined not by heredity and environment but only internally would be the product of a core self, a miniature self within the self, as R.E. Hobart says (1934/1984). But how could that core self be free from external influences? Only by its character having been determined by a further internal miniature self, and so on in preposterous infinite regress. "To cause his original self a man must have existed before his original self. Is there something humiliating to him in the fact that he is not a contradiction in terms?" (Hobart 1934/1984, p. 505).

In some respects, of course, a person's earlier self does partially shape his later self: his earlier decisions and actions affect his capacity for and inclinations toward later experiences, decisions, and actions. But if a person does improve his qualities, what could merit praise but the ingredient of aspiration and resolution in him that made his effort possible (Hobart 1934/1984, p. 505)? What could merit praise except features of an already existing character that could not have been fully its own creation? One praiseworthy character trait is the capacity to respond suitably to praise, blame, and the concept of responsibility.

Any consistently conceivable self must to at least some extent, then—and experience suggests a large extent—be the product of external forces. What implications follow concerning the freedom, autonomy, dignity, and responsibility of the individual? Hobart faces the question: How can anyone be praised or blamed if heredity and circumstance have ultimately given him his qualities? Does the fact that a person did not create himself bar recognizing his character for what it is? If—inconceivably—someone had somehow made his own "original character," and a fine one, and if we praised him for it, we would be ascribing a still earlier character to him. Praise or blame for decisions or actions refers to what kind of person took them; there is nothing else for praise or blame to refer to (Hobart 1934/1984, p. 505).

A person's character at a particular time is what it is. It inclines him to the kinds of intentions and decisions and actions that it does incline him toward; so it meaningfully exposes him to admiration or reprehension, praise or blame. This is true regardless of just how his character came to be what it is. A reprehensible character remains reprehensible even though it can be explained, or explained away, as the product of adverse heredity and environment. The notion of character being admirable or reprehensible only to the extent that it is internally determined, free of external influences, is a self-contradictory notion.

An analogy of sorts holds with a person's wants and tastes. J.K. Galbraith (1958, esp. chap. XI) made much of what he called the "dependence effect": many of an individual's wants in modern society are not wants that he would experience spontaneously if left to himself. Instead, his wants are created by the process of satisfying them. The consumption patterns of other members of society, and notoriously advertising, create wants. Wants that are artificial in this sense cannot be urgent or important, so the implication runs (and, in Galbraith's view, incomes that might nevertheless be spent on meeting them may properly be taxed heavily to finance really important services of the kinds supplied by government).

F.A. Hayek (1961/1967) calls this argument a *non sequitur*. Suppose that people would indeed feel no need for something if it were not produced. If that fact did prove the thing of small value, then the highest products of human endeavor, including the arts, literature, and the marvels of high technology, would be of small value. Standards of hygiene and the demand for products with which to meet them, instead of arising spontaneously within each separate individual, are likewise social products.

More generally, the individual himself is the product of social forces, operating largely through language, which conditions his thoughts, values, and activities. Recognizing the individual as a social product in no way denies that happiness and misery, success and frustration, are experienced by individuals; there is no such thing as collective happiness distinct from and transcending the happiness of individuals. Recognizing how society shapes its members in no way imposes collectivist or communitarian rather than individualist thinking and policies.

The analogy, in brief, amounts to this: A person's tastes are what they are and their gratification or frustration causes him pleasure or unhappiness, even though his tastes are themselves largely the product of external influences. Similarly, a person's character is what it is and does expose him to admiration and praise or reprobation and blame, even though his character, like his tastes, is itself largely the product of external influences.

Praise and reward, blame and punishment, are appropriate to the extent that they are capable in principle of influencing actions, decisions, and character traits, inappropriate otherwise—so Moritz Schlick persuasively argues. Having grown up in ghetto poverty is no valid excuse for robbery, mayhem, or murder; on the other hand, it is pointless to blame a person for actions imposed by congenital deformity or actual insanity. Reward and punishment, praise and blame, all implicitly acknowledge a partial determinism operating in human affairs. (Sometimes, however, a distinction holds between punishment and blame, as in the case of the unruly dog. Individual or collective self-defense against criminally insane persons, as against mad dogs, is not the same as assigning moral culpability. "Punishment" in such a case, like quarantine of a disease-carrier, is not punishment in the fullest sense.)

Praise or blame, reward or punishment, is appropriate for an act committed freely, even and especially for one committed in accordance with the agent's moral character. Its appropriateness does not hinge on the agent's character being totally uncaused, whatever that might mean. Praise or blame would be inappropriate if it would have no effect on acts of the type in question and no effect on propensities to commit them.

Partial determinism, which responsibility presupposes, is fundamentally different both from full determinism and from complete (perhaps stochastic) indeterminism. It recognizes that causality does operate in human affairs, as in the rest of the universe. It recognizes that how an individual will decide when facing a particular choice may be heavily or decisively influenced by his genetic makeup and by his past experiences. These influences include the arguments he has heard and the thoughts that have been aroused in his mind, including the concept of responsibility and prospects of praise and blame. Partial determinism does not maintain, however, that absolutely everything is fully predetermined in the minutest detail. It allows some scope for chance and possibly, also, some scope for the autonomy (or whatever it might be called) that doctrines of free will allude to.

Unlike full determinism, the doctrine of only partial determinism, recognizing scope for some sort of free will, does *not* enjoy built-in immunity to adverse evidence and is *not* devoid of practical implications. If people never experienced feelings of autonomy in making decisions—if they never experienced situations in which they felt that they personally were weighing conflicting considerations and themselves making decisions, free of *total* outside compulsion and constraint, and if, on the contrary, they always perceived themselves under identifiable tight compulsions and constraints—then the doctrine of free will would falter. Or if people sometimes did experience feelings of autonomy but could be shown in each case that the feelings were illusory and shown in detail just how their supposed free choices were in fact externally predetermined in full, again the free-will doctrine would be undermined. Most obviously, the doctrine would be discredited if people were always keenly aware of being mere links in a causal chain and if they recognized in detail just what causes were operating on them, including recognizing just how various facts and arguments came to their attention and what weight each of these commanded.

Discrediting evidence of this sort is conceivable, and the free-will doctrine itself does not rule out its significance. That very fact shows that the doctrine is not empty. The absence of such discrediting evidence suggests, furthermore, that the doctrine may be correct. But it does not, of course, prove that it is right; no doctrine about empirical reality can ever be proved absolutely.

CONCLUSION

Discussing free will versus determinism was necessary because many philosophers consider the issue genuine and important, intertwining with the question of moral responsibility and so with ethics in general. The fatalist doctrine of an unbroken chain of tight causal determination operating from the beginning of time, of apparently ever more complex states of the world having been fully specified in advance by the apparently less complex earlier states—that doctrine is practically incredible. The idea of some kind of sheer chance almost imposes itself. Chance enters ethical discussion not because it itself provides scope for responsible human choice but because it undermines the claims of full, fatalistic determinism. Once determinism is shaken, the idea of some sort of free will, operating along side of both causation and chance, gains a possible foothold. Everyday personal experience supports some such idea.

One question, however, remains dangling: *Can* a person's will be shaped in any manner other than by chance and by external influences such as heredity, environment, and experiences (including exposure to ideas concerning responsibility, praise, and blame)? Is reflection in one's own mind such an "other" manner? No, or not unequivocally; for although ample experience testifies to its reality, that reflection is itself conditioned by external influences, including the actions and ideas of other people. Yet some such "other" manner of determination seems to be what the cheerleaders for free will are postulating.

One approach to a solution—to reconciling free will with the sort of determinism that science deals in—appeals to the notion of emergent properties. "Specific combinations, arrangements or interactions of components can give rise to totally new attributes. The whole is more than the sum of its parts." Diamond and charcoal possess properties quite different from those of their component carbon atoms. A drum made from flat planks can roll. An essay has meaning not contained in the individual ink dots on the printed page. Laws of grammar are quite different from but not incompatible with laws of physics. Similarly, somehow, the human mind is able "to make choices not determined solely by external or genetically fixed factors; the mind is self-programming—it modifies its own processes" (Voss 1995/1996).

I admittedly cannot form a satisfactorily definite conception of what suggestions like that may be getting at. I claim, then, not to have settled the free-will issue but to have kept alive the possibility that if it is not merely a pseudo-problem after all, it anyway is not a problem subversive of ethics. The determinist thesis appears meaningless in the sense of carrying built-in immunity to any conceivable adverse evidence. Since no observations about the world could conceivably clash with it, the thesis does not really say anything about the world and about whether any free will operates in it.

While the free-will/determinism issue thus dangles unsettled, we all find ourselves seized with ineradicable impressions (or illusions) that we enjoy some freedom of action and choice and even of will. When we write as scholars, we simply cannot believe that our every word is precisely predetermined and will draw precisely predetermined reactions from our fellow scholars.

Sometimes we find two or more strands of theory applicable to certain phenomena without our being able—yet, anyway—to reconcile those strands, which may even appear inconsistent. An example concerns the apparent dual nature (wave and particle natures) of light and of electrons. The principle of complementarity, introduced to physics by Niels Bohr, condones applying each strand of theory where it does good service while still hoping to reconcile the different strands, perhaps by modifying one or all (Teller 1980, pp. 93, 105–106, 138–140). Economists formerly did not know, and some would say still do not know, how fully to reconcile three strands of balance-of-payments analysis, the elasticities, absorption, and monetary approaches. It makes sense anyway to apply each approach where it does good service while still seeking a fuller reconciliation among them.

Similarly, in analyzing the worlds of nature and human affairs, we find it reasonable to believe in tight causality or in causality loosened by an element of sheer chance. We also find reason—or at least the pressure of compelling personal experience—to believe in a loosening by some element of free will. The corresponding strands of theory are complementary. Since we cannot really believe that ethics is a field deprived of subject matter, let us continue investigating it.[7]

Let us condemn, though, the tactic of offering mere cheerleading for free will in the guise of argument. (Free will is good, those who doubt it are scoundrels, and we are on the side of the good.) As David Hume said, "this question should be decided by fair arguments before philosophers, [rather] than by declamations before the people" (1739–1740/1961, Bk. II, Pt. III, last paragraph of Sec. II).

---

[7] Edward N. Lorenz (1993, pp. 159–160) reminds us that we should believe even in an uncomfortable truth rather than in an appealing falsehood. That premise recommends believing in free will. If it is a reality, our choice is correct. If it is not, we still shall not have made an incorrect choice, since, lacking free will, we shall not have made any choice at all.

REFERENCES

Boyle, Joseph M., Jr., Germain Grisez, and Olaf Tollefsen. *Free Choice: A Self-Referential Argument.* Notre Dame, Ind.: University of Notre Dame Press, 1976.

Campbell, C.A. "Is 'Freewill' a Pseudo-Problem?" 1951. In *Free Will and Determinism*, edited by Bernard Berofsky, 112–135. New York: Harper & Row, 1966.

Dworkin, Gerald. "Acting Freely." 1970. In *Reason at Work: Introductory Readings in Philosophy*, edited by Steven M. Cahn, Patricia Kitcher, and George Sher, 509–522. New York: Harcourt Brace Jovanovich, 1984.

Eucken, Walter. *The Foundations of Economics.* Translated by T.W. Hutchison. London: Hodge, 1950.

Galbraith, John Kenneth. *The Affluent Society.* Boston: Houghton Mifflin, 1958.

Georgescu-Roegen, Nicholas. *The Entropy Law and the Economic Process.* Cambridge, Mass.: Harvard University Press, 1971.

Gigerenzer, Gerd, Zeno Swijtink, Theodore Porter, Lorraine Daston, John Beatty, and Lorenz Krüger. *The Empire of Chance.* 1989. Cambridge and New York: Cambridge University Press, 1993.

Hayek, F.A. "The Non Sequitur of the 'Dependence Effect'." 1961. In *Studies in Philosophy, Politics and Economics.* Chicago: University of Chicago Press, 1967.

———. *The Constitution of Liberty.* Chicago: University of Chicago Press, 1960.

Hazlitt, Henry. *The Foundations of Morality.* 1964. Los Angeles: Nash, 1972.

Hobart, R.E. "Free Will as Involving Determination and Inconceivable Without It." 1934. In *Reason at Work: Introductory Readings in Philosophy*, edited by Steven M. Cahn, Patricia Kitcher, and George Sher, 494–508. New York: Harcourt Brace Jovanovich, 1984.

Hospers, John. "What Means this Freedom?" 1961. In *Free Will and Determinism*, edited by Bernard Berofski, 26–45. New York: Harper & Row, 1966.

Hume, David. *A Treatise of Human Nature.* 1739–1740. Garden City: Doubleday Dolphin, 1961.

Kant, Immanuel. *Groundwork of the Metaphysic of Morals.* 1785. Translated by H.J. Paton. New York: Harper Torchbooks, 1964.

Lorenz, Edward N. *The Essence of Chaos*. Seattle: University of Washington Press, 1993.

Meyerson, Émile. *Explanation in the Sciences*. 1921. Translated by Mary-Alice Sipfle and David A. Sipfle. Dordrecht and Boston: Kluwer, 1991.

Mills, Frederick C. *Statistical Methods Applied to Economics and Business*. Rev. ed. New York: Holt, 1938.

Peirce, Charles S. *Values in a Universe of Chance*. 1877. Edited by Philip P. Wiener. Garden City: Doubleday Anchor Books, 1958.

———. "The Scientific Attitude and Fallibilism." 1891. In *Philosophical Writings of Peirce*, edited by Justus Buchler, 42–59. New York: Dover, 1955.

Popper, Karl. "Indeterminism Is Not Enough." Lecture at the Mont Pélerin Society meeting in Munich, September 1972. Printed in *The Open Universe*, 30–36. Totowa, N.J.: Rowan and Littlefield, 1982.

———. *Unended Quest*. Rev. ed. La Salle, Ill.: Open Court, 1982.

———. *Popper Selections*. Edited by David Miller. Princeton, N.J.: Princeton University Press, 1985.

Schlick, Moritz. *Problems of Ethics*. 1930. Translated by David Rynin, 1939. New York: Dover, 1961.

Slote, Michael. "Ethics without Free Will." *Social Theory and Practice* 16 (Fall 1990): 369–383.

Squire, John Collings, ed. *If, or History Rewritten*. New York: Viking, 1931.

Teller, Edward. *The Pursuit of Simplicity*. Malibu: Pepperdine University Press, 1980.

van Inwagen, Peter. "Response to Slote." *Social Theory and Practice* 16 (Fall 1990): 385–395.

Voss, Peter. "Freewill and Determinism." 1995. Revised 1996. http://mol.redbarn.org/objectivism/writing/PeterVoss/FreeWillAndDeterminism.html.

CHAPTER 16

Elementos del Economia Politic*

Le economia politic jace al intersection del sciencia economic, theoria politic, e philosophia. Io conduceva un seminario in iste campo durante multe annos al Universitate de Virginia e postea al Universitate Auburn. Le studentes e io revideva le conception libertari del governamento e conceptiones plus collectivista. Ma non preoccupa vos: mi proposito hodie non es recrutar vos a mi proprie puncto de vista politic. Como altere parlatores e como io ipse a previe reuniones del UMI, io vole illustrar le interlingua parlate e un vocabulario anque technic in discuter un large varietate de themas.

PROPOSITIONES POSITIVE E NORMATIVE

Mi studentes e io comenciava per explorar le rolo de judicios de valor in recommendar e decider politicas public (como regulationes economic e impostos). On debe distinguer inter judicios de valor, anque appellate propositiones normative, e propositiones positive, que es observationes de factos o inferentias de logica. Exemplos de propositiones de factos e logica es illos del stricte theoria economic. Le philosopho e economista David Hume (Scotia, 1711–1776) insisteva super iste distinction, postea appellate le «Furca de Hume»: on non pote derivar un conclusion super que es bon o recommendabile, o le contrario, solo per le factos e le logica. Brevemente, on non pote derivar un *debe* de un *es*. Per exemplo, solo ab le facto medical que il *es* periculose pro le sanitate del infante si un femina gravide bibe alcohol, on non pote arrivar at judicio que un femina gravide *debe* abstiner se del alcohol. Pro un tal conclusion, on besonia non solo le factos medical

---

*This introduction to political economy and the Public Choice school was a talk at the Interlingua conference, Prague, 7 August 1995, published as a pamphlet by Union Mundial pro Interlingua, Bilthoven, Netherlands, 1995.

ma anque le judicio normative que le sanitate de infantes es desirabile, e mesmo plus desirabile que le placeres momentari de lor matres in biber alcohol. Un altere exemplo: solo del proposition factual e de logica que un certe politica economic conducerea al miseria de personas in general e que un politica alternative conducerea al felicitate general, on non pote judicar le prime politica mal e le secunde bon; on besonia anque un judicio normative contra le miseria e pro le felicitate.

Como iste exemplos suggere, on pote discuter judicios relativemente specific—como pro e contra politicas specific—per invocar e factos e logica e altere e plus profunde judicios de valor. On pote condemnar le mentir, le defraudar, e le furar per demonstrar que tal conductos tende a subverter le felicitate general, *juncte con* un judicio in favor del felicitate. Le judicio in favor del felicitate es pro le plus de personas, probabilemente, un judicio de valor *fundamental*, como on dice. Per le definition de un judicio fundamental, on non pote arguer in su favor; on es al fin de argumentation; on debe appellar al observation o intuition directe. Ma como iste exemplo anque suggere, disputas super judicios fundamental de valor es rar. Quasi nemo dubitarea que le miseria es mal e le felicitate es bon, ma quasi nemo pensarea a *demonstrar* lo; un tal demonstration exigerea un appello a un judicio ancora plus fundamental, le qual on pote a pena imaginar.

Nos non ha le tempore hic pro approfundar nos in iste distinctiones inter factos, logica, e valores e inter valores relativemente specific e valores fundamental. Io pote solo sublinear que iste themas philosophic es importante in identificar le fontes exacte de disaccordo in disputas super politicas governamental como in le vita personal.

LE ETHICA

Judicios de bon e mal es materias de ethica, e le ethica es a base del conceptos de philosophia politic e le derectos del homine. In plus, le fundamento de ethica pote a pena esser altere que utilitari. Le criterio quasi-ultimate de actiones, regulas, tractos de character, etc. es le cooperation social, o como alicunos dice, le societate civil. Illo es un societate ben functionante in le qual le individuos pote viver insimul in pace, beneficiante mutualmente de lor interactiones e lor commercio. Le analyse del cooperation social es le grande campo commun inter le ethica e le scientia social. Actiones, regulas, e tractos de character se judica bon o mal secundo que illos tende a appoiar o subverter le cooperation social. Io appella isto le criterio *quasi*-ultimate proque illo es solmente un medio, ben que le medio indispensabile, al desideratum final, que es le felicitate human (in un senso convenibilemente extendite del parola «felicitate»).

COOPERATION E RECIPROCITATE

In mi seminarios nos discuteva le perspicacias de David Hume, F.A. Hayek, Robert Alexrod, David Gauthier, Loren Lomasky, e alteres super le possibile evolution «spontanee» del cooperation inter homines. Axelrod empleava torneos e simulationes per computator pro explorar le joco repetite del «dilemma del prisioneros». (On lo appella assi ab un certe exemplo standard del joco.) In un singule session o reprisa del joco, sin reguardo a eventual repetitiones, le action plus avantagiose e strictemente rational pro cata un del duo jocatores es cercar exploitar le altere (non cooperar), sin reguardo a su action. Infortunatemente, quando ambes age assi, rationalmente in le sense stricte, le resultato es mal pro ambes. Quando, al contrario, cata un age cooperativemente, le resultato es assatis bon pro ambes Ma, como jam stipulate, quando cata uno decide su strategia separatemente, su action strictemente rational es cercar exploitar le altere; alteremente, on se trova le victima. Alora, le problema es: que incentivo ha cata jocator prender un perspectiva plus large e non perseguer su proprie stricte avantage immediate?

Le solution appare in un joco repetite in multe reprisas. Cata jocator apprende que su actiones transmitte signales al altere. In le experimentos de Axelrod, le strategia plus successose es render le par (anglese: «tit-for-tat»). Isto vole dicer: on comencia jocar cooperativemente; ma si le opponente age exploitevemente, on retalia in le reprisa sequente. Si le opponente recomencia jocar cooperativemente, on lo face anque. Le principio successose es cooperar, ma non lassar se dupar: jocar reciprocamente.

Iste strategia se distingue del principio christian de verter le altere gena. Ille conducta christian pote semblar confortabile in le singule caso, e on pote illuder se que illo es mesmo nobile e philanthropic. Al contrario, tal vertimento del altere gena facilita le via pro le predatores; illo tende a traher le predation non solo a se ipse ma anque a altere personas innocente. Dunque, illo es *anti*-social. On debe non premiar ma punir e discoragiar le aspirante predatores. Le strategia vermente social pro le longe termino es le reciprocitate: responder al cooperation e benevolentia con le mesmo, ma punir le predation.

Obviemente, le joco del dilemma del prisioneros e le experimentos de Axelrod es un metaphora pro le sociatate. Mesmo si cata individuo proseque solo su proprie interesse, un reguardo pro le longe termino e pro le reactiones de altere personas pote inducer le a ager reciprocamente. Le cooperation pote evolver «spontaneamente».

Le metaphora de Axelrod e altere recercatores in su tradition es un mer profilation de certe aspectos del societate, e on debe evitar misinterpretation del concepto «reciprocitate». Reciprocar non vole dicer insister super un stricte excambio de beneficios recipite e beneficios fornate, toto mesurate in moneta. Le reciprocitate in societate es le bon voluntate a tractar altere personas con un certe benevolentia generalisate e expectar un simile tractamento ab le alteres, ma non le voluntate a tolerar le maltractamento, que invitarea le predation non solo contra se ipse ma anque contra altere personas. Reciprocitate es le excambio—non necessarimente strictemente calculate—de attitudes e actiones appropriate. (De modo similar, le parola «mercato» non se restringe sempre a transactiones strictemente economic. In un senso extendite, le «mercato» es un metaphora pro omne relationes voluntari inter homines, in contrasto con relationes imponite per fortia o fraude o costumes rigide e oppressive.)

Multo economicamente productive, pro recoltar le ganios del specialisation e commercio, es le grande processo national e mundial de excambios multilateral de benes e servicios inter milliones e billiones de personas qui non se cognosce le un le altere. In iste processo de cooperation impersonal, evaluationes monetari es indispensabile. Ma non omne relationes inter homines es relationes del mercato commercial e del moneta. Como dice F.A. Hayek, laureato Nobel e celebre campion del economia del mercato, un ethica de solidaritate es debite in parve gruppos special contenite in le grande societate de intercambios economic mundial—gruppos como le familia, bon amicos, e forsan enthusiastas devote a un causa commun. In un certe grado, on poterea adder, le mesmo pote applicar se anque inter collegas professional e inter empleatos e empleatores associate desde longe tempore. In un grande societate o «ordine extendite» (como lo appella Hayek), le individua appertine a ordines de plure typos. Le intimitate attingite intra parve gruppos special ha un grande valor psychologic. Persequer su interesse personal stricte e immediate, insister super calculos monetari de costos e beneficios, e insister super reciprocitate strictemente concipite anque inter membros de tal gruppos—tote isto destruerea grande valores. «Si nos sempre applicava le regulas del ordine extendite a nostre gruppamentos plus intime, *nos los applattarea*. Dunque nos debe apprender viver in duo species de mundo simul». ("If we were always to apply the rules of the extended order to our more intimate groupings, *we would crush them.* So we must learn to live in two sorts of world at once." Hayek, *The Fatal Conceit*, 1989, p. 18.) Le mercato e le moneta es onstitutiones indispensabile al superviventia e conforto human. Ma non omne aspectos del vita debe o pote esser transationes monetari.

LE GOVERNAMENTO E POLITICAS PUBLIC

Infortunatemente, non omne personas observa le regulas de cooperation social; alicunos es predatores, criminales. Il se besonia un agentia del societate pro restringer les e punir les. Assi argumenta Thomas Hobbes in su libro *Leviathan* de 1651. Pro le disveloppamento economic e assi pro un vita confortabile—pro un modo commode de viver, como dice Hobbes—il se besonia le pace e securitate, comprendente le securitate de proprietate private protegite per un governamento adequate. Sin illo, le vita del homine es—e hic seque, in le libro de Hobbes, un description citate tanto frequentemente in anglese que illo deveni toto enoiose. Ma io vole traducer le parolas in interlingua. Alora, sin le protection del pace e securitate, dice Hobbes, le vita del homine es «solitari, povre, nauseabunde, brutal, e breve». De facto, nos observa tal conditiones hodie in plure paises del Tertie Mundo, e pro le rationes explicate per Hobbes.

David Hume enuncia tres regulas necessari pro un societate prospere: le securitate de possessiones, lor transferentia ab un proprietario ad un altere solo per consentimento (e non per fortia o fraude), e le fidelitate a promissas. Sin le observation general de iste regulas, le gente ha incentivos relativemente debile pro facer planos pro le futuro, pro interprender projectos cooperative complicate e extendite in tempore, pro sparniar, e pro investir.

Inter le attitudes philosophic circa le quales se ragia disputas super politicas plus specific, uno notabile es le equalitarismo. Iste attitude incargarea le governamento a facer le conditiones economic del individuos e del stratas del societate minus differente que illos alteremente esserea. Pauco controverse es le idea de un rete social de securitate, que vole dicer le institutiones pro adjutar le plus povre e infortunate membros del societate. Plus controverse es le idea que le equalitarismo debe extender se al supposite problema del troppo grande ricchessas e que le governamento debe anque diminuer le fortunas del familias plus ric. In discuter le equalitarismo, on debe considerar le relationes inter le equalitate e le libertate personal. Esque il es possibile perseguer politicas de redistribution, e specialmente politicas pro punir le plus ric personas, sin ulle costo in le libertate personal e sin ulle periculo de un governamento troppo potente?

CONFUSIONES DE PAROLAS: LIBERTATE E DEMOCRATIA

Discussiones de libertate es confundite per varie interpretationes. Per exemplo, un lector (Angus Sibley) scribe al magazine *The Economist* (numero del 21 de januario de 1995):

> Conflicto inter libertate e communitate es inevitabile ubi le libertate es simplemente prendite significar «... le derecto del individuo de non suffrer imposition per alteres». Compara le opinion de un eminente moderne theologo, Patre Bernard Haring: «In essentia, le libertate es le poter de facer le bon». Hic es un plus large e plus ric concepto de libertate que cohere melio con le necessitate basic de communitate.

Alora, ille lector e le Patre Haring interpreta le libertate como le poter de facer lo que se considera bon e conforme al necessitates de communitate. Per iste interpretation, quando le stato preveni un individuo de ager in un modo considerate mal, on *non* infringe su libertate (o su *ver* libertate). Como equivoc! Ma tal equivocationes es assatis commun in discussiones de philosophia politic, como demonstra Sir Isaiah Berlin in un famose conferentia.

Un interpretation del libertate plus franc e plus conforme al linguage ordinari es suggerite per plure philosophos politic: Le libertate de un persona es le *absentia* de restrictiones e compulsiones super su activitates imponite per altere personas (includente agentes del stato). Iste definition admitte considerar varie typos e grados de restriction del libertate; on pote investigar eventual incompatibilitates inter varie libertates specific de differente personas; on pote investigar relationes inter libertate personal e mesuras pro promover le equalitate.

On debe distinguer inter le libertate de un pais ab un governamento estranie e le libertate personal de su habitantes, i.e., le absentia de plure intrusiones, typicamente governamental, in le vita del individuo. Le citatanos de plure paises in le Tertie Mundo, specialmente in Africa, ha experimentate le ganio de libertate national (per le decolonisation) ma le perdita de grande partes de lor libertates personal.

Un altere parola multo abusate per confusiones sentimental es «democratia». Frequentemente on include in su signification non solo un forma o modo particular de governamento ma anque varie species de bon conditiones como «libertate, equalitate, fraternitate», varie conceptiones de justitia social, varie derectos del individuo e del societate, e mesmo le stilo de vita american. Assi on confunde distincte conceptiones sub un singule etiquetta e impedi considerar in que grado le varie bon conditiones es compatibile le un con le altere. Per exemplo, que tensiones existe inter le dominantia del majoritate e le libertate personal? On glissa ab pensar que le democratia es bon a pensar que plus de democratia es melior e que, dunque, il es bon facer plus e plus decisiones democraticamente, que vole dicer lassar los facer per le governamento democratic, que vole dicer que le governamento los face.

Un adjuta al clar pensamento es le definition de democratia suggerite per Joseph Schumpeter (inter alteres). Le democratia es un methodo particular pro seliger, influer, e reimplaciar le governatores politic; illo es le methodo de libere competition pro le scrutinios de un large electorato in electiones periodic. Como mer methodo pro seliger le governatores, le democratia non pote esser un scopo final, un desideratum in su proprie derecto. In particular, le governamento del majoritate non es bon in se. Plus vicin a un tal scopo es le cooperation social con pace, securitate, e libertate personal. Con le conception stricte del democratia como un specific methodo politic, on pote considerar le tensiones e compatibilitates inter iste methodo e altere conditiones desirate como «libertate, equalitate, fraternitate» e le bon functionamento del economia. On recognosce que le democratia non es le mesmo que libertate personal e que anque governamentos democratic pote infringer le libertate personal e le derectos del homine. On pote comparar le democratia con altere methodos politic; e si on trova que illo es minus mal que le alteres, iste conclusion non justifica le continue extension del poteres e activitates de un governamento democratic. Il se besonia limitationes anque al activitates de un tal governamento.

Como dice Schumpeter, le democratia es un mer methodo pro attinger fines ulterior. Totevia, le Consilio de Registratores de Votantes del Contato Lee (ubi io vive) ha annunciate in le jornal local (Lee County *Eagle* de 14 e 21 augusto 1994): «Il non ha un plus grande derecto in un societate libere que le derecto, honor, e deber de votar». William Bradford ha diagnosticate iste specie de confusion in un essayo super «Le Nove Religion Civic». E on pensa al fatuitates que circulava un anno retro super le «restauration del democratia» a Haiti, pais ubi il nunca ha habite le democratia.

LE PROCESSO DEMOCRATIC

Le democratia es preferibile a altere formas de governamento, ma isto non vole dicer que facer le cosas democraticamente, illo es, per governamento democratic, es preferibile a altere methodos a ager, como per transactiones voluntari in le mercato. Non plus vole illo dicer que limitationes super le democratia es necessarimente mal (in despecto del epitheto «antidemocratic»). Considera, per exemplo, le objectiones commun ma mal concipite contra le limitationes a terminos legislative in le Statos Unite o a un amendamento constitutional pro le budget equilibrate. Io critica le superstitiones re le democratia in arguer pro *limitar* le sphera e le poteres del governamento e non pro le autoritarismo o alicun altere forma de governamento. In comparation con altere formas, le democratia ha importante avantages (cf. *The Economist* del 27 augusto 1994). (Totevia, il ha argumentos rationabile pro un rege o regina constitutional intra un regime principalmente democratic.)

SELECTION PUBLIC

Le themas que io revide hodie forma parte—lontan del toto—del materias de recerca del economistas del Schola de Selection Public ("public choice school"). Io non ha le tempore pro describer le extension e subtilitate de lor recercas; io pote solo mentionar alicun aspectos o themas. Lor recercas applica le conceptos e methodos del analyse economic al investigar le functionamento de institutiones sin scopo lucrative, super toto le governamento e su varie partes, nivellos, e institutiones. On preme le analyse usque al actor individual. Le idea central, banal ma decisive, es que le individuos es fundamentalmente le mesme in institutiones governamental que in le vita private. Solo per devenir politico o empleato public, le individuo non acquire plus de spirito social o plus de distachamento que le persona integral qui ille jam es. Cata individuo ha su preferentias e scopos personal (que non debe esser strictemente egoista); e in persequer su scopos, cata uno responde a opportunitates e incentivos (includente resultatos e costos expectate).

Le prime grande obra de iste schola (ultra, forsan, un libro de Anthony Downs de 1957) es *Le Calculo del Consentimento* (*The Calculus of Consent*), publicate in 1962 per James M. Buchanan e Gordon Tullock. Le Professor Buchanan, qui ganiava le Premio Nobel in le Scientia Economic in 1986, es le prime Associato Distinguite del Union Mundial pro Interlingua.

Chapter 16: Elementos del Economia Politic

LE VOTANTE ORDINARI E INTERESSES SPECIAL

In considerar le actores individual in le processo politic, on non debe oblidar le votante ordinari (le elector, e anque le non-votanter proque non omne citatanos exerce lor derecto a votar). On recognosce su «ignorantia rational»: al individuo, ordinarimente, il non vale le pena expender tempore e energia in informar se ben del questiones politic proque su action personal in acquirer information non cambiara le resultato del election.

On pote demandar: viste que le singule voto del individuo non determina le resultato, proque mesmo votar? On suggere varie explicationes. Alicun votantes pensa a lor supposite responsibilitate in prender parte in un ceremonia civic e assi exprimer solidaritate con ideales democratic. Alicunos trova le acto de votar un modo personalmente incostose de exprimer emotiones de benevolentia—o de malitia. Precisemente proque su influentia es tanto diluite, quasi nulle, le votante individual pote ager sin senso de responsabilitate personal.

On remarca le basse qualitate de discussiones del politica public, specialmente politicas economic. On concentra le attention at troppo breve termino; on non pensa al consequentias al longe termino de politicas que superficialmente pote semblar attractive. On tende a creditar o blasmar le presidente o partito in poter pro le bon o mal stato currente del cyclo conjunctural; on non comprende que iste mesme cyclo resulta ab institutiones que persiste trans le varie administrationes. On comprende mal le moneta. Per exemplo, le notion prevale que le taxas de interesse es mer parametros fixate per le banca central, fixate a basse nivello quando le banca se senti benevolente e a alte nivello quando illo se senti malevolente. Le subtilitates del relationes inter le inflation de precios e le crescimento del production total se perde in le discussion public. Le publico non comprende le stato precari del dollar, que remane sin definition.

Iste basse nivello de discussion seque del ignorantia rational del votante individual e del realismo del politicos in tractar le votantes como illes vermente es e vermente pensa. Lor ignorantia lassa grande campo pro le demogogia. Ordinarimente il non servi le interesse del politicos predicar bon senso economic.

Thomas Sowell ha dicite; «Le prime lection del scientia economic es le raritate: il nunquam ha assatis de alique pro satisfacer a omnes qui lo vole. Le prime lection del politica es disdignar le prime lection del scientia economic». ("The first lesson of economics is scarcity: There is never enough of anything to satisfy all those who want it. The first lesson of politics is to disregard the first lesson of economics." Citate in *CEI UpDate*, julio de 1994).

Ultra le votante rationalmente ignorante, nos considera le membros e representantes de interesses economic special, qui ha rationes pro informar se ben e exercer pression super le politicos. Simile in iste respecto es illes que on pote denominar «hobbyistas», qui, per exemplo, cerca regulationes plus rigorose contra supposite periculos in activitates de sport o in le dieta del homine medie o qui vole plus grande fundos governamental pro recercas contra le syndrorna de immunodeficientia acquirite (SIDA) o altere maladias particular o qui conduce un cruciada contra le aborto o pro le derecto del femina a seliger. On comprende proque tal interesses special e tal hobbyistas ha multo plus de influentia politic que le citatano ordinari, cuje interesses es relativemente negligite.

POLITICOS

Un altere classe de participantes in le processo politic es, obviemente, le politicos mesme. Duo seculos retro in le Statos Unite, le officiales public e le legislatores esseva, al minus idealmente, citatanos de spirito civic qui occupava lor officios temporarimente o solo un parte del tempore e postea retornava a lor fermas o altere occupationes normal. (On pensa al ancian romano Cincinnatus e a George Washington.) Hodie le politica ha devenite un profession de horario complete e un carriera del vita. Le politicos ipse ha devenite un interesse special, con su particular desiros e puncto de vista. Isto es un del rationes pro le proposition de poner limites a quante annos on pote servir in un officio determinate. (Iste reforma certo non sanarea omne defectos del systema politic, ma il ha un certe senso.) Il ha conflictos inter le interesse personal del politico e le interesse general del pais.

Le politicos ha breve horizontes de tempore e vision restringite como in un tunnel. Como mentionate, illes exploita le ignorantia del votante ordinari. Pro le publicitate e probabilemente anque pro un senso de amor proprie e de importantia, illes tende a inventar ideas brillante e cercar impler los per le fortia del lege. On perveni a pensar del governamento como Fee Benefic. On glissa a pensar que si alique es bon o desirabile, le governamento debe provider o promover o subsidiar lo. Si alique es mal, le governamento debe supprimer o discoragiar lo. On glissa a attribuer iste responsibilitates specialmente al governamento national, oblidante que sub le Constitution american su poteres es strictemente limitate e

Chapter 16: Elementos del Economia Politic 317

que le plus grande parte del poteres e responsabilitates es restringite al cinquanta Statos e su subdivisiones politic e al populo mesme. On tende a pensar que opposition a un proponite action del governamento national es opposition al ben ipse e consentimento al mal ipse.

Exemplos de benes e males que le governamento debe promover o rernediar, secundo le caso, listate in nulle ordine special, es: education, repastos pro infantes, systemas de pension, drogas, pornographia, discimination inter le racias e altere manifestationes del pensamento pauco nobile, consideration special pro personas con handicaps corporal o mental, le congedo ab le empleo in caso de problemas familial, le securitate physic in le empleo e in le sport, preservation de terras humide, e le supposite alte cultura in le artes, television, e radio. In martio de 1995, per le posta, le assi denominate Gente pro le Via American (People for the American Way) me ha invitate a «inrolar me in le battalia contra le censura» ("join in the battle against censorship")—per contribuer moneta, il va sin dicer. Le «censura» in ille appello se refere al propositiones pro discontinuar le subsidios del governamento national al television.

On se rememora rarmente del Lege de Consequentias Non Intendite. On non da debite attention a effectos lateral non desirate e a alternativas al action governamental.

Iste generalisationes re breve horizontes, legislation de ideas supposite brillante, e vision de tunnel es documentate in libros de James L. Payne, Robert Higgs, e Richard Epstein e in studios caso per caso del systema politic in le Statos Unite, e specialmente del Congresso, studios scribite per jornalistas, empleatos in le officios al Collina del Capitolio in Washington, e altere proxime observatores. Io recommenda Alan Ehrenhalt, *The United States of Ambition*, John Jackley, *Hill Rat*, e Eric Felten, *The Ruling Class*.

BUREAUCRATES E PARTICIPANTES IN PROCESSOS AL LEGE

Le theoria del selection public explora le positiones e incentivos special anque del bureaucrates. Mesmo si su motivation es purmente le ben del publico, un bureaucrate sape plus del nobile mission de su proprie bureau que de altere usos, public e private, del moneta e ressources necessari. Ille vole incrementar le grandor e le budget de su bureau. Un bureau tende a formar alliantias inter se, le sector private affectate, e le committees parlamentari cargate con su supervision. Tote isto contribue al crescimento del governamento.

On debe considerar le situationes special anque de advocatos, litigantes, judices, e juratos. Le processos de lege pro traher judicamentos financiari ab «tascas profunde» deveni ancora un maniera de abusar le governamento ad in un organo de redistribution de ricchessas, mesmo dum impedir lor creation.

INEXACTITUDES DEL PROCESSO DEMOCRATIC

Mesmo si il es desirabile implementar le preferentias del populo, on constata que le mechanismo democratic los registra pauc accuratemente. On parla frequentemente del fallimentos del processo del mercato economic. A causa de tal appellate «externalitates», le personas qui decide le natura e extension de varie activitates non debe prender in consideration tote le costos e beneficios. On mira al governamento pro remediar tal situationes.

Alora, le fallimentos del processo democratic es ancora plus grave. Decisiones facite sin adequate comparation de costos e beneficios es ancora pejor. Isto se explica non solo per le considerationes jam indicate super le positiones de individuos ma anque per certe technicalitates. Plure «paradoxos de votation» es ben cognoscite. On construe exemplos con listas monstrante le ordines in le quales le votantes o gruppos de votantes prefere le politicos o candidatos alternative. Secundo le detalios del processo, on demonstra como un politica o candidato con minus appoio que un alternativa pote nonobstante prevaler. (Per exemplo, suppone que plus de membros del electorato o del legislatura prefere le option A al option B e anque un majoritate prefere option B al option C. Logicamente, per le «transitivitate de preferentias», on pensarea que le option C perde, ma il es ben possibile que illo gania.)

Io non ha le tempore pro presentar tal exemplos in detalio. Io mentionara solo alicun phenomenos simile. Uno es le phenomeno de «minoritates governa» (assi appellate per Robert Dahl): ni «le majoritate» ni «le minoritate», ma «minoritates», plural, governa. Typicamente, le majoritate in favor de un particular candidato o partito es un coalition de diverse minoritates, cata un con su desiros particular. Il pote facilemente evenir que un particular projecto de lege es adoptate contra le desiros de un majoritate del populo o del legislatores proque su preferentias super iste particular projecto es relativemente debile e illo forma parte de un pacchetto assemblate per implicite or explicite commercio in votos. Post toto, le politicos es interprenditores in questa de votos; e illes functiona per assemblar coalitiones pro servir un multiplicitate de interesses special cuje desiros, anque contra illos del population in general, es relativemente intense.

Iste paradoxo de «minoritates governa» es un aspecto del confusion de questiones o themas in le processo politic. Rarmente selige le votantes inter distincte e clar accostamentos a cata singule question. Plus tosto illes debe seliger inter *pacchettos* de positiones mal definite re un varietate de questiones. In plus, le candidatos e partitos politic evita formular su positiones e pacchettos de positiones innecessarimente clarmente proque illes es anxiose de non alienar le electores qui poterea esser perdite per clar positiones re singule questiones. Brevemente, le candidatos e partitos ha rationes pro confunder le questiones. Il ha un tendentia verso un mal definite centro del cammino, un position centristic. E proque on evita clar formulationes in le processo politic, le location de iste centro flotta al deriva trans le annos. Illo que se considera realista—politicamente possibile flotta al deriva, e le populo ha pauc opportunitate a determinar le resultato a longe termino.

LE AMBITION EXCESSIVE DEL GOVERNAMENTO

Partialmente a causa de iste manco de precision, le participantes in le processo politic non ha incentivos pro cercar comparationes accurate del beneficios e costos de programmas governamental. Le deficits chronic del budgets governamental in le Statos Unite e a ver dicer in le plus grande parte del paises es un grande exemplo e consequentia de iste manco de incentivos appropriate e le fragmentation de responsabilitate.

De plus in plus on considera le governamento como mechanismo del redistribution, e non solo per un rete de securitate social contra le grande e nonprevisibile infortunitates del vita. Le litigation—le avide recurso al processos al lege—es un note exemplo. Le notion de responsabilitate financiari pro productos allegate esser defectuose se ha expandite quasi in le notion que nemo debe suffrer un mal fortuna sin que alicun altere paga le expensas, recompensation, e frequentemente anque penalitate. On da attention inadequate al effectos super le disposition de facer innovationes e currer riscos in interprisas industrial e commercial.

On non considera que le activitate governamental in iste varie campos pote obstruer alternativas melior. Si le governamento non se habeva inmiscite, qui sape lo que interprenditores private haberea inventate in su loco? On debe rememorar se de lo que Frédéric Bastiat (1801–1850) scribeva super lo que on vide e lo que on non vide. Si le governamento cessava bloccar le via, alternativas melior poterea disveloppar se (ben que, confessemente, con difficultates transitional, que se derivarea del involvimento initial del governamento).

Il es ironic que nos nos ha habituate a expectar tanto del governamento, viste le triste historia de su excessive ambitiones. Le chronic deficit governamental duce a expectar un quasi-repudiation del debito governamental o quasi-bancarupta del governamento. Io dice «quasi» proque isto evenira non aperternente ma per le collapso inflationari del dollar. Io non dice que isto evenira jam intra pauc annos, ma finalmente. E il es theoricamente possibile que le governamento cambia curso a bon tempore.

CONCLUSION

Mi conclusion es: Nos non debe lassar nos dupar per irreflexive laudes del democratia. Nos debe guardar le governamento, mesmo governamento democratic, con un oculo realistic. Nos debe prestar attention re quante aspectos del vita incargar al governamento. Re le futuro, il ha mesmo alicun rationes pro sperantia. Un es le comprension del governamento e del economia politic que cresce in le mundo academic, gratias specialmente al labores del Schola de Selection Public, e que poterea finalmente prevaler in le grande publico. Mesmo le pubtico ordinari comencia devenir sage al trucos del governamento, que, como dice Harry Brown, candidato pro le nomination presidential del Partito Libertari in le Statos Unite, perde spatio pro manovrar.

CHAPTER 17
Is There a Bias Toward Overregulation?*

WHAT IS "TOO MUCH" GOVERNMENT?

Often it is appropriate to consider the question of government regulation industry by industry or problem by problem, focusing on specific facts. Heaven knows there has been enough of the opposite: adopting regulations lightheartedly, as if good intentions were justification enough. On the other hand, sometimes it is appropriate to step back from a narrowly factual focus and consider a broader question. Preoccupation with the immediate and specific is part of the problem with government action.[1]

A broader view suggests that our political system harbors a bias toward overactivity. Regulation is just one of several things that government does probably too much of. Such a bias, if it does exist, argues for seeking—or restoring—constitutional restraints on regulatory activity and for not letting each particular issue be decided on its own narrow apparent merits. Despite the scorn of hard-nosed positivists, human rights belong in the discussion.

Strictly speaking, perhaps, what argues for restraint is not an incontestable bias toward too much regulation but a structure of government

---
*From *Rights and Regulation*, eds. Tibor R. Machan and M. Bruce Johnson (San Francisco and Cambridge, Mass.: Pacific Institute for Public Policy Research and Ballinger, 1983), 99–126.

[1] As F.A. Hayek notes, "we are not fully free to pick and choose whatever combination of features we wish our society to possess, or to ... build a desirable social order like a mosaic by selecting whatever particular parts we like best." Yet this idea "seems to be intolerable to modern man." The suggestion draws scorn that unwanted developments may necessarily stem from earlier decisions. "I am myself now old enough," Hayek continued, "to have been told more than once by my elders that certain consequences of their policy which I foresaw would never occur, and later, when they did appear, to have been told by younger men that these had been inevitable and quite independent of what in fact was done" (1973, pp. 59–60).

321

decisionmaking in which prospective costs and benefits escape accurate confrontation. The result may be too much regulation in some directions and, in some sense, too little in others. Errors of omission do not cancel out errors of hyperactivity, though, and a case for restraint remains.

What might the ideal amount of government mean? Even without being able to say (and without facing the anarchists' challenge to any government at all), one can still recognize aspects of decisionmaking processes that tilt the outcome toward too much government. Some utterly familiar facts suggest this conclusion. Admittedly, I may have overlooked some powerful and even overriding biases working in the opposite direction. As a contribution to discussion, though, I report the biases I see and challenge the reader to explain any opposite ones that might override them.

FRAGMENTED DECISIONS AND AGGLOMERATED ACTIVITIES

Almost everyone who plays a part in governmental decisionmaking, from the average citizen on up, has a fragmentary view. No one has, or has reason to seek, a full view of the prospective costs and benefits of a contemplated activity. (Just one kind of relatively specific and obvious example concerns federal sharing in the costs of many state and local projects, with the result that the local authorities are deciding on expenditure of what, from their points of view, are "ten-cent dollars" or "fifty-cent dollars.") Nothing in government corresponds to the market process of spontaneous coordination of decentralized decisions; nothing corresponds to its way of bringing even remote considerations to the attention of each decentralized decisionmaker in the form of prices.[2] Knowledge, authority, incentives, and responsibility are largely fragmented and uncoordinated in the political and governmental process. Far-reaching and long-run consequences of decisions receive skimpy attention.

One aspect of this fragmentation, noted by Samuel Brittan, is that "the cost of a political decision is borne by people other than the voter. A customer buying a suit or a washing machine has to bear the cost himself." Someone voting for a candidate who makes some attractive promise, however, usually—and realistically—assumes "that others will bear the cost" (Brittan 1978, pp. 165–166).

---

[2] Obviously, I have in mind Hayek 1945.

Of course, externalities, transactions costs, and all that keep the price system from operating with all imaginable perfection. But what is a fringe "imperfection" of the market economy is a central characteristic of governmental decisionmaking.

Any number of government activities might each seem desirable by itself in the absence of most of the others, but it does not necessarily follow that the whole agglomeration of them is also desirable. To suppose so would be to commit the fallacy of composition, of supposing that anything true of the part or individual must also be true of the whole or group. Adding any particular government function to all the others complicates the tasks of choosing, operating, and supervising those others.[3] The more functions the government takes on and the more complicated they are, the more they must be left to the "experts"; and the people's elected representatives, let alone the people themselves, are less able to exercise close and informed control. The elected representatives, who supposedly should monitor the experts, must largely depend on them for information; and the experts have their own special views about their work.

Particular government programs, and especially agglomerations of them, have remote, unforeseen consequences. The current inflation is one example. Burgeoning programs—including, ironically, ones intended to help make the citizens economically secure—have led to federal deficits, government borrowing, upward pressures on interest rates, Federal Reserve actions to restrain their rise, consequent excessive expansion of the monetary base and money supply, price inflation, further allowance for inflation in interest rates, further short-run efforts to restrain their rise by monetary expansion, establishment of a momentum in prices and wages such that an antiinflationary turn in monetary policy would not bring quick success but would bring a recession, monetary accommodation of the rising wages and prices, and so on. The result is all the *in*security that inflation brings, and all the disruption of economic calculation. A still more pervasive example—so one might argue—is that the accumulation of government activities and their repercussions brings a drift in the whole character of our social, political, and economic system; yet that drift was never squarely faced and decided on as a political issue.

THE "FLAW" AND THE CASE FOR LIMITS

Overregulation stems from a "basic flaw" in our political system closely related to the flaw noted in current arguments for a constitutional limit to government taxing or spending.[4] Because of its close relation to the

---

[3] See, in part, Friedman 1962, p. 32. In the technical jargon, government activities have external diseconomies.

[4] One presentation of the diagnosis appears in Rickenbacker and Uhler 1977, chap. 1.

present topic, the central argument is worth reviewing. The alternative to such a limit—letting total spending emerge as the sum of individually enacted appropriations—is biased upward. Some people are especially interested in government spending on rivers and harbors and military installations, others in spending for schools and teachers, others in housing subsidies, and still others in energy-research contracts. Because of its special interest, each group is well informed about the government action it wants and has arguments for it readily at hand. Furthermore, since the benefits of its favorite program will be relatively concentrated on itself rather than diluted over the entire population, its members have incentives to incur the trouble and expense of pressing the group's views on the legislators. A candidate or legislator, for his part, knows that each special interest cares intensely about what concerns it and fears that losing the support of only a few such interests could cost him election or reelection; so he tends to be responsive.[5]

The links between particular government expenditures and particular tax collections are loose. No one really knows who will ultimately pay for a government program. The voter can drift into thinking that someone else, perhaps "the rich" or the big corporations, will pay or ought to pay. (Not even economists know who ultimately pays the corporate income tax.) It is easy to drift into thinking that the government gets resources out of some sort of fourth dimension. Politicians will not hasten to disabuse voters of this "fiscal illusion." Nowadays, with taxes and inflation being what they are, this illusion is evaporating; but the very fact that the present state of affairs could develop suggests that some such illusion has been at work until recently.

An art-loving journalist has unwittingly illustrated the sort of attitude that expands government activity—and thereby also illustrated the logic of the sort of limit he was complaining against (Sansweet 1978, p. 11). State and local government actions taken after passage of Proposition 13 in California reveal, he complained, that many officials see the arts as an expendable elitist pursuit. The recent tremendous growth in public funding for the arts had suddenly been thrown into reverse. A 60 percent slash in the budget of a state agency making grants to art programs and individual artists had lowered California to 44th place among all states in per capita funding for the arts. Yet, he continued, the arts pay the wages of hundreds

---

[5]See "Single-Issue Politics," in *Newsweek* 1978, pp. 48–60, and, on congressmen's feelings of insecurity, see Mann 1978.

of thousands of people, directly and indirectly. How many restaurants near the Music Center in downtown Los Angeles would remain open without the audiences that the Center draws? The arts offer pleasure and entertainment and stimulation. State and local governments have made too much of a commitment to them to back out now without seriously retarding their progress. "A society that considers it a frill to nourish its soul is in deep trouble." In reply, a reader asked: "What kind of trouble can be expected by a society that depends on government to nourish its soul?" (Beaver 1978, p. 12). The journalist tacitly accepts the notion that not to finance particular activities by taxes—by compulsion—is to be neglectful of them. Also noteworthy is his misuse, regarding downtown Los Angeles, of the overworked theoretical argument about externalities—here, spillover benefits.

Much the same points that apply to spending apply also to regulation. Some economic interest groups benefit from regulation (perhaps it protects them against competition) and automatically have the information and incentives to press candidates and legislators for what they want. The latter, for their part, are rationally more responsive to special-interest pressures than to the general interest of the average voters, who are rationally ignorant and apathetic about the details of public policy. Furthermore, citizens who identify themselves with some cause—protecting the environment, cracking down on health and safety hazards, developing exotic energy sources, fostering the arts, remedying supposedly unjust inequalities, suppressing (or facilitating) abortion, improving the eating habits of school children, or whatever—take on the political characters of special interests and, like them, tend to have disproportionate influence with politicians or the relevant bureaucrats. The much discussed "new class" of activist intellectuals and publicists belongs in the story. Legislators, bureaucrats, and other members of the government themselves have personal stakes in government activism, though many of them are no doubt sincerely motivated to do good as they conceive of doing good in their own special niches in life.

METHODOLOGICAL INDIVIDUALISM IN ANALYZING GOVERNMENT

None of this amounts to casting aspersions on the moral characters of the people who take part in deciding on government activities. I am simply drawing implications from the fact that these people decide and act within particular frameworks of information, incentives, tests of performance, and rewards.[6] Economists, long successful with methodological individualism in their own field, are now applying that approach to understanding how people behave in the governmental framework. We, the analysts, project ourselves into the role of businessman, consumer, bureaucrat, legislator, political candidate, or whoever it is whose decisions and actions we are trying to understand. We consider his motivations and incentives, perhaps even including the circumstances affecting his self-esteem, as well as the opportunities and constraints he faces. We can draw relevant information from our own personal thoughts, actions, and experiences. Such an approach does not depend on the profundities of psychology. It draws inferences from familiar facts about human nature and about decisionmaking situations.

CIRCUMSTANCES AND IDEAS OF THE AVERAGE VOTER

The "average voter" is the voter considered at random, otherwise than as a member of any special interest group. (To take account of *non*voting, perhaps the term should be "average citizen.") He does not automatically possess the information needed to weigh the pros and cons of more or less spending on each special group's favorite project. Furthermore, obtaining such information would cost him money, time, and trouble better devoted to other purposes. He profits more from a day spent learning the strong and weak points of different makes of car or refrigerator, when he wants to buy a new one, than from a day spent trying to learn the advantages and disadvantages of increased government spending on aircraft carriers or urban renewal.

Acquiring and acting on information about public issues has a low payoff because it is a "public good." The standard rationale for having any government at all is that it is necessary to provide public goods, such as national defense, police protection, and the legal system. Their benefits cannot be confined to people who voluntarily contribute money or effort for them. Each person might as well sit back and enjoy a free ride on

---

[6]Kenneth N. Waltz makes an analogous point, which illuminates this one, in his *Theory of International Politics* (1979). Almost regardless of the internal character of its regime, we can say much about how a country behaves in the arena of international politics in view of the situation confronting it—in particular, according to whether or not it is a dominant power and, if it is, whether it is one of several or one of only two dominant powers.

the expenditures or efforts of others. So government sells public goods compulsorily, for taxes. But no such solution, imperfect as it may be, has been found for the public good of monitoring the government itself.[7] If an average voter should go to the trouble of keeping informed and politically active, most of the benefits, in the form of sounder policy, would accrue to others. While reaping only a very minor share of these benefits, he would have to bear all of his own costs. He has about as little reason to incur them as he would have to stop driving his car to hold down air pollution. He has little incentive to work for what is in the general interest.[8]

Exhorting citizens to study the issues and take an active role in politics largely ignores these facts. It tacitly regards concern with governmental affairs as a noble activity holding a special claim on each citizen's attention. Actually, badgering him to divert his money, time, and energy from work or recreation to political studies that perplex or bore him will contribute little to wise policymaking. It is an imposition, too, if holding down the range of government decisions in the first place could have held down these demands on his attention.

Even if, implausibly, the voter should become well informed and vote accordingly, he cannot express himself on each program separately. If he is voting on issues at all when choosing between candidates, he is voting on policy positions all jumbled together in vaguely specified packages, along with the candidates' actual or advertised personalities. Furthermore, his own monitoring of the government through informed voting (and lobbying) would do little good unless other voters joined him. He is only one out of many, and his own informed vote would hardly be decisive for the outcome of an election or for the decision on some program. It is rational for him to content himself with superficial notions about election issues, voting for a party label out of habit or for a well-packaged

---

[7]The concept of monitoring as a public good is due, I believe, to Roland McKean.

[8]The weakness of personal incentives to seek collective rather than individual benefits is a leading theme of Mancur Olson, Jr., *The Logic of Collective Action* (1965). The free-ride motivation of the average voter also characterizes the individual member of a special interest group. It operates, though, to a lesser degree. The group member belongs to a smaller group with a more intense and concentrated interest than the average voter does; his own interest is less diluted by being shared with others. Furthermore, as Olson notes, an organized interest group may be able to command the support of its members by supplying services of value to them individually, such as business information and other trade-association services, in addition to its collectively desired lobbying function.

personality out of whim.[9] His position is different from that of people who would reap concentrated benefits from particular programs and have good prospects of promoting government *activism* in their favor. Average and special-interest voters alike, though, enjoy an apparent freedom from personal responsibility in the voting booth; each is acting anonymously along with many others.

It is doubtful that businessmen, as such, have any strong interest in working to limit government intervention. Just because they are the key actors in a free-market economy, it does not follow that the individual businessman finds it in his self-interest to work to preserve such an economy. Businessmen can cope with regulation. Its burdens may not be much worse than those of competition, which, anyway, some kinds of regulation restrain. The prospects for businessmen of ordinary ability relative to the prospects of the most dynamic entrepreneurs may even be better in a highly regulated economy than under substantial laissez faire; enjoying the quiet life may be easier. Hence the pointlessness of businessmen exhorting each other to do a better job of communicating their case to the public. Businessmen as such, rather than simply as human beings, are not the main beneficiaries of a free economy.

With little personal incentive really to understand public affairs, the average voter tends to work with ideas that are in the air. The attitude does seem to prevail widely these days that if anything is bad—pornography, or small children's eating medicine that they shouldn't have, or junk food in the schools—then it is the government's job to suppress it. Similarly, if anything is good—housing, arts, effective drugs, good nutrition—then government ought to promote or subsidize it. This attitude parallels the doctrine of altruism, which receives wide lip service, the doctrine that one ought to be primarily concerned with the (supposed) interests of other people. It is wickedly selfish, then, to oppose a program for doing good, even if it does cost tax money. (Government programs in one's own special interest can readily be rationalized in altruistic terms, as good for other people also. It is a routine theoretical exercise for economists to concoct "externality" arguments for government interventions.) The altruist doctrine meshes well with the idea that it is slightly indecent to be a rightist and the presumption that the decent and humane position on any issue is at least a little left of center (Ellul 1968, pp. 215–219).

---

[9] "Rational ignorance" is a leading theme of Anthony Downs, *An Economic Theory of Democracy* (1957).

Chapter 17: Is There a Bias Toward Overregulation? 329

The psychological roots[10] of interventionism include people's tendency to believe what they want to believe and the readiness of politicians to exploit this tendency. In political argumentation, plausibility counts. Mere slogans and name-calling sometimes work. The acceptance of merely plausible arguments is aided by a trait of contemporary thought roughly equivalent to what F.A. Hayek has called "scientism."[11] Just as Chanticleer thought his crowing made the sun rise, so voters and politicians seem to think that their laws are what make good things happen. People are unaccustomed to conceiving of how good results will occur unless they are explicitly sought; the invisible hand is not universally appreciated. When a problem has become politically fashionable, to suggest leaving its solution to private initiative seems callous.[12] Action is considered "positive" and therefore good, while opposition is "negative" and therefore bad.

Support for activism intertwines with the idea that democracy is a good thing. That idea slides into the belief that doing things democratically, that is, through democratic government, that is, through government, is a good thing.

Another reason for the widespread appeal of government intervention is disregard of the incompleteness of knowledge and the costs of information, transactions, and decisionmaking in the public sector while emphasizing such "imperfections" of the private sector. Tacitly, the government is regarded as a philosopher-king, totally benevolent, omniscient, efficient, and effective.[13] Handing over a problem to such an entity seems like solving it.

SPECIAL INTERESTS AND SYNTHETIC MAJORITIES

So far we have been considering the average voter, his circumstances and attitudes, and the appeals directed toward him. Next we turn to special interests and then to "hobbyists." Politicians are tempted to appease each

---
[10] Here I am falling into temptation—into amateur psychologizing—and what follows should perhaps be discounted.
[11] His articles on "Scientism and the Study of Society" are reprinted in *The Counter-Revolution of Science* (Hayek 1952, Pt. 1).
[12] See below in the section on "crowding out."
[13] George Stigler quotes a pair of rather typical passages on the defects of a private market economy that could readily be overcome by "a socialist economy" (Oskar Lange) or by "the State" (A.C. Pigou). Then he substitutes "Almighty Jehovah" and "his Serene Omnipotence" for the words here in quotation marks—with amusing and telling effect. See Stigler 1975, pp. 112–113. The assumption illustrated is now being undermined by the application of methodological individualism to the study of government.

clamoring interest by helping it get what it wants and to compensate the others by doing the same for them. Under these circumstances, logrolling (explicit in legislatures and implicit in political platforms) assembles majorities out of essentially unrelated minorities. "Minorities rule"[14] (Dahl 1963, pp. 125–130)—not *the* minority, but an implicit coalition of several minorities. Suppose that for each of three programs, 25 percent of the voters favor it so intensely that they would vote for whichever candidate supports it, regardless of his position on other issues. Seventy-five percent of the voters oppose each program, but only mildly. Suppose, further, that the minority favoring each of the three programs is a distinct group. (To recognize that two or three of the groups have some members in common would complicate the example without affecting its point.) A candidate supporting all three programs would be elected overwhelmingly and be put in a position to work for their enactment, even though 75 percent of the electorate opposed each program. The same sort of implicit logrolling operates, though less clearly than in this example, in the growth of government budgets. As the example suggests, by the way, the political process affords scope for political entrepreneurship and not just for passive response to existing demands.

Particularly as the vote-trading process spreads out over time and over numerous separate ballots, spurious consensus becomes possible. Policy combinations get adopted that could not have commanded a majority if considered as a whole. The procedure of making decisions year by year leads to commitments to the future growth of spending that are not seen or not appreciated when made, yet are hard to reverse later. Furthermore, the automatic growth of revenue as the economy grows and as inflation proceeds, pushing taxpayers into higher brackets, allows the government to avoid an *explicit* decision to raise taxes to cover increased spending (Stein 1978, p. 20).

The politics of abortion illustrates the influence of intensely concerned minorities. The California and Massachusetts legislatures were so embroiled in controversy over public funding of abortions in July 1978 that they failed to finish their budget work in time for the new fiscal year. A single issue fought over intensely by small but well-organized groups can distract politicians' attention from matters of broad but unfocused public concern. Similarly, a vast majority may grumble about high taxes, but its concern is so diffuse (or has been, until recently) that it can seldom

---

[14]"Minorities Rule" is the title of the reprinted version of Dahl 1963, pp. 124–134, in Fein 1964, pp. 125–130.

counterbalance powerful minority pressures working for specific spending programs (*Wall Street Journal* 1978, p. 20).

HOBBYISTS

Activists on all sides of the abortion issue are examples of what I call "hobbyists," who engage in political study and activity not so much for obvious material gain as because they have identified themselves with some mission or are seeking an outlet for their energies or a sense of participation in admirable causes. Hobbyists include people who want a federal crash program to cure a disease that killed a relative, or who have lost a child in a boating accident and therefore seek federal regulation, or want subsidies for art or music, or want preservation of the unspoiled wilderness. People acting out of disinterested public spirit count among the hobbyists; the term is not meant disparagingly. Stretched a bit, the term also covers "consumer advocates," who, for the publicity they thrive on, require "a constant supply of new charges against new villains ... suitably printed in the hot ink of outrage" (Stigler 1975, p. 188).

By the very nature of their "hobbies," just as by the very nature of special economic interests, most hobbyists are pressing for more government activity. A belief in laissez faire or limited government is itself a hobby for some people, to be sure; but it is just one among a great many hobbies, most of which do tend toward interventionism. It is no real embarrassment for this argument that some intellectuals do take an *anti*interventionist stand. Of course some are libertarians, but psychological factors and aspects of the democratic process make it difficult for their view to prevail in practice.

Hobbyists are charmed at having one central focus, Washington, for their persuasive efforts and charmed by the prospect of using the force of government to *impose* what they want. Success seems easier along that route than along the route of persuading myriads of individuals voluntarily to observe, for example, stricter standards of boating safety. Hobbyists seeking entertainment or a sense of participation are inclined to want to be in fashion. If altruist and interventionist doctrines prevail, they will go along.

THE POLITICIAN

The politician, to thrive in his career, must recognize the voters as they are—the average voters with their susceptibilities, the special interests and hobbyists with their particular concerns. Like most people, he wants to think well of himself; he wants to think he is accomplishing something. His particular mission in life is to perceive problems and get government programs enacted to solve them.[15] Even when out of office, the politician does not typically strive to limit the scope for doing good in the office he hopes to win at the next election.[16] In office, he wants to carry forth his uncompleted programs and continue serving the public better than his opponents could do.

Publicity is helpful in the quest for votes. (So is having patronage with which to reward supporters, and to which government expansion contributes.) One way to gain favorable publicity is to become identified with one or more problems and with proposals for their solution—pollution, unemployment, the urban crisis, the energy crisis, the expenses of medical care, poverty, inequality, or whatever. It may even count as a solution that the proposed legislation merely creates a new agency assigned to deal with the problem.[17] One reason for delegating work to regulatory agencies is that the legislature has too much to do to consider problems and solutions in detail; legislating, along with the bargaining necessary for it, is a high-cost activity with steeply rising marginal costs (Posner 1974). Furthermore, the vagueness inherent in handling a problem by turning it over to a new agency can itself be helpful in lulling possible opposition, just as vagueness in the wording of a proposed international agreement may be helpful in getting all parties to accept it.

The individual advocate of one particular bit of government expansion has little personal incentive to consider the external diseconomies that may result in the form of the enhanced role of inadequately supervised experts and the worsened difficulties of monitoring government. Neither he nor the voters will recognize any responsibility of his for such long-run consequences. Later on, after such pseudosolutions have enhanced the power of administrators, reduced the relative power of the people and

---

[15] "[T]he people's representatives seem to be enchanted with the notion that they are not doing their job unless they are manufacturing laws" (McClellan 1974, p. 66).

[16] See Benjamin Constant, *Cours de Politique Constitutionnelle* (1818–1820), as quoted in Bertrand de Jouvenel 1949, p. 384; and also de Jouvenel himself, p. 10.

[17] Relevant here is Amitai Etzioni 1972, pp. 88–92, 142–143. Headed "Got a problem ... ? ... call or write The Grand Shaman," the article notes people's propensity to look to the federal government for solutions to all sorts of problems. Its main concern, however, is the empty, symbolic character of many ostensible solutions. Speeches are made, conferences held, commissions appointed, bills passed, agencies established, funds appropriated, and programs launched, often doing little of substance to treat the problems involved.

their elected representatives, increased the difficulties of monitoring the government, and expanded the scope for court cases, these unintended results will hardly be traced to and blamed on the original sponsors of the legislation. Meanwhile, they get credit for being *concerned* with problems.

Politicians and government officials tend to have short time horizons. Unlike corporation executives, who may hold stock or stock options of their companies and whose performance tends to be assessed and reported on the stock market anyway, government officials hold no shares of stock whose current prices might reflect assessments of the *long-run* consequences of their actions; hence, short-run electoral concerns tend to prevail. How much incentive, for example, do mayors have to mount strong resistance to the demands of unionized city employees? Mayor John Lindsay of New York "took the attitude that he would not be around in ten years. He thought he would be either in the White House or doing something else, so he decided to pay people off with promises of pensions that would come due when he was no longer mayor" (Bork 1978, p. 13).

The personal qualities useful in gaining favorable publicity and in political wheeling and dealing are not likely to coincide with the personal qualities of a competent, far-sighted, and courageous statesman. Neither are the qualities of a successful campaigner, which include adroitness in projecting an appealing personality and in cleverly stating or obscuring issues.[18] Similarly, a competent and devoted public servant would have rather different qualities than a personally successful bureaucrat, whose abilities might run more toward cultivating superiors by promoting their personal ambitions.

Exceptions do occur. Why can't a politician see it as his mission in life to do good by resisting and reversing the trend toward ever more government? If that resistance really is in the interest of the average citizen, why

---

[18] See Ellul 1967, pp. 150–151: "The politician is generally not competent with regard to the problems that are his to solve, particularly if, as it is now inevitable, he has become a specialist in political affairs.... The political leader must be a politician by trade, which means to be a clever technician in the capture and defense of positions.... desire for power clearly has priority ... because he cannot undertake just and desirable reforms or guard the common good unless he *first* obtains power and keeps it.... The two forms of politics ... demand radically different personal qualities and contrary preoccupations. To be a clever maneuverer in arriving at the summit is no qualification for perceiving the common good, making decisions, being politically enlightened, or mastering economic problems. Conversely, to have the moral qualities and intellectual competence to be capable of genuine thought and of eventually putting a genuine political program into operation in no way ensures having the equipment to reach the top."

can't the politician both serve his self-esteem and win votes by campaigning on such a platform?

Conceivably he might. But these questions, instead of refuting the argument about activist biases, merely note a possible offset. For several reasons, this offset is unlikely to be strong. (The exceptional politician to whom the following remarks do not apply stands at a disadvantage in winning elections and wielding influence.) First, a political career would generally have been less appealing in the first place to a skeptic about government than to a man who saw great opportunities in it for doing good. Opportunities for also gaining personal success in that endeavor are greater for a politician, as for a bureaucrat, if government is big and growing than if it is kept small. Secondly, winning elections on a platform of *restricting* government activities depends on a greater degree of sophisticated understanding among voters than they are likely to have (although hope on this score is now emerging). Even if a politician is concerned with enlightening the citizens over the long run, he must realize that his chances of providing enlightenment are poor if the voters remove him from political life. He directs his campaigning to the citizens as they are and as they think, not to the economists and political philosophers that they are not.

A third line of rebuttal denies the common idea that politicians try to sell their programs to voters for votes quite as businessmen try to sell their wares to consumers for dollars. The analogy is defective in many respects. For example, candidates go beyond direct appeals to the electorate. They also seek votes indirectly by appealing to influential opinionmakers and to other politicians. Alliances are essential for getting nominations, getting allocations of party funds and other help in campaigns, and logrolling the enactment of one's favorite projects (and thereby gaining in personal status). The individual politician has to tailor his appeal partly to other politicians, most of whom incline toward an activist government for the reasons under discussion. Even the exceptional politician is restrained, then, from advocating as much limitation of government power as he might otherwise personally favor.

Our amateur psychologizing about politicians should pay some attention to the members of legislators' staffs. With government expansion and legislative burdens making increasing demands on their employers' time and ability to absorb information, staff members have growing influence. They further their own careers by helping their employers gain prominence. Bright ideas help. Although a few ideas may focus on repealing laws and abolishing agencies, activism generally offers more scope for brightness, as well as for maintaining political alliances, especially in an intellectual atmosphere predisposed to activism.

THE BUREAUCRAT

The bureaucrat, like the politician, may well see his mission in life as doing good through the agency of government. He is likely, though, except at the highest levels, to be a specialist. (At the highest levels, he is likely to be mobile between government positions and to be judged more by his reputed abilities and performance in the short run than by the long-run consequences of how he runs any particular agency.) The specialist identifies with the mission of his bureau, appreciates the value of its services, but appreciates less clearly the alternative results obtainable from devoting the necessary money and resources to other purposes, public or private. Like most people, he wants to think that his job is important and demanding and that he is doing it well. With a bigger budget and a larger staff, he could serve the public still better. Fortunately for his ambitions, the legislators must depend largely on what he and his fellow experts tell them about the benefits and costs of his agency's activities. Because his job is specialized and complicated and because they have other tasks also, the legislators cannot monitor him closely. Furthermore, alliances tend to form among the agency, the members of the legislative committee monitoring it, and the constituency in the private sector that benefits from the agency's services or regulations.[19]

THE COURTS

Judges, like other government decisionmakers, are often in a position to take a narrow view, doing what seems good or benevolent in the particular case at hand without having to weigh costs against benefits carefully and without having to exercise adequate foresight about the long-run

---

[19]William A. Niskanen (1971) argues that bureaucrats strive to maximize their budgets. Years earlier, Ludwig von Mises had stressed the contrast between a profit-seeking firm and a bureau. In a firm, the higher executives can monitor the performance of their subordinates by financial accounting and the test of profit and loss. Monitoring is more complicated in a nonprofit organization. Especially in one that gets its funds from budget appropriations rather than by selling goods or services to willing customers, the financial tests are necessarily weakened, and detailed "bureaucratic" rules and regulations must take their place as best they can (Mises 1945).

repercussions of a particular decision. Of course, judges are under an obligation to decide according to the law, including precedent; but when legislation, administrative decrees, lawsuits, and court decisions have vastly proliferated, the judge—cued by the litigants' attorneys—has all the more decisions to hunt among for the precedent that will rationalize the decision he wants to make.

Nathan Glazer (1975) describes several factors contributing to a tide of judicial activism. Powerful new interests are at work, including public-advocacy law centers supported by government or foundations. "Law—for the purpose of the correction of presumed evils, for changing government practices, for overruling legislatures, executives, and administrators, for the purpose indeed of replacing democratic procedures with the authoritarian decisions of judges—became enormously popular" (p. 123). Second, the courts must work out the logic of positions once taken and cannot easily withdraw from their implications. New decisions create precedents whose applications and extensions cannot be fully foreseen; case law evolves with a momentum of its own. Examples concern the concepts of "standing" to sue, of due process, and of equal protection. Third, expansion of government activity provides all the more subject matter for court cases. The "facts" relevant to court decisions become all the more numerous and complex. Social science becomes relevant; and as it changes, so may the law. The judges acquire all the more opportunities for second-guessing not only ordinary citizens but also the legislative and executive branches of government.[20] In short, the courts well illustrate the main theme of this paper: the fragmentation, on the governmental scene, of cost-benefit calculation, decisions, and responsibility.

A POSSIBLE COUNTERARGUMENT

Considering the circumstances and incentives of voters, politicians, bureaucrats, and judges does seem to reveal a bias toward hyperactive government. Yet Anthony Downs (1960), who had lucidly explained the rationality of voter ignorance, went on to offer a supposed explanation of "why the government budget is too small in a democracy." The core of his argument is that the rationally ignorant voter does not appreciate all the remote and problematical benefits that government programs would provide. As society becomes wealthier and more complex, the potential scope for remote

---

[20] Glazer cites numerous specific examples of judicial activism. I have rearranged and interpreted Glazer's points.

and poorly understood but genuine government benefits expands. Public goods do not enjoy the advertising that private goods do. The average voter is highly aware, however, of the costs of government programs as reflected in his taxes. Catering to such voters, politicians hold taxing and spending down to levels at which the benefits of additional spending would still exceed the costs.

Several things are wrong with this argument. First, taxes are not all that evident to the individual voter. Excise taxes are concealed in the prices of products, and just which persons ultimately bear the burden of the corporation income tax is even more obscure. Even personal income taxes can be made less conspicuous by withholding. Downs does not take adequate account of these tax concealments. He does not adequately recognize the several distinct ways in which inflation can bring what amounts to hidden tax increases. He does not recognize how easy it is for government to spend the incremental tax revenues generated by economic growth. He does not take "fiscal illusion" seriously enough. Second, politicians have discovered the beauties of deficit spending; and working as they do with short time horizons, they do not agonize over an ultimate day of reckoning. Third, Downs gives only unconvincing examples of government activities that have thin but widespread benefits, or benefits that are great in the long run but unnoticed in the short run. In fact, his chief example seems to be foreign aid. Although he notes the coercive nature of dealings with government, he seems not to recognize that private activities carried out with resources not taxed away might themselves have remote benefits and that the coercive nature of the expansion of government activity makes that expansion less likely to leave a net excess of benefit over cost than the alternative of voluntary expansion of private activity. He does not recognize the differential incentives that special private interests have to press exaggerated claims about the benefits of the government programs that they are seeking.

Fourth, while Downs applies the approach of methodological individualism to the voter, he does not apply it consistently to bureaucrats, politicians, judges, and litigants. In some passages, he refers to "the governing party" or even "the government" as if it were a monolithic entity making coordinated choices rather than an assemblage of individual persons each working with his own drives, motives, opportunities, incentives, constraints, and special point of view. He does not take heed of how individual legislators or candidates can call for particular spending programs without calling for the taxes to pay for them. He supposes that each bureau would submit its budget requests to, in effect, "the directors of the governing party," who, anxious for votes, would develop suitable checks on the bureau's expansionism. He does not recognize, as William Niskanen (1971) later explained, that self-aggrandizing bureaus are in fact not supervised by a sufficiently authoritative central budgeting agency. On the contrary, they are likely to develop cozy relations with the congressional committees that are supposed to monitor them. In short, Downs fails to grasp the full implications of fragmented government decision-making.

POLICY DRIFT

The fragmentation of decisions over time contributes to an unintended drift of the character of the whole economic and political system. Especially under a two-party system, platform-builders and campaigners often avoid drawing issues in a clear-cut way.[21] A candidate opposed to protective tariffs would not call for complete free trade for fear of losing some protectionist voters who would support him on other issues. He realizes that many a voter will choose the lesser evil rather than "waste his vote" on a third party even if one happened to mirror his own set of views more accurately. Political straddling, together with the jumbling together of unrelated issues (and even the candidates' personalities) in every election, water down the issue of interventionism versus the free market into an uninspiring choice between parties leaning just a little more one way or a little more the other. Incentives and prejudices favoring a middle-of-the-road position leave the direction of cumulative policy drift to whoever are most active in locating the two sides of the road, or even just one side. The kinds of choices that voters and politicians consider feasible (and, similarly, the positions they consider unrealistically extreme) are conditioned by how policy has been drifting. Resistance to drift weakens when not only politicians but even scholars make a fetish of recommending only policies they consider politically "realistic."[22] Under such circumstances, discussion does not adequately consider long-run repercussions and long-run compatibilities and clashes among various goals and measures. Major choices, such as ones affecting the general character of the

---

[21]An early explanation was provided by Harold Hotelling (1929) in an article basically dealing with economic matters.

[22]On the harmfulness and even immorality of such "realism," see Clarence E. Philbrook 1953.

economic and social system, may get made by default as the cumulative result of piecemeal decisions whose combined tendencies were not realized when they were made.

FRAGMENTATION BAD AND GOOD

Closely related to dispersion of decisionmaking among persons and over time is dispersion of responsibility. Things that would be considered morally reprehensible if done by a single decisionmaker escape moral condemnation when done by government, since it is not apparent where the responsibility lies. Examples are our inflation mess, the quasi-repudiation of government debt, the taxation of phantom earnings and phantom capital gains, even when the taxpayer has suffered a real loss and even when he has suffered it on bonds of the government itself, and the government's continued pushing of its savings bonds.

Fragmentation of decisionmaking is not to be condemned *tout court*. In many cases, keeping decisions close to the affected level will improve the cost-benefit confrontation. Furthermore, it helps preserve freedom. In fact, this is one of the chief arguments for the market as opposed to government control.[23]

CROWDING OUT

Another disadvantage of routine reliance on government to suppress all bad and promote all good is that it tends to freeze out alternative solutions to the problems tackled. It can hamper diverse initiatives and experimentation. It can crowd out private activity by taxing away funds that

---

[23]"The system of direct regulation cannot allow flexibility in the application to individual cases because favoritism cannot be distinguished from flexibility and diversity of conditions cannot be distinguished from caprice. The price system, however, possesses this remarkable power: if we make an activity expensive in order to reduce its practice, those who are most attached to the practice may still continue it. It is the system which excludes from an industry not those who arrived last but those who prize least the right to work in that industry. It is the system which builds roads by hiring men with an aptitude for road-building, not by the corvée of compulsory labor" (Stigler 1975, p. 36).

The recent gasoline shortage and proposals to deal with it by rationing or by making everybody forgo driving one day a week, or the nonsystem of rationing by inconvenience, all illustrate Stigler's points about regulation versus the market. Regulation cannot take into account the detailed personal knowledge that people have about their own needs and wants and circumstances.

people would otherwise spend themselves on satisfying their wants, by transferring real resources from the private to the public sector, by creating or threatening subsidized competition with private approaches, and by stifling imagination with the thought that the problem in question is already being taken care of. It is instructive to ponder what the state of affairs in education, health and retirement programs, housing, transportation, the mails, and other fields would be today if government had not gotten so heavily involved as it has in fact. One frequent advantage of private over government financing is that it can take better account of how strongly people desire an activity on the whole and in its various possible forms. Far from the importance of an activity arguing for its being taken over by the government, one should think that its importance argues against its being dominated by one big supplier. It is all the more regrettable when various monopolized activities are monopolized by the same monopolist and when economic and political power are combined, with all that implies about potentialities for coercion.

What crowding out means is illustrated in the field of energy. Proposals abound for government action and subsidies to develop non-conventional sources. Taxpayers would in effect have to pay the difference between the high cost and lower price of subsidized fuels; and they could not, acting individually, escape this burden by energy conservation. Production from conventional sources and potential production from unsubsidized new sources will suffer as producers find it easier and less risky to take government handouts. Not only money but also talent and ingenuity will be diverted from other types of production, exploration, and research into those favored by the government. Business firms and investors will shy away from risky, expensive, long-term-oriented projects not only for fear of future government-subsidized competition but also for fear of future infringements on property rights. The history of energy policy, together with current demogogy, provides ample grounds for the latter fear: firms and investors must recognize the prospect that even after risking heavy losses, they will not be allowed to collect exceptionally large profits from successful hunches and good luck.[24] Government reassurances, even if made, would nowadays not be credible. This example bears on a broader point about remote repercussions—remote in time and in sector affected. A violation of property rights—perhaps restrictions on use of

---

[24]Paul L. Joskow and Robert S. Pindyck develop points like these in "Those Subsidized Energy Schemes" (1979, p. 12).

property rather than outright public purchase—may seem the economical and expedient thing to do in the individual case. Yet in contributing to an atmosphere of uncertainty, it can have grave repercussions in the long run.

An advocate of limited government cannot specify just what non-governmental solution to a problem might have been found if it had not been crowded out. An economist sympathetic to the market can explain how entrepreneurs have incentives to seek unfilled wants and ways of filling them, but he cannot predict what unfilled wants are going to be filled, and how and when.[25] Hence his position seems complacent; it reeks of the ivory tower. In contrast, the interventionist position looks concrete, active, practical, and down-to-earth.

Here I am in danger of being misunderstood. While I deplore regulating voluntary transactions that are not immoral and that adults are undertaking with their eyes open, the case is different with hidden safety or health hazards or with the imposition of costs onto innocent third parties. I have qualms about cold-turkey deregulation in such cases. Yet over the long run, phasing out government regulation could open the way for entrepreneurial discovery of alternatives that we can hardly imagine in advance. Such alternatives might, for example, include inspection and certification by specialist firms, as well as regulations imposed by insurance companies as a condition of insurance. My emphasis, however, is not on predicting alternative approaches but on their unpredictability and on how central control can forestall their discovery.[26]

---

[25] See Hayek 1973, especially the section headed "Freedom can be preserved only by following principles and is destroyed by following expediency," pp. 56–59. Hayek reminds us that the benefits of civilization rest on using more knowledge than can be deployed in any deliberately concerted effort. "Since the value of freedom rests on opportunities it provides for unforeseen and unpredictable actions, we will rarely know what we lose through a particular restriction of freedom." Any restriction will aim at some foreseeable particular benefit, while what it forecloses will usually remain unknown and disregarded. Deciding each issue on its own apparent merits means overestimating the advantages of central direction.

[26] Israel M. Kirzner explains how regulation can impede the process of discovery. His concern, however, is not so much with alternative solutions to problems taken under the government's wing as, rather, with discovery of new and better goods and services and production methods. Furthermore, regulation diverts entrepreneurs' energies from seeking discoveries of these constructive kinds into coping with or circumventing the regulations themselves. See Kirzner 1979, esp. chap. 4.

STILL BROADER COSTS OF REGULATION

Costs (and conceivably benefits) of regulatory measures include effects on the whole social, political, and economic climate and on people's attitudes. One example of what I have in mind concerns how even the vaguest hints about discriminatory enforcement of myriad regulations can be used to encourage "voluntary" compliance with the wage and price controls decreed by the president, without legal authority, in October 1978.[27] Another hard-to-fathom cost is the danger (already alluded to in the section on "The Courts") of undermining the rule of law and the law's objectivity, predictability, and worthiness of respect.

My worries do not hinge on any particular one of the several theories of regulation that are in circulation.[28] I am not, for example, adopting as the central story the theory that regulated industries "capture" their regulatory authorities. No doubt some aspects even of the public-interest theory of regulation enter into the explanation of why we have so much of it. Numerous pressures, motivations, and governmental decisionmakers interact.[29]

The issue of regulation falls under the broader question of whether policy should serve principle or expediency, the latter meaning to act on the supposed merits of each individual case, narrowly considered. Elements of an answer to that question argue for framing policy with prime attention, instead, to the general framework of rules within which persons and companies can pursue their own goals. (In philosophical terminology, the argument favors rules-utilitarianism over act-utilitarianism.)

Some types of regulation are even open to objection on ethical grounds. Notions of human rights properly belong in the discussion, including rights of people to make open-and-above-board voluntary transactions

---

[27] Referring to this program, one Federal Reserve economist has written as follows: "Violators are explicitly threatened with bad publicity and loss of government contracts. Implicitly, possible violators must be aware of potential retaliation by regulatory agencies not formally incorporated in the wage-price control program.... Due to the magnitude of discretionary authority possessed by the Internal Revenue Service, Environmental Protection Agency, Federal Trade Commission, Occupational Safety and Health Administration, etc., a large potential for retaliation confronts any business" (Webb 1979, p. 14 n.).

[28] See Stigler 1975; Richard A. Posner 1974; and Sam Peltzman 1976.

[29] "More generally, different types of constitutionally empowered agents on the political scene—bureaucrats, judges, legislators, and elected executives—each bring distinct motivations, authorities, and constraints into the process of political exchange that leads to the final regulatory outcome" (Hirshleifer 1976, p. 242).

with each other and to use and deal in their own property.[30] It is a questionable view to accord equal respect to people's use of their own property and forcible interference with that use. That view sets aside the question of who has a right to do what in favor of the question of which expected pattern of property use and resource allocation appeals more to politicians and other outside observers.

POLICY IMPLICATIONS

What implications follow from my argument, if it is broadly correct? Most generally, it recommends alertness to activist bias, and an appropriate constitutional attitude. Proposals have been made for a regulatory budget: included in the annual limit to each regulatory agency's expenses would be not only its own cash outlays but also the estimated costs that compliance with its regulations would impose on the private sector. Admittedly, implementing such a proposal would run into practical difficulties, but it is mainly its spirit that concerns us here.

It is instructive to review the rationale for the analogous proposal of placing a constitutional limit on federal government taxing or spending. The opportunity to enact such a limit would give the public at large the hitherto lacking means to vote on the total of the government budget. By voting for a limit, a majority could override the spending bias that arises from the accumulation of smaller special-interest decisions.[31] The people assign a budget to the legislature and require it spend the limited amount of money in the most effective way. (Supporters of a limit ask: if families have to operate within income ceilings, why shouldn't the government also?) Overall limitation would force choices among the many spending programs that might be separately desirable. To argue persuasively in the face of a given budget total, a group wanting a particular program would have to point out other budget items that could and should be cut. Special interests would then be forced to work for the general interest rather than against it.

Regulatory activity is not as quantifiable as taxing and spending. But it would be premature to give up on ingenuity. Perhaps a quantitative specification will prove impossible and procedural restraints will have to serve as a substitute. A constitutional amendment might require that enactment of

---

[30] See Tibor R. Machan 1979.
[31] See *Wall Street Journal* 1978 and, in particular, Milton Friedman 1978, pp. 7–14.

new regulatory measures be coupled with repeal of others of comparable scope (perhaps as judged by numbers of regulators involved, or number of persons or dollar volume of activities in the private sector directly affected). Perhaps it would be necessary to settle for some vaguer and more nearly only hortatory restraint. Anyway, good intentions would not be enough to justify a new regulation; the proposed measure would have to be shown to be not merely desirable but exceptionally so, desirable even against the background of an already overgrown government. The objective is a framework of constraints and opinion in which different government activities are seen to be in rivalry with one another, each costing the sacrifice of others. Ideally, advocates of each new regulatory measure would accept the obligation of showing it to be so desirable as to be worth the sacrifice of specified existing regulations.

Opponents sometimes charge that a budget limit would undemocratically tie the hands of democratic government, and a similar objection would no doubt be made to constitutional restrictions on regulation. Yet the purpose of either limit is not to undercut democracy but to make it more effective by remedying a flaw that has so far kept the people from controlling the overall consequences of piecemeal decisions. A budget limit or a regulatory limit no more subverts democracy than the First Amendment does by setting limits to what Congress may do. Without that amendment, popular majorities might have placed many particular restrictions on freedom of speech, but our Founding Fathers rolled all these issues up together instead of letting each one be decided by a separate majority vote (Friedman 1978, pp. 8–10).

Just as proponents of tax cuts or budget limits face the supposedly embarrassing demand that they draw up lists of specific expenditure cuts, so proponents of limits to regulation might encounter a similar demand. This one might well be easier to comply with than the demand about spending cuts. Either demand, however, is unreasonable. It in effect invites the limitationists to shut up unless they exhibit detailed knowledge of government (and private) activities that they cannot realistically be expected to have. It tacitly denies that the principle of specialization and division of labor applies in public policymaking as in other areas of life. It tacitly supposes that general knowledge—namely, knowledge of bias in the current system—is worthless unless accompanied by detailed further knowledge on the part of the same persons. Yet the very purpose of an overall limit is to bring the detailed knowledge of its possessors to bear in coping with that bias.

SUMMARY

The private sector is routinely made the target of regulation because of externalities, meaning cases in which the persons who decide on some activity or its scale decide wrongly because they do not themselves bear or take full account of all of its costs and benefits.[32] How ironic, then, routinely to expect a solution from government! Government is the prototypical sector in which decisionmakers do *not* take accurate account of all the costs as well as all the benefits of each activity. The fragmentation of decisionmaking and responsibility goes part way toward explaining this condition, along with the kinds of opportunities and incentives that bureaucrats, politicians, legislative staff members, judges, and citizens have.

It is difficult to compare even the relatively direct and obvious costs and benefits of an individual government policy action. It is practically impossible to assess the indirect and long-run consequences of individual actions and of their aggregate, including their effects on the drift of policy and on the character of the economic and social system. The aggregate of activities all appearing individually desirable may itself turn out quite undesirable. Hence the importance of frankly allowing considerations of political philosophy into policy discussions. Broad principles should count, including a principle of skepticism about government activity. Even when no strong and obvious disadvantages are apparent, there is presumption (though a defeasible one) against each new government function. The pragmatic, "realistic" approach of considering each individual function separately and narrowly, on its own supposed merits, is fatally flawed.

Our Founding Fathers accepted the concept of human rights that government should not violate. That concept need not be based on mysticism. It follows from a version of rules-utilitarianism (as distinguished from act-utilitarianism). As John Stuart Mill argued (in *Utilitarianism*, chapter 5, writing when the word "justice" had not yet been stretched into uselessness for all but emotive purposes), unswervingly to put respect for justice ahead of what might be called narrow expediency is a rule of topmost utility (or expediency in a broad and deep sense). I believe it can be shown that respect for and basing policy on certain rights and values, like justice,

---

[32] Externalities are due, anyway, not to the very logic of the market system but to difficulties and costs of fully applying that system, including property rights, to the cases in question.

accords with human nature and with the sort of society in which people have good chances for cooperating effectively as they pursue happiness in their own specific ways. Ludwig von Mises and Henry Hazlitt, following David Hume, have persuasively argued that social cooperation is such an indispensable means to people's pursuit of their own diverse specific goals that it deserves recognition practically as a goal in its own right.[33] Considerations like these merit respect again in appraisals of government regulation.

REFERENCES

Beaver, Roy A. Letter to *Wall Street Journal*, 26 July 1978.

Bork, Robert. *Taxpayers' Revolt: Are Constitutional Limits Desirable?* American Enterprise Institute Round Table, July 1978. Washington, D.C.: American Enterprise Institute, 1978.

Brittan, Samuel. *The Political Economy of Inflation*. Edited by Fred Hirsch and John H. Goldthorpe. Cambridge, Mass.: Harvard University Press, 1978.

Dahl, Robert A. *A Preface to Democratic Theory*. Chicago: University of Chicago Press, 1963.

de Jouvenel, Bertrand. *On Power*. New York: Viking, 1949.

Downs, Anthony. *An Economic Theory of Democracy*. New York: Harper, 1957.

———. "Why the Government Budget is Too Small in a Democracy." *World Politics* 3 (July 1960): 541–563.

Ellul, Jacques. *The Political Illusion*. Translated by Konrad Kellen. New York: Knopf, 1967.

———. *A Critique of the New Commonplaces*. Translated by Helen Weaver. New York: Knopf, 1968.

Etzioni, Amitai. "The Grand Shaman." *Psychology Today* 6 (November 1972): 88–92, 142–143.

Fein, Leonard J., ed. *American Democracy*. New York: Holt, Rinehart and Winston, 1964.

---

[33] See Ludwig von Mises 1949 and 1957, esp. pp. 57–58; and Henry Hazlitt 1964. An emphasis on social cooperation as a near-ultimate criterion, if not the use of the term, traces back at least as far as Thomas Hobbes.

Friedman, Milton. *Capitalism and Freedom*. Chicago: University of Chicago Press, 1962.

———. "The Limitations of Tax Limitation." *Policy Review* 5 (Summer 1978): 7–14.

Glazer, Nathan. "Towards an Imperial Judiciary?" *The Public Interest* 41 (Fall 1975): 104–123.

Hayek, F.A. "The Use of Knowledge in Society." *American Economic Review* 35 (September 1945): 519–530.

———. *The Counter-Revolution of Science*. Glencoe, Ill.: Free Press, 1952.

———. *Rules and Order*. Vol. 1 of *Law, Legislation and Liberty*. Chicago: University of Chicago Press, 1973.

Hazlitt, Henry. *The Foundations of Morality*. Princeton, N.J.: D. Van Nostrand, 1964.

Hirshleifer, Jack. "Comment" on "Toward a More General Theory of Regulation," by Sam Peltzman. *Journal of Law and Economics* 19 (August 1976): 242.

Hotelling, Harold. "Stability in Competition." *Economic Journal* 39 (March 1929): 41–57.

Joskow, Paul L., and Robert S. Pindyck. "Those Subsidized Energy Schemes." *Wall Street Journal*, 2 July 1979.

Kirzner, Israel M. *The Perils of Regulation: A Market-Process Approach*. Law and Economics Center Occasional Paper. Coral Gables, Fla.: Law and Economics Center of the University of Miami, 1979.

Machan, Tibor R. "Some Normative Considerations of Deregulation." *Journal of Social and Political Studies* 3 (Winter 1979): 363–377.

Mann, Thomas E. *Unsafe at Any Margin*. Washington, D.C.: American Enterprise Institute, 1978.

McClellan, James. "The Tyranny of Legalism." A review of Bruno Leoni, *Freedom and the Law*. *University Bookman* (Spring 1974): 66.

Mises, Ludwig von. *Bureaucracy*. London: Hodge, 1945.

———. *Human Action*. New Haven, Conn.: Yale University Press, 1949.

———. *Theory and History*. New Haven, Conn.: Yale University Press, 1957.

Niskanen, William A. *Bureaucracy and Representative Government.* Chicago: Aldine-Atherton, 1971.

Olson, Mancur, Jr. *The Logic of Collective Action.* Cambridge, Mass.: Harvard University Press, 1965.

Peltzman, Sam. "Toward a More General Theory of Regulation." *Journal of Law and Economics* 19 (August 1976): 211–240.

Philbrook, Clarence E. "'Realism' in Policy Espousal." *American Economic Review* 43 (December 1953): 846–859.

Posner, Richard A. "Theories of Economic Regulation." *Bell Journal of Economics and Management Science* 5 (Autumn 1974): 335–358.

Rickenbacker, William F., and Lewis K. Uhler. *A Taxpayer's Guide to Survival: Constitutional Tax-Limitation.* Briarcliff Manor, N.Y.: National Tax-Limitation Committee, 1977.

Sansweet, Stephen J. "Proposition 13's Impact on the Arts." *Wall Street Journal*, 14 July 1978.

"Single-Issue Politics." *Newsweek*, 6 November 1978.

Stein, Herbert. "The Real Reasons for a Tax Cut." *Wall Street Journal*, 18 July 1978.

Stigler, George J. *The Citizen and the State.* Chicago: University of Chicago Press, 1975.

Wall Street Journal. Editorial. 12 July 1978.

Waltz, Kenneth N. *Theory of International Politics.* Reading, Mass., and Menlo Park, Calif.: Addison-Wesley Publishing Company, 1979.

Webb, Roy H. "Wage-Price Restraint and Macroeconomic Disequilibrium." Federal Reserve Bank of Richmond *Economic Review* 65, no. 3 (May/June 1979).

CHAPTER 18

Economics and Principles*

The title does not announce a talk about the Principles of Economics course. Instead, I am going to deliver a sermon—and I use the word in a self-deprecatory sense. So far as my sermon champions principle over expediency, it is directed more toward academics in their roles as self-appointed policy advisers than toward practicing politicians. Politicians could not function without making compromises. Senator Everett Dirksen used to say, quite aptly, "I am a man of principle, and my chief principle is flexibility."

Now, a sermon is not required on an occasion like this one. Some of my predecessors have talked about technicalities of their special fields. On the other hand, there is plenty of precedent for talking more about the interrelations of topics than about the details of any, for making broad observations and sweeping conjectures, and for including a personal element.

My theme is the two-way relation that exists between economics and general principles of behavior. Economics helps us understand the nature and basis of such principles, their serviceability, and the conditions that tend to support or undermine them.[1]

THE ECONOMICS OF PRINCIPLES

Economists can help explain the value of respecting principles not only in the realm of economic policy but also in other interactions among human beings. Relevant strands of economic theory refer to: the concept, made familiar by Hayek (1967, chap. 6) of "results of human action but not of human design" (ethical codes and languages, as well as money and other economic institutions, being prime examples); the importance, for

---

*Presidential address at meetings of the Southern Economic Association, printed in *Southern Economic Journal* 42 (April 1976): 559–571.
[1]The section "Principles and Policy" in the original version of this article was removed for brevity. Its major points are addressed in chapter 17, "Is There a Bias Toward Overregulation?".

a functioning society, of people's having some basis for predicting each other's actions; the inevitable imperfection, incompleteness, dispersion, and costliness of knowledge; the costs of making transactions and of negotiating, monitoring, and enforcing agreements, and the consequent usefulness of tacit agreements and informally enforced rules; applications of methodological individualism and of property-rights theory to analysis of nonmarket institutions and activities; concepts of externalities and collective goods and the supposed free-rider problem; and the principle of general interdependence.

Such concepts enter into explaining the usefulness of ethical rules and even of concern with people's characters.[2] Statutory law cannot prevent all bad and enforce all good behavior. Laws attempting that would be prohibitively costly to frame and enforce, as would the mobilization of the necessary information. They would have to be sweeping and vague, would leave dangerous scope for administrative discretion, and would violate the principle of *nulla poena sine lege*. The law could not enforce ordinary decency, let alone actual benevolence. ("Ordinary decency" means such things as honesty, respect for other people's rights, and being considerate, as in not throwing bottles into the street or making too much noise.) The very attempt at legal enforcement of decency, though doomed to failure, would spell totalitarian control over people's lives. This is not to deny that properly enforceable ethical standards exist—far from it, and I shall have more to say about enforcement later on—, but the case is overwhelming for keeping those standards and their enforcement outside the realm of government and for keeping them informal, flexible, and subject to piecemeal, gradual, decentralized reform (Hazlitt 1964, esp. pp. 184–185).[3]

---

[2] A social scientist may take interest in how ethical principles relate to the functioning of a social and economic system without imagining himself to possess superior moral character. It is no coincidence that many eminent economists have pursued such an interest—David Hume, Adam Smith, John Stuart Mill, Henry Sidgwick, J.M. Keynes, and James Buchanan, to mention a few. Without implicating him in any mistakes of mine, I should particularly like to mention my colleague Roland McKean, a former president of our Association, with whose ideas on the economics of morality mine run largely in parallel. See, for example, his two papers of 1974. I should also like to acknowledge a significant parallelism (despite some differences) with the thinking of another former president and a former colleague, James Buchanan, whose *The Limits of Liberty* (1975) I have read since delivering this address.

[3] The most basic principles of morality, I would argue, are relatively unchanging, deriving as they do from human nature, including man's nature as a social animal. But the specific rules that are appropriate do change as factual circumstances and knowledge change. Furthermore, as Hazlitt suggests, there may be such a thing as progress in moral

(Vagueness and flexibility are undesirable, however, as characteristics of government law.)

For insight into the respective merits of voluntarism and law in various aspects of life, let us consider the familiar kind of appeal for voluntary restraint in pricing, in wage demands, in energy consumption, and in spending and investing abroad. Such an approach tends, I argue, to undermine ordinary morality. By and large, it is in a person's long-run self-interest to behave with ordinary decency and to cultivate the kind of character that leads him to do so.[4] For this proposition to hold true, social institutions should be such as to hold down tension between self-interest and social interest (ostensible or actual), allowing the invisible hand to work. While legal rules and penalties do have a role in such arrangements, it is tremendously important for social cooperation that people generally be able to trust each other anyway. Voluntary decency is a scarce resource not to be wasted.

"Wasting" voluntary decency means putting an excessive strain on the implicit contract existing among members of society to treat each other decently. Such a strain occurs when, as is likely to be true in the context of appeals to "voluntary" economic self-denial, behavior in the supposed social interest does in fact clash with self-interest. A counter-argument to my contention is often more implicit than explicit. It sees value in giving people exercise for their moral muscles—habit-forming exercise in setting aside self-interest in the social interest. I conjecture, though, that plenty of occasions for moral exercise arise anyway in everyday life, when an excessively narrow and short-run conception of self-interest clashes with a fuller conception. I am warning against the kind of exercise that strains and damages moral muscles because the clash between self-interest and supposed social interest is genuine and not merely apparent.

---

understanding, with a minority of individuals leading the way. In morality as in law, continuity and modifiability both have value. Change is desirable in view of changing circumstances and knowledge, but not change so rapid that people cannot act and form expectations on the basis of a known moral code.

[4] Or so argue writers whom I respect, such as Moritz Schlick (1930/1962), Mortimer Adler (1970), and Ayn Rand (1957 and other novels). In effect they argue that the best prospects for a satisfying life hinge on having the sort of character that sometimes leads one to subordinate one's immediate narrow interest or whim to one's more enduring interest. Yet exceptions do occur; and in rare cases, decency will cost a man his life. Still, while a decent character does not guarantee happiness—nothing can—it tends to improve the probabilities. See Schlick 1930/1962, pp. 185–199, but esp. pp. 193–194.

Expecting people to act against their own economic interest tends to undercut the signaling function of prices and the incentive of loss-avoidance and profit. How are people to know, then, when it is legitimate and when illegitimate to pursue economic gain?[5] Why should they suppose that the President of the United States knows best? Why should they respect an attempt to obtain the results of possibly momentous legislation by bypassing the constitutional process?[6] To exhort people to think of compliance as in their own interest when it plainly is not, or to appeal to self-sacrifice as if it were the essence of morality, is to undercut the rational basis of morality and even rationality itself.[7] It obscures the compatibility between social interest and rational self-interest that can generally hold under appropriate social institutions. This educative effect is especially perverse when the ostensible social interest is not genuine and when the economic controls would be damaging even if enforced by law.

Appeals to voluntary sacrifice promote perverse selection by penalizing the people who do comply to the benefit of others. Mine is similar to Garrett Hardin's point (1968/1969) about the voluntary approach to population control in an overpopulated country:[8] the people who comply thereby contribute to the population relatively few persons exposed in their formative years to their own moral standards (and also having whatever genes may be relevant). The noncompliers will have relatively many children, who will grow up exposed to the lower moral standards of their parents (as well as having any relevant "bad" genes). Over time, these others will outbreed the decent people. In economic affairs, similarly, the compliant businessman who holds his selling price below the market-clearing level will

---

[5] I am referring, of course, to the pursuit of gain as such, not to the methods used. Lying, cheating, and stealing do not become right by being used in the pursuit of otherwise honorable ends.

[6] Furthermore, the voluntary approach tends to obscure responsibility for the unsatisfactory conditions occasioning the appeals to restraint and sacrifice. Appeals to ordinary citizens to "Stop Inflation" by restraint in consumption or in paying increased prices (appeals such as were frequent late in 1971) tend to draw attention away from the real source of trouble.

[7] As Robert G. Olson says (1965, pp. 12, 126), "the probable effect of urging a man to act contrary to what he rationally regards as his own best interests is either to embitter him or to inspire contempt for reason." "If ... an economic system is such that honesty puts an individual at a serious competitive disadvantage, the system is at least as much at fault as the dishonest individual, for honesty ought to pay not only with prestige but with profits."

[8] I cite Hardin only to clarify my point, not to echo his specific recommendation on an issue rather far afield from my present topic.

have to turn away some customers, who will then buy from his noncomplying rivals. In earning profits and winning control over resources, then, the less public-spirited businessmen will prevail over the more public-spirited. By practicing restraint in driving, public-spirited car owners will leave more gasoline available, and at a lower price than otherwise, to drivers less public-spirited than themselves. Eventually such effects become evident, further supporting the perverse idea that morality is for suckers and dupes.

In contrast with "voluntary" controls, legally enacted penalties against specifically defined violations do tend to make compliance serve the individual's self-interest. The contrast weakens, though, if supposedly compulsory controls, by their nature, are easy to evade, so that any compliance must in effect be voluntary. The contrast also weakens if the law makes crimes out of actions not otherwise morally wrong, or if the controls become so extensive and complicated that the individual can hardly know just what is expected of him.

My criticism of voluntary economic controls does not imply opposition to voluntarism in all aspects of life. Quite the contrary: precisely because voluntarism is indispensable, we must beware of misusing and subverting it. Far from denying that there are valid distinctions between right and wrong, I am stressing the alternatives to detailed governmental compulsion and prohibition. Many types of wrongdoing can be discouraged, if at all, only in an informal, de-centralized way. Discouragement consists in part of an atmosphere in which wrongdoers bear certain costs, including, perhaps, that of being regarded with appropriate revulsion.

Although dealing with relatively trivial cases, a memorable *Newsweek* column by Stewart Alsop (1970, p. 100) contains valuable insights. "[T]he man who makes a justified fuss," said Alsop, "does a public service."[9] Alsop cited examples of indifference of clerks at railroad ticket counters and hotel desks as long queues formed, the surliness of waiters, the dishonoring of confirmed air reservations. Professor David Klein of Michigan State University practices rendering the kind of public service that Alsop praised. When a Montreal hotel tried to dishonor his confirmed reservation, Klein gave the desk clerk three minutes to find him a room; otherwise, he would change to his pajamas in the lobby and go to sleep on a sofa. Klein got his room. Klein also makes it his practice to bill business

---

[9] Alsop deplored "the sheepish docility of most American customers." "In the public interest, the pricks should be kicked against at every opportunity."

firms for time spent coping with errors on their part. A quiet, well-bred scene does not embarrass him. "[I]f more people did what I do," he says, "business practices might improve." If middle-class people used their clout "in the right way, they could make enormous changes in retailing, and in other practices" (Nemy 1974).[10]

Alsop and Klein were suggesting that the exceptional victim who does protest deserves admiration for imposing costs on abuses and thereby discouraging their repetition. Because this service is a public good, as Alsop noted, the protester unfortunately reaps only a fraction at best of the total benefit from his action.

A further reason why incentives to protest are inadequate emerges from Helmut Schoeck's analysis of a case less trivial than those reported by Alsop and Klein. Schoeck's case may even afford insight into why totalitarian regimes can often enjoy apparent mass support. Schoeck supposes that a new center of power has come into being in some organization, perhaps by foul means. It seeks to bring "under its domination those groups and persons who have not yet submitted to it." Some groups or persons will already have lined up behind it, "whether out of greed, cowardice, stupidity or genuine enthusiasm. But these men ... are not satisfied with conforming, themselves, and almost invariably develop intense feelings of hostility towards those who continue to stand aside.... Tension, usually originating with the conformists, then arises between those who conform and those who do not." A conformist "begrudges others their courage, the freedom they still enjoy." He "sees both himself and his chosen power group endangered by those who obviously prefer ... to keep their distance. Those at the periphery of the power center ... now begin to exert pressure on other people ... with the object of getting them to conform as well" (Schoeck 1966/1970, pp. 89–90).

Schoeck could have strengthened his analysis by invoking Leon Festinger's theory of cognitive dissonance (1957, p. 4, chap. 4 and passim). Those who resist evil not only fail to reap the full benefits of their public service but even risk being reviled for performing it. Others will prefer to

---

[10]The Southern Economic Association has been victimized by the double-booking of hotel rooms for convention sessions. Vigorous protest in every such case would presumably hold down this sort of abuse, thus conferring external benefits. On the external benefits of what Buchanan calls "strategic courage" in tough individual cases and the external costs of what he calls "pragmatic compassion"—but "pragmatic compliance" might be a better term—, see his 1972/1975. Strategic courage is related to acting on principle, while pragmatic compliance follows from treating each case on its own narrow merits.

be "realistic," to "get along." Those who conform out of cowardice or calculation (to use Schoeck's words) shun facing that fact; such a cognition would be dissonant with their self-image as decent human beings. They have to adjust their cognitions. They come to believe that conformity is proper and moral, that the usurping power is worthy and its tactics honorable. The nonconformists pose an obstacle to this adjustment of cognitions, so the adjustment proceeds until the collaborators can really believe that the others are scoundrels. A further strand to the theory of cognitive dissonance is ironic but understandable: the more nearly just barely adequate was the inducement to collaborate, the stronger is the internal pressure on the collaborator to adjust his cognitions until he believes, sincerely, that he has lent his support to a worthy cause. No one likes to believe that he has betrayed his principles for small stakes, although as Elliot Aronson (1972) says, if a man sells out for a large amount of money, then he has as many cognitions as dollars that are consonant with his having taken a stand he does not really believe in.

For reasons like these, then, prospective resisters may decide not to make the necessary sacrifice in the first place. Why not cultivate a kind of stoicism instead?[11] Why not sit back, possibly enjoying a free ride if other people do raise the "justified fuss"?

Such passiveness is reinforced if people actually believe in "turning the other cheek" and in not passing judgment on other people's actions. Passiveness can create external diseconomies by almost inviting repetition of the wrongs tolerated. There is such a thing as culpable blindness to evil. Harold Macmillan had a point in saying of a certain British cabinet member of the 1930s who remained pacifistic in the face of the Nazi menace that "he was a good man in the worst sense of the word" (quoted in Davis 1975, p. 338).

Let me be clear. I am not calling for promiscuous meddling. I am not calling on everyone to go around hunting for misbehavior to condemn. Instead, I am referring to the role of people directly acquainted with abuses. Silent acquiescence on their part is no virtue.[12] Still, I would not say that

---

[11] In effect, though not in so many words, this is the advice of such writers as Albert Ellis (1968, esp. chap. 13), and, with Robert Harper (Ellis and Harper 1961), and Harry Browne (1974), the best-selling amateur economist and gold bug.

[12] The Honor System at the University of Virginia depends on the willingness of students who know of violations to accuse the offenders. Silence in such cases is considered dishonorable, subversive of the system. The system applies only to students, not to faculty members and administrators.

they have an actual obligation to speak out at great personal cost. I am urging a good deal less. Anyone who does render that public service deserves at least sympathetic understanding.

Worse than free riding on other people's carrying the burden of protest against injustices is the free-riding of the culprits themselves. The more prevalent and well based is the belief that people are generally decent and honest, the greater is the chance that culprits have to benefit from the presumption that they too have these virtues. They will enjoy a free ride on, while posing unfair competition with, the warranted credibility of other people. I conjecture that a general atmosphere of decency and trust in society is unstable for at least two reasons. The more prevalent knavery becomes, the stronger is the temptation on the individual to behave likewise, rather than lie down like a doormat (Hazlitt 1964, pp. 155–156). On the other hand, as I have just been arguing, when morality does generally prevail, the individual violator has a correspondingly high chance of profiting from the presumption that he is decent and honest though he is not.[13]

Just as X-inefficiency probably causes more economic loss than allocative inefficiency,[14] so, I conjecture, does the impairment of social cooperation through erosion of the presumption of decency and honesty. That presumption—and its basis in fact—is practically indispensable for coordination of individuals' diverse activities and so for an economically progressive society. What economists are capable of contributing to analysis of this connection may well have more significance for welfare than further refinements of the analysis of deviations from Pareto-optimality. Already, some of the best writings on economic backwardness and economic development do lay stress on the ethos of society.[15]

---

[13] Furthermore, as Buchanan (1965) has explained, largeness of the society or group concerned probably increases the temptation on the individual to behave immorally.

[14] The standard reference to a burgeoning literature on this topic is Leibenstein 1966.

[15] Banfield 1958 has shown the role of "amoral familism" (an excessively narrow and short-run concern for the material welfare of the nuclear family), together with dishonesty, suspiciousness, and envy, in impeding social cooperation and economic development in a town of southern Italy around 1955. The importance of attitudes and culture for development or backwardness is the main theme of Zinkin 1963. While Zinkin does not particularly emphasize trustworthiness and honesty, he does recognize their importance in several contexts. He also notes the importance of bureaucrats' abiding by principle rather than undercutting predictability by deciding each case on its own merits. See also Wraith and Simpkins 1964, particularly pp. 155, 157, 189, where the authors note the role of business and accounting in deterring corruption.

CONCLUSION

In conclusion and in summary, economic theory helps clarify the usefulness and necessity of leaving much in the realm of good and evil to informal principles and their decentralized, nongovernmental enforcement. It also points out dangers to such principles and obstacles to such enforcement. It helps explain the role of broad principles in assessing economic policies and helps explain why the merits of each specific government intervention, narrowly assessed, are not the only relevant considerations. We should appraise each proposed intervention, as best we can, for its likely legal, political, social, and ethical repercussions—for its repercussions on the system as a whole. If we avoid appraising and comparing alternative economic systems as wholes, if we avoid forming and acting on a coherent conception of the good society, we shall make momentous choices in ignorance and by default. The opposite approach, respecting principles, would go far, I believe, toward reinstating the wisdom of the Founding Fathers regarding the scope and power of government.

REFERENCES

Abelson, Philip H. "Federal Intervention in Universities." *Science* 190 (17 October 1975): editorial page.

Adler, Mortimer J. *The Time of Our Lives.* New York: Holt, Rinehart and Winston, 1970.

Alsop, Stewart. "Let's Raise More Hell." *Newsweek*, 9 March 1970.

Aronson, Elliot. *The Social Animal.* San Francisco: Freeman, 1972.

Banfield, Edward C., assisted by Laura C. Banfield. *The Moral Basis of a Backward Society.* New York: Free Press, 1958.

Browne, Harry. *How I Found Freedom in an Unfree World.* New York: Avon Books, 1974.

Browning, Edgar K. "Why the Social Insurance Budget Is Too Large in a Democracy." *Economic Inquiry* 13 (September 1975): 373–388.

Buchanan, James M. "Ethical Rules, Expected Values, and Large Numbers." *Ethics* 76 (October 1965): 1–13.

———. "America's Third Century in Perspective." *Atlantic Economic Journal* 1 (November 1973): 3–12.

―――. *The Limits of Liberty.* Chicago: University of Chicago Press, 1975.

―――. "The Samaritan's Dilemma." Manuscript, 1972. In *Altruism, Morality, and Economic Theory*, edited by E.S. Phelps. New York: Russell Sage Foundation, 1975.

Dahl, Robert. "Minorities Rule." 1963. In *American Democracy*, edited by Leonard J. Fein, 123–130. New York: Holt, Rinehart and Winston, 1964.

Davis, Joseph S. *The World between the Wars, 1919–39: An Economist's View.* Baltimore: Johns Hopkins University Press, 1975.

Downs, Anthony. *An Economic Theory of Democracy.* New York: Harper, 1957.

―――. "Why the Government Budget is Too Small in a Democracy." *World Politics* 3 (July 1960): 541–563.

Ellis, Albert. *Is Objectivism a Religion?* New York: Lyle Stuart, 1968.

Ellis, Albert, and Robert Harper. *A Guide to Rational Living in an Irrational World.* Englewood Cliffs, N.J.: Prentice Hall, 1961.

Etzioni, Amitai. "The Grand Shaman." *Psychology Today* 6 (November 1972): 88–92, 142–143.

Festinger, Leon. *A Theory of Cognitive Dissonance.* Evanston, Ind. and White Plains, N.Y.: Row, Peterson, 1957.

Friedman, Milton. *Capitalism and Freedom.* Chicago: University of Chicago Press, 1962.

Glazer, Nathan. "Towards an Imperial Judiciary?" *The Public Interest*, no. 41 (Fall 1975): 104–123

Greenfield, Meg. "Food for Thought." *Newsweek*, 10 November 1975.

Hardin, Garrett. "The Tragedy of the Commons." 1968. In *Population, Evolution, and Birth Control*, 2nd ed., edited by Hardin, 367–381. San Francisco: Freeman, 1969.

Hayek, F.A. *Studies in Philosophy, Politics and Economics.* Chicago: University of Chicago Press, 1967.

―――. *Rules and Order.* Vol. 1 of *Law, Legislation and Liberty.* Chicago: University of Chicago Press, 1973.

Hazlitt, Henry. *The Foundations of Morality.* Princeton, N.J.: D. Van Nostrand, 1964.

Hotelling, Harold. "Stability in Competition." *Economic Journal* 39 (March 1929): 41–57.

Kahn, Robert L., Barbara A. Gutek, Eugenia Barton, and Daniel Katz. "Americans Love their Bureaucrats." *Psychology Today* 9 (June 1975): 66–71.

Leibenstein, Harvey. "Allocative Efficiency vs. 'X-Efficiency'." *American Economic Review* 56 (June 1966): 392–415.

McKean, Roland N. "Collective Choice." In *Social Responsibility and the Business Predicament*, edited by James W. McKie, 109–134. Washington, D.C.: Brookings Institution, 1974.

———. "Economics of Ethical and Behavioral Codes." Manuscript, 1974.

Mises, Ludwig von. *Bureaucracy*. London: Hodge, 1945.

Nemy, Enid. "Professor Rebels Against System." New York Times News Service dispatch, *Charlottesville Daily Progress*, 15 December 1974.

Niskanen, William A., Jr. *Bureaucracy and Representative Government*. Chicago: Aldine, 1971.

Olson, Mancur, Jr. *The Logic of Collective Action*. Cambridge, Mass.: Harvard University Press, 1965.

Olson, Robert G. *The Morality of Self-Interest*. New York: Harcourt Brace & World, 1965.

Ortega y Gasset, José. *The Revolt of the Masses*. 1930. New York: Norton, 1957.

Philbrook, Clarence H. "'Realism' in Policy Espousal." *American Economic Review* 43 (December 1953): 846–859.

Rand, Ayn. *Atlas Shrugged*. New York: New American Library, 1957.

Rawls, John. *A Theory of Justice*. Cambridge, Mass.: Harvard University Press, 1971.

Schlick, Moritz. *Problems of Ethics*. 1930. Translated by D. Rynin. New York: Dover, 1962.

Schoeck, Helmut. *Envy: A Theory of Social Behaviour*. 1966. Translated by Michael Glenny and Betty Ross. New York: Harcourt Brace & World, 1970.

Smith, Adam. *The Theory of Moral Sentiments*. 1759. In *Adam Smith's Moral and Political Philosophy*, edited by Herbert W. Schneider. New York: Harper Torchbook, 1970.

Viner, Jacob. "The Short View and the Long in Economic Policy." 1940. In *The Long View and the Short*, 103–130. Glencoe, Ill.: Free Press, 1958.

Vining, Rutledge. "On Two Foundation Concepts of the Theory of Political Economy." *Journal of Political Economy* 77 (March/April 1969): 199–218.

———. *On Appraising the Performance of an Economic System*. Cambridge, U.K., and New York: Cambridge University Press, 1984.

Wilson, James O. "The Rise of the Bureaucratic State." *The Public Interest*, no. 41 (Fall 1975): 77–103.

Wraith, Ronald, and Edgar Simpkins. *Corruption in Developing Countries*. New York: Norton, 1964.

Zinkin, Maurice. *Development for Free Asia*. New ed. New York: Oxford University Press, 1963.

CHAPTER 19
American Democracy Diagnosed*

Alan Ehrenhalt earned a master's degree in journalism, has worked as a political reporter, editor, and columnist, has been a Nieman Fellow at Harvard and a visiting scholar in political science at Berkeley, and is now executive editor of *Governing* magazine in Washington. His new book, *The United States of Ambition*, shapes his keen observations into an intelligible pattern.

The U.S. political system has changed vastly from what it was several decades ago. Old-style machines like the one bossed in Utica, New York, by Rufus Elefante (never elected to anything) are gone. Political parties have lost their organized character. Experienced politicians and party leaders no longer have much chance to screen potential candidates. Success no longer belongs to team players. The political process has become much more open to leaderless individuals seeking office on their own. "The skills that work in American politics at this point in history are those of entrepreneurship. At all levels of the political system ... it is unusual for parties to nominate people. People nominate themselves" (p. 17).

Those who gain and keep office tend to be people who like politics, see it as a full-time career, and either enjoy campaigning or dislike its rigors less than most people would. They bask in publicity and put a relatively low value on privacy. As careerist professionals, they develop expertise in fundraising and in exploiting technology and the media. Furthermore, people who have these tastes tend to be people who believe in activist government. Even out of genuine public spirit, they work to expand their scope for doing good in their favorite way, through exercising governmental power.

---
*From *Liberty* 5 (January 1992): 69–71. Review of Alan Ehrenhalt, *The United States of Ambition: Politicians, Power, and the Pursuit of Office* (New York: Times Books, 1991).

People with a negative image of government, seeing it as overly meddlesome, or whatever, tend to shun politics. Exceptions do exist, but they are just that, exceptions; and they tend not to persevere in politics as tenaciously as career-oriented devotees of activist government. Under our current system, furthermore, a party's success depends on steadily recruiting full-time talent. Government-bashing does not build majorities. Ronald Reagan's antigovernment rhetoric reinforced a distaste for political careers among young Republicans.

When conservatives occasionally come to power, they do not do much to roll back activist programs already in place. "Government programs acquire an inertia and a set of constituencies that make repeal look like onerous and politically costly work, even for a newly installed conservative regime that finds them unattractive" (p. 64).

> [T]hrough the 1970s and 1980s, the Democratic party strengthened itself as the vehicle for people who grew up interested in government and politics and wanted to make a career of them. And the Republican party was forced to compete as the vehicle of those who felt that government was a dirty business and that they were demeaning themselves to take part in it. (p. 222)

Ehrenhalt illustrates his points with case studies of local government (Concord, CA.; Utica, N.Y.; Greenville county, S.C.), state government (South Carolina, Alabama, Connecticut, Colorado, Wisconsin), and members of Congress.

In Wisconsin, for example, the people

> have never chosen the Democratic party *en bloc* to be the legislative majority. The question is not put to the electorate that way.... Wisconsin's voters have elected individual Democrats who outperformed their opposition at the tasks a modern political career requires. The electorate has not sent them to govern; it has merely maintained the conditions under which they could send themselves. (p. 142)

In Wisconsin, "the GOP has become the party of Cincinnatus—the party of those who, in the final analysis, would rather be doing something else for a living. The Democrats are the party of those who believe, with [Assemblyman] David Clarenbach, that 'I can't think of anything I'd rather devote my life to'" (p. 126).

As Ehrenhalt recognizes, his observations do not fully apply to the general election for President. For a brief period every four years, after the self-nomination process is over, the opinions and values of the electorate are decisive. However little the voters know about the vast majority of political choices confronting them, "they do have enduring images of what the two major parties are about in presidential politics" (p. 270). They apply these images and they pay attention to the campaign as they choose between the two major candidates—or many of the voters do, so the qualification should run. Another qualification should be that the voters are choosing only between two candidates that they have not themselves deliberately nominated.

Ehrenhalt identifies a "central contradiction" of the U.S. political system that cries out for explanation: although voters have shown a clear preference for Republican presidential candidates over the last twenty years, this has done nothing to give the GOP a majority in the country as a whole (p. 208). Yet his own method of analysis suggests how to explain this "contradiction," as well as the common observation (if it is correct) that voters tend to disdain Congress in general while admiring their own particular representative.

Presidential elections deal with the big picture. Voters are interested and informed—relatively. They have a chance to express conservatism more effectively than in local and Congressional elections.

Voters may dislike the performance of Congress as a whole. Taking the system as given, though, they can sensibly elect a representative who knows how to manipulate it in defense of their interests. Forbearance from grabbing their own supposed share of federal largesse would not appreciably turn the system around. Responsible government—government responsible to the general public interest rather than overresponsive, piecemeal, to numerous local and special interests—is a public good; pursuing it has prisoners'-dilemma aspects. Why should one's own representative behave responsibly when few others would follow the example and when the payoff to himself and his or her constituents would be so slight and conjectural? Furthermore—as is one of the book's main themes—their representative tends to be a specialist in providing services to constituents and in projecting an attractive personal image.

Ehrenhalt mentions the chronic U.S. government budget deficit as an example of irresponsibility or dissipation of responsibility in the political and legislative processes (although he does not phrase the matter just that way; see pp. 245–250). More generally, the political system has developed a critical flaw: "It has allowed power and leadership, at many levels, simply to evaporate" (p. 38).

What accounts for changes in the political system over the past few decades? Ehrenhalt makes or hints at several suggestions. Skill in communicating—in town meetings, in door-to-door canvassing, on television, in direct-mail literature—has gained in importance (p. 19). "The more campaigning becomes a science unto itself, the more public offices and rewards flow to people who have mastered its details" (p. 206).

Air conditioning and jet planes helped change the character of Congress. More so than before, serving in it can and must be a year-round, full-time occupation; yet members can keep in touch with their constituents. But long weekends back in the district, together with heavier work loads, have further eroded camaraderie among the members (p. 234 in particular). On local as well as congressional levels, an explosion in staffing has changed the legislative process, making legislatures both more competent and more active (p. 138).

Redistricting under the 1962 Supreme Court decision and the civil-rights movement contributed to opening up the political system. Changed convention rules and the increased importance of primaries have altered the presidential race. Vietnam and Watergate created opportunities for antiestablishment, antiorganization types (pp. 152, 209–210).

Some of these points, obviously, are just as much features as explanations of the new system and require explanation themselves. Ehrenhalt does not, and does not claim to, provide anything approaching a full, well-articulated, persuasive explanation.

Still, he has made a praiseworthy contribution to political science. It meshes nicely with the work of public-choice economists. Perhaps more academically oriented researchers will build on his work, figuring out, for example, how to obtain statistics on the personal characteristics of politicians and how to test his insights in ingenious ways.

The book's two final paragraphs state a brief conclusion. Our political system is deficient in leadership, discipline, and the willingness to seek accommodation of divergent personal preferences. It generates a politics of posturing and stalemate. Yet it will not do simply to blame ambitious professional politicians for "this mess":

> We understand more than we might like to admit about city councils that can't defer to leadership; about state legislatures where every individual is a faction unto himself; about a Congress that lacks any sort of meaningful community among its members. We understand these problems, or should, because they are all around us in American life. For all

our ignorance as voters and inattentiveness as citizens, we have a politics that is, in the end, appropriate to its time and place.

This rather lame conclusion overlooks the insights of Anthony Downs in *An Economic Theory of Democracy* (1957): It is perfectly rational for the individual citizen ordinarily to remain ignorant of political issues and give them only superficial attention. Any reform effort that hopes to succeed must take this circumstance to heart.

Ehrenhalt neither fully explains our political malady nor gives advice on how to cure it. Yet even unaccompanied by an etiology and a prescription, his diagnosis is well worth having. Although Ehrenhalt is not pushing any particular ideological line, his analysis tempts me to offer some libertarian embroidery.

Sheer eloquence, I conjecture, including a knack for devising memorable slogans, succeeds better in the political arena than competent concern for the sizes or importance of various supposed problems and of the benefits and costs of remedies offered. Knowing economics can hobble the honest politician, while the pangs of conscience spare the economic ignoramus as he prevails with promises and eloquence. Concern for the long run is a similar handicap, since looking good at election time is what counts.

These are among the reasons why the qualities and skills of a successful political campaigner do not coincide with those of a good government executive or legislator (as Ehrenhalt noted in Concord, CA., p. 55). "The ability to canvass for votes in Iowa or New Hampshire does not have much to do with the qualities that make a successful president. But it has come to be a virtual prerequisite for anyone who wants the job" (p. 206).

Ehrenhalt further helps us understand why the outcome of the political process does not necessarily represent the will of the people. It is a fallacy to say (as George Will and Herbert Stein did) that people must be pretty well satisfied with government as a whole; otherwise they would vote to change it. The voters do not have an opportunity to express themselves, and express themselves knowledgeably, on the character of government and its overall scale of activity. The political process operates with a bias toward bigness. Furthermore, voters are probably trapped in a kind of prisoners' dilemma (as suggested in remarks about Congress above).

Ehrenhalt's readers will see further reasons for skepticism about democracy as a good in its own right. Democracy is a particular political method, a method of choosing, replacing, and influencing our rulers.

Ideally it offers us a way of avoiding or dismissing rulers who would destroy our individual rights. It is a radically inaccurate method of implementing the desires of the people, but the alternative political methods are even worse. It is a gross fallacy to slide from the case for democracy as the least bad political method into admiring political methods as such and into a supposed case for throwing more and more aspects of life into the political—meaning governmental—arena. Ehrenhalt's observations bolster the case for strictly limiting the scope of government.

Although reforms in the democratic process will not dispel the dangers of big government, Ehrenhalt's book should arouse interest in exploring them. The case for limiting the terms of governmental office looks better. So does the case for choosing legislators, or some of them, by lot rather than by election. So, perhaps, do the radical reforms suggested by F.A. Hayek in *The Political Order of a Free People* (1979).

Prospects for reforming politics and restraining government may look bleak just now. In the long run, though, experience, reason, and the growth of organized knowledge can change what is politically feasible. (The historical and intellectual demise of socialism is a case in point.) Ehrenhalt has made a solid contribution to this growth of knowledge. So doing, he provides grounds for optimism.

CHAPTER 20

Civic Religion Reasserted*

In recent decades the public-choice school has been applying economic analysis to political institutions and activities. People are fundamentally the same in government as in private life. In trying to achieve their purposes (which need not be narrowly egoistic ones), individuals respond to opportunities and incentives. The specifics of these are different in politics than in the marketplace of business.

One implication is that the ordinary voter seldom finds it worth while to become well informed on a wide range of political issues. Almost never would his trouble change an election result or the policies adopted. He has better uses for his time and energy. The private market gives him a better chance than politics does to satisfy his own preferences, even quirky ones. Similarly, he has only slight opportunities and incentives to monitor the performance of his supposed servants in government. Special interest groups have better opportunities to steer government policies in their own favorite directions.

For these and other reasons—only some of them noticed in the book under review—the democratic political process responds inaccurately to what the citizens would desire if they were well informed. Modern democratic government has a bias toward counterproductive hyperactivity.

An extensive literature making such points meets sweeping rejection by a Berkeley Ph.D. graduate, former assistant professor of political science at the University of Chicago, and now professor of economics at the University of California at Santa Cruz. In an earlier article now expanded into the book, Donald Wittman claimed that "democratic markets work as well as economic markets" (1989, p. 1395). The book (1995, p. 1) weakens this claim into "both political and economic markets work well." In article and book alike, Wittman claims that the democratic process is "efficient,"

---

*From *Liberty* 10 (January 1997): 57–60, there titled "We Many, We Happy Many." Review of Donald A. Wittman, *The Myth of Democratic Failure: Why Political Institutions Are Efficient* (Chicago: University of Chicago Press, 1995).

scarcely bothering to describe what his standard of comparison might be. He does invoke, but only ritualistically, the criteria of Pareto optimality and wealth maximization (pp. 3–6, 22 n., chap. 11). Relative to what is democracy "efficient"? Relative to other forms of government? Relative to leaving wide aspects of life outside the political arena, as the American Founders evidently intended? Wittman does not say.

Wittman argues his efficiency claim feebly. He scarcely goes beyond asserting that the positions he attacks are incorrect or have been "exaggerated." ("I have already argued that the degree of opportunism by politicians has been greatly exaggerated," p. 33.) Such claims are hard to confront and are correspondingly limp, since some exaggerations occur on almost any side of any issue. Furthermore, Wittman relies heavily on the analogy—hardly more than that—between economic markets and democratic politics ("this book develops an invisible-hand theory of efficient democratic markets," p. 3). Gordon Tullock, Richard Posner, and others had argued that spending to curry government favors will tend to dissipate the rents sought. Wittman replies that rules will develop to minimize the social cost. Campaign contributions are not dead losses; they help provide valuable information. Besides, rent-seeking goes on in the business sector also. Pet stores push sales of bird feeders, which redistributes income from humans to birds. If rent-seeking is not viewed as a serious problem in the business sector, it probably should not be so viewed in political markets either (p. 36).

Wittman provides many more examples of trying merely to talk away points made by public-choice analysts. Political entrepreneurs, like business entrepreneurs, can gain from discovering and exploiting unknown demands, providing related information, and clearing up confusion. So doing, they help solve the supposed problems of the "rational ignorance" of voters and the differential information of special interests. As for principal-agent problems (problems of monitoring by voters of their supposed political servants), well, they are mitigated by institutions such as government structure, political parties, and candidate reputation. Besides, if the principal cannot monitor his political agent, then neither can the academic researcher. Competition for office reduces politicians' potential for opportunism and shirking. The party is the analogue in politics of the franchise in the business sector. Party labels, accumulated reputations, interest-group endorsements, and comparative political advertising also provide good substitutes for specific knowledge about particular candidates. Voters discount information from sources known to be biased. As for the allegation that "diffuse taxpayers" are insensitive to spending for concentrated interests, well, uninformed people may even exaggerate the extent and harm of pork-barrel projects. Even if some voters do make incorrect choices, the law of large numbers is likely to yield the correct majority choice anyway. Political institutions, including legislatures much smaller than the constituencies represented, reduce transactions costs and facilitate efficient policy deals. Despite supposed problems of transitivity, externalities, localism, and pressure groups, efforts to gain a majority push a government toward achieving efficient outcomes. Local zoning, for example, is likely to be efficient.

Here are three more examples of Wittman's style of argument. (1) Do voters shift some of the burden of current government spending onto future generations through debt-financed deficits? Three short sentences assuming that taxes fall on land introduce a sweeping conclusion: "The burden of the debt falls on the present generation, and they will therefore choose the optimal discount rate, just as they choose the optimal policy in other areas" (p. 159). (2) "[E]fficient economic markets constrain the behavior of democratic markets. If vote-maximizing politicians try to monkey with the economy, it backfires—the economy becomes less efficient, and workers and capitalists vote them out of office. So politicians are restrained from such maneuvers in the first place" (p. 176). (3) In making consumption-versus-investment decisions in a socialist economy, "Vote-maximizing politicians would again be constrained in their choices by requirements of an efficient economy. Making different choices would ultimately yield fewer votes" (p. 176). "Ultimately"—perhaps so, if freedom and democracy survive under socialism; but why should the individual politician care about "ultimately"?

Wittman provides little sustained reasoning to support his positions, and scant evidence beyond airy references to the existence of elections, parties, ideologies, rivalries, campaigning, Congressional hearings, and so forth. He does cite many books and articles claimed to support his position, but he cites them sweepingly, without detailed discussion. He spends more space on the supposed methodological and other flaws of studies that reach contrary conclusions. One whole chapter criticizes psychological studies casting doubt on how dependably people behave "rationally" as economists understand the term.

Wittman pays little or no attention to major strands of public-choice literature. While he does paw away at the concept of voter ignorance, he seems not deeply to appreciate why superficiality is rational for the individual voter (and nonvoter). Other such phenomena include: the fuzzing of issues in a two-party system (the Hotelling effect), and the associated drift over time in what positions are considered respectably mainstream; the jumbling together of diverse issues in often incoherent packages; the chasm between the personal qualities of an effective campaigner and those of a sound statesman; various rather mechanical inaccuracies of the political process (including several paradoxes of voting and what Robert Dahl labeled "minorities rule"); the fragmentation of decisionmaking power and responsibility among levels and branches of government and among individual politicians, bureaucrats, and judges; the analogous intertemporal fragmentation of responsibility; the associated reasons why politicians and bureaucrats have short time horizons; the forestalling of market solutions to problems by governmental preemption; the way that government activism, far from just remedying externalities in the private sector, creates major externalities in government decisionmaking itself; the lesser scope for prices to function in government than in markets; and the coercive aspect of government that is absent from private business. He does not draw the implications of politicians' and bureaucrats' constituting special interests of their own (he should have taken to heart such case studies as Alan Ehrenhalt, *The United States of Ambition*, 1991; John Jackley, *Hill Rat*, 1992; and Eric Felten, *The Ruling Class*, 1993).

One wonders what world Wittman has been living in. Hasn't he noticed examples of government irresponsibility and failure in policy on crime, education, welfare, regulation, litigation, money, and budgeting? Can voters diagnose who is responsible for current poor economic performance, especially given lags in the effects of policies? Hasn't Wittman noticed voters' tendency to blame or credit the administration in power for the current stage of the business cycle? Hasn't he noticed the wretched quality of arguments on economic policy issues presented by all major sides and reported on television and in the popular press? Doesn't he recognize that the quality of political discussion is so low because politicians appeal to voters as they actually are, with their short attention spans in their actual circumstances?

Although Wittman neglects most such counterevidence, his treatment of what he does notice suggests how he would deal with the rest of it. It is all too easy, he says, to point to such standard examples of supposed government inefficiency as rent control, tariffs, tobacco and other farm subsidies, and agricultural-marketing orders. But some observers complain about too much foreign aid or too much support for right-wing dictators; others complain about too little. "So, while just about everyone has her [sic] theory of government failure, at least half must be wrong." "[M]any examples of political-market failure are mutually contradictory and methodologically unsound" (chap. 13, quotations from pp. 182 and 181).

Wittman's arguments are not only feeble but sometimes inconsistent. "[O]pportunism by politicians is mitigated when they are paid above-market salaries and then threatened with losing office if they shirk. The fact that candidates engage in very costly election campaigns is consistent with the hypothesis that holding office pays above-market salaries" (p. 27). What, then, has become of the much trumpeted competition? Don't the costly campaigns dissipate wealth? And how does Wittman's judgment about politicians' salaries square with his equally blithe judgment (p. 106) that bureaucrats' wages *are* kept at the competitive level?

Ironically, Wittman's book, like the precursor article, was published at the University of Chicago, a citadel of positivism in economic theory and of insistence that theories be falsifiable. (I interpret this, perhaps charitably, as insistence that theories have actual content, as opposed to being formulated with built-in immunity to any adverse evidence.) Wittman himself makes self-congratulatory remarks about sound and unsound methodologies. His two concluding chapters, totaling only 13 pages, bear the titles "The Testing of Theory" and "Epilogue: The Burden of Proof." (Page 2 had already placed "the burden of proof... on those who argue that democratic political markets are inefficient.") The reader expects Wittman at last to say what he would recognize as weighty evidence or argument against his thesis and say how it stands up to the test.

Yet he does not follow through. Even so, he ends his book claiming to have "carried over to models of political-market failure" the suspicion about underlying assumptions that economists properly apply to assertions of failure in the business sector. "I have argued that voters make informed judgments and that democratic markets are competitive" (p. 192). "Economists do not dwell on business error or pathological consumer behavior." Instead, they "analyze the normal and look for efficiency explanations for abnormal market behavior. Similarly, political scientists should not dwell on the mistakes made by political markets" (p. 193 n.). But he does not claim to have actually shown that democracy is efficient. The fuzziness that remains renders his thesis even less testable than it might have been if more sharply formulated. Again he insinuates that the burden of proof lies on those who would deny the presumption of efficiency to economic markets and political markets alike.

That something as inadequate and perverse as this book (and its predecessor article) has been written and published under prestigious academic auspices is a phenomenon crying out for explanation. Tackling the puzzle is important, for the book's mere existence and academic trappings will carry some weight. Along with like-minded academics, politicians and bureaucrats relish support from what "studies have shown."

Before exploring possible explanations, I should confess to indignation dating back to the 1989 article. Perhaps my judgment must be discounted. I used to criticize that article in my graduate seminars in political economy. What called my attention to the book was Donald Boudreaux's excellent, and properly adverse, review article on it in the first issue (Spring 1996) of *The Independent Review*. (In hopes of avoiding duplication, I set Boudreaux's review aside while reading the book and drafting my own review.)

I must also confess to embarrassment. It is a commonplace remark that one should not ask about people's motives. Yet sometimes such inquiry is necessary. A detective in a murder case must conjecture about motives while formulating rival hypotheses and trying to rule out all but one of them. The intellectual puzzle of a curious book requires a roughly similar procedure.

My first hypothesis must be that Wittman is driven by passion for truth. Conceivably he is quite right: the now-familiar public-choice theories of bureaucracy and democratic politics are radically deficient, and in the ways he diagnoses. Democratic processes do indeed closely resemble competitive processes in markets for goods and services. It is I who am wrong, blinded by mindless indignation to the merits of Wittman's brilliant revisionism.

But other hypotheses suggest themselves. The thought did cross my mind that Wittman's book (and article) might be a sustained spoof, like physicist Alan Sokal's article on "postmodern gravity" in *Social Text*, or if not a spoof, at least a move in an academic game. Wittman does acknowledge (p. ix) that he has been playing a "game," that latecomers to an intellectual controversy enjoy an advantage, and that he has "had a lot of fun."

Or perhaps Wittman was trying, as an exercise, to make the best case for democratic government he could devise. "Democratic decisions should be treated as innocent until proven guilty," he says, "and they deserve a lawyer arguing their side of the case" (p. 193). With ample talent already making the prosecution's case, perhaps Wittman chose to write the legal brief for the defense. Letting someone else recognize how weak even that best case is—provoking the reader toward a judgment of his own—might be an effective way to reinforce public-choice-type skepticism about activist democratic government.

One variant of the hypothesis about an intellectual exercise is that Wittman saw an opportunity to fill a vacant niche in the academic landscape. From that hitherto unoccupied "intellectual foxhole" (as Charles Peirce said), he might sally forth in battle with holders of other positions. Evidently the marketplace of ideas had left room for an academically credentialed rehabilitation of what R.W. Bradford (1993, pp. 159–165) has called "The New Civic Religion"—pop wisdom about the virtue and efficacy of voting and about the mandates conferred by elections. I do not know about Wittman, but as a general proposition, holding a distinctive intellectual position can draw invitations to attend scholarly conferences and contribute chapters to collective works. Serving as a foil for other positions is not necessarily disreputable: as John Stuart Mill said in *On Liberty*, truth may sometimes strengthen its appeal by struggle against error, even contrived error.

The hypothesis about niche-filling meshes with one about the state of academic economics (at least as diagnosed by several eminent participants). Academics feel pressure to publish and be noticed. Latching onto a fad is one way. Delivering shock value—being an iconoclast, challenging established beliefs—is another way, which can even add to the "fun" of the game. Occasionally the two approaches can even blend into a kind of routine originality: extend a fad so as to challenge yet another widely accepted belief. I have observed plenty of faddism, iconoclasm, and their combination in my own field of macroeconomics. Certain strands of Chicago and UCLA economics cultivate the fad of arguing that whatever institution or practice has long endured thereby demonstrates a certain efficiency, whether or not its rationale has hitherto been spelled out. Such iconoclastic faddism (or chic iconoclasm) purports to rationalize forms of protection and rent-shifting long condemned by mainstream economists. Wittman's work could be another example, whether intentionally or not I do not know.

Following academic practice in one or several of these ways need not indicate insincerity or other personal immorality. Besides, Leon Festinger's principle of cognitive dissonance may be at work. If one feels uncomfortable as a gamesman saying things one does not really believe, one can remove or forestall the dissonance by coming quite sincerely to believe those things.

I do not know which of the hypotheses mentioned is correct; maybe some other one is. Pending further evidence, we should perhaps opt for a charitable one. Meanwhile, Wittman's judgments remain puzzlingly perverse. If they should succeed in making a great splash, that would reflect adversely on academic social science and on popular discourse infected by it.

REFERENCES

Bradford, R.W., ed. *It Came from Arkansas*. Port Townsend, Wash.: Liberty Publishing, 1993.

Wittman, Donald A. "Why Democracies Produce Efficient Results." *Journal of Political Economy* 97 (December 1989): 1395–1424.

Wittman, Donald A. *The Myth of Democratic Failure*. Chicago: University of Chicago Press, 1995.

CHAPTER 21

A Libertarian Case for Monarchy*

DEMOCRACY AND OTHER GOOD THINGS

Clear thought and discussion suffer when all sorts of good things, like liberty, equality, fraternity, rights, majority rule, and general welfare—some in tension with others—are marketed together under the portmanteau label "democracy." Democracy's core meaning is a particular method of choosing, replacing, and influencing government officials (Schumpeter 1950/1962). It is not a doctrine of what government should and should not do. Nor is it the same thing as personal freedom or a free society or an egalitarian social ethos. True enough, some classical liberals, like Thomas Paine (1791–1792/1989) and Ludwig von Mises (1919/1983), did scorn hereditary monarchy and did express touching faith that representative democracy would choose excellent leaders and adopt policies truly serving the common interest. Experience has taught us better, as the American Founders already knew when constructing a government of separated and limited powers and of only filtered democracy.

As an exercise, and without claiming that my arguments are decisive, I'll contend that constitutional monarchy can better preserve people's freedom and opportunities than democracy as it has turned out in practice.[1]

---

*From *Liberty* 18 (January 2004): 37–42, where this article was titled "Monarchy: Friend of Liberty."

[1] I do not know how to test my case econometrically. The control variables to be included in equations regressing a measure of liberty or stability or prosperity or whatever on presence or absence of monarchy of some type or other are too ineffable and too many. We would have to devise variables for such conditions as history and traditions, geography, climate, natural resources, type of economic system, past forms of government, ethnicity and ethnic homogeneity or diversity, education, religion, and so on. Plausible historical data points are too few. Someone cleverer than I might devise some sort of econometric test after all. Meanwhile, we must weigh the pros and cons of monarchy and democracy against one another qualitatively as best we can.

My case holds only for countries where maintaining or restoring (or conceivably installing) monarchy is a live option.[2] We Americans have sounder hope of reviving respect for the philosophy of our Founders. Our traditions could serve some of the functions of monarchy in other countries.

An unelected absolute ruler could conceivably be a thoroughgoing classical liberal. Although a wise, benevolent, and liberal-minded dictatorship would not be a contradiction in terms, no way is actually available to assure such a regime and its continuity, including frictionless succession.

Some element of democracy is therefore necessary; totally replacing it would be dangerous. Democracy allows people some influence on who their rulers are and what policies they pursue. Elections, if not subverted, can oust bad rulers peacefully. Citizens who care about such things can enjoy a sense of participation in public affairs.

Anyone who believes in limiting government power for the sake of personal freedom should value also having some nondemocratic element of government besides courts respectful of their own narrow authority. While some monarchists are reactionaries or mystics, others (like Erik von Kuehnelt-Leddihn and Sean Gabb, cited below) do come across as genuine classical liberals.

SHORTCOMINGS OF DEMOCRACY

Democracy has glaring defects.[3] As various paradoxes of voting illustrate, there is no such thing as any coherent "will of the people." Government itself is more likely to supply the content of any supposed general will (Constant 1814–1815/1988, p. 179). Winston Churchill reputedly said: "The best argument against democracy is a five-minute conversation with the average voter" (BrainyQuote and several similar sources on the Internet). The ordinary voter knows that his vote will not be decisive and has little reason to waste time and effort becoming well informed anyway.

This "rational ignorance," so called in the public-choice literature, leaves corresponding influence to other-than-ordinary voters (Campbell

---

[2]Monarchist organizations exist in surprisingly many countries; a few of their web sites appear in the References. Even Argentina has a small monarchist movement, described in the September 1994 issue of *Monarchy* at the site of the International Monarchist League.

[3]Barry 2003 partially summarizes them. Hayek 1979 describes the defects at length and proposes an elaborate reform of the system of representation, not discussing monarchy. James Buchanan and the Public Choice school analyze democracy in many writings.

1999). Politics becomes a squabble among rival special interests. Coalitions form to gain special privileges. Legislators engage in logrolling and enact omnibus spending bills. Politics itself becomes the chief weapon in a Hobbesian war of all against all (Gray 1993, pp. 211–212). The diffusion of costs while benefits are concentrated reinforces apathy among ordinary voters.

Politicians themselves count among the special interest groups. People who drift into politics tend to have relatively slighter qualifications for other work. They are entrepreneurs pursuing the advantages of office. These are not material advantages alone, for some politicians seek power to do good as they understand it. Gratifying their need to act and to feel important, legislators multiply laws to deal with discovered or contrived problems—and fears. Being able to raise vast sums by taxes and borrowing enhances their sense of power, and moral responsibility wanes (as Constant, 1814–1815/1988, pp. 194–196, 271–272, already recognized almost two centuries ago).

Democratic politicians have notoriously short time horizons. (Hoppe 2001 blames not just politicians in particular but democracy in general for high time preference—indifference to the long run—which contributes to crime, wasted lives, and a general decline of morality and culture.) Why worry if popular policies will cause crises only when one is no longer running for reelection? Evidence of fiscal irresponsibility in the United States includes chronic budget deficits, the explicit national debt, and the still huger excesses of future liabilities over future revenues on account of Medicare and Social Security. Yet politicians continue offering new plums. Conflict of interest like this far overshadows the petty kinds that nevertheless arouse more outrage.

Responsibility is diffused in democracy not only over time but also among participants. Voters can think that they are only exercising their right to mark their ballots, politicians that they are only responding to the wishes of their constituents. The individual legislator bears only a small share of responsibility fragmented among his colleagues and other government officials.

Democracy and liberty coexist in tension. Nowadays the United States government restricts political speech. The professed purpose of campaign-finance reform is to limit the power of interest groups and of money in politics, but increased influence of the mass media and increased security of incumbent politicians are likelier results. A broader kind of tension is that popular majorities can lend an air of legitimacy to highly illiberal measures. "By the sheer weight of numbers and by its ubiquity the rule of 99 per cent is more 'hermetic' and more oppressive than the rule of 1 per cent" (Kuehnelt-Leddihn 1952, p. 88). When majority rule is thought good in its own right and the fiction prevails that "we" ordinary citizens are the government, an elected legislature and executive can get away with impositions that monarchs of the past would scarcely have ventured. Louis XIV of France, autocrat though he was, would hardly have dared prohibit alcoholic beverages, conscript soldiers, and levy an income tax (pp. 280–281)—or, we might add, wage war on drugs. Not only constitutional limitations on a king's powers but also his[4] *not* having an electoral mandate is a restraint.

At its worst, the democratic dogma can abet totalitarianism. History records totalitarian democracies or democratically supported dictatorships. Countries oppressed by communist regimes included words like "democratic" or "popular" in their official names. Totalitarian parties have portrayed their leaders as personifying the common man and the whole nation. German National Socialism, as Kuehnelt-Leddihn reminds us, was neither a conservative nor a reactionary movement but a synthesis of revolutionary ideas tracing to before 1789 (Kuehnelt-Leddihn 1952, pp. 131, 246–247, 268). He suggests that antimonarchical sentiments in the background of the French Revolution, the Spanish republic of 1931, and Germany's Weimar Republic paved the way for Robespierre and Napoleon, for Negrin and Franco, and for Hitler (p. 90). Winston Churchill reportedly judged that had the Kaiser remained German Head of State, Hitler could not have gained power, or at least not have kept it (International Monarchist League). "[M]onarchists, conservatives, clerics and other 'reactionaries' were always in bad grace with the Nazis" (p. 248).

SEPARATION OF POWERS

A nonelected part of government contributes to the separation of powers. By retaining certain constitutional powers or denying them to others, it can be a safeguard against abuses.[5] This is perhaps the main modern justification of hereditary monarchy: to put some restraint on politicians

---

[4] I hope that readers will allow me the stylistic convenience of using "king" to designate a reigning queen also, as the word "koning" does in the Dutch constitution, and also of using "he" or "him" or "his" to cover "she" or "her" as context requires.

[5] "[T]he first and indispensable condition for the exercise of responsibility is to separate executive power from supreme power. Constitutional monarchy attains this great

rather than let them pursue their own special interests complacent in the thought that their winning elections demonstrates popular approval. When former president Theodore Roosevelt visited Emperor Franz Joseph in 1910 and asked him what he thought the role of monarchy was in the twentieth century, the emperor reportedly replied: "To protect my peoples from their governments" (quoted in both "Thesen pro Monarchie" and Purcell 2003). Similarly, Lord Bernard Weatherill, former speaker of the House of Commons, said that the British monarchy exists not to exercise power but to keep other people from having the power; it is a great protection for British democracy (interview with Brian Lamb on C-Span, 26 November 1999).

The history of England shows progressive limitation of royal power in favor of parliament; but, in my view, a welcome trend went too far. Almost all power, limited only by traditions fortunately continuing as an unwritten constitution, came to be concentrated not only in parliament but even in the leader of the parliamentary majority. Democratization went rather too far, in my opinion, in the Continental monarchies also.

CONTINUITY

A monarch, not dependent on being elected and reelected, embodies continuity, as does the dynasty and the biological process.

> Constitutional monarchy offers us ... that neutral power so indispensable for all regular liberty. In a free country the king is a being apart, superior to differences of opinion, having no other interest than the maintenance of order and liberty. He can never return to the common condition, and is consequently inaccessible to all the passions that such a condition generates, and to all those that the perspective of finding oneself once again within it, necessarily creates in those agents who are invested with temporary power.

It is a master stroke to create a neutral power that can terminate some political danger by constitutional means (Constant 1814–1815/1988, pp. 186–187). In a settled monarchy—but no regime whatever can be guaranteed perpetual existence—the king need not worry about clinging to power. In a republic, "The very head of the state, having no title to his office save that which lies in the popular will, is forced to haggle and bargain like the lowliest office-seeker" (Mencken 1926, p. 181).

---

aim. But this advantage would be lost if the two powers were confused" (Constant 1814–1815/1988, p. 191).

Dynastic continuity parallels the rule of law. The king symbolizes a state of affairs in which profound political change, though eventually possible, cannot occur without ample time for considering it. The king stands in contrast with legislators and bureaucrats, who are inclined to think, by the very nature of their jobs, that diligent performance means multiplying laws and regulations. Continuity in the constitutional and legal regime provides a stable framework favorable to personal and business planning and investment and to innovation in science, technology, enterprise, and culture. Continuity is neither rigidity nor conservatism.

The heir to the throne typically has many years of preparation and is not dazzled by personal advancement when he finally inherits the office. Before and while holding office he accumulates a fund of experience both different from and greater than what politicians, who come and go, can ordinarily acquire. Even when the king comes to the throne as a youth or, at the other extreme, as an old man with only a few active years remaining, he has the counsel of experienced family members and advisers. If the king is very young (Louis XV, Alfonso XIII) or insane (the elderly George III, Otto of Bavaria), a close relative serves as regent.[6] The regent will have had some of the opportunities to perform ceremonial functions and to accumulate experience that an heir or reigning monarch has.

OBJECTIONS AND REBUTTALS

Some arguments occasionally employed for monarchy are questionable. If the monarch or his heir may marry only a member of a princely family (as Kuehnelt-Leddihn seems to recommend), chances are that he or she will marry a foreigner, providing international connections and a cosmopolitan way of thinking. Another dubious argument (also used by Kuehnelt-Leddihn) is that the monarch will have the blessing of and perhaps be the head of the state religion. Some arguments are downright absurd, for example: "Monarchy fosters art and culture. Austria was culturally much richer around 1780 than today! Just think of Mozart!" ("Thesen pro Monarchie").

---

[6]Otto von Habsburg blames the risk that an incompetent might occupy the throne on an inflexible legitimism—preoccupation with a particular dynasty—that displaced safeguards found in most classical monarchies. He recommends that the king be assisted by a body representing the highest judicial authority, a body that could if necessary replace the heir presumptive by the next in line of succession (1958/1970, pp. 262, 264, 266–267).

But neither all arguments for nor all objections to monarchy are fallacious. The same is true of democracy. In the choice of political institutions, as in many decisions of life, all one can do is weigh the pros and cons of the options and choose what seems best or least bad on balance.

Some objections to monarchy apply to democracy also or otherwise invite comments that, while not actual refutations, do strengthen the case in its favor. Monarchy is charged with being government-from-above (Kuehnelt-Leddihn 1952, p. 276). But all governments, even popularly elected ones, except perhaps small direct democracies like ancient Athens, are ruled by a minority. (Robert Michels and others recognized an "iron law of oligarchy"; Jenkin 1968, p. 282.) Although democracy allows the people some influence over the government, they do not and cannot actually run it. Constitutional monarchy combines some strengths of democracy and authoritarian monarchy while partially neutralizing the defects of those polar options.

Another objection condemns monarchy as a divisive symbol of inequality; it bars "an ideal society in which everyone will be equal in status, and in which everyone will have the right, if not the ability, to rise to the highest position" (Gabb 2002, who replies that attempts to create such a society have usually ended in attacks on the wealthy and even the well-off). Michael Prowse (2001), calling for periodic referendums on whether to keep the British monarchy, invokes what he considers the core idea of democracy: all persons equally deserve respect and consideration, and no one deserves to dominate others. The royal family and the aristocracy, with their titles, demeanor, and self-perpetuation, violate this democratic spirit. In a republican Britain, every child might aspire to every public position, even head of state.

So arguing, Prowse stretches the meaning of democracy from a particular method of choosing and influencing rulers to include an egalitarian social ethos. But monarchy need not obstruct easy relations among persons of different occupations and backgrounds; a suspicious egalitarianism is likelier to do that. In no society can all persons have the same status. A more realistic goal is that everyone have a chance to achieve distinction in some narrow niche important to him. Even in a republic, most people by far cannot realistically aspire to the highest position. No one need feel humbled or ashamed at not ascending to an office that simply was not available. A hereditary monarch can be like "the Alps" ("Thesen pro Monarchie"), something just "there." Perhaps it is the king's good luck, perhaps his bad luck, to have inherited the privileges but also the limitations of his office; but any question of unfairness pales in comparison with advantages for the country.

Prowse complains of divisiveness. But what about an election? It produces losers as well as winners, disappointed voters as well as happy ones. A king, however, cannot symbolize defeat to supporters of other candidates, for there were none. "A monarch mounting the throne of his ancestors follows a path on which he has not embarked of his own will." Unlike a usurper, he need not justify his elevation (Constant 1814–1815/1988, p. 88). He has no further political opportunities or ambitions except to do his job well and maintain the good name of his dynasty. Standing neutral above party politics, he has a better chance than an elected leader of becoming the personified symbol of his country, a focus of patriotism and even of affection.

The monarch and his family can assume ceremonial functions that elected rulers would otherwise perform as time permitted. Separating ceremonial functions from campaigning and policymaking siphons off glamor or adulation that would otherwise accrue to politicians and especially to demagogues. The occasional Hitler does arouse popular enthusiasm, and his opponents must prudently keep a low profile. A monarch, whose power is preservative rather than active (pp. 191–192), is safer for people's freedom.

Prowse is irritated rather than impressed by the pomp and opulence surrounding the Queen. Clinging to outmoded forms and ascribing importance to unimportant things reeks of "collective bad faith" and "corrosive hypocrisy." Yet a monarchy need not rest on pretense. On the contrary, my case for monarchy is a utilitarian one, not appealing to divine right or any such fiction. Not all ritual is to be scorned. Even republics have Fourth of July parades and their counterparts. Ceremonial trappings that may have become functionless or comical can evolve or be reformed. Not all monarchies, as Prowse recognizes, share with the British the particular trappings that irritate him.

A case, admittedly inconclusive, can be made for titles of nobility (especially for close royal relatives) and for an upper house of parliament of limited powers whose members, or some of them, hold their seats by inheritance or royal appointment (e.g., Constant 1814–1815/1988, pp. 198–200). "The glory of a legitimate monarch is enhanced by the glory of those around him.... He has no competition to fear.... But where the monarch sees supporters, the usurper sees enemies" (p. 91; on the precarious position of a nonhereditary autocrat, compare Tullock 1987). As long as the nobles are not exempt from the laws, they can serve as a kind of framework of the monarchy. They can be a further element of diversity in the social structure. They can provide an alternative to sheer wealth or notoriety as a source of distinction and so dilute the fawning over celebrities characteristic of modern democracies. Ordinary persons need no more feel humiliated by not being born into the nobility than by not being born heir to the throne. On balance, though, I am ambivalent about a nobility.

A KING'S POWERS

Michael Prowse's complaint about the pretended importance of unimportant things suggests a further reason why the monarch's role should go beyond the purely symbolic and ceremonial. The king should not be required (as the Queen of England is required at the opening of parliament) merely to read words written by the cabinet. At least he should have the three rights that Walter Bagehot identified in the British monarchy: "the right to be consulted, the right to encourage, the right to warn. And a king of great sense and sagacity would want no others. He would find that his having no others would enable him to use these with singular effect" (Bagehot 1867/1966, p. 111).

When Bagehot wrote, the Prime Minister was bound to keep the Queen well informed about the passing politics of the nation. "She has by rigid usage a right to complain if she does not know of every great act of her Ministry, not only before it is done, but while there is yet time to consider it—while it is still possible that it may not be done."

A sagacious king could warn his prime minister with possibly great effect. "He might not always turn his course, but he would always trouble his mind." During a long reign he would acquire experience that few of his ministers could match. He could remind the prime minister of bad results some years earlier of a policy like one currently proposed. "The king would indeed have the advantage which a permanent under-secretary has over his superior the Parliamentary secretary—that of having shared in the proceedings of the previous Parliamentary secretaries.... A pompous man easily sweeps away the suggestions of those beneath him. But though a minister may so deal with his subordinate, he cannot so deal with his king" (Bagehot 1867/1966, pp. 111–112). A prime minister would be disciplined, in short, by having to explain the objective (not merely the political) merits of his policies to a neutral authority.

The three rights that Bagehot listed should be interpreted broadly, in my view, or extended. Constant (1814–1815/1988, p. 301) recommends the right to grant pardons as a final protection of the innocent. The king should also have power: to make some appointments, especially of his own staff, not subject to veto by politicians; to consult with politicians of all parties to resolve an impasse over who might obtain the support or acquiescence of a parliamentary majority; and to dismiss and temporarily replace the cabinet or prime minister in extreme cases. (I assume a parliamentary system, which usually does accompany modern monarchy; but the executive could be elected separately from the legislators and even subject to recall by special election.) Even dissolving parliament and calling new elections in an exceptional case is no insult to the rights of the people. "On the contrary, when elections are free, it is an appeal made to their rights in favor of their interests" (p. 197). The king should try to rally national support in a constitutional crisis (as when King Juan Carlos intervened to foil an attempted military coup in 1981).

KINGS AND POLITICIANS

What if the hereditary monarch is a child or is incompetent? Then, as already mentioned, a regency is available. What if the royal family, like some of the Windsors, flaunts unedifying personal behavior? Both dangers are just as real in a modern republic. Politicians have a systematic tendency to be incompetent or worse.[7] For a democratic politician, understanding economics is a handicap.[8] He either must take unpopular (because misunderstood) stands on issues or else speak and act dishonestly. The economically ignorant politician has the advantage of being able to take vote-catching stands with a more nearly clear conscience. Particularly in these days of television and of fascination with celebrities, the personal characteristics necessary to win elections are quite different from those of a public-spirited statesman. History does record great statesmen in less democratized parliamentary regimes of the past. Nowadays a Gresham's Law operates: "the inferior human currency drives the better one out of circulation" (Kuehnelt-Leddihn, pp. 115, 120). Ideal

---

[7] Consider the one Republican and nine Democrats currently (October 2003) competing for the U.S. presidency. The day after the televised debate among the Democrats in Detroit, Roger Hitchcock, substitute host on a radio talk show, asked: "Would you like to have dinner with any of those people? Would you hire any of them to manage your convenience store?"

[8] "The first lesson of economics is scarcity: There is never enough of anything to satisfy all those who want it. The first lesson of politics is to disregard the first lesson of economics" (Sowell 1994).

democratic government simply is not an available option. Our best hope is to limit the activities of government, a purpose to which monarchy can contribute.

Although some contemporary politicians are honorable and economically literate, even simple honesty can worsens one's electoral chances. H.L. Mencken wrote acidly and with characteristic exaggeration: "No educated man, stating plainly the elementary notions that every educated man holds about the matters that principally concern government, could be elected to office in a democratic state, save perhaps by a miracle.... It has become a psychic impossibility for a gentleman to hold office under the Federal Union, save by a combination of miracles that must tax the resourcefulness even of God.... [T]he man of native integrity is either barred from the public service altogether, or subjected to almost irresistible temptations after he gets in" (Mencken 1926, pp. 103, 106, 110). Under monarchy, the courtier need not "abase himself before swine," "pretend that he is a worse man than he really is." His sovereign has a certain respect for honor. "The courtier's sovereign ... is apt to be a man of honour himself" (Mencken 1926, p. 118, mentioning that the King of Prussia refused the German imperial crown offered him in 1849 by a mere popular parliament rather than by his fellow sovereign princes).

Mencken conceded that democracy has its charms: "The fraud of democracy ... is more amusing than any other—more amusing even, and by miles, than the fraud of religion.... [The farce] greatly delights me. I enjoy democracy immensely. It is incomparably idiotic, and hence incomparably amusing" (pp. 209, 211).

CONCLUSION

One argument against institutions with a venerable history is a mindless slogan betraying temporal provincialism, as if newer necessarily meant better: "Don't turn back the clock." Sounder advice is not to overthrow what exists because of abstract notions of what might seem logically or ideologically neater. In the vernacular, "If it ain't broke, don't fix it." It is progress to learn from experience, including experience with inadequately filtered democracy. Where a monarchical element in government works well enough, the burden of proof lies against the republicans (cf. Gabb 2002). Kuehnelt-Leddihn, writing in 1952 (p. 104), noted that "the royal, non-democratic alloy" has supported the relative success of several representative governments in Europe. Only a few nontotalitarian republics there and overseas have exhibited a record of stability, notably Switzerland, Finland, and the United States.[9]

Constitutional monarchy cannot solve all problems of government; nothing can. But it can help. Besides lesser arguments, two main ones recommend it. First, its very existence is a reminder that democracy is not the sort of thing of which more is necessarily better; it can help promote balanced thinking. Second, by contributing continuity, diluting democracy while supporting a healthy element of it, and furthering the separation of government powers, monarchy can help protect personal liberty.

REFERENCES

Bagehot, Walter. *The English Constitution*. 1867, 1872. Ithaca, N.Y.: Cornell Paperbacks, 1966.

Barry, Norman. "What's So Good About Democracy?" *Ideas on Liberty* 53 (May 2003): 44–48.

Campbell, Colin M. "Large Electorates and Decisive Minorities." *Journal of Political Economy* 107 (December 1999): 1199–1217.

Constant, Benjamin. *Political Writings*. 1814–1815. Translated and edited by Biancamaria Fontana. Cambridge, U.K., and New York: Cambridge University Press, 1988.

Gabb, Sean. "In Defence of the Monarchy." *Free Life Commentary*, no. 83 (9 December 2002). http://www.seangabb.co.uk/flcomm/flc083.htm.

Gray, John. *Post-Liberalism: Studies in Political Thought*. London and New York: Routledge, 1993.

Habsburg, Otto von. "Monarchy or Republic." 1958. In *The Conservative Tradition in European Thought*, edited by Robert Schuettinger, 258–267. New York: Putnam, 1970.

Hayek, F.A. *The Political Order of a Free People*. Vol. 3 of *Law, Legislation and Liberty*. Chicago: University of Chicago Press, 1979.

Hoppe, Hans-Hermann. *Democracy: The God That Failed*. New Brunswick, N.J.: Transaction Publishers, 2001.

---

[9]Compare Lewis and Woolsey 2003: "[O]f the nations that have been democracies for a very long time and show every sign that they will remain so, a substantial majority are constitutional monarchies (the U.S. and Switzerland being the principal exceptions)."

International Monarchist League. "The Case for Monarchy."

Jenkin, Thomas P. "Oligarchy." In *International Encyclopedia of the Social Sciences*, edited by David L. Sills, vol. 11: 281–283. New York: Macmillan and Free Press, 1968.

Kuehnelt-Leddihn, Erik von. *Liberty or Equality*. Edited by John P. Hughes. London: Hollis & Carter, 1952. http://www.scribd.com/doc/3917515/KuehneltLeddihn-Liberty-or-Equality.

Lewis, Bernard, and R. James Woolsey. "King and Country." *Wall Street Journal*, 29 October 2003.

Mencken, H.L. *Notes on Democracy*. New York: Knopf, 1926.

Mises, Ludwig von. *Nation, State, and Economy*. 1919. New York: New York University Press, 1983.

Paine, Thomas. *The Rights of Man*. Part First, 1791, and Part Second, 1792. In *Two Classics of the French Revolution: Edmund Burke's* Reflections on the Revolution in France *and Paine's* The Rights of Man, pp. 267–515. New York: Doubleday, Anchor Books, 1973, 1989.

Prowse, Michael. "Why Britain Should Hold 'Royal Referendums'." *Financial Times*, 21–22 April 2001.

Purcell, Frank. "All Hail the House of Habsburg!" *LiveJournal*, 18 August 2003. http://arisbe.livejournal.com/42592.html.

Schumpeter, Joseph A. *Capitalism, Socialism, and Democracy*. 1950. 3rd ed. New York: Harper and Row, 1962.

Sowell, Thomas. Quoted (without indication of source) in "Endnotes." *CEI UpDate* 7 (July 1994): 8.

"Thesen pro Monarchie." http://rasputin.de/Monarch/thesen.html. Tradition und Leben e.V. http://www.pro-monarchie.de/

Tullock, Gordon. *Autocracy*. Dordrecht and Boston: Kluwer, 1987.

CHAPTER 22

Uchronia, or Alternative History*

The history that didn't happen can be just as interesting as the history that did.
This article is a small example of its own topic. Except by chance, I wouldn't now be writing it. Not finding what I wanted while browsing in our library's magazine aisles, I came across mention of "uchronie" in *Le Nouvel Observateur*. The philosopher Charles Renouvier chose this word as the title of his novel of 1857 and 1876; he coined it from Greek roots meaning "no-time." He was following the pattern set by St. Thomas More, whose *Utopia* derives from roots meaning "no-place." Utopia is a place that does not exist; uchronia is a time that did not exist. Uchronian works—to introduce the English adjective—are also called "what-if," alternative, conjectural, or counterfactual history. They consider what would have happened if something else had chanced to happen.

Such works fall into two categories. The distinction is fuzzy but useful. Writings of the first kind, unlike actual history or a standard historical novel, are sheer fiction. They are not speculations about real events; they are stories that stand on their own. The *Star Wars* movies and Tolkien's tales are good examples. Another is *Islandia*, a novel by Austin Tappan Wright, published posthumously in 1942. Wright describes events and personalities in a country on a fictional continent in the southern hemisphere before World War I. The people of Islandia, while highly civilized and advanced in philosophy and psychology, prefer their old ways, rejecting railroads and most other modern technology and narrowly limiting contact with the outside world. The reader (this one, anyway) drifts with the author into sympathy with the Islandian way of thinking.

---

*From *Liberty* 23 (September 2009): 31–34. I thank the editor, Stephen Cox, for suggestions and some of the wording.

388

Edward Bellamy's *Looking Backward* (1887) projects an opposite vision, one intended as backward only in an ironic sense; it imagines a prosperous and happy socialist utopia of 2000. This uchronia actually exerted some influence in its time, converting many readers to socialism because they wanted to live in the world of Bellamy's vision. A less satisfying example of the first category of uchronian works is *Hadrian VII* (1904), a rather amateurish fantasy by Frederick Rolfe, the self-appointed Baron Corvo. Its hero is a frustrated would-be priest whom a deadlocked College of Cardinals implausibly elects as pope, the second English pope in history. Pope Hadrian radiates his benevolence right up to World War I or, rather, to its avoidance. His ministrations successfully adjust the world's important political conflicts. This story also had real-world effects. The oddness of the book and its author inspired a famous work of literary detection, *The Quest for Corvo* (1934), in which A.J.A. Symons discovered how strange the "Baron" actually was.

The second (and my preferred) category of uchronian literature is more strictly what-if history. It concerns actual events or circumstances that might plausibly have been different. *If: Or History Rewritten*, edited by J.C. Squire (1931), samples the genre with stories by many writers. Phillip Guedalla supposes that the Christian Reconquista of Spain had somehow not gone far enough to absorb the Moorish Kingdom of Grenada, leaving it a power in international affairs into the twentieth century and presumably beyond. Hendrik Willem van Loon supposes that the Dutch had retained Nieuw Amsterdam until, by a treaty with a curiously libertarian provision, it joined the United States in 1841. André Maurois supposes that Louis XVI had been firm enough to keep Turgot, his liberalizing finance minister, until and beyond 1789 (when the French Revolution began, in the real world), instead of dismissing him in 1776. Hillaire Belloc supposes that the cart that blocked Louis's path when he tried to flee from France in 1791 had gotten stuck before reaching the crucial spot at Varennes. Emil Ludwig asks what if German Emperor Frederick III, liberal-minded and married to a daughter of Queen Victoria, instead of dying after only ninety-nine days on the throne in 1888, had survived and exerted his moderating influence until 1914. Winston Churchill, in a double twist, writes as a historian in a world in which Lee had actually won the battle of Gettysburg and who speculates about his not having won. Milton Waldman supposes that Booth's shot missed Lincoln. G.K. Chesterton imagines Don John of Austria married to Mary Queen of Scots; Harold Nicholson, Byron enthroned as King of Greece; and

H.A.L. Fisher, Napoleon escaped to America and become a prosperous planter. Squire, the editor, postulates discovery of proof that Lord Bacon wrote Shakespeare's works.

Such speculation need not be frivolity. Contrasts with what really happened can deepen our understanding of actual history and of theories of economics, psychology, political science, international relations, military affairs, theology, medicine, and even natural science as applied by decisionmakers of the past. History for us was the unknown future for them. And each of us has undoubtedly experienced choices in his own life very differently from the way in which a biographer would describe them. He would know the results; we didn't.

One subcategory of conjectural history doesn't much appeal to me. Like Guedalla's Grenada scenario, it speculates about *major* trends or conditions that turned out different from the actual ones. What if the dinosaurs or the Roman Empire hadn't disappeared? What if Europe had never discovered America? So sweeping a conjecture is unsatisfying because it focuses on general frameworks of history instead of particular events, ones that may have seemed unimportant in themselves but had major consequences. (Just what might have enabled Grenada to survive the Reconquista?) Likewise, it seems out of the spirit of the genre to use some event or nonevent as a take-off point for sheer fiction, as about Napoleon's imaginary exploits in the New World.

Divergences between what did happen and what might have happened sometimes trigger momentous domino or butterfly effects. Several may particularly interest libertarians. What if the Civil War had been avoided, and with it the federal government's domination of the monetary system? What if the Federal Reserve System had never been created? What if Chancellor of the Exchequer Winston Churchill had heeded warnings against returning Great Britain to the gold standard in 1925 at the no longer viable prewar parity? What if (as Milton Friedman and Anna Schwartz have speculated) Benjamin Strong, Governor of the Federal Reserve Bank of New York, dominant figure in the Federal Reserve System, and a better intuitive economist than most of his colleagues, had not died prematurely in 1928? What if Harry Gunnison Brown or Irving Fisher had headed the System, or if his advice had prevailed around 1929? Would an ordinary recession have turned into the Great Depression, creating opportunities both for the New Deal and for Hitler? I think not.

But we can carry speculations further. What if Giuseppe Zangara's shot at President-elect Roosevelt in February 1933 hadn't killed Chicago's

Mayor Cermak instead? What if the United States hadn't adopted the silver-purchase program of the 1930s, which benefited domestic silver interests but ruined China's monetary system and thus improved the chances of the Communists? What if von Papen and his associates, early in 1933, had not expected to manage Hitler and make him a safe choice for Chancellor? What if Hitler had decided to finish off England in 1940–1941 before tackling Russia? What if FDR, seriously ill, had died before the Yalta conference of February 1945—or earlier, while Henry Wallace was still vice president? What if Hitler had died in the nearly successful attempt to assassinate him in 1944? What if Lee Harvey Oswald had proved a poor marksman at Dallas in 1963? How would Gerald Ford and the country have fared if he had not pardoned Richard Nixon? Or what would Nixon's refusal of a pardon have meant? What if the tight vote in Florida in 2000 had gone the other way, as it might well have gone, were it not for hanging chads, misaligned ballots, and accidental votes for Pat Buchanan? A Gore administration would have been a disaster, but of a different sort from the disaster Bush brought us. And would today's financial crisis be less or more severe if the rescue of Long-Term Capital Management, orchestrated by the Federal Reserve in 1998, and of other institutions before and later hadn't worsened the dilemma of moral hazard?

Sure, history has its deterministic aspects; Marx stressed technology. But the possibilities inherent in many junctures of history discredit overemphasis on determinism and underline the element of chance. Suppose that Pontius Pilate had saved Jesus Christ, forestalling his crucifixion and the resurrection story. Would Jesus still have become the focus of a religion dominating, for good and ill, most of the Western world? Or would he have remained an itinerant preacher scarcely mentioned in the history of religion? Would one of the mystery religions of the Eastern Mediterranean have become dominant instead of Christianity?

Consider an episode of British history. Queen Anne had 18 children, more or less, counting miscarriages and stillbirths as well as live births. If better medical care had managed to save even one of these potential heirs beyond Anne's death in 1714, the Protestants of her family, the Stuarts (the Catholics among them being ineligible by law), would have retained the British crown. But Anne died without leaving a Protestant Stuart heir, so the crown passed to the distantly related House of Hanover. Hanoverians had very different interests and political traditions. It was among them that the British developed what came to be the characteristically modern party-and-prime-minister system. Would it have developed in a similar way under a Stuart succession?

Here we are speculating about the latent potential of people and movements that we can identify. But what about the multitude of what-if cases that never had a chance to come to our attention? Were it not for the accident of dying early, how many men and women would have survived to change the course of cultural and political history? This is a theme of Gray's "Elegy Written in a Country Churchyard":

> Perhaps in this neglected spot is laid
> Some heart once pregnant with celestial fire,
> Hands that the rod of empire might have swayed,
> Or waked to ecstasy the living lyre.

Here, perhaps, speculation ceases with our lack of knowledge. But events that are too certain are not fruitful subjects of speculation, either. Historical struggles make poor examples of uchronia when the advantage was decisively on one side. They become more interesting when the details could easily have gone the other way. "My kingdom for a horse!" cries Shakespeare's Richard III at Bosworth Field. To me, even more interesting than battles that might have gone either way are wars that might have gone either way—in the sense that they might have been avoided.

If American war hawks had not misrepresented the explosion of the Maine in Havana harbor in 1898, Spain might well have remained a substantial power; and the United States might have avoided its deeper colonial and geopolitical burdens. Suppose that hotheads had been less influential in Charleston in April 1861 or that Jefferson Davis had restrained them. The Confederates could have been more patient, not falling for Lincoln's provocative move to resupply Fort Sumter. Without their firing on the fort, Lincoln could not have whipped up war fever in the North. How would a few more months or even years of a Union garrison in Charleston harbor have impaired Confederate independence, thus far succeeding? After all, the garrison had been allowed to buy supplies in Charleston even after secession. Neither side expected four years of tragic bloodshed. The issue of slavery might have been resolved at much less cost for either side.

France in 1870 is an example of not taking "yes" (compliance) for an answer. The Spanish provisional government had invited a Hohenzollern prince to become the country's new king. The government of the French Emperor, Napoleon III, objected; and the German prince, a member of the house then ruling Prussia, withdrew. Events could easily have stopped there, but they didn't. Not content with this diplomatic triumph, the French foreign ministry tried to humiliate the Prussians further. It instructed the French ambassador to accost Prussia's King William I at a spa and press for written assurance that no such candidacy would ever be renewed. The king politely refused. Bismarck, the Prussian prime minister, published the king's report of the episode after tendentiously editing it to give the impression to the French that the king had insulted their ambassador and to the Prussians that the ambassador had been impolite to their king. Empress Eugenie of France, a leading war hawk, expected that victory would further consolidate the Napoleonic dynasty. So the French enthusiastically let themselves be tricked into declaring war, even though they were militarily unprepared and lacked even adequate maps of the likely theaters of operations. Napoleon III lost his throne, the Bonapartist Second Empire collapsed, France lost Alsace-Lorraine, revanchisme emerged as a political force in France, and danger of another war developed. What if soberer minds had prevailed in the French government? What if the Spaniards had invited some non-German as their king in the first place?

As the end of the Second Empire hinged on chance, so did its beginning. Louis-Napoleon Bonaparte, as he was then known, staged a generally unforeseen coup d'etat on December 2, 1851. His term as president of the republic (won by name recognition) would soon expire, and the constitution barred his reelection. Hence he seized power. But his cruel stroke might well have failed, and with it the train of events that led France and Germany to the wars of 1870 and 1914.

The Great War was a tragic and unnecessary modern turning point. Think of its consequences—economic, political, military, and psychological. In 1914 no power desired or foresaw a war so long and bloody. Although a complicated network of alliances did pose danger, events on the scale that later developed were not predicted. They did not stop with the armistice of 1918. World War II followed, largely as a consequence of and sequel to the first war. One of the causal connections was the fact that Germany's defeat and the ensuing Treaty of Versailles gave Hitler material for domestic propaganda. But what if advice not to punish Germany so severely had prevailed at Versailles? Or what if Britain and France had acted decisively when Hitler first violated the treaty in 1934–1936?

The fateful significance of June 28, 1914—the date when the Austrian Archduke Franz Ferdinand was assassinated at Sarajevo and the curtain began to rise for the world conflict of 1914–1918 and then of

1939–1945—led me, along with a friend's young son who was accompanying me to a conference in Italy, to make a side trip to Sarajevo. There we saw where Gavrilo Princip stood when firing the shot that killed Franz Ferdinand—by a building where a laudatory commemorative plaque was subsequently mounted and a museum established. I wondered: what if the Archduke's car had not made a wrong turn? What if Princip's shot had missed, if even only by inches? An assassination attempt had already failed earlier the same day, just barely. This one might also have failed.

Still, the assassination did not make war inevitable. Suspecting Serbian complicity, Austria-Hungary sent Serbia an ultimatum imposing drastic conditions: it must collaborate in an investigation and suppress further terrorist agitation. Serbia came surprisingly close to agreeing completely; but Austria-Hungary, unwilling (like France in 1870) to take a near-yes for an answer, started a war, and alliances fed contagion. What if Austria-Hungary had been satisfied with the near-yes, or if Serbia had totally complied?

Beyond the questions it poses, conjectural history can contribute to understanding oneself as well as the roles of other people and of chance in human affairs. When I was in high school I bought *Hugo's Spanish Simplified* and a few of the Haldeman-Julius Company's cheap little books on religion and on the international language Esperanto. Miss Connor, my history teacher, steered me to the economics of Henry George and to a book about Italian history. These little episodes affected my later life in unforeseeable ways. Miss Connor was what we would now call an outspoken left-liberal; still, she was a conscientious and inspiring teacher. Without her influence, I might not have majored in economics in college and gone on for a Ph.D. in economics. Meanwhile, the little Haldeman-Julius books aroused my interests in religion and in an international language, both of which I have discussed in *Liberty* (October 2007 and January/February 2008).

Perhaps most accidental, yet significant, was the influence of Hugo's Spanish book. I went on learning Spanish, entirely without any formal classes. At Auburn University I joined the "Friends of Guatemala," a dormant then resurrected weekly Spanish conversation group, the origin of whose name nobody could remember. All but two of our group's members soon dropped out, but Luis Dopico and I carried on, eventually having our Spanish conversations at dinner once a week. I visited him once in his home city in Spain. He now lives in North Carolina and has dual citizenship. I talk with him by phone in Spanish for about an hour almost every Sunday, then for about 15 minutes in English with his wife, Stephanie Crofton. If I hadn't been turned onto Spanish by Hugo's book, I would never have made these two close friendships. This is a prime example of a microstochastic event—an instance of randomness on a very small scale—with major consequences for me.

And what if I had failed, like some of my colleagues, in a Japanese language course during the war? What if I had followed my father's (bad) advice, offered because I had lost three years in the Army, to skip returning to college and go directly into the business world? What if I had not happened onto books by Ludwig von Mises in the Oberlin College library and by Wilhelm Röpke in a New York bookstore, works that greatly influenced my understanding of economics and of libertarianism or quasi-libertarianism? What if I had chosen the problem of innovation under socialism as my dissertation topic in 1950–1952, instead of the other topic I was considering, "An Evaluation of Freely Fluctuating Exchange Rates," which I did choose? (I know I would have had trouble finding much to say about innovation under socialism.) What if I hadn't taught at Texas A&M for one year and at the University of Maryland for five, making a few close friends at the two schools? A year in Maryland's European program came at just the right time of my life. What if an article of mine had not brought me an invitation to move to the University of Virginia in 1957? By happening to take part in an Institute for Humane Studies program in the summer of 1981, I met a valued academic collaborator, Robert Greenfield. In 1984, the idea of buying a big house with a big mortgage as an inflation hedge tipped my agonizingly close decision toward moving from Virginia to Auburn University. (Yes, not only inflation but uncertainty about it can disrupt even personal planning.) Speculation not only about episodes in world history but also about turning points in a single life can make for lively but serious conversation—with others, and with oneself.

I've saved for last an example of uchronia that, for two reasons, is my favorite. Like many of the examples above and as best I can remember, I thought of it myself. More importantly, it is an extreme example of its type; arguably, it even bears on the philosophical issue of free will and determinism. Suppose that in 1818 Queen Victoria had been conceived as a male rather than a female. Her (or his) sex determination was surely a microstochastic event. Except only for this accident of sex, the crowns of Great Britain and Hanover would have remained united after the death of Victoria's uncle, William IV, in 1837. Women could succeed to the throne of Britain, but the medieval Salic Law excluded all females from the throne of Hanover so long as any male heirs were to be found. So another of Victoria's uncles, Ernest Augustus, became king of Hanover, separating the two crowns.

Now, if the new monarch of Britain had been a male, he would also have been king of Hanover. A kingdom in the heart of northern Germany sharing the same English-speaking, English-educated monarch with Great Britain would have greatly hampered Bismarck's efforts toward German unification. The Seven Weeks War of 1866 (Prussia against Austria), having in its background the 1864 war of Prussia and Austria against Denmark over the north-German Schleswig-Holstein issue, might never have taken place. As its result, however, Hanover, an ally of defeated Austria, lost its independence in 1866 and was absorbed into Prussia. Without Victoria's conception as a female, then, the wars of 1866 and 1870–1871, the establishment of the German Empire, World War I, and the Bolshevik revolution of 1917 might never have occurred, at least not at their actual times and in their actual ways. Would our lives be different? It's difficult to argue otherwise.

Small chance events can indeed sway history. This is how uchronia becomes reality.

CHAPTER 23

Hayek on the Psychology of Socialism and Freedom*

INTRODUCTION (BY HERBERT STEIN)

Nineteen eighty-four is the eighty-fifth anniversary of the birth of Friedrich Hayek, Nobel laureate and one of this century's great economists. This year is also the fortieth anniversary of Hayek's best-known book, *The Road to Serfdom*.

The Road to Serfdom was published at a critical time. The 1930s had been a decade of exceptionally rapid increase of the economic role of government in the Western democracies, including the United States and Britain. In 1944, as the war was coming to an end, the common, expectation was that this trend would be resumed in the postwar period. The usual term for the postwar economic environment was "postwar planning," meaning planning by government.

During the 1930s there had been little objective intellectual resistance to the movement toward increasing government controls. In the United States resistance came from Republicans, Southern Democrats, and business organizations and could be dismissed as partisan, nostalgic, or self-interested.

Hayek's book was the opening—and the most important—shot in the intellectual resistance to the trend toward government control. Hayek argued that military victory over the Nazis and Fascists would not permanently ensure the triumph of freedom. The repulsive features of the Nazi and Fascist regimes were not the results of peculiarly German and Italian characteristics. Rather they were the results of carrying out fully the implications of a socialist way of thinking that was already present in Britain and the United States. He warned that unless we rejected that way of thinking we could follow along the same road to serfdom.

*From *AEI Economist* (November 1984): 1–5.

The book was an immediate sensation. It had an enormous popular audience, partly through a condensation in the *Reader's Digest*, and has been translated into some sixteen languages.

If we are not now on the road to serfdom—and we do not seem to be—some of the credit for that must go to Friedrich Hayek. In salute to him we publish the following article by a distinguished student of Hayek's work, Professor Leland Yeager of the University of Virginia.

HAYEK ON THE PSYCHOLOGY OF SOCIALISM AND FREEDOM

Now, forty years after its publication, is a good time to reconsider Friedrich Hayek's *The Road to Serfdom* (1944). George Orwell's *1984* also deserves mention, since Orwell had written a kind review of Hayek's book before writing his own.[1]

Someone reading a book again after a long interval is likely to receive a rather different message. This fact illustrates the thesis that Hayek develops in *The Sensory Order* (published in 1952 but derived from a paper drafted over thirty years earlier). I'd like to explain my point, and also hail Hayek's inadequately remembered work in psychology, by first surveying that book. A further link between his books of 1944 and 1952 is that Hayek often deployed psychological insights in *The Road to Serfdom* to explain, for example, why certain wrong ideas nevertheless have wide appeal. Fully appreciating Hayek's work in economics and political science requires knowing of his interest in psychology.

HAYEK'S PSYCHOLOGICAL DOCTRINES

Although *The Sensory Order* does not stress the connection, Hayek's psychological doctrines do mesh well with his methodology in economics and his approach to practical affairs. A sharp distinction between theory and fact or between theory and practice is not tenable. All our actions, all our observations of fact, even all our supposedly ultimate or irreducible sense perceptions are shot through with theory. Even at the level closest to bare fact, theory is indispensable to making sense out of the world and even to perceiving it.

We never perceive unique properties of individual objects but only properties that objects have in common. Perception always involves

---

[1] Hayek mentions Orwell's review in a new foreword to *The Road to Serfdom* (Hayek 1944/1956, p. viii n.).

interpretation ascribing impulses received to one or more classes. This classification is at least rudimentary theory. The qualities we attribute to experienced objects belong, actually, to the relations by which we classify them.

Examples may help. When I hear a sound or see a patch of red, neither simply exists as a distinct part of objective reality impressing itself on my nervous system. Rather, my nervous system selects certain aspects of reality accessible to my sense organs, classifies them, and organizes them into my perception of the sound or the red patch. Far from playing a purely passive role, my nervous system impresses order or character onto my perceptions and thus shapes and in a way even creates them.

What aspects of reality can affect my sense organs and how its effects shape themselves into perceptions depend on the state of those organs, of my nervous system, and indeed of my entire body. The role of the physical body is obvious. Unlike a dog, I cannot perceive certain smells or high-pitched sounds. Unlike me, the dog cannot recognize and so cannot perceive words in a conversation or on a printed page.

Biological processes and natural selection have presumably shaped organisms in such ways that their perceptions possess an order corresponding to whatever order may exist in the world. Organisms that frequently confused hot and cold, small and large, near and far, up and down, hunger and satiety, wolf and bush would be less likely to survive and reproduce than ones whose perceptions corresponded better to reality. Among higher organisms, actions conforming to principles of logic would have greater survival value than actions clashing with logic.

We see some possible truth, then, in Immanuel Kant's contention that human beings can have knowledge prior to experience. Quibbling, we might narrow that contention down. People do not have any a priori knowledge in an articulated form. What they more plausibly have are predispositions to behave as if they had certain knowledge and predispositions to recognize and become able to articulate it.

In Hayek's interpretation, experience is involved in knowledge, after all, but it is not restricted to experience obtained by the individual organism itself. Rather, it includes the experience of the species and its ancestors as embodied, through biology and natural selection, in each individual's genetic and physiological makeup. The individual human being inherits the experience of his ancestors not only through biological but also through cultural processes, notably through language. Language increases his capacity for discrimination in dealing with new experience.

Language is itself the product of interwoven biological and cultural evolution.

Still another type of experience besides his own direct current experience helps shape the individual's current perceptions. His own past experience does so by having affected physical and chemical conditions within his body, such as nerve connections governing the travel of impulses to and from the brain. People do not first have sensations that are then preserved by memory. Rather, it is as a result of physiological memory that physiological impulses received are converted into sensations.

We need not go into what Hayek says further about physiology and about what experiments do or would tend either to support or to refute his theory. It is worth mentioning, though, that while Hayek (like almost all scientists) is a mechanist as opposed to a vitalist, he is no reductionist. He does not believe that the life sciences and social sciences can be "reduced" to physics and chemistry in such a way as to recommend banishing the language of seeing, hearing, thinking, consciousness, purposes, intentions, decisions, and actions and requiring all propositions about such matters to be phrased exclusively in physical and chemical terms instead.

Hayek argues, in short, that the individual's cognitive apparatus, shaped by his biological and cultural inheritances and by his own past experiences, brings a predisposition to each new situation to perceive it and organize its aspects in particular ways. No such thing operates as raw, pure, unfiltered perception. Rather, the observer largely shapes what he perceives.

Knowledge does indeed have an a priori aspect then (though its nature and sources are not quite what Kant had supposed). It is not true that all we know must be subject to confirmation or contradiction by sense experience, that is, by current or future sense experience. At least part of what we know at any moment about the external world is implicit in the means through which we can obtain experience.

Many observations tend to support or illustrate Hayek's theory, or at least to provide illuminating parallels. George Stigler and Gary Becker (1977), in a well-known methodological article, tacitly accept something like the theory. They warn against hastily chalking up a change in a person's behavior to a change in his tastes. They recommend postulating a stable basic structure of tastes within which the accumulation of experience may alter the response even to otherwise unchanged circumstances. A person may respond differently than before to a given set of opportunities, including perhaps prices, if in the interval he has acquired, for example, more "music appreciation capital."

When one uses a foreign language, particularly over the telephone, what he hears—not just understands, but even hears—depends on how well he knows the language, that is, on his previous experience.

Hayek's theory, along with Leon Festinger's theory of cognitive dissonance, helps explain why many people cannot recognize the worst source of cruelty, predation, and mortal peril in the world today and instead dump the blame onto those Western statesmen who do identify the evil and call for adequate defense. Those theories also help explain why certain economists who trumpet their supposed empirical orientation nevertheless cannot see which of their favorite postulates are falsified by facts and cannot see how substantial or how slight the results are that their favorite methods have yielded. Admittedly, it may be I, not the people I am criticizing, who is wrong; but then my errors would still illustrate the central point that the experiences and the mind set one brings to a cognitive situation affect not only one's interpretation of it but even what one can see.

Many writers have presumably been criticized, as I have, for views they had not expressed. Their readers evidently could not perceive, unfiltered, what they were saying. Rather, the readers classified the material in their own preexisting pigeonholes. They then reacted to what their filing systems accommodated, not just to any bare substance of what had been said.

The message that a reader draws from a book follows partly from the experiences he brings to it, including his past reading. That is why a book reread after a long interval may make a different impression than before.

THE ROAD TO SERFDOM

That is how *The Road to Serfdom* has affected me. The book's central message is, of course, hard to miss: Socialism, in the sense of collective ownership of the means of production and central direction of economic life, entails loss of personal freedom. What came more strongly to my attention is Hayek's concern with political institutions and incentives and also with linkages of ideas. Since I had also been sensitized in the meanwhile to Hayek's interest in psychology, the same is true of his many psychological insights.

These, in *The Road to Serfdom*, are insights of "literary" psychology ("thymology," as Ludwig von Mises called it) rather than of the technical discipline. Hayek stresses the influence of beliefs and attitudes and explores reasons why people hold them.

Specialists tend to be enthusiastic for central planning because they tacitly assume that the planners will, like themselves, be intelligent persons having sensible scales of values and so understanding the special importance of each particular specialist's favorite goal. (Examples might be education, environmental protection, high technology, mass transportation, or more nearly equal distribution of income and wealth.) Accordingly, an apparent consensus in favor of planning is likely to be spurious, for the different enthusiasts will have different visions of the plan to adopt.

What "gives the demand for planning its strongest impetus," says Hayek, is "the resentment of the frustrated specialist" (1944/1956, p. 55). No single economic factor has contributed more to help Fascist and National Socialist movements "than the envy of the unsuccessful professional man, the university-trained engineer or lawyer, and of the 'white-collared proletariat' in general, of the engine driver or compositor and other members of the strongest trade unions whose income was many times theirs" (p. 116).

Another source of discontent with the market economy is a vague resentment at often having to pay a material cost to serve higher values—"life and health, beauty and virtue, honor and peace of mind." People resent "having the higher values of life brought into the 'cash nexus'." At bottom, and without realizing it, what they resent is the economic problem—the inexorable fact of scarcity and the need to make choices (pp. 97–98).

Hayek describes the attitude, cultivated in the Germany that eventually put Hitler in power, that something disreputable attaches to taking economic risks and making profit: "to employ a hundred people is represented as exploitation but to command the same number as honorable" (pp. 130–131).

In a complex civilization with a developed market economy, many people will not understand why they must adjust to changes of unknown source and nature, as by shifting occupations, or why some things they desire should become harder to obtain than in the past. They do not understand that "the only alternative to submission to the impersonal and seemingly irrational forces of the market is submission to an equally uncontrollable and therefore arbitrary power of other men" (p. 205).

One famous piece of Hayek's psychologizing is his chapter on "Why the Worst Get on Top." In a system in which achieving wealth and position depends less than it does in a market economy on satisfying the wants of one's fellows through voluntary transactions, ambitious people have more scope for pandering to popular resentments and prejudices and to the vanity and power-hunger of their superiors. Opportunities for the unscrupulous, ruthless, and uninhibited (including people not inhibited by concern for truth) will be relatively greater. Hayek (p. 152) quotes Frank Knight: "the probability of the people in power being individuals who would dislike the possession and exercise of power is on a level with the probability that an extremely tender-hearted person would get the job of whipping-master in a slave plantation."

It helps describe *The Road to Serfdom* to compare it with a book published in Switzerland four years later whose author repeatedly cites Hayek: Walter Adolf Jöhr (1948), *Ist ein freiheitlicher Sozialismus möglich?* (Is Socialism with Freedom Possible?). Hayek's is the longer book, though both are short (248 pages plus introductions versus 137 pages). Jöhr sticks more closely to systematic analysis of what economic and other aspects of society are or are not likely to be compatible with one another; he aims rather narrowly at answering the question posed. His answer turns out "No." He cites, and rejects, published efforts to reconcile socialism and freedom by redefining one or both terms. He explains why a centrally directed economy would destroy economic freedoms, why economic and other freedoms cannot be sharply separated, and why political and cultural freedoms would therefore suffer also. He shows why losses of some freedoms are unlikely to be outweighed by gains of others. Decentralized socialism and partial socialism would have difficulties of their own and would experience pressures to evolve toward fuller-fledged socialism.

The two books are complementary. Hayek covers much the same ground as Jöhr, but in a looser, more discursive, less narrowly analytical way; he argues more by piling up plausible insights. He also ranges more widely. He diagnoses more trends and draws more parallels. He points out, for example, that the rise of fascism and Nazism was not a reaction against socialist trends but rather their extension.

> The intensity of the moral emotions behind a movement like that of National Socialism or communism can probably be compared only to those of the great religious movements of history. Once you admit that the individual is merely a means to serve the ends of the higher entity called society or the nation, most of those features of totalitarian regimes which horrify us follow of necessity.... When German philosophers again and again represent the striving for personal happiness as itself immoral and only the fulfilment of an imposed duty as praiseworthy, they are perfectly sincere, however difficult this may be to understand

for those who have been brought up in a different tradition. (Hayek 1944/1956, p. 149)

Besides delving into psychology, Hayek goes further than Jöhr into the history and interconnections of ideas. He makes more allusions to people, events, and literature. He considers the allegedly inexorable decline of competition and the supposed necessity of planning for that reason. He describes the positive accomplishments of a price system. Anticipating chapter 6 of his *The Constitution of Liberty* (1960), he presents the case for allowing market incentives to guide the allocation of resources, effort, and risk-bearing rather than trying to make the distribution of income correspond somehow to judgments of moral merit.

The Road to Serfdom foreshadows many of Hayek's later writings and could serve as an introduction and summary. Over his lifetime his work shows continuity. In his writings, as I know them, he has had to reverse himself on remarkably little. This is not to say that he is stuck in a rut, reciting earlier formulations—not at all. His thought has developed, but largely through his deepening of earlier insights and extending them to new fields. With regard to the degree of economic intervention he favors, he has evolved if anything in a laissez-faire direction, as illustrated by his proposals for taking even the monetary system out of the clutches of government.

The Road to Serfdom explains the perverse consequences of government measures to shelter individual sectors of the economy against the adverse impact of change. Already in 1944, Hayek had begun to grasp some points later elaborated by Mancur Olson in his *The Rise and Decline of Nations* (1982). The longer a society enjoys peace and stability, the better organized economic interest groups become and the more successful in lobbying the government for special privilege and for protection against domestic and foreign competition. Economies become sclerotic, with adverse consequences for productivity, growth, and macroeconomic performance. Olson was able to explain much recent economic history with this simple insight.

Hayek had already explained how anticompetitive restrictions impose all the more of the burden of change on occupations outside the favored ones.

> In consequence, instead of prices, wages, and individual incomes, it is now employment and production which have become subject to violent fluctuations.... Few catchwords have done so much harm as the ideal of

a "stabilization" of particular prices (or wages), which, while securing the income of some, makes the position of the rest more and more precarious. (1944/1956, p. 129; cf. p. 45).

Hayek's warning that socialism endangers freedom is widely recognized as valid nowadays. Already in the foreword to his 1956 edition, Hayek recognized that "hot socialism is probably a thing of the past" and that a "hodge-podge of ill-assembled and often inconsistent ideals" labeled the Welfare State had "largely replaced socialism as the goal of the reformers" (p. ix). Few prominent English-speaking economists actually advocate socialism any longer. Exceptions like J.K. Galbraith and Robert Lekachman do come to mind, but it is not clear—not to me, anyway—just what they mean by socialism. Politicians still advocating socialism in developed countries, like François Mitterrand in France, no longer mean full-fledged socialism, but rather a welfare state, with redistributionist measures and only limited nationalization of industry. Hayek is right: hot socialism is dead.

I do not say that people now reject socialism because they have directly absorbed Hayek's message. Rather, his arguments have been in the air and have worked indirectly. Experience at first or second or *n*th hand has oozed into people's consciousness. In the forty years since 1944, the world has observed socialism in Soviet-bloc and third world countries. But it has not seen personal freedom coexisting with full-fledged socialism. As Hayek wrote already in 1944, "'liberal socialism' as most people in the Western world imagine it is purely theoretical, while the practice of socialism is everywhere totalitarian" (p. 141). Failure to observe freedom under socialism is no mere accident.

If we in the developed countries eventually wind up socialist after all, we will have done so unintentionally. Especially in his later writings (Hayek 1978 and 1979), Hayek has foreseen how this might happen. The irresponsibility flourishing in democratic politics could accommodate excessive demands for special governmental favor and protection against competition, hamper enterprise, swell government budgets and deficits, bring debt monetization and price inflation, and bring counterproductive attempts to fight inflation with direct controls. Capitalism could seem to have failed, and opportunistic politicians would offer governmental remedies. Actually, what would have failed would be the inflation-prone, intervention-ridden economy and the political system responsible for those ills.

Hayek (1973/1979) has recognized such dangers and has recommended political reforms. Already in *The Road to Serfdom* he anticipated his later and fuller diagnoses of flaws in the political system. He explained the nature of democracy and why one should not make a fetish of it (pp. 70–71), the impossibility of working out a coherent economic plan democratically (pp. 61–68), and why planning is incompatible with the rule of law (pp. 72–87).

Will we still blunder into socialism and totalitarianism through the back door—through exploitation of government power by special-interest groups run amok, overburdening of government, rigidification of the economy, inflation and stagflation and misconceived measures against them, slowdown of productivity growth, and, in general, a botch from which demagogues and power-seekers can make hay? Our chief hope is that we will combine and absorb the teachings of F.A. Hayek and of the public-choice school, led by James Buchanan, and put them into practice before the opportunity runs out.

REFERENCES

Hayek, F.A. *The Sensory Order*. London: Routledge & Kegan Paul, 1952.

———. *The Road to Serfdom*. 1944. Chicago: University of Chicago Press, Phoenix Books, 1956.

———. *The Constitution of Liberty*. Chicago: University of Chicago Press, 1960.

———. *New Studies in Philosophy, Politics, Economics, and the History of Ideas*. Chicago: University of Chicago Press, 1978.

———. *The Political Order of a Free People*. Vol. 3 of *Law, Legislation, and Liberty*. 1973. Chicago: University of Chicago Press, 1979.

———. *A Tiger by the Tail*. Compiled by Sudha R. Shenoy. San Francisco: Cato Institute, 1979.

Jöhr, Walter A. *Ist ein Freiheitlicher Sozialismus Möglich?* Bern: Francke, 1948.

Olson, Mancur. *The Rise and Decline of Nations*. New Haven, Conn.: Yale University Press, 1982.

Stigler, George, and Gary Becker. "De Gustibus Non Est Disputandum." *American Economic Review* 67 (March 1977): pp. 76–90.

CHAPTER 24

Kirzner on the Morality of Capitalist Profit*

Israel Kirzner develops insights into the moral legitimacy of capitalism and especially of entrepreneurial profit. This paper tries to echo or strengthen Kirzner's points by relating them more closely than he does to the foundations of ethics. Although I have no reason to suppose so, Kirzner may conceivably resist being linked with one version of utilitarianism, a version tracing as far back in the history of philosophy as David Hume and even earlier, forthrightly expounded by Kirzner's mentor Ludwig von Mises and by Henry Hazlitt, and employed at least tacitly by Friedrich A. Hayek.[1] If Kirzner should think I am trying to draft him into an unwelcome alliance, I can only apologize and only hope that he will nevertheless accept my contribution to a dialogue that he himself has actively advanced.

KIRZNER'S POSITIVE ANALYSIS

As I just implied, Kirzner does not claim to be setting forth a novel ethical position or to be contributing to ethical theory as distinct from economics (1992b, chap. 13; 1989, p. 98; but see 1979, p. 211). He does not try to show that the critics of capitalism have used morally flawed criteria. For his immediate purposes, he accepts existing and widely shared ethical intuitions without challenge. He recognizes that someone might reject his conclusions, independently of the economics, on different ethical

---

*From *Advances in Austrian Economics*, vol. 2A, eds. Peter J. Boettke and Mario J. Rizzo (Greenwich, Conn.: JAI Press, 1995), 197–209.

[1] See Hazlitt 1964 and, for discussion of Mises's and Hayek's writings, Yeager 1993 and Yeager 1985.

Kirzner does mention Mises's utilitarianism (1989, pp. 63–64). Unfortunately, he seems to imply that Mises was little concerned with ethics and defended capitalism simply on the grounds that it delivers the goods.

grounds. (This characterization of his views derives from 1992b, p. 209; 1989, pp. 129–130; and, more broadly, from all his writings listed in the references.)

Kirzner argues, as positive economic analysis, that capitalism works otherwise than its critics and most of its defenders believe. He traces the entrepreneur's pure profit to generally unappreciated facts. The entrepreneur *creates* wealth, practically *ex nihilo*, by discovering and exploiting opportunities. Kirzner sharply distinguishes these acts of discovery from acts of deliberate production (1989, p. 166). Instead of taking resources away from anyone else, the entrepreneur creates what did not exist before, benefiting other persons as well as himself. The prior physical existence of a diamond discovered on a remote mountain is irrelevant to the creative act and the moral entitlement it engenders. Kirzner sees the discoverer/producer as entitled to the product not because he transformed and combined inputs over which he already held just title but because he genuinely originated it. No one has any right to deprive the creator of the enjoyment of his creation (1989, pp. 150, 153).

Of course, an entrepreneur does not create *ex nihilo* the *entire* market value of the products of his discoveries. Typically, he combines his creativeness with the services of already existing resources and factors of production, paying their owners for them. Kirzner focuses on the net value of results remaining to the entrepreneur beyond all necessary factor payments. This pure profit deriving from the entrepreneur's creation is the subject of Kirzner's distinctive theory.

Allegedly, as Kirzner notes, discoveries depend on good luck, which seems a weak basis for capitalist property rights. But luck does not operate alone; motivated alertness also enters into discovery (1989, pp. 161–162; 1992b, pp. 221ff.; F.A. Hayek speaks somewhere of *Findigkeit*).

Kirzner does not maintain that a factual account of discovery and creation by itself constitutes a *justification* of capitalism; he does not claim to be dissolving the dichotomy between "is" and "ought." He appeals not only to economics but also, as he must, to moral intuitions (about which I say more below).

APPROPRIATION AND ENTITLEMENT

Kirzner finds the "entitlement" theories of John Locke, John Bates Clark, and Robert Nozick not downright wrong but incomplete or inadequate. These theorists tacitly take the economic pie, or the resources used to produce it, as given. They deal with the supposed issue of justice in appropriating what already exists. Once, though, we recognize the creativeness of entrepreneurial discovery, "we can no longer be satisfied with a moral philosophy which, in its consideration of property rights and property institutions, treats the world as if the future is an unending series of fully perceived manna-deposits waiting to be assigned and distributed" (1989, p. 150; cf. p. 161). As for pure profit, John Bates Clark's purported marginal-productivity defense of capitalist distribution does not even claim to deal with it.

Nozick's theory is unsatisfactory in a further way. It relies on John Locke's justification of private appropriation of previously unowned resources from nature. The appropriator acquires just title by mixing his own labor with them, labor assumed to be unquestionably his property. Locke hedges this justification with the proviso that the appropriator leave "enough and as good" resources available for latecomers. This proviso can scarcely ever be met, however, since appropriating resources from an unowned common stock brings closer a stage at which a subsequent appropriator simply could not leave "enough and as good" available for still later would-be appropriators (1989, pp. 156–157). It is no answer to postulate that the resources are so superabundant in relation not only to present human wants but even to all future wants that they would never become economically scarce. Few if any resources meet such a specification, leaving Locke's theory relevant only to an imaginary world. If any resources were inexhaustibly abundant and destined to remain free goods forever, they would hardly be resources in an economic sense; and making them private property would be pointless in the first place. It is only in a world of scarcity that private property matters.

Since Kirzner's doctrine does not pertain to appropriation of already existing things, it is unencumbered by any Lockean proviso (1992b, p. 225). In seeing that some hitherto unrecognized and valueless aspect of nature might be put to economic use, the alert entrepreneur in effect *creates* the result. He cannot deprive anyone of what did not previously exist. No question arises of leaving "enough and as good" for others.

David Schmidtz (1991, chap. 2) confronts the Lockean proviso in a way different from but reconcilable with Kirzner's. Schmidtz reformulates it as justifying an appropriation of resources from nature if it does not worsen and especially if it improves the *opportunities* open to other persons. Instituting private property does in general do so, while leaving things owned by no one or owned in common practically ensures their ruin through a "tragedy of the commons" (as Hardin 1968/1969 called it). A commons is tragic precisely when things are economically scarce and leaving "enough and as good" for everyone just is not possible. By avoiding the tragedy, private property gives even people other than the initial appropriators more and better opportunities to prosper from specialization, trade, the prudent administration of resources, and the accumulation of wealth.

Beyond his own distinctive contributions, Kirzner well understands other strands in the justification of private property and profit. Pure profit, or the lure of it, helps mobilize entrepreneurial alertness, including alertness to potential wants of consumers, and helps transfer control over resources out of relatively less into relatively more competent hands. Kirzner knows about decentralized decisionmaking, the use of scattered knowledge, and the productivity of a capitalist system. But he does not dwell on these familiar themes because he wants to answer criticisms of capitalism made on moral grounds.

CASES OF QUESTIONABLE ENTITLEMENT

Defense of the capitalist system does not extend to whatever occurs within it. Kirzner would contend (I am confident) that transfer-seeking through government, even when done by entrepreneurs, is not capitalism. Business alertness does not justify just anything (1989, p. 177). We may moralize against traders who exploit the impossibility of sharply delineating the legal from the illegal, or even the moral from the immoral. No system can make legal, moral, and actual behaviors fully coincide. Part of the rationale of ethics is that it can deal, flexibly, with innumerable individual cases that could not be foreseen in detail and for which detailed rules could not be laid out in advance.

Kirzner is uneasy at the imaginary case of one of several travelers in a desert who races ahead to appropriate a waterhole so he can charge the others an exorbitant price for water (1979, pp. 222–223). He seems less uneasy, though, than I would expect. Racing ahead implies already existing knowledge about the waterhole and its importance. Instead of making a creative discovery, the racer seizes a hold on his fellows by blocking them from an opportunity.

More fundamentally, economic rivalry and market transactions are not appropriate to all human relations. Not all behavior conforming to the logic and ethics of the capitalist system is ethically acceptable for that reason alone. Part of the rationale of an ethical code is that it would be impossible for the law to codify and enforce all desirable character traits and all desirable lines of behavior in all imaginable and unimaginable circumstances. The logic of an ethical code requires adhering to its spirit rather than to minutely specified rules; it requires a certain flexibility in its application. People's moral obligations toward one another depend on many circumstances, including what kind and degree of solidarity or loyalty among them are appropriate.

In the impersonal market relations of the nationwide and worldwide "great society" or "extended order" (as Hayek 1989 calls it), no special solidarity or loyalty is appropriate—nothing beyond honorable dealing and refraining from lying, cheating, stealing, and coercion. The situation is different within relatively small and intimate groups—family, friends, and perhaps enthusiasts devoted to some shared cause. In such groups, the attitudes of solidarity and altruism, presumably inherited biologically from the prehistoric days of life in small hunter-gatherer bands, are more appropriate. Even or especially within an impersonal extended order, the intimacy available within small, close-knit groups has great psychological value. Within them, emulating market behavior, pursuing narrow self-interest, and insisting on cost/benefit calculations and careful measurements of quid pro quo would be destructive. Such market-oriented behavior would subvert the solidarity and loyalty appropriate to such groups and would tend to "crush" them (Hayek 1989, p. 18).

Venturers on an expedition through a hazardous desert, like explorers in Antarctica, are in a sense colleagues, even if they happen not to belong to the same organized group, or so it seems to me. They owe a certain extra respect, solidarity, and loyalty to one another. Character traits conducive to recognizing this special obligation are praiseworthy on broadly the same utilitarian grounds that underpin ethical principles in general. To turn the adventure into a zero-sum struggle, to "race ahead" for a chance to exploit one's colleagues, manifests antisocial traits. To condone such behavior in the name of the ethics of capitalism would ill serve both capitalism and ethics.

In another case, also, Kirzner implies some unease about the moral legitimacy of profit. He repeatedly (e.g., 1989, pp. 49–50) mentions Paul Samuelson's example of a commodity speculator who reaps a big profit by learning about a crop failure just minutes before other traders do. True enough, speculators perform a socially useful function in acquiring information relevant to the timing of the consumption of scarce goods and in using that information to affect prices appropriately. But just what justifies the big profit of Samuelson's slightly early speculator?

If we agree that his windfall is unjustified, we agree with fuller knowledge of the situation—after all, we ourselves *thought it up*—than people in a comparable real-world situation would possess before hindsight became available. Anyway, what do we morally disapprove of in such a case? We probably would feel revulsion at profiting through somehow delaying the availability of information to others. Obstructing the transfer of information is the opposite of productive.

Someone who is in the business of bearing risks, however, hoping to profit on average over time from his superior instincts and decisiveness, is rendering a public service. If on occasion he is alert enough or even just lucky enough to receive profitable information early, well, that is part of the game. We could hardly expect speculators to operate if they had to stand their losses from bad luck themselves but were never allowed to keep the fruits of good luck.

Differences in knowledge of prices enter into the question, faced by Kirzner (e.g., 1989, p. 104), whether transactions made in ignorance of the full potential values of the things exchanged are nevertheless truly voluntary. Robert Nozick (1974) linked the moral legitimacy of holdings of property to their acquisition in voluntary transactions. Suppose—my example, not Kirzner's—that an art dealer sees the great value of an old painting brought to him by its uninformed owner. Is the dealer morally justified in exploiting its owner's ignorance by buying the painting cheap?

Possibly he is, provided he had made it clear that he was a sharp trader greedy even for questionable gains. Ordinarily, though, or so I understand, art dealers at least tacitly represent themselves as experts combining the roles of brokers, dealers on their own account, and de facto advisers; and they want to deserve a long-run reputation for honorable dealing in all these professional capacities. Ordinarily, then, the dealer has some fiduciary obligation to a novice who comes to him possibly for a business deal but also partly for advice. More generally, it may be in a business firm's own long-run interest to lean over backwards in being honest, telling not just the truth but the whole relevant truth. The just price is not an entirely nonsensical notion. (Kirzner is indeed aware, e.g., 1979, p. 209, of notions of honor, fiduciary responsibility, and just price.)

Similar issues arise about the moral legitimacy of stock-market profits deriving from inside information. Much depends on the details, including how the trader came by the information and what fiduciary obligations he might have to the various parties involved.

What policy implications follow from imagined cases like those of the person who races ahead to the oasis, Samuelson's commodity speculator, the art dealer, and the insider trader? It would be extremely difficult to draw up specific rules that would suitably cover all such conceivable cases. Much behavior must be left to the informal pressures of moral judgments and reputation effects. We scarcely want—do we?—to establish a government authority charged with appraising everyone's moral entitlement to each bit of his income and with rectifying allocations of income deemed unjustified. Institutions and policies simply cannot be devised to guarantee ethically appealing detailed outcomes in each individual case. As Rutledge Vining (1984) emphasizes, legislators do not have a handle on ultimate outcomes; they can only tinker with rules and institutions.

A discoverer does not in general have an obligation to share the fruits of his discovery just because a rival would soon have made the same discovery on his own anyway. In Kirzner's example (1989, pp. 167–169), one person on a beach stealthily but legitimately snatches a spectacular seashell from beneath the nose of someone entranced by the sunset. He has not "blocked discovery" by the sunset-watcher; he has simply been more alert.

In other cases, however, one transactor may have a moral duty to divulge information to another, although failure to do so does not necessarily entitle the other person to claim that he was robbed or cheated (1989, p. 170). "There appear to be a number of moral gradations, in regard to the reprehensibility of gaining benefit by failure to disclose available information" (1989, pp. 170–171). Doubts about the decency of benefiting from the removable ignorance of others seem to recede the more impersonal the relation is between the parties (1989, p. 171). Although we may well sympathize with persons whose ignorance is exploited, we should consider that they would probably be even less well informed and less well-off than under some system in which entrepreneurial profit were not allowed to provide the driving motivation (1989, p. 171).

ENTITLEMENT FURTHER CONSIDERED

Let us step back from our dubious or borderline cases and focus on wealth that the holder indisputably has created or has received by indisputably voluntary transactions untainted by ignorance. Even then, can we be sure that the holder is morally entitled to his wealth? Kirzner (1989, pp. 101–102) mentions Robert Nozick's (1974, pp. 161–163) hypothetical example of Wilt Chamberlain, who arranges for spectators to pay an additional 25 cents earmarked for him beyond the regular price of admission to his basketball games. Nozick holds Chamberlain fully entitled to this income. Still, one might disagree. By paying voluntarily, the spectators are not necessarily approving the financial arrangements and the additional inequality of income distribution that results; they are not necessarily indicating opposition to a supposed remedy through redistributionary taxation. The individual spectator might realize that he alone could not thwart the antiegalitarian result by boycotting the game, so he might as well attend if he values the performance sufficiently more than the ticket price plus Chamberlain's 25 cents. Partly because, in economists' jargon, an externality is operating, the voluntariness of the transactions does not automatically confer moral legitimacy on Chamberlain's wealth. James Buchanan (1977, chap. 4) argues, in part, that Chamberlain's large income is an economic rent, itself largely attributable to the society in which he has the good fortune of performing, and that other, equally voluntary, arrangements could distribute this rent much differently. Although I myself dislike the attitude of my hypothetical spectator, neither that critic nor Buchanan commits a logical fallacy.

In *The Mirage of Social Justice* (1976) and other works, F.A. Hayek dismissed "social justice" as an empty pair of words. Although one might speak of the justice or injustice of a deliberate parceling out of an existing stock of goods, such an evaluation cannot pertain to the pattern of distribution of income and wealth that results, unplanned by anyone, from the market process of innumerable decentralized decisions. (The result of the market process is not even a "distribution" in the strict, etymological sense.) One might as well discuss the justice or injustice of natural phenomena.

Although I have not looked up adverse reviews of Hayek's work, I can well imagine a critic replying that it is unjust to leave a particular distribution of income and wealth uncorrected, however spontaneous it is and however little it is anyone's fault, if it can be corrected without unacceptable side effects. Bad luck, or unfair shakes from nature, can in some circumstances and to some extent be remedied by being shared. Leaving remediable bad luck nevertheless unremedied might reasonably—I do not say conclusively—be deemed unfair.

Defenders of capitalism will have to do better than simply dismiss discussions of social justice and injustice as having no subject matter but

Chapter 24: Kirzner on the Morality of Capitalist Profit   415

mirages. John Rawls (1971) may have been wrong in writing about rectification of the natural distribution and in setting forth his "difference principle" of distribution, but he was not writing nonsense.

Let us milk the Wilt Chamberlain example further. Chamberlain's large income flows from no special moral merit; he just enjoys the good luck of possessing talents that happen to command a high price. We might further complain about the bad taste among fans that confers big rewards on not particularly meritorious sports figures.

In *The Constitution of Liberty* (1960, chap. 6) F.A. Hayek does face the criticism that a free-market economy confers material rewards in an unjust way. The market values of the services of people and their property depend on many circumstances and seldom correspond to people's moral merit. Some defenders of the market system deny the charge, replying that the market does indeed, if only in a rough and ready way, distribute rewards in proportion to merit. Hayek warns against this reply:

> Any attempt to found the case for freedom on this argument is very damaging to it, since it concedes that material rewards ought to be made to correspond to recognizable merit and then opposes the conclusion that most people will draw from this by an assertion which is untrue. The proper answer is that in a free system it is neither desirable nor practicable that material rewards should be made generally to correspond to what men recognize as merit and that it is an essential characteristic of a free society that an individual's position should not necessarily depend on the views that his fellows hold about the merit he has acquired. (1960, pp. 94–95)

Hayek goes on to examine the concepts of value and merit. He considers the advantages (connected with information and incentives) of letting market values guide people's decisions about how to use their creativity and their other abilities. He asks what institutions would be required for trying to implement the alternative principle of distribution according to moral merit. He explores the psychological consequences of a state of affairs in which material rewards were supposed to be clear indicators of moral merit. His exercise in comparative-institutional analysis leaves the thoughtful reader recoiling in horror at the consequences of radically non-market-oriented methods of distribution. His whole chapter 6 is worth pondering at length.

On ethical grounds, nevertheless, a critic might question whether a person is truly entitled to whatever he has created through alert discovery or created in some more literal and pedestrian way. One might even question a person's Lockean self-ownership of his own body. After all, John Rawls (1971) argued that each person's physical and mental capacities are in some respects a morally arbitrary gift of nature and the environment and so are properly at the disposal of society in general.

I myself do not deny a person's entitlement to his body and his creations; I do not agree with Rawls. I object, though, to prematurely resting judgments on such issues on undiscussable sheer intuitions. The judgments in question are not *fundamental* value judgments (to use a term that will become clearer in what follows). They are relatively specific judgments that themselves require grounding in the facts of reality and in one or more value judgments that are more nearly fundamental.

ORIGIN AND APPRAISAL OF ETHICAL INTUITIONS

Appraising capitalism on ethical grounds necessarily involves both the facts about how the system operates and the ethical standards themselves. Kirzner specializes, quite legitimately, in the positive economics of the issue; but room remains to consider the sources and force of the prevailing ethical intuitions taken for granted in his writings reviewed here.

Where did these intuitions come from? It seems plausible to trace them to social and perhaps biological evolution: acting in accordance with them conferred advantages on societies and individuals. On the account of F.A. Hayek (1989 and other writings), practices based on those intuitions have stood the test of social and perhaps biological evolution. Groups adhering to ethical precepts and institutions and kinds of behavior conducive to survival of the group and reproduction of its members do tend to flourish, while others wither. Groups have a better chance to prosper under traditions that conduce to the accumulation of wealth and to trade, including trade with outsiders. These traditions concern private property, saving, voluntary exchange, truthfulness, promise-keeping, and contract. Favorable traditions gain ground not only through transmission to successive generations but also by being imitated.[2]

---

[2] Hayek knows that cultural natural selection works through trial and error and through mere tendencies toward eventual decline of societies with inexpedient institutions and traditions—unless they reform themselves, perhaps by imitating more successful societies. He thereby recognizes that errors do occur and can persist. He also knows that deliberate attention, within a society, to how well or poorly its institutions are functioning plays a role in the evolutionary process. Still, the process as a whole is not directed by a

Explanation of origins is not appraisal. *Should* one indeed approve of intuitions, precepts, and practices that conduce to the flourishing of groups and individuals? Well, it is the essence of value judgments—this one included—that they cannot be established purely by facts and logic. Some element of sheer moral intuition or emotion necessarily enters into the story.

SOCIAL COOPERATION

A plausible sweeping intuition (though not an irreducibly fundamental one) recommends what Ludwig von Mises and Henry Hazlitt, among others, have emphasized under the label *social cooperation*. Social cooperation characterizes a well-functioning society; it is the complex of institutions, practices, shared ethical standards, and even attitudes that foster peace, security, specialization, and the gains from trade and so ease fruitful cooperation among individuals striving to make good lives for themselves in their own diverse ways. Private property, the market, contractual liberty, voluntary associations, and the rule of law are key elements of it in successful modern societies. The idea, though not the actual term, goes back to David Hume and even to Thomas Hobbes, pioneers in the utilitarian tradition. Social cooperation is much the same as what John Gray calls "civil society" and Michael Oakeshott called "civil association" (Gray 1993, pp. 246, 275, and passim).

A version of utilitarianism centering on this concept appraises ethical precepts, kinds of personal conduct, traits of character, institutions, and policy choices according to how likely they are to serve or subvert social cooperation. It is practically the same thing as a comparative-institutions approach to evaluation. An adherent of this doctrine tries to contemplate and compare alternative sets of mutually compatible institutions. The criterion of social cooperation, together with positive analysis in economics, psychology, and other disciplines, recommends the precepts, attitudes, behaviors, and so forth conducive to an extended order, as Hayek calls it, and to many kinds of intimate relationships embedded in a healthy extended order. The criterion recommends truth-telling, promise-keeping, justice, respect for persons and individual rights, respect for private property, the transfer of property by consent, and even, within limits, honest partiality towards oneself and one's compatriots, friends, and associates.

single mind or committee, and not all the knowledge operating in it has been consciously articulated.

But social cooperation is only a *nearly* ultimate criterion. It is instrumental toward something more completely ultimate, something for which no further argument is possible, something taken as desirable by sheer intuition or emotion. That ultimately desirable "something" is individuals' success in living, or fulfillment, or life appropriate to human potential. No single word is an adequate label; but when a single word is required, the traditional choice is "happiness," understood in a suitably stretched sense.[3]

A UTILITARIAN CONCLUSION

Kirzner goes far toward justifying capitalist principles of ownership and distribution, as well as the system itself, by positive analysis combined with appeal to simple and widely accepted ethical intuitions. A person is entitled to what he himself creates or discovers[4] and to what he obtains in a voluntary transaction from a previous owner whose title is undisputed. These, however, are fairly specific intuitions. When they are questioned, a social theorist relying on them should be able to defend them (conceivably

---

[3] Hayek (1989) appears to make survival, not happiness, the ultimate criterion. It does seem plausible that the processes of biological and cultural selection have operated through the survival or elimination of individuals and groups, not through their happiness or unhappiness. Again, though, we must distinguish between explanation and appraisal. In the context of appraisal, we need not decide between survival and happiness as ultimate criteria. Since social cooperation is prerequisite to both, it can serve as a surrrogate criterion. Only on a particularly rarefied level of philosophizing must we try to choose between rival ultimate criteria.

[4] *Why* is he entitled to his creation or discovery? A short answer, presumably, is that such a rule holds down disputes and fosters social cooperation and creativity better than any alternative would do.

Kirzner calls his view of entitlement a "finders-keepers ethic" (e.g., 1992, p. 222; 1989, pp. 110–111, 166). While agreeing with the substance of his doctrine, I regret that label. In my own childhood experience, anyway, the full slogan was "finders keepers, losers weepers." It conveyed a certain graspingness combined with a rather cynical unconcern for whoever had lost or been unfairly done out of some item. Kirzner evokes the second part of the slogan by mentioning the finder's entitlement to a coin that someone else had lost in Times Square (1989, p. 153). I am confident, though, that Kirzner does not hold the attitude that the full slogan brings to my mind.

Since drafting this paper and this note in particular, I have seen Ricketts's 1992 paper. Ricketts aptly calls Kirzner's "finders-keepers ethic" a "graspers-keepers ethic" (p. 80). He also questions Kirzner's position on the traveler who races ahead to appropriate the waterhole (pp. 76–78). Ricketts objects that Kirzner pays inadequate attention to the nature of property rights, even though his description of his imaginary situation suggests that the waterhole, instead of being simply "unheld," is already regarded as a communal asset that individuals are entitled to *use*.

modified in their details) by further positive analysis and by appeal to further and more nearly fundamental ethical intuitions. This further analysis will almost surely emphasize social cooperation and rely on a fundamental value judgment against misery and for happiness in a suitably stretched sense of the latter term.

Kirzner appears to adopt this utilitarian (indirect utilitarian) approach, which might also be called a comparative-institutions approach.[5] Alternatives to it are conceivable—just barely, in my judgment. Since Kirzner shows no sympathy for them, however, there is no need to review them here.

The ultimate basis of Kirzner's conclusions about entitlements to capitalist wealth and profit must be that a society operating with different (more collectivist) principles would function less well than a society embodying broadly classical liberal principles. It would "function less well" in the sense of affording its individual members inferior prospects of the successful pursuit of happiness.

In conclusion, I quote one of several passages (1989, p. 177) suggesting Kirzner's agreement with the position just sketched out:

> A defense of capitalist justice has not declared it innocent of all moral flaws. It certainly has not declared all behaviour under historical capitalism to have been moral or even to have been just. A defense of capitalist justice suggests, however, that the system that has been so extraordinarily productive in raising the standards of human life need not be rejected out of hand on the grounds of innate unfairness. Moral improvement may be sought within the capitalist framework, without harboring a guilty sense of participation in an inevitably and fundamentally flawed form of social organization.

REFERENCES

Buchanan, James M. *Freedom in Constitutional Contract*. College Station: Texas A&M University Press, 1977.

Gray, John. *Mill on Liberty: A Defence*. London: Routledge, 1983.

---

[5]This approach is far from an "act utilitarianism" that would require making each large or small decision according to the apparent merits of the individual case and without regard to further principles or to individual rights. Such a crude version of utilitarianism has by now, one hopes, become hardly more than a straw man beaten by superficial critics. What John Gray (1983) calls *indirect* utilitarianism recognizes the great utility of abiding by general principles and *not* practicing case-by-case expediency.

———. *Post-Liberalism: Studies in Political Thought.* London and New York: Routledge, 1993.

Hardin, Garrett. "The Tragedy of the Commons." 1968. In *Population, Evolution, and Birth Control*, 2nd ed., edited by Hardin, 367–381. San Francisco: Freeman, 1969.

Hayek, F.A. *The Constitution of Liberty.* Chicago: University of Chicago Press, 1960.

———. *The Mirage of Social Justice.* Vol. 2 of *Law, Legislation, and Liberty.* Chicago: University of Chicago Press, 1976.

———. *The Fatal Conceit.* Edited by W.W. Bartley, III. Chicago: University of Chicago Press, 1989.

Hazlitt, Henry. *The Foundations of Morality.* Princeton, N.J.: D. Van Nostrand, 1964.

Kirzner, Israel M. *Perception, Opportunity, and Profit.* Chicago: University of Chicago Press, 1979.

———. *Discovery and the Capitalist Process.* Chicago: University of Chicago Press, 1985.

———. *Discovery, Capitalism, and Distributive Justice.* Oxford and New York: Basil Blackwell, 1989.

———. "Commentary" on Martin Ricketts's paper. In *Austrian Economics: Tensions and New Directions*, edited by Bruce J. Caldwell and Stephan Boehm, 85–102. Boston: Kluwer, 1992a.

———. *The Meaning of Market Process.* London and New York: Routledge, 1992b.

Nozick, Robert. *Anarchy, State, and Utopia.* New York: Basic Books, 1974.

Rawls, John. *A Theory of Justice.* Cambridge, Mass.: Belknap Press of Harvard University Press, 1971.

Ricketts, Martin. "Kirzner's Theory of Entrepreneurship—A Critique." In *Austrian Economics: Tensions and New Directions*, edited by Bruce J. Caldwell and Stephan Boehm, 67–84. Boston: Kluwer, 1992.

Schmidtz, David. *The Limits of Government: An Essay on the Public Goods Argument.* Boulder, Colo.: Westview Press, 1991.

Vining, Rutledge. *On Appraising the Performance of an Economic System.* New York: Cambridge University Press, 1984.

Yeager, Leland B. "Mises and His Critics on Ethics, Rights, and Law." In *The Meaning of Ludwig von Mises*, edited by Jeffrey M. Herbener, 321–344. Norwell, Mass., and Dordrecht, Netherlands: Kluwer, 1993. Reprinted here as chapter 25.

———. "Utility, Rights, and Contract: Some Reflections on Hayek's Work." In *The Political Economy of Freedom: Essays in Honor of F. A. Hayek*, edited by Kurt R. Leube and Albert H. Zlabinger, 61–80. Munich and Vienna: Philosophia Verlag, 1985.

CHAPTER 25
Mises and His Critics on Ethics, Rights, and Law*

MISES'S UTILITARIANISM

Ludwig von Mises was a utilitarian and has been criticized for being one. Utilitarianism is a particular approach to ethics in personal life and public affairs. It compares alternative sets of institutions, laws, traditions, patterns and maxims and rules of behavior, and traits of personal character. It approves of those that support and disapproves of those that subvert the kind of society that affords people relatively good opportunities to make satisfying lives for themselves. Institutions and practices and attitudes that facilitate fruitful cooperation among individuals as they pursue their own diverse specific ends score ahead of ones that make for destructive clashes. "Social cooperation" (so called by Mises and other thinkers in the utilitarian and libertarian traditions) is so nearly essential to individuals' success in their own diverse pursuits that it is a nearly ultimate criterion of institutions, ethical precepts, character traits, and so forth. On this criterion, truth-telling and promise-keeping command approval. So does respect for justice, property rights, and other human rights.

These words are mine, not Mises's; but his stance on economic policy does rest on an ethical underpinning like the one just sketched out. Mises wrote bluntly. The theory of social cooperation elaborated by British political economy from Hume to Ricardo, he says,

> consummated the spiritual, moral and intellectual emancipation of mankind inaugurated by the philosophy of Epicureanism. It substituted an autonomous rational morality for the heteronomous and intuitionist ethics of older days. Law and legality, the moral code and social

*From *The Meaning of Ludwig von Mises*, ed. Jeffrey M. Herbener (Auburn, Ala., and Norwell, Mass.: Ludwig von Mises Institute and Kluwer, 1993), 321–344. A few pages have been cut out here.

institutions are no longer revered as unfathomable decrees of Heaven. They are of human origin, and the only yardstick that must be applied to them is that of expediency with regard to human welfare. The utilitarian economist does not say: Fiat justitia, pereat mundus. He says: Fiat justitia, *ne* pereat mundus. He does not ask a man to renounce his well-being for the benefit of society. He advises him to recognize what his rightly understood interests are. In his eyes God's magnificence does not manifest itself in busy interference with sundry affairs of princes and politicians, but in endowing his creatures with reason and the urge toward the pursuit of happiness. (Mises 1949/1963, p. 147)

The ultimate yardstick of justice is conduciveness to the preservation of social cooperation ... [,] for almost every man the great means for the attainment of all ends. An eminently human common interest, the preservation and intensification of social bonds, is substituted for pitiless biological competition, the significant mark of animal and plant life. Man becomes a social being.... Other people become his fellows.... As social cooperation is ... a means and not an end, no unanimity with regard to value judgments is required to make it work.... [S]ocial cooperation is for man a means for the attainment of all his ends.... The characteristic feature of a free society is that it can function in spite of the fact that its members disagree in many judgments of value. (1979/1985, pp. 54–61)

By its recognition that social cooperation is for the immense majority a means for attaining all their ends, [utilitarianism] dispels the notion that society, the state, the nation, or any other social entity is an ultimate end and that individual men are the slaves of that entity. It rejects the philosophies of universalism, collectivism, and totalitarianism. In this sense it is meaningful to call utilitarianism a philosophy of individualism. (1979/1985, p. 58)

As Murray Rothbard has correctly pointed out (1982, p. 212), no one can ever advocate any policy whatsoever on a *purely* scientific, value-free basis. Mises would agree. No one can approve or disapprove of a particular policy or of anything at all without holding at least one ultimate or fundamental value judgment. A judgment is ultimate in the sense that its holder, in expressing it, has come to the end of being able to give factual and logical reasons for his attitudes.[1] For Mises and other utilitarians, the fundamental value judgment is approval of happiness and disapproval of misery. (One can argue for or against particular policies, lifestyles, and so

---

[1]On fundamental value judgments, see Paul Edwards 1965; Sidney S. Alexander 1967, esp. pp. 105–107 and 114–115; and Amartya K. Sen 1970, esp. pp. 62–64.

forth by trying to show that they tend toward happiness or misery; but I cannot imagine how one could argue for happiness and against misery themselves. But if one could so argue, the argument would necessarily invoke some further, deeper, value judgment, which would then be the fundamental one.)

Mises hastens to disavow hedonism in the narrow sense: despite superficial critics, "happiness" does not mean mere material, bodily pleasures. Advanced utilitarians, he says, interpret pleasure and pain, utility and disutility, in the "purely formal" senses of those words, emptying them of all specific content. They refer to whatever individuals in fact try to achieve or avoid (Mises 1933/1960, pp. 52, 151; Mises 1979/1985, pp. 12–13; Mises 1949/1963, p. 21). Mises recognizes that many people, especially creative workers, are not driven by material desires or narrow self-interest alone. They may also be expressing competence and strength and even heroism (Mises 1919/1983, pp. 193, 213). "There are people whose only aim is to improve the condition of their own ego. There are other people with whom awareness of the troubles of their fellow men causes as much uneasiness as or even more uneasiness than their own wants" (1949/1963, p. 14).

Mises's remarks about the merely formal content of "happiness" hardly settle all questions about fundamental value judgments. Room remains for discussing whether the utilitarian criterion should be the true happiness of individuals or instead, if there is a difference, the satisfaction of whatever desires individuals suppose they have. Still, Mises is on the right track. "Happiness," before being unpacked, is an inadequate term for the ultimate utilitarian value judgment. I can only take stabs at labeling what is ultimately desirable: it is individuals' success in making good lives for themselves, or fulfillment, or satisfaction, or life appropriate to human potentiality. No single word is an adequate label; but when a single word is required as shorthand, "happiness" is the traditional choice.

This formulation might be criticized as being all-encompassing to the point of vacuousness. Yet it is not vacuous: alternative criteria are conceivable. They include conformity to the supposed will of God; or performance of duty for duty's sake alone, with no analysis of consequences entering into the identification of duties; or conformity to intuited ethical precepts for conformity's sake alone; or respect for individual rights that have simply been postulated rather than argued for on utilitarian or any other grounds, and again regardless of consequences; or conduciveness to the flourishing of the highest or noblest specimens of the human race, however ordinary people might then fare (a view sometimes attributed, rightly or wrongly, to Nietzsche). Or instead of taking the "happiness" of people in general as the criterion of institutions and precepts and so forth, one might conceivably urge the happiness of oneself or some other specific person.

That these alternatives are conceivable shows that the utilitarian criterion is not vacuous, while their implausibility strengthens its own appeal. As a practical matter, furthermore, utilitarianism does not hinge on any *exact* spelling out of its fundamental value judgment. Its fulfillment is served by social cooperation—a well-functioning network of beneficial relations among individuals. Institutions, precepts, and so forth may be appraised according to how they support or subvert this crucial means to happiness, without constant appeal to any precise interpretation of "happiness" itself.

With characteristic bluntness, Mises denies that utilitarian philosophy has anything to do with the doctrine of natural rights. He has a point: respect for rights is ill served by a faulty defense. Rights are not merely conferred by government; rather, they derive from ethical precepts, which in turn have a rational underpinning. Utilitarianism, Mises says, recommends "popular government, private property, tolerance, and freedom not because they are natural and just, but because they are beneficial.... [S]ocial cooperation and division of labor ... is beneficial." With apparent approval, Mises quotes Bentham: "*Natural rights* is simple nonsense: natural and imprescriptible rights, rhetorical nonsense." In investigating what ought to be right, Bentham "does not care about preconceived ideas concerning God's or nature's plans and intentions, forever hidden to mortal men; he is intent upon discovering what best serves the promotion of human welfare and happiness" (1949/1963, p. 174).

Mises occasionally slipped into repeating slogans about "the greatest happiness for the greatest number" (1919/1983, p. 183). Such a formulation, taken literally, has no precise meaning, of course. All that Mises presumably meant by it is that the happiness to be furthered by social institutions and practices is the happiness of people in general—of the member of society chosen at random, in F.A. Hayek's formulation (Hayek 1967, p. 163; Hayek 1976, pp. 129–130)—rather than the differential happiness of specific persons or classes. Mises specifically repudiated any numerical utilitarianism such as critics enjoy attacking. He denied that "it is the task of economics to establish how in the whole of society the greatest possible satisfaction of all people or of the greatest number could be attained.... [T]here is no method which would allow us to measure the state of satisfaction attained by various individuals" and make "comparison[s] between various people's happiness"(Mises 1949/1963, p. 242).

CRITICISM

Mises's utilitarianism has drawn criticism even from students and others inspired by his work. I do not maintain that Mises expounded the subtlest versions of utilitarianism, complete with distinctions between act utilitarianism and the various "rule" or "indirect" versions. He was writing before most philosophical treatments of these subtleties were published. Furthermore, the subtleties were not essential to his main concerns, theoretical and applied economics. Still, his basic philosophical stance is worth defending (Hazlitt 1964 offers an admirably detailed defense).

One of his critics, Karen Vaughn regretted that

> Mises, unfortunately, attempted to refute the collectivists and authoritarians by accepting the terms of their argument and arguing for the superior ability of the free market to provide for the economic well-being of the populace.... Such an attempt to defend freedom is dangerous on two counts. First, it is open to empirical refutation. (Vaughn 1976, p. 109)

Second, such a defense is dangerous because of "nonmaterial items in individual utility functions" (1976, p. 109). Bureaucrats may enjoy controlling and regulating. If their utilities should be taken into account and if interpersonal comparisons are not possible, how can we be sure that a nonliberal system will not provide "maximum social welfare"?

Vaughn seems to approve of the reported intellectual outlook in seventeenth-century England, when liberalism was emerging. Then, she says, "freedom was considered ... desirable for its own sake [as] a natural condition of human beings.... It was a moral value that, as a bonus, also happened to lead to the well-being of society." The utilitarian argument simply provided "additional fire power." "By the time of John Stuart Mill, however, the argument became reversed, and freedom was espoused, not because it was a good in itself, but because it led to the 'greatest good for the greatest number'" (p. 108).

Possibly I have misunderstood her, but Vaughn does seem to say that Mises was wrong to develop arguments for freedom because they might conceivably be refuted and the case for freedom thereby embarrassed. To forestall embarrassment, it is better not to argue any case but simply to postulate freedom as a supreme value. Admittedly, someone who mounts no arguments need fear no refutations; but why, then, should he expect anyone to pay attention? As for freedom's supposedly just happening, as a bonus, to promote "the well-being of society," Mises might well ask what could constitute that well-being except the well-being of individuals. And how, apart from entering into or contributing to their well-being, could freedom be a supreme value?

Murray Rothbard repeatedly criticizes utilitarianism, including Mises's formulations. One of his criticisms is similar to Vaughn's. The utilitarian

> will rarely adopt a principle as an absolute and consistent yardstick to apply to the varied concrete situations of the real world. He will only use a principle, at best, as a vague guideline or aspiration, as a *tendency* which he may choose to override at any time.... [N]ineteenth-century laissez-faire liberals came to use laissez-faire as a vague tendency rather than as an unblemished yardstick, and therefore increasingly and fatally compromised the libertarian creed. To say that a utilitarian cannot be "trusted" to maintain libertarian principle in every specific application may sound harsh, but it puts the case fairly. A notable contemporary example is ... Professor Milton Friedman who ... holds to freedom as against state intervention as a general tendency, but in practice allows a myriad of damaging exceptions, exceptions which serve to vitiate the principle almost completely. (Rothbard 1973, p. 24)

This charge is first, and rather inconsistently, utilitarian itself: utilitarianism tempts its adherents into considering and sometimes even recommending unwise, nonlibertarian, policies. Second, the charge suggests that an alternative philosophical stance can guard its adherents from falling into error. Unfortunately, no doctrine can provide such built-in protection against its being misunderstood or misused or improperly set aside. It is an illegitimate test of a doctrine to expect it to do what no doctrine can do. Nothing can substitute for the constant discipline of fact and logic.

Rothbard called Mises "an opponent of objective ethics" (1976, p. 105). I wonder if this is a fair description. Certainly Mises was not an ethical relativist or nihilist, scornful of all judgments of right and wrong and complacent about however individuals might behave, even violating the rights of others, in pursuit of narrow and short-run self-interest. On the contrary, Mises was concerned with whether behavior and precepts of behavior tended to serve or subvert social cooperation and so serve or subvert happiness. Much scope exists for positive—objective—investigation into the likely consequences of various kinds and precepts of behavior, and the scope for purely subjective ethical judgments is correspondingly narrow.

Mises, says Rothbard, was willing to make only one value judgment: "he joined the majority of the people in favoring their common peace, prosperity, and abundance"; he endorsed "the desirability of fulfilling the subjectively desired goals of the bulk of the populace" (p. 105). Actually, Mises's fundamental value judgment, instead of simply favoring whatever a majority wanted or thought it wanted, favored the actual happiness of people in general. Nevertheless, Rothbard poses a case in which the great majority wants to murder the redheads. "How could Mises rebut this proposed policy either as a praxeologist or as a utilitarian liberal? I submit that he could not do so"[2] (p. 108). Or someone might "desire to see an innocent person suffer.... Yet a utilitarian must hold that [such preferences], fully as much as the most innocuous or altruistic preferences, must be included in the quantitative reckoning" (1982, p. 213 n. 5).

Who says so? Mises supposedly "*cannot* quarrel with the ethical nature of [people's] chosen goals, for, as a utilitarian, he must confine himself to the *one* value judgment that he favors the majority achieving their chosen goals" (1982, p. 210). (Rothbard makes sweeping references to Mises; but instead of dealing with his actual statements, he criticizes what Mises, as a utilitarian, supposedly must believe.) Now, what even half-way sophisticated utilitarian maintains that preferences and attitudes and character traits must be immune from appraisal? Mises, to my knowledge, never said any such thing.

A rules or indirect utilitarianism is indeed concerned with how attitudes and even character traits, so far as they are amenable to encouragement or discouragement, tend to affect the health of a society and so the happiness of its members (on John Stuart Mill's indirect utilitarianism, see Gray 1983). For fear of adverse side-effects and for other reasons, a utilitarian does not want to enlist the state's coercive powers in suppressing all unfortunate preferences and attitudes and traits; but this in no way means that he considers all of them equally worthy of respect and equally entitled to influence public policy. Neither as a utilitarian nor as a libertarian must

---

[2]This example of the redheads turns up repeatedly in Rothbard's writings against utilitarianism.

I myself, for example, deplore psychological and sociological and other positive inquiry into what sorts of preferences and attitudes and lifestyles tend in fact to serve or to undercut social cooperation and happiness. But saying so in no way commits me to wanting the state to implement the supposed findings of such inquiries.

The utilitarian, says Rothbard, "has *no conception* let alone theory of justice."[3] With regard to property rights in particular, the utilitarian "must fall back on the pragmatic, *ad hoc* view that all titles to private property currently existing at any time or place must be treated as valid and accepted as worthy of defense against violation" (Rothbard 1982, p. 52). "[U]tilitarians ... plac[e] an arbitrary and indiscriminate ethical blessing upon every current property title" (1982, pp. 58–59). If the tyrannical king of Ruritania dissolves his rule but first divides up the whole country into the private property of himself and his relatives, "consistent utilitarians ... must bow to this subterfuge" (1982, p. 54).

But where does Rothbard get this notion that utilitarianism requires respect for even patently spurious titles?[4] Mises's discussion in *Socialism* (1922/1951) is quite sophisticated and hardly bears out the suspicion that he would defend even the ethically shabbiest status quo.

To make the case for laissez faire and the free-market economy, says Rothbard,

> one must go beyond economics and utilitarianism to establish an objective ethics that affirms the overriding value of liberty and morally condemns all forms of statism, from egalitarianism to the murder of redheads, as well as such goals as the lust for power and the satisfaction of envy. To make the full case for liberty, one cannot be a methodological slave to every goal that the majority of the public might happen to cherish. (Rothbard 1976, p. 109)

But why would anyone want to make a case for liberty, the free market, and laissez faire and against statism, envy, and the lust for power except out of concern for the character of society and, more fundamentally, for the happiness of its members? And *how could* anyone go about making such a case except in some broadly utilitarian way? It seems backwards to desire a foundation for a particular policy stance before

---

[3]Rothbard 1982, p. 52,—but what about John Stuart Mill's *Utilitarianism*, 1863/1968, chap. 5?
[4]Rothbard 1982, p. 60 n. 2, does cite Mises's *Socialism* 1922/1932/1951, pp. 45–47.

having some idea of its consequences. But Rothbard does think he has another way.

ROTHBARD'S AXIOMS ABOUT RIGHTS

Rothbard identifies three broad types of philosophical basis for libertarianism, first is utilitarianism. Second is emotivism: it adopts liberty, or the libertarian nonaggression axiom, as its premise on purely subjective, emotional grounds. As Rothbard suggests, such a stance abandons the realm of rational discourse (1973, pp. 23–24).

Third is Rothbard's own approach, emphasizing natural rights embedded in natural law. Each entity, including the species man, has its own distinct nature.

> Since men can think, feel, evaluate, and act only as individuals, it becomes vitally necessary for each man's survival and prosperity that he be free to learn, choose, develop his faculties, and act upon his knowledge and values. This is the necessary path of human nature; to interfere with and cripple this process by using violence goes profoundly against what is necessary by man's nature for his life and prosperity. (1973, pp. 25–26)

To appeal to what is necessary for man's life and prosperity, given his nature, sounds like a utilitarian argument. Anyway, Rothbard begins with the right to self-ownership, with the axiom that each man or woman owns his or her own body. Alternatives are conceivable, though barely. One caste of persons might belong to another, an arrangement hardly compatible with an objective, impartial ethics. Or each person might own a tiny equal share of himself and all other persons. Trying to manage people's lives on such a basis, however, would quickly bring inefficiency and starvation. (Here is another tacitly utilitarian argument.) With these alternatives ruled out, self-ownership remains (1973, pp. 26–28; and 1982, pp. 45–46).

Rothbard's second axiom concerns ownership of products and land. Everyone has a right to the goods he has produced and to hitherto unowned land that he has transformed by his labor. A person does not acquire this "homesteading" right in all the unowned land that he may *claim*; his right is limited to the amount of land he actually puts into use. But once is enough. Here Rothbard avowedly follows the doctrine of John Locke, but with modifications; for example, he rejects the "Lockean proviso" that homesteading leave "enough and as good" land available for latecomers (1973, pp. 28–37; and 1982, pp. 46–50, 63–65, 240). People may of course acquire and dispose of ownership rights in goods and land through honest trading.

These principles of property rights, especially of homesteading, look detailed or specific enough to raise doubts about whether they are truly axioms. Don't they have some utilitarian underpinning after all? Rothbard does make comments about ownership of land similar to his comments about ownership of human beings.

> [I]f the land is to be used at all as a resource in any sort of efficient manner, it must be owned or controlled by *someone* or some group, and we are again faced with our three alternatives: either the land belongs to the first user, the man who first brings it into production; *or* it belongs to a group of others; *or* it belongs to the world as a whole, with every individual owning a quotal part of every acre of land.... In practice, again, it is obviously impossible for every person in the world to exercise effective ownership of his four-billionth portion (if the world population is, say, four billion) of every piece of the world's land surface. (1973, pp. 33–34)

Notice Rothbard's references—utilitarian references—to efficiency, practicality, and effectiveness.

Nevertheless, Rothbard maintains that his "two axioms, the right of self-ownership and the right to 'homestead,' establish the complete set of principles of the libertarian system. The entire libertarian doctrine then becomes the spinning out and the application of all the implications of this central doctrine" (1973, p. 40).

PECULIARITIES OF THE AXIOMATIC APPROACH

One peculiarity of this approach appears at the beginning, in the supposed axiom that each person owns himself, his body. An argument phrased in such a peculiar way is suspect for that very reason. A utilitarian argument can readily show the importance of property rights; but to put property rights at the very beginning, even ahead of considerations of human personality, seems odd indeed. Someone not intent on a particular chain of deductive reasoning would describe human nature and the human condition more straightforwardly. He would probably speak not of each person's *owning* himself but of each person's *being* his own self and having his own consciousness and purposes and capacity to feel pleasure and pain, satisfaction and frustration. He would probably assert or argue for each person's right to personal freedom. Property rights would come into the argument, but not as its very foundation.

A more pervasive peculiarity is the attempt, openly avowed—recall the quotation above—to spin out positions on all sorts of specific issues from the two axioms about ownership of selves and other property. (Although utilitarian points occasionally creep into Rothbard's arguments, they do not characterize his approach.) Rothbard's positions on crime, extortion, blackmail, contracts, and bankruptcy provide striking examples, calling his whole approach into question, as I shall try to show. For brevity, I forgo commenting on how self-confidently he spins out firm positions on abortion, boycotts, children's rights, animal rights, and other issues. Again, my purpose is not to attack Rothbard but to defend Mises.

Meanwhile, let us note, a utilitarian would not try to derive all sorts of specific judgments by deducing them in one direction only from a very few initial axioms. Instead, he would check his tentative specific judgments and his tentative generalizations (rules) against one another. In a way, judgments about specific cases would serve as data—tentative, corrigible data—for reaching generalizations. The utilitarian would stand ready to modify any or all of his specific and general judgments until he had achieved consistency among them, as well as consistency with his fundamental value judgment about happiness and misery. He would seek consistency between his judgment about some specific provision of the bankruptcy laws, for example, and his generalizations about honesty, promises, and property rights. At each stage, facts of reality, including the principles of psychology and economics and other disciplines, would be eligible to enter into his reasoning.[5]

Crime provides my first example of the peculiar positions that Rothbard deduces. He regards crime as, in effect, a private transaction between culprit and victim.[6] Suppose someone mugs me. By his aggression, the mugger has violated my property right in my own person and, if he has taken any valuables, my property right in them also. I am entitled to restitution or compensation. If, however, I waive this right and forgive the mugger, then I have made him a gift of the use (or abuse) he has

---

[5]This method of seeking consistency between specific judgments and general rules is what John Rawls, not himself an avowed utilitarian, has called the method of reflective equilibrium; Rawls 1971, esp. pp. 20–21, 48–51.

[6]Rothbard 1982, chap. 13. I hope it is legitimate to draw, also, on personal correspondence with Rothbard.

made of my body and also, if I so choose, of the property he has taken. Because these were mine to give away, the situation becomes the same as if no crime had occurred. No authority has any right to prosecute him, on Rothbard's view—not if I object (and if the mugger happened to kill me, it is my heirs who have the option of forgiving him, subject to any applicable provisions of my will).

But let's face reality. In all probability the mugger did not intend to make his "transaction" with me in particular. It just happened to be I who was in the wrong place at the wrong time. By his actions and attitudes, the mugger is a threat to society, to people in general; he contributes to undermining the peace and security and social cooperation on which practically everyone's well-being depends. Because of the menace he constitutes, and for other reasons, he deserves to be restrained and punished. The accident that I rather than someone else was his victim does not entitle me to forgive him and thereby contribute to perpetuating the general menace that he and people like him pose. In fact—though this is not the main point—I probably do not want the option of forgiving him. Particularly in cases involving criminal organizations, the option to forgive would expose the victim to unwanted pressure. (It is not always true that a wider range of options is preferable to a narrow one. When I was teaching at the University of Virginia, I welcomed the rule that forbade me to change a grade, once reported, except to correct an actual error. That rule sheltered me from appeals to my compassion by students "needing" a higher grade.)

Now for extortion.[7] Suppose a scoundrel pressures me to pay him $100,000 or to sell him my business firm for a token price; otherwise he will beat me up—or perhaps he just threatens to kick me in the shins or trample my tomato plants. In any case, he is violating my rights in my person or property (for the threat, like the threatened act, is itself a violation). He is properly subject to restraint or punishment. But suppose he makes a different threat, which I find more ominous: he will spread vicious lies to ruin my business and my personal life. He may add, rightly or wrongly, that his credibility with a wide circle of influential contacts will make his lies especially effective. Yet in this case he is not properly subject to legal restraint, for he is violating no property right of mine. I have no right to an unsullied reputation, no matter how much I may have in some sense earned it; for it is other people, not I, who have property

---

[7]On this and the closely related topic of blackmail, see Rothbard 1982, chap. 16; here too I draw on personal correspondence.

rights in the contents of their own minds, even including their opinions of me.

It seems strange that a member of the Austrian school of economists, who put such emphasis on the radically subjective nature of benefits and costs, goods and bads (Yeager 1987), should make such a momentous distinction between threats according to whether they do or do not involve *physical* harm to persons or objects. But that is what Rothbard deduces from his two axioms.

Rothbard takes a similar position on blackmail, defined as obtaining or trying to obtain money or goods in exchange for silence on some matter.[8] Again, the supposedly decisive question is who has a property right to the contents of the minds of the blackmailer and other people with whom he might share his information (or misinformation). Not the victim—so runs Rothbard's answer. It is irrelevant to Rothbard's judgment that the victim might be better off if the blackmailer had never been born. Rothbard brushes aside the contention that the blackmailer's activity might be judged unproductive in some sense. Rights, not assessments of productivity, must prevail. A utilitarian side point enters in: the victim may be better off with than without the opportunity to give the possessor of information an incentive not to blab. The presumption still holds that voluntary transactions—in this case, an exchange of money for silence—benefits all concerned. I would reply (not taking space here to develop the argument) that such a proposition about gains from trade is no more universally valid than the proposition about more options always being preferable to fewer.

Rothbard's conception of property rights also determines his position on what contracts are properly enforceable at law (1982, chap. 19). Suppose a performer agrees with an impresario to take part in a concert tour for a specified compensation, and the impresario proceeds with costly arrangements. Or suppose a retailing chain agrees to buy 100,000 tables over the following two years at a specified price, thereby inducing the manufacturer to construct a new factory to be able to deliver. Now, for no extenuating reason (whatever one might be), the performer or the retailer defaults on his part of the bargain, leaving the impresario or the manufacturer with heavy expenses that he can hardly recoup. In neither case, we stipulate, has any money or other property yet changed hands between the contracting

---

[8]Rothbard 1982, chap. 16 and pp. 241–243; similar arguments appear in Block and Gordon 1985 and Block 1986.

parties. Tough luck, Rothbard says in effect; the aggrieved party should have drawn up the contract more warily in the first place. The law cannot properly require the defaulter to keep his promise or pay compensation. The reason is that the default does not constitute stealing property (remember, no money has been paid); the defaulter has violated no property right. If, however, the contract had read in such a way that default did count as taking property by force or fraud, then Rothbard's judgment would be different.

A utilitarian must wonder. Why, especially with "subjectivist" Austrian economists, should so great a difference hinge on the relatively materialistic issue of whether and when property had actually changed hands? The opportunity for people to make enforceable contracts in which promises serve as consideration for each other serves social cooperation, just as it undermines it to urge peculiar axioms as reasons for tolerating default on such contracts.

Rothbard condemns bankruptcy laws. They "compel the discharge of a debtor's voluntarily contracted debts, and thereby invade the property rights of creditors. The debtor who refuses to pay his debt has stolen the property of his creditor." Fraudulent concealment of assets makes the offense even worse. "But even if the defaulting debtor is not able to pay, he has *still* stolen the property of the creditor." Bankruptcy laws "virtually confer a license to steal upon the debtor." Instead, the legal system should enforce payment through, for example, attachment of the debtor's future income (1982, p. 142).

Of course default is regrettable. So is resort to bankruptcy; so is the poor planning or bad luck that results in its appearing necessary. But regrettable things do happen. Instead of just condemning them with simplistic axioms, the utilitarian considers how best to forestall them and how best to deal with them if they do happen anyway. He asks how the world would work and how social cooperation would flourish or would suffer if no legal means were available for distributing the assets of a hopelessly indebted debtor in an orderly way and for clearing away obstacles to his future productive activity.

MORALITY AND LAW

Murray Rothbard and Walter Block try to ward off outrage over their positions on crime and blackmail and other issues by distinguishing between rights and the morality of exercising them and between law and morality

(1982, pp. 23–24; Block and Gordon 1985, pp. 47, 53; Block 1986, p. 73). To say that I have a right to exempt a mugger from prosecution is not at all to say that I should do so. To say that it should not be illegal for a scoundrel to extort money from me by threatening to spread scurrilous stories, whether false or true, is not to deny that he is indeed a scoundrel. On the view of Rothbard and Block, apparently, two categories coincide—the violation of rights and what should be illegal. Immorality is a separate question. Rothbard and Block apparently believe they can hold to their distinctive theories of rights and law while holding fairly standard ethical views and waxing just as indignant as any of the rest of us over the forgiving of muggers, extortion accomplished by threats of verbal as well as physical action, blackmail, and default on contractual promises.

I wonder if their theories can be rescued so easily. The trouble is too deep-seated: it stems from trying to deduce all sorts of specific policy positions from the two axioms about property, with no more than incidental attention to the consequences of alternative rules and policies.

I see a closer relation between ethics and law than Rothbard and Block do. (Mises 1922/1951, pp. 397–399, makes sensible comments on this relation, as does Hazlitt 1964, chap. 9.) A long process of evolution and selection has yielded ethical precepts that, by and large, praise or condemn kinds of behavior and traits of character according as they tend to serve or subvert human survival, social cooperation, and happiness. By a similar process of evolution, which in some cultures involves the accretion of precedents set in court decisions, law has come to reinforce the observance and penalize the violation of ethical precepts in the relatively most clear-cut cases. This evolved law has been codified and modified by legislatures. Ideally, these strands of law proscribe acts that are "wrong in themselves." Other strands establish acts that are "wrong because they are prohibited." Ideally, their purpose is to improve each person's opportunities to predict other people's actions and so to mesh his own actions with theirs. Traffic laws are the standard example (driving on the left side of the road is wrong not intrinsically but because the law prohibits it and because the violation would now infringe the warranted expectations and the rights of other people and endanger their lives). Technicalities of real-estate and inheritance law also provide examples of law intended to improve coordination.

Here, though, we are emphasizing the relation between law and ethics. Why shouldn't reinforcement be total, with the law prohibiting and punishing absolutely all immoral behavior? Imagining such a state of affairs—a utilitarian exercise—provides the answer. Legally prohibiting all sorts of undesirable actions, including inappropriate sulkiness, and legally requiring all sorts of desirable actions, including kind words when appropriate, would be downright impossible. The very attempt to make law completely coincide with ethics, though doomed to failure, would bring an oppressive totalitarianism and would give the rulers vast opportunities to prosecute individuals selectively and arbitrarily. We should be chary about applying and threatening violence, on which enforcement of the law ultimately rests. Use and threat of force is tolerable only when—but not whenever—the cases in which it is applied are clearly specified and when individuals can know how they must behave to avoid having force applied to them. The law must content itself, therefore, with proscribing and punishing acts that can be defined fairly definitely and detected fairly straightforwardly, without unacceptable side effects.

The greatest range of human behavior must remain outside the direct purview of the law—kind words and charitable actions on the one hand, perverted ambition, careless gossip, and malicious lies on the other hand. Encouragement and discouragement of most actions and attitudes must be left to the flexible, informal, and decentralized application of ethical precepts. Ethics, by its very logic, must be flexible in its application to particular cases and capable of evolving as knowledge grows and conditions change (Hazlitt 1964, pp. 184–185). Whether the law should forbid certain unethical actions, such as blackmail and default on contractual promises, cannot sensibly be decided directly from first principles alone. Utilitarian considerations must carry weight, including the importance of keeping the law definite and concentrated power constrained.

Why don't we want to go to the other extreme, with law so divorced from ethics as not to exist at all? Not even actual anarchists like Rothbard would go that far. (Rothbard expects law to persist even in the absence of government; private enterprises would ascertain and enforce it; 1973, chap. 11.) Allowing even murder and theft to go legally unpunished would put relatively ethical people at the mercy of the unethical, and a Hobbesian war of all against all would rage. When it can be framed and applied fairly definitely, furthermore, the law has educative value: it can help teach ethically rather dense people that certain acts are wrong, or at least that committing them puts themselves at risk.

On one point I emphatically agree with what I think is Rothbard's and Block's position: the law does not and should not be expected or thought to *determine* morality. It is not true that whatever the law permits is morally right and whatever it forbids morally wrong. Ethics is prior to law, logically and probably also historically. Ideally, law serves a good society by reinforcing the precepts of morality in certain clear-cut cases, doing so through the duly restricted exercise and threat of governmental coercion.

Unfortunately, actual law is not ideal law. Particular laws can be unwise in their conception and wicked in their consequences and even in their intent. Laws should always be subject to appraisal on ethical grounds. For reasons I won't take space to develop here (see Yeager 1985, pp. 280–283), a strong presumption runs in favor of obeying the law, even laws one thinks should be changed. In cases of exceptionally wicked laws, however (a particular U.S. law of 1850 comes to mind), ethical considerations may call for disobedience. In some such cases, furthermore, it may even be the lesser evil for judges to render decisions contrary to the actual law; at least I can sympathize with arguments to that effect.

The foregoing is what sense I can make of the concepts of "natural law" or a "higher law." So interpreted, I do not disparage those concepts; they are legitimate and important—enough so to deserve a sensible grounding. Actual laws, merely by being actual, do not acquire ethical force beyond what their content warrants and beyond the force of the general presumption in favor of obeying them. Laws are always properly subject to appraisal not only in view of their purposes, consequences, and side effects but also on broader ethical grounds. They should ordinarily be changed only by regular legislative and judicial processes; but in exceptional and extreme cases, to repeat, ethical considerations may properly lead ordinary citizens and perhaps even judges to disobey them.

These truths should not be perverted into supposing that actual common law or statutory law is not actual law after all if it is deemed contrary to some natural or higher law. For the sake of clear thinking, we should maintain the distinctions between actual and ideal law and between law and ethics.

Although, then, I accept and insist on a distinction between law and ethics, mine is not the one that Rothbard and Block make. They invoke theirs, it seems to me, in an unsuccessful attempt to confer plausibility on their highly questionable positions concerning crime, blackmail, and other topics mentioned above. Their errors are not so easily plastered over, since they stem from trying to deduce all sorts of detailed positions from two supposed axioms; and their errors threaten to spread from their legal theory to their ethical theory.[9]

I am tempted to deliver a sermon, particularly to Walter Block, author of *Defending the Undefendable*, who portrayed the pimp, the drug pusher, the litterbug, and other unsavory types as heroes (Block 1976; also Block 1986 and Block and Gordon 1985). Much speaks in support of a society's prevailing ethical norms, the norms that support social cooperation. A certain "squareness" is admirable. To recognize this is not to want to dictate people's lifestyles. Still, honesty and civility, including a decent respect for other people's rights and even their feelings, do deserve encouragement. The more generally people behave decently out of respect for ingrained ethical precepts, the less is the need or apparent need for applying the coercive force of law. For these reasons, someone who wishes well for mankind should avoid writing in a style that appears, though unintentionally, to disparage traditional ethical values.

UTILITARIANISM AGAIN

I have reviewed Rothbard's "natural rights" approach because it seems to be the leading alternative to utilitarianism as a philosophical basis for policy espousal. (I do not regard the "contractarianism" of James Buchanan and his school as a genuine alternative, for it seems to me to be a version of utilitarianism disguised by fictions; see my 1985.) In rejecting Rothbard's approach, I do not at all ridicule or dismiss the concept of rights. It is vital to a healthy society and thus to happiness that rights (very roughly, the ones mentioned in the U.S. Declaration of Independence and Bill of Rights) be respected in public policy and private life. Conducting public policy or living one's own life according to what seems narrowly expedient in each particular case would be disastrous.

The question that separates utilitarians from other theorists of rights is how to ground them philosophically. Rothbard (1982) observes that Robert Nozick (1974) does not give rights any grounding; he simply intuits them. Rothbard does attempt a grounding, which, however, fails, as suggested by the peculiar policy positions that his approach grinds out. The utilitarian, in contrast, compares alternative institutions; he investigates what conceptions of rights and justice, what rules, what restraints

---

[9] Rothbard's 1982, by the way, is not really a book on ethics; it is a book advocating a particular type of libertarian political philosophy.

on government, and what other institutions are most conducive to a good society and so to happiness.

Obviously I am referring to so-called "rules" or "indirect" utilitarianism. The supposed utilitarian who goes around looking for opportunities to frame and execute innocent men to pacify raging mobs, or to torture redheads for the amusement of the multitude, or to approve of rape when the rapist's pleasure outweighs the victim's distress, is an invention of superficial critics. The shallow, act-oriented versions of utilitarianism occasionally encountered may once have offered critics a target, but one must wonder why anyone still pursues worthless triumphs over doctrines that are hardly better than straw men.

Nevertheless, cheap shots at utilitarianism continue. Years ago, already, Mises noted the phenomenon.

> Hedonism, eudaemonism, and utilitarianism were condemned and outlawed, and whoever did not wish to run the risk of making the whole world his enemy had to be scrupulously intent on avoiding the suspicion that he inclined toward those heretical doctrines. This must be kept in mind if one wants to understand why many economists went to great pains to deny the connections between their teachings and those of utilitarianism. (Mises 1933/1960)

Mises was forthright, even courageous, in his utilitarianism. For this his reputation continues to suffer even among eminent economists and social philosophers who in other respects are carrying on his work. I urge them to reconsider. I am not saying that Mises developed the distinction between the act and rules or indirect versions of utilitarianism and fully articulated the latter version. I am not saying that he examined and demolished the axiomatic rights approach offered as an alternative by some of his disciples. Doing all this was not necessary for his work in economics. However, a sophisticated utilitarianism does fit within and extend the philosophical framework that Mises adopted. Hazlitt, for one, extended it. Mises was on the right track.

REFERENCES

Alexander, Sidney S. "Human Values and Economists' Values." In *Human Values and Economic Policy*, edited by Sidney Hook. New York: New York University Press, 1967.

Block, Walter. *Defending the Undefendable*. New York: Fleet, 1976.

———. "Trading Money for Silence." *University of Hawaii Law Review* 8 (Spring 1986): 57–73.

Block, Walter, and David Gordon. "Blackmail, Extortion and Free Speech." *Loyola of Los Angeles Law Review* 19 (November 1985): 37–54.

Edwards, Paul. *The Logic of Moral Discourse*. New York: Free Press, 1965.

Gray, John. *Mill on Liberty: A Defence*. London and Boston: Routledge & Kegan Paul, 1983.

Hayek, Friedrich A. *Studies in Philosophy, Politics and Economics*. Chicago: University of Chicago Press, 1967.

———. *The Mirage of Social Justice*. Chicago: University of Chicago Press, 1976.

Hazlitt, Henry. *The Foundations of Morality*. Princeton, N.J.: D. Van Nostrand, 1964.

Mill, John Stuart. *Utilitarianism*. 1863. In *Selected Writings of John Stuart Mill*, edited by Maurice Cowling. New York: New American Library, 1968.

Mises, Ludwig von. *Socialism: An Economic and Sociological Analysis*. 1922. New enlarged ed. Translated by J. Kahane. New Haven, Conn.: Yale University Press, 1951.

———. *Epistemological Problems of Economics*. 1933. Translated by George Reisman. Princeton, N.J.: D. Van Nostrand, 1960.

———. *Human Action*. 1949. 2nd ed. New Haven, Conn.: Yale University Press, 1963.

———. *Nation, State, and Economy*. 1919. Translated by Leland B. Yeager. New York: New York University Press, 1983.

———. *Theory and History*. 1979. Auburn, Ala.: Ludwig von Mises Institute, 1985.

Nozick, Robert. *Anarchy, State, and Utopia*. New York: Basic Books, 1974.

Rawls, John. *A Theory of Justice*. Cambridge, Mass.: Belknap Press of Harvard University Press, 1971.

Rothbard, Murray N. *For a New Liberty*. New York: Macmillan, 1973.

———. "Praxeology, Value Judgments, and Public Policy." In *The Foundations of Modern Austrian Economics*, edited by Edwin G. Dolan. Kansas City, Kans.: Sheed and Ward, 1976.

———. *The Ethics of Liberty*. Atlantic Highlands, N.J.: Humanities Press, 1982.

Sen, Amartya K. *Collective Choice and Social Welfare*. San Francisco: Holden-Day, 1970.

Vaughn, Karen I. "Critical Discussion of the Four Papers." In *The Economics of Ludwig von Mises*, edited by Laurence S. Moss. Kansas City, Kans.: Sheed and Ward, 1976.

Yeager, Leland B. "Rights, Contract, and Utility in Policy Espousal." *Cato Journal* 5 (Spring/Summer 1985): 259–294.

———. "Why Subjectivism?" *Review of Austrian Economics* 1 (1987): 5–31. Reprinted here as chapter 2.

CHAPTER 26

The Moral Element in Mises's *Human Action*[*]

SCIENCE AND VALUES

Israel Kirzner recently asked how Ludwig von Mises could claim to be pursuing value-free science while at the same time showing "enormous *passion*" to communicate its truths (Kirzner 1998, pp. 582–586). "Passion" in that context implies moral judgment, a concern for truth over falsehood and right over wrong. I will embroider a bit on how Kirzner answered his own question, which, by the way, recognizes the fact/value or is/ought distinction. Further, I will review Mises's insights into the basis of morality.

As Kirzner argued, the passionate pursuit of value-free truths involves no contradiction. Mises wanted people to have the opportunity to pursue happiness successfully. That opportunity presupposes what he called "social cooperation," meaning a secure and peaceful society in which people can interact to their mutual benefit while pursuing their own diverse specializations, projects, and kinds of excellence. Such a society presupposes policies that serve, rather than undercut, social cooperation; and they in turn presuppose that policymakers and the public have some understanding of economics—value-free science. It is too much to expect that most people should actively understand economics; perhaps it suffices if they have the humility to recognize their ignorance and refrain from destructively imposing its consequences.

Still, it is important that enough people do get economics straight and disseminate its teachings. That requires subtle insights and a perspective different from those of the layperson. Its conclusions are counterintuitive, and fallacies pervade public opinion. Most do not understand the law of

---

[*]This lecture was presented as one in a series at Hillsdale College and published in *Human Action: A 50-Year Tribute*, ed. Richard M. Ebeling (Hillsdale, Mich.: Hillsdale College Press, 2000).

unintended consequences. Economic ignorance is so widespread and its consequences so frightening that, as Kirzner said, reducing it "becomes a goal invested with independent moral worth." Economic education serves a human goal of such importance that "passionate concern becomes ... a morally natural phenomenon." Kirzner insists on "a fundamental difference between economic education" and promoting "'libertarian' ideology or rhetoric." Passion need not and dare not "compromise the detachment and objectivity of the *content* of ... economic education" (1998, pp. 582–586).

I will make one clarification. We cannot expect the whole of any science to be value-free and expect researchers to pursue their work with no heed to values. Values guide scientists toward questions that they find interesting and worth investigating. Values guide the application of scientific findings. What *can* be value-free is the *content* of scientific propositions. The distinction between value-free and value-loaded pertains not to whole fields of study or to professional careers but to propositions, to sentences. Some value-free propositions are that snow is white, that demand curves slope downward, that expanding the quantity of money beyond what people are willing to hold at existing prices causes price inflation, and that private property and genuine markets are necessary (as Mises and Hayek explained) for economic calculation.

Does insisting on a distinction between normative and positive propositions disparage ethics? No. Normative propositions can be argued for and against. All value judgments have descriptive as well as normative content, except only for fundamental value judgments. Examples of relatively specific judgments are that lying, cheating, and stealing are wrong. A fundamental judgment, in contrast and by definition, is one that one cannot argue for because one has reached the end of arguing and must appeal to direct observation or intuition instead. Probably the most familiar example is the judgment that misery is bad and happiness is good; scarcely anyone would try to *demonstrate* that judgment.

UTILITARIANISM

Utilitarianism rests on that one fundamental intuition or, in other words, on approval of human flourishing, of people's success in making good lives for themselves, and disapproval of the opposite conditions. This is a tame value judgment, to be sure; but combined with positive knowledge of the world and human affairs, it goes a long way in ethics. What fundamental value judgment or criterion could be more plausible?

One great insight of Mises, following David Hume and elaborated by Henry Hazlitt (1964), is that direct appeal to the criterion of happiness over misery is seldom necessary. A surrogate criterion is more tractable. Actions, institutions, rules, principles, customs, ideals, dispositions, and character traits count as good or bad according to whether they support or undercut social cooperation, which is prerequisite to the happiness of a society's members. Economics and the other social and natural sciences have much to say about what does support or undercut it.

Hazlitt gives powerful reasons for repudiating the variety of utilitarianism that calls for whatever action seems most likely, on each particular occasion, to contribute most to the sum total of happiness. That brand, called "act-utilitarianism," has now sunk almost to the status of a mere strawman. Even so, it remains the favorite target of superficial critics. Hazlitt advocates "rules-utilitarianism" instead, which might better be named "indirect utilitarianism." I won't spell out his reasons for espousing this version of utilitarianism here. Suffice it to say that he rejects case-by-case expediency and calls for adherence, almost without exception, to traditional precepts of morality, ethical principles that do satisfy the utilitarian criterion. Utilitarian philosophers can give reasons, grounded in reality, for respecting cherished values.

ETHICS IN *HUMAN ACTION*

Henry Hazlitt, and Mises before him, forthrightly and courageously avowed utilitarian ethics in a hostile intellectual atmosphere. Let us look more closely at what Mises wrote. He identifies ethical doctrines as normative disciplines concerned with what ought to be. Praxeology and economics, in contrast, recognize that ultimate ends are purely subjective. They judge means by whether or not they are suitable to attain the desired ends (Mises 1949/1966).

Does Mises say that a widely accepted ethical code is essential to a decently functioning economy? I do not find that he says so explicitly—perhaps because the point is almost too obvious to need saying. He says so implicitly, however, when he emphasizes that social cooperation, including market relations, is essential to prosperity and happiness and when he expounds the ethics of social cooperation.

Chapter VIII of *Human Action* explains that the moral rules necessary for social cooperation constitute an autonomous, rationalistic, and voluntaristic ethic. They stand in contrast with the heteronomous doctrines both of intuitionism and of revealed commandments (Mises 1949/1966, p. 833). Earlier we read, "Society and the state are ... the primary means for all people to attain the ends that they aim at of their own accord." Society is the great means for attainment of all the individual's ends (pp. 148, 165). The division of labor and the exchange of people's specialized outputs enhance productivity. The principle of comparative advantage, which Mises calls the Ricardian Law of Association, goes far toward explaining how. In a world without this enhancement of productivity, there would be no sentiments of benevolence and good will (pp. 144, 159–164).

The operation of the market coordinates individuals' actions. No special orders or prohibitions are necessary. Noncooperation penalizes itself. The market economy does not ask anybody to deviate from those lines of conduct that best serve his own interests (pp. 734–736).

Beyond the sphere of private property and the market, organized society has built dams to protect private property and the market against violence, malice, and fraud (pp. 734–736). Such misbehavior does occur because some persons are too narrow-minded or too weak in moral strength and willpower to adjust themselves on their own to the conditions of social life. They yield to temptations; they seek fleeting advantage by actions harmful to the smooth functioning of the social system. Society could not exist if the majority were not ready to apply or threaten force to keep these others from destroying the social order. Although anarchists overlook this regrettable truth, the state is essential to crush the onslaughts of peace-breakers (p. 149). "[T]he only purpose of the laws and the social apparatus of coercion and compulsion is to safeguard the smooth functioning of social cooperation" (p. 722).

In some passages Mises is quite explicit about his utilitarianism. The theory of social cooperation elaborated by British political economy from Hume to Ricardo extended the Epicurean philosophy. "It substituted an autonomous rational morality for the heteronomous and intuitionist ethics of older days." The only yardstick to be applied to law, the moral code, and social institutions is expediency with regard to human welfare. God endowed "his creatures with reason and the urge toward the pursuit of happiness" (p. 147).

Mises presents a utilitarian case for democracy and classical liberalism. Liberalism is not itself a theory, he says, but an application of economic and other theories to policy. It attaches a concrete—not purely formal—meaning to happiness and removal of uneasiness. It supposes that people prefer life, health, nourishment, and abundance to their opposites;

and it teaches how to act in accordance with these valuations (pp. 149–150, 153–154).

If an economist states that a certain policy measure is bad, he is not pronouncing a value judgment; he is simply saying that it is inappropriate for the desired goal (p. 883).

Reformers want to replace what they call selfishness, acquisitiveness, and profit-seeking, Mises observes, with altruism, charity, and fear of God. But in urging people to substitute "considerations of public welfare for those of private profit, one does not create a working and satisfactory social order.... [H]ow should the 'altruistic' entrepreneur proceed?" (pp. 725–726).

Flexibility of prices and wages is the vehicle of adjustment, improvement, and progress. Those who condemn price and wage changes as unjust are working against endeavors to make economic conditions more satisfactory (p. 728).

Is profit to be morally condemned? "The marvelous economic improvements of the last two hundred years were an achievement of the capitalists who provided the capital goods required and of the elite of technologists and entrepreneurs. The masses of the manual workers were benefited by changes which they not only did not generate but which, more often than not, they tried to cut short" (p. 301).

Mises identifies connections between interventionism and the corruption of government officials. In administering many interventionist measures, for example, import licenses, favoritism simply cannot be avoided. Whether or not money changes hands does not matter; licenses can be awarded to people who supply campaign help. "Corruption is a regular effect of interventionism." Mises also identifies the mindset of redistributionists. "They reject all traditional notions of law and legality in the name of a 'higher and nobler' idea of justice. Whatever they themselves do is always right because it hurts those who selfishly want to retain for themselves what, from the point of view of this higher concept of justice, ought to belong to others" (pp. 734–736).

ETHICS IN MISES'S OTHER WRITINGS

Beyond *Human Action*, Mises wrote on ethics elsewhere. In *Theory and History* (1979/1985, pp. 54–61) we read:

> The ultimate yardstick of justice is conduciveness to the preservation of social cooperation.... [S]ocial cooperation is for man a means for the

attainment of all his ends.... As social cooperation is ... a means and not an end, no unanimity with regard to value judgments is required to make it work.... The characteristic feature of a free society is that it can function in spite of the fact that its members disagree in many judgments of value.

Utilitarianism "dispels the notion that society, the state, the nation, or any other social entity is an ultimate end and that individual men are the slaves of that entity. It rejects the philosophies of universalism, collectivism, and totalitarianism. In this sense it is meaningful to call utilitarianism a philosophy of individualism" (Mises 1979/1985, p. 28).

In an essay of 1950 Mises wrote:

> Social cooperation under the division of labor is the ultimate and sole source of man's success in his struggle for survival and his endeavors to improve as much as possible the material conditions of his well-being. But as human nature is, society cannot exist if there is no provision for preventing unruly people from actions incompatible with community life. In order to preserve peaceful cooperation, one must be ready to resort to violent suppression of those disturbing the peace. (1990, p. 303)

The following comes from an essay of 1945:

> The sacrifice that a man or a group makes in renouncing some short-run gains, lest they endanger the peaceful operation of the apparatus of social cooperation, is merely temporary. It amounts to an abandonment of a small immediate profit for the sake of incomparably greater advantages in the long run.
>
> Such is the core of the moral teachings of nineteenth-century utilitarianism. Observe the moral law for your own sake, neither out of fear of hell nor for the sake of other groups, but for your own benefit. Renounce economic nationalism and conquest, not for the sake of foreigners and aliens, but for the benefit of your own nation and state.
>
> It was the partial victory of this philosophy that resulted in the marvelous economic and political achievements of modern capitalism....
>
> The scientific basis of this utilitarian ethics was the teachings of economics. Utilitarian ethics stands and falls with economics.
>
> [But our age witnesses a] revolt against rationalism, economics, and utilitarian social philosophy; it is at the same time a revolt against freedom, democracy, and representative government.
>
> [The anti-liberals call their adversaries names.] Rationalism is called superficial and unhistoric. Utilitarianism is branded as a mean system

Chapter 26: The Moral Element in Mises's Human Action 449

of stockjobber ethics ... "peddler mentality," "dollar philosophy." [Economics is scorned.] (1990, pp. 209–210)

Writing probably in 1949 or 1950, Mises recognizes that science does not have the duty to tell people what to seek as their chief good. In assessing a doctrine, we have to ask only whether it is logically coherent or self-contradictory and whether its practical application will help people attain their desired ends. We have to consider doctrines as recipes for action and apply no other standard than that of whether they will work (1990, pp. 300–301).

Utilitarianism has rejected all standards of a heteronomous moral law, which has to be accepted and obeyed regardless of the consequences arising therefrom. For [sic] the utilitarian point of view a deed is a crime because its results are detrimental to society and not because some people believe that they hear in their soul a mystical voice which calls it a crime. We do not talk about problems of ethics. (1990, p. 301)

In various writings Mises disavows hedonism in the narrow sense. Notwithstanding superficial critics, "happiness" does not mean mere material, bodily pleasures. Advanced utilitarians, he says, interpret pleasure and pain, utility and disutility in "purely formal" senses, referring to whatever individuals in fact try to achieve or avoid (1933/1960, pp. 52, 151; 1979/1985, pp. 12–13; and 1949/1966, p. 21).

Mises recognizes that many people, especially creative workers, are not driven by material desires or narrow self-interest alone. They may also be expressing competence and strength and even heroism (1919/1983, pp. 193, 213). Besides people concerned only with their own egos, there are "people with whom awareness of the troubles of their fellow men causes as much uneasiness as or even more uneasiness than their own wants" (1949/1966, p. 14).

Mises occasionally slipped into repeating slogans about "the greatest happiness for the greatest number" (1919/1983, p. 183). Such a formulation has no precise meaning, of course. All that Mises presumably meant by it is that the happiness to be furthered by morality and other social institutions and practices is the happiness of people in general—of the random member of society—rather than the differential happiness of specific persons or classes at the expense of others. Mises specifically repudiated any idea—such as critics enjoy attacking—of trying to maximize any numerical aggregate of measurable individual utilities (1949/1966, p. 242).

Some passages from his *Nation, State, and Economy* document Mises's rejection of slogans and intuitions as a basis for policy and his focus on likely consequences.

> Rationalist utilitarianism rules out neither socialism nor imperialism on principle. Accepting it provides only a standpoint from which one can compare and evaluate the advantages and disadvantages of the various possibilities of social order; one could conceivably become a socialist or even an imperialist from the utilitarian standpoint. But whoever has once adopted this standpoint is compelled to present his program rationally. (1919/1983, p. 211)

Utilitarianism has been reproached for aiming only to satisfy material interests and for neglecting higher human goals. It is true that liberalism and utilitarianism aim at the highest possible productivity of labor. But they know "that human existence does not exhaust itself in material pleasures. They strive for welfare and for wealth not because they see the highest value in them but because they know that all higher and inner culture presupposes outward welfare.... Utilitarian policy is indeed policy for this earth. But that is true of all policy" (1919/1983, pp. 214–215).

It is an absurd confusion of values and positive knowledge, Mises wrote, when insistence on the economics relevant to some policy issue is criticized as "insensitive." If dispelling economic fallacies "is inhuman, then so is every expression of truth. If to say this is inhuman, then the physicians who exploded the myth of the healing power of mandrake were inhuman, too, because they hurt the people employed in gathering mandrake" (1990, p. 234).

Mises used to say that various interventionist measures could be rejected on the basis of economic analysis and the value judgments of their advocates.

> [A]ll the methods of interventionism are doomed to failure. This means: the interventionist measures must needs result in conditions which *from the point of view of their own advocates* are more unsatisfactory than the previous state of affairs they were designed to alter. These policies are therefore contrary to purpose. (1922/1981, p. 486)

CRITICISM OF MISES'S POSITION

For many decades, utilitarian ethics has had a bad press, not least in libertarian circles. It draws scorn as the mindset of crass, grasping, unprincipled people. It supposedly invites government hyperactivity aimed at maximizing some misconceived aggregate welfare. Ethics and policy must be grounded instead in noble and intuitively obvious principles such as unswerving respect for human dignity and human rights.

Mises the utilitarian has drawn his share of criticism, even from some of his own disciples. I do not maintain that Mises expounded the subtlest version of the doctrine, distinguishing between act utilitarianism and rules or indirect utilitarianism. He wrote mostly before detailed philosophical treatments of these subtleties were published, and, anyway, they were not central to his main concerns. Still, his basic philosophical stance is worth defending. Confronting it with the arguments of critics and would-be reinterpreters helps clarify it and, I think, strengthen its appeal.

Murray Rothbard called Mises "an opponent of objective ethics" (1976, p. 105). This charge is scarcely fair. Certainly Mises was not an ethical relativist or nihilist, scorning all judgments of right and wrong and complacent even when some individuals violate others' rights in pursuit of narrow and short-run self-interest. On the contrary, he was concerned with whether behavior and precepts and character traits tend to serve or subvert social cooperation and people's happiness.

According to Rothbard, Mises made one fundamental value judgment: He hoped that the bulk of the population would get whatever it wanted or thought it wanted. But what if the great majority wants to murder redheads or wants to see innocent persons suffer for its own amusement? A utilitarian such as Mises would include such preferences "fully as much as the most innocuous or altruistic preferences, ... in the quantitative reckoning" (1976, pp. 105, 108, 182, 210, 213). Instead of citing specific statements by Mises, Rothbard criticizes what he supposes Mises, as a utilitarian, must believe.

Murray Rothbard has called Mises "an opponent of objective ethics" and has even trotted out his own standard remark about possibly murdering all the redheads to gratify a majority. Instead of citing specific statements by Mises, however, Rothbard criticizes what he thinks a utilitarian must believe. Also, like Karen Vaughn, he criticizes Mises on the grounds that he could not be trusted to hew to the libertarian line in absolutely all cases. Actually, it seems backward to criticize ethical systems according to whether they unswervingly support preconceived policy positions. It is more sensible to appraise policies according to how they accord with a well-grounded ethics. (On these criticisms, recall the preceding chapter, number 25).

Rothbard implies that utilitarians hold preferences and attitudes and character traits immune from appraisal. But Mises, to my knowledge, never said any such thing. A rules or indirect utilitarianism is indeed concerned with how attitudes and character traits, so far as they are open to influence, tend to affect the health of a society and the happiness of its individual members. For fear of adverse side effects and for other reasons, a utilitarian does not want to enlist the state's coercive powers in suppressing all unfortunate preferences and attitudes and traits; but this in no way means that he considers all of them equally worthy of respect and of influence on policy.

Other criticism is policy-oriented. Rothbard objected that the utilitarian will rarely apply an absolute principle to real-world situations. The utilitarian regards principle as no more than a vague and overridable guideline. He "cannot be 'trusted' to maintain libertarian principle in every specific application" (1973, p. 24). Karen Vaughn regretted that Mises accepted the collectivists' and authoritarians' terms of debate by stressing how efficiently the free market provides well-being. Such a defense of freedom is doubly dangerous. "First, it is open to empirical refutation." Second, the utilitarian calculus might tip in favor of a nonliberal system if it counted the bureaucrats' enjoyment from controlling and regulating. A less risky course simply postulates freedom as supremely "desirable for its own sake" and as "a moral value that, as a bonus, also happen[s] to lead to the well-being of society" (1976, pp. 108–109).

But it seems backward to criticize ethical systems according to whether they unswervingly support preconceived policy positions. It is more sensible to appraise policies according to how they accord with a well-grounded ethics. Furthermore, such criticisms distinguish sharply, if sometimes only implicitly, between ethically principled and utilitarian approaches to policy. They interpret the latter as unprincipled, case-by-case direct calculation of gains and losses of utility. Actually, far from rejecting principles, utilitarianism seeks their sound basis.

On the charge that utilitarians cannot be trusted to hew to the libertarian line in absolutely all cases, compare Mises's remark:

> It may be that socialism represents a better form of organization of human labor. Let whoever asserts this try to prove it rationally. If the proof should succeed, then the world, democratically united by liberalism, will not hesitate to implement the communist community. In a democratic state, who could oppose a reform that would be bound to bring the greatest gain to by far the overwhelming majority? Political rationalism does

not reject socialism on principle. But it does reject in advance the socialism that hinges not on cool understanding but rather on unclear feelings, that works not with logic but rather with the mysticism of a gospel of salvation, the socialism that does not proceed from the free will of the majority of the people but rather from the terrorism of wild fanatics. (1919/1983, p. 221)

Mises means that rationalism does reject socialism, yes, but from the scientific comparison of alternative systems.

NATURAL LAW AND NATURAL RIGHTS

One widely admired doctrine in supposed rivalry with utilitarianism insists on adherence to natural law and natural rights. Rothbard tries to derive many detailed propositions about ethics and law from his conception of rights, purportedly derived in turn from John Locke's axioms of self-ownership and homesteading (1973; 1982). (Yet even for these he offers utilitarian arguments, without acknowledging the label.) John J. Piderit (1993), a Georgetown University economist, argues for what he calls a natural-law approach: correct reason ascertains what actions are "natural" and therefore ethically acceptable by reflecting on the nature of human beings, their shared aspirations and fundamental values, and their interactions in community. Yet Piderit can scarcely mean that whatever is natural is right and good. Civilization is largely an exercise in taming natural behavior. Of course, any acceptable doctrine must conform to nature in the sense of not requiring impossible actions or behavior enforceable only at excessive cost. Respecting the facts of nature and human interaction does not distinguish the natural-law approach from utilitarianism.

Natural-law doctrine does make sense if it means merely that all sorts of behavior and precepts, notably including laws made by legislatures and judges, are open to appraisal on moral grounds. Nothing becomes ethically acceptable merely by enactment into positive law. That interpretation of natural law does not rule out a utilitarian grounding of morality. But if the doctrine says that whatever is morally right (or wrong) has all (or none) of the force of positive law, it fatuously denies a live distinction.

As for natural (or human or individual) rights, the meaning that seems to fit the typical context is this: A right is a person's entitlement to others' treatment of him that is binding on those others with compelling moral force. Some rights are positive entitlements, like a child's right to support by his parents or each party's right to performance by the other party to a contract. The rights mentioned in the Declaration of Independence are negative rights, rights to forbearances, rights not to be coerced or victimized by other persons, notably including agents of the state. One reason why negative rights are especially stringent is that they are relatively easy to honor—simply by not interfering.

Rights, being moral entitlements, *presuppose* an ethical system or tradition and cannot provide its very grounding. On what principles or intuitions provide the basis of rights, "the rhetoric of rights sheds no light whatever" (Hare 1989, chaps. 7–9, p. 194). Richard Epstein finds a utilitarian grounding for natural law and natural rights, sensibly interpreted, and even for the Lockean axioms of self-ownership or personal autonomy and homesteading or first possession (1989, pp. 713–751, 769–773; and 1995, pp. 30, 55, 68, 311–313, and passim).

Making natural rights the very foundation of ethics substitutes intuition for factual research and reasoning. Furthermore, some strands of "rights talk" debase political discussion, making absolutistic and moralistic demands, and subverting a creative search for mutually beneficial accommodations.

In the words of Donald Livingston, interpreting David Hume, corrupt modes of philosophizing are undercutting whatever fragments of *sensus communis* could discipline radical self-determination. Philosophical resentment spawns

> an endless stream of self-created victims. Someone's self determination is met with the violent protest that someone else's rights have been violated. Ever more numerous rights are generated to protect ever more numerous desires.... "I want"... has become an argument of practical reason.... Thus a form of the Hobbesian state of nature is renewed in the most advanced civilization, and society is held together not by the enjoyment and cultivation of an inherited *sensus communis* but by *legalism* enforced by an increasingly consolidated and bureaucratic modern state. Consolidation must occur as power is transferred from dismantled, independent social authorities to the center in order to service an ever-increasing number of antinomic individual rights. (1998, pp. 398–399)

As Mises says, declarations about disagreements hinging on irreconcilably and unnegotiably different worldviews

> describe the antagonism as more pointed than it really is. In fact, for all parties committed to pursuit of the people's earthly welfare and thus

approving social cooperation, questions of social organization and the conduct of social action are not problems of ultimate principles and of world views, but ideological issues. They are technical problems with regard to which some arrangement is always possible. No party would wittingly prefer social disintegration, anarchy, and a return to primitive barbarism to a solution which must be bought at the price of the sacrifice of some ideological points. (1949/1966, p. 181)

MISES AND NATURAL RIGHTS

Mises's own position on natural law and rights is an embarrassment for some of his disciples. Nature is alien to the idea of right and wrong, he observes, questioning the notion of an eternally established standard. Right and wrong are utilitarian judgments. As for natural law, people deduce clashing implications from their arbitrary notions of it. "*De lege ferenda* there is no such a thing as justice. The notion of justice can logically only be resorted to *de lege lata*." In enacting or changing laws, the issue is not justice but social expediency and social welfare. "There is neither right nor wrong outside the social nexus.... The idea of justice always refers to social cooperation" (Mises 1949/1966, pp. 720–721).

Utilitarian philosophy and classical economics have nothing to do with the doctrine of natural rights, says Mises. All that matters for them is social utility. Mises even quotes Bentham on the "nonsense" of natural rights. Utilitarians recommend democratic government, private property, freedom, and equality under the law not on illusory grounds of natural law and human equality but because they are beneficial (1949/1966, p. 475).

Elsewhere,[1] Mises insisted, "Utilitarian Liberalism had nothing to do with these natural rights fictions. The Utilitarians themselves must be credited with the merit of having once and for all refuted them" (1990, p. 228).

To quote Henry Hazlitt, who wrote largely under Mises's inspiration, the inviolability of rights rests "not ... on some mystical yet self-evident 'law of nature'... [but] ultimately (though it will shock many to hear this) on utilitarian considerations" (1964, p. 264).

Some of the formulations quoted above are sharper than I myself would have expressed them, but Mises was nothing if not forthright. Precisely because human rights and human dignity are important values, they

---

[1] A 1945 essay commenting on ideas not only of natural law, but also of government by social contract.

deserve a more solid grounding than mere intuitions reported in noble-sounding language. Mises of course did not reject natural law in the scientific sense; and he did not reject natural law and human rights as ethical precepts if they are interpreted in the tame sense that I sketched out earlier, the sense compatible with utilitarianism. What Mises rejected was the exaggerated, foundationalist, almost mystical status that some writers have accorded to them.[2]

HOPPE'S SUPPOSEDLY VALUE-FREE APPROACH TO LIBERTARIANISM

Hans-Hermann Hoppe presents a curious supposed alternative to utilitarian ethics (1988a, pp. 56–76; 1988b, pp. 20–22; and contribution to a symposium, "Hoppe's Rights Theory" 1988, pp. 4–53, 53–54). He purportedly dispenses with any appeal to value judgments at all, even such a tame one as wishing people happy rather than miserable lives. He does not have to try to get an "ought" from an "is" because the libertarian policy position rests entirely on logic and facts and not at all on value judgments.

Reason, Hoppe says, can prove moral laws valid a priori. It makes explicit what the sheer fact of discussion already implies. The libertarian private-property ethic can be justified morally and by argumentation and without invoking any value judgments. Proposing any alternative ethic contradicts what inheres in the very act of engaging in argumentation; nonlibertarian proposals are falsified by the very act of making them.

Argumentation—discussion—requires employing scarce means, privately owned. Argumentation presupposes that the participants recognize each one's exclusive control over one's own body. Furthermore, argumentation could not be sustained for any length of time without private property in things beyond one's own body, property ultimately tracing to Lockean homesteading. Without private property defined in objective, physical terms, life, acting, and proposition-making would be impossible. "By being alive and formulating any proposition, then, one demonstrates that any ethic except the libertarian ethic is invalid." Hoppe further says he has proved "that it is impossible to propositionally justify nonlibertarian property principles without falling into contradictions.

---

[2]A section is omitted below because it confronts a reinterpretation of Mises too strained to be worth the space needed to refute it. For the omitted material, see the original version of this chapter.

Empirical evidence has absolutely no bearing on it." He explicitly rejects utilitarianism; his approach is an alternative ("Hoppe's Rights Theory" 1988).

Murray Rothbard had been preaching for over thirty years that economists cannot arrive at any policy conclusion in a strictly value-free way; they have to come up with some kind of ethical system. Then Rothbard said that Hoppe had proven him wrong. "[H]e has deduced an anarcho-Lockean rights ethic from self-evident axioms.... Hoppe has managed to establish the case for anarcho-capitalist-Lockean rights in an unprecedentedly hard-core manner, one that makes my own natural law/natural rights position seem almost wimpy in comparison.... [I]t is impossible to disagree with the anarcho-Lockean rights ethic without falling immediately into self-contradiction and self-refutation." Hoppe appeals to the concept of the "ethics of argumentation." "[A]ny argument whatsoever ... must imply self-ownership of the body of both the arguer and the listeners, as well as a homesteading of property right so that the arguers and listeners will be alive to listen to the argument and carry it on" (contribution to the symposium on "Hoppe's Rights Theory," 1988).

Hoppe seems to say that espousing nonlibertarian policy positions commits self-refutation in the same sense that I would be refuting myself if I wrote a letter saying that it is impossible to write a letter or made an oral statement saying it is impossible for anybody to speak. The self-contradiction of a nonlibertarian ethic may be more complicated and require more attention to expose, but it still is a self-contradiction, and of the same general type. The exposure of self-contradiction is a neat kind of argument and has great appeal—when it works.

In the present case, it just does not work. Hoppe simply asserts, but does not demonstrate, a logical contradiction. Being emphatic and repetitious is not enough. A slaveowner and his slave might conceivably engage in an intellectual discussion, even about the moral status of slavery itself, without either necessarily falling into self-contradiction.

THE SIGNIFICANCE OF RIVAL DOCTRINES

One reason for mentioning Hoppe's and other alternatives to Mises's utilitarianism (and, more broadly, to the indirect utilitarianism of David Hume, Mises, and Henry Hazlitt) is to show that utilitarianism is not so plastic and all-encompassing as to be vacuous. The existence of rival positions defuses that charge. One envisages a just society in the sense of

John Rawls (1971), who rejects viewing justice as a mere means to happiness. Other rival doctrines center on duty or religion. Still others posit conformity to traditional ethical precepts, even if only intuition, rather than analysis of consequences, has tested the precepts; or respect for individual rights that have simply been postulated rather than argued for; or conduciveness to the special flourishing of the few highest and noblest specimens of the human race. One might also conceivably make the criterion the happiness not of people in general but of oneself discriminatorily or of some other specific person or class.

Some of these ostensibly rival doctrines, and perhaps others that do not now come to mind, may turn out, on examination, not to be truly *rival* doctrines. The criteria they appeal to either may not be as ultimate as happiness or may be equivalent to it after all. (In putting forth his axioms of self-ownership and Lockean homesteading, even Rothbard introduces utilitarian considerations.) Some of these doctrines, on the other hand, really are different. Their very existence shows that utilitarianism is not vacuous. If they are too unattractive to be realistic contenders, that fact further supports utilitarianism.

INTUITIONISM

The most urged alternatives to utilitarianism turn out to be varieties of intuitionism, which Mises quite properly spoke out against. Let me quote and paraphrase from his *Socialism*. (First I should explain a term that Mises uses. Eudaemonistic ethics is, loosely speaking, a system that applies the criterion of happiness.) Philosophers had been arguing about the ultimate Good for a long time, Mises wrote, before modern investigation settled it. All the arguments used in favor of an anti-eudaemonistic ethics were unable to dissociate the concept of Morality from that of Happiness. The vain efforts of these philosophers

> were necessary to expose the problem in all its wide ramifications and so enable a conclusive solution to be reached.... [T]he tenets of intuitionist ethics ... are irreconcilable with scientific method [and] have been deprived of their very foundations.... [E]udaemonistic ideas lie concealed in every train of aprioristic-intuitive ethical thought.... Every ethical system built upon the idea of duty ... is finally obliged to yield so much to Eudaemonism that its principles can no longer be maintained. In the same way every single requirement of aprioristic-intuitive ethics displays ultimately an eudaemonistic character. (1922/1981, p. 360)

CONCLUSION

The fact/value or is/ought distinction, which I introduced at the beginning, is indeed a sound one. Nevertheless, "ought" judgments can be discussed and soundly made (except only for fundamental value judgments, and even for them, considerations can be adduced that incline people to accept them; Mill 1863/1968, chap. 1). The soundest, most appealing approach to value judgments and to their use, as in policy recommendations, has been shown by Hume, Mises, Hazlitt, and other writers in their tradition (or in parallel, as by R.M. Hare). This approach is indirect utilitarianism.

Mises was forthright, even courageous, in espousing utilitarianism and repudiating intuitionist alternatives. For this his reputation continues to suffer even among disciples who otherwise are carrying on his work. I urge them to reconsider. I am not saying that Mises developed the distinction between the act version and the rules or indirect version of utilitarianism and fully articulated the latter. I am not saying that he anticipated and demolished in advance the axiomatic or intuitionist rights approach that some of his disciples would urge. Doing all that was not possible in his time and was not necessary for his work in economics. However, a sophisticated utilitarianism does fit in with and extend his philosophical framework. Henry Hazlitt, for one, extended it. Mises was on the right track.

REFERENCES

Epstein, Richard A. "The Utilitarian Foundations of Natural Law" and "Postscript: Subjective Utilitarianism." *Harvard Journal of Law & Public Policy* 12 (1989): 713–751, 769–773.

———. *Simple Rules for a Complex World*. Cambridge, Mass.: Harvard University Press, 1995.

Hare, R.M. *Essays on Political Morality*. Oxford: Clarendon Press, 1989.

Hazlitt, Henry. *The Foundations of Morality*. Princeton, N.J.: D. Van Nostrand, 1964.

Hoppe, Hans-Hermann. "From the Economics of Laissez Faire to the Ethics of Libertarianism." In *Man, Economy, and Liberty: Essays in Honor of Murray N. Rothbard*, edited by Walter Block and Llewellyn H. Rockwell, Jr., 56–76. Auburn, Ala.: Ludwig von Mises Institute, 1988a.

———. "The Ultimate Justification of the Private Property Ethic." *Liberty* 2 (September 1988b): 20–22.

"Hoppe's Rights Theory: Breakthrough or Buncombe?" A symposium by various authors, with a response by Hoppe. *Liberty* 2 (November 1988): 4–53, 53–54.

Kirzner, Israel. "The Nature and Significance of Economic Education." *The Freeman* 48 (October 1998): 582–586.

Livingston, Donald W. *Philosophical Melancholy and Delirium: Hume's Pathology of Philosophy*. Chicago: University of Chicago Press, 1998.

Mill, John Stuart. *Utilitarianism*. 1863. Reprinted in *Selected Writings*, edited by Maurice Cowling, 243–304. New York: New American Library, 1968.

Mises, Ludwig von. *Nation, State, and Economy*. 1919. Translated by Leland B. Yeager. New York: New York University Press, 1983.

———. *Socialism: An Economic and Sociological Analysis*. 1922. Translated by J. Kahane. Indianapolis: Liberty Classics, 1981.

———. *Epistemological Problems of Economics*. 1933. Translated by George Reisman. Princeton, N.J.: D. Van Nostrand, 1960.

———. *Human Action*. 1949. 3rd ed. Chicago: Regnery, 1966.

———. *The Ultimate Foundation of Economic Science*. 1962. 2nd ed. Kansas City, Kans.: Sheed Andrews and McMeel, 1977.

———. *Theory and History*. 1979. Reprinted Auburn, Ala.: Ludwig von Mises Institute, 1985.

———. *Money, Method, and the Market Process*. Essays selected by Margit von Mises. Edited and with an introduction by Richard M. Ebeling. Norwell, Mass.: Kluwer, 1990.

Piderit, John J. *The Ethical Foundations of Economics*. Washington, D.C.: Georgetown University Press, 1993.

Rawls, John. *A Theory of Justice*. Cambridge, Mass.: Belknap Press of Harvard University Press, 1971.

Rothbard, Murray N. *For a New Liberty*. New York: Macmillan, 1973.

———. "Praxeology, Value Judgments, and Public Policy." In *The Foundations of Modern Austrian Economics*, edited by E.G. Dolan. Kansas City, Kans.: Sheed and Ward, 1976.

———. *The Ethics of Liberty.* Atlantic Highlands, N.J.: Humanities Press, 1982.

Vaughn, Karen. "Critical Discussion of the Four Papers." In *The Economics of Ludwig von Mises*, edited by L.S. Moss, 101–110. Kansas City, Kans.: Sheed and Ward, 1976.

CHAPTER 27

Can a Liberal Be an Egalitarian?*

An answer to the question posed by my title depends, obviously, on how its terms are defined.

I shall deny that a liberal can consistently advocate government action to chop down high incomes or especially favorable opportunities out of zeal for a closer approach to material equality as a goal in its own right.[1]

Instead of using the term "liberal" as it is used in modern American politics, I use it, as Professor Mises and the "Austrian" and "Chicago" economists do, in the traditional sense. Liberalism is a doctrine that rejects any supposed social or national purpose transcending the purposes of individuals. Instead, it seeks to allow each individual a wide range of free choice among purposes and pursuits. (While emphasizing the goals of each individual, it in no way denies the healthy fact that he may largely relate his own interests and satisfactions to those of many people beyond himself.) Liberalism calls for preserving, adopting, and devising the social, political, and economic institutions likeliest to minimize the frictions that inevitably arise to some extent among the pursuits and the specific freedoms of different individuals. Yet it cannot give an equal blessing to whatever goals individuals might have. Malicious enjoyment of the misfortunes of other people, or envy, or a sheer delight in meddling—all are hard to square with liberalism. This judgment holds even when such tastes are gratified through voluntary transactions among all persons concerned. More about this later.

---

*From *Toward Liberty*, vol. II, Festschrift for Ludwig von Mises (Menlo Park, Calif.: Institute for Humane Studies, 1971), 422–440. Here, in the article's title and throughout, the word "egalitarian" replaces the original "equalitarian."

[1] I shall obviously be dealing in value judgments. While it is impossible to classify value judgments scientifically as right or wrong, it is possible to investigate relations among them, revealing compatibilities and clashes and striving for a consistent and economical articulation. Showing people that certain of their less fundamental value judgments clash demonstrates the need for a more careful ranking and articulation of their values.

As for egalitarianism, instead of defining it explicitly, I want to distinguish between leveling up and leveling down. Consider a minority of people whose wealth or income or opportunities are distressingly inferior to those of most people. Redistribution to help them, perhaps through the government budget, is leveling up. With that I have no quarrel in principle. Such relief of actual poverty—of definitely sub-modal circumstances—is not meddlesomeness. Rather, it is an effort to remedy a situation almost universally recognized as bad. (This is not to say that monks and nuns and other ascetics should be barred from choosing a life of poverty.) Involuntary but eradicable poverty is a blemish, making a society less attractive for practically everyone who comes in contact with or even is keenly aware of it. Its elimination would be in the recognized interest of almost everyone.

Redistribution to *level down* unusually great wealth or incomes or unusually favorable opportunities is quite a different thing. Great wealth is the opposite of something that almost everyone would consider bad for himself. It, or the opportunity to achieve it, broadens the range of alternatives open to people, as we can recognize without supposing that material abundance must form the very core of the good life. Ideally, a liberal would like each person to have the opportunity for it if that is what he wants. A policy aimed at leveling down the exceptionally wealthy few would deprive some people of their good fortune—a good fortune that a liberal would welcome for everyone—because other people are less fortunate. If everyone cannot be very lucky, no one shall be. This attitude may be a human one; but it is an unlovely one, unworthy of being sanctified in public policy.

But do any people who consider themselves traditional liberals really advocate leveling down as distinguished from leveling up? Does any liberal really favor tax progression of such a degree that direct benefits to poor people are doubtful or trivial? It is true that this idea seldom appears unequivocally in print. But it crops up often in discussions. And it seems to underlie the ubiquitous slogan that "Equality is an end in its own right." Henry Simons, who ranks as one of the saints of the Chicago School, has expressed his preference

> for rather steep progression. The tax system should be used systematically to correct excessive economic inequality and to preclude inordinate, enduring differences among families or economic strata in wealth, power, and opportunities. (1950, p. 144)

According to Simons,

> Sound meliorative measures must yield not mere leveling of incomes but leveling accretions of capacity, capital, and possessed power. Equality of opportunity is an ideal that free societies should constantly pursue, even at much cost in terms of other ends. (1948, p. 6)

According to Allan T. Peacock,

> Liberal support for such measures as progressive taxation does not rest on the utilitarian belief that an extra pound is more "valuable" or will "afford a greater utility" to a poor man than to a rich man. It rests on a positive dislike of gross inequality. (Quoted in Hayek 1960, p. 518)

Frank H. Knight has repeatedly likened social life to a "game" or "contest," has talked about the "distribution of prizes," has mused on what arrangements tend to make the contest "interesting to participants and spectators," and has considered the imposition of "handicaps."[2] His thought is so rich and complex that a reader cannot be sure whether Knight really favors some degree of leveling down for the sake of equality as an end in its own right. Qualifications can also be found in Simons's writings. But whatever the correct interpretations may be, Knight and Simons have furnished intellectual stimulation for some of their more forthrightly egalitarian Chicago School disciples. Ideas of the kind under consideration abound, of course, in the works of writers who do not even claim to be traditional liberals.

I wonder whether liberals who speak of equality as an end in its own right have really examined their values thoroughly. *Why* is equality an end? Perhaps some people honestly have no idea of how to answer this question because they consider equality as an ultimate desideratum that they cannot describe as a means of serving any more basic values. But this position must be rare. Most egalitarians presumably consider equality a means to more basic values with which the connection is obvious.

What might these still more basic values be?[3] One might be the avoidance of concentrated power. But great wealth is not great power. Being

---

[2] For example, in Knight 1936, pp. 60–66, 292–293, 302–304.

[3] The ones to be considered here still are not absolutely basic. An absolute value would presumably be something comprehensive and vague such as "human happiness" or "human self-fulfillment." Not only economics but also political science, sociology, psychology, philosophy, and other disciplines presumably have much to contribute to investigation of which *intermediate* ends, or the policies and social and political and economic

wealthy does not enable a person to coerce others or to restrict the opportunities open to them. His ability to offer them financially attractive deals is not the same as power to deprive them of alternatives they would have had anyway. The situation would be different if one person or group, or a very few of these, accounted for a large enough fraction of national income or wealth to possess monopoly power in dealing with other people. Then, however, the unsatisfactory condition would be precisely this monopoly power and it would confuse the issue to talk about inequality instead. When a country has several thousand separate individuals or families of great wealth, it is almost a contradiction in terms to speak of *concentration* of wealth or power in their hands. On the contrary, the existence of several thousand pillars of economic strength, many of them able and some of them willing to support causes and persons that may be unpopular with the general public and with the government, may be of great value in preserving a free society.

Another motive for egalitarianism might be the belief that a marginal dollar adds less to the utility of a rich person than of someone else and that redistribution might accordingly increase total social utility. Besides taking some old-fashioned strands of economic theory too seriously, this argument blinks the ethical question whether an involuntary transfer can be justified by the mere fact or conjecture that the gainers gain more than the losers lose. A more plausible version of the argument is that the surplus of the rich can be taken for such socially important purposes as building and running schools and hospitals. In considering this argument, we must distinguish between two cases, though the analysis does not hinge on any exact dividing line between them. First, suppose that those who benefit from the schools and hospitals[4] are so poor that they could not pay for them without trenching painfully on consumption of still more urgent necessities: they could not pay by ordinary private purchase of schooling and hospitalization, through premiums on private or governmental insurance, by taxes, or in any other way. The problem is then one of their actual poverty, and rhetoric about schools and hospitals in particular beclouds the issue. Most liberals would favor measures to relieve actual poverty; but precisely because it is in almost everyone's interest to live in a society

---

arrangements adopted in their pursuit, do and which do not conduce to the irreducibly basic end of human happiness.

[4]These beneficiaries are of course likely to include people beyond those who actually use the schools and hospitals—the externalities involved are familiar—and I am not necessarily implying that the entire cost should be charged to the actual users alone.

free of actual poverty, it is not clear—at least, not without further argument—why the cost should be concentrated on a rich minority. Secondly, suppose that the beneficiaries of the schools and hospitals are not especially poor and could afford to pay for their services in one of the ways mentioned. Why, then, should a rich minority have to pay a share of the costs out of proportion to their share of the benefits? So far as the beneficiaries of the schools and hospitals escape the cost, they have money left over to spend on other things. Redistributive taxation may thus in effect make the rich help pay for the clothing, automobiles, entertainment, and liquor of people who are not poor. Perhaps this is defensible; but what, then, becomes of the special emotional aura of schools and hospitals?

Perhaps egalitarianism is an extension of the liberal case for relief of actual poverty. For, redistributionists might argue, the dividing line between poverty and adequate income is vague. Even persons in the modal or typical income brackets may suffer *relative* poverty; they may be uncomfortable about not being able to live on the same material plane as the wealthy minority. If relieving the discomfort of actual poverty is urgent, then relieving the mental discomfort of relative poverty may be somewhat advantageous.[5] In reply, it may be pointed out that while a line between poverty and material comfort cannot be drawn precisely, a general basis for the distinction exists. In the United States, the persons to be considered actually poor are a fairly small minority in material circumstances well below what is typical. Redistribution to benefit this poor minority is different in principle from leveling down a rich minority in the supposed interest of a modal majority. Principle, not definite tax schedules, is what is at issue here. A further aspect of the issue is whether public policy should recognize the notion of *relative* poverty and should dignify whatever uneasiness some people may feel about the better fortune of others by basing tax legislation upon it. It is not enough to consider what attitudes may in fact prevail, causing mental pain or pleasure; social philosophers also have the job of considering what sorts of attitudes should or should not be encouraged because they do or do not tend to promote a good society, coherently conceived.

---

[5] Admittedly I cannot cite a clear statement of this position. The grounds for egalitarianism or redistributionism are so generally regarded as self-evident that a critic must try to figure out for himself just how the redistributionist case might look if spelled out in detail in the strongest version he can conceive. This is what I am trying to do, rather than concocting and refuting flimsy arguments as a debating tactic.

Perhaps the redistributionist case rests less on any of the foregoing arguments than on inchoate notions about what makes for a healthy tone of society—notions about avoiding social distinctions and feelings of inferiority and about promoting solidarity and brotherhood. Slogans about equality as part of the democratic ideal support this conjecture. I admittedly would consider it a good thing—though I would be hard pressed to explain just *why*—if the distributions of physical and mental talent and energy, personal ambition and inclination, inherited property, advantageous family backgrounds, and so forth meshed with the derived demands for material and human factors of production in such a way that the personal incomes created on the free market were not conspicuously unequal. Spontaneous equality of this sort could perhaps be furthered by measures to break down any contrived restrictions on economic opportunity.

Spontaneous equality would still contrast sharply with deliberately leveling down the rich. Deliberate leveling would be likely to do the reverse of overcoming incentives to envy, embarrassments to social intercourse, and obstacles to brotherhood and mutual respect. The degree of envy and so forth would probably not correlate at all closely with the size of inequalities remaining under an avowed program of equalization; sometimes the smallest distinctions are the most keenly resented. More important, the idea of deliberate leveling seems dangerously akin to ideas that all men are *not* equal in those respects which concern the State, that men with different incomes are different in intolerable ways, and that differences in people's material wealth and lifestyle—differences going beyond the discomforts of actual poverty—are conditions to emphasize, to be suspicious of, and to take action about. To work against poverty is admirable, but to be concerned about other people's exceptional good fortune and to want to interfere strikes me as hardly compatible with a coherent liberalism. People are all too ready, anyway, to pass judgment on their fellows. They are all too ready to display intolerance, bitterness, Puritanism, a busybody spirit, and suspicion of other people and their personalities and lifestyles. Many redistributionists, it is true, are moved by humanitarian motives; they do not want to promote suspiciousness or pander to resentment. But "good intentions are not enough." The spirit of live-and-let-live, so crucial to a free society, is fragile. Any policy that dignifies and reinforces the less lovely traits of human nature, however unintentionally, deserves bad marks on this score.

The leveler philosophy may rest in part on the feeling that extremely high incomes are undeserved. Of course not all large incomes derive from hard work, ingenuity, or alertness in meeting consumer tastes. Large incomes obtained by force, fraud, restraint on competition, or dishonest advertising and salesmanship are indeed open to question. More precisely, it is the illegal or immoral activities themselves that deserve attention; to focus on the sheer size of the resulting incomes beclouds the issue. Large incomes due to inheritance of talent or energy or beauty or connections or wealth, or to sheer luck, pose a trickier question: why should some not particularly virtuous people enjoy luxury while millions of harder-working and worthier people must scrape to make ends meet? In partial reply, one may ask another question: If the processes of allocating the services of persons and property into the lines of most intense consumer demand yield very large incomes for some not especially deserving persons and for their heirs, who is actually hurt and entitled to complain? In an innovating, enterprising society, total real income is not a fixed pie; larger slices for some do not necessarily mean smaller slices for others. Perhaps people with lower incomes are harmed in the sense that their taxes would be lower if the rich paid still higher taxes. But this "harm" is different from harm positively inflicted by the rich. As for rich persons innocent of illegal or immoral activities, the demand that they justify or forgo their exceptional incomes raises fundamental questions about what prerogatives of organized society are compatible with liberalism. Like busybodiness, it is perhaps a human trait to begrudge one's fellows whatever exceptional good luck may come their way—I say "perhaps" because the general public does not seem to bear grudges against lottery winners and against the exceptionally glamorous rich—but grudges about good luck are unworthy of being dignified as the basis of public policy.

Note that I am not accepting—instead, I explicitly reject—the "marginal productivity ethics" of John Bates Clark and his followers, a doctrine rightly dissected by Frank Knight and other liberal economists. The mere fact that a man's own work or the services of his property happen to have an exceptionally high market value does not mean that he is especially deserving, in any ethical sense, of an exceptionally large income. Market value is not a measure of ethical merit, and people in general would be happier if this fact were explicitly recognized.[6] My concern is with what sort of a politico-economic system would replace capitalism if productivity and market-value considerations were set aside as a basis of income distribution. More specifically, in this paper, I am concerned about the

---

[6] On this point, see Hayek 1960, chap. 6.

implicit redistributionist conception of the State as an agency that, while not allotting individuals their fates outright, at least takes a decisive hand in readjusting that allotment. I am rather horrified at the idea of the State as a dispenser of "justice" in the concrete, material sense, and as a God that passes judgment on what people deserve and steps in not merely to allay the unfortunate consequences of bad luck but also to strip people of the fruits of what it considers too much good luck.

Before returning to the question of equality of opportunity, I shift now from examining possible strands in a rationale of leveling down to expressing some actual doubts. A much-discussed problem in political ethics arises when people who expect material or psychological gain from redistributionary taxation act as judges in their own cause. By imposing higher tax rates than they themselves are willing to pay, the majority of voters ask a rich minority to "work more days out of the year for the government" than they themselves are willing to do. As Hayek (1960, p. 314) has said, "That a majority, merely because it is a majority, should be entitled to apply to a minority a rule which does not apply to itself is an infringement of a principle much more fundamental than democracy itself, a principle on which the justification of democracy rests."[7]

This "discrimination" argument infuriates redistributionists, who suspect that its user's heart is bleeding for people who will have more income and wealth per head, even after taxes, than their alleged despoilers. The critic has a hard time proving that his real worry is over the attitude that might makes right—the sheer might of numerous votes.

The "discrimination" argument would lose much of its force if leveling down were enacted not merely by an overall majority but also by a majority of even those persons who would have to pay the exceptionally high tax rates. But then why not rely on voluntary redistribution? One reason, apparently, is the "public-good" character of redistribution: the typical rich person might be willing to redistribute only if all other rich persons did the same; only compulsion could achieve the general redistribution assumed

---

[7]I am aware that a case of sorts can be made out for redistributive taxation as a kind of mutual insurance arrangement: not knowing how rich or poor they will be in the future, individual voters may agree to a scheme that will redistribute income away from them if they turn out to be rich but in their favor if they turn out to be poor. One trouble with this argument is that voters do in fact have a pretty good idea of their current and future positions in the national income distribution. Furthermore, the argument hardly applies to the philosophy of leveling down for its own sake, leveling carried to the point where additional tax revenue for redistribution to the poor is relatively insignificant.

to be desired by the rich themselves. But if this coerced action would be noble and praiseworthy, would it not be still more so for each rich person to redistribute independently? A generous act is tarnished by being made compulsory and by satisfaction in seeing other persons coerced along with oneself. Those who failed to respond to a campaign for voluntary redistribution—I am setting aside, for the sake of argument, doubts about the desirability of even such a campaign—could be left unmolested as monuments to the toleration of eccentricity so essential in a free society. Apart from the matter of voluntary action versus coercion, much can be said for distribution from numerous individual sources and in favor of a great variety of independent purposes rather than through the monolithic agency of the State.

The doctrine of coercive redistribution has a subtle affinity with materialism. Why should it disturb us that some people are very wealthy? If we are unwilling to tolerate great superiorities in income and wealth, how do we feel about superiorities in talent, physical and mental strength and health, influence through family connections and personal friendships, ability and time to appreciate conversation and art and music and sports, amount of formal education, experience gained through travel, and so forth? People's circumstances can be different in innumerable ways. Why do redistributionists single out material inequality unless they think that money is—and should be—the prime measure of a man's capacity to enjoy life and of his worth to himself and other people, his social status, and his personal dignity? The reason cannot be that material inequality is the only kind susceptible of being leveled down. We could partially level out advantages of early training by requiring all children to attend democratically standardized public schools. (Even some self-styled liberals are perverse enough to recommend compulsory military training for similar reasons.) We could level down physical attractiveness by requiring everybody to wear masks and shapeless uniforms, or we could put especially heavy taxes on beauty as well as on brains.

Auréle Kolnai has perceptively said:

> the true Christian is inclined to feel a certain disdain for the wealthy inasmuch as he disdains wealth, more or less factitious goods of which the rich man is a slave, while the believer in the "social gospel" will call for the elimination of the wealthy for the gain of all because wealth seems to him to be the sole good that counts. (1946, p. 7)

> In the old liberal democratic conception, a poor man seemed invested with human dignity, had a claim to honour and was entitled to freedom

no less than a prosperous one; the refurbished ideology denies him the capacity for freedom unless or until he is also made wealthy.[8] (1949, p. 82)

In doubting whether the pursuit of material equality will achieve any of the more decent motives of its proponents, I can quote Frank Knight on my side:

> the significance of consumption itself is largely symbolic; the inequality which really "hurts" is the unequal distribution of dignity, prestige, and power. Neither abstract reasoning nor the evidence of experience affords ground for belief that, given the moral drive toward such values as the dominant motive in society, democratic political process could fail to distribute them even more unequally still than does competitive business. (1936, pp. 308–309)

Furthermore, pursuit of an unattainable material equality will foster attitudes and political behavior incompatible with a quasi-equality of a more human and more nearly attainable type. Ideally, people should not have to be ranked above or below each other according to the fields in which their accomplishments lie. Each person should have a chance to excel in *something*, with the different types of excellence regarded as incommensurable. Adventure, scholarship, conviviality, self-effacing service to mankind—all should be as respectable as the amassing of fortunes. People of modest talents or ambitions who do routine work and content themselves with inexpensive pleasures should be regarded as contributing to a desirable diversity in personalities, modes of thinking, and styles and goals of life. A teacher could continue associating without embarrassment with congenial former colleagues or students who had become business tycoons not because progressive taxation had lopped off their larger monetary incomes but because scholarly values and monetary values were regarded as incommensurate but of equal dignity. As Herbert W. Schneider has noted, the equality of the egalitarians implies measurement; he emphasizes, instead, what he calls "the incommensurability of human beings" (1956, p. 97; cf. pp. 100, 118).

"All men are created equal" and statements like that are obviously not meant literally. They use poetic language legitimate in their contexts. They are meant as normative prescriptions for social actions and attitudes. They express disapproval of trying to classify individuals as more or less worthy, more or less entitled to pursue happiness in their own ways, and more or

---

[8]My quoting these passages is not meant as an endorsement of the attitude of "the true Christian."

less entitled to have their views or interests considered in the forming of public policy.

We should not exalt materialism, but neither should we despise it. Just as a healthy society needs statesmen, humanitarians, esthetes, and eggheads, so it also needs money-minded Philistines. It takes all kinds of (decent) people to make a world. Each person's freedom to choose the niche in life that best accords with his own talents and inclinations gains from the willingness of other people to fill other niches.

Erosion of monetary incentives unleashes pressures toward conformity. One of the individual's best protections against the arbitrary whims of the business firm employing him is the fact that his employer and other employers are seeking profit in a competitive market. Policy that weakens the profit motive or the competitiveness of markets is likely to reduce the cost to employers of tyrannizing over employees. (This fact, in the academic world, leads teachers to demand other forms of protection.) Furthermore, to the extent that the tax structure leads companies to compensate their executives in kind rather than in freely spendable money—stock options, club memberships, pleasure travel in the guise of business travel, use of company cars, planes, apartments, vacation lodges, and expense accounts—to this extent business and private lives become intermingled. We see the rise of the Organization Man. From the liberal point of view, this state of affairs seems questionable not only or not even especially for the Organization Men themselves but also for members of society in general.

I offer as a mere conjecture one more doubt about egalitarianism. Especially if it is dignified by serving as a basis for public policy, the philosophy that encourages people to brood about whether wealthier people "deserve" their material abundance, and whether they themselves are not "entitled" to a larger share, may well have something to do with crime. Even relatively poor people are likely to suffer in the long run from the far-reaching consequences of a philosophy that undermines respect for personal safety and property rights.

The postponed topic of equality of opportunity serves as a transition to the concluding sections of this paper. Ideally, everyone should have a decent start in life, free from the cumulative disadvantages of initial poverty. But should the State go so far as to try to deprive fortunate young people of whatever advantages they might enjoy from bodily or mental or financial inheritance or from family background and contacts? Much could be done, after all, towards offsetting even the nonfinancial aspects of exceptionally favorable opportunity. Any really close approach to equality of opportunity is, however, impossible. Liberals should shun a slogan—"equality of opportunity"—whose implementation is impossible, especially since even an attempt to implement it approximately would entail totalitarianism. Furthermore, it is hard to see equality of opportunity as a desideratum distinct from equality of income or status, since unequal attainments in income or status must be due either to unequal luck or to unequal endowments of the abilities and inclinations conducive to achieving income or status. From an egalitarian standpoint, inequality of results would show that unequal luck had not been properly compensated for or that opportunities had not been properly equalized.

From the liberal standpoint, the whole discussion would be simplified by calling for *adequacy* rather than equality of opportunity. Removal of actual poverty and of caste and race restrictions that arbitrarily hamper people in the pursuit of their own goals is quite different from chopping down advantages.

Why, incidentally, might anyone want to chop down advantages rather than merely remove disadvantages? I wonder whether one of the objectives of egalitarians who consider themselves liberals might not be to make the outcome of the market process a more nearly plausible indicator of personal worth. Their likening of life to a "game" or "race" and their talk of imposing "handicaps" to make the game "interesting" certainly suggests so (recall Frank Knight, quoted above). Everyone is to have the same purpose in life, overriding the diverse purposes that individuals might otherwise have; and this common purpose is to succeed in the game. Everyone is to engage in it, if necessary be drafted into it. The score will be kept, especially in money and status. No one will have an excuse for not taking this rivalry seriously, for proper handicaps will have been imposed. By persuading themselves that the "game" has been made "fair," the self-styled liberal egalitarians will have more of a supposed basis than ever for indulging a propensity to pass judgment on their fellows, smugly dispensing praise and scorn.

This view of society as an organized activity, with the government as a busybody game-master or social director imposing handicaps and otherwise trying to drum up "interesting" rivalry, strikes me as profoundly anti-liberal. It is putting things backwards to regard the game—or the market of the textbooks—as a supreme value in its own right, with the diverse values of individuals taking second place.

Here I have admittedly drifted into considering the possible *motives* of the egalitarians. Questioning motives is often bad form. It is rank antiintellectualism, in particular, to dismiss purportedly factual or logical propositions by a mere sneer at the alleged motives of their propounders. But when policy goals and conceptions of the good society are at issue, motives are at the core of the discussion. If we ask why someone advocates certain policies, the reason is that we are trying to understand his conception of the good society. The tastes gratified by leveling policies—the taste for making a goal out of the social and economic game itself, the taste for smugly passing judgment on other persons, the taste for sheer meddling—clash with the spirit of liberalism.

Am I denying that liberalism accords equal esteem to all tastes of individuals, regardless of what they are? Should liberalism discriminate between worthy and unworthy tastes, ones that "ought" and others that "ought not" to count in a liberal social order? Yes. As a conception of the good society, liberalism cannot, with consistency, give its blessing to all kinds of taste, indifferent to the kind of society that emerges in response. If social philosophy has any role at all, it is to investigate and promote consensus about what social institutions and policies and attitudes are conducive to human happiness. Its job is to paint a coherent picture of the good society. It cannot just offer a ticket instead of a picture, a ticket reading that the good society looks like whatever a substantially unanimous opinion thinks it looks like. There may be no substantially unanimous opinion. Prevalent opinion may be unenlightened. Social philosophy shirks its job when it offers no positive guidance. Quite properly, de Tocqueville and John Stuart Mill inveighed in the name of liberalism not only against governmental tyranny but also against the conformist pressures of public opinion.

Suppose one man were to buy the fawning submissiveness of another, or even the other's submission to torture, to gratify the sadism of the first. Can liberalism bless such transactions in the name of the free market? Of course not. Voluntary though they may be, they gratify and encourage attitudes subversive of an enduring liberal social order. Practical reasons, to be sure, tell against making them illegal. On the other hand, public policy should not provide examples that sanctify tyrannical and meddlesome private tastes. Policymakers should recognize that State actions today may well influence what private attitudes prevail tomorrow.

Does liberalism sanctify illiberal practices freely agreed upon? Does tolerance include toleration of intolerance? Does democracy imply the right of the people to vote democracy out and dictatorship in? Such questions are reminiscent of certain logical paradoxes discussed by Bertrand Russell and untangled by his distinction between levels of discourse. We have to be clear whether we are talking "in" or "about" language, "within" or "about" democracy, "within" or "about" liberalism. An action or policy that embodies or sanctifies meddlesomeness cannot properly be called liberal merely by postulating that it is freely agreed to, perhaps in some market transaction or by some democratic procedure. Liberalism is defined, instead, by the nature and motivation and probable consequences of policies and institutions. For the word to have any content, we must recognize the possibility that people may freely choose the negation of liberalism. To define liberal policies in terms of negotiating procedures or of degree of agreement is to empty the word of meaning. The choices that emerge from political or market processes may quite conceivably not be coherent; they may not fit in with a coherent picture of the good society. One reason among many is that the choices may not be sufficiently enlightened.[9] A decision-making process is no substitute for a social philosophy. If totalitarianism were adopted by unanimous consent, would this decision be a liberal one? Of course not, for liberalism values arrangements that enable individuals to pursue their own diverse ends with a minimum of interference with each other.

In conclusion, I recognize that some would-be levelers of income, wealth, and opportunity are honorable men. They do not believe that numerical might makes right; they do not want to aggrandize the power of the State; they do not pander to envy; they do not make money the measure of all things; they do not savor the prospect of feeling superior to the losers in a suitably handicapped contest. But in appraising a line of policy, it is not enough to satisfy oneself about the motives of the more honorable among its proponents; one must also consider what type of society it tends to promote. One must consider that a policy may exert some of its effects over a long period of time through its influence on what attitudes prevail. If I am a good judge of my own motives, I oppose fiscal leveling because I want the kind of society that respects but puts no special emphasis on material values, one that allows niches for people with diverse drives and goals in life, one characterized by tolerant attitudes, and one whose

---

[9]This is one among many reasons for rejecting the currently fashionable concept of "Pareto optimality" as a touchstone for economic policy. There is no substitute for considering how the probable consequences of each contemplated policy will mesh or will clash with one's conception of a good society.

institutions facilitate voluntary cooperation while minimizing the scope for clashes among the freedoms of its members.

REFERENCES

Hayek, F. A. *The Constitution of Liberty*. Chicago: University of Chicago Press, 1960.

Knight, Frank H. *The Ethics of Competition*. 2nd ed. New York: Harper, 1936.

Kolnai, Auréle. "Le culte de l'homme commun et la gloire des humbles." *Laval Théologique et Philosophique* 2, no. 1 (1946).

———. "Privilege and Liberty." *Laval Théologique et Philosophique* 5, no. 1 (1949).

Schneider, Herbert W. *Three Dimensions of Public Morality*. Bloomington: Indiana University Press, 1956.

Simons, Henry. *Economic Policy for a Free Society*. Chicago: University of Chicago Press, 1948.

———. *Federal Tax Reform*. Chicago: University of Chicago Press, 1950.

CHAPTER 28

Rights, Contract, and Utility in Policy Espousal*

RIVAL CRITERIA

This paper defends one version of utilitarianism against supposed alternatives to it as a policy criterion. First it reviews the natural rights doctrine, contractarianism, and criticisms of each. Several sections state and defend a broad version of utilitarianism. Examples follow of writings about rights and contract that tacitly accept utilitarianism. A summary concludes the paper.

NATURAL RIGHTS

Clear-cut examples of the antiutilitarian rights doctrine are rare. One reason, apparently, is that doctrines ostensibly of that kind are in fact tacitly utilitarian—a point developed later. Murray Rothbard (1973, pp. 23–25) observes that most libertarians have adopted natural rights and rejected both emotivism and utilitarianism as the foundation for their nonaggression principle. Their basic axiom is the "right to self-ownership," absolute property in one's own body. Accordingly, everyone has the right to perform actions necessary for surviving and flourishing without coercive molestation. Rothbard then develops a theory of property in nonhuman objects by appealing to John Locke's concept of a person's rightful ownership of previously unused natural resources that he first transforms by his labor (1973, pp. 26ff.). "These two axioms, the right of self-ownership and right to 'homestead,' establish the complete set of principles of the libertarian system" (p. 40).

---

*From *Cato Journal* 5 (Spring/Summer 1985): 259–294. Some sections overlap other chapters of this book and have been deleted or shortened here.

Rights theorists reject the approach that would take a stand on each specific policy issue, such as deregulation of a particular industry or imposition of wage and price controls or government credit allocation, according to the apparent merits of the individual case; they reject narrowly focused cost-benefit calculations. Instead of being framed by case-by-case expediency, policy should conform to persons' rights.

And those rights should not be defended on a utilitarian basis, for doing so supposedly opens the door to all sorts of pragmatic demands for government intervention. The utilitarian, Rothbard complains (1973, p. 24), will rarely adopt a principle as an absolute and consistent yardstick. Instead, he regards it as a vague guideline or aspiration or tendency that may well be overridden. Milton Friedman, for example, although devoted to the free market as a general tendency, in practice allows many damaging exceptions to freedom against state intervention (Rothbard 1973, p. 24). Utilitarianism—or rather, in my view, its exaggerated pragmatist version—contrasts sharply with a pure doctrine of rights. Rights theorists derive positions even on quite specific policy issues from a very few propositions taken as axiomatic.

Unfortunately, the door is open to interventionist demands anyway. Libertarians cannot keep it closed by issuing methodological pronouncements or by reporting their intuitions about endangered rights. A pure rights position, untainted by utilitarian aspects, might serve for warding off illegitimate or undesirable interventions if it enjoyed general acceptance. Although it might be convenient if a particular doctrine were true and generally accepted, that convenience alone is no evidence, unfortunately, that the doctrine is in fact true. To make the best of reality, which often is inconvenient, we must face it as it is.

In reality, no doctrine will automatically protect us from bad interventions. Abuse of utilitarian arguments cannot be prevented by rejecting utilitarianism *tout court*. Instead, one must enter into discussion with one's pragmatist opponents, demonstrating how acting on an excessively narrow utilitarianism violates rights as intelligibly conceived and convincingly defended and so impedes the pursuit of happiness.

RIGHTS AND VALUE JUDGMENTS

What I am rejecting is a *pure* rights doctrine scornful of any utilitarian underpinning. I accept a pro-rights doctrine, provided that propositions about rights are recognized not as positive propositions of fact and logic but rather as normative propositions. A definite list of rights is unnecessary here. Suffice to say that rights are persons' entitlements to freedom from coercive interference by their fellows and by government; they concern life, liberty, property, and the pursuit of happiness. (When embodied in constitutions or statutes, of course, normative propositions like that take on an additional, legal, status.)

To identify assertions of rights as value judgments is emphatically not to disparage them as mere expressions of emotion or whim. It is instead the claim of imprescriptible ontological status for them that disparages them by exposing them to easy ridicule, as in Jeremy Bentham's remark (1843/1973, p. 269) about "nonsense upon stilts." Although they are normative, assertions of rights can be supported by appeal to facts of human nature and other aspects of reality and to the findings of psychology, economics, and other disciplines.

As the philosopher Paul Edwards (1965) and the economists Sidney Alexander (1967, esp. pp. 105–107, 114–115) and A.K. Sen (1970, esp. pp. 62–64) have argued explicitly and as many other writers have recognized, fact and logic can be brought to bear in trying to clear up disagreement over all but fundamental value judgments. (Supporting considerations appear in Adler 1970.) It can be a constructive enterprise to try to clear up disagreement over specific or nonfundamental values. (Examples are the judgments that Jones should be sent to jail, that lying, cheating, and stealing are wrong, that private property is a desirable institution, and that specified rights should be recognized and respected.) It is anti-intellectual simply to chalk disagreement up to irresolvable emotional differences. We can give and discuss *reasons* for value judgments.

Reasons for and against specific value judgments might include positive analysis showing why accepting some tends to promote and accepting others to subvert a society of a kind conducive to its members' successful pursuits of happiness. An important objective element, utilitarian in a broad sense, thus enters into the vindication of human rights. Only when we finally have nothing left to appeal to beyond some such fundamental value judgment as one favoring happiness and abhorring misery have we exhausted the relevance of facts and logic, investigation and discussion. But bona fide disagreements in the real world seldom if ever center on fundamental values, openly avowed. For practical purposes of policymaking, then, the fact-value distinction fades away.

ABSTRACT REASONING IN FAVOR OF RIGHTS

The most immaculately antiutilitarian version of the rights doctrine boils down all too soon to simply promulgating rights and even to anathematizing disagreement as a sign of moral deficiency. Some antiutilitarian proponents of rights (Rothbard 1973, Rothbard 1982, Gewirth 1978, Mack 1978, Paul 1978) do offer arguments, after all, but arguments of peculiarly abstract kinds—appealing (as already noted) to self-ownership and Lockean homesteading or, alternatively, to what one must say about rights to avoid logical error.

Consider, for example, what Alan Gewirth does with his Principle of Generic Consistency, which, "unlike utilitarian and material deontological theories, ... contains within itself the ground of its necessity; it is self-justifying" (1978, quotation from p. 203). Certain rights must be respected if each person, a purposive being, is to strive effectively for his purposes. He cannot consistently claim these rights for himself while denying them to persons affected by his actions when the very reasons he gives for claiming the rights for himself also apply to those other persons. He would be uttering logically contradictory propositions. In effect he would be saying: All persons for whom such-and-such reasons hold, including me, have such-and-such rights; yet he would deny, when expedient for himself, that other persons have those rights even though the stated reasons do hold for them also.

I question the supposed logical *contradiction*. An egoist might consider it expedient to claim certain rights for himself and deny them to others when he can get away with it. *He* is not necessarily accepting certain statements about rights as objectively true; *he* is not committing logical error. Instead, he considers it expedient to encourage other persons to hold certain beliefs about rights, beliefs in which those others might perceive contradictions if they were astute enough. If he can thereby further his own purposes, why should he care about the contradictions in other persons' beliefs? (In taking up what he calls "the Machiavellian case," pp. 196–198, Gewirth does try, but ineffectually, to rebut a counterargument similar to but not the same as mine.) We might consider the person a scoundrel, but that is not the same as his being a poor logician.

Eric Mack (1978) tries to derive the existence of rights from the proposition that coercion is deontically wrong—wrong because of its very character and not just because of its consequences. Because each person is an end in himself, it is deontically wrong for others to cause his actions to be out of accord with his own purposes, which is what coercion does. The deontic wrongness of coercion condemns any destruction of freedom by it. Contractual rights and property rights can also be vindicated by recognition of their violation as essentially coercive. Mack recognizes that utilitarian reasons for respecting rights could be grafted onto his argument but maintains that his argument does not depend on them.

ARGUMENTS, NOT JUST INTUITION

The examples already given illustrate how antiutilitarian ethicists stop short, before a utilitarian would, with mere propounding or with appeal to irreducible intuition (even if they do not use the term). But what is intuition based on? Perhaps on an unarticulated recognition of consequences—tacit utilitarianism. Conceivably humans have an innate propensity, elaborated by natural selection, to develop such intuitions. If so, the consequences of having or not having them must have figured in the biological process.

Why not, then, strive to clarify those intuitions by disciplined observation and reasoning? It seems inadequate to rest everything on the assertion, for example, that individuals, as ends in themselves, simply should not be coerced. Such a line of argument does not take adequate account of the social context in which questions about rights arise. The utilitarian, however, does press on with an empirically oriented investigation into what sorts of institutions and practices do and what sorts do not accord well with human nature and the human condition.

Supposed axioms about rights cannot serve as the ultimate foundation of one's conception of desirable social arrangements. Instead, propositions about rights must be argued for, along with other propositions about what makes for a good society. John Gray (1983, esp. pp. 59–60, 66, 68) maintains that John Stuart Mill in effect sought—successfully, Gray implies—to provide a utilitarian underpinning for respect for rights.

Another ethicist-economist who does so is Henry Hazlitt (1964, pp. 286–287). Within necessary qualifications, he says,

> legal rights are or ought to be *inviolable*. And so, of course, should moral rights be.
>
> This inviolability does not rest on some mystical yet self-evident "law of nature." It rests ultimately (though it will shock many to hear this) on utilitarian considerations. But it rests, not on *ad hoc* utilitism [sic], on expediency in any narrow sense, but on *rule* utilitism, on the recognition that

the highest and only permanent utility comes from an unyielding adherence to *principle*. Only by the most scrupulous respect for each other's imprescriptible rights can we maximize social peace, order, and cooperation.

Elsewhere Hazlitt (1978, pp. 22–23) describes natural rights as "simply the rights that people ought to have." He notes the idea that rights gain in sanctity and respect by being called "natural," as if they were "something built into the universe, prior to creation, prior to existence." Actually, "natural rights" is "a mystical phrase. It's simply an unnecessary concept."

Before noting expositions of the rights doctrine that are tacitly utilitarian, we must consider the latter doctrine. First, though, a review of another rival doctrine is in order.

CONTRACTARIANISM

A "contractarian" approach or attitude toward public policy has won respectful attention. Its most forceful and prolific advocate has been James M. Buchanan. (See the bibliography and, for some criticism, Gordon 1976 and Samuels 1976.) Buchanan and other contractarians often also cite John Rawls (1971) with approval.

Contractarians exalt the individual over "society," agreement over coercion, and application of consent as the overriding criterion of desirability not merely to small-scale interpersonal relations but also in the large—to the broad framework of social, political, and economic institutions. A social contract—if not an actual one, at least a "conceptual" one—figures prominently in their vision.

Quotations from James Buchanan will help convey the contractarians' case and their objections to the allegedly opposed "truth-judgment" approach.

> To the contractarian that law is legitimate, and just, which might have emerged from a genuine social contract in which he might have participated. That law is illegitimate, and unjust, which finds no such contractual basis. (1977, p. 127)

> My point is mainly that of emphasizing the use of process, as opposed to end-state results.... For Rawls, as for contractarians generally, that which emerges from contractual agreement is just. (1977, p. 1)

> That is "good" which "tends to emerge" from the free choices of the individuals who are involved. It is impossible for an external observer to lay

down criteria for "goodness" independent of the *process* through which results or outcomes are attained. The evaluation is applied to the means of attaining outcomes, not to outcomes as such. (1975a, p. 6)

Many more passages of similar import can be found in Buchanan's writings. He would have us approve or disapprove of states of affairs or sets of rules not primarily by considering their substance but overridingly by appraising the process employed to reach decisions about them.

SOME PRELIMINARY DOUBTS ABOUT CONTRACTARIANISM

That idea seems odd to me. It resembles the idea that whatever people freely choose is in fact good for them. Broome (1978) exposes this fallacy. One of his examples concerns "Jane," who, perhaps out of a sense of duty somehow absorbed from her surroundings, chooses to sacrifice an independent life of her own to care for her aged mother. It does not necessarily follow that Jane's free choice best serves her own interest or fulfillment or happiness or even that it maximizes her and her mother's utilities combined. Broome is simply warning against an invalid inference, of course, and not saying that some authority should impose on Jane the lifestyle it thinks best for her.

Price theory and welfare economics may legitimately, as blackboard exercises or for other purposes, assume that people make choices so as to maximize their utilities on the basis of definite utility functions. It does not in the least follow, however, that freedom of choice is the very criterion of what to choose. A libertarian might deplore forcible interference with the use of addictive drugs. Yet this attitude does not commit him to the view that drugs serve the happiness of those who choose to take them. He would not be inconsistent in wanting to legalize them while considering their use harmful and deplorable.

Similarly, voluntary agreement is not itself the criterion of what to agree on. To value voluntary agreement and the democratic process in no way commits an economist or social philosopher to value whatever institutions or policies such processes may grind out. Why should he feel obliged to withhold any criticism? Decisionmaking procedure is itself properly an object of approval or disapproval, but it cannot sensibly be taken as the sole criterion of what to decide.

Rather than suppose that proper procedure exhausts the content of the good society, it would seem reasonable to emphasize proper procedure as an important part of that conception. But it is hard to see how a procedure can be deemed good utterly apart from some consideration of its likely results.

As Scott Gordon observed in reviewing *The Limits of Liberty*, Buchanan was trying to derive "moral principles without the aid of any moral premise" by carrying over positive analysis of collective decisionmaking into fundamental political philosophy. Buchanan might reply that he does have a moral premise, a weak one favoring individualism. Anyway, in Gordon's view (1976, p. 583), Buchanan's attempt to get normative conclusions from analysis that is entirely (or almost entirely) positive "cannot succeed.... [T]ry as one will, that troublesome word 'ought' cannot be excised from political philosophy and no degree of sophisticated 'is' can take its place."

Striving for clarity may justify some harshness. Except in brief and untypical passages, Buchanan obscures his employment of and shirks his responsibility for values that he, like anyone, *must* be employing when he recommends anything, even when what he recommends is process rather than substance as the criterion for appraising institutions and policies.

Viktor Vanberg (n.d.) also raises apt questions about a supposedly purely procedural criterion. Can we appraise a process or a set of rules solely by the procedure of establishing and changing it, and so on? How do we avoid infinite regress? Isn't some substantive criterion needed somewhere? Furthermore, doesn't an "agreement test" unavoidably muddle together observations of people's preferences and of their theories about how alternative institutions would work? (Vanberg attributes the latter point to Karen Vaughn. As Vaughn has also said somewhere, or so I am told, choosing constitutional principles is not as easy as choosing a toaster.) One implication, I should think, is that economists and social philosophers have a legitimate role explaining and preaching what social arrangements they consider best, and why.

"Contractarianism gets its name," says one commentator (Pettit 1980, pp. 147–148), "from the device which it uses to filter out people's enlightened preferences." It identifies just social arrangements as those that answer to people's preferences—not the sort recorded by ordinary voting, however, but rather the preferences that people would have if they were not influenced by narrow self-interest and bias.

But on what grounds would people—people in real life and even or especially people stripped of distinctive self-interests, as by being placed behind a Rawlsian "veil of ignorance"—prefer one set of social arrangements over others? On what basis can a social philosopher hope to distinguish between laws or constitutions that could and those that could not have been agreed upon under either actual or idealized conditions? The only plausible basis, I submit, is that people stripped of narrow self-interest would consider the preferred arrangements as coming closer to an impartial conception of the good society, that is, as being more conducive to happiness, than the alternatives. A contractarian might say: No; impartial people would prefer those arrangements because they were *fair*. But why is fairness so desirable? Either because it just is, because a compelling intuition insists on it, because the question is not further discussable; or else because people's treating each other fairly is conducive to their effective pursuit of happiness.

I assert not that contractarianism is flatly wrong but that it disguises its affinities with utilitarianism by repulsive and unnecessary fictions (about which I shall have more to say).

THE ATTACK ON "TRUTH JUDGMENT"

Yet Buchanan sharply contrasts his contractarian vision with the "truth-judgment" approach, as he disparagingly labels a position akin to the utilitarianism defended here. This scorned approach tends to "assume that there is a unique explanation, a unique set of rules which defines the elements of a good society and which, once discovered, will come to be generally accepted by informed and intellectually honest men" (1977, p. 75; the words quoted occur in interrogative sentences, but the context leaves little doubt that Buchanan is characterizing the approach he condemns).

Buchanan distinguishes further between his own approach and its rival. His contractarian conception is analogous to market activity, a search for agreement to the mutual benefit of the participants. The truth-judgment approach is analogous to the deliberations of a jury (1984, pp. 29–30). Earlier (1975a, p. 164) he had distinguished, similarly, between the politician and the judge. The politician seeks consensus and acceptable compromises.

> He is not engaged in a search for some one "true" judgment, and he is not properly behaving if he seeks to further some well-defined ideal drawn from the brains of his academic mentors. The judge is in a distinctly different position. He does seek "truth," not compromise.

As applied to politics, Buchanan deplores the judge or jury conception. It conduces to intolerance by those who think they have attained political truth. Implicitly they claim the right to impose truth on persons mired in error (1977, pp. 76–77). Their view entails

> a demonstrated willingness to impose nonvoluntary changes on the existing pattern of entitlements in social order.... Once truth is found, there is no moral argument to be raised against its implementation. Consent is meaningless in this context. Opposition can be variously characterized as stemming from ignorance, folly, or the exercise of selfish interest. In any case, the views of those who actively oppose the truth-carrying zealots are not treated as worthy of respect. And any requirement to compromise with such views arises only because the reformists might otherwise lack the power to impose "truth" unilaterally. (1977, pp. 143–144)

Buchanan (1975a, p. 167) sees many social philosophers exhibiting

> intellectual and moral arrogance. An attempt to describe the social good in detail seems to carry with it an implied willingness to impose this good, independently of observed or prospective agreement among persons. By contrast, [his] natural proclivity as an economist is to place ultimate value on process or procedure, and by implication to define as "good" that which emerges from agreement among free men, independently of intrinsic evaluation of the outcome itself.

Passages abound in which Buchanan dwells on this theme of the arrogance, the itch to play God, of those who presume to employ their own value judgments in trying to frame a coherent conception of a good society.

For contractarians, process and consent, not outcome or substance, form the criterion of goodness or desirability in human institutions and relations. "'Truth,' in the final analysis, is tested by agreement. And if men disagree, there is no 'truth'" (1977, p. 113). "A scientist may advance an argument to the effect that a proposition is 'true.' His argument ... may succeed in establishing a consensus among his fellow scientists. But the 'truth' of the proposition emerges only from this agreement and not from some original objective reality" (1977, p. 145 n.).

AUTHORITARIANISM, RELATIVISM, FALLIBILISM

This extreme relativism is remarkable, yet Buchanan finds adopting it necessary to avoid authoritarianism with regard to truth. Actually, these are not the only alternatives.

Harry Davis (1967–1968) has described a third position distinct from the two between which Buchanan evidently thinks the choice must lie.

The first of those is the authoritarian position of one who believes he possesses an infallible pipeline to objective truth. That is the position of the baseball umpire who insists that he calls balls and strikes as they objectively *are*. The second is a relativist-nominalist position of rejecting all absolutes and embracing a radical relativism or skepticism. An umpire holding this view says that pitches are neither balls nor strikes until he calls them. The third position, "fallibilism," combines metaphysical or ethical objectivism with epistemological relativism. The fallibilist umpire says, "I call 'em as I see 'em." On this view, it makes sense to seek objective truths about reality, even including truths about what is morally valuable and politically desirable. Yet no person or group is entitled to claim infallible possession of such knowledge. Each searcher contributes what he can, aware that his contribution is incomplete and perhaps erroneous. In science, culture, and philosophy, fallibilism calls for free discussion open to the competition of all ideas, evidences, and arguments. (Davis recognizes fallibilism as a central concept in the philosophy of Charles Sanders Peirce. See also Wiener 1968 and Peirce 1955.)

Far from being subversive of constructive discussion, a willingness to state clearly what one believes and why, exposing one's views to inspection and possible refutation, is essential to it.

The fallibilist position adopts the scientific attitude and method. Belief in the meaningfulness or at least the heuristic value of the concept of objective truth to be sought through research and discussion need not entail arrogance, elitism, and an eagerness forcibly to impose one's beliefs. Belief, for example, that one type of society is more conducive to human happiness than another in no way entails an eagerness to implement one's vision by force. A concern for process and for how decisions are made and implemented, an extreme aversion to having policies, even good ones, rammed down one's own throat or down other people's throats, may well be a major element in one's conception of the good society. An adherent of the truth-judgment approach may well harbor this strong concern for due process; it is not the private property of the contractarians.

Yet the contractarians tend to suppose that a policy not commanding a strong consensus in its favor (or whose adoption would not at least be in accordance with an underlying constitution deemed to command unanimous consent) is thereby revealed to be bad or undesirable. (Passages to this effect in Buchanan and Tullock 1962 are quoted in Yeager 1978, p. 200 and n. 17.)

The contractarians overlook a vital distinction: What is undesirable in such a case is not necessarily the policy itself but rather its imposition by antidemocratic means. It is not necessarily inconsistent or antidemocratic or elitist for an economist or social philosopher, while deploring imposition of the policy, to continue advocating it and trying to explain its virtues. In short, the nihilistic relativism of the contractarians is by no means the only alternative to a repulsive authoritarianism.

CONTRACTARIAN FICTIONS

Contractarians understand, of course, that specific policy measures cannot in practice be enacted only with unanimous consent. They therefore try to find constitutional authority for non-unanimous enactments. The constitution need not necessarily be a written document; it may consist of the fundamental features of the existing society. That broad constitution is deemed to command substantially unanimous consent by virtue of its actual existence and people's living under it. (See, for example, Buchanan and Tullock 1962, pp. 254, 260–261.) Yet David Hume had long before mocked such notions of passive, tacit consent with his much-quoted example of the shanghaied sailor who, merely by refraining from jumping overboard, does not thereby consent to the captain's supposed authority over him ("Of the Original Contract," reprinted in Hume 1752/1965, p. 263).

Buchanan and Tullock (1962, pp. 260–261) conceived of the "social contract" as

> a dynamic one.... We do not conceive the "constitution" as having been established once and for all. We conceive the contractual aspects to be continuous, and the existence of a set of organizational rules is assumed to embody consensus. We think of the individual as engaging continuously both in everyday operational decisions within the confines of established organizational rules and in choices concerned with changes in the rules themselves, that is, constitutional choices. The implicit rule for securing the adoption of changes in these organizational rules (changes in the structure of the social contract) must be that of unanimity. This is because only through the securing of unanimity can any change be judged desirable on the acceptance of the individualistic ethic.

In later writings Buchanan also treats a supposed implicit social contract as if it had actual force. He refers (1975a, p. 96) to the "existing and

Chapter 28: Rights, Contract, and Utility in Policy Espousal 489

ongoing implicit social contract, embodied and described in the institutions of the status quo." At greater length (1975a, pp. 84–85), he argues that the status quo must be evaluated as if it were legitimate contractually, even

> when an original contract may never have been made, when current members of the community sense no moral or ethical obligation to adhere to the terms that are defined in the status quo, and ... when such a contract, if it ever existed, may have been violated many times over.... Does the presence of any one or all of these negations remove legitimacy from the status quo?
>
> Again it is necessary to repeat the obvious. The status quo defines that which exists. Hence, regardless of its history, it must be evaluated as if it were legitimate contractually. Things "might have been" different in history, but things are now as they are.

The interpretation conveyed by the foregoing quotations finds support in a book by one of Buchanan's former students. The social-contract theory of the state, Randall Holcombe (1983) explains, is an attempt to describe the legitimacy of the government's power. It views society as "a type of club, where all individuals conceptually agree to become members and adhere to the club rules." Actually, individuals are born into society and must adhere to its rules whether they agree to or not. "Here, the social contract theory of the state must fall back upon the conceptual agreement of all members of society. The state operates as if all members of society had agreed to its rules—as if there is unanimous approval of the constitution" (Holcombe 1983, pp. 124–125; compare passages of similar import on pp. 9, 123, 125–126, 134).

Holcombe does not accept Buchanan's formulations wholly without reservation. "Since all of the members of the society did not actually agree to a social contract, ... some type of conceptual agreement must be fabricated if the theory is to have any connection with reality" (1983, p. 155). The words "must be fabricated" deserve emphasis.

The writings of Buchanan and other contractarians (including Holcombe 1983, esp. chap. 8) bristle with words like "conceptual" and "conceptually"—"conceptually agree," "conceptual agreement," "conceptual social contract," "conceptual unanimous approval," and the like. The very use of the words indicates that a "conceptual" agreement is not an actual one, that a "conceptually" true proposition is not actually true. It is no mere joke to say that "conceptually" is an adverb stuck into contractarians' sentences to immunize them from challenge on the grounds of their not being true.

Buchanan (1975b, pp. 123, 125) distinguishes between constitutional and postconstitutional stages of decisionmaking and envisages agreement or "conceptual" agreement at the constitutional stage as authorizing "apparent coercion" and "apparent redistribution" at the postconstitutional stage. By such fictions, realities like actual coercion and actual redistribution are interpreted away. They vanish into the realm of the merely "apparent" by being deemed in accordance with some agreement that may itself be merely "conceptual."

Even punishment, in Buchanan's view (1975a, p. 192 n.) implements a contract. "In a genuine contractarian theory, there is no problem raised concerning the 'right' of some persons to punish others, since, in effect, individuals who find themselves in the implicit social contract that any social order presupposes have presumably chosen to be punished as the law directs when they violate law." Here the word "presumably" seems to mean "conceptually" in Buchanan's sense.

Further evidence of the contractarians' reliance on fictions is that Buchanan and many other commentators accept John Rawls's (1971) characterization of his own method as contractarian. Actually, no social contract at all is involved in Rawls's derivation of his principles of justice. Instead, Rawls employs elaborate fictions (about deliberations behind a "veil of ignorance") in more or less disguising—perhaps even from himself—his total reliance on his own intuitions. (It astonishes me how many eminent scholars swallow Rawls's own characterization of his approach. Among the apparent minority who do identify what Rawls actually does are Hare n.d., and Gray 1978.)

No one need object to fictions if they are heuristically useful—if they stimulate the flow of ideas. Nor is it necessarily objectionable to employ fictions and figures of speech for expository and stylistic purposes. But a doctrine should not *depend* on them. Ideas that defy expression in straightforward, nonmetaphorical language incur deserved doubt by that very fact.

Contractarians might strengthen their case by occasionally presenting it, if they can, without resort to their favorite fictions. In doing so, however, they would be bound to erase sharp distinctions between their approach and the supposedly despicable truth-judgment approach. The version of the latter advocated in this paper does lead to much the same individualistic values as contractarianism, but its conceptual apparatus and expository style are quite different—more straightforward, and charier of fictions.

UTILITARIANISM UNDER ATTACK

Utilitarianism is routinely caricatured and scorned nowadays, and some versions do deserve scorn. It is said to be lowbrow, crass, and subversive of personal rights. The Benthamites, says Joseph Schumpeter (1954, pp. 133, 407–408), created "the shallowest of all conceivable philosophies of life."

That assessment might well apply if utilitarianism really did recommend that people spend their lives pursuing immediate pleasure. The utilitarianism defended in this paper, however, concerns the appraisal of social arrangements—policy espousal, as Philbrook (1953) would say.

Jeffrie G. Murphy (1977, p. 232) criticized a version that he attributed, wrongly, to John Stuart Mill:

> This theory is so obviously morally bankrupt that very few contemporary moral philosophers take it at all seriously.... [It] fails to pay attention to ... important *autonomy* values ... and thus fails to articulate a satisfactory conception of *justice* or *respect for persons*. It does not ... rule out the sacrifice of persons *for* the general good.

Walter Grinder (1978, pp. 9–10) bewails "the tired and woefully pragmatic doctrines of end-state utilitarianism—the cursed Benthamism in all its permutations, that has proved the bane of liberty's existence for almost 200 years. During the 19th century, utilitarianism almost single handedly short-circuited the great classical liberal revolution." Frank S. Meyer (1962, pp. 1–2, 32–33) perceived a fatal flaw in the philosophical underpinnings of utilitarianism. Nineteenth-century liberalism "deserted its heritage of defense of freedom of the person" and "denied the validity of moral ends firmly based on the constitution of being. Thereby, with this denial of an ultimate sanction for the inviolability of the person, liberalism destroyed the very foundations of its defense of the person as primary in political and social matters." To utilitarians, "Human beings considered as the objects of operations are no more nor less than objects. Kant's imperative is reversed. Our humanitarians of the welfare society take as their maxim: treat no person as an end, but only as a means to arrive at a general good."

The criterion of the greatest sum of the utilities of individuals is collectivistic, as John Rawls says; it regards individuals as processing stations for converting goods and services and experiences into increments to aggregate social utility. The ideal utilitarian legislator, in allocating rights and duties and scarce means of satisfaction, makes decisions similar to those of a maximizing entrepreneur or consumer; his correct decision is essentially a matter of efficient administration. "This view of social cooperation is the consequence of extending to society the principle of choice for one man, and then, to make this extension work, conflating all persons into one through the imaginative acts of the impartial sympathetic spectator. Utilitarianism does not take seriously the distinction between persons" (Rawls 1971, p. 27; cf. pp. 178–192, 449, 450, 572–573).

This last objection ties up with reference to the nonoperationality of the aggregate-utility criterion. Can one conceive of operationally meaningful rules for sacrificing individuals for the greater good of "society"? How good, how conducive to the pursuit of happiness, would a society with such rules be? And how would the utilities of different persons be measured and compared and added anyway? (Perhaps the clearest example of accepting the maximum-aggregate utility criterion is Edgeworth 1881/1961. Edgeworth already pointed out, p. 136, as Rawls did later, that this version of utilitarianism requires extreme altruism; it connotes *"Vivre pour autrui."*)

Act-utilitarianism, as distinguished from rules-utilitarianism, is particularly objectionable. It calls on the individual to choose, in each separate case, the action appearing likely to contribute to the greatest excess of pleasure or happiness or good over the opposite. No notion of rights or principles should bar such a calculation, for respecting them is not an independent objective. Respecting them is fine when it happens in the individual case to serve the greatest total excess of pleasure over pain, but that excess alone remains the final criterion.

Perhaps the clearest recent example of wanting each case handled on its own merits, with no presumption in favor of respecting rights or principles, occurs in Joseph Fletcher's *Situation Ethics* (1966). Fletcher departs from act-utilitarianism as ordinarily conceived only in making "love" rather than happiness the criterion and in making the altruism it calls for more blatant and cloying. Even this substitution makes little difference, since Fletcher interprets "love" as conduciveness to well-being, especially of persons other than oneself. In the coalition that he recommends between the love ethic and the utilitarianism he attributes to Bentham and Mill, "the hedonistic calculus becomes the agapeic calculus, the greatest amount of neighbor welfare for the largest number of neighbors possible." Fletcher "holds flatly that there is only one principle, love, without any prefabricated recipes for what it means in practice, and that *all other* so called principles or maxims are relative to particular, concrete situations! If it has any rules, they are only rules of thumb." "The situationist holds that whatever is the most loving thing in the situation is the right and good thing" (quotations from pp. 95, 36, 65 respectively).

No wonder critics reject utilitarianism understood as something like that. It betrays remarkable arrogance to take it for granted that the actor in the individual case, tacitly endowed with the omniscience of the act-utilitarian or act-agapeic philosopher himself, can foresee all the immediate and remote and all the direct and indirect consequences of his actions, even including those working through reinforcing or undermining principles and habits and through affecting persons' moral characters, and can assess the good and bad values of all these consequences and strike a balance. As Peter S. Prescott (1973) has said, "what was recently called 'situation ethics' can be defined as action based on invincible trust in one's own moral perspective."

An extreme act-utilitarianism or situation ethics might indeed countenance framing and executing an innocent man to pacify an angry mob and so avoid worse outrages—to mention the example so routinely trotted out (for example, by McCloskey 1969, p. 181; compare Rothbard 1973, pp. 24–25, on the execution of all redheads to delight the rest of the population).

SOME ANSWERS TO THE CRITICS

John Rawls comments perceptively on this sort of attack on a strawman version of utilitarianism. Rawls (1955/1968), writing before McCloskey (1969) and before his own book of 1971, attributed the standard horrible example to E.F. Carritt. Rawls (1955/1968, pp. 76–78) also answered the question, raised in a similar vein, whether it is acceptable to break one's promise when the consequences of doing so appear good on balance. The very point of promising "is to abdicate one's title to act in accordance with utilitarian and prudential considerations in order that the future may be tied down and plans coordinated in advance.... The promisor is bound because he promised: weighing the case on its merits is not open to him." The institution of promising and promise-keeping itself has obvious utilitarian advantages. That the promisor's obligation may be overridden in exceptional hard cases does not mean that the obligation does not exist at all.

How conducive to happiness would a society be, Rawls (1955/1968) asks in effect, in which truth and rights were treated as contemptuously as in the hackneyed horrible example? More specifically, in what context might a judgment be made in favor of sacrificing the innocent victim to pacify the mob? It is vague to say that it would be a good idea if somebody did something to save many innocent lives by sacrificing one. How could such acts be institutionalized? Just who would be authorized, and in what circumstances and under what rules, to inflict "telishment" (by which Rawls apparently means ostensible punishment inflicted for ulterior purposes)? Several reasons are obvious, and Rawls suggests some, why an institution of telishment could hardly be justified on utilitarian grounds.

Does this dismissal of the telishment case simply postulate out of existence the difficulties that it is meant to illustrate? Am I denying that any single case could ever arise in which sacrificing an innocent person might appear to promise greater good on the whole? Well, can one ever be confident that such a case has in fact arisen? The consequences of supposing so and acting accordingly are unfathomable. Approving the violation of rights whenever the decisionmaker thinks it would be beneficial on the whole would reinforce unhealthy temptations and undercut the very concept of rights. A society tolerating such violations would hardly be one in which people enjoyed relatively favorable opportunities to make good lives for themselves. Taking account of the associated institutions, habits, attitudes, and personality traits, as well as the fact that each person has a life and consciousness and purposes of his own, requires rejecting such a society. Endorsement of personal rights instead follows precisely on utilitarian grounds.

In the abstract, though hardly in convincing detail, one can contrive a case in which an act ordinarily deemed wrongful would have a net balance of good consequences, even with any undermining of respect for rules and rights counted on the negative side in the assessment. Perhaps the wrongful act can be kept secret, and its victim would have died soon of agonizing disease anyway. The contrived assumptions would rule out such adverse consequences as impairment of the agent's attitudes and moral character. The assumptions would render the proposition about the acceptability of the otherwise wrong act an empty tautology. *If* the act really would lead to the greatest net utility, absolutely all things accurately considered, and *if* the greatest net utility is one's criterion of what ought to be done, then the act ought to be done. But in what actual context could these *if*s be met? When could one have absolutely all the relevant knowledge of consequences, including the consequences of violation of valued principles, certainty that one's knowledge was accurate and complete, and certainty of one's accuracy in weighing opposing considerations? The assumptions required negate the real-world context that in fact recommends rules-utilitarianism over act-utilitarianism.

Suppose for the sake of argument, nevertheless, and quite implausibly, that a clear case of the postulated kind did arise. Suppose, further, that arranging compensation acceptable to the prospective victim or victims was for some reason impossible and that the burden of decision fell on me. Then I would have to face up to that case. I cannot commit myself in advance, ignorant of the specific facts, to insisting on observance of rules and rights even though the heavens should crumble. And neither could a self-styled antiutilitarian champion of rights.

A DEFENSIBLE UTILITARIANISM

A sounder version of utilitarianism than the one routinely pilloried has been called rules-utilitarianism or indirect utilitarianism. (John Gray, 1983, esp. pp. 11–15, 31–32, 38–39, 46–47, attributes an indirect utilitarianism to John Stuart Mill and tries to distinguish it from rules-utilitarianism; for present purposes the distinction is inessential.)

According to McCloskey, however, rules-utilitarianism arises from awareness that the act version will not do; yet it is only pseudo-utilitarianism. It opts for "irrational" conformity to rules even though no intrinsic moral significance attaches to them and even when conforming to them brings greater total evil. The rules-utilitarian prefers conformity to a rule to maximization of good. If he replies that "his is the best way of promoting the greatest good, he is abandoning rule for act utilitarianism" (McCloskey 1969, p. 188).

Why, though, does McCloskey speak of *irrational* conformity to rules? Rules serve human welfare. Utilitarianism of course recognizes dilemma cases—they figure in the human predicament—in which applicable rules clash and in which some must be overridden to permit conforming to others more demanding in the particular case. To recognize such cases is not to lapse back into act-utilitarianism or situation ethics. The rules version does stress the advantages of habituation to rules and does caution against excessive readiness to override a rule (especially against the temptation to make an exception in one's own favor). If the idea of framing the innocent man to pacify the mob so shocks us, it is because we rightly find it so hard to imagine cases in which the rule of justice should be the one to be overridden. The quality of McCloskey's debating tactics is evident in his example (p. 191) of choosing between abiding by Australia's drive-on-the-left rule and colliding with a car in the wrong lane.

As for rules having no "intrinsic" moral significance, well, what is so suspect about there not being irreducible ultimates for which no arguments can be offered? Of course utilitarianism does not and cannot insist that rules be followed for their own sakes. On the contrary, rules are *instrumental* to a good society and thereby to people's happiness. To treat rules as absolute ultimates would undermine respect for them by making them appear ridiculous.

Let us consider the question of justice and injustice a bit further. Victimizing an innocent person or minority for the supposed greater gain of others is indeed unjust. But we need not stop short with reporting our intuition to that effect; we can give reasons for our judgment. We do not downgrade justice by not regarding it as an undiscussable ultimate. Injustice subverts social cooperation and the pursuit of happiness. Sir James MacIntosh argued *(Vindiciae Gallicae*, quoted in Halévy 1955, p. 185) that the extreme usefulness of general principles of justice makes them morally obligatory.

> Justice is expediency, but it is expediency, speaking by general maxims, into which reason has concentrated the experience of man kind.... When I assert that a man has a right to life, liberty, &c. I only mean to annunciate *a moral maxim* founded on *general interest*, which prohibits any attack on these possessions.... [A Declaration of Rights is an expedient] to keep alive the Public vigilance against the usurpation of partial interests, by perpetually presenting the general right and the general interest to the Public eye.

John Stuart Mill (Mill 1968, p. 299) said: "Justice is a name for certain classes of moral rules which concern the essentials of human well-being more nearly, and are therefore of more absolute obligation, than any other rules for the guidance of life."

SOCIAL COOPERATION AND COMPARATIVE INSTITUTIONS

As an approach to understanding what sorts of individual conduct and especially what institutions and policies are desirable, rules- or indirect utilitarianism amounts to much the same thing as the comparative-institutions or good-society approach. These all have an affinity with the "truth-judgment" approach disparaged by James Buchanan.

For present purposes it matters little whether these different labels apply to exactly the same doctrine; if not identical, the doctrines do share a common orientation. Their adherents try to form a conception of the good society by contemplating and comparing alternative sets of mutually compatible social institutions. Their ideal is whatever arrangements best facilitate the success of individuals seeking to make good lives for themselves in their own diverse ways. (Strictly speaking, their ultimate criterion is human happiness, however best served. It is a researchable and discussable empirical judgment that happiness is served by institutions that facilitate voluntary cooperation, including ones that secure the rights mentioned in the U.S. Declaration of Independence.)

This approach recognizes the importance of mutually beneficial cooperation among individuals—through peace and security and through the gains from specialization and exchange. (Adam Smith pointed out that man is a social animal: he makes contracts. As Scott Gordon, 1976, p. 586, notes perceptively, "the most important feature of that word is the final letter, which makes it plural. There is a world of difference between the conception of society as consisting of contracts and the conception of it as based upon a contract.")

The approach recommended here appraises particular principles, rules, institutions, and policies according to whether they are likely to serve or subvert social cooperation in the sense just indicated. (The concept if not the term is prominent in the philosophies of Thomas Hobbes and, as F.A. Hayek has emphasized, of David Hume. See Hobbes, *Leviathan*, 1651/1952, chap. 15, and Kemp 1970. The term "social cooperation" is prominent in the writings of Herbert Spencer, Ludwig von Mises, and Henry Hazlitt.)

Social cooperation counts as a near-ultimate criterion, since it is an indispensable means to individuals' effective pursuit of their own happiness in their own diverse ways (Hazlitt 1964, esp. p. 36). Cooperation is facilitated by rules that improve people's chances of predicting each other's behavior and achieving coordination. Voluntary cooperation accords better than coercion with each person's having purposes and ideals of his own and with his having only one life to live. Emphasis on voluntary cooperation warns against authorizing any agency to impose unfair sacrifices on individuals for the supposed greater good of a greater number. But this approach does not simply postulate voluntary cooperation and deplore coercion. It investigates and compares the types of society likely to emerge from having alternative sets of institutions and rules and, in particular, from whether or not personal rights are recognized and respected.

The term "utilitarianism" as used here applies to any critical examination of social rules and institutions, their functioning, and their implications for happiness. In this wide sense, F.A. Hayek says (1976, pp. 17–18), anyone prepared to examine existing values rather than accept them unquestioningly is a utilitarian; Aristotle, Thomas Aquinas, and David Hume would so count.

In rejecting act-utilitarianism for rules-utilitarianism—but the terms are not his—Hayek explains (1969, pp. 45–46) why it may be rational to disregard known particular circumstances when making decisions. Accidental and partial bits of information might not change the probability that if we knew and could process all information about the circumstances, the net advantage would lie on the side of following the applicable rule. We should not decide each case on the basis of the limited number of individual facts that we happen to know.

One reason for abiding by rules, then, is that we simply cannot assess all the consequences and costs and benefits—direct and remote, immediate and delayed—of alternative actions in each particular case. One might object that this position is anti-intellectual, making a virtue of ignorance. How can we know that advances in theory and technology may not make possible those allegedly impossible assessments? Part of the answer, I conjecture, is that the critic has not really seen the point. Rules-utilitarianism does not glorify ignorance. Rather, it perceives the rationality of acting, in certain cases and aspects of life, on generally applicable abstract principles instead of on the fragmentary and probably accidentally biased bits of concrete information that one may happen to possess. Furthermore, complexity and ignorance by no means form the entire case for rules-utilitarianism. Acting by rule or on principle often contributes to *overcoming* ignorance, namely people's ignorance of each other's probable behavior. General acceptance of principles contributes to predictability in the world and thus to people's chances of coordinating their activities to their mutual benefit.

As a utilitarian in the tradition of Hume rather than Bentham, Hayek does not envision maximization of some aggregate of numerical measures. He says (1976, pp. 129–130) that the aim in developing or altering rules of just conduct "should be to improve as much as possible the chances of anyone selected at random." He speaks of *chances* rather than *probabilities* "because the latter term suggests numerical magnitudes which will not be known." Equivalently, "the best society would be that in which we would prefer to place our children if we knew that their position in it would be determined by lot" (1976, p. 132; similar passages occur in 1967, p. 163; 1978, pp. 62–63; 1976, p. 114).

Hayek's formulations are similar to those of John C. Harsanyi, an avowed utilitarian, who considers a person contemplating alternative social arrangements in ignorance or at least in disregard of what his personal situation would be. On Harsanyi's theory, that person "would have to choose the social situation yielding him a higher expected utility, which in this case would mean choosing the situation providing a higher *average utility level* to the individual members of the society." (Harsanyi 1976, chap. 5, p. 67; cf. Harsanyi 1955/1973, pp. 276–277. If Harsanyi's method resembles Rawls's 1971 notion of choice behind a veil of ignorance, the similarity goes to show that such a conception of impartiality need not be a distinctively contractarian one, as Rawls seems to think.)

The version of utilitarianism here attributed to Hayek, among others, might also, as already suggested, be called a comparative-institutions or good-society approach. Although Hayek repeatedly emphasizes how spontaneously evolved rules and institutions may serve an order that tends to reduce conflicts and ease cooperation among persons pursuing their own diverse ends, he does not discourage looking critically at those rules and institutions and sometimes deliberately modifying them.

Consciously designing a society from scratch, however, is not a live option. No one knows enough for such an undertaking. Through trial and error and survival of what works, our existing society incorporates much unarticulated knowledge. Throwing that knowledge away merely because of its being unarticulated and therefore unappreciated would be reckless. We should have a certain humility in undertaking reform—so Hayek in effect argues—but not reject all thought of reform.

UTILITARIANISM AND POLITICAL OBLIGATION

The comparative-institutions strand of utilitarianism does not try to ground government and political obligation in contractarian fictions. The notion of consent—tacit consent—may have heuristic value, admittedly; but arguments using it should, if sound, be amenable to translation into straightforward English. In such arguments, tacit consent alludes to considerateness, reciprocity, and self-esteem, all of which are valuable on broadly utilitarian grounds. Most of us believe that we should ordinarily practice the everyday little courtesies toward one another, accepting trivial inconveniences for ourselves to spare others substantial ones. Ordinarily, for example, we do not complain about reasonable noise incidental to useful activity ("reasonable" is admittedly a weasel word here); for we ourselves benefit from a society in which such noise is tolerated. The point is not that we and others have agreed, or are "deemed" to have agreed, to suffer noise. Such a fiction is unnecessary. Rather, each of us refrains from complaining about reasonable noise in the expectation of others' similar forbearance and in the interest of the social cooperation from which we all benefit.

Each of us would be uneasy constantly and belligerently insisting on our "rights," refusing consideration of others at the cost of even the slightest momentary inconvenience, and insisting that others either refrain from activities exerting the slightest adverse externality or else pay compensation. That would be a nerve-wracking way to live. We would be inconsistent in being intolerant and inconsiderate of others while expecting them to be tolerant and considerate of us. Such behavior would emit messages to others about our own character.

For most of us, furthermore, it serves our self-esteem to think of ourselves as consistent, considerate persons who play fair and who support rather than subvert a decent society. Each of us benefits from courtesy and ease in relations with our fellows. It does not serve our self-esteem or interest to undercut that spirit. Thus, we need not interpret tolerant and considerate behavior toward others as compliance with a contract.

Much the same considerations argue for respecting the legitimacy of government and an obligation to obey its laws. The argument also explains why the legitimacy and obligation are not total. Most of us feel obliged to obey a reasonably decent government on the grounds that doing so contributes to our own and our fellows' welfare—in view of the Hobbesian alternative. Consideration of our fellows, which ordinarily serves our self-esteem, requires our not contributing to the subversion of a generally useful institution (which government is, even though a "necessary evil"). Unfairly arrogating special privilege to oneself, picking and choosing which laws to obey, and making exceptions in one's own favor does something toward undermining the legitimacy and authority of a government from which we ourselves derive net advantages. (I distinguish, of course, between a government that is decent on the whole and, on the other hand, a tyrannical one that ought, on the same grounds of concern for ourselves and our fellows, to be overthrown.)

On grounds involving one's own and other persons' happiness as served through social cooperation, then, one can make a case for people's (1) according everyday courtesies to one another, and (2) practicing considerateness and reciprocity in yet another way, through respecting political obligation toward a reasonably decent government.

Much of the following ties in with possible answers to what Brand Blanshard calls the fundamental question of political theory: "Why should I obey the law? An adequate answer to that question would carry with it the answer to such questions as, Why should there be a government at all? What are the grounds of its rights against me and my rights against it and how in principle are those rights to be limited?" (Blanshard 1961, chap. 14, "Reason and Politics," quotation from p. 376).

According to the first theory that Blanshard reviews, political rights and duties are based on nothing. This anarchist view is "doctrinaire idealism of a pathetically irresponsible sort" (1961, p. 378). Second is the doctrine that might makes right; it sets ethics aside. The third appeals to divine authority, the fourth, the doctrine of Hobbes and Rousseau, to a social contract.

Contractarianism begs the question, Blanshard explains. If, before entering into the social contract, I do not have an obligation to keep contracts, then the social contract to keep future contracts is not binding, nor are future contracts supposedly made under it. But if I do have an obligation in the first place to keep contracts or to honor certain other duties, then the theory is superfluous.

Fifth is the doctrine of the Declaration of Independence: the self-evident truths that men have certain unalienable rights, that governments are instituted to secure these rights, and that if a government becomes destructive of them, the people have the right to alter or abolish it. This doctrine, says Blanshard, comes close to the correct one. He does not deny the existence of natural rights resting on no government and no convention and identifiable by reason, but he doubts that the doctrine of self-evidence states their true ground. Natural rights can break down: cases are conceivable in which the community can legitimately exercise coercion. All sorts of rights would be desirable—here I am embroidering on Blanshard a bit—if recognizing them did not cost too much in various ways. Now, considering costs means going beyond what is supposedly self-evident.

Sixth comes Blanshard's doctrine of "rational will":

that men have a common moral end which is the object of their rational will, that the state is a contrivance that they have worked out [that has evolved, Hayek would probably say] to help them realize that end, and that its authority over them rests on its being necessary for that end. If it is politically obligatory at times to obey a law that one regards as bad, that is because the state could not be run at all if the citizens could pick and choose which laws they would obey. Ultimately, therefore, political obligation, even that of obeying a morally bad law, *is* a moral obligation; and when, as occasionally happens, it become [sic] a duty to disobey, the ground is still the same. (1961, p. 395)

Four propositions elaborate this doctrine:

First we can distinguish within our own minds between the end of our actual or immediate will, and the end of our rational will, which is what on reflection would commend itself as the greatest good. Secondly, this rational end is the same for all men. Thirdly, this end, because a common end, is the basis of our rights against each other. Fourthly, the justification of the state, and its true office, lie in furthering the realization of this end.... [T]he theory of a rational will provides a natural and intelligible ground both for obedience in normal cases and for disobedience in abnormal cases. (pp. 395, 402)

Briefly interpreted, Blanshard's rational-will doctrine says that the obligation to support government is binding because—and to the extent that—it serves social cooperation. The obligation to support rather than subvert social cooperation rests, in turn, on ordinary ethical precepts. (I do not maintain, however, that Blanshard would himself accept the utilitarian label.)

We have no need for contractarian fictions. I might well obey the laws of an absolute monarchy, and even consider such obedience in the general interest and morally obligatory, while disapproving of that government's nondemocratic character and of some of its actions.

A UTILITARIAN CONCEPTION OF GOVERNMENT

A restatement is worth attempting. We go along with the existing form of government and generally obey its laws because, first, we have no real alternative. For an individual, revolt would be fruitless and moving abroad too

Chapter 28: Rights, Contract, and Utility in Policy Espousal

costly. (Besides, where would we go?) We individuals have not agreed even to having a government at all, much less to the particular constitution in force. We have not even been asked whether we agree (and asking us now would be a mockery). Rather, we of the current generation find ourselves living under a form of government and under laws that have evolved over time without our individually having had any effective say. Government and laws are *not* primarily results of an organized and deliberate process of collective decisionmaking, certainly not of one in which we the living have taken decisive part.

A second reason for acquiescence is that we find the existing system preferable to general lawlessness. Peace and security and a stable legal framework serve social cooperation and thus happiness. We individuals benefit from others' abiding by the law and feel that we in turn should do the same. We feel that it would be morally wrong to make exceptions in our own favor at others' expense. In self-defense we apply force against criminals who flout such of the moral code as has been reinforced by law.

The most—which is perhaps too much—that can be said for a social-contract theory is that most of us abide by the law and refrain from unconstitutional subversion of existing government in expectation or in consideration of others' doing the same. But this very nebulous contract, if it is a contract at all, is of the same sort as the one in accordance with which we generally observe ordinary ethical precepts. We ordinarily show some consideration for other people and their rights because we expect them to show similar consideration for us and because behaving with this consistency and decency serves our own self-esteem. Considerateness for each other yields gains from trade.

It would really be reaching, however, to interpret this sort of implicit trading as a social contract, and particularly as a contract whereby each of us has consented to the existing constitution and is thus deemed to have consented to government decisions made in accordance with the constitution. It is an exaggeration to call the government's laws and actions the result of collective decisionmaking in any literal sense. Let's face it: government decisions are made by government officials (and the composite of those decisions undergoes some unintended drift over time); we ordinary citizens are not the government.

Under democracy, it is true, we have some influence on those decisions through voting, through helping shape public opinion, and thus through influencing what decisions public officials will consider in their own interest. But our control over government is less precise and effective than our control over economic activity through our "voting in the marketplace." Some analogy does hold between political and economic decisions, but we should not delude ourselves about how closely it holds.

Is the state a product of its citizens' voluntary consent, a mechanism voluntarily established to attend to their common concerns? Nonsense. I have no choice about being subjected to its laws. True enough, I am glad that the state exists; I prefer it to anarchy; but the state is there whether I want it or not. My welcoming certain arrangements does not mean that they are not compulsory. I am glad to have seat belts in my car and would probably have bought them willingly if I had had a free choice, but the fact remains that I did not have a free choice and that the belts were installed under compulsion of law.

Far from the state's being a voluntary arrangement, then, its essence is compulsion. It relies as a last resort on its power to seize goods and persons, to imprison, and to execute. If obedience to government is not compulsory, then what is? What does the word "compulsory" mean? What happens to the distinction between the voluntary and the compulsory?

To say this is not to glorify the compulsory aspects of government. I concede their necessity only with regret. I want to keep them tightly restrained, as the cause of human liberty requires. One serves that cause poorly if one deludes oneself into thinking that government embodies free exchange and that compliance with its orders is voluntary. Hard-headedness or tough-mindedness better serves one's values.

While libertarians want to extend the voluntary aspects of society and government, they should not delude themselves about reality and the human condition. Society and government are not and cannot be the results of a social contract. Their justification rests on other considerations.

The key element in the case for democracy, as I see it, is that democracy lessens the necessity or desirability of violent rebellion. It makes the alternative, discussion, relevant. If a policy or a law really is oppressively bad, citizens and their political representatives may come to understand why and may change it peacefully. This case for democracy is a far cry from asserting that all decisions made under democratic government are therefore made in accordance with each citizen's will, or his real will, or are to be "considered" as having been so made. We need not appeal to any fiction about unanimous constitution agreement to waive unanimous agreement on specific issues.

TACIT UTILITARIANISM AMONG RIGHTS THEORISTS

Even several rights theorists who disavow utilitarianism do tacitly employ a version similar to the one recommended in this paper. I ask them to conduct a mental experiment. Suppose, just for the sake of argument, it could be demonstrated that insistence on the inviolability of human rights as they conceive of them would lead to general misery, whereas a pragmatic policy of respecting rights or not as conditions seemed to recommend would lead to general happiness. Would those theorists still insist on the inviolability of rights as the supreme goal to be upheld even at the cost of prevalent human misery?

Perhaps they would reply that this is a preposterous supposition and that respect for rights promotes human fulfillment and happiness, whereas a pragmatic attitude toward rights is an obstacle. Well, I think so too. But unless the rights advocates do answer "yes" to the question, insisting on rights even at the cost of general misery, they are taking a broadly utilitarian stance. If they answer as I think they must, they are insisting on rights because of the good consequences of upholding them and the bad consequences of disregarding or overriding them. At the back of their minds, at least, they must have some notion of a workable social order as an indispensable means to happiness.

Why do I care about the word "utilitarian"? Why am I anxious to pin that label onto everyone? Well, I do not care about the word as such. (And I do distinguish between versions of utilitarianism, although I do not find the supposed distinction between utilitarianism and consequentialism of much importance.) However, when a doctrine that plausibly and in accord with established usage bears the label "utilitarian" comes under attack, it serves clear thinking and communication to defend that doctrine under its own name rather than cast about for a new one. Playing the latter game is like trying to defend capitalism by inventing a new name for it. The game seems to admit that the doctrine or system defended really is so odious that it must be referred to only by euphemisms.

Robert Nozick, who avowedly just postulates rights without developing an argument for them, provides an example of tacit utilitarianism in the way he handles the question of blackmail. Murray Rothbard, another rights theorist, had put blackmail on a par with any other economic transaction; it would not be illegal in a free society (1962, vol. 1: p. 443 n. 49). Nozick counters that blackmail is wrong, akin to the protection racket. He takes a step toward assessing its effect on the character of society by noting that it, like the racket, is an unproductive activity, whereas bona fide protective services are productive (Nozick 1974, pp. 85–86). (Rothbard 1977, pp. 53–55, rejects Nozick's distinction, but with arguments that strike me as feeble, even though they too are in part, unavowedly, utilitarian.)

Tacit utilitarianism creeps into the discussion of risky activities also. Suppose that your neighbor handles explosives recklessly or plays Russian roulette with a cannon mounted on a turntable. Even if he has liability insurance, he harms you, probably by raising your own insurance rates, lowering the value of your property, and striking fear and apprehension into you. You might plausibly argue that your neighbor is infringing on your rights, even though no explosion or cannon ball happens to damage your house. Rothbard appears to brush aside such problems by asking, in effect: If "fear" of others' "risky" activities is allowed to justify action against them, won't *any* tyranny become justified? What about the greater risk of having a state empowered to control activities it deems risky? (Rothbard 1977, esp. pp. 48–50. The particular example used here is mine, not Rothbard's or Nozick's, but it suits the general tenor of their discussion.)

Nozick (1974, pp. 74–75, 78), on the other hand, candidly recognizes that "Actions that risk crossing another's boundary pose serious problems for a natural-rights position.... Imposing how slight a probability of a harm that violates someone's rights also violates his rights?... It is difficult to imagine a principled way in which the natural-rights tradition can draw the line to fix which probabilities impose unacceptably great risks upon others." Many kinds of actions do impose some degree of risk on others. A society that prohibited them all unless the actors had adequate means or adequate insurance to pay for possible harm would "ill fit a picture of a free society as one embodying a presumption in favor of liberty, under which people permissibly could perform actions so long as they didn't harm others in specified ways."—Again, the good-society approach, utilitarianism!

Other utilitarian strands are evident in Nozick's book. His flexibility about property rights is an example. He supposes that a natural disaster destroys the entire supply of water except one man's, which is sufficient for everyone. Under these circumstances, other persons may take the water or at least are not obliged to pay whatever exorbitant price its owner may demand. Nozick appeals to the Lockean proviso that one man's appropriation of a resource is justified only if it leaves enough and as good of that resource for others. He is not, in his own view, saying that recognized property rights may be overridden. Instead, "Considerations internal to the theory of property itself, to its theory of acquisition and appropriation, provide the means for handling such cases" (1974, pp. 180–181). Nozick adds another example: "Similarly, an owner's property right in the only island in an area does not allow him to order a castaway from a shipwreck off his island as a trespasser, for this would violate the Lockean proviso."

It is mere word play, however, to wonder whether rights are overridden or are defined in the first place to be appropriate even for the catastrophe case. Nozick misapplies the Lockean proviso anyway, since it concerns someone's original acquisition of property, not its retention in the face of changed circumstances of other persons (Hodson 1977, esp. pp. 221, 224–227).

Nozick tacitly appeals to utilitarian considerations in framing his conception of property rights in a sufficiently complicated and flexible way to allow the actions that intuition and utility would suggest in the catastrophe case. He would have us permit acts that threaten to cross our boundaries—loosely speaking, violate our property rights—when certain conditions are satisfied, including those of the case in which the benefits in harm prevented or good produced far outweigh the costs of fully compensating the person whose boundaries are crossed (Rabinowitz 1977, p. 93). Lawrence A. Scaff (1977, p. 202) looks behind Nozick's assertion that moral theory has priority in political discussions and finds his language of moral theory consisting of "economic terms, calculations, categories, and assumptions. Moral discourse is suffused with cost-benefit analysis. Thus, even in the realm of morality, all values carry a price tag."

Nozick (p. 79) adduces similar considerations in recommending cost-benefit analysis and the test of compensation (actual or merely potential?) in decisions on which polluting activities to forbid and which to permit. He recognizes (p. 182) that he cannot derive a definite position on patents from considerations of rights alone. Although a patent does not deprive others of what would not exist if not for the inventor's work, knowledge of the patented invention does tend to discourage independent efforts to reinvent it. "Yet ... in the absence of the original invention, sometime later someone else would have come up with it. This suggests placing a time limit on patents, as a rough rule of thumb to approximate how long it would have taken, in the absence of knowledge of the invention, for independent discovery."

Tibor Machan, avowedly a rights theorist, is another tacit utilitarian. Instead of simply postulating or intuiting rights, he inquires into the political principles of a good society—good for man's pursuit of happiness or perhaps excellence, given his nature and his character as a moral agent.

Machan seeks to demonstrate that since "each person is responsible to achieve his own happiness, that society that is suited for him is one in which his individual liberty is fully secured.... [I]t is only in such a free society that the moral agency, the freedom and the dignity, of each person can be respected. Thus only in that kind of community can the moral life flourish" (1975, p. 100).

Machan asks why someone who has the option of either taking from another person or producing and trading on his own should support the institution of private property. He suggests essentially utilitarian answers, reasons why respecting the institution of ownership is generally advantageous even for the person in question. He concludes "that ownership is a morally appropriate institution for human beings in general.... [T]o rely on *his* own work (and/or trade, creativity, ingenuity, etc.) is better for the person than to live off the work of others" by stealing or confiscating (pp. 133–134). Finally, Machan's approving characterization of Ayn Rand's doctrine is tacitly utilitarian. Rand, he says, defends "capitalism as morally right because human beings can work (trade, create, risk) for their own good only when and where it prevails." She advocates it as "a system that is good for human beings, morally good for them, to choose for themselves" (Machan 1975, p. 136).

Even Murray Rothbard has at least once (1973, pp. 23–25) lapsed into a tacit utilitarianism, seeing it as "vitally necessary for each man's survival and prosperity that he be free to learn, choose, develop his faculties, and act upon his knowledge and values.... [T]o interfere with and cripple this process by using violence goes profoundly against what is necessary by man's nature for his life and prosperity."

TACIT UTILITARIANISM AMONG CONTRACTARIANS

In the contractarian camp, John Rawls in effect says we should ask: "If a group of ideally rational beings came together in order to pick rules to govern their mutual relations, which rules would they be compelled (by the power of their rationality) to pick?" (restatement by Murphy 1977, p. 233). Well, what do those beings rationally take into account? Facts of reality and applicable economic and other theories, presumably, together with a value judgment in favor of happiness, especially their own. Rawls assumes that the parties negotiating in the original position already accept a "thin theory of the good," according to which "liberty and opportunity, income and wealth, and above all self-respect are primary goods," goods conducive to happiness for persons almost regardless of their specific personality traits and plans of life. This list of primary goods "is one of the premises from which the choice of the principles of right is derived" (Rawls 1971, pp. 397, 433–434, and passim).

When Rawls considers what principles would help make primary goods available and so serve persons' pursuit of their life plans, he is appealing to broadly utilitarian considerations. The same is true when he rhapsodizes over the benefits of public commitment to avowed principles of justice: "deliberate injustice invites submission or resistance. Submission arouses the contempt of those who perpetuate injustice and confirms their intention, whereas resistance cuts the ties of community" (p. 384). In discussing the problem of envy, Rawls notes the advantages of having a plurality of associations and many noncomparing groups. His "principles of justice are not likely to arouse ... envy ... to a troublesome extent.... What a social system must not do clearly is to encourage propensities and aspirations it is bound to repress and disappoint. So long as the pattern of special psychologies elicited by society either supports its arrangements or can be reasonably accommodated by them, there is no need to reconsider the choice of a conception of justice.... [T]he principles of justice as fairness pass this test" (1971, pp. 536–537, 541; Rawls's discussion of envy covers pp. 530–541). Furthermore, Rawls's whole method of reflective equilibrium—testing tentative principles by how they are likely to work out in practice and adjusting both principles and judgments about particular cases to achieve consistency between them—is a kind of utilitarianism.

Rawls himself rejects this label. He recognizes that the parties in the original position might adopt some form of utility principle in defining the principles of social cooperation. Still, he says, it would be "a mistake to call these principles—and the theory in which they appear—utilitarian. In fact, the case for the principles of justice is strengthened if they would be chosen under different motivation assumptions." Contract theory could eventually lead "to a deeper and more roundabout justification of utilitarianism" (1971, pp. 181–182). In saying so, Rawls is forgetting that his notion of a contract negotiated in an original position is utter fiction.

Buchanan's wing of contractarianism has already been described sufficiently to suggest how it is tacitly utilitarian. According to its tenets, an economist is entitled to recommend a policy only tentatively, only as a hypothesis that it is in accord with a unanimously made contract, or that it conceptually commands agreement, or that it could command agreement, presumably after a sufficient amount of sufficiently enlightening public discussion. Well, on what basis could the economist expect or hope for the necessary degree of agreement? The probable effects of the contemplated policy must surely figure prominently in the answer.

Contractarians like Buchanan distinguish between propounding hypotheses about what policies could ideally command agreement and recommending policies because they are expected to enhance social cooperation and so serve human happiness. The distinction seems operationally empty to me.

CONCLUSION

The pure doctrine of natural or human rights cuts analysis short either by merely postulating rights as axioms or by questionably deriving rights from supposedly axiomatic propositions that in fact require further examination themselves. In truth we cannot infer one infallibly best set of institutions and policies from one or more first principles whose implications are guaranteed never to clash. It is a "great illusion" in political philosophy to seek "solutions to insoluble problems.... [T]here is more than one basic principle that appeals to moral sense and for which good argument can be made.... We live in a morally messy world. But it is the one we are stuck with" (Gordon 1976, p. 589).

Contractarianism rests on farfetched fictions. Or if it does not exactly rest on them, its rhetoric does abound in them; and if it is stripped of its fictions and translated into straightforward language, contractarianism turns out to be not much different from a form of utilitarianism.

We can hardly make progress in social philosophy or policy analysis by adopting *fictions* as our first principles. While wishing to enhance the voluntary and market-like aspects of government, for example, we must not blind ourselves to its essentially coercive character. Instead of beguiling ourselves with attractive myths, we can better serve our fundamental values by trying to compare alternative sets of institutions, alternative big pictures, avoiding excessively narrow and short-run focus. Investigation, analysis, and discussion of the features and probable consequences of contemplated institutions and policies all are indispensable aspects of the search for agreement—assuming, for the sake of argument, that agreement were the touchstone of policy. Actually, agreement itself cannot form the decisively appealing substance of a state of affairs capable of commanding it.

Discussion in search of agreement relies ideally on investigation, reasoning, and checking and comparison—the ordinary scientific process.

This process is poles apart from dictatorship and from appeals to infallible insight. In this process, we can communicate better and guard better against misunderstandings if we employ straightforward language. Conceivably the rights doctrine and contractarianism are not the only alternatives to the approach to policy espousal that I recommend. If so, those other alternatives deserve further investigation and discussion. Meanwhile, I submit, a rules-utilitarianism or indirect utilitarianism—in other words, a good-society/comparative-institutions approach—turns out to be the only one that stands up under critical inspection.

REFERENCES

Adler, Mortimer J. *The Time of Our Lives.* New York: Holt, Rinehart, and Winston, 1970.

Alexander, Sidney S. "Human Values and Economists' Values." In *Human Values and Economic Policy*, edited by Sidney Hook. New York: New York University Press, 1967.

Bentham, Jeremy. "A Critical Examination of the Declaration of Rights." 1843. In *Bentham's Political Thought*, edited by Bhikhu Parekh, 257–290. New York: Barnes & Noble, 1973.

Blanshard, Brand. *Reason and Goodness.* New York: Macmillan, 1961.

Broome, John. "Choice and Value in Economics." *Oxford Economic Papers*, n.s. 30 (November 1978): 313–333.

Buchanan, James M. "Who Should Distribute What in a Federal System?" In *Redistribution Through Public Choice*, edited by H. Hochman and G. Peterson. New York: Columbia University Press, 1974.

———. *The Limits of Liberty.* Chicago: University of Chicago Press, 1975a.

———. "Utopia, the Minimal State, and Entitlement." Review of *Anarchy, State, and Utopia*, by Robert Nozick. *Public Choice* 23 (Fall 1975b): 121–126.

———. *Freedom in Constitutional Contract.* College Station: Texas A&M University Press, 1977.

———. "Sources of Opposition to Constitutional Reform." In *Constitutional Economics*, edited by Richard B. McKenzie. Lexington, Mass.: Lexington Books, 1984.

———. "Natural and Artifactual Man." Manuscript.

———. "Why Does Justice Have Value?" Manuscript.

Buchanan, James M., and Gordon Tullock. *The Calculus of Consent*. Ann Arbor: University of Michigan Press, 1962.

Davis, Harry B. "Toward Justifying Democracy." *The Key Reporter* 33 (Winter 1967–1968): 2–4, 8.

Edgeworth, Francis Y. *Mathematical Psychics*. London: Kegan Paul, 1881. Photo reprint, New York: Kelley, 1961.

Edwards, Paul. *The Logic of Moral Discourse*. New York: Free Press, 1965.

Fletcher, Joseph. *Situation Ethics*. 1st British ed. London: SCM Press, 1966.

Gewirth, Alan. *Reason and Morality*. Chicago: University of Chicago Press, 1978.

Gordon, Scott. "The New Contractarians." *Journal of Political Economy* 84 (June 1976): 573–590.

Gray, John N. "Social Contract, Community and Ideology." In *Democracy, Consensus & Social Contract*, edited by Pierre Birnbaum, Jack Lively, and Geraint Parry. London and Beverly Hills: Sage Publications, 1978.

———. *Mill on Liberty: A Defense*. London and Boston: Routledge & Kegan Paul, 1983.

Grinder, Walter. "Cross Currents." *Libertarian Review* (May 1978): 9–10.

Halévy, Élie. *The Growth of Philosophic Radicalism*. Translated by Mary Morris. Boston: Beacon Press, 1955.

Hare, R.M. "Rawls' Theory of Justice." In *Reading Rawls*, edited by Norman Daniels. New York: Basic Books, n.d. (circa 1974).

Harsanyi, John C. "Cardinal Welfare, Individualistic Ethics and Interpersonal Comparisons of Utility." 1955. In *Economic Justice*, edited by E.S. Phelps, 266–285. Baltimore: Penguin Books, 1973.

———. *Essays on Ethics, Social Behavior, and Scientific Explanation*. Dordrecht and Boston: D. Reidel Publishing Company, 1976.

Hayek, Friedrich A. *The Constitution of Liberty*. Chicago: University of Chicago Press, 1960.

———. *Studies in Philosophy, Politics and Economics*. Chicago: University of Chicago Press, 1967.

Chapter 28: Rights, Contract, and Utility in Policy Espousal 513

———. *Freiburger Studien.* Tübingen: Mohr, 1969.

———. *New Studies in Philosophy, Politics, Economics, and the History of Ideas.* Chicago: University of Chicago Press, 1978.

———. *Law, Legislation and Liberty.* Vols. 1–3. Chicago: University of Chicago Press, 1976.

Hazlitt, Henry. *The Foundations of Morality.* Princeton, N.J.: D. Van Nostrand, 1964.

———. "An LR Interview." *Libertarian Review* (November 1978): 22–23.

Hobbes, Thomas. *Leviathan.* 1651. In *Great Books of the Western World,* vol. 23. Chicago: Encyclopaedia Britannica, 1952.

Hodson, John D. "Nozick, Libertarianism, and Rights." *Arizona Law Review* 19, no. 1 (1977): 212–227.

Holcombe, Randall G. *Public Finance and the Political Process.* Carbondale and Edwardsville: Southern Illinois University Press, 1983.

Hume, David. "Of the Original Contract." 1752. In *Hume's Ethical Writings,* edited by A. MacIntyre. New York: Collier Books, 1965.

Kemp, J. *Ethical Naturalism: Hobbes and Hume.* London: Macmillan, 1970.

Machan, Tibor. *Human Rights and Human Liberties.* Chicago: Nelson Hall, 1975.

Mack, Erie. "An Outline of a Theory of Rights." Manuscript, 1978.

McCloskey, H.J. *Meta-Ethics and Normative Ethics.* The Hague: Martinus Nijhoff, 1969.

Meyer, Frank S. *In Defense of Freedom.* Chicago: Regnery, 1962.

Mill, John Stuart. *Utilitarianism.* 1863. In *Selected Writings,* edited by M. Cowling. New York: New American Library, 1968.

Mises, Ludwig von. *Human Action.* New Haven, Conn.: Yale University Press, 1949.

———. *Theory and History.* New Haven, Conn.: Yale University Press, 1957.

Murphy, Jeffrie C. "Rights and Borderline Cases." *Arizona Law Review* 19, no. 1 (1977): 228–241.

Nozick, Robert. *Anarchy, State, and Utopia.* New York: Basic Books, 1974.

Paul, Jeffrey. "On the Foundations of Natural Rights." Manuscript, 1978.

Peirce, Charles S. "The Scientific Attitude and Fallibilism." In *Philosophical Writings of Peirce*, edited by Justus Buchler, 42–59. New York: Dover, 1955.

Pettit, Philip. *Judging Justice*. London and Boston: Routledge & Kegan Paul, 1980.

Philbrook, Clarence. "'Realism' in Policy Espousal." *American Economic Review* 43 (December 1953): 846–859.

Prescott, Peter S. Review of *Theophilus North*, by Thornton Wilder. *Newsweek*, 22 October 1973.

Rabinowitz, Joshua T. "Emergent Problems and Optimal Solutions." *Arizona Law Review* 19, no. 1 (1977): 61–157.

Rawls, John. "Two Concepts of Rules." 1955. In *Contemporary Utilitarianism*, edited by M.D. Bayles, 59–98. Garden City: Anchor Books, 1968.

———. *A Theory of Justice*. Cambridge, Mass.: Belknap Press of Harvard University Press, 1971.

Rothbard, Murray. *Man, Economy, and State*. 2 vols. Princeton, N.J.: D. Van Nostrand, 1962.

———. *For a New Liberty*. New York: Macmillan, 1973.

———. "Robert Nozick and the Immaculate Conception of the State." *Journal of Libertarian Studies* 1 (Winter 1977).

———. *The Ethics of Liberty*. Atlantic Highlands, N.J.: Humanities Press, 1982.

Samuels, Warren J. "The Myths of Liberty and the Realities of the Corporate State: A Review Article." *Journal of Economic Issues* 10 (December 1976): 923–942.

Scaff, Lawrence A. "How Not to Do Political Theory: Nozick's Apology for the Minimal State." *Arizona Law Review* 19, no. 1 (1977): 193–211.

Schumpeter, Joseph A. *History of Economic Analysis*. New York: Oxford University Press, 1954.

Sen, Amartya K. *Collective Choice and Social Welfare*. San Francisco: Holden-Day, 1970.

Spencer, Herbert. *The Principles of Ethics*. 1897. 2 vols. Indianapolis: Liberty Classics, 1978.

Vanberg, Viktor. "Liberty, Efficiency and Agreement: The Normative Element in Libertarian and Contractarian Social Philosophy." Manuscript, George Mason University, n.d. (circa 1984 or 1985).

Wiener, Philip P. "Charles Sanders Peirce." In *International Encyclopedia of the Social Sciences*, vol. 11: 511–513. New York: Macmillan, 1968.

Yeager, Leland B. "Pareto Optimality in Policy Espousal." *Journal of Libertarian Studies* 2 (Fall 1978): 199–216.

———. "Utility, Rights, and Contract: Some Reflections on Hayek's Work." In *The Political Economy of Freedom: Essays in Honor of F. A. Hayek*, edited by Kurt B. Leube and Albert H. Zlabinger. Munich and Vienna: Philosophia Verlag, 1984–1985.

Index

A

Abortion issue, example of special interests, 330
Absorption approach, balance-of-payments, 276
Academic game
  economics, 251–254
  methodology and rigor, 233
Activism. *See also* Regulation
  and democracy, 329
  hobbyists, 331
  judicial activism, 336
Alexander, Sidney S., elasticities, 276
Allais, Maurice
  academic incentives and games, 252
  changes in tastes, taxes or policies, 215, 216
  inflation, 220
  land: diversion and willingness to wait, 212–214
  savers and money, 219
Allocation effects, inflation, 220
America. *See* United States of America
Anarcho-capitalist-Lockean rights, 457
Anderson, Benjamin M., gold standard, 202
Appropriation. *See* Entitlements; Social justice; Taxation
Armchair theorizing, George, 65
Arts, public funding of, 324

Austria, gold standard, 191, 195
Austrian School of Economics, 100–115
  attention to process, 137
  business cycle, 149
  complementary schools, 113
  coordination, 131
  criticisms of, 103–105
  George, 51–53, 54
  macroeconomics, 152
  marketplace of ideas, 107–113
  neoclassical economics, 105–107
  strengths, 100–103
Authoritarianism, relativism, fallibilism, 486–488
Axioms
  rights, 481
  Rothbard: rights, 430–435

B

Balance-of-payments, tautology, 274–277
Bartley, William Warren, III, justificationism, 235
Bellamy, Edward, uchronia, 389
Biology, tautologies, 271
Blackmail, Rothbard: property rights, 434
Blanshard, Brand, political rights and duties, 501
Block, Walter, morality and law, 435–439
Bohr, Niels, principle of complementarity, 275

Booms. *See* Business cycle
Boyle, Joseph M., determinism: self-referential problem of, 297
Britain, Hutt on postwar Britain, 179
Brockway, George, Keynes, 161
Broome, John, contractarianism, 483
Brown, E.H. Phelps, general equilibrium theory equation systems, 14
Buchanan, James
  academic incentives and games, 251–254
  contractarianism, 482, 509
  neoclassical economics, 106
  social contract, 488–490
  truth judgment, 485
Budget constraints
  limits on government expenditures, 343
  as tautologies, 273
Bureaucracy
  and government regulation, 335
  political economy, 317
Business cycle
  econometrics, 241
  macroeconomics, 138–142, 149
  money: Hutt, 181

C

Cagan, Philip, money: econometrics, 242
Calculation
  knowledge, 93–99
  Mises and Hayek, 131
  socialism, 86
Campbell, C.A., descriptive and prescriptive laws, 285
Capital
  capital formation: money and, 217–222
  and interest theory: subjectivism, 36–38
  land and international capital movements, 211
  macroeconomics, 149
  willingness to wait, 212
Capital-import-and-export arguments for trade intervention, general equilibrium theory, 12
Capitalism, Kirzner: morality of capitalism and profit, 407–421
Cassel, Gustav
  general equilibrium theory equation systems, 13
  subjectivism, 46
Causality
  determinism, 291
  general equilibrium theory, 10
Chamberlin, T.C., competing hypotheses, 246
Chance, ethics, 292–295
Churchill, Winston, on voters and democracy, 376
Citation indexes, measuring academic excellence, 111, 119
Classical school. *See also* New Classical school
Classification, tautologies, 271
Clower, Robert
  coordination, 130
  on general equilibrium theory, 4
  Keynes, 159, 177, 180
  methodology, 232
Coase-Buchanan concept of cost, 42
Coase, R.H., pricing and socialism, 78
Cognitive dissonance, 354
Collateral effects, general equilibrium theory, 12
Collectibles, 217
Comparable worth fallacy, subjectivism, 25
Competing hypotheses, methodology, 246–248
Complementarily, principle of, 275

Complexity
    ethics, 289–292
    general equilibrium theory, 7
Concepts, role in economics, 349
Constitutional monarchy, versus democracy, 375–387
Consumers
    consumer-surplus: general equilibrium theory, 11
    consumers' sovereignty: subjectivism, 29
    knowledge and coordination, 28
Contagion. See Business cycle
Contractarianism
    about, 482–485
    fictions, 488–490
    tacit utilitarianism, 508–510
Contracts, utilitarianism: rights, contract and utility in policy espousal, 477–515
Conventions, science, 268
Cooperation, political economy, 309–311
Coordination
    George, 59–62
    intertemporal, 145
    macroeconomics, 130–134
    and subjectivism, 27–30
Costs. See also Opportunity cost
    Coase-Buchanan concept of, 42
    general equilibrium theory, 7
    of government regulation, 342
Courts. See Judicial process
Credit, and money, 144
Credit-allocation, subjectivism, 26
Credit-default swaps, 141
Crowding out, government regulation and, 339–341
Crypticism, subjectivism, 41
Custom unions, trade, 213
Customer service, Klein: how to ensure hotel reservations are honored, 353

D

Darrow, Clarence, determinism as fatalism, 289
Davenport, H.J., monetary of depression, 164
Decentralization, Austrian Economics, 101
Decreasing-cost, general equilibrium theory, 11
Deficit financing, subjectivism, 33
Democracy. See also United States of America
    and liberty, 312–314
    process, 318
    versus constitutional monarchy, 375–387
Democratic markets, Witmann, 367–374
Dependence effect, Galbraith, 300
Descriptive and prescriptive laws, 285
Determinism
    about, 283
    extreme positions and partial determinism, 299–302
    irrefutability of, 297–299
    Schlick, 284–286
    self-referential problem of, 297
Discrimination argument, redistribution, 469
Disequilibrium
    methodology, 230
    monetary theory, 129, 144, 163
    theories: Hutt, 176–178
Diversion, land and willingness to wait, 211–214
Draft, military draft and subjectivism, 24
Duhem, Pierre, models, 238
Dynamic subjectivism, Lachmann, 45
Dynasties. See Constitutional monarchy

E

Econometrics, methodology, 241–245
Economics
  and principles, 349–360
  tautologies, 272–274
Economies-of-scale, general equilibrium theory, 11
Efficiency
  socialism, 72–92
  subjectivism, 27
Egalitarianism, and liberalism, 462–476
Ehrenhalt, Alan, U.S. political system, 361–366
Elasticities, balance-of-payments and exchange rates, 276
Endogeneity, money, 243
Energy crisis of 1974 and 1979, subjectivism and, 22
Energy industry, example of crowding out, 340
Enthoven, Alain, general equilibrium theory equation systems, 15
Entitlements, Kirzner, 408–416
Entrepreneurship
  Austrian Economics on, 105
  Kirzner: morality of capitalism and profit, 407–421
Equation of exchange, 265–268
Equation systems
  equilibrium and socialism, 75–77
  general equilibrium theory, 13–16
Equilibrium. *See also* Disequilibrium; General equilibrium theory
  Keynes, 160, 165
  methodology, 229, 231
  neoclassical economics, 105
  simultaneous equations and socialism, 75–77
Ersatz standards, 118–121
Essentialism, about, 283

Ethics, 283–306
  chance, 292–295
  complexity, 289–292
  determinism, 288, 297–302
  ethical judgments and determinism: Slote, 287
  free will, 286–288, 295–297
  Kirzner: morality of capitalism and profit, 407–421
  Mises: ethics, rights and law, 422–442
  political economy, 308
  Rothbard and Block: ethics and law, 435–439
  Schlick on, 284–286
Euken, Walter, theory, 238
Exchange rates
  elasticities, 276
  fluctuating, 198
Expectations, subjectivism, 32, 34, 35
Exports, versus imports, 21
External-economy arguments for protection, general equilibrium theory, 12
Extortion, Rothbard: property rights, 433

F

Fallacy-mongering, methodology, 248–350
Fallibilism, authoritarianism, relativism, 486–488
Fatalism, determinism as, 288
Fluctuating exchange rates, 198
Fragmentation
  government regulation, 322
  policy drift and government regulation, 338
France, alternative histories, 392
Frank, Robert, intersection of economics, psychology and ethics, 237
Free will
  about, 283

determinism and free will:
  Schlick, 284–286
  ethics, 295–297
Freedom. *See also* Liberty
  Hayek, 397–406
Fry, Maxwell J., land: changes in tastes, taxes or policies, 216
Fundamentalist Keynesianism
  about, 128
  savings, investment and money, 146

G

Galbraith, J.K., dependence effect, 300
General equilibrium theory, 3–18. *See also* Equilibrium
  about, 3
  arguments in favor, 6–9
  criticism, 4–6
  equation systems, 13–16
  fallacies clarified by, 9–13
  Mises, 137
  Walras's Law, 265
General Theory (Keynes), 160–163, 167, 174
Generic Consistency, Principle of, 480
George, Henry, 51–71
  Austrian School of economics, 51–53
  independence of, 54
  knowledge, coordination and unplanned order, 59–62
  methodology, 64–66
  social philosophy, 66–69
  socialism, 63
  value theory, 55–58
Germany, alternative histories, 393
Gerwirth, Alan, Principle of Generic Consistency, 480
Giere, Ronald, models, 239
Glazer, Nathan, judicial activism, 336

Gold standard, 191–208
  appeal of, 201–203
  arguments pro and con, 192–196
  attitudes, 204–206
  climates of opinion, 196–198
  Hutt, 184
  noneconomic motives, 198–201
Government. *See also* Deficit financing; Policy; Regulation
  budget constraints, 273
  growth of, 319
  Hutt, 178
  utilitarian conception of, 502–504
Granger-causality tests, 243
Great Britain, alternative histories, 395
Grinder, Walter, utilitarianism, 491
Grisez, Germain, determinism: self-referential problem of, 297

H

Halmos, Paul, writing style, 256
Hansen, Gary D., business cycle: econometrics, 242
Hardin, Garrett, information glut, 252
Hayek, F.A.
  business cycle, 149
  calculation, 93, 97, 131
  cooperation and reciprocation, 310
  dependence effect: Galbraith, 300
  free-market values, 415
  money, 143
  social justice, 414
  on socialism and freedom, 397–406
  subjectivism, 28
  utilitarianism, 498
Hazlitt, Henry
  determinism and free will, 284–286

ethics in *Human Action*, 445
free will and responsibility,
  286–288
natural rights, 482
Health and safety, government
  regulations, 341
High, Jack, on general equilibrium
  theory, 4
History. *See* Narratives
Hobart, R.E., extreme positions and
  partial determinism, 299
Hobbes, Thomas, government and
  public policy, 311
Hobbyists, government regulation
  and, 331
Hoppe, Hans-Hermann, libertarianism and utilitarian ethics,
  456
Hotel reservations, Klein: how to
  ensure hotel reservations are
  honored, 353
Hotelling-Lerner pricing, socialism,
  79
Huerta de Soto, Jésus, on general
  equilibrium theory, 4
Human Action (Mises), 443–461
Human capital, subjectivism, 25
Hume, David, government and
  public policy, 311
Hungary, gold standard, 193, 195,
  196–201
Hutt, William H., 173–190
  disequilibrium theories, 176–178
  enduring value of message, 187
  Keynes: demand theory, 174
  Keynes: selling ideas, 186
  market processes, 178
  micro orientation, 174
  money, 180–184
  style of argument, 184–186
Hypotheses, competing, 246–248

I

Identification problem, general
  equilibrium theory, 10
Imports, versus exports, 21
Incentives, for protesting poor
  injustices and poor customer
  service, 354
Income distribution, marginal-productivity theory: George,
  57
Incomes, general equilibrium theory,
  7
Individualism, government regulation and methodological
  individualism, 325
Inflation, Allais: allocation effects,
  220
Insider information, Kirner, 412
Institutions
  Austrian Economics and, 101
  macroeconomics, 150
  monetary system, 147
  prices, 135
  social cooperation, 496–499
Interdependence, general equilibrium theory, 6
Interest
  capital theory: subjectivism,
    36–38
  willingness to wait, 212
Interventionism. *See also* Regulation
  psychological roots of, 329
Intuitionism
  Kirzner and Hayek on, 416
  Mises, 458
Investment, macroeconomics,
  146–149
Ireland, Peter N., models, 236

J

Jobs, rationing and subjectivism, 25
Judicial process
  and government regulation,
    335–338

Mises: ethics, rights and law, 422–442
Rothbard: axioms, rights and natural law, 430–435
and voluntary economic behavior, 350
Justificationism, Bartley, 235

K
Kant, Immanuel, free will and the laws of nature, 283
Keynes, John Maynard, 157–172
 appraisal, 168
 crowding out other intellectual developments, 158
 Hutt on, 173–190
 investment, 149
 a Keynesian?, 160–163
 lasting appeal, 167
 lingering Keynesianism, 164
 a monetarist?, 163
 overreaction and label-shifting, 165–167
 reinterpretation of, 159
 the salesman, 157
Keynesianism. *See also* Fundamentalist Keynesianism; New Keynesian school
 about, 128
King, Robert G., attitudes and pressures in macroeconomics, 251
Kings. *See* Constitutional monarchy
Kirzner, Israel, on morality of capitalism and profit, 407–421, 443
Klein, David, how to ensure good customer service, 353
Knight, Frank H., redistribution, 464
Knowledge
 calculation, 93–99
 George, 59–62
 and subjectivism, 27–30

Krugman, Paul, methodology, 232

L
Laband, David, market test of ideas, 116–126
Lachmann, Ludwig, dynamic subjectivism, 45
Land, 209–219
 changes in tastes or policies, 214–217
 diversion and willingness to wait, 211–214
 George: rent, 58
 international capital movements, 211
 ownership of, 209–211, 223
Landesberger, Julius, gold standard, 194
Lange-Taylor solution, socialism, 81
Laws. *See* Judicial process
Leadership, U.S. political system, 361–366
Leijonhufvud, Axel, Keynes, 159, 177, 180
Lerner, Abba P.
 money and price stickiness, 136
 socialism, 83
Liberalism
 attitudes to gold standard, 204
 and egalitarianism, 462–476
Libertarians
 constitutional monarchy versus democracy, 375–387
 Hoppe and utilitarian ethics, 456
 utilitarian conception of, 504
Liberty. *See also* Freedom
 coexistence with democracy, 377
 and democracy, 312–314
Liquidity preference
 Hutt, 176
 Keynes, 161
Loan guarantees, general equilibrium theory, 12
Lucas Project, 232

Lucas, Robert E., Jr., models, 231
Lucas supply function, 229

M

Machan, Tibor, utilitarianism, 507
Macroeconomics, 128–156
 about, 128–130
 appraisal and opportunities, 151–153
 attitudes and pressures, 250
 business cycle, 138–142, 149
 capital and interest, 149
 coordination, 130–134
 credit and money, 144
 imperfections of reality, 134–136
 institutions, 150
 macroeconomic disorder: Hutt, 182
 methodology, 229–232
 monetary disorder, 142–144
 money and price stickiness, 136–138
 savings, investment and money, 146–149
 time element, 145
Marginal-cost-pricing
 general equilibrium theory, 11
 socialism, 78, 79
Marginal-productivity theory of functional income distribution, George, 57
Market value, for property seized under eminent domain: subjectivism, 25
Marketplace of ideas, 116–127
 about, 116
 Austrian School of Economics, 107–113
 influence of Laband-and-Tollison-type thinking, 123
 methodology, 254
 standards and ersatz standards, 118–121
 style of argument, 124
 truth and games, 117
 worries about, 121
Marshall, Alfred, socialism, 78
Materialism, versus subjectivism in policy, 19–27
Mathematical physics, conventions in science, 268
Mathematics
 methodology and rigor, 234
 tautologies, 272
McCloskey, Donald
 clarity versus obscurantism, 255
 fallacy-mongering, 248
 methodology, 226
 models, 236
 utilitarianism, 495
Meltzer, Allan, Keynes, 161
Menger, Anton, gold standard, 191, 193, 198
Menger, Carl, gold standard, 192, 200
Merit, Hayek, 415
Methodology, 225–262
 academic incentives and games, 251–254
 attitudes and pressures, 250
 Austrian Economics, 102
 clarity versus obscurantism, 255–258
 competing hypotheses, 246–248
 econometrics, 241–245
 fallacy-mongering, 248–250
 George, 53, 64–66
 macroeconomics, 229–232
 market analogy, 254
 models, 235–241
 other evidence, 245
 preaching and countermethodology, 225–228
 rigor, 233–235
Micro orientation, Hutt, 174
Military draft, subjectivism, 24

Mises, Ludwig von
  business cycle, 140, 149
  calculation and socialism, 96
  calculation debates, 131
  economic theory as an "a priori" science, 104, 138
  ethics, rights and law, 422–442, 443–461
  general equilibrium theory, 137
  prices, 135, 136, 137
  propositions, 240
  socialism, 72–74
Models
  Lucas, 231
  methodology, 235–241
Modigliani, Franco, socialism, 87
Monarchy, constitutional monarchy versus democracy, 375–387
Monetary system, United States of America, 147
Monetary theory
  balance-of-payments, 276
  capital and investment, 149
  disorder, 142–144
  general equilibrium theory, 8
  monetary disequilibrium theory, 129, 144, 163
  narrative and statistical history, 139
Money
  business cycle: econometrics, 241
  capital formation and, 217–222
  costs: subjectivism, 44
  and credit, 144
  econometrics, 242
  endogeneity, 243
  Hayek, 143
  Hutt, 180–184
  macroeconomics, 146–149
  price stickiness, 136–138
Money prices, general equilibrium theory, 7
Morality. *See* Ethics

N

Narratives
  and statistical history: monetarists, 139
  urchronia and alternative history, 388–396
Natural law, 430, 438, 453–457
Natural rights, Rothbard, 477
Natural sciences, tautologies, 270–272
Neoclassical school of economics, Rosen on, 102
New Classical school
  about, 129
  coordination, 134
New Keynesian school
  about, 130
  attitudes and pressures, 250
  coordination, 134
Nihilism, subjectivism, 45
Nonempiricism, Austrian Economics, 104
Normative and positive propositions, 307
Nozick, Robert
  entitlements, 408
  utilitarianism, 505–507

O

Objective ethics, Rothbard and Mises on, 451
Obscurantism versus clarity, 255–258
Opportunity cost, general equilibrium theory, 8
Optimum conditions, socialism, 74
Overregulation. *See* Regulation

P

Partial determinism, extreme positions and, 299–302
Partial-equilibrium theory, general equilibrium theory, 11
Pigou effect, 217

Platt, John R., competing hypotheses, 246
Poincaré, Henri
conventions in science, 268
science compared to a library, 269
Policy
government and public policy, 311, 343
landownership, 214–217
policy drift and government regulation, 338
subjectivism, 33–35
utilitarianism: rights, contract and utility in policy espousal, 477–515
Political economy, 307–320. *See also* Regulation
bureaucracy, 317
cooperation and reciprocation, 309–311
democratic process, 318
ethics, 308
government and public policy, 311, 319
liberty and democracy, 312–314
political process, 316
positive and normative propositions, 307
voting and special interests, 315
Political obligation, utilitarianism, 499–502
Political philosophy. *See also* Social philosophy
Blanchard: political rights and duties, 501
socialism, 89
Political system. *See also* United States of America
politicians and government regulation, 331–335
Wittman: democratic markets, 367–374

Popper, Karl
chance and ethics, 293
on essentialism, 283
ethics and complexity, 292
Population control, 352
Positive and normative propositions, 307
Preaching and methodology, 225–228
Predictions, Austrian Economics on, 105
Prescott, Edward C., business cycle: econometrics, 242
Prescriptive and descriptive laws, 285
Prices. *See also* Money prices
calculation, 94
Hayek on free-market values, 415
Hutt, 178
institutions, 135
Kirzner and Nozick on, 412
Mises, 135
prices system and subjectivism, 31
socialism, 76, 78–86
stickiness, 136–138
subjectivism, 28
Principle of complementarity, Bohr, 275
Principle of Generic Consistency, Gerwirth, 480
Principles, economics and, 349–360
Priorities, subjectivism, 22
Process, Austrian School of Economics attention to, 137
Productivity, George, 55–58
Profit, Kirzner: morality of capitalism and profit, 407–421
Property, subjectivism and market value when seized under eminent domain, 25
Property rights
crowding out and government regulation, 340
George, 68

Rothbard: axiomatic approach,
    431–435
  subjectivism, 35
Propositions
  Mises, 240
  positive and normative propositions, 307
Protection, general equilibrium theory, 12
Prowse, Michael, constitutional monarchy, 383
Publication of articles
  Austrian School of Economics, 107
  market test of ideas, 121
Purchasing-power argument, general equilibrium theory, 11

R
Rand, Ayn, market test of ideas, 110
Randomness, ethics, 292–295
Rational expectations
  Hutt, 183
  methodology, 229
Rational ignorance, 376
Rawls, John, utilitarianism, 491, 493, 508–510
Real-balance effect, 217
Real-bills doctrine, general equilibrium theory, 12
Real-business-cycle school, 129
Real disturbances, 139
Recoordination, 133
Redistribution
  discrimination argument, 469
  egalitarianism and liberalism, 463
Regulation, 321–348
  bureaucracy and, 335
  costs, 342
  courts' role in, 335–338
  crowding out, 339–341
  flaw in political system, 323–325
  fragmented decisions and agglomerated activities, 322
  hobbyists and, 331
  methodological individualism, 325
  policy drift, 338
  policy implications, 343
  politicians, 331–335
  special interests and synthetic majorities, 329
  voters, 326–329
Relative poverty, 466
Relativism, fallibilism, authoritarianism, 486–488
Rights
  Mises: ethics, rights and law, 422–442
  Rothbard: axioms, 430–435
  Rothbard: natural law and natural rights, 453
  utilitarianism: rights, contract and utility in policy espousal, 477–515
  value judgments, 478
The Road to Serfdom (Hayek), 397, 401–406
Robbins, Lionel, socialism, 75
Rockoff, Hugh, gold standard, 202
Rosen, Sherwin, Austrian Economics, 100–112
Rothbard, Murray
  axioms about rights, 430–435
  Hoppe and anarcho-Lockean rights, 457
  landownership, 209
  Mises and objective ethics, 451
  Mises and utilitarianism, 427–430, 452
  morality and law, 435–439
  natural law and natural rights, 453–455, 477
  on subjectivism, 38
Russia, gold standard, 194, 197, 200

S

Salerno, Joseph T.
    calculation, 93
    prices and calculation, 94
Samuelson, Paul, tautologies, 273
Sargent, Thomas, on general equilibrium theory, 5
Savings
    land and willingness to wait, 214
    macroeconomics, 146–149
    real capital formation, 218
    saving preference: Hutt, 176
Say's Law, Hutt on, 175
Scarcity
    applied to methodology, 256
    Sowell: politics and economics of scarcity, 315
Schlick, Moritz
    determinism and free will, 284–286
    extreme positions and partial determinism, 301
Schmidtz, David, entitlements, 409
Schoeck, Helmut, incentives for protesting poor injustices and poor customer service, 354
Schumpeter, Joseph
    George, 69
    liberty and democracy, 313
Science, conventions in, 268
Scientism, subjectivism, 24
Scott, Anthony, land: changes in tastes, taxes or policies, 216
Secondary effects, general equilibrium theory, 12
Secondhandism, 124
Separation of powers, 378
Shock effect, general equilibrium theory, 11
Simultaneous equations. See Equation systems
Slote, Michael, ethical judgments and determinism, 287
Slumps. See Business cycle

Social contract, Buchanan, 488–490
Social cooperation
    about, 417
    comparative institutions, 496–499
    market test of ideas, 116
Social justice, Hayek, 414
Social philosophy. See also Political philosophy
    George, 66–69
    socialism, 89
Socialism
    calculation, 96
    efficiency, 72–92
    George, 63
    Hayek, 397–406
    subjectivism, 34
Sowell, Thomas, politics and economics of scarcity, 315
Special interests, and government regulation, 329
Standards and ersatz standards, 118–121
Subjectivism, 19–50
    about, 19
    capital and interest theory, 36–38
    concluding thoughts, 46
    degrees of, 38–46
    economic theory, 30–33
    George, 55–58
    knowledge and coordination, 27–30
    materialism versus subjectivism in policy, 19–27
    policy, 33–35
Subsidies, general equilibrium theory, 11

T

Tariffs, general equilibrium theory, 12
Tastes, landownership, 214–217
Tautologies, 263–279
    about, 263–265

balance-of-payments, 274–277
conventions in science, 268
economics, 272–274
examples in the natural sciences, 270–272
Walras's Law, 265–268
Taxation
land, 215
link to expenditures, 324
tax cuts and budget limits, 343
Theory, Euken, 238
Thrift, landownership, 210
Time
Austrian Economics and, 101
George, 55–58
macroeconomics, 145
Tollefsen, Olaf, determinism: self-referential problem of, 297
Tollison, Robert, market test of ideas, 116–126
Trade, custom unions, 213
Trade interventions, general equilibrium theory, 12
Truth. *See* Marketplace of ideas
Truth judgment, Buchanan, 485

U

Uchronia, 388–396
Ultrasubjectivists, 39
United States of America
alternative histories, 392
democratic process, 314, 361–366
monetary system, 147
political process, 316
Unplanned order, George, 59–62
Utilitarianism
Mises, 422, 444, 448–450
political obligation, 499–502
rights, contract and utility in policy espousal, 477–515
Rothbard and natural rights, 439

V

Value judgments
rights, 478
and value-free propositions: Austrian Economics, 102
Value theory
George, 55–58
Hayek, 415
Vandberg, Viktor, contractarianism, 484
VAR technique, 243
Vaughn, Karen
contractarianism, 484
Mises and utilitarianism, 426
Vickrey, William, multi-part pricing and socialism, 80
Voluntary compliance, 352
Voting
and special interests, 315
vote-trading process, 330
voters and government regulation, 326–329
Winston Churchill on voters and democracy, 376

W

Waiting, land and the willingness to wait, 211–214
Walras's Law, 263, 265–268, 275
Warburton, Clark, Keynes, 158
Wealth effect, 217
Welfare properties, subjectivism, 34
Williamson, Steve, models, 237
Winks, Robin, historical evidence, 246
Wittmann, Donald, democratic markets, 367–374
Workers' sovereignty, subjectivism, 29
World War I and II, alternative histories, 393
Wright, Randall, models, 237
Writing style, Halmos, 256